Lecture Notes in Artificial Intelligence 8736

Subseries of Lecture Notes in Computer Science

Lecture Notes in Artificial Intelligence   8736

Subseries of Lecture Notes in Computer Science

LNAI Series Editors

Randy Goebel
    University of Alberta, Edmonton, Canada
Yuzuru Tanaka
    Hokkaido University, Sapporo, Japan
Wolfgang Wahlster
    DFKI and Saarland University, Saarbrücken, Germany

LNAI Founding Series Editor

Joerg Siekmann
    DFKI and Saarland University, Saarbrücken, Germany

Carsten Lutz   Michael Thielscher (Eds.)

KI 2014: Advances in Artificial Intelligence

37th Annual German Conference on AI
Stuttgart, Germany, September 22-26, 2014
Proceedings

 Springer

Volume Editors

Carsten Lutz
Universität Bremen, Germany
E-mail: clu@informatik.uni-bremen.de

Michael Thielscher
University of New South Wales
Sydney, NSW, Australia
E-mail: mit@cse.unsw.edu.au

ISSN 0302-9743   e-ISSN 1611-3349
ISBN 978-3-319-11205-3   e-ISBN 978-3-319-11206-0
DOI 10.1007/978-3-319-11206-0
Springer Cham Heidelberg New York Dordrecht London

Library of Congress Control Number: 2014948038

LNCS Sublibrary: SL 7 – Artificial Intelligence

Typesetting: Camera-ready by author, data conversion by Scientific Publishing Services, Chennai, India

Printed on acid-free paper

Springer is part of Springer Science+Business Media (www.springer.com)

Preface

Welcome to the proceedings of the 37th German Conference on Artificial Intelligence (KI 2014)! Known as the German Workshop on Artificial Intelligence at its inauguration in 1975, this annual conference brings together academic and industrial researchers from all areas of AI, providing the premier forum in Germany for exchanging news and research results on theory and applications of intelligent system technology. For the first time, the conference comes to Stuttgart, a metropolitan area that is one of the leading hubs for high-tech innovation and development in Europe.

KI 2014 received 62 submissions with authors from 21 countries. Each submission was reviewed by at least three Program Committee members or external referees. A lively and intense discussion ensued among the reviewers, Program Committee members, and program chairs. After this thorough assessment, 21 submissions (34%) were finally accepted to be published as full papers in the proceeding and an additional 7 (11%) as short papers.

KI 2014 featured three exciting keynote speeches by distinguished scientists: Wolfram Burgard (Freiburg University, Germany) gave an overview of Probabilistic Techniques for Mobile Robot Navigation. Hans van Ditmarsch (LORIA Nancy, France) spoke about Dynamic Epistemic Logic and Artificial Intelligence. Toby Walsh (NICTA and UNSW Sydney, Australia) talked about Allocation in Practice.

Three workshops with their own proceedings were held on the first two days of the conference: the 8th Workshop on Emotion and Computing — Current Research and Future Impact; the 28th Workshop Planen/Scheduling und Konfigurieren/Entwerfen (PuK); and the workshop on Higher-Level Cognition and Computation. The workshops were complemented by two tutorials: Probabilistic Programing by Angelika Kimmig, KU Leuven; and Human Computation by François Bry, LMU Munich. Together these tutorials and workshops, which were overseen by the workshop and tutorial chair Frieder Stolzenburg, provided an excellent start to the event.

KI 2014 would not have been successful without the support of authors, reviewers, and organizers. We thank the many authors for submitting their research papers to the conference and for their collaboration during the preparation of final submissions. We thank the members of the Program Committee and the external referees for their expertise and timeliness in assessing the papers. We also thank the organizers of the workshops and tutorials for their commitment and dedication. We are very grateful to the members of the Organizing Committee for their efforts in the preparation, promotion, and organization of the conference, especially Andrés Bruhn for coordinating with INFORMATIK 2014 and Maximilian Altmeyer for setting up and maintaining the conference webpage. We acknowledge the assistance provided by EasyChair for conference management, and we appreciate the professional service provided by the Springer LNCS editorial and publishing teams.

September 2014   Carsten Lutz
                                                                Michael Thielscher

Organization

Program Chairs

Carsten Lutz   University of Bremen, Germany
Michael Thielscher   University of New South Wales, Australia

Workshop and Tutorial Chair

Frieder Stolzenburg   Hochschule Harz, Germany

Doctoral Consortium Chair

Markus Krötzsch   TU Dresden, Germany

Local Arrangement Chair

Antonio Krüger   Saarland University, Germany

Program Committee

Sven Behnke   University of Bonn, Germany
Ralph Bergmann   University of Trier, Germany
Mehul Bhatt   University of Bremen, Germany
Philipp Cimiano   University of Bielefeld, Germany
Cristobal Curio   TWT GmbH Science & Innovation, Germany
Kerstin Dautenhahn   University of Hertfordshire, UK
Stefan Edelkamp   University of Bremen, Germany
Stefan Funke   University of Stuttgart, Germany
Johannes Fürnkranz   TU Darmstadt, Germany
Christopher Geib   Drexel University, USA
Birte Glimm   University of Ulm, Germany
Christian Guttmann   IBM Research, Australia
Malte Helmert   University of Basel, Switzerland
Gabriele Kern-Isberner   Technical University of Dortmund, Germany
Thomas Kirste   University of Rostock, Germany
Roman Kontchakov   Birkbeck, University of London, UK
Oliver Kramer   University of Oldenburg, Germany
Ralf Krestel   University of California at Irvine, USA

Torsten Kroeger	Stanford University, USA
Gerhard Lakemeyer	RWTH Aachen University, Germany
Andreas Lattner	Otto Group Hamburg, Germany
Volker Lohweg	inIT - Institute Industrial IT, Germany
Robert Mattmüller	University of Freiburg, Germany
Till Mossakowski	University of Magdeburg, Germany
Ralf Möller	Hamburg University of Technology, Germany
Marco Ragni	University of Freiburg, Germany
Jochen Renz	Australian National University, Australia
Stephan Schiffel	Reykjavik University, Iceland
Malte Schilling	CITEC Bielefeld, Germany
Ute Schmid	University of Bamberg, Germany
Lutz Schröder	Friedrich-Alexander University Erlangen-Nürnberg, Germany
Daniel Sonntag	German Research Center for Artificial Intelligence (DFKI), Germany
Steffen Staab	University of Koblenz-Landau, Germany
Hannes Strass	University of Leipzig, Germany
Heiner Stuckenschmidt	University of Mannheim, Germany
Thomas Stützle	Free University of Brussels (ULB), Belgium
Moritz Tenorth	University of Bremen, Germany
Matthias Thimm	University of Koblenz-Landau, Germany
Ingo Timm	University of Trier, Germany
Johanna Völker	University of Mannheim, Germany
Toby Walsh	NICTA and UNSW, Australia
Dirk Walther	Technical University of Dresden, Germany
Stefan Wölfl	University of Freiburg, Germany

Additional Reviewers

Albrecht, Rebecca
Asmus, Josefine
Bader, Sebastian
Classen, Jens
Dörksen, Helene
Gessinger, Sarah
Goerke, Nils
Görg, Sebastian
Hein, Albert
Hué, Julien
Klinger, Roman
Klinov, Pavel
Krüger, Frank
Kuhnmünch, Gregory

Kutz, Oliver
Lee, Jae Hee
Ma, Yue
Mailis, Theofilos
Mccrae, John P.
Mkrtchyan, Tigran
Müller, Gilbert
Nyolt, Martin
Özcep, Özgür Lütfü
Pommerening, Florian
Ponomaryov, Denis
Rizzardi, Enrico
Rodriguez-Muro, Mariano

Schultz, Carl
Schulz, Hannes
Schwering, Christoph
Siebers, Michael
Slaney, John
Stückler, Jörg
Tran, Trung-Kien
Ul-Hasan, Adnan
Unger, Christina
van Delden, André
Westphal, Matthias
Wirth, Christian

Table of Contents

Knowledge Representation and Reasoning

Machine Learning and Data Mining

Planning and Scheduling

The Ditmarsch Tale of Wonders

Hans van Ditmarsch

LORIA — CNRS, Université de Lorraine
hans.van-ditmarsch@loria.fr

Abstract. We propose a dynamic logic of lying, wherein a 'lie that φ' (where φ is a formula in the logic) is an action in the sense of dynamic modal logic, that is interpreted as a state transformer relative to φ. The states that are being transformed are pointed Kripke models encoding the uncertainty of agents about their beliefs. Lies can be about factual propositions but also about modal formulas, such as the beliefs of other agents or the belief consequences of the lies of other agents.[1]

1 Introduction

I will tell you something. I saw two roasted fowls flying; they flew quickly and had their breasts turned to Heaven and their backs to Hell; and an anvil and a mill-stone swam across the Rhine prettily, slowly, and gently; and a frog sat on the ice at Whitsuntide and ate a ploughshare.

Four fellows who wanted to catch a hare, went on crutches and stilts; one of them was deaf, the second blind, the third dumb, and the fourth could not stir a step. Do you want to know how it was done? First, the blind man saw the hare running across the field, the dumb one called to the deaf one, and the lame one seized it by the neck.

There were certain men who wished to sail on dry land, and they set their sails in the wind, and sailed away over great fields. Then they sailed over a high mountain, and there they were miserably drowned.

A crab was chasing a hare which was running away at full speed; and high up on the roof lay a cow which had climbed up there. In that country the flies are as big as the goats are here.

Open the window that the lies may fly out.

My favourite of Grimm's fairytales [9] is 'Hans im Glück' (Hans in Luck). A close second comes 'The Ditmarsch Tale of Wonders', integrally cited above. In German this is called a 'Lügenmärchen', a 'Liar's Tale'. A passage like "A crab was chasing a hare which was running away at full speed; and high up on the roof lay a cow which had climbed up there." contains very obvious lies. Nobody considers it possible that this is true. Crabs are reputedly slow, hares are reputedly fast.

In 'The Ditmarsch Tale of Wonders', none of the lies are believed.

---

[1] This contribution is based on [27].

C. Lutz and M. Thielscher (Eds.): KI 2014, LNCS 8736, pp. 1–12, 2014.

In the movie 'The Invention of Lying' the main character Mark goes to a bank counter and finds out he only has $300 in his account. But he needs $800. Lying has not yet been invented in the 20th-century fairytale country of this movie. Then and there, on the spot, Mark invents lying: he tells the bank employee assisting him that there must be a mistake: he has $800 in his account. He is lying. She responds, oh well, then there must be a mistake with your account data, because on my screen it says you only have $300. I'll inform system maintenance of the error. My apologies for the inconvenience. And she gives him $800! In the remainder of the movie, Mark gets very rich.

Mark's lies are not as unbelievable as those in Grimm's fairytale. It is possible that he has $800. It is just not true. Still, there is something unrealistic about the lies in this movie: new information is believed instantly, even if it is inconsistent with prior information, or with direct observation. There are shots wherein Mark first announces a fact, then its negation, then the fact again, while all the time his extremely credulous listeners keep believing every last announcement. New information is also believed if it contradicts direct observation. In a café, in company of several of his friends, he claims to be a one-armed bandit. And they commiserate with him, oh, I never knew you only had one arm, how terrible for you. All the time, Mark is sitting there drinking beer and gesturing with both hands while telling his story.

In the movie 'The Invention of Lying', all lies are believed.

In the real world, if you lie, sometimes other people believe you and sometimes they don't. When can you get away with a lie? Consider the well-known consecutive numbers riddle, often attributed to Littlewood [14].

> *Anne and Bill are each going to be told a natural number. Their numbers will be one apart. The numbers are now being whispered in their respective ears. They are aware of this scenario. Suppose Anne is told 2 and Bill is told 3. The following truthful conversation between Anne and Bill now takes place:*
> *— Anne: "I do not know your number."*
> *— Bill: "I do not know your number."*
> *— Anne: "I know your number."*
> *— Bill: "I know your number."*
> *Explain why is this possible.*

Initially, Anne is uncertain between Bill having 1 or 3, and Bill is uncertain between Anne having 2 or 4. So both Anne and Bill do not initially know their number. Suppose Anne says to Bill: "I know your number." Anne is lying. Bill does not consider it possible that Anne knows his number, so he tells Anne that she is lying. However, Anne did not know that Bill would not believe her. She considered it possible that Bill had 1, in which case Bill would have considered it possible that Anne was telling the truth, and would then have drawn the incorrect conclusion that Anne had 0. I.e., if you are still following us... It seems not so clear how this should be formalized in a logic interpreted on epistemic modal structures, and this is the topic of our contribution.

In everyday conversation, some lies are believed and some are not.

1.1   The Modal Dynamics of Lying

What is a lie? Let p be an atomic proposition (propositional variable). You lie to me that p, if you believe that p is false while you say that p, and with the intention that I believe p. The thing you say, we call the announcement. If you succeed in your intention, then I believe p, and I also believe that your announcement of p was truthful, i.e., that you believed that p when you said that p. In this investigation we abstract from the intentional aspect of lying. We model lying as a dynamic operation, and in that sense we only model the realization of the intention. This is similar to the procedure in AGM belief revision [1], wherein one models how to incorporate new information in an agent's belief set, but abstracts from the process that made the new information acceptable to the agent. Our proposal is firmly grounded in modal logic. We use dynamic epistemic logic [28].

What are the modal preconditions and postconditions of a lie? Let us for now assume that p is a Boolean proposition, and two agents a (female) and b (male). The precondition of 'a is lying that p to b' is $B_a \neg p$ (i.e., 'Agent a believes that p is false', where B_a stands for 'a believes that' and $\neg$ for negation). Stronger preconditions are conceivable, e.g., that the addressee considers it possible that the lie is true, $\neg B_b \neg p$, or that the speaker believes that, $B_a \neg B_b \neg p$; or even involving common belief. These conditions may not always hold while we still call the announcement a lie, because the speaker may not know whether the additional conditions are satisfied. We therefore will (initially) only require precondition $B_a \neg p$.

We should contrast the *lying announcement* that p with other forms of announcement. Just as a lying agent believes that p is false when it announces p, a truthful agent believes that p is true when it announces p. The precondition for a lying announcement by a is $B_a \neg p$, and so the precondition for a *truthful announcement* by a is $B_a p$. Besides the truthful and the lying announcement there is yet another form of announcement, because in modal logic there are always three instead of two possibilities: either you believe p, or you believe $\neg p$, or you are uncertain whether p. The last corresponds to the precondition $\neg(B_a p \lor B_a \neg p)$ ($\lor$ is disjunction). An announcement wherein agent a announces p while she is uncertain about p we call a *bluffing announcement*.

We now consider the postconditions of 'a is lying that p to b'. If a's intention to deceive b is successful, b believes p after the lie. Therefore, $B_b p$ should be a postcondition of a successful execution of the action of lying. (If the precondition of the lie is $B_a \neg p$, then the postcondition becomes $B_b B_a p$ instead of $B_b p$. In the presence of common belief the postcondition should clearly be $B_b C_{ab} p$.) Also, the precondition should be preserved: $B_a \neg p$ should still be true after the lie. Realizing $B_b p$ may come at a price. In case the agent b already believed the opposite, $B_b \neg p$, then b's beliefs are inconsistent afterwards. (This means that b's accessibility relation is empty.) There are two different solutions for this: either b does not change his beliefs, so that $B_b \neg p$ still holds after the lie (this we call the *skeptical* agent), or the belief $B_b \neg p$ is given up in order to consistently incorporate $B_b p$ (which in our treatment corresponds to the *plausible* agent).

The action of lying is modelled as a dynamic modal operator. The dynamic modal operator for 'lying that p' is interpreted as an epistemic state transformer, where an epistemic state is a pointed Kripke model (a model with a designated state) that encodes the beliefs of the agents.

The belief operators B_a do not merely apply to Boolean propositions p but to any proposition φ with belief modalities. This is known as higher-order belief. The preconditions and postconditions of lying may be such higher-order formulas. In the semantics, the generalization from 'lying that p' to 'lying that φ' for any proposition does not present any problem. But in the syntax it does: we can no longer require that the beliefs of the speaker a remain unchanged, or that, after the lie, the addressee b believes the formula of the lie. For a typical example, suppose that p is false, that a knows the truth about p, and that b is uncertain whether p. Consider the lie by a to b that $p \wedge \neg B_b p$ (a Moorean sentence). This is a lie: a knows (believes correctly) that p is false, and therefore that the sentence $p \wedge \neg B_b p$ is false. But a does not want b to believe $p \wedge \neg B_b p$! Of course, a wants b to believe p and thus no longer to be ignorant about p.

1.2   A Short History of Lying

Philosophy. Lying has been a thriving topic in the philosophical community for a long time [21,5,16]. Almost any analysis quotes Augustine on lying:

> "that man lies, who has one thing in his mind and utters another in words" and "the fault of him who lies, is the desire of deceiving in the uttering of his mind."

In other words: lying amounts to saying that p while believing that $\neg p$, with the intention to make believe p, our starting assumption. The requirements for the belief preconditions and postconditions in such works are illuminating. For example, the addressee should not merely believe the lie but believe it to be believed by the speaker. Gettier-like scenarios are presented, including delayed justification [18]: Suppose that you believe that $\neg p$ and that you lie that p. Later, you find out that your belief was mistaken because p was really true. You can then with some justification say "Ah, so I was not really lying." Much is said on the morality of lying [5] and on its intentional aspect, that we do not discuss.

Cognitive science and economics. Lying excites great interest in the general public [23]. In psychology, biology, and other experimental sciences, lying and deception are related. In economics, 'cheap talk' is making false promises. Your talk is cheap if you do not intend to execute an action that you publicly announced to plan. It is therefore a lie, it is deception [8,11].

Logic. Papers that model lying as an epistemic action, inducing a transformation of an epistemic model, include [2,22,4,26,13,29,19]. Lying by an external observer has been discussed by Baltag and collaborators from the inception of dynamic epistemic logic onward [2]; the later [4] also discusses lying in logics with plausible belief, as does [26]. In [29] the conscious update in [7] is applied to model lying by an external observer. In [20] the authors give a modal logic of lying and bluffing, including intentions. Instead of bluffing they call this bullshit, after [6]. In [19], various modal logics combining knowledge and intention are listed, where the philosophically familiar themes of how to stack belief preconditions and belief postconditions reappear. The recent [15] allows explicit reference in the logical language to truthful, lying and bluffing agents, thus enabling some form of self-reference.

2   Agent Announcements

In this section we present *agent annoucement logic*, in order to model lying by one agent to another agent, where both are modelled in the system. (An example is lying in the consecutive numbers riddle.) Let us retrace this agent announcement logic to better known logics. It can be seen as a version of a logic of truthful and lying public announcements [29], which in its turn is based on the logic of so-called 'arrow elimination' public announcements [7], and that, finally, can be seen as an alternative for the better known 'state elimination' logic of truthful public announcements [17,3].

In public announcement logics, the announcing agent is an outside observer and is implicit. Therefore, it is also implicit whether it believes that the announcement is false or true. (The usual assumption is that it is true.) In dynamic epistemic logic, it is common to formalize 'agent a truthfully announces φ' as 'the outside observer truthfully announces $B_a\varphi$'. However, 'agent a lies that φ' cannot be modelled as 'the outside observer lies that $B_a\varphi$'. What do we want?

Consider an epistemic state (with equivalence relations, encoding knowledge) where b does not know whether p, a knows whether p, and p is true. (We underline the actual state.) Agent a is in the position to tell b the truth about p. A truthful public announcement of $B_a p$, in the usual semantics where we eliminate states that do not satisfy the announcement, has the following effect ($!B_a p$ stands for 'truthful public announcement of $B_a p$').

$$ab \left(\circlearrowright \; \neg p \xleftarrow{\;\;b\;\;} \underline{p} \; \circlearrowright \right) ab \quad \overset{!B_a p}{\Rightarrow} \quad \left(\underline{p} \; \circlearrowright \right) ab$$

In the alternative arrow-eliminating semantics the result is slightly different. But also now, truthful public announcement of $B_a p$ indeed simulates that a truthfully and publicly announces p. (From the perspective of the actual state, the results are bisimilar.)

$$ab \left(\circlearrowright \; \neg p \xleftarrow{\;\;b\;\;} \underline{p} \; \circlearrowright \right) ab \quad \overset{!B_a p}{\Rightarrow} \quad \neg p \xrightarrow{\;\;b\;\;} \underline{p} \; \circlearrowright \; ab$$

Given the same model, now suppose p is false, and that a lies that p. In a lying public announcement of φ we eliminate all arrows pointing to φ states, on condition that $\neg\varphi$ is true in the actual state [29]. A lying public announcement of $B_a p$ (it is lying, because it satisfies the required precondition $\neg B_a p$) does not result in the desired information state for a lying to b that p, because this makes agent a believe her own lie. And as she already knew $\neg p$, this makes a's beliefs inconsistent ($¡B_a p$ stands for 'lying public announcement of $B_a p$').

The problem here is that, no matter how complex the formula of the announcement, both lying and truthful public announcements will always similarly affect the (accessibility relations and thus) beliefs of the speaker and the addressee. This is because the announcements are public actions.

To model one agent lying to another agent we need a more complex form of model change than uniform restriction of the accessibility relation for all agents. We need to differentiate between the relation encoding the uncertainty of the speaker and the relation encoding the uncertainty of the addressee. A lie by a to b that p should have the following effect. ($¡_a p$ stands for 'lying agent announcement —by agent a— of p').

After this lie we have that a still believes that $\neg p$, but that b believes that p. (We even have that b believes that a and b have common belief of p.) We see that lying does not affect the accessibility relation of the speaker but only of that of the addressee. This implements the intuition that the speaker a can say φ *no matter what*, whether she believes what she says, believes the opposite, or is uncertain (as in the truthful, lying, and bluffing announcement). Whereas the addressee b takes φ to be the truth *no matter what*.

These requirements for agent announcements are embodied by the following language, structures, and semantics. Given are a finite set of agents A and a countable set of propositional variables P (let $a \in A$ and $p \in P$).

Definition 1. *The* language of agent announcement logic *is defined as*

$$\mathcal{L}(!_a, ¡_a, !¡_a) \ni \varphi ::= p \mid \neg\varphi \mid (\varphi \wedge \psi) \mid B_a\varphi \mid [!_a\varphi]\psi \mid [¡_a\varphi]\psi \mid [!¡_a\varphi]\psi$$

Other propositional connectives are defined by abbreviation. For $B_a\varphi$, read 'agent a believes formula φ'. Agent variables are $a, b, c, \ldots$. The inductive constructs $[!_a\varphi]\psi$, $[¡_a\varphi]\psi$, and $[!¡_a\varphi]\psi$ incorporate modalities for the *agent announcements* $!_a\varphi$, $¡_a\varphi$, and $!¡_a\varphi$ that stand for, respectively, a truthfully announces φ, a is lying that φ, and a is bluffing that φ; where agent a addresses all other agents b. We also define by abbreviation $[_a\varphi]\psi$ as $[!_a\varphi]\psi \wedge [¡_a\varphi]\psi \wedge [!¡_a\varphi]\psi$.

Definition 2. *An epistemic model $M = (S, R, V)$ consists of a domain S of states (or 'worlds'), an accessibility function $R : A \to \mathcal{P}(S \times S)$, where each $R(a)$, for which we write R_a, is an accessibility relation, and a valuation $V :$ $P \to \mathcal{P}(S)$, where each $V(p)$ represents the set of states where p is true. For $s \in S$, (M, s) is an epistemic state.*

An epistemic state is also known as a pointed Kripke model. We often omit the parentheses in (M, s). The model class without restrictions we call $\mathcal{K}$, the one where all accessibility relations are transitive and euclidean $\mathcal{K}45$, and if they are also serial $\mathcal{K}D45$; if accessibility relations are equivalence relations we get $\mathcal{S}5$. Class $\mathcal{K}D45$ is said to have the *properties of belief*, and $\mathcal{S}5$ to have the *properties of knowledge*. We target $\mathcal{K}D45$.

Definition 3. *Assume an epistemic model $M = (S, R, V)$.*

$$
\begin{array}{lll}
M, s \models p & \textit{iff} & s \in V_p \\
M, s \models \neg\varphi & \textit{iff} & M, s \not\models \varphi \\
M, s \models \varphi \wedge \psi & \textit{iff} & M, s \models \varphi \text{ and } M, s \models \psi \\
M, s \models B_a\varphi & \textit{iff} & \text{for all } t \in S : R_a(s, t) \text{ implies } M, t \models \varphi \\
M, s \models [!_a\varphi]\psi & \textit{iff} & M, s \models B_a\varphi \text{ implies } M_a^\varphi, s \models \psi \\
M, s \models [\mathsf{i}_a\varphi]\psi & \textit{iff} & M, s \models B_a\neg\varphi \text{ implies } M_a^\varphi, s \models \psi \\
M, s \models [!\mathsf{i}_a\varphi]\psi & \textit{iff} & M, s \models \neg(B_a\varphi \vee B_a\neg\varphi) \text{ implies } M_a^\varphi, s \models \psi
\end{array}
$$

where M_a^φ is as M except for the accessibility relation R' defined as ($a \neq b$)

$$
R'_a := R_a \qquad R'_b := R_b \cap (S \times [\![B_a\varphi]\!]_M).
$$

The principles for a making a truthful, lying, or bluffing announcement to b are as follows. The belief consequences for the speaker a are different from the belief consequences for the addressee(s) b.

Definition 4 (Axioms for agent announcements).

$$
\begin{array}{ll}
[!_a\varphi]B_b\psi \leftrightarrow B_a\varphi \to B_b[!_a\varphi]\psi & [\mathsf{i}_a\varphi]B_a\psi \leftrightarrow B_a\neg\varphi \to B_a[_a\varphi]\psi \\
[!_a\varphi]B_a\psi \leftrightarrow B_a\varphi \to B_a[_a\varphi]\psi & [!\mathsf{i}_a\varphi]B_b\psi \leftrightarrow \neg(B_a\varphi \vee B_a\neg\varphi) \to B_b[!_a\varphi]\psi \\
[\mathsf{i}_a\varphi]B_b\psi \leftrightarrow B_a\neg\varphi \to B_b[!_a\varphi]\psi & [!\mathsf{i}_a\varphi]B_a\psi \leftrightarrow \neg(B_a\varphi \vee B_a\neg\varphi) \to B_a[_a\varphi]\psi
\end{array}
$$

To the addressee, the announcement always appears to be the truth. Therefore (in the third axiom), after the lie by a that φ the *addressee* b believes ψ, iff, on the condition $B_a\neg\varphi$ that it is a lie, the addressee believes that ψ holds after the truthful announcement by a that φ. Whereas after the lie that φ by a the *speaker* a herself believes ψ, iff, on the condition $B_a\neg\varphi$ that it is a lie, the speaker believes that ψ holds after *any* (either truthful or lying or bluffing) announcement by a that φ. All other axioms and rules are as usual in dynamic epistemic logics. By way of an embedding into action model logic [3] it is easy to prove that:

Proposition 1 ([27]). *The axiomatization of the logic of agent announcements is sound and complete.*

3   Lying in the Consecutive Numbers Riddle

The consecutive numbers riddle (see the introduction) illustrates very well the agent announcements. The standard analysis, in terms of $S5$ knowledge, is by [30] and played an important role in the development of the area of dynamic epistemic logic. The initial model encodes that the numbers are consecutive and consists of two disconnected countable parts, one where the agents have common knowledge (correct common belief) that a's number is odd and b's number is even, and another one where the agents have common knowledge that a's number is even and b's number is odd. For simplicity of the presentation we only display the part of the model where a's number is even. States are pairs (x, y) where x is a's number and y is b's number. The transitions are as follows. (The fourth announcement, by b, does not have an informative consequence.) Symmetry and reflexivity are assumed in the figures.

A: "I do not know your no."
B: "I do not know your no."
A: "I know your no."

$$(0,1) \text{ --- } b \text{ --- } (2,1) \text{ --- } a \text{ --- } (2,3) \text{ --- } b \text{ --- } (4,3) \quad \cdots$$
$$(2,1) \text{ --- } a \text{ --- } \overline{(2,3)} \text{ --- } b \text{ --- } (4,3) \quad \cdots$$
$$\overline{(2,3)} \text{ --- } b \text{ --- } (4,3) \quad \cdots$$
$$\overline{(2,3)}$$

Next, we show two different scenarios for the consecutive numbers riddle with lying. With lying, the riddle involves a speaker feigning knowledge and consequently an addressee incorrectly believing something to be knowledge, so we move from knowledge to belief. In the communication, only the sentences 'I know your number' and 'I do not know your number' occur. Bluffing can therefore not be demonstrated: introspective agents believe their uncertainty and believe their beliefs. As beliefs may be incorrect, we show (again) all arrows.

First scenario. The first scenario consists of Anne lying in her first announcement. Bill does not believe Anne's announcement: his accessibility relation from actual state $(2, 3)$ has become empty. Bill's beliefs are therefore no longer consistent. (We can adapt the example to model Bill as a 'skeptical agent' thus preserving consistency. See Section 4.) Here, the analysis stops. We do not treat Bill's 'announcement' "That's a lie" as a permitted move in the game. On the assumption of initial common knowledge Bill *knows* that Anne was lying and not mistaken.

– Anne: "I know your number." *Anne is lying*

– Bill: "That's a lie."

Second scenario. In the second scenario Anne initially tells the truth, after which Bill is lying, resulting in Anne mistakenly concluding (and truthfully announcing) that she knows Bill's number: she believes it to be 1. This mistaken announcement by Anne is informative to Bill. He learns from it (correctly) that Anne's number is 2, something he didn't know before. Bill gets away with lying, because Anne considered it possible that he told the truth. Bill knows (believes correctly and justifiably) that Anne's second announcement was a mistake and not a lie. The justification is, again, common knowledge in the initial epistemic state.

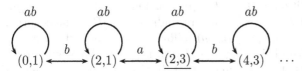

– Anne: "I do not know your number."

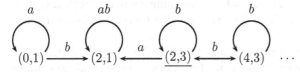

– Bill: "I know your number." *Bill is lying*

– Anne: "I know your number." *Anne is mistaken.*

4 Some Results for Agent Announcements

Public announcements are agent announcements. Consider a depiction of an epistemic model. The outside observer is the guy or girl looking at the picture: you, the reader. She can see all different states. She has no uncertainty and her beliefs are correct. It is therefore that her truthful announcements are true and that her lying announcements are false. It is also therefore that 'truthful public announcement logic' is not a misnomer, it is indeed the logic of how to process new information that is true. We can model the outside observer as an agent *gd*, for 'god or the *devil*', with as its associated accessibility relation the identity on the domain. And therefore, public announcements are a special form of agent announcements.

Lying about beliefs. Agents may announce factual propositions (Boolean formulas) but also modal propositions, and thus be lying and bluffing about them. In the consecutive numbers riddle (Section 3) the announcements 'I know your number' and 'I do not know your number' are modal propositions, and the agents may be lying about those.

For agents that satisfy introspection (so that $B_a B_a \varphi \leftrightarrow B_a \varphi$ and $B_a \neg B_a \varphi \leftrightarrow \neg B_a \varphi$ are validities) the distinction between bluffing and lying seems to become blurred. If I am uncertain whether p, I would be bluffing if I told you that p, but I would be lying if I told you that I believe that p. This is how: The announcement that p satisfies the precondition $\neg(B_a p \vee B_a \neg p)$. It is bluffing that p (it is $!_{!_a} p$). But the announcement that $B_a p$ satisfies the precondition $B_a \neg B_a p$, the negation of the announcement. (From $\neg(B_a p \vee B_a \neg p)$ follows $\neg B_a p$, and with negative introspection we get $B_a \neg B_a p$.) It is lying that $B_a p$ (it is $_{!_a} B_a p$). We would prefer to call both bluffing, and that 'a announces that $B_a p$' is *strictly* 'a announces that p'. One can define a notion of 'strictness' that avoid this ambuity and then show, by employing the alternating disjunctive forms proposed in [10], that for each formula there is an equivalent strict formula [27].

Mistakes and lies. I am lying that φ if I say φ and believe $\neg \varphi$ (independently from the truth of φ), whereas I am mistaken about φ (I mistakenly but truthfully announce φ) if I say φ and believe φ, but φ is false. Let a be the speaker, then the precondition of lying that φ is $B_a \neg \varphi$ and the precondition of a mistaken truthful announcement that φ is $\neg \varphi \wedge B_a \varphi$. The speaker can therefore distinguish a lie from a mistake.

If both knowledge and belief play a role, then the addressee can distinguish a lie from a mistake (and otherwise, not). In 'fair games' there is initial common knowledge of what agents know about each other. For a player b in that game, a mistake is that player a says φ when $K_b(\neg \varphi \wedge B_a \varphi)$, whereas a lie is that a says φ when $K_b K_a \neg \varphi$ (where K_a means 'a knows that'). The consecutive numbers riddle gave an example.

Action models. Action models [3] are a familiar way to formalize different perspectives on 'what the real action is'. The action model for truthful public announcement (state elimination semantics) can be viewed as a singleton action model. This is well-known. We can view truthful and lying public announcement ('believed announcement', the arrow elimination semantics) as the different points, respectively, of a two-point action model. This is somewhat less well-known [24,12]. We can also view truthful, lying and bluffing agent announcement as the respective different points of a three-point action model [27].

Unbelievable lies and skeptical updates. If I tell you φ and you already believe the opposite, accepting this information will make your beliefs inconsistent. This is not merely a problem for lying ('unbelievable lies') but for any form of information update. One way to preserve consistent beliefs is to reject new information if it is inconsistent with your beliefs. Such agents may be called *skeptical*. By a minor adaptation of the semantics (replace condition $B_a \neg \varphi$ of the lie by a to

b that φ, by $B_a\neg\varphi \wedge \neg B_b\neg\varphi$) we can model announcements to skeptical agents [22,13,27].

Plausible reasoning. Going mad is too strong a response (credulous agents), not ever accepting new information seems too weak a response (skeptical agents), a solution in between (plausible agents), also resulting in consistency preserving belief change, involves distinguishing stronger from weaker beliefs when revising beliefs. To achieve that, we need to give epistemic models more structure: given a set of states all considered possible by an agent (its epistemic equivalence class), it may consider some states more plausible than other states, and belief in φ can then be defined as the truth of φ in the most plausible states that are considered possible. We now have more options to change beliefs. We can change the sets of states considered possible by the agent, but we can also change the relative plausibility of states within that set. Such approaches for belief change involving plausibility have been proposed in [25,24,4], and are applied in [27].

Future research. We envisage future research involving the integration of common knowledge in our framework, on the comparative complexity of reasoning without considering lies and reasoning while keeping track of possible lies, and on modelling the liar paradox in a dynamic epistemic logic. Many others actively pursue novel results in the area of lying and logic. Chiaki Sakama is working on lying in argumentation, and investigates the 'white lie'. You truthfully announce p knowing that your opponent falsely believes $p \to q$ and thus will incorrectly deduce q. Is this a lie? Yanjing Wang models lying in the setting of protocol analysis. His convincing lying example involves you telling both your feet-dragging friends that the other is going to accept the invitation for a party, thus successfully managing that both will indeed accept. Thomas Ågotnes investigates the syntactic characterization of the 'true lie' that is a lie indeed but that will always become true when announced. Rineke Verbrugge and her group investigate lying and deception in higher-order cognition, see the workshop series 'Reasoning about other minds'.

References

1. Alchourrón, C.E., Gärdenfors, P., Makinson, D.: On the logic of theory change: Partial meet contraction and revision functions. Journal of Symbolic Logic 50, 510–530 (1985)
2. Baltag, A.: A logic for suspicious players: Epistemic actions and belief updates in games. Bulletin of Economic Research 54(1), 1–45 (2002)
3. Baltag, A., Moss, L.S., Solecki, S.: The logic of public announcements, common knowledge, and private suspicions. In: Proc. of 7th TARK, pp. 43–56. Morgan Kaufmann (1998)
4. Baltag, A., Smets, S.: The logic of conditional doxastic actions. In: New Perspectives on Games and Interaction. Texts in Logic and Games 4, pp. 9–31. Amsterdam University Press (2008)
5. Bok, S.: Lying: Moral Choice in Public and Private Life. Random House, New York (1978)

6. Frankfurt, H.G.: On Bullshit. Princeton University Press (2005)
7. Gerbrandy, J.D., Groeneveld, W.: Reasoning about information change. Journal of Logic, Language, and Information 6, 147–169 (1997)
8. Gneezy, U.: Deception: The role of consequences. American Economic Review 95(1), 384–394 (2005)
9. Grimm, J.L.K., Grimm, W.K.: Kinder- und Hausmärchen. Reimer (1814), vol. 1 (1812) and vol. 2 (1814)
10. Hales, J.: Refinement quantifiers for logics of belief and knowledge. Honours Thesis, University of Western Australia (2011)
11. Kartik, N., Ottaviani, M., Squintani, F.: Credulity, lies, and costly talk. Journal of Economic Theory 134, 93–116 (2006)
12. Kooi, B.: Expressivity and completeness for public update logics via reduction axioms. Journal of Applied Non-Classical Logics 17(2), 231–254 (2007)
13. Kooi, B., Renne, B.: Arrow update logic. Review of Symbolic Logic 4(4), 536–559 (2011)
14. Littlewood, J.E.: A Mathematician's Miscellany. Methuen and Company (1953)
15. Liu, F., Wang, Y.: Reasoning about agent types and the hardest logic puzzle ever. Minds and Machines 23(1), 123–161 (2013)
16. Mahon, J.E.: Two definitions of lying. Journal of Applied Philosophy 22(2), 21–230 (2006)
17. Plaza, J.A.: Logics of public communications. In: Proc. of the 4th ISMIS, pp. 201–216. Oak Ridge National Laboratory (1989)
18. Rott, H.: Der Wert der Wahrheit. In: Mayer, M. (ed.) Kulturen der Lüge, pp. 7–34. Böhlau-Verlag, Köln und Weimar (2003)
19. Sakama, C.: Formal definitions of lying. In: Proc. of 14th TRUST (2011)
20. Sakama, C., Caminada, M., Herzig, A.: A logical account of lying. In: Janhunen, T., Niemelä, I. (eds.) JELIA 2010. LNCS (LNAI), vol. 6341, pp. 286–299. Springer, Heidelberg (2010)
21. Siegler, F.A.: Lying. American Philosophical Quarterly 3, 128–136 (1966)
22. Steiner, D.: A system for consistency preserving belief change. In: Proc. of the ESSLLI Workshop on Rationality and Knowledge, pp. 133–144 (2006)
23. Trivers, R.: The Folly of Fools – the logic of deceit and self-deception in human life. Basic Books (2011)
24. van Benthem, J.: Dynamic logic of belief revision. Journal of Applied Non-Classical Logics 17(2), 129–155 (2007)
25. van Ditmarsch, H.: Prolegomena to dynamic logic for belief revision. Synthese (Knowledge, Rationality & Action) 147, 229–275 (2005)
26. van Ditmarsch, H.: Comments on 'The logic of conditional doxastic actions'. In: New Perspectives on Games and Interaction. Texts in Logic and Games 4, pp. 33–44. Amsterdam University Press (2008)
27. van Ditmarsch, H.: Dynamics of lying. Synthese 191(5), 745–777 (2014)
28. van Ditmarsch, H., van der Hoek, W., Kooi, B.: Dynamic Epistemic Logic. Synthese Library, vol. 337. Springer (2007)
29. van Ditmarsch, H., van Eijck, J., Sietsma, F., Wang, Y.: On the logic of lying. In: van Eijck, J., Verbrugge, R. (eds.) Games, Actions and Social Software 2011. LNCS, vol. 7010, pp. 41–72. Springer, Heidelberg (2012)
30. van Emde Boas, P., Groenendijk, J., Stokhof, M.: The Conway paradox: Its solution in an epistemic framework. In: Truth, Interpretation and Information: Selected Papers from the Third Amsterdam Colloquium, pp. 159–182. Foris Publications, Dordrecht (1984)

Allocation in Practice*

Toby Walsh

NICTA and UNSW, Sydney, Australia
toby.walsh@nicta.com.au

Abstract. How do we allocate scarce resources? How do we fairly allocate costs? These are two pressing challenges facing society today. I discuss two recent projects at NICTA concerning resource and cost allocation. In the first, we have been working with FoodBank Local, a social startup working in collaboration with food bank charities around the world to optimise the logistics of collecting and distributing donated food. Before we can distribute this food, we must decide how to allocate it to different charities and food kitchens. This gives rise to a fair division problem with several new dimensions, rarely considered in the literature. In the second, we have been looking at cost allocation within the distribution network of a large multinational company. This also has several new dimensions rarely considered in the literature.

1 Introduction

The next decade will throw up some fundamental and deep challenges in resource and cost allocation that computer science can help solve.

Environmental challenges: the world's resources are under increasing pressure with threats like global warning, and with the impact of an increasing population. This will require us to find ways to allocate scarce resource more efficiently and more fairly. There will also be increasing pressure to allocate costs fairly to those consuming these resources.

Economic challenges: the fall out from the global financial crisis will continue, with fresh shocks likely to occur. With growth faltering, both government and industry will increasingly focus on efficiency gains. As wealth concentrates into the hands of a few, a major and highly topical concern will be equitability.

Technological challenges: new markets enabled by the internet and mobile devices will emerge. These markets will require computational mechanisms to be developed to allocate resources and share costs fairly and efficiently.

As an example of one of these new markets, consider users sharing some resources in the cloud. How do we design a mechanism that allocates CPU and memory to those users that reflects their different preferences, and that is fair and efficient? Such a mechanism needs to be computational. We will want to implement it so that it is highly

---

* The work described here is joint with many colleagues including: Martin Aleksandrov, Haris Aziz, Casey Cahan, Charles Grettom, Phil Kilby, Nick Mattei. NICTA is supported by the Australian Government through the Department of Communications and the Australian Research Council through the ICT Centre of Excellence Program. The author receives support from the Federal Ministry for Education and Research via the Alexander von Humboldt Foundation.

C. Lutz and M. Thielscher (Eds.): KI 2014, LNCS 8736, pp. 13–24, 2014.

responsive and runs automatically in the cloud. And users will want to implement computational agents to bid for resources automatically. As a second example of one of these new markets, consider sharing costs in a smart grid. How do we design a mechanism that shares costs amongst users that is fair and encourages efficiency? Such a mechanism again needs to be computational. We will want to implement it so that it is highly responsive and runs automatically over the smart grid. And users will again want to implement computational agents to monitor and exploit costs in the smart grid as they change rapidly over time.

There are a number of ways in which computation can help tackle such resource and cost allocation problems. First, computation can help us set up richer, more realistic models of resource and cost allocation. Second, within such computational models, users will be able to express more complex, realistic, combinatorial preferences over allocations. Third, computation can be used to improve efficiency and equitability, and to explore the trade off between the two. And fourth, users will increasingly farm out decision making to computational agents, who will need to reason rapidly about how resources and costs are allocated.

Central to many allocation problems is a trade off between equitability and efficiency. We can, for example, give each item to the person who most values it. Whilst this is efficient, it is unlikely to be equitable. Alternatively, we can allocate items at random. Whilst this is equitable, it is unlikely to maximise utility. Rather than accept allocations that are equitable but not efficient, or efficient but not equitable, we can now use computing power to improve equitability and efficiency. Computing power can also be used to explore the Pareto frontier between equitability and efficiency.

One related area that has benefitted hugely of late from the construction of richer computational models is auctions. Billions of dollars of business have been facilitated by the development of *combinatorial* auctions, transforming several sectors including procurement and radio spectrum allocation. We expect rich new models in resource and cost allocation will drive similar transformations in other sectors. It is perhaps not surprising that a transformation has already been seen in auctions where efficiency (but not equitability) is one of the main drivers. By comparison, many of the examples we give here are in the not-for-profit and public sector where criteria like equitability are often more important. Indeed, equitability is looking increasingly likely to be a major driver of political and economic reform over the next few decades. In the not-for-profit and public sector, research like this can quickly inform both practice and policy and thereby impact on society in a major way. Indeed, such richer models are now starting to be seen in one area of resource allocation, namely kidney exchange (e.g. [1]).

2 Allocation in Theory

The theoretical foundations of resource and cost allocation have been developed using simple abstract models. For example, one simple model for resource allocation is "cake cutting" in which we have a single resource that is infinitely divisible and agents with additive utility functions [2]. As a second example, a simple model for cost allocation in cooperative game theory supposes we can assign a cost to each subset of agents. As we will demonstrate shortly, abstract models like these ignore the richness and structure of many allocation problems met in practice. For example, allocation problems are often repeated. The problem we meet today is likely to be similar to the one we will meet tomorrow. As a second example, allocation problems are often online. We must start allocating items before all the data is available. As a third example, cost functions are often complex, and dependent on time and other features of the problem. Such real world features offer both a challenge and an opportunity. For instance, by exploiting the repeated nature of an allocation problem, we may be able to increase equitability without decreasing efficiency. On the other hand, the online nature of an allocation problem makes it harder both to be efficient and to be equitable.

Our long term goal then is to develop richer, more realistic computational models for resource and cost allocation, and to design mechanisms for such models that can be fielded in practice. Many of the new applications of such models will be in distributed and asynchronous environments enabled by the internet and mobile technology. It is here that computational thinking and computational implementation is necessary, and is set to transform how we fairly and efficiently allocate costs and resources. Hence, a large focus of our work is on applying a computational lens to resource and cost allocation problems. To this end, we are concentrating on designing mechanisms that work well in practice, even in the face of fundamental limitations in the worst case.

3 Allocation in Practice

We have two projects underway in NICTA which illustrate the richness of allocation problems met in practice.

3.1 Case Study #1: The Food Bank Problem

Consider the classical fair division problem. Fair division problems can be categorised along several orthogonal dimensions: divisible or indivisible goods, centralised or decentralised mechanisms, cardinal or ordinal preferences, etc [3]. Such categories are, however, not able to capture the richness of a practical resource allocation problem which came to our attention recently. FoodBank Local is a social startup founded by students from the University of New South Wales that is working with food bank charities around the world, as well as with us, to improve the efficiency of their operations. FoodBank Local won the Microsoft Imagine Cup in Australia in 2013, and were finalists worldwide for their novel and innovative approach to using technology for social good. After supermarkets, catering companies and the public have donated food, the food bank must allocate and distribute this food to charities in the local area. This requires solving a fair division problem. Fairness is important as charities often cater to different sectors of the population (geographical, social and ethnic), whilst efficiency is important to maximise the overall good. This fair division problem has several new dimensions, rarely considered in the literature.

Online: Offers of donated food arrive throughout the day. The food bank cannot wait till the end of the day before deciding how to allocate the donated food. This means we have an *online* problem, where decisions must be made before all the data is available.

Fig. 1. FoodBank Local's app for donating, allocating and distributing food

Repeated: Each day, a food bank repeats the task of allocating, collecting and distributing food with a similar amount of donated food and set of charities. The *repeated* nature of the problem provides fresh opportunities. For example, we can be somewhat unfair today, in the expectation that we will compensate tomorrow.

Unequal entitlements: The different charities working with the food bank have different abilities at feeding their clients. The allocation of food needs to reflect this.

Combinatorial: The different charities had complex, combinatorial preferences over the donated food. A charity might want the donated apples or the bananas but not both. Models based on simple additive utilities, like those often considered in the literature, are inadequate to describe their true preferences.

Constrained: There are various constraints over the allocations. For example, we must allocate all the foods requiring refrigeration to charities served by the same truck. As a second example, certain combinations of food cannot be put together for health and safety or religious reasons.

Mixed: Each allocation problem induces a new pickup and delivery problem. This means that we have a *mixed* problem that combines resource allocation and logistics. We need to both ensure a fair division whilst at the same time optimising distribution.

To reason about such issues, we need to develop more complex and realistic models of resource allocation that borrow techniques from related areas like constraint programming [4]. Note that some of these features have individually been considered in the past. For example, we recently initiated the study of online cake cutting problems [5] in which agents being allocated the cake arrive over time. In the FoodBank problem, by comparison, it is the goods that arrive over time. Our model of online cake cutting also has none of the other features of the FoodBank problem (e.g. the FoodBank problem is repeated and preferences are combinatorial, whilst in online cake cutting, the cake is cut only once and preferences are described by a simple additive utility function). As a second example, Guo, Conitzer and Reeves have looked at repeated allocation problems [6] but their study was limited to just to one indivisible good and had none of the other features of the FoodBank problem.

We now describe our first step in building a richer model for online fair division. We stress that this is only the *first* step in putting together a richer model that has more of the features required by FoodBank Local. There are many more features which we need to add before we have a model that is close to the actual requirements. Our online model supposes items arrive over time and each item must be allocated as soon as it arrives. For simplicity, we suppose one new item arrives at each time step. Again, as a first step, we also suppose that the utility of an agent for each item is either 0 or 1. A next step would be to consider more general utilities. A simple mechanism for this model is the *like* mechanism. Agents declare whether they like an item, and we allocate each item uniformly at random between the agents that like it.

We can study the axiomatic properties of such an online fair division mechanism. For instance, it is strategy proof (the agents have an incentive to like all items with non-zero utility and no incentive to like any item with zero utility)

Proposition 1. *The like mechanism is strategy proof.*

The like mechanism is also envy free as an agent will not have greater expected utility for another agent's items.

Proposition 2. *Supposing agents bid sincerely, the like mechanism is envy free ex ante.*

However, ex post, agents can have considerable envy for the actual allocation of items given to another agent. For example, one agent could get unlucky, lose every random draw and end up being allocated no items. This agent would then envy any agent allocated item which they like. We have therefore been designing more sophisticated mechanisms which are fairer ex post. A challenge is to do so without losing a good property like strategy proofness. We also need to explore how such mechanisms work in practice, and not just in the worst case. For example, in real world problems, agents' preferences are likely to be correlated. A tool that is likely useful in such studies is identifying computational phase transitions (e.g. [7–11]), as well as related phenomena like backbones and backdoors (e.g. [12–14]).

3.2   Case Study #2: Cost Allocation in a Complex Distribution Network

We have come across similar rich features in real world cost allocation problems. In particular, we have been working with a large multinational company which spends hundreds of millions of dollars each year on distributing fast moving consumer goods to 20,000 customers using a fleet of 600 vehicles. They face a very challenging problem of allocating costs between customers[1]. By working with us, they have saved tens of millions of dollars per annum.

A standard method to allocate costs is to use co-operative game theory and one of the well defined cost allocation mechanisms like the Shapley value which considers the marginal cost of a customer in every possible subset of customers. In reality, the

---

[1] These are not the actual costs charged to the customer but the costs used to decide if a customer is profitable or not. They are used as the basis for reorganising their business (e.g. changing distribution channels, renogiating contracts).

problem is much richer than imagined in a simple abstract model like the Shapley value which supposes we can simply and easily cost each subset of customers. This richness raises several issues which are rarely considered in the literature. Several of these issues are similar to those encountered in the last example. For instance, the cost allocation problem is repeated (every day, we deliver to a similar set of customers), and constrained (since we must deliver to all supermarkets of one chain or none, we must constrain the subsets of customers to consider only those with all or none of the supermarkets in the chain). However, there are also several new issues to consider:

Computational complexity: we need a cost allocation method that is computationally easy to compute. As we argue shortly, the Shapley value is computationally challenging to compute.

Heterogeneous customers: the Shapley value supposes customers are identical, which is not the case in our problem as different customers order different amounts of product. In addition, the trucks are constrained by volume, weight, and the number of stops. We therefore need principled methods of combining the marginal cost of each unit of volume, of each unit of weight, and of each customer stop.

Complex cost functions: a cost allocation mechanism like the Shapley value supposes a simple cost function for every subset of customers. However, the cost function in our cost allocation problem is much more complex. For example, it is made up of both fixed and variable costs. As a second example, the cost function is time dependent because of traffic whilst a mechanism like the Shapley value ignores time. As a third example, the cost function depends not just on whether we deliver to a customer or not but on the channel and delivery frequency.

Strategic behaviour: cooperative game theory supposes the players are truthful and are not competing with each other. In practice, however, we have business alliances where two or more delivery companies come together to share truck space to remote areas and must then share costs. We must consider therefore that the players may game the system by misrepresenting their true goals or costs.

Sensitivity analysis: in some situations, a small change to the customer base has a very large knock-on effect on marginal costs. We are therefore interested in cost allocations that are robust to small changes in the problem.

As before, some of these features have been considered individually in the past, but combinations of these features have not. For example, [15] looked at cost allocation in a vehicle routing game with a heterogeneous fleet of vehicles. However, this study considered the solution concepts of the core and the nucleolus rather than the Shapley value. The study also ignored other features of the actual real world problem like the repeated nature of the delivery problems and the full complexity of the cost function.

A naive method to allocate costs is simply to use the marginal cost of each customer. However, such marginal costs will tend to under-estimate the actual cost. Consider two customers in the middle of the outback. Each has a small marginal cost to visit since we are already visiting the other. However, their actual cost to the business is half the cost of travelling to the outback. Cost allocation mechanism like the Shapley value deal with such problems. The Shapley value equals the average marginal cost of a customer in *every* possible subset of customers. It has nice axiomatic properties like efficiency (it allocates the whole cost), anonymity (it treats all customers alike) and monotonicity (when the overall costs go up, no individual costs go down). However, we run into several complications when applying it to the our cost allocation problem.

One complication is that the Shapley value is computationally challenging to compute in general [16]. It involves summing an exponential number of terms (one for each possible subset of customers), and in our case each term requires solving to optimality a NP-hard routing problem. One response to the computational intractability of computing the Shapley value, is to look to approximate it. However, we have proved [17] that even finding an approximation to the Shapley value of a customer is intractable in general.

Proposition 3. *Unless P=NP, there is no polynomial time α-approximation to the Shapley value of a customer for any constant factor $\alpha > 1$.*

We have therefore considered heuristic methods based on Monte Carlo sampling [18, 19], and on approximating the cost of the optimal route. We have also considered simple proxies to the Shapley value like the depot distance (that is, allocating costs proportional to the distance between customer and depot). Unfortunately we were able to identify pathological cases where there is no bound on how poorly such proxies perform. These pathologies illustrate the sort of real world features of routing problems like isolated customers which can cause difficulties.

Proposition 4. *There exists a n customer problem on which Φ_{depot}/Φ goes to 0 as n goes to ∞, and another on which Φ/Φ_{depot} goes to 0 where Φ is the true Shapley value for a customer and Φ_{depot} is the estimate for it based on the proxy of distance from depot.*

Despite such pathological problems, we were able to show that more sophisticated proxies, especially those that "blend" together several estimates, work well in practice on real world data. Figure 1 illustrates the performance of two different sampling methods. It shows that in just a few iterations we can converge on estimates that are within 5-10% of the actual Shapley value.

There are other complications that we run into when allocating costs in this domain. For example, costs are not simple but made up of fixed and variable costs which depend on the size of the delivery. As a second example, costs depend on the time of day as traffic has a large impact on the problem. As a third example, customers should not be treated equally as they order different amounts of product, and delivery vehicles are limited by both the weight and volume of product that they can deliver. As a fourth example, there are supermarket chains that require us to deliver to all their supermarkets or none. We cannot choose some profitable subset of them. All these features need ultimately to be taken into account. We are thus only at the beginning of developing richer models of cost allocation for this domain. Nevertheless, we are encouraged by these preliminary results which have resulted in significant cost savings and greatly increased profits for our business partner.

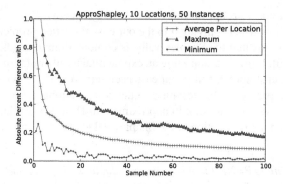

Fig. 2. Performance of the ApproShapley method [19] for Monte Carlo sampling to estimate the Shapley value in a distribution costs game. After just 100 iterations ApproShapley achieves an average error of less than 10% per location with a maximum error of less than 20%.

4 Related Work

A limited number of richer models for resource and cost allocation have been considered previously. However, such models have only considered a small number of the additional features that we have described here.

One sided markets: In an one sided market, we allocate items to agents based on the preferences of the agents. The market is one sided as the items do not have preferences over the agents. It covers the allocation of goods, the division of chores, roommates and other related problems. For example, in the roommates problems, agents express preferences over each other, and the goal is to pair these agents up subject to these preferences. There has been some work already to look at more realistic models of resource allocation in one sided markets. For example, we have proposed an online version of the cake cutting problem in which agents arrive over time [5]. As a second example, [6] looked at repeated allocation problems with a single indivisible good. As a third example, [20] studied the fair division problems of indivisible goods when agents do not have completely ordered preferences over the goods, but instead have dichotomous and other succinctly specified types of preferences. As a fourth example, [21] considered roommate problems in which agents can express ties in their preference lists rather than the basic assumption of completed ordered preferences. As a fifth example, [22] set up a dynamic version of fair division, proposed some desirable axiomatic properties for such dynamic resource allocation, and designed two mechanisms that satisfy these properties. However, real world features like those met in these five examples have usually been considered in isolation. For instance, there has not been proposed a model of resource allocation in an one sided market that is simultaneously online, repeated and involves preferences that go beyond totally ordered lists.

Two sided markets: In a two sided market, both sides of the market can have preferences over each other. For example, in a stable marriage problem, the women have preferences over the men they marry and vice versa. Another example of a two sided market is kidney exchange. There has been some work already to look at more realistic models in two sided markets. For example, in the hospital residents problem, a two sided problem in which we allocate residents to hospitals according to the preferences of the residents for the hospitals and of the hospitals for the residents, a number of real world features have been considered like couples [23], and ties in preference lists [24]. As a second example, in kidney exchange problems, a number of real world features have been considered like dynamic allocation [1], and probabilistic models of clearing (since many transplants never take place due to unforeseen logistical and medical problems) [25]. As a third example, the student-project allocation problem [26] generalises the hospital residents problem by adding capacity constraints. However, as with one side markets, such real world features have usually been considered in isolation and not in combination.

Cost allocation: Cost allocation has been widely studied in game theory and combinatorial optimisation [27–29]. Due to its good axiomatic properties, the Shapley value has been used in many domains [30]. A number of special cases have been identified where it is tractable to compute (e.g. [31]). However, due to the computational challenges we outlined, the Shapley value has rarely been used in the past in the sort of complex problems like the distribution problem discussed earlier. An exception is [32] which introduced the cooperative travelling salesperson (TSP) game. This also introduced the *routing game* in which the locations visited in a coalition must be traversed in a (given) fixed order. This gives a polynomial time procedure for computing cost allocations [33]. [34] developed a column generation procedure to allocate costs for a homogeneous vehicle routing problem. [15] extended this to a more practical setting of distributing gas using a *heterogeneous* fleet of vehicles. However, this study considered the solution concepts of the core and the nucleolus rather than the Shapley value. It also ignored other real world features like the repeated nature of such delivery problems. More recently [35] developed cost allocation methods for *inventory routing* problems in which customers have a capacity to hold stock, consume product at a fixed rate and the goal is to minimise costs whilst preventing stock-outs. Whilst this model has many real world features, it continues to miss others like inventory and delivery costs.

Related problems: There have been a number of complex markets developed to allocate resources which use money. For example, in a combinatorial auction, agents express prices over bundles of items [36]. Our two projects, however, only consider allocation problems where money is not transfered. Nevertheless, there are ideas from domains like combinatorial auctions which we may be able to borrow. For example, we expect the bidding languages proposed for combinatorial auction may be useful for compactly specifying complex, real world preferences even when money is not being transferred. As a second example, as occurs in some course allocation mechanisms used in practice, we can give agents virtual "money" with which to bid and thus apply an auction based mechanism [37, 38].

Finally, computational phase transitions have been observed in a number of related areas including constraint satisfaction [39–43], number partitioning [44, 45], TSP [46], social choice [47–49], and elsewhere [50–54]. We predict that a similar analysis of phase transitions will provide insight into the precise relationship between equitability and efficiency in allocation problems.

5 Conclusions

I have discussed two recent projects at NICTA involving resource and cost allocation. Each is an allocation problem with several new dimensions, rarely considered in the literature. For example, our resource allocation problem is online, repeated, and constrained, whilst our cost allocation problem is also repeated and constrained, and additionally involves a complex cost function. These projects suggest that models for allocation problems need to be developed that are richer and more complex than the abstract models which have been used in the past to lay the theoretical foundations of the field.

References

1. Dickerson, J., Procaccia, A., Sandholm, T.: Optimizing kidney exchange with transplant chains: Theory and reality. In: Proceedings of the 11th International Conference on Autonomous Agents and Multiagent Systems, AAMAS 2012, vol. 2, pp. 711–718. International Foundation for Autonomous Agents and Multiagent Systems (2012)
2. Brams, S., Taylor, A.: Fair Division: From cake-cutting to dispute resolution. Cambridge University Press, Cambridge (1996)
3. Chevaleyre, Y., Dunne, P., Endriss, U., Lang, J., Lemaitre, M., Maudet, N., Padget, J., Phelps, S., Rodriguez-Aguilar, J., Sousa, P.: Issues in multiagent resource allocation. Informatica (Slovenia) 30(1), 3–31 (2006)
4. Rossi, F., van Beek, P., Walsh, T. (eds.): Handbook of Constraint Programming. Foundations of Artificial Intelligence. Elsevier (2006)
5. Walsh, T.: Online cake cutting. In: Brafman, R.I., Roberts, F., Tsoukiàs, A. (eds.) ADT 2011. LNCS (LNAI), vol. 6992, pp. 292–305. Springer, Heidelberg (2011)
6. Guo, M., Conitzer, V., Reeves, D.M.: Competitive repeated allocation without payments. In: Leonardi, S. (ed.) WINE 2009. LNCS, vol. 5929, pp. 244–255. Springer, Heidelberg (2009)
7. Gent, I., Walsh, T.: Phase transitions from real computational problems. In: Proceedings of the 8th International Symposium on Artificial Intelligence, pp. 356–364 (1995)
8. Gent, I., Walsh, T.: Easy problems are sometimes hard. Artificial Intelligence, 335–345 (1994)
9. Gent, I., Walsh, T.: The SAT phase transition. In: Cohn, A.G. (ed.) Proceedings of 11th ECAI, pp. 105–109. John Wiley & Sons (1994)
10. Gent, I., Walsh, T.: The hardest random SAT problems. In: Proceedings of KI 1994, Saarbrucken (1994)
11. Gent, I., Walsh, T.: The satisfiability constraint gap. Artificial Intelligence 81(1-2) (1996)
12. Slaney, J., Walsh, T.: Backbones in optimization and approximation. In: Proceedings of 17th IJCAI, International Joint Conference on Artificial Intelligence (2001)
13. Kilby, P., Slaney, J., Thiebaux, S., Walsh, T.: Backbones and backdoors in satisfiability. In: Proceedings of the 20th National Conference on AI. Association for Advancement of Artificial Intelligence (2005)
14. Kilby, P., Slaney, J., Walsh, T.: The backbone of the travelling salesperson. In: IJCAI, pp. 175–180 (2005)

15. Engevall, S., Göthe-Lundgren, M., Värbrand, P.: The heterogeneous vehicle-routing game. Transportation Science 38(1), 71–85 (2004)
16. Chalkiadakis, G., Elkind, E., Wooldridge, M.: Computational aspects of cooperative game theory. Synthesis Lectures on Artificial Intelligence and Machine Learning 5(6), 1–168 (2011)
17. Aziz, H., Cahan, C., Gretton, C., Kilby, P., Mattei, N., Walsh, T.: A study of proxies for Shapley allocation of transport costs. Journal of Artificial Intelligence Research (Under review, 2014)
18. Mann, I., Shapley, L.S.: Values for large games IV: Evaluating the electoral college by monte carlo. Technical report, The RAND Corporation, Santa Monica, CA, USA (1960)
19. Castro, J., Gomez, D., Tejada, J.: Polynomial calculation of the Shapley value based on sampling. Computers & Operations Research 36(5), 1726–1730 (2009)
20. Bouveret, S., Lang, J.: Efficiency and envy-freeness in fair division of indivisible goods: Logical representation and complexity. Journal of Artificial Intelligence Research (JAIR) 32, 525–564 (2008)
21. Irving, R., Manlove, D.: The stable roommates problem with ties. J. Algorithms 43(1), 85–105 (2002)
22. Kash, I., Procaccia, A., Shah, N.: No agent left behind: Dynamic fair division of multiple resources. In: Proceedings of the 2013 International Conference on Autonomous Agents and Multi-agent Systems, AAMAS 2013, pp. 351–358. International Foundation for Autonomous Agents and Multiagent Systems, Richland (2013)
23. McDermid, E., Manlove, D.: Keeping partners together: algorithmic results for the hospitals/residents problem with couples. Journal of Combinatorial Optimization 19(3), 279–303 (2010)
24. Irving, R.W., Manlove, D.F., Scott, S.: The hospitals/residents problem with ties. In: Halldórsson, M.M. (ed.) SWAT 2000. LNCS, vol. 1851, pp. 259–271. Springer, Heidelberg (2000)
25. Dickerson, J., Procaccia, A., Sandholm, T.: Failure-aware kidney exchange. In: Proceedings of the Fourteenth ACM Conference on Electronic Commerce, EC 2013, pp. 323–340. ACM, New York (2013)
26. Abraham, D., Irving, R., Manlove, D.: Two algorithms for the student-project allocation problem. Journal of Discrete Algorithms 5(1), 73–90 (2007)
27. Koster, M.: Cost sharing. In: Encyclopedia of Complexity and Systems Science, pp. 724–753 (2009)
28. Curiel, I.: Cooperative combinatorial games. In: Chinchuluun, A., Pardalos, P., Migdalas, A., Pitsoulis, L. (eds.) Pareto Optimality, Game Theory and Equilibria. Springer Optimization and Its Applications, vol. 17, pp. 131–157. Springer, New York (2008)
29. Young, H.P.: Producer incentives in cost allocation 53(4), 757–765 (1985)
30. Young, H.P.: Cost allocation. In: Handbook of Game Theory with Economic Applications, vol. 2, pp. 1193–1235 (1994)
31. Mann, I., Shapley, L.S.: Values for large games IV: Evaluating the electoral college exactly. Technical report, The RAND Corporation, Santa Monica, CA, USA (1962)
32. Potters, J.A., Curiel, I.J., Tijs, S.H.: Traveling salesman games. Mathematical Programming 53(1-3), 199–211 (1992)
33. Derks, J., Kuipers, J.: On the core of routing games. International Journal of Game Theory 26(2), 193–205 (1997)
34. Göthe-Lundgren, M., Jörnsten, K., Värbrand, P.: On the nucleolus of the basic vehicle routing game. Mathematical Programming 72(1), 83–100 (1996)
35. Özener, O.O., Ergun, O., Savelsbergh, M.: Allocating cost of service to customers in inventory routing. Oper. Res. 61(1), 112–125 (2013)

36. Cramton, P., Shoham, Y., Steinberg, R.: Combinatorial Auctions. MIT Press (2006)
37. Sonmez, T., Unver, M.: Course bidding at business schools. International Economic Review 51(1), 99–123 (2010)
38. Budish, E., Cantillon, E.: The Multi-Unit Assignment Problem: Theory and Evidence from Course Allocation at Harvard. American Economic Review 102(5), 2237–2271 (2012)
39. Gent, I., MacIntyre, E., Prosser, P., Walsh, T.: Scaling effects in the CSP phase transition. In: Montanari, U., Rossi, F. (eds.) CP 1995. LNCS, vol. 976, pp. 70–87. Springer, Heidelberg (1995)
40. Gent, I., MacIntyre, E., Prosser, P., Walsh, T.: The constrainedness of search. In: Proceedings of the 13th National Conference on AI, pp. 246–252. Association for Advancement of Artificial Intelligence (1996)
41. Gent, I., MacIntyre, E., Prosser, P., Walsh, T.: The scaling of search cost. In: Proceedings of the 14th National Conference on AI, pp. 315–320. Association for Advancement of Artificial Intelligence (1997)
42. Walsh, T.: The constrainedness knife-edge. In: Proceedings of the 15th National Conference on AI. Association for Advancement of Artificial Intelligence (1998)
43. Gent, I., MacIntyre, E., Prosser, P., Smith, B., Walsh, T.: Random constraint satisfaction: Flaws and structure. Constraints 6(4), 345–372 (2001)
44. Gent, I., Walsh, T.: Phase transitions and annealed theories: Number partitioning as a case study. In: Proceedings of 12th ECAI (1996)
45. Gent, I., Walsh, T.: Analysis of heuristics for number partitioning. Computational Intelligence 14(3), 430–451 (1998)
46. Gent, I., Walsh, T.: The TSP phase transition. Artificial Intelligence 88, 349–358 (1996)
47. Walsh, T.: Where are the really hard manipulation problems? The phase transition in manipulating the veto rule. In: Proceedings of 21st IJCAI, International Joint Conference on Artificial Intelligence, pp. 324–329 (2009)
48. Walsh, T.: An empirical study of the manipulability of single transferable voting. In: Coelho, H., Studer, R., Wooldridge, M. (eds.) Proc. of the 19th European Conference on Artificial Intelligence (ECAI 2010). Frontiers in Artificial Intelligence and Applications, vol. 215, pp. 257–262. IOS Press (2010)
49. Walsh, T.: Where are the hard manipulation problems? Journal of Artificial Intelligence Research 42, 1–39 (2011)
50. Walsh, T.: Search in a small world. In: Proceedings of 16th IJCAI, International Joint Conference on Artificial Intelligence (1999)
51. Gent, I., Walsh, T.: Beyond NP: the QSAT phase transition. In: Proceedings of the 16th National Conference on AI. Association for Advancement of Artificial Intelligence (1999)
52. Gent, I., Hoos, H., Prosser, P., Walsh, T.: Morphing: Combining structure and randomness. In: Proceedings of the 16th National Conference on AI. Association for Advancement of Artificial Intelligence (1999)
53. Walsh, T.: Search on high degree graphs. In: Proceedings of 17th IJCAI, International Joint Conference on Artificial Intelligence (2001)
54. Walsh, T.: From P to NP: COL, XOR, NAE, 1-in-k, and Horn SAT. In: Proceedings of the 17th National Conference on AI. Association for Advancement of Artificial Intelligence (2002)

Applying Inductive Program Synthesis to Induction of Number Series – A Case Study with IGOR2*

Jacqueline Hofmann[1], Emanuel Kitzelmann[2], and Ute Schmid[3,**]

[1] University of Constance, Germany
jacqueline.hofmann@uni-konstanz.de
[2] Adam-Josef-Cüppers-Berufskolleg Ratingen, Germany
ekitzelmann@gmail.com
[3] Faculty Information Systems and Applied Computer Science,
University of Bamberg, 96045 Bamberg, Germany
ute.schmid@uni-bamberg.de

Abstract. Induction of number series is a typical task included in intelligence tests. It measures the ability to detect regular patterns and to generalize over them, which is assumed to be crucial for general intelligence. There are some computational approaches to solve number problems. Besides special-purpose algorithms, applicability of general purpose learning algorithms to number series prediction was shown for E-generalization and artificial neural networks (ANN). We present the applicability of the analytical inductive programming system IGOR2 to number series problems. An empirical comparison of IGOR2 shows that IGOR2 has comparable performance on the test series used to evaluate the ANN and the E-generalization approach. Based on findings of a cognitive analysis of number series problems by Holzman et al. (1982, 1983) we conducted a detailed case study, presenting IGOR2 with a set of number series problems where the complexity was varied over different dimensions identified as sources of cognitive complexity by Holzman. Our results show that performance times of IGOR2 correspond to the cognitive findings for most dimensions.

1 Introduction

The ability to reason inductively is one of the core features of any intelligent system (Holland, Holyoak, Nisbett, & Thagard, 1986; Schmid & Kitzelmann, 2011). In cognitive science research, inductive reasoning is considered as basic mechanism for knowledge expansion by exploiting previous experience (Tenenbaum, Griffiths, & Kemp, 2006). Inductive reasoning is also a central component of intelligence tests – often completion of number series is used to measure inductive reasoning ability. In the context of research on the Turing test

---

* The work reported here was conducted by Jacqueline Hofmann in her bachelor thesis in Applied Computer Science at University of Bamberg, Dec. 2012.
** Corresponding author.

C. Lutz and M. Thielscher (Eds.): KI 2014, LNCS 8736, pp. 25–36, 2014.

to evaluate machines, researchers proposed algorithms which are able to solve number series as one of several problems (Dowe & Hernández-Orallo, 2012).

Typically, a number series completion problem is presented as a series of numbers whose elements feature a special relation among one another which can be described algorithmically. To solve the series, a generalized pattern has to be identified in the given series and this pattern has then to be applied to generate the most plausible successor number. In the 1980s, Holzman et al. analyzed the influence of several characteristics of number series – like the magnitude of the starting value and the kind of operator involved in the series – on human performance (Holzman, Pellegrino, & Glaser, 1982, 1983). These characteristics can be used for systematic evaluation of computational approaches to number series problems and their comparison to human performance.

In general, computational approaches for number series induction can be intended as a cognitive model or as a general AI approach, they can be based on symbolic or sub-symbolic computation, and they can be designed specifically to solve number series or they can be realized as a specific application of a general induction algorithm. For example, Strannegård, Amirghasemi, and Ulfsbäcker (2013) proposed a special-purpose, symbolic, cognitive model which relies on pre-defined patterns and which addresses the (small) class of number series problems used in IQ tests. Siebers and Schmid (2012) presented a symbolic AI algorithm based on a pre-defined set of numerical operators (addition, subtraction, division, multiplication and exponentiation). Patterns which capture the regularity in a series are generated by analysis of the given numbers and hypotheses are enumerated based on a heuristics. Ragni and Klein (2011) presented an application of an artificial neural network (ANN) which was trained with a large number of examples of different partial sequences of a number series and learned to (approximately) predict the next number. Burghardt (2005) demonstrated that E-generalization can be applied to generate rules which capture the regularities in number series.

E-generalization extends the notion of anti-unification by the use of equational theories as background knowledge. For an equational theory E, a term t is the E-generalization or E-anti-unification of two terms t_1, t_2, if there are two substitutions σ_1, σ_2, such that $t\sigma_1 =_E t_1$ and $t\sigma_2 =_E t_2$, where $=_E$ denotes the smallest congruence relation containing all equations from E. Given equational theories for $+, *, if$ and *even*, examples can be generalized to patterns such as $v_p * v_p$ for $0, 1, 4, 9$, or *if(even(v_p), v_p, 1)* for $0, 1, 2, 1, 4, 1$ where v_p represents the current position.

Providing specialized algorithms which can deal with inductive reasoning problems typically used to measure human intelligence is interesting for cognitive science research. However, in our opinion, demonstrating that a general purpose machine learning algorithm can be successfully applied to such a task is of interest not only to cognitive AI research but for AI in general. Comparing the two general-purpose systems which have been applied to number series problems, in our opinion, E-generalization is the more convincing approach: In E-generalization, the generalization is based on the identification of the regularities in the number series and the most simple pattern which covers the series is constructed. In contrast, the ANN application is trained with many partial sequences of the original input. Furthermore, E-generalization learns a generalized rule which can not only be applied to predict the next number in the sequence but which can also be presented as an explanation for the proposed solution. In the ANN approach, on the other hand, the output is an approximative prediction of the next number in the sequence only.

Analytical approaches to inductive programming can be considered as a generalization of the E-generalization approach proposed by Burghardt. Inductive programming systems address the problem of generalizing recursive functional or logical programs from small numbers of input/output examples (Flener & Schmid, 2009). Like E-generalization, analytical approaches generate hypothetical programs by identifying regularities in the given examples and generalize over the found regularities. However, since the hypothesis language is a subset of the set of possible programs, the hypothesis space is larger than for E-generalization and therefore, inductive programming approaches have a larger scope. A current analytical system is IGOR2 (Kitzelmann, 2009). The authors of IGOR2 already demonstrated the applicability of IGOR2 to cognitive domains such as learning from problem solving, reasoning, and natural language processing (Schmid & Kitzelmann, 2011). For that reason, we identified IGOR2 as a suitable inductive programming system to investigate its applicability to automated induction of number series.

The rest of this paper is organized as follows: We shortly introduce IGOR2 and propose some ideas for the representation of number series as an inductive programming problem. Afterwards, we demonstrate that IGOR2 can be successfully applied to number series problems which were investigated by (Ragni & Klein 2011) and (Burghardt, 2005). We present a detailed case study we conducted to ascertain the specific characteristics of number series – including characteristics identified in psychological research – which influence the performance of IGOR2. We conclude with a short evaluation and discussion of future research.

2   Solving Number Series with IGOR2

IGOR2 is an inductive programming system which learns functional (MAUDE or HASKELL) programs from small sets of input/output examples. For instance, given examples for reversing a list with up to three elements, IGOR2 generalizes the recursive *reverse* function together with helper functions *last* and *init* (see Figure 1). IGOR2 relies on constructor-term-rewriting (Baader & Nipkow, 1998). That is, besides the examples for the target function, the data types have to be declared. For lists, the usual algebraic data type [a] = [] | a:[a] is used.

The algorithm of IGOR2 was developed from IGOR1 (Kitzelmann & Schmid, 2006) which is in turn based on Summers's inductive system THESYS (Summers, 1977). While many inductive programming systems are based on generate-and-test strategies (Quinlan & Cameron-Jones, 1993; Olsson, 1995; Katayama, 2005), IGOR2 uses an analytical, example-driven strategy for program synthesis. That is, generalized programs are constructed over detected regularities in the

I/O Examples

```
reverse  []  =  []        reverse  [a,b]    = [b,a]
reverse  [a] =  [a]       reverse  [a,b,c] = [c,b,a]
```

Generalized Program

```
reverse    []    = []
reverse (x:xs) = last (x:xs) : reverse(init (x:xs))
```

Automatically Induced Functions (*renamed* from $f1$, $f2$)

```
last [x]    = x           init [a]    = []
last (x:xs) = last xs     init (x:xs) = x:(init xs)
```

Fig. 1. Inductive Programming with IGOR2: Generalizing *reverse* from Examples

examples. IGOR2 incorporates concepts introduced in inductive logic programming (Muggleton & De Raedt, 1994), mainly, the possibility to use background knowledge (in form of additional functions which can be used while synthesizing a program besides the pre-defined constructors) and the invention of additional functions on the fly (see *init* and *last* in Figure 1). A detailed description of IGOR2 is given by Kitzelmann (2009), an empirical comparison of the performance of IGOR2 with other state-of-the-art inductive programming systems is given by Hofmann, Kitzelmann, and Schmid (2009).

The task of solving number series with IGOR2 differs from its primary application area, that is, induction of recursive functions over lists. However, IGOR2 was already applied successfully to several domains of cognitive rule acquisition, namely learning from problem solving, reasoning, and natural language processing (Schmid & Kitzelmann, 2011). Therefore, we consider the system a good candidate for an approach to solving number series. To apply IGOR2 for induction of a constructor-function which correctly describes and continues a given number series, as a crucial first step, we have to decide how to represent the needed data types, equations, and background knowledge.

Data Types. IGOR2 is able to handle any user defined data type. For our purpose, to represent sequences containing natural numbers, we needed constructors for numbers and for lists. Numbers are defined recursively by the base case 0 and the successor of a natural number, s. The list constructors are defined in the established form of the empty list and a constructor adding an element to an existing list.

Input/Output Equations. To make IGOR2 generalize over the given number series, the sequences have to be presented as input/output equations. There are different possibilities to represent number series in such a way: (1) The input can be presented as a list and the output as successor number, (2) the input can be presented as index position in the list and the output as number sequence up

(1) Input List – Output Successor Value

```
eq Plustwo((s 0) nil) = s^3 0
eq Plustwo((s^3 0) (s 0) nil) = s^5 0
eq Plustwo((s^5 0) (s^3 0) (s 0) nil) = s^7 0
```

(2) Input Position – Output List

```
eq Plustwo(s 0) = (s 0) nil
eq Plustwo(s^2 0) = (s^3 0)(s 0) nil
eq Plustwo(s^3 0) = (s^5 0)(s^3 0)(s 0) nil
eq Plustwo(s^4 0) = (s^7 0)(s^5 0)(s^3 0)(s 0) nil
```

(3) Input Position – Output Value

```
eq Plustwo(s 0) = s 0
eq Plustwo(s s 0) = s s s 0
eq Plustwo(s s s 0) = s s s s s 0
eq Plustwo(s s s s 0) = s s s s s s s 0
```

Fig. 2. Different Representations for the Number Series Problem PlusTwo (For representations (1) and (2) successor sequences are abbreviated for better readability)

to this position or (3) as the value at this position. An example for the number series PlusTwo $(1, 3, 5, 7)$ is given in Figure 2. To generalize a recursive function from the equations it is necessary to explicitly state every equation which could result from a recursive call of one of the given equations. Therefore, an example series $1, 3, 5, 7$ has to be represented by three equations for representation 1 and four equations for representations 2 and 3.

Background Knowledge. In the context of number series, IGOR2 has to be provided with knowledge about arithmetic operations. These operations can be specified as background knowledge (BK). BK is presented in the same manner as the input/output equations – with the only difference that there is no generalization on the BK equations. This means that every equation which could occur while inducing the series has to be defined explicitly. For example, for the series $2, 4, 8, 16$ we need to define $2 * 2 = 4$, $2 * 4 = 8$ and $2 * 8 = 16$, if we want IGOR2 to be able to use this BK by pattern matching. In this context, the BK given to IGOR2 corresponds to the way arithmetic knowledge is handled in other symbolic approaches such as action planning (Ghallab, Nau, & Traverso, 2004) or in cognitive architectures such as ACT-R (see, e.g., the model discussed in (Lebiere, 1999)). However, the number of equations – input/output as well as background knowledge – is critical for performance.

3   Comparing IGOR2 with E-Generalization and ANNs

We conducted a first test with IGOR2 on solving number series on the sequences which were tested with the ANN (Ragni & Klein 2011) and E-generalization

Table 1. Sample of series tested with ANN and IGOR2

By ANN and IGOR2:	7,10,9,12,11	$f(n-1)+3, f(n-1)-1$
By IGOR2 but not by ANN:	3,7,15,31,63	$2 * f(n-1)+1$
By ANN but not by IGOR2:	6,9,18,21,42	$f(n-1)+3, f(n-1)*2$
Not by ANN and not by IGOR2:	2,5,9,19,37	$f(n-1)*2+1, f(n-1)*2-1$

Table 2. Series solved by E-generalization and IGOR2

0,1,4,9	$v_p * v_p$	0,1,2,1,4,1	$if\ (ev(v_p); v_p; 1)$
0,2,4,6	$s(s(v_p))$	0,0,1,1,0,0,1,1	$ev(v_2)$
0,2,4,6	$v_p + v_p$	0,1,3,7	$s(v_1 + v_1)$
1,1,2,3,5	$v_1 + v_2$	1,2,2,3,3,3,4,4,4,4	—

(Burghardt, 2005) approaches. To examine the general ability to solve these number series we decided to test representations 1 and 2 for the input/output equations and set the time-out to 30 minutes.[1]

Ragni and Klein (2011) presented an initial evaluation of their ANN approach with 20 selected number series as well as an extensive evaluation with over 50,000 number series from the Online Encyclopedia of Integer Sequences (OEIS[2]). We tested IGOR2 with the initial 20 number series. The ANN approach could solve 17, IGOR2 14 of these series correctly. However, IGOR2 was able to correctly generalize two number series which no configuration of the networks was able to predict. Example series are given in Table 1. Here, the first problem was solved by IGOR2 without background knowledge, the second problem with multiplication as background knowledge. Note that the 14 problems were solved with *one instance* of IGOR2 while for ANN 840 network configurations were run where the highest number of series solved by one single network was 14.

To compare IGOR2 with the E-generalization approach we used the 8 example series reported in Burghardt (2005). The results show that both systems solve the same 7 series (see Table 2). Background knowledge for IGOR2 was addition and multiplication. Background knowledge for E-generalization was addition, multiplication, conditional expression, and even.

During this first test we were able to find some general constraints for IGOR2 on the task of correctly generalizing number series. Due to the chosen constructor-symbols which define a natural number as a successor of 0, we found that there is no elegant way to represent *negative numbers*. Even defining a predecessor constructor and binding it with the successor via background knowledge did not lead to success.

Another difficulty came up with *descending number series*. IGOR2 was able to solve these sequences with the needed background knowledge (e.g., division), but

---

[1] Note that run-times for IGOR2 are typically below 100 ms. Detailed performance results for IGOR2 on all three representations are given in section 4.

[2] https://oeis.org/

not with every kind of representation. Even if representation 1 (input: list, output: successor) is the most intuitive one, the input format restricts the solvability of number series. As the input represents the whole number series, it automatically restricts the possible input for the generalized function. If we want IGOR2 to generalize over $16, 8, 4$, the generalized function accepts as lower bound 4, because this is the smallest number presented in the input. This problem results from the definition of natural numbers as successors of natural numbers, which makes it easy for IGOR2 just to count up, but difficult to subtract some s from the given number.

The last limitation appeared by trying to solve *alternating sequences*. To date we were not able to implement some kind of separating function to split functions or divide them by the parity of the current position. Therefore, IGOR2 has only very restricted ability to solve alternating number series, yet. Solving alternating series is possible for IGOR2, if it is able to find a global operation of two or more alternating operations. E.g., for a number series alternating adding 3 and subtracting 1 (see first line in Table 1), IGOR2 induces the operation *add 2* to the pre-predecessor in the sequence. Otherwise, if one alternating sequence could be split up in two individual and independent series without intersection, IGOR2 is able to generalize the original sequence by simply pattern matching over the given elements. E.g., a constructor-function for the series $1, 2, 1, 4, 1$ (see Table 2) can be correctly induced by checking if the predecessor is 1 and if so, adding 2 to the pre-predecessor. If not, the induced function just appends 1 to the number series.

4   A Case Study on Solving Number Series

For a systematic evaluation of the performance of IGOR2 we systematically constructed number series varying in different characteristics. Several of these series are included in OEIS. The evaluation was conducted on a computer with Windows 7, Intel Core i5-2410M with 2.3 GHz and 8 GB RAM.

4.1   Materials

Holzman et al. defined a set of characteristics of number sequences which influence humans on their performance when solving such sequences (Holzman et al., 1982, 1983). Based on these findings we generated a set of 100 number series, varying in the following features: *Operator* $(+, *, */+, =)$, *Number of Operators* (1 or 2), *Magnitude of Starting Value* (low, high), *Magnitude of Argument* (low, high, variable), *Recursion* (linear, cascading), *Reference* (pre-/prepre-/prepreprepre-decessor, pre- and prepredecessor), *Position* (yes or no).

To be able to compare all three kinds of representation, we omitted operators producing descending number series, like $-$ or $/$. We had to distinguish the *magnitude of argument* for the operators. Multiplication by 2 was considered as low, multiplication by 3 as high. For addition, low is in the range of $2-4$ and high $11-13$. For the equivalence operator $(=)$ the argument is variable. *Magnitude of starting value* was defined as low in the range of $1-4$ for all operators and high in the range of $14-17$ for addition and $3-8$ for multiplication. *Reference* specifies the element in the number series from which the current value is calculated.

We used mostly number series of a length of five elements. Seven elements were used, if the reference is the preprepredecessor. The background knowledge for every number series was explicitly given and optionally used by IGOR2.

4.2 Hypotheses

Although this was the first time IGOR2 was applied on solving number series, we tried to formulate some assumptions of how it performs:

Assumption for Representations. As representation 1 offers the whole list to IGOR2 as input and just asks for the successor as output, we considered it to be the fastest representation. Furthermore, we expected representation 2 to be much slower than representation 3, because the output of the second version is the whole list, which means additional computation time.

Assumption for Reference. We expected IGOR2 to perform more slowly for larger distances between the reference value and the actual value. As the predecessor is available to IGOR2 before the preprepredecessor, IGOR2 will first try to build the constructor-function with the value which is available earlier before moving left in the sequence.

4.3 Results

Every number series was solved ten times by IGOR2 while we recorded the needed time to solve it in milliseconds. Although IGOR2 is a deterministic approach, some variations in run time typically occur, e.g., due to processes of the operating system.

Differences in Representations. With respect to the different representations, the results show that the means of the running times of representation 1 and 3 are quite similar (36 ms vs. 33 ms). Pairwise t-tests showed that there is no significant difference. However, there is a much higher variance in the running times of representation 1 than representation 3 (standard deviations 198 for representation 1 and 74 for representation 3). That is, representation 3 does not differ strongly in its individual results and is therefore more predictable. Representation 2 turned out to be significantly ($p < 0.001$) slower than the others with a mean of 83 ms.

Furthermore, we examined the interaction between the kind of representation and a) the operator and b) the reference in the series with two-factorial ANOVAs and Tukey post-hoc tests. Interaction-analysis showed significant ($p < 0.001$) differences for the *representations* and *operators*. As the Tukey post-hoc analysis showed, the operators $=$ and $+$ differed significantly within the representations.

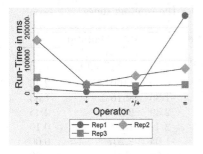
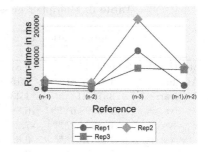

Fig. 3. Interaction of Representation Format and Operator (a) / Reference (b)

This result is illustrated in Figure 3(a). The interaction between *representation* and *reference* in the sequence showed no significant effect. As shown in Figure 3(b), the shapes of the graphs look quite similar, except for the reference point of pre- and pre-predecessor, where inference times for representation 3 were slightly (but not significantly) slower than for representation 1.

Regression Model To Predict Running Time. To assess the relative influence of the different characteristics of the number series, we conducted a multiple regression analysis for the varied characteristics. We excluded the features recursion and number of operators because they can be explained completely through other features (like reference and operator). The parameter position was also ignored because of an imbalanced distribution of the frequencies of its characteristics. The coefficients of the analysis are shown in table 3. As we used dummy variables for all parameters within the model, there are no different scales whereby the coefficients can be directly compared. The model explains 23.98%, 32.48% and 26.40% of the variances of representations 1, 2, and 3.

The magnitude of sequence elements has a comparable impact for all three representations. A higher magnitude of the starting value leads to a significant rise of the mean running time. The magnitude of the argument, however, shows less impact, but also the tendency for higher running times for higher magnitudes.

Regarding the kind of operator, the influence on different representations differ from each other. As interaction-analysis has already shown, the running times of representation 1 are significantly higher for the equivalence operator than for the others. In contrast, representation 3 shows the tendency to be faster for the equivalence operator than for the others. However, this tendency becomes only significant in comparison to addition. For representation 2, running times for addition are significantly higher than for the equivalence-relation, whereas multiplication could be solved significantly faster.

The coefficients for the references were much more surprising. In contrast to our initial assumption, the nearer the reference the faster the algorithm, the regression analysis shows different results. The running times for referring to the pre-predecessor instead of the predecessor do not show significant differences. Even a

Table 3. Multiple regression-analysis for the running times

	Representation 1		Representation 2		Representation 3	
	B	t	B	t	B	t
Starting Value	69343.9***	6.31	127320.7***	11.21	52832.8***	13.07
Arg_high	1905.3	0.15	10659.6	0.80	11601.1*	2.43
Arg_var	33752.1	1.43	-33008.2	-1.36	8916.3	1.03
+ vs. =	-188598.6***	-6.89	67657.0*	2.39	24700.3*	2.45
* vs. =	-198261.2***	-7.24	-68438.0*	-2.42	1587.0	0.16
*/+ vs. =	-199648.3***	-6.69	-59873.6	-1.94	2.207	0.00
(n-2)	-72.65	-0.00	-10445.2	-0.69	-9711.4	-1.80
(n-3)	120029.7***	8.17	192171.5***	12.66	48409.7***	8.96
((n-1),(n-2))	6682.1	0.24	54458.6	1.92	34595.5***	3.42
β_0	128650.5***	3.97	-16099.1	-0.48	-22568.5	-1.89

Table 4. *

* $p < 0.05$ ** $p < 0.01$ *** $p < 0.001$
B = unstandardized coefficient

small tendency to faster running times for the pre-predecessor can be seen (as co-efficients are negative). By moving the reference one step further left, the running times become significantly slower than before for all three representations.

4.4   Interpretation

The results of the ANOVAs as well as the regression analysis illustrate in general that with higher values within the number series the running times rise. The fact that the magnitude of the starting value has a much higher influence than that of the argument can be explained by the use of background knowledge. As mentioned above, we decided to explicitly give the needed background knowledge to IGOR2. Therefore, if the argument to be added to an existing value is 3 or 13 does not make a strong difference. Nevertheless, the model shows a tendency towards faster running times for lower arguments, which results from the general increasing values in the number series if a larger argument is added.

Regarding the results of the influence of the kind of operator, the discovered differences are not very evident. The significant increase of the running time for representation 1 for the equivalence operator resulted from the very high running times for two number series with the operator =. Unfortunately, we were not able to detect the reason for these values.

Only about a third of the existing variance within the independent variable running time can be explained with the presented model. However, we expected these values to be a lot higher because we have generated the series completely from the parameters covered in the model. Deeper analyses of the concrete running time values for each number series did not reveal any further systematic variance. We recognized that IGOR2s performance varied strongly by minimal changes of the values of the elements. As our model represents the magnitudes nominally instead of metrically, we developed a second model for a subset of the number series to see if this explains more variance within the variable. The new model explained a total of 32,12% of the existing variance for representation 1.

5   Conclusions and Further Work

We could demonstrate that the general-purpose inductive programming system IGOR2 can be applied to solve number series problems. To our knowledge, most approaches to number series induction are based on algorithms specifically designed for this problem class. Two applications of general-purpose algorithms previous to our IGOR2 experiments are the ANN approach of Ragni and Klein (2011) and the application of E-generalization by (Burghardt, 2005). We could demonstrate that IGOR2 can solve a superset of series solvable with E-generalization. Even compared to the ANN approach, its scope is acceptable and IGOR2 can solve some types of series not solvable by the ANN.

Performance constraints of IGOR2 are due to the use of background knowledge and its limited ability to deal with negative numbers and alternating sequences. In our evaluation we presented only those arithmetic operations in background knowledge which were necessary to solve a series. This is necessary because matching examples against background knowledge results in exponential growth of run time. This problem could be reduced by providing a pre-filtering of the possibly needed background knowledge. To deal with negative numbers, one could think of an extra implementation of integers and not only natural numbers. For solving alternating series, it is necessary to implement some kind of query to rely on invariances, such as the parity of the actual position. As a next step, we plan to introduce such extensions.

In our opinion, the generic induction algorithm underlying IGOR2 can be seen as one possible realization of a cognitive rule acquistion device. In Schmid and Kitzelmann 2011 we could show that IGOR2 can be applied to learn generalized strategies for Tower of Hanoi and other problem solving puzzles. In this paper we demonstrated that the same algorithm can be applied to number series problems.

References

Baader, F., Nipkow, T.: Term rewriting and all that. Cambridge University Press (1998)

Burghardt, J.: E-generalization using grammars. Artificial Intelligence 165, 1–35 (2005)

Dowe, D.L., Hernández-Orallo, J.: IQ tests are not for machines, yet. Intelligence 40(2), 77–81 (2012)

Flener, P., Schmid, U.: An introduction to inductive programming. Artificial Intelligence Review 29(1), 45–62 (2009)

Ghallab, M., Nau, D., Traverso, P.: Automated planning: Theory and practice. Morgan Kaufmann, San Francisco (2004)

Hofmann, M., Kitzelmann, E., Schmid, U.: A unifying framework for analysis and evaluation of inductive programming systems. In: Goerzel, B., Hitzler, P., Hutter, M. (eds.) Proceedings of the Second Conference on Artificial General Intelligence (AGI 2009), Arlington, Virginia, March 6-9, pp. 55–60. Atlantis Press, Amsterdam (2009)

Holland, J., Holyoak, K., Nisbett, R., Thagard, P.: Induction – Processes of inference, learning, and discovery. MIT Press, Cambridge (1986)

Holzman, T.G., Pellegrino, J.W., Glaser, R.: Cognitive dimensions of numerical rule induction. Journal of Educational Psychology 74(3), 360–373 (1982)

Holzman, T.G., Pellegrino, J.W., Glaser, R.: Cognitive variables in series completion. Journal of Educational Psychology 75(4), 603–618 (1983)

Katayama, S.: Systematic search for lambda expressions. Trends in Functional Programming, 111–126 (2005)

Kitzelmann, E.: Analytical inductive functional programming. In: Hanus, M. (ed.) LOPSTR 2008. LNCS, vol. 5438, pp. 87–102. Springer, Heidelberg (2009)

Kitzelmann, E., Schmid, U.: Inductive synthesis of functional programs: An explanation based generalization approach. Journal of Machine Learning Research 7, 429–454 (2006)

Lebiere, C.: The dynamics of cognition: An ACT-R model of cognitive arithmetic. Kognitionswissenschaft 8(1), 5–19 (1999)

Muggleton, S., De Raedt, L.: Inductive logic programming: Theory and methods. Journal of Logic Programming, Special Issue on 10 Years of Logic Programming 19-20, 629–679 (1994)

Olsson, R.: Inductive functional programming using incremental program transformation. Artificial Intelligence 74(1), 55–83 (1995)

Quinlan, J.R., Cameron-Jones, R.M.: FOIL: A midterm report. In: Brazdil, P.B. (ed.) ECML 1993. LNCS, vol. 667, pp. 3–20. Springer, Heidelberg (1993)

Ragni, M., Klein, A.: Predicting numbers: An AI approach to solving number series. In: Bach, J., Edelkamp, S. (eds.) KI 2011. LNCS, vol. 7006, pp. 255–259. Springer, Heidelberg (2011)

Schmid, U., Kitzelmann, E.: Inductive rule learning on the knowledge level. Cognitive Systems Research 12(3), 237–248 (2011)

Siebers, M., Schmid, U.: Semi-analytic natural number series induction. In: Glimm, B., Krüger, A. (eds.) KI 2012. LNCS, vol. 7526, pp. 249–252. Springer, Heidelberg (2012)

Strannegård, C., Amirghasemi, M., Ulfsbäcker, S.: An anthropomorphic method for number sequence problems. Cognitive Systems Research 22-23, 27–34 (2013)

Summers, P.D.: A methodology for LISP program construction from examples. Journal ACM 24(1), 162–175 (1977)

Tenenbaum, J., Griffiths, T., Kemp, C.: Theory-based Bayesian models of inductive learning and reasoning. Trends in Cognitive Sciences 10(7), 309–318 (2006)

Algorithmic Debugging and Literate Programming to Generate Feedback in Intelligent Tutoring Systems

Claus Zinn

Department of Computer Science, University of Konstanz
claus.zinn@uni-konstanz.de

Abstract. Algorithmic debugging is an effective diagnosis method in intelligent tutoring systems (ITSs). Given an encoding of expert problem-solving as a logic program, it compares the program's behaviour during incremental execution with observed learner behaviour. Any deviation captures a learner error in terms of a program location. The feedback engine of the ITS can then take the program clause in question to generate help for learners to correct their error. With the error information limited to a program location, however, the feedback engine can only give remediation in terms of what's wrong with the current problem solving step. With no access to the overall hierarchical context of a student action, it is hard to dose scaffolding help, to explain why and how a step needs to be performed, to summarize a learner's performance so far, or to prepare the learner for the problem solving still ahead. This is a pity because such scaffolding helps learning. To address this issue, we extend the meta-interpretation technique and complement it with a program annotation approach. The expert program is enriched with terms that explain the logic behind the program, very much like comments explaining code blocks. The meta-interpreter is extended to collect all annotation in the program's execution path, and to keep a record of the relevant parts of the program's proof tree. We obtain a framework that defines sophisticated tutorial interaction in terms of Prolog-based task definition, execution, and monitoring.

1 Introduction

The core part of an intelligent tutoring system can be based upon logic programming techniques. The expert knowledge that learners need to acquire is represented as a Prolog program, and the meta-interpretation technique *algorithmic debugging* is used to diagnose learners' problem solving steps. Algorithmic debugging meta-interprets the expert program in an incremental manner. At any relevant stage, it compares its behaviour with the behaviour of the student by making use of a mechanised Oracle. Any deviation between observed learner behaviour to Prolog-encoded expert behaviour is captured in terms of a program location. The deviation can be used by the feedback component of the ITS to address learners' incorrect or incomplete answers. Given the program

C. Lutz and M. Thielscher (Eds.): KI 2014, LNCS 8736, pp. 37–48, 2014.

clause in question, the feedback engine generates remediation or hints to help learners overcome the error. The feedback engine, however, has no access to the overall hierarchical context of the program clause in question, and also has no information about a learner's past performance and the problem solving steps still ahead. An engine deprived of such information is not capable of generating more sophisticated feedback to further support student learning and motivation. It is also a pity because Prolog's hierarchical encoding of expert knowledge must surely be beneficial to tackling this issue quite naturally. If, in addition, the expert program would be annotated with terms that explain the role of each relevant clause in the overall context, we could further harness the potential of logic programming techniques for computer-aided education. In this paper, we:

- define a simple program annotation language. Each relevant program clause modeling a skill can be associated with a term that describes its use and role in the overall program;
- extend algorithmic debugging to collect all annotations it encounters on the execution path, and to keep a record of all skills tackled; and
- specify a feedback engine that exploits the wealth of information provided by the algorithmic debugger.

A prototype has been implemented to test and show-case our innovative approach to authoring intelligent tutoring systems, and which defines tutorial interaction in terms of task definition, execution and monitoring.

2   Background

Shapiro's algorithmic debugging technique defines a systematic manner to identify bugs in programs [6]. It is based upon a dialogue between the programmer (the author of the program) and the debugging system. In the top-down variant, using the logic programming paradigm, the program is traversed from the goal clause downwards. At each step during the traversal of the program's AND/OR tree, the programmer is taking the role of the *Oracle*, and answers whether the currently processed goal holds or not. If the Oracle and the buggy program agree on the result of a goal G, then algorithmic debugging passes to the next goal on the goal stack. Otherwise, the goal G is inspected further. Eventually an *irreducible disagreement* will be encountered, hence locating the program's clause where the buggy behaviour is originating from.

Algorithmic debugging can be used for tutoring [7] when Shapiro's algorithm is turned on its head: the expert program takes the role of the buggy program, and the student takes on the role of the programmer. Now, any irreducible disagreement between program behaviour and given answer indicates a *student's* potential error.

We give an example. For this, consider multi-column subtraction as domain of instruction. Fig. 1 depicts the entire cognitive model for multi-column subtraction using the decomposition method. The Prolog code represents a subtraction problem as a list of column terms (M, S, R) consisting of a minuend M, a subtrahend S, and a result cell R. The main predicate subtract/2 determines the

subtract(*PartialSum*, *Sum*) ←
   length(*PartialSum*, *LSum*),
   mc_subtract(*LSum*, *PartialSum*, *Sum*).

mc_subtract(_, [], []).
mc_subtract(*CurCol*, *Sum*, *NewSum*) ←
   process_column(*CurCol*, *Sum*, *Sum1*),
   shift_left(*Sum1*, *Sum2*, *ProcessedColumn*),
   CurCol1 **is** *CurCol* − 1,
   mc_subtract(*CurCol1*, *Sum2*, *SumFinal*),
   append(*SumFinal*, [*ProcessedColumn*], *NewSum*).

process_column(*CurCol*, *Sum*, *NewSum*) ←
   last(*Sum*, *LastColumn*), **allbutlast**(*Sum*, *RestSum*),
   subtrahend(*LastColumn*, *Sub*), **minuend**(*LastColumn*, *Min*),
   Sub > *Min*,
   CurCol1 **is** *CurCol* − 1,
   decrement(*CurCol1*, *RestSum*, *NewRestSum*),
   add_ten_to_minuend(*CurCol*, *LastColumn*, *LastColumn1*),
   take_difference(*CurCol*, *LastColumn1*, *LastColumn2*),
   append(*NewRestSum*, [*LastColumn2*], *NewSum*).

process_column(*CurCol*, *Sum*, *NewSum*) ←
   last(*Sum*, *LastColumn*), **allbutlast**(*Sum*, *RestSum*),
   subtrahend(*LastColumn*, *Sub*), **minuend**(*LastColumn*, *Min*),
   Sub =< *Min*,
   take_difference(*CurCol*, *LastColumn*, *LastColumn1*),
   append(*RestSum*, [*LastColumn1*], *NewSum*).

shift_left(_CurCol, *SumList*, *RestSumList*, *Item*) ←
   allbutlast(*SumList*, *RestSumList*), **last**(*SumList*, *Item*).

add_ten_to_minuend(*CurCol*, (*M*, *S*, *R*), (*NM*, *S*, *R*)) ←
   irreducible, *NM* **is** *M* + 10.

decrement(*CurCol*, *Sum*, *NewSum*) ← **irreducible**,
   last(*Sum*, (*M*, *S*, *R*)), **allbutlast**(*Sum*, *RestSum*),
   M == 0,
   CurCol1 **is** *CurCol* − 1,
   decrement(*CurCol1*, *RestSum*, *NewRestSum*),
   NM **is** *M* + 10, *NM1* **is** *NM* − 1,
   append(*NewRestSum*, [(*NM1*, *S*, *R*)], *NewSum*).

decrement(*CurCol*, *Sum*, *NewSum*) ← **irreducible**,
   last(*Sum*, (*M*, *S*, *R*)),
   allbutlast(*Sum*, *RestSum*),
   ⊬ (*M* == 0)
   NM **is** *M* − 1,
   append(*RestSum*, [(*NM*, *S*, *R*)], *NewSum*).

take_difference(*CurCol*, (*M*, *S*, _R), (*M*, *S*, *R*)) ← **irreducible**,
   R **is** *M* − *S*.

minuend((*M*, _S, _R), *M*).
subtrahend((_M, *S*, _R), *S*).

irreducible.

Fig. 1. The Decomposition Method for Subtraction

number of columns and passes its arguments to `mc_subtract/3`.[1] This predicate processes columns from right to left until all columns have been processed and the recursion terminates. The predicate `process_column/3` receives a partial sum, and processes its right-most column (extracted by `last/2`). There are two cases. Either the column's subtrahend is larger than its minuend, when a borrowing operation is required, or the subtrahend is not larger than the minuend, in which case we can subtract the former from the latter (calling `take_difference/3`). In the first case, we add ten to the minuend (`add_ten_to_minuend/3`) by borrowing from the left (calling `decrement/3`). The decrement operation also has two clauses, with the second clause being the easier case. Here, the minuend of the column left to the current column is not zero, so we simply reduce the minuend by one. If it is zero, we need to borrow again, so `decrement/3` is called recursively. When we return from recursion, we add ten to the minuend, and then reduce it by one.

Consider three solutions to the task of solving the subtraction '32 – 17': Fig. 2(a) depicts the correct solution, Fig. 2(b) an instance of the no-payback error, and Fig. 2(c) a situation with no problem solving steps.

	2	12			12			
	~~3~~	~~2~~		3	~~2~~		3	2
-	1	7	-	1	7	-	1	7
=	1	5	=	2	5	=		
(a) correct			(b) no payback			(c) no steps		

Fig. 2. A correct and two incorrect answers

For the solution shown in Fig. 2(b), our variant of algorithmic debugging generates this dialogue between expert system and the learner:

```
> algo_debug(subtract([(3,1,S1),(2,7,S2)], [(3,1,2),(12,7,5)],ID).

do you agree that the following goal holds:
 subtract([(3,1,R1),(2,7,R2)],          [(2,1,1),(12,7,5)])        |: no.
 mc_subtract(2,[(3,1,R1),(2,7,R2)],     [(2,1,1),(12,7,5)])        |: no.
 process_column(2,[(3,1,R1),(2,7,R2)],  [(2,1,R1),(12,7,5)])       |: no.
 decrement(1,[(3,1,R1)],[(2,1,R1)])                                |: no.

ID = (decrement(1,[(3,1,R1),(2,1,R1)]),missing)
```

The dialogue starts with the program's top clause, where a disagreement is found, follows the hierarchical structure of the program, until it ends at a leaf node with an irreducible disagreement that locates the learner's "no payback" error in the decrement skill.

[1] The argument `CurCol` is passed onto most other predicates; it is used to help automating the Oracle and to support the generation of feedback.

With the mechanisation of the Oracle [7], it is not necessary for learners to respond to Prolog queries (or more readable variants thereof). All answers to Oracle questions can be derived from a learner's (potentially partial) answer to a subtraction problem.

Once a program clause has been identified as irreducible disagreement, our previous system used a template-based mechanism for verbalisation, mapping *e.g.*, the disagreement `decrement(1,[(3,1,R1),(2,1,R1)]),missing)` to the natural language feedback "you need to decrement the minuend in the tens" [7].

Note however, that the learner's partial answer in Fig. 2(c) has algorithmic debugging to return the same irreducible disagreement, also by traversing the same intermediate nodes of the proof tree. Consequently, we also generated the same feedback, which left us with a feeling of unease and pedagogical inadequacy. A learner giving the solution in Fig. 2(b), a full albeit incorrect answer, should get a different response than the learner in Fig. 2(c) who provided none of the steps. In general, we believe that the analysis of learner input could profit from embedding the irreducible disagreement in the overall task context. Hence, we will need to enhance our algorithmic debugger to collect *all* relevant information from the program's proof tree. Moreover, we will annotate the expert model with additional information about the logic behind each relevant program clause.

3   Program Annotation Language

Comments are a construct that allow programmers to annotate the source code of a computer program. Comments are used, *e.g.*, to outline the logic behind the code rather than the code itself, to explain the programmer's intent, or to summarize code into quick-to-grasp natural language. In general, comments are ignored by compilers and interpreters, and this also holds for Prolog.

We will use comments in the spirit of the literate programming idea [4]. Our comments construct is a regular Prolog predicate with no effect on the program's semantics. Each comment goal is bound to succeed, and has access to variable bindings in its vicinity:

@comment(*Str*, *Arg*) ← (**format**(*Str*, *Arg*), !) ; **true**.

The predicate `@comment/2` is thus mostly syntactic sugar for Prolog's built-in `format/2` predicate. It has two arguments: a string with format specifications, and a list of associated arguments.

Fig. 3 shows a fragment of the expert model for multi-column subtraction, now enriched with comments. Consider the first clause `process_column/3`, which has two comments. Both comments make use of the Prolog goal `get_label/2` that converts the number denoting the current column to a natural language label such as "ones" or "tens" and writes it to the `current_output` stream. The string is then inserted in the result string of `@comment/2`.

The feedback engine assumes that `@comment/2` constructs within the same clause are ordered from low to high specificity. The first occurrence of `@comment/2` in `process_column/3` gives away less information than its second occurrence.

With the annotation, we obtain this execution trace of the expert model:

subtract(*PartialSum*, *Sum*) ← **length**(*PartialSum*, *LSum*),
  @comment('Subtract␣the␣two␣numbers␣with␣the␣decomposition␣method.',[]),
  @comment('Columns␣are␣processed␣from␣left␣to␣right.', []),
  mc_subtract(*LSum*, *PartialSum*, *Sum*).

mc_subtract(_, [], []) ← @comment('Problem␣solved.~n', []).
mc_subtract(*CurCol*, *Sum*, *NewSum*) ←
  @comment('Now,␣process␣the␣~@␣column.~n', get_label(*CurCol*)),
  process_column(*CurCol*, *Sum*, *Sum1*), *CurCol1* **is** *CurCol* − 1,
  shift_left(*CurCol1*, *Sum1*, *Sum2*, *ProcessedColumn*),
  mc_subtract(*CurCol1*, *Sum2*, *SumFinal*),
  append(*SumFinal*, [*ProcessedColumn*], *NewSum*).

process_column(*CurCol*, *Sum*, *NewSum*) ← **last**(*Sum*, *LastColumn*), [...],
  subtrahend(*LastColumn*, *Sub*), [...], *Sub* > *Min*, *CurCol1* **is** *CurCol* − 1,
  @comment('In␣the␣~@,␣cannot␣take␣away␣~d␣from␣~d.',
          [get_label(*CurCol*), *Sub*, *Min*]),
  @comment('Need␣to␣borrow␣from␣the␣~@␣before␣taking␣differences.~n',
          [get_label(*CurCol1*)]), [...]

Fig. 3. Annotation of the Expert Program (Fragment)

Subtract the two numbers with the decomposition method. Columns are processed from right to left. Now, process the units column. In the units, cannot take away 7 from 2. Need to borrow from the tens before taking differences. Reduce the minuend in the tens. Do this by scoring out the 3 and writing a small 2. Add ten to the minuend. For this, put the figure 1 (representing one tens = 10 units) in front of the 2 units to obtain 12 units. Subtract 7 from 12 to yield 5. Put the figure 5 in the units column. Now, process the tens column. In the tens, the minuend is larger or equal to the subtrahend. Subtract 1 from 2 to yield 1. Put the figure 1 in the tens column. Problem solved.

Clearly, only selected, situation-specific, parts will be required for tutoring.

4   Extension of Meta-interpretation

The algorithmic debugger that meta-interprets the expert program to identify a learner's error needs to be augmented in three ways:

- rather than terminating with the first irreducible disagreement found, it now traverses the entire program;
- it must keep a record of all the goals visited during code walking;
- it must collect all program annotation attached to goals.

Fig. 4 depicts the enhanced meta-interpreter. The predicate adebug/5 gets five arguments: a goal, and input and output arguments for agreements and disagreements, respectively. Four cases are distinguished. If the goal is a goal structure (Goal1, Goal2), then the goal Goal1 is processed first. The results of the first recursive call, updated values for agreements AINTER and disagreements DINTER,

adebug(($Goal1$, $Goal2$), AIN, $AOUT$, DIN, $DOUT$) ←
  adebug($Goal1$, AIN, $AINTER$, DIN, $DINTER$),
  adebug($Goal2$, $AINTER$, $AOUT$, $DINTER$, $DOUT$).

adebug($Goal$, AIN, $AOUT$, DIN, $DOUT$) ←
  on_discussion_table_p($Goal$), !,
  copy_term($Goal$, $CopyGoal$), **call**($Goal$),
  ask_oracle($Goal$, $Answer$),
  ($Answer$ = **yes**
  →
    (**get_annotation**($Goal$, Ann),
      $AOUT$ = [**agr**($Goal$, Ann, DIN)|AIN], $DOUT$ = DIN))
  ;
    (**get_applicable_clause**($CopyGoal$, $Clause$, Ann),
     (**irreducible_clause**($Clause$)
     →
      ($AOUT$ = AIN, $DOUT$ = [**irrdis**($Goal$, Ann)|DIN])
     ;
      adebug($Clause$, AIN, $AOUT$, [**dis**($Goal$, Ann)|DIN], $DOUT$)
     )))

adebug($Goal$, A, A, D, D) ←
  system_defined_predicate($Goal$), !, **call**($Goal$).

adebug($Goal$, AIN, $AOUT$, DIN, $DOUT$) ←
  clause($Goal$, $Clause$), **adebug**($Clause$, AIN, $AOUT$, DIN, $DOUT$).

Fig. 4. Extended Meta-Interpreter

are passed on to the recursive call to process `Goal2`. The other tree cases process atomic goals. If the `Goal` is relevant enough to be discussed with the Oracle (`on_discussion_table_p/1` holds), we check whether expert behaviour and Oracle agree on the results of calling `Goal`. If we obtain an agreement, we update `AOUT` and `DOUT` accordingly. A record is kept on the agreement, its annotation as well as its history, *i.e.*, its path to the root node, where each node on the path has been disagreed upon. If expert program and Oracle disagree, the disagreement must be examined further. We identify an applicable clause that corresponds to `Goal` – a clause is applicable when its body succeeds when evaluated. If the goal belongs to a clause marked `irreducible`, the disagreement is atomic, and we update the variables `AOUT` and `DOUT` accordingly. Otherwise, we continue to explore the execution tree below `Goal` to identify the irreducible disagreement. The last two clauses of `adebug/5` handle the cases where `Goal` is a built-in predicate, and where `Goal` is not on the discussion table. In the latter, the goal's body is investigated.

If we run algorithmic debugging with an expert program, the learner's answer, and the Oracle, we obtain all the program clauses where learner behaviour matches expert behaviour, and all program clauses where there is no such match. Each agreement and each irreducible disagreement is decorated with the execution path and its annotations.

5   Feedback Engine

We illustrate the design rationale of the feedback engine by reconsidering the two erroneous learner's solutions to the task of solving the subtraction '32 − 17'.

5.1   Rationale

For the first solution in Fig. 2(b), the new algorithmic debugger returns two irreducible disagreements: a missing payback operation located at `decrement/3`, and an incorrect difference in the tens at `take_difference/3`. Also, there are two irreducible agreements: the learner correctly added ten to the minuend in the ones at `add_ten_to_minuend/3`, and also took the correct difference in this column at `take_difference/3`. For Fig. 2(c), the algorithmic debugger returns four irreducible disagreements: there are missing operations for decrementing the minuend in the tens, adding ten to the minuend in the ones, taking differences in the ones, and taking differences in the tens. Each of the (dis)-agreements is embedded in its hierarchical structure, and is associated with its annotations.

Both solutions share the same first irreducible disagreement, with the same path to the expert model's top clause. Our old approach, where algorithmic debugging terminates with the first irreducible disagreement, generated only a single feedback candidate to both learners:

`decrement/3` *Reduce the minuend in the tens. Do this by scoring out the 3 and writing a small 2.*

Our new approach exploits the hierarchical context of the first irreducible disagreement and we get these candidates for both of Fig. 2(b) and Fig. 2(c):

`decrement/3` *Reduce the minuend in the tens. Do this by scoring out the 3 and writing a small 2.*
`process_column/3` *In the units, cannot take away 7 from 2. Need to borrow from the tens before taking differences.*
`mc_subtract/3` *Now, process the ones column*
`subtract/2` *Subtract the two numbers using the decomposition method. Columns are processed from left to right.*

For Fig. 2(c), it is rather inappropriate to start with the first and most specific feedback candidate. There is no single agreement in the proof tree, and all irreducible disagreements are of type missing. Here, it is rather better to start with the least-specific feedback associated with the top node, and then to proceed downwards, if necessary.

For Fig. 2(b), it is more appropriate to consider more specific feedback early. Rather than starting with the most specific feedback at `decrement/3`, we back-up to its parent node, which has two child nodes that expert and learner behaviour agree upon. We consider such feedback to be more natural as it acknowledges a learner's past achievements. For Fig. 2(b), we obtain these candidates:

`process_column/3` *In the units, cannot take away 7 from 2. Need to borrow from the tens before taking differences.*

  `add_ten_to_minuend/3` *Add(ten to the minuend.*

  `take_difference/3` *Subtract 7 from 12 to yield 5.*

`decrement/3` *Reduce the minuend in the tens. Do this by scoring out the 3 and writing a small 2.*

Whenever there is a candidate node that is parent to child nodes that have been agreed upon, the annotations attached to all nodes are verbalised together. For each child node, however, only the least specific feedback is given to learners.

5.2 Algorithm

Whenever the learner asks for help, the current problem solving state is read and sent to the algorithmic debugger for analysis. The list of agreements and disagreements returned are then passed onto the feedback engine, see Fig. 5. The engine's task is to process all information and to compute a sequence of candidate nodes and their associated annotations. For this, `feedback_engine/3` will use the first irreducible agreement and its hierarchical embedding `DPath`. If there is a path to a parent node with agreement children, it will use these nodes as candidate nodes; otherwise it will take the path to the top node and use it in reverse order. The engine takes the first element from the candidate list that does not appear in the dialogue history. Once a `@comment/2` is realized, it is added to the dialogue history. When a user repeatedly clicks on help without advancing the problem solving state, a bottom-out hint will be eventually generated that advances the problem solving state. A subsequent run of the algorithmic debugger will hence return other (dis-)agreement structures, until the task at hand is solved.

give_feedback(*As*, *Ds*) ← **feedback_engine**(*As*, *Ds*, *Acts*),
  realize_acts(*Acts*).

feedback_engine(*As*, *Ds*, *Acts*) ←
  get_first_disagreement_path(*Ds*, *DPath*),
  (**path_to_parent_with_agr**(*As*, *DPath*, *ParentPath*, *AgrNodes*)
  → **combine_nodes**(*ParentPath*, *AgrNodes*, *CandidateNodes*)
  ; **reversePath**(*DPath*, *CandidateNodes*)
  ),
  extract_comments(*CandidateNodes*, *Acts*).

realize_acts(*Acts*) ← **member**(*A*, *Acts*),
  dialogue_history(*DH*), ⊬ **member**(*A*, *DH*), **realize_act**(*A*).

Fig. 5. Feedback Engine

6   Discussion

There is little recent research in the ITS community that builds upon logic programming. In [2], Beller & Hoppe use a fail-safe meta-interpreter to identify student error. A Prolog program, encoding the cognitive model, is executed by instantiating its output parameter with the student answer. While standard Prolog interpretation would fail, a fail-safe meta-interpreter can recover from execution failure, and can also return an execution trace. Beller & Hoppe formulate error patterns which are then matched against the execution trace, and where each successful match indicates a plausible student bug.

In [7], we have presented our first meta-interpreter approach to analyse learner input in intelligent tutoring systems. In this initial version, algorithmic debugging terminated with the first irreducible disagreement between Prolog-encoded expert and observed learner behaviour. The disagreement was then directly verbalised by the feedback engine to help learners correct their error. All student actions that were in line with the expert model were ignored. In this paper, we address the drawback and keep a record of all agreements and deviations between expert and learner behaviour and also maintain their hierarchical embedding. Also, we now attach comments to each clause of the expert model.

The association of feedback messages to cognitive models is nothing new. In tutoring systems driven by production rules, expert skills are represented as expert rules and anticipated erroneous behaviour is being simulated by an encoding of buggy rules. Fig. 6 depicts a production rule taken from the the CTAT tutor [1]. It represents one of the skills for adding fractions. The rule's IF-part lists a number of conditions that are checked against the content of a global working memory that captures the current problem solving state. If all conditions are met, the actions in the THEN-part are carried out, usually changing the contents of the working memory. In the THEN part, we find a message construct that is directly used for the generation of remedial feedback. Tutoring systems based on production rules systems perform *model tracing*. After each and every student step, the rule system is executed to identify a rule that can reproduce a learner's action. When such a rule if found, its associated feedback is produced. Each student action is thus being commented on, advancing a tutorial dialogue context by continually tracking student actions. Model-tracing tutors thus keep learners on a tight leash. They have little opportunity to explore different solutions paths; with every step, they are exposed to potentially corrective feedback.

In constraint-based tutors, the correctness of learner input in diagnosed in terms of a *problem state*, given a set of constraints that test whether relevant aspects of the state are satisfied or not. Each relevant but unsatisfied constraint is flagged as potential source of error; its associated feedback message is given to the learner, see Fig. 7. As constraint-based models do not model learner action, there is no hierarchy of skills. Also, developers of constraint-based systems must cope with situations where more than a single relevant constraint is unsatisfied. In ASPIRE's fraction addition tutor, this is addressed by artificially partitioning the problem solving state into discrete units, where the next unit can only be tackled when the current one has been successfully completed. The set of constraints is

```
(defrule one-denominator-multiple-of-other
    (declare (salience 200))
    ?problem <- (problem
        (given-fractions $? ?f1 $?)
        (subgoals))
    ?problem <- (problem (given-fractions $? ?f2 $?))
    (test (not (eq ?f1 ?f2)))
    ?f1 <- (fraction (denominator ?denom1))
    ?f2 <- (fraction (denominator ?denom2)
        (has-converted-form ?conv))
    ?denom1 <- (textArea (value ?d1&:(neq ?d1 nil)))
    ?denom2 <- (textArea (value ?d2&:(neq ?d2 nil)))
    (test (= 0 (mod ?d1 ?d2)))
=>
    (bind ?sub1 (assert (convert-fraction-goal (fraction ?f2)
        (denominator-value ?d1))))
    (bind ?sub2 (assert (add-fractions-goal (fractions ?f1 ?conv))))
    (modify ?problem (subgoals ?sub1 ?sub2))
    (construct-message
        "[ What denominator could you use to add the two fractions? ]"
        "[ Since " ?d1 " is a multiple of " ?d2 ", use " ?d1 " as the
        denominator of the sum fraction.   ]"
    ))
```

Fig. 6. A Production Rule, see [1]

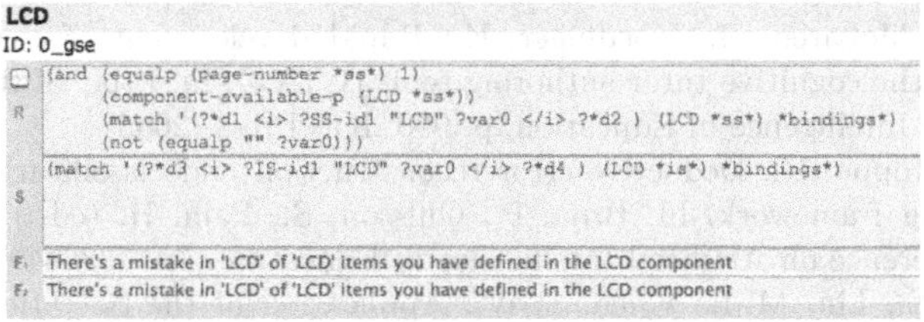

Fig. 7. An ASPIRE constraint, see [5]

de facto divided into subsets that correspond to units. Similar to model tracing, this restricts learners exploring the solution space.

In our approach, learners only get feedback when they explicitly ask for it, and learners may ask for help early or late in their problem solving process. Each help request starts algorithmic debugging anew, now taking into account and acknowledging all learner actions. Hence, we can now create a more natural tutorial dialogue context, which is a huge improvement to our earlier work [7].

7   Conclusion

In this paper, we extend our previous work on using logic programming and meta-level techniques for the analysis of learner input in intelligent tutoring systems. We modified algorithmic debugging to traverse the entire proof tree, and to mark each node as agreeing or disagreeing with learner behaviour. Following the spirit of literate programming, we enrich the expert model with comments that explain the role of each relevant clause in natural language. This is a rather straightforward idea, and very much in line with the feedback structures attached to production rules or constraints. In combination with algorithmic debugging, the anytime-feedback capability, and the hierarchical representation of expertise, this simple idea is rather powerful, yielding to the generation of sophisticated feedback that is very hard to replicate in the other two approaches.

In the future, we would like to use a fully-fledged natural language generation engine to make generation more flexible (*e.g.*, variation in lexicalisation; tense and formality of language). Also we would like to extend learners' ability to contribute to the dialogue. Instead of pressing the help button, they shall be able to click on any subtraction cell to get help specific to the cell in question. Moreover, we would like to manage multi-turn Socratic dialogues were learners are lead to discover and correct their misconceptions (*e.g.*, [3]). Here, we anticipate the need for additional annotations of the task structure. To further test-drive, validate and fine-tune our approach, we will also implement different domains to explore the use of hierarchically organised annotations and their use to support learning.

References

1. Aleven, V., McLaren, B., Koedinger, K.: Rapid development of computer-based tutors with the cognitive tutor authoring tools (CTAT). In: Proc. of the Int'l Conf. on Artificial Intelligence in Education, p. 990. IOS Press (2005)
2. Beller, S., Hoppe, U.: Deductive error reconstruction and classification in a logic programming framework. In: Brna, P., Ohlsson, S., Pain, H. (eds.) Proc. of the World Conference on Artificial Intelligence in Education, pp. 433–440 (1993)
3. Chang, K.-E., Lin, M.-L., Chen, S.-W.: Application of the Socratic dialogue on corrective learning of subtraction. Computers & Education 31, 55–68 (1998)
4. Knuth, D.E.: Literate programming. Computer Journal 27(2), 97–111 (1984)
5. Mitrovic, A., Martin, B., Suraweera, P., Zakharov, K., Milik, N., Holland, J., McGuigan, N.: Aspire: An authoring system and deployment environment for constraint-based tutors. Int. J. of Artif. Intell. in Educ. 19(2), 155–188 (2009)
6. Shapiro, E.Y.: Algorithmic Program Debugging. ACM Distinguished Dissertations. MIT Press (1983), Thesis (Ph.D.) – Yale University (1982)
7. Zinn, C.: Algorithmic debugging to support cognitive diagnosis in tutoring systems. In: Bach, J., Edelkamp, S. (eds.) KI 2011. LNCS (LNAI), vol. 7006, pp. 357–368. Springer, Heidelberg (2011)

A Note on Chances and Limitations of Psychometric AI

Tarek Richard Besold

Institute of Cognitive Science, University of Osnabrück,
49069 Osnabrück, Germany
tbesold@uni-osnabrueck.de

Abstract. Human-level artificial intelligence (HAI) surely is a special research endeavor in more than one way: In the first place, the very nature of intelligence is not entirely clear; there are no criteria commonly agreed upon necessary or sufficient for the ascription of intelligence other than similarity to human performance (and even this criterion is open for a plethora of possible interpretations); there is a lack of clarity concerning how to properly investigate HAI and how to proceed after the very first steps of implementing an HAI system; etc. In this note I assess the ways in which the approach of Psychometric Artificial Intelligence [1] can (and cannot) be taken as a foundation for a scientific approach to HAI.

1 Introduction

From a certain perspective AI seems to stand out between the modern sciences for more than one reason: Neither is there agreement upon what shall be AI's overall objective (i.e., whether the purpose of AI is the implementation of technical systems supporting humans in their everyday tasks and facilitating human intellectual activity, or if the purpose of AI is the creation of a computer system exhibiting general intelligence — in doing so possibly outperforming humans in tasks requiring reasoning and thought —, or something in between these two extremes), nor is there a commonly accepted methodology for conducting research in AI, nor is there consensus concerning the valuation of previous developments and of the actual status quo in AI as a story of success or perpetual failure.

These and related observations repeatedly caused philosophers of science and even some researchers from within AI to wonder about AI being a special type of science, or to even question (and occasionally finally deny) the status of AI as a science. In this note, specifically focussing on the subbranch of AI dealing with human-level AI (HAI), I want to undertake a critical review of Psychometric AI (PAI) [1] which has been proposed as a strictly scientific approach and conceptual framework suitable for measuring, evaluating, and guiding progress during the development of an HAI system.

2 Introducing Psychometric AI

Psychometric AI [1] aims to apply the full battery of techniques from psychometrics to an HAI context, setting its internal standard by declaring an agent as intelligent if and only if it does well in all established, validated tests of intelligence.[1] PAI as a dedicated

---

[1] This definition of PAI actually only is approximate and partially incomplete. For the actual detailed phrasing see the following section introducing and discussing PAI in detail.

C. Lutz and M. Thielscher (Eds.): KI 2014, LNCS 8736, pp. 49–54, 2014.

research program was first explicitly institutionalized a decade ago in [1] and has been actively worked on since (as, e.g., documented by the articles collected in [2]).

2.1 Psychometrics and Intelligence

Psychometrics as a field is by definition concerned with analyzing and developing means of psychological measurement as, for instance, personality assessments or questionnaires for measuring certain abilities or knowledge. For doing so, psychometrics engages in the study of theoretical approaches to measurement as well as in the active development and implementation of the corresponding concrete instruments and procedures. For a long time special interest has been taken in the measurement of the phenomena commonly subsumed under the term "intelligence": There is a wide variety of psychometric tests of intelligence, ranging from tests with only one type of item to varied batteries of different questions, combining verbal and non-verbal items and requiring subjects to perform qualitatively very different tasks (e.g., spatial tasks as opposed to language-related tasks).

2.2 Psychometrics and Artificial Intelligence

The goal of PAI now is to carry over the quantitative assessment of intelligence from the realm of classical psychometrics into artificial intelligence. In his programmatic papers [1,3,4], Bringsjord introduces PAI as a research program and discusses various objections critics might have.

Naive Psychometric AI: The first attempt at defining what it means for an agent (human or artificial) to be intelligent, given in [1] and repeated in the later publications, reads as follows: "*Some agent is intelligent if and only if it excels at all established, validated tests of intelligence.*"

So in this account, which I will refer to as "naive PAI" (nPAI) in the following, AI in its entirety is reduced to a strictly psychometric core, namely the construction of a system which outperforms most humans in all currently available intelligence tests. Clearly, as also noticed by Bringsjord, this definition is overly narrow and insufficient for the purpose of building an HAI. Even the most advanced and broad battery of items has to be considered as too narrow when compared to the full range of cognitive capacities seen in humans. And also from a system engineer's perspective, given that at any point in time there will only be a finite number of commonly accepted tests of intelligence available, the maxim underlying nPAI seems dubious: Each of the individual capacities could be addressed by a specifically dedicated standalone subsystem, so that intelligence would actually be reduced to correctly selecting and executing the respective module from a finite number of available subprograms based on a finite number of possible input categories. But this could hardly be considered satisfactory as an answer to the intelligence puzzle for anyone but diehard followers of Descartes: At least the Cartesian would be comforted in that the resulting AI — being an almost ideal instantiation of a "type-c machine" [5] — might be able to pass any test for a particular set of cognitive capacities, whilst still failing a test for any mental power whatsoever.

General Psychometric AI: A second, more commonly used definition of PAI, to which I will henceforth refer as "general PAI" (gPAI), is also introduced in [1]: "*Psychometric*

AI is the field devoted to building information-processing entities capable of at least solid performance on all established, validated tests of intelligence and mental ability, a class of tests that includes not just the rather restrictive IQ tests, but also tests of artistic and literary creativity, mechanical ability, and so on."

Clearly, gPAI intuitively feels a lot like the classical Turing Test [6]. And this impression is not unfounded: Having a look at Harnad's Total Turing Test (TTT; [7]) as modernized and (possibly) broadened version of Turing's original proposal, we notice that — due to the simple mass of possible test methods, presentation modalities and required modes of interaction — a solution to gPAI would most likely also serve as an important step towards solid performance on the TTT. Conversely, a system convincingly solving the TTT most likely would also encompass the ability to solve gPAI.

So instead of focusing exclusively on the classical psychometric battery of tests for intelligence, gPAI widens its focus to also encompass all other available tests for cognitive capacities whatsoever. As there are now at least two possible reading to this claim. In order to avoid misunderstandings, let us clarify what in all probability is the intended meaning of this statement: Although the definition could be read as universally quantified statement in a strong sense, demanding from a system trying to accomplish gPAI to solve all possible tests for all conceivable mental capacities which might be validated at some point, this does not seem meaningful as a standard for evaluation.[2] In light of these considerations what is meant by the description of gPAI quoted above is the requirement for an AI system to pass, at a given point in time, all available validated psychometric tests for any kind of mental ability. So although the number of possible tests would still be enormous, gPAI would in this reading (contrary to the first possible interpretation) nonetheless be dealing with a finite and well-defined set of tests; the significant difference to nPAI resulting from opening up the scope of the tests from a strict focus on tests of intelligence to also include other mental abilities in general.

3   (Dis)Advantages of Psychometric AI for Guiding HAI

Let us return to the initial considerations concerning the use of PAI as means of guidance and assessment for the development of human-level artificial intelligence.

3.1   The Beauty of Numbers: What PAI Can Do

The great advantage of an approach such as PAI over, for instance, the (Total) Turing Test is the quantitative nature of the used evaluation method. Psychometric methods and tests are metric by their very nature, they are designed to provide assessments in terms of numbers on a scale. This clearly has already two advantages by itself: On the one hand, if psychometrics is applied in the evaluation of an artificial agent the result is a number which is at first glance directly comparable to the results of other systems on the same test(s). There is no question of how to compare outcomes of different evaluation

---

[2] Especially not since gPAI claims superiority over the Turing Test/Total Turing Test amongst others also for being — from an engineering perspective — in its goals and conditions of success less elusive and for almost automatically enforcing a more feasible and manageable approach by gPAI's test-based nature (see [1] for details).

runs, the standardized nature of the testing technique is meant to take care of these and similar issues. On the other hand, this also allows for a fairly unquestionable measure of progress, both due to the applied evaluation method as well as due to the overall goal of the PAI approach. A higher score on a particular battery of tests simply and straightforwardly indicates that the examined agent has advanced towards the target of performing decently on the respective tests. And, in turn, the term "decently" is (at least for HAI) also clearly defined by, for example, the average outcome human test subjects achieve on the tests under consideration; so even problems surrounding optimality criteria and/or the choice of an appropriate normative dimension seem to be addressable by the framework.

These advantages should by no means be underappreciated. Research in HAI has in many ways suffered from a lack of quantitative assessment methods for its systems: Neither could researchers easily compare the performance of their different agents and AIs, nor could they themselves know whether and how well they were advancing in the outcomes of their work. In summary, PAI does offer several very pleasant properties which many other paradigms lack and, I believe, can with a clear conscience be recommended for consideration as a solution to everyone whose main concern lies with having a research program with completely transparent and hard-to-question means of evaluation. Still, as will be discussed in the following subsection, this comes at a price which casts serious doubt on the applicability of PAI in HAI, and even the satisfiability of PAI's own goals by means of PAI.

3.2   A (Possibly) Fatal Flaw: What PAI Cannot Do

HAI has been characterized as the endeavor to create computer systems that exhibit intelligence at a level similar to humans. This by itself is ambiguous in many ways as neither "exhibit" nor "intelligence" are well-defined in the given context. Against this background, PAI[3] now offers clear specifications for both terms, equating a system's exhibition of intelligence with its performance on a huge variety of psychometric tests for different mental capacities — the act of solving the tests becomes the active demonstration, the resulting scores define the (level of) intelligence. But it is here where a quite troublesome conceptual flaw in the PAI framework comes to light.

[1] justifies the reliance on psychometrics as crucially defining criterion of an agent's intelligence as follows: *"What's intelligence? (...) [M]ost thinkers seem to forget that there is a particularly clear and straightforward answer available, courtesy of the field that has sought to operationalize the concept in question; that field is psychometrics. Psychometrics is devoted to systematically measuring psychological properties, usually via tests. These properties include the one most important in the present context: intelligence."*

But this reading of psychometrics and the relation between its tests and the respective objects of investigation unfortunately turns out to be overly simplistic. Psychometric tests do not directly measure any mental ability as, for example, intelligence or creativity. There even is no unanimously agreed upon definition of what exactly intelligence is

---

[3] As already discussed above, nPAI (when seen in an HAI context) clearly seems to be overly simplistic in many ways. As, moreover, it is trivially subsumed under the notion of gPAI I will in the following argument without loss of generality only refer to the latter notion.

as a mental faculty and what its defining characteristics would be; and the same holds for many other high-level cognitive capacities. Psychometric measures are correlational measures, measuring the performance of traits which are commonly associated (and assumed to be strongly positively correlated) with what is considered intelligence — and even these correlations are in part justified merely by plausibility arguments and general agreement within the respective research community.

Therefore, what PAI actually trains its systems on (and measures them against) is not a standard for human-like intelligence of what form soever, but are benchmarks for better defined, more or less clearcut cognitive capacities which are quite plausibly intimately related and/or part of what is considered human intelligence. But even when taking the entirety of available psychometric tests available at a specific point in time (as proposed by gPAI) and having a system succeed on them, we still would only be dealing with placeholders and parts without any guarantee at all that an immediate measure of "human intelligence" would implicitly or explicitly have emerged from within the collection of different tests (leaving . In a way similar to the case of a person suffering from the savant syndrome [8], when an AI should exceed human performance on all available psychometric means of assessment of intelligence or other high-level mental abilities, all we would know for sure is that the system performs better on the tested correlated tasks — but nothing would be revealed about whether the system is "truly intelligent" in the general way typically developing humans are deemed to be.

Clearly, a strict behaviorist would disagree with this conclusion as at least from the exclusively behavior-oriented point of view human and machine would be indistinguishable in their performance on the applied psychometric tests. But at the same time, even from this perspective, it could not be excluded that there might still be the possibility of some aspect of intelligence that simply had not yet been accounted for in the available battery of measures — so even under a behaviorist angle the verdict that solving PAI guarantees that human-level intelligence has been achieved by an artificial intelligence would require a considerable leap of faith.

4   Comparison to Related Work and Conclusion

Trying to establish an adequate standard for ascertaining the level of human-like intelligence an artificial agent has achieved goes back to the very beginning of AI research — one might even say that the field started out from this question in [6]. Thus it should not come by surprise that by now there is a remarkable variety of tests on the market, two of them being the above mentioned original Turing Test and Harnad's expansion of it, the Total Turing Test. As already discussed, Total Turing Test and gPAI seem to share a close relationship in terms of their generality and requirements. Unfortunately, this closeness also makes them share a weakness usually brought forth against the Turing Test (and thus even more applicable to the more general TTT): Amongst others, [9,10] remark that the Turing Test might be effectively useless as a test of machine intelligence as for passing it something similar to a "*human subcognitive substrate*" [9] would be needed. For a task like the Turing Test this seems fairly straightforward, as the machine would have to make sure that it can reflect all the behaviors produced by low- and mid-level cognitive structures in humans. And to a lesser degree, this also holds for PAI:

Amongst the battery of eligible psychometric tests there also are items which assess not only high-level capacities, but which move down in the cognitive hierarchy.

Still, PAI indeed has at least one advantage over the Turing Test, the TTT, and most (if not all) other versions and variants thereof: Contrary to them, due to its reliance exclusively on quantitative psychometrics tests, PAI offers a well-defined goal and the option of quantifying progress towards meeting it, getting rid of the seemingly unavoidable vagueness and ambiguity in the evaluation of a system's performance. From a purely engineering-oriented perspective, this argument should not be dismissed too easily — it should just always be kept in mind at which price this clarity is obtained.

Going back to the original undertaking of this note, trying to address the question whether PAI can serve as a guiding force for HAI, tying it even closer to standard scientific procedures, the answer as so often is not a simple "Yes." or "No.", but rather a "Up to a certain point.". On the one hand, it surely will have to be the case that an actual HAI system eventually must be able to perform well on psychometric tests, so using a wide variety of the latter as means of quantitatively assessing progress in HAI has to be seen as beneficial. On the other hand, it cannot be presumed that excelling on all available validated psychometrical measures at any point in time will guarantee that an artificial system has reached human-level intelligence. In summary, PAI unfortunately still will not serve as a final methodological answer deciding the question for human-level intelligence in artificial systems and, thus, falls fundamentally short of its own promises.

References

1. Bringsjord, S., Schimanski, B.: What is Artificial Intelligence? Psychometric AI as an Answer. In: Proceedings of the 18th International Joint Conference on Artificial Intelligence (IJCAI 2003). Morgan Kaufmann (2003)
2. Bringsjord, S.: Psychometric artificial intelligence. Journal of Experimental & Theoretical Artificial Intelligence, JETAI 23(3) (2011)
3. Bringsjord, S., Schimanski, B.: "Pulling it All Together" via Psychometric AI. In: AAAI Technical Report of the AAAI Fall 2004 Symposium on Achieving Human-Level Intelligence Through Integrated Systems and Research, pp. 9–17. The AAAI Press (2004)
4. Bringsjord, S.: Psychometric artificial intelligence. Journal of Experimental & Theoretical Artificial Intelligence 23(3), 271–277 (2011)
5. Wheeler, M.: God's Machines: Descartes on the Mechanization of Mind. In: Husbands, P., Holland, O., Wheeler, M. (eds.) The Mechanical Mind in History, pp. 307–330. MIT Press, Cambridge (2008)
6. Turing, A.: Computing Machinery and Intelligence. Mind LIX(236), 433–460 (1950)
7. Harnad, S.: Other Bodies, Other Minds: A Machine Incarnation of an Old Philosophical Problem. Minds and Machines 1, 43–54 (1991)
8. Treffert, D.A.: The savant syndrome: An extraordinary condition. A synopsis: Past, present, future. Philosophical Transactions of the Royal Society B: Biological Sciences 364(1522), 1352–1357 (2009)
9. French, R.: Subcognition and the Limits of the Turing Test. Mind 99, 53–65 (1990)
10. Cullen, J.: Imitation Versus Communication: Testing for Human-Like Intelligence. Minds and Machines 19, 237–254 (2009)

Applying AI for Modeling and Understanding Analogy-Based Classroom Teaching Tools and Techniques

Tarek Richard Besold and Kai-Uwe Kühnberger

Institute of Cognitive Science,
University of Osnabrück,
49069 Osnabrück, Germany
{tbesold,kkuehnbe}@uos.de

Abstract. This paper forms the final part of a short series of related articles[1,2] dedicated to highlighting a fruitful type of application of cognitively-inspired analogy engines in an educational context. It complements the earlier work with an additional fully worked out example by providing a short analysis and a detailed formal model (based on the Heuristic-Driven Theory Projection computational analogy framework) of the Number Highrise, a tool for teaching multiplication-based relations in the range of natural numbers up to 100 to children in their first years of primary school.

1 Introduction

With this paper we want to complete a line of work dedicated to showing an additional way of how methods and technology developed in AI, and more precisely in the subfield of cognitive systems, can provide valuable support in the learning sciences and education studies on a conceptual level: Based on the theoretical underpinnings presented in [1], this paper complements the earlier [2] by presenting a second large-scale application case for the use of computational analogy engines in modeling, simulating, and analyzing analogy-related tools and scenarios from classroom teaching. We thus propose to apply intelligent systems not only at the stage of implementation and deployment but already earlier at the level of research and conceptualization of teaching methodology and tools.

As case study we first provide a description and short analysis of the analogy-based Number Highrise [3] used for teaching multiplication-based relations in the range of natural numbers up to 100 to children attending basic mathematics classes in primary school, before showing how a computational analogy-making framework as Heuristic-Driven Theory Projection (HDTP; [4]) can be used to provide a formal computational reconstruction of the highrise as an example of targeted analogy-use taken from a real-life teaching situation.

2 Case Study: The Number Highrise

In this section we develop and analyze the HDTP-based model for the Number Highrise. By constructing this kind of model we hope to identify underlying principles and factors

C. Lutz and M. Thielscher (Eds.): KI 2014, LNCS 8736, pp. 55–61, 2014.

Table 1. An idealized form of the children's initial conception of the $[0; 100]$ integer number space $(n_0 - n_{99})$ and the times tables up to 10 $(n_{100} - n_{390})$. *multiply* represents multiplication over $[0; 100]$, laws $n_{391} - n_{393}$ define the successor and the lower and greater ordering relations.

Sorts:
  natural_number, operation, relation.
Entities:
  zero, one, two, ..., one_hundred, N_1, N_2, N_3 *: natural_number.*   *multiply : operation.* $<, >$ *: relation.*
Functions:
  apply : operation $\times$ *natural_number* $\times$ *natural_number* $\rightarrow$ *natural_number.*
Predicates:
  succ : natural_number $\times$ *natural_number.*   *holds : relation* $\times$ *natural_number* $\times$ *natural_number.*
Facts:
  (n_0) *succ(zero, one).* (n_1) *succ(one, two).* (n_2) *succ(two, three).*   ... (n_{99}) *succ(ninety-nine, one_hundred).*
  (n_{100}) *apply(multiply, one, one) = one.* (n_{101}) *apply(multiply, one, two) = two.*
  (n_{102}) *apply(multiply, one, three) = three.*   ... (n_{199}) *apply(multiply, one, one_hundred) = one_hundred.*
  (n_{200}) *apply(multiply, two, one) = two.* (n_{201}) *apply(multiply, two, two) = four.*   ...
  (n_{249}) *apply(multiply, two, fifty) = one_hundred.*
  (n_{250}) *apply(multiply, three, one) = three.*   ... (n_{282}) *apply(multiply, three, thirty-three) = ninety-nine.*
  (n_{283}) *apply(multiply, four, one) = four.*   ... (n_{390}) *apply(multiply, ten, ten) = one_hundred.*
Laws:
  (n_{391}) *succ*$(N_1, N_2) \rightarrow$ *holds*$(<, N_1, N_2).$
  (n_{392}) *holds*$(<, N_1, N_2) \wedge$ *holds*$(<, N_2, N_3) \rightarrow$ *holds*$(<, N_1, N_3).$
  (n_{393}) *holds*$(<, N_1, N_2) \leftrightarrow$ *holds*$(>, N_2, N_1).$

---

which shed light on some of the basic mechanisms of human developmental learning and knowledge transfer.

2.1 Discovering the Number Space from 0 to 100

As described in [3], the Number Highrise is a mathematical toy world designed for exploring the space of the natural numbers up to 100 making explicit use of multiplication-based relations. It consists of 10 so called hallways each made up by 100 pearls. In each hallway the pearls are connected in chunks going in accordance with one of the basic times tables for numbers between 1 and 10 (the leftmost hallway corresponding to the one times table, the one to its right corresponding to the two times table, etc.). The resulting segments within each hallway are marked by separating slices of acrylic glass, the so called platforms (similar to half landings in a hallway). Not all of the hallways terminate in a platform, depending on the respective times table there might be some remaining pearls needed for reaching the 100.

The children interact with toy figures which can travel the different hallways up and down. Fitting with the difference in the number of pearls between two platforms, the toy figures can be equipped with different pairs of number shoes (having the respective segment size written on them). Wearing a specific pair of number shoes allows a toy figure to navigate from platform to platform within one specific hallway, namely the hallway with the corresponding distance between platforms. If two or several differently shod toy figures within their respective hallway can reach platforms on equal height with each other, they are called neighbors and can celebrate a party together. If this is the case, an elevator mechanism within the Number Highrise allows the toy figures to actually meet at the height of their platforms: The elevator is a horizontal batten movable vertically along the row of hallways. It can be stopped at each point along the height of the highrise and can be used for checking for numerical factor relations.

Table 2. Partial formalization of the Number Highrise focusing on multiplication-based relations

---

Sorts:
  pearl, hallway, platform, number_shoe, toy_figure, batten, operation, relation, time, natural_number.
Entities:
  zero, one, two, three, . . . , one_hundred, P_1, P_2, P_3 : *pearl.* $h_1, h_2, h_3, . . . , h_{10}, H_1, H_2$: *hallway.*
  $pl_1, pl_2, . . . , pl_n$: *platform.* $s_1, s_2, s_3, . . . , s_{10}, S_1$: *number_shoe.* $fi_1, fi_2, . . . , fi_m, F_1, F_2$: *toy_figure.*
  elevator : *batten.*   *climb* : *operation.*   *below, above* : *relation.* T_1, T_2 : *time.*
Functions:
  value : *pearl* → *natural_number.*   *location* : *hallway* → *natural_number.*   *caption* : *number_shoe* → *natural_number.*
  apply : *operation* × *natural_number* × *natural_number* → *natural_number.*
Predicates:
  holds : *relation* × *pearl* × *pearl.*   *platf_at* : *hallway* × *pearl.*   *stands_on* : *toy_figure* × *hallway* × *pearl* × *time.*
  wears : *toy_figure* × *number_shoe.*   *meets* : *batten* × *hallway* × *platform* × *time.*   *on_top_of* : *pearl* × *pearl.*
  party_location : *hallway* × *pearl* × *time.*   *neighbors* : *toy_figure* × *toy_figure.*
Facts:
  (h_0) *on_top_of*(*base, one*). (h_1) *on_top_of*(*one, two*).   . . . (h_{99}) *on_top_of*(*ninety-nine, one_hundred*).
  (h_{100}) *platf_at*(h_1, *one*). (h_{101}) *platf_at*(h_1, *two*).   . . . (h_{199}) *platf_at*(h_1, *one_hundred*).
  (h_{200}) *platf_at*(h_2, *two*). (h_{201}) *platf_at*(h_2, *four*).   . . . (h_{249}) *platf_at*(h_2, *one_hundred*).
  (h_{250}) *platf_at*(h_3, *three*).   . . . (h_{390}) *platf_at*(h_{10}, *one_hundred*).
  (h_{391}) *value*(*base*) = 0. (h_{392}) *value*(*one*) = 1. (h_{393}) *value*(*two*) = 2.   . . . (h_{491}) *value*(*one_hundred*) = 100.
  (h_{492}) *location*(h_1) = 1.   . . . (h_{501}) *location*(p_{10}) = 10.
  (h_{502}) *caption*(s_1) = 1.   . . . (h_{511}) *caption*(s_{10}) = 10.
Laws:
  (h_{512}) *on_top_of*(P_1, P_2) → *holds*(*below*, P_1, P_2).
  (h_{513}) *holds*(*below*, P_1, P_2) ∧ *holds*(*below*, P_2, P_3) → *holds*(*below*, P_1, P_3).
  (h_{514}) *holds*(*below*, P_1, P_2) ↔ *holds*(*above*, P_2, P_1).
  (h_{515}) $T_1 < T_2$: *platf_at*(H_1, P_1) ∧ *stands_on*(F_1, H_1, P_1, T_1) ∧ *wears*(F_1, S_1) ∧ *location*(H_1) = *caption*(S_1) ∧ *value*(P_2) =
  value(P_1) + *caption*(S_1) ∧ *apply*(*climb*, 1, *caption*(S_1)) → *stands_on*(F_1, H_1, P_2, T_2).
  (h_{516}) $T_1 < T_2, \forall n \in [0; 100]$: *platf_at*(H_1, P_1) ∧ *stands_on*(F_1, H_1, P_1, T_1) ∧ *wears*(F_1, S_1) ∧ *location*(H_1) =
  caption(S_1) ∧ *value*(P_2) = *value*(P_1) + *caption*(S_1) ∧ *apply*(*climb*, *n*, *caption*(S_1)) → *stands_on*(F_1, H_1, P_2, T_2) ∧
  apply(*climb*, *n* − 1, *caption*(S_1)).
  (h_{517}) *platf_at*(H_1, P_1) ∧ *platf_at*(H_2, P_2) ∧ *meets*(*elevator*, H_1, P_1, T_1) ∧ *meets*(*elevator*, H_2, P_2, T_1) →
  party_location(H_1, P_1, T_1) ∧ *party_location*(H_2, P_2, T_1).
  (h_{518}) *stands_on*(F_1, H_1, P_1, T_1) ∧ *stands_on*(F_2, H_2, P_2, T_1) ∧ *meets*(*elevator*, F_1, P_1, T_1) ∧ *meets*(*elevator*, F_2, P, T_1) →
  neighbors(F_1, F_2).
  (h_{519}) *neighbors*(F_1, F_2) ↔ *neighbors*(F_2, F_1).

In class the Number Highrise can be used in several ways: From teaching the basic conception of the natural number space, through the discovery of concepts like the least common multiple and the greatest common factor, to finding and exploring the notion of prime numbers.

2.2   An HDTP-Based Model of the Number Highrise

We now reconstruct the Number Highrise as an analogy-based model for discovering and experiencing the space of natural numbers between 0 and 100, together with multiplication-based relations within this number space.

The analogy uses the Number Highrise as a base domain, transferring the structure and relational conception children acquire by playing with it into their previously acquired knowledge about natural numbers as target domain. Although already populated with previous knowledge, the latter domain is most likely initially relatively poor (especially with regard to the internal relational structure) as compared to the Number Highrise domain as only limited internal structure or relations have been acquired. The pre-existing relational concepts are most likely rather simple in that they are either based on equality between magnitues (i.e., "=") and ordering relations for simple magnitudes — as commonly represented by the "<" and ">" relations — or that they are based on

Table 3. Generalized theory of the Number Highrise and the children's conception of the non-negative integers, expanded by the generalized forms of the candidate elements for analogical transfer from base to target domain (marked with $*$)

Sorts:
pearl/natural_number, hallway, platform, number_shoe, toy_figure, batten, operation, relation, time, natural_number.
Entities:
$zero, one, \ldots, one\_hundred, P_1, P_2, P_3$: pearl/natural_number.   Climb/Multiply : operation.
Below/<, Above/> : relation.
$(*)\ h_1, h_2, h_3, \ldots, h_{10}, H_1, H_2$: hallway. $(*)\ pl_1, pl_2, \ldots, pl_n$: platform. $(*)\ s_1, s_2, s_3, \ldots, s_{10}, S_1$: number_shoe.
$(*)\ fi_1, fi_2, \ldots, fi_m, F_1, F_2$: toy_figure. $(*)$ elevator : batten. $(*)\ T_1, T_2$: time.
Functions:
apply : operation $\times$ natural_number $\times$ natural_number $\to$ natural_number.
$(*)$ value : pearl/natural_number $\to$ natural_number. $(*)$ location : hallway $\to$ natural_number.
$(*)$ caption : number_shoe $\to$ natural_number.
Predicates:
holds : relation $\times$ pearl/natural_number $\times$ pearl/natural_number.
GenSucc : pearl/natural_number $\times$ pearl/natural_number.
$(*)$ platf_at : hallway $\times$ pearl/natural_number. $(*)$ stands_on : toy_figure $\times$ hallway $\times$ pearl/natural_number $\times$ time.
$(*)$ wears : toy_figure $\times$ number_shoe. $(*)$ meets : batten $\times$ hallway $\times$ platform $\times$ time.
$(*)$ party_location : hallway $\times$ pearl/number $\times$ time. $(*)$ neighbors : toy_figure $\times$ toy_figure.
Facts:
(g_0) GenSucc(zero, one). (g_1) GenSucc(one, two). $\ldots$ (g_{99}) GenSucc(ninety-nine, one_hundred).
$(g_{100}*)$ platf_at(h_1, one). $(g_{101}*)$ platf_at(h_1, two). $\ldots$ $(g_{199}*)$ platf_at(h_1, one-hundred).
$(g_{200}*)$ platf_at(h_2, two). $(g_{201}*)$ platf_at(h_2, four). $\ldots$ $(g_{249}*)$ platf_at(h_2, one-hundred).
$(g_{250}*)$ platf_at(h_3, three). $\ldots$ $(g_{390}*)$ platf_at(h_{10}, one-hundred).
$(g_{391}*)$ value(zero) = 0. $(g_{392}*)$ value(one) = 1. $\ldots$ $(g_{491}*)$ value(one_hundred) = 100.
$(g_{492}*)$ location(h_1) = 1. $\ldots$ $(g_{501}*)$ location(p_{10}) = 10.
$(g_{502}*)$ caption(s_1) = 1. $\ldots$ $(g_{511}*)$ caption(s_{10}) = 10.
Laws:
(g_{512}) GenSucc(P_1, P_2) $\to$ holds(Below/<, P_1, P_2).
(g_{513}) holds(Below/<, P_1, P_2) $\land$ holds(Below/<, P_2, P_3) $\to$ holds(Below/<, P_1, P_3).
(g_{514}) holds(Below/<, P_1, P_2) $\leftrightarrow$ holds(Above/>, P_2, P_1).
$(g_{515}*)$ $T_1 < T_2$: platf_at(H_1, P_1) $\land$ stands_on(F_1, H_1, P_1, T_1) $\land$ wears(F_1, S_1) $\land$ location(H_1) = caption(S_1) $\land$ value(P_2) = value(P_1) + caption(S_1) $\land$ apply(Climb/Multiply, 1, caption(S_1)) $\to$ stands_on(F_1, H_1, P_2, T_2).
$(g_{516}*)$ $T_1 < T_2, \forall n \in [0; 100]$: platf_at(H_1, P_1) $\land$ stands_on(F_1, H_1, P_1, T_1) $\land$ wears(F_1, S_1) $\land$ location(H_1) = caption(S_1) $\land$ value(P_2) = value(P_1) + caption(S_1) $\land$ apply(Climb/Multiply, n, caption(S_1)) $\to$ stands_on(F_1, H_1, P_2, T_2) $\land$ apply(Climb/Multiply, $n-1$, caption(S_1)).
$(g_{517}*)$ platf_at(H_1, P_1) $\land$ platf_at(H_2, P_2) $\land$ meets(elevator, H_1, P_1, T_1) $\land$ meets(elevator, H_2, P_2, T_1) $\to$ party_location(H_1, P_1, T_1) $\land$ party_location(H_2, P_2, T_1).
$(g_{518}*)$ stands_on(F_1, H_1, P_1, T_1) $\land$ stands_on(F_2, H_2, P_2, T_1) $\land$ meets(elevator, F_1, P_1, T_1) $\land$ meets(elevator, F_2, P, T_1) $\to$ neighbors(F_1, F_2).
$(g_{519}*)$ neighbors(F_1, F_2) $\leftrightarrow$ neighbors(F_2, F_1).

---

the arithmetic operations of addition and subtraction. The notion of multiplication is known on a mostly abstract basis (as are the corresponding times tables), but has not yet been developed into a grounded, constructively applicable conceptualization. Also, the more complex multiplication-based concepts as, e.g., the least common multiple or prime numbers are not yet present.

An idealized version (i.e., a version featuring complete times tables, which in reality should be assumed to be rather incomplete or sparse) of the students' initial conceptualization of the natural number space can formally be represented as shown in Table 1, whilst Table 2 gives a partial formal HDTP-style model of the Number Highrise (on the relational side focusing only on the multiplication-based aspects).

We shortly want to focus on some aspects of the respective formalizations. The formalization of the target domain of the later analogy, i.e., of an idealized version of the children's initial conception of the integer number space $[0; 100]$, contains mostly facts the children have learned by heart, namely the order of the number terms between zero

Table 4. Analogically enriched conception of the non-negative integers

---

Sorts:
natural_number, operation, relation, hallway, platform, number_shoe, toy_figure, batten, time.
Entities:
zero, one, ..., one_hundred, N_1, N_2, N_3 : natural_number.   multiply : operation.   <, > : relation.
(*) $h_1, h_2, h_3, \ldots, h_{10}$: hallway.   (*) $pl_1, pl_2, \ldots, pl_n$: platform.   (*) $s_1, s_2, s_3, \ldots, s_{10}$: number_shoe.
(*) $fi_1, fi_2, \ldots, fi_m$: toy_figure.   (*) elevator : batten.   (*) T_1, T_2 : time.
Functions:
apply : operation × natural_number × natural_number → natural_number.
(*) value : natural_number → natural_number.   (*) location : hallway → natural_number.
(*) caption : number_shoe → natural_number.
Predicates:
holds : relation × natural_number × natural_number.   succ : natural_number × natural_number.
(*) platf_at : hallway × natural_number.   (*) stands_on : toy_figure × hallway × natural_number × time.
(*) wears : toy_figure × number_shoe.   (*) meets : batten × hallway × platform × time.
(*) party_location : hallway × natural_number × time.   (*) neighbors : toy_figure × toy_figure.
Facts:
(e_0) succ(zero, one).   (e_1) succ(one, two).   ...   (e_{99}) succ(ninety-nine, one_hundred).
(e_{100}) apply(multiply, one, one) = one.   (e_{101}) apply(multiply, one, two) = two.   ...
(e_{390}) apply(multiply, ten, ten) = one_hundred.
(e_{391}*) platf_at(h_1, one).   (e_{392}*) platf_at(h_1, two).   ...   (e_{490}*) platf_at(h_1, one-hundred).
(e_{491}*) platf_at(h_2, two).   (e_{492}*) platf_at(h_2, four).   ...   (e_{540}*) platf_at(h_2, one_hundred).
(e_{541}*) platf_at(h_3, three).   ...   (e_{681}*) platf_at(h_{10}, one_hundred).
(e_{682}*) value(zero) = 0.   ...   (e_{782}*) value(one_hundred) = 100.
(e_{783}*) location(h_1) = 1.   ...   (e_{792}*) location(h_{10}) = 10.
(e_{793}*) caption(s_1) = 1.   ...   (e_{802}*) caption(s_{10}) = 10.
Laws:
(e_{803}) succ(N_1, N_2) → holds(<, N_1, N_2).
(e_{804}) holds(<, N_1, N_2) ∧ holds(<, N_2, N_3) → holds(<, N_1, N_3).
(e_{805}) holds(<, N_1, N_2) ↔ holds(>, N_2, N_1).
(e_{806}*) $T_1 < T_2$: platf_at(H_1, N_1) ∧ stands_on(F_1, H_1, N_1, T_1) ∧ wears(F_1, S_1) ∧ location(H_1) = caption(S_1) ∧ value(N_2) = value(N_1) + caption(S_1) ∧ apply(multiply, 1, caption(S_1)) → stands_on(F_1, H_1, N_2, T_2).
(e_{807}*) $T_1 < T_2, \forall n \in [0; 100]$: platf_at(H_1, N_1) ∧ stands_on(F_1, H_1, N_1, T_1) ∧ wears(F_1, S_1) ∧ location(H_1) = caption(S_1) ∧ value(N_2) = value(N_1) + caption(S_1) ∧ apply(multiply, n, caption(S_1)) → stands_on(F_1, H_1, N_2, T_2) ∧ apply(multiply, n − 1, caption(S_1)).
(e_{808}*)   platf_at(H_1, N_1) ∧ platf_at(H_2, N_2) ∧ meets(elevator, H_1, N_1, T_1) ∧ meets(elevator, H_2, N_2, T_1) → party_location(H_1, N_1, T_1) ∧ party_location(H_2, N_2, T_1).
(e_{809}*) stands_on(F_1, H_1, N_1, T_1) ∧ stands_on(F_2, H_2, N_2, T_1) ∧ meets(elevator, F_1, N_1, T_1) ∧ meets(elevator, F_2, N_2, T_1) → neighbors(F_1, F_2).
(e_{810}*) neighbors(F_1, F_2) ↔ neighbors(F_2, F_1).

---

and one hundred, and the times tables up to 10 within this range. In reality it has to be assumed that the times tables are significantly more sparsely populated than in our formalization, corresponding to incomplete recall of the memorized full tables.

The base domain of the later analogy, i.e., the formalization of the Number Highrise, exhibits a rich structure concerning facts and laws alike. The facts represent the easily accessible structure of the highrise, namely the order of succession of the pearls, the distinction between the different hallways, and the placement of the platforms within the respective hallways. The laws cover the rules of the transformational and constructive process by which the children can interact with the highrise: For instance (h_{515}) and (h_{516}) encompass the process of having the toy figure climb the highrise, and (p_{517}) to (p_{519}) add the notion of several figures meeting on the same level and celebrating a party together.

The HDTP mechanism can now be used for computing a common generalization of both domains, yielding a generalized theory like given in Table 3. The main domain elements defining the alignment of formulae are the matching between the entities of sort *pearl* and *natural_number*, between the *apply* functions, the matching of the *holds* predicates, the thus induced alignment of the respective *operation* and *relation* entities, as well as the alignment between the *successor* and *on_top_of* predicates (in turn induced by the alignment of the *operation* and *relation* entities and the resulting structural similarity between predicates).

In conclusion, the generalized theory forms the basis for transferring knowledge in an analogy-based way from the (originally richer) Number Highrise domain to the children's number domain, resulting in an expanded theory for the numbers as given in Table 4. The important aspect in this expanded version is the availability of the constructive relations and insights obtained in the interaction with the Number Highrise. These give, for instance, meaning to the multiplication relation via the assignment of the constructive process of climbing the highrise and the corresponding platforms for the intermediate steps and the result. Furthermore laws $(e_{806}*)$ and $(e_{807}*)$ allow for the independent computation of parts of the times tables that might not be obtainable from memory (i.e., that would not explicitly be present as a fact in a more realistic formalization of the number domain).

2.3   Example: Discovering the Least Common Multiple

We now can reconstruct, for instance, the children's discovery of the least common multiple of three numbers documented in [3]: At the cognitive level the analogy-based process of transfer of the gained insights from the Number Highrise into the children's conception of the $[0; 100]$ number space can be exemplified in the given HDTP model. Taking the definition of the least common multiple lmc of two natural numbers x and y (i.e., $lmc|x$ and $lmc|y$ and $\nexists a \in \mathbb{N} : a < lmc, a|x, a|y$), it becomes obvious that the concept of a party location and the notion of neighborhood between toy figures (i.e., laws $(e_{808}*)$ to $(e_{810}*)$ in the analogically enriched formalization in Table 4, together with the game-immanent concept of having the toy figures start at level zero of the hallways and the task to find the first possible party location between all three neighbors, naturally induces the least common multiple concept in the children's number domain. Via analogical transfer from the Number Highrise, building upon the already pre-existing basic structure of natural numbers and times tables, the more complex idea of the least common multiple has been acquired by the children — experience-grounded concept learning has taken place in a rather abstract domain.

3   Conclusion

In general, this work is an example for the application of AI techniques and tools in gaining deeper understanding of the mechanisms underlying analogy-based teaching material. Modeling educational analogies, on the one hand, sheds new light on a particular analogy, in terms of which information is transferred, what the limitations of the analogy are, or whether it makes unhelpful mappings; and what potential extensions might be needed. On the other hand, it also contributes to a deeper general understanding of the basic principles and mechanisms underlying analogy-based learning (and subsequently teaching) in fairly high-level and abstract domains.

References

1. Besold, T.R.: Analogy engines in classroom teaching: Modeling the string circuit analogy. In: AAAI Spring Symposium: Creativity and (Early) Cognitive Development. AAAI Technical Report, vol. SS-13-02. AAAI (2013)
2. Besold, T.R., Schmidt, M., Pease, A.: Analogy and Arithmetics: An HDTP-Based Model of the Calculation Circular Staircase. In: Proceedings of the 35th Annual Conference of the Cognitive Science Society (CogSci 2013), pp. 1893–1898 (2013)
3. Schnalle, K., Schwank, I.: Das Zahlen-Hochhaus [ZH]: Multiplikative Zusammenhänge im Hunderterraum. In: Beiträge zum Mathematikunterricht. Franzbecker (2006)
4. Schmidt, M., Krumnack, U., Gust, H., Kühnberger, K.-U.: Heuristic-driven theory projection: An overview. In: Prade, H., Richard, G. (eds.) Computational Approaches to Analogical Reasoning: Current Trends. SCI, vol. 548, pp. 163–194. Springer, Heidelberg (2014)

Automatic Identification of Human Strategies by Cognitive Agents

Felix Steffenhagen, Rebecca Albrecht, and Marco Ragni

Center for Cognitive Science,
University of Freiburg, Germany
{steffenhagen,ragni}@cognition.uni-freiburg.de,
albrechr@informatik.uni-freiburg.de

Abstract. So far most cognitive modeling approaches have concentrated on modeling and predicting the actions of an "average user" – a user profile that in reality often does not exist. User performance is highly dependent on psychological factors like working memory, planning depth, search strategy etc. that differ between users. Therefore, we propose a combination of several AI methods to automatically identify user profiles. The proposed method assigns each user a set of cognitive agents which are controlled by several psychological factors. Finally, this method is evaluated in a case study on preliminary user data on the PSPACE-complete planning problem Rush-Hour.

Keywords: Identification of Heuristics, Cognitive Modeling, Spatial Planning, Data Analysis in Planning Domains, Strategy Analysis.

1 Introduction

Identifying common move and strategy patterns of agents in planning problems can be difficult, especially if the state space is large. If, furthermore, human agents are considered, these patterns (or planning profiles) will also depend on psychological factors that are known to restrict the performance of human agents, e.g., working memory capacity [6]. In this work, we combine different methods to identify such cognitive planning patterns and evaluate this method on preliminary results from a case study.

The proposed method consists of three steps. Firstly, for a given planning domain, so-called *strategy graphs* for single problem instances are introduced. A strategy graph represents all strategies used by a group of agents. We define a strategy of an agent in a problem instance as a path from a given initial state to one or many given goal states. Secondly, a group of artificial agents programmed to comply to restricting psychological factors (controlled by parameters) is introduced. These factors include, for example, working memory capacity and planning depth. Thirdly, to each human agent a set of best replicating artificial agents is assigned. We define the notion best replicating agent based on the maximal path similarity for a human agent and a set of artificial agents. The values of parameters which are used to control the best replicating

C. Lutz and M. Thielscher (Eds.): KI 2014, LNCS 8736, pp. 62–67, 2014.

agents' planning behavior is identified as the planning profile of the assigned human agent.

The presented method is evaluated in a case study in the Rush Hour planning domain. We introduce a group of human and a group of artificial agents which both solved selected Rush Hour instances. In order to identify best replicating artificial agents for each human agent we use the Smith-Waterman algorithm [8] as a similarity measure. The quality of the presented approach is evaluated based on the mean similarities of human agents with best replicating artificial agents.

2 Methodology

Strategy Graphs. In this section we describe the data structure used to represent all strategies used by a group of agents A, in a problem instance p of a planning domain D. We identify a strategy s for a problem instance p as a path from a initial state to a goal state in the problem space induced by the planning domain D.

A *strategy graph* with respect to a problem instance p is a directed, labelled multigraph $G_p = (V_p, E_p, S_p, G_p)$. The set of vertices V_p represents all states traversed by any agent in A in the solution of problem p. The set of edges $E_p \subset V_p \times V_p \times \mathbb{N} \times \mathbb{N}$ represents the application of legal actions in the planning domain D including information about an agent's $id \in \mathbb{N}$ and a step number in the solution process $t \in \mathbb{N}$. Additionally, a strategy graph includes a set of initial states $S_p \subset V_p$ and a set of goal states $G_p \subset V_p$. Note that the strategy graph may include multiple edges between two states, each labelled with an agent id and a step number.

As we evaluate human agents' strategies, we have to account for several factors which do not contribute to identifying human planning profiles. Therefore, we propose several graph reduction mechanisms. Firstly, we automatically identify and remove cycles of a certain length. This is important to exclude moves which are immediately retracted. We define a cycle in the strategy graph as a path $s \to s' \to \ldots \to s'' \to s$, where $s \neq s' \neq s''$, and for edges (s, s', id, t) and (s'', s, id, t') it holds that $t < t'$.

Secondly, we remove outlier strategies for each problem instance p with respect to threshold values τ_p. An outlier is a strategy which is only used by a very small number of agents. In order to detect these outlier strategies we use a significance measure $Sig_p : V_p \times V_p \to \mathbb{N}$, which for two given states returns the number of edges between these states. With respect to a threshold τ_p, we remove all edges (s, s', id, t) where $Sig_p((s, s')) < \tau_p$.

Thirdly, we merge partial strategies which are equivalent wrt. partial order planning [7]. The basic idea is to exclude strategies which correspond to subsequent moves here it does not matter in which sequence they are played (cp. move transpositions in chess). The term strategy equivalence is defined with respect to a parameter ϵ (also called epsilon equivalence). We call two strategies $s_0^1 \to s_1^1 \to \ldots \to s_n^1$ and $s_0^2 \to s_1^2 \to \ldots \to s_m^2$ $n - \epsilon$ equivalent iff $n \leq m$, $s_0^1 = s_0^2$, $s_n^1 = s_m^2$, $s_n^1, s_m^2 \notin \{s_1^1, \ldots, s_{n-1}^1, s_1^2, s_{m-1}^2\}$, and $m - n \leq \epsilon$. For every detected $n - \epsilon$ equivalence we exclude all involved edges and include a new edge given by the start and the goal state, e.g. (s_0^1, s_m^2, id, t).

Agent Similarity. In this section we show how strategy graphs are used to identify a set of best replicating artificial agents for one human agent. As a first step, we will introduce the notion of strategy similarity generally for two arbitrary sets of agents A_1 and A_2. The motivation is to allow for different similarity measures to be used. An agent is given by a partial strategy graph, i.e. a path from a start to a goal state. We define that A_1 and A_2 are pairwise disjoint sets, i.e. the same agent is not in both sets. However, two agents from different sets may use the same planning strategy. We denote the similarity between two agents a_1 and a_2 for one problem instance p as $0 \leq Sim_p(a_1, a_2) \leq 1$, and the similarity for two agents a_1 and a_2 over all instances in the problem domain D as $Sim_D(a_1, a_2) = \frac{\sum_{p \in D} Sim_p(a_1, a_2)}{|D|}$. Furthermore, we denote the set of similarity values for one agent $a_1 \in A_1$ and a group of agents A_2 as $Sim(a_1, A_2) = \{Sim(a_1, a_2) \mid a_2 \in A_2\}$, where Sim is either Sim_p or Sim_D.

- For each agent $a_1 \in A_1$ we identify the set of best replicating agents for agent a_1 in one problem instance $p \in D$ as

$$bra_p(a_1) = \{a_2 \in A_2 \mid max(Sim_p(a_1, A_2))\}$$

- For each agent $a_1 \in A_1$ we identify the set of best replicating agents for agent a_1 over all problem instances $p \in D$ as

$$bra_D(a_1) = \{a_2 \in A_2 \mid max(Sim_D(a_1, A_2))\}$$

We denote the set of best replicating agents from group A_2 for all agents in group A_1 for one problem instance p as $bra_p(A_1) = \bigcup_{a_1 \in A_1} bra_p(a_1)$, and over all problem instances in D as $bra_D(A_1) = \bigcup_{a_1 \in A_1} bra_D(a_1)$, respectively. Note that the considered search space is restricted to moves applied by agents.

3   Case Study

Planning Domain. As planning domain D we consider the planning problem *Rush Hour* developed by Nob Yoshigahara[1]. *Rush Hour* is a two-dimensional puzzle game where a specified object (exit car) has to be moved out of the grid. The (generalized) computational complexity of this game is known to be PSPACE-complete [2]. Other characteristics are that it is well-defined, solvable, decomposable, not dynamic and has only one goal (to free the red car) to be reached [3].

Agent Groups. In the following, we consider two groups of agents, one group only consisting of human agents A_H and one consisting of artificial agents A_A. Both groups were tested on the same problem set selected from the "Junior

---

[1] A description of RushHour can be found at http://www.thinkfun.com/
instructions

Edition" problem set of the Rush Hour game[2]. The problem selection was based on different problem attributes: (1) existing classification of the tasks (beginner, intermediate, and advanced), (2) the optimal solution length, (3) number of moves of the exit car. This includes 22 problem instances.

The human group A_H consisting of 20 participants (or agents) was tested in a psychological experiment. The experiment was conducted using a computer-based version of Rush Hour[3] for recording selected actions and response times during the solution process. The problems were presented in a randomized order. Human agents had three minutes to solve each trial.

The group of artificial agents A_A is programmed to use Means-End-Analysis [1, 4, 5] particularly tailored to the Rush Hour planning domain. We identified seven parameters to control the agent's local planning behavior based on psychological factors to identify planning profiles of human agents. Parameter values characterize the planning profiles of the artificial agents. Most importantly, these parameters include the move distance for game objects, the goal stack capacity (corresponding to human working memory capacity), and several parameters controlling the greedy selection of sub goals.

Rush Hour Strategy Graphs. In order to construct Rush Hour strategy graphs, we use the graph reduction mechanisms described in Section 2. Cycle detection is restricted to cycles of length two. For human agents, this corresponds to moves which are immediately retracted. For outlier detection parameters τ_p were determined based on statistical evaluation of strategy frequencies for each problem instance p. We remove equivalent strategies with respect to the introduced $n - \epsilon$ measure with $\epsilon = 2$. The choice of these parameters is highly specific to Rush Hour and the used problem instance in particular. These decisions were made based on a detailed analysis of the planning domain and problem instances.

Similarity Measure. In Section 2 we defined the notion of best replicating agents based on similarity measures for two agents a_1, a_2 in one problem instance p, denoted by $Sim_p(a_1, a_2) \in \mathbb{R}$. In this paragraph, we will define this value. For measuring the similarity between the two agent groups we use the Smith-Waterman Algorithm (SW) algorithm for local sequence alignment used in bioinformatics [8]. In this approach we compare sequences of states to find the optimal local alignment of the two sequences, i.e. the longest state sequence occurring in both strategies. The SW algorithm computes a scoring matrix H based on weights for sequence matches (w_m), insertions (w_i) and deletions (w_d). In this approach, we use the weights $w_m = 1$, $w_i = -1$, and $w_d = -1$, as we do not have insertions and deletions. The maximum value of H is the similarity score of the local alignment with the highest similarity. With respect to the chosen weights, this score reflects the length of the longest local alignment. We define the similarity of two agents a_1 and a_2 for problem instance p as $Sim_p(a_1, a_2) = \frac{Sim(a_1, a_2)}{max(|a_1|, |a_2|)}$, where $|a_i|$ is the path length of the strategy used by agent a_i.

---

[2] https://portal.uni-freiburg.de/cognition/alte-seite/research/
projects/cspace/rushhour
[3] By courtesy of the Dept. of Theoretical Psychology, University of Heidelberg.

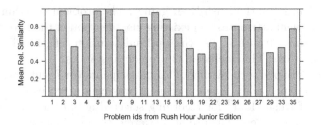

Fig. 1. Mean similarities of all human agents A_H and best replicating artificial agents in $bra_p(A_H)$ for each of the 22 tested Rush Hour problem instances

Results. We evaluated the average similarity for each of the 22 tested problem instances for both the best replicating artificial agents for human agents over all problem instance $(bra_D(A_H))$ and the best replicating artificial agents with respect to single problem instances $(bra_p(A_H))$. The best replicating agents in $bra_D(A_H)$ are assigned based on the maximum mean similarity of human agents and artificial agents over all 22 tasks. Therefore, the best replicating agents in this group correspond to planning profiles for a human agent which are constant over all problem instances. The mean similarity for all best replicating agents in $bra_D(A_H)$ and over all problem instances is 44%.

The best replicating agents in $bra_p(A_H)$ are assigned based on the maximum mean similarity of human agents and artificial agents for each task separately. Therefore, the best replicating agents in this group correspond to different planning profiles for a human agent in every problem instance. The mean similarity for all best replicating agents in $bra_p(A_H)$ and over all problem instance is 76%. Figure 1 shows the average similarities for each problem instance for artificial agents in $bra_p(A_H)$.

4   Discussion

In this work, we present a method to automatically identify psychological planning profiles for human agents. A planning profile is given by a set of parameters used to control the planning behavior of artificial agents. A planning profile for one human agent is identified as the values of parameters of artificial agents which best replicated human planning strategies.

We report preliminary results on a case study based on this method in the Rush Hour planning domain. The results show that best replicating agents which are assigned to human agents constantly over all problem instances can be identified as planning profiles for only half of the human agents. Best replicating agents assigned to human agents for each problem instance separately can be identified as planning profiles for three quarter of the agents. A possible explanation is that human planning profiles are not only different for each user but also different for each user in each task.

Another possible explanation for the results, especially for planning constantly assigned planning profiles, is the conservative similarity measure used. This measure only considers the longest sequence alignment of states in two different strategies. However, if two strategies only deviate in one state, the shorter sequence is not considered.

Further extension of the presented methods include, for example, the automatic identification of branching points, i.e. states where agents choose different successor states, to further classify different strategies. This can be used to identify and analyze preferred user strategies. Another possible extension is the introduction of a measure to describe deviations from optimal strategies as a measure of success.

To conclude, we believe that the presented preliminary methods are a first step for automatically analyzing large and heterogeneous data sets generated by human planners. Especially the strategy graphs are useful for an abstraction of large data sets. In order to analyze this method further, other similarity measures, for example based on all local sequence alignments or based on the number of deviating states, and additional psychological factors should be considered.

Acknowledgement. This work has been supported by a grant to Marco Ragni within the project R8-[CSpace] within the SFB/TR 8 "Spatial Cognition".

References

1. Faltings, B., Pu, P.: Applying Means-ends Analysis to Spatial Planning. In: Proceedings of the International Workshop on Intelligent Robots and Systems, pp. 80–85 (1992)
2. Flake, G.W., Baum, E.B.: Rush Hour is PSPACE-complete, or "Why you should generously tip parking lot attendants". Theoretical Computer Science 270, 895–911 (2002)
3. Helmert, M.: Understanding Planning Tasks. LNCS (LNAI), vol. 4929. Springer, Heidelberg (2008)
4. Mcdermott, D.: A Heuristic Estimator for Means-Ends Analysis in Planning. In: Proceedings of the Third International Conference on AI Planning Systems, pp. 142–149 (1996)
5. Newell, A., Simon, H.A.: Computer Simulation of Human Thinking. Rand Corporation (1961)
6. Owen, A.M., Downes, J.J., Sahakian, B.J., Polkey, C.E., Robbins, T.W.: Planning and spatial working memory following frontal lobe lesions in man. Neuropsychologia 28(10), 1021–1034 (1990)
7. Russell, S.J., Norvig, P.: Artificial Intelligence: A Modern Approach, 2nd edn. Prentice Hall, Englewood Cliffs (2003)
8. Smith, T.F., Waterman, M.S.: Identification of Common Molecular Subsequences. Journal of Molecular Biology 147, 195–197 (1981)

Environment-Adaptive Learning: How Clustering Helps to Obtain Good Training Data

Shoubhik Debnath[1,2], Shiv Sankar Baishya[1,2], Rudolph Triebel[1],
Varun Dutt[2], and Daniel Cremers[1]

[1] Computer Vision Group, Technical University Munich, Germany
[2] Indian Institute of Technology Mandi, India
{debnath,baishya,triebel,cremers}@in.tum.de,
varun@iitmandi.ac.in

Abstract. In this paper, we propose a method to combine unsupervised and semi-supervised learning (SSL) into a system that is able to adaptively learn objects in a given environment with very little user interaction. The main idea of our approach is that clustering methods can help to reduce the number of required label queries from user interaction, and at the same time provide the potential to select useful data to learn from. In contrast to standard methods, we train our classifier only on data from the actual environment and only if the clustering gives enough evidence that the data is relevant. We apply our method to the problem of object detection in indoor environments, for which we use a region-of-interest detector before learning. In experiments we show that our adaptive SSL method can outperform the standard non-adaptive supervised approach on an indoor office data set.

Keywords: Semi-supervised learning, active learning.

1 Introduction

Current machine perception systems often rely on their capabilities to automatically learn a mapping from the set of potential observations to a set of semantic annotations, for example class labels from a natural language. The biggest challenges for the employed learning algorithms are the large amount of labelled data they usually require, and their potential to adapt to new, unseen environments and situations. In many applications, and particularly in mobile robotics, this adaptability is an important requirement, because it is impossible to anticipate all situations that the robot might encounter before deployment. Therefore, we investigate learning mechanisms that are capable of adapting to new observations by updating their internal representation as new information arrives. This implies that the learning step is performed during operation of the system and not beforehand, and that the data used for training is acquired online. However, the main question is: what are good data to train on? A good answer to this

C. Lutz and M. Thielscher (Eds.): KI 2014, LNCS 8736, pp. 68–79, 2014.

question directly leads to a shorter training time and in a reduced amount of required human data annotations.

In this paper, we address this question using a simple, but effective idea: Before asking the human supervisor for a semantic label, we group the observed data into clusters using unsupervised learning. Then, our algorithm queries one common label for each cluster from the supervisor and uses the so obtained training data in a semi-supervised learning step. This approach has two major advantages: first, it further reduces the amount of human intervention significantly by asking labels for multiple instances at the same time. And second, it gives us the potential to pre-select interesting data to train on, for example by asking labels only for clusters that are significantly represented. We apply our method to the problem of object detection in indoor office environments, and we show in experiments that this adaptive way of learning can outperform the standard approach, where a purely supervised classifier is learned before observing the actual test data.

2   Related Work

Our work is mostly related to the area of semi-supervised learning (SSL) and transductive learning methods, which have become very popular in the last decade. A good overview of this field is given by Zhu [1,2], who also proposed a graph-based SSL method named Label Propagation. Other methods include the sparse Gaussian Process classifier with null category noise model [3], semi-supervised boosting [4] and the transductive Support Vector Machine (tSVM) [5]. In our work, we also use unsupervised learning as in [6] and combine it with a tSVM to reduce the required interaction with the human supervisor even further. Example applications of SSL in computer vision include image classification from labelled and unlabelled, but tagged images [7], object recognition [8], and video segmentation [9].

Furthermore, our work is also related to the area of active learning, because it involves a user interaction step, for which queries for class labels are actively generated. A good overview on the active learning literature is given by Settles [10]. One interesting example of active learning is the work of Kapoor *et al.* [11] on object categorization using a GP classifier (GPC), where data points possessing large uncertainty (using posterior mean and variance) are queried for labels and used to improve the classification. Triebel *et al.* [12] use active learning for semantic mapping where a sparse GP classifier actively learns to distinguish traffic lights from background. In contrast to classical active learning methods, our approach chooses the data to be asked for labelling based on a relevance criterion rather than, e.g. based on the entropy of the underlying classifier.

3   Combined Unsupervised and Semi-supervised Learning

Fig. 1 gives an overview of our proposed semi-supervised learning method. We start with a sequence of input images and determine first an appropriate set of

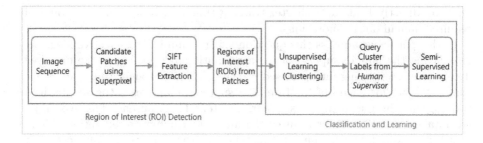

Fig. 1. Flow chart of our proposed system. From a sequence of images, regions of interest are detected using super pixel segmentation and by comparing the segments based on SIFT features. Then the resulting patches are clustered. From each cluster, a subset of patches is used to query object labels from a human supervisor. The resulting hand-labelled data together with some unlabelled samples is then used to train a semi-supervised classifier.

rectangular regions of interest named *patches*. From these patches, we extract SIFT features ("Scale-invariant feature transform", [13]) and use them to define a similarity measure between patches. Based on these similarities, we cluster the patches using spectral clustering. Then, we select a subset of appropriate patches from each cluster and query object labels from a human supervisor as described below. The resulting labelled patches, together with the remaining unlabelled ones are then passed into a multi-class transductive SVM, which then returns predicted labels for the unlabelled patches. In the following sections we describe each step in more detail and give motivations for our algorithm design.

3.1 Region of Interest Detection

Object detection for a given image of a scene is much harder than pure object recognition, because it is not even known to the algorithm *if* the object to be recognized exists in the scene and *where* it is. The common approach to this problem is to determine small sub-windows within the image which potentially contain the object(s) to be classified. In the simplest case, these so-called *regions of interest* (ROI) are obtained using a sliding-window approach. However, to reduce the number of potential ROIs, we use a different method: Given an image sequence, we first compute a superpixel segmentation for each image based on the SLIC algorithm [14]. Then, we compute the bounding box for each segment in every image. For each such resulting candidate patch, we extract SIFT features [13] and compare the patches across the image sequence using a similarity measure s. The motivation for the choice of SIFT descriptor is their high expressive power and their ability to find good matches even under changes of illumination, orientation and scale. In our application, object instances do not vary much in color or texture, which is an ideal condition for the SIFT descriptor. Of course, in a more general setting, where the appearance between the objects of a class

Fig. 2. Example result of our ROI detector. From left to right: 1. Original image 2. SLIC superpixels with boundaries in red, 3. Bounding boxes of the super pixels, 4. Detected ROIs after threshold.

may vary more, other descriptors, for example based on the geometry may be more appropriate.

To compute the similarity measure s, we first define a distance function d between two patches A and B as:

$$d(A, B) = \frac{1}{n} \sum_{i=1}^{n} \|\tilde{\mathbf{x}}_i - \tilde{\mathbf{y}}_i\|^2,\qquad(1)$$

where n is the number of matches found by the SIFT algorithm and i iterates over all these matches. The vectors $\tilde{\mathbf{x}}_i$ and $\tilde{\mathbf{y}}_i$ denote the 128-dimensional descriptor values computed at the key points found by the SIFT method in patches A and B, respectively. From this distance measure, we define the similarity s between two patches as:

$$s(A, B) = 1 - \frac{d(A, B)}{\max\limits_{A', B'} d(A', B')},\qquad(2)$$

thus, s gives values between 0 and 1, where 1 corresponds to maximal similarity. To find patches that contain potentially interesting objects, we compute a similarity score p for patch A as follows:

$$p(A) = \sum_{B \neq A} s(A, B),\qquad(3)$$

i.e. the score is defined by the sum of similarities to all other patches. The intuition here is that patches that are very similar to many others more likely contain objects of interest, because they give evidence that there are many instances of the same object class. Note that our formulation implicitly deals with the problem that background patches containing walls, the floor, etc., despite occurring very often will not give a high score, because their appearance is usually much more uniform, which means that much less SIFT key points are detected on them.

Using these score values, an ROI is then detected as the patches A for which $p(A)$ exceeds the average score over an entire image. This simple statistical method finds patches that stick out in terms of their similarities and has the advantage that it does not require to introduce a threshold parameter. In our experiments, this gave good results (see Fig. 2 for an example sequence of our detector), but of course other methods could be used here.

3.2   Clustering of Patches

The main contribution of our work is the idea of using unsupervised learning *before* employing a semi-supervised method for classification. The motivation of this approach is two-fold: first, the number of required user interactions, i.e. label queries, is further reduced compared to standard semi-supervised learning, because we query only one common label for an entire group (cluster) of data instances. And second, the clustering step gives us the opportunity to pre-select interesting data to train on, because typically some clusters can be easily identified as more relevant for the learning task based on simple characteristics such as cluster size or similarities of elements within a cluster. The intuition here is that only those data instances should be learned by the classifier, for which there is enough evidence that they correspond to a meaningful object class. For example, in an office environment, usually there are many instances of classes like telephone, chair or monitor, and the mere fact that there are many very similar instances makes them highly relevant, for example for a mobile robotic system operating in the environment. In contrast, in a home environment, there might be other types of relevant objects, and our approach particularly aims at finding such relevant classes adaptively.

To perform the clustering step, we use the same SIFT descriptors computed earlier for each patch and rely on the same similarity measure s to cluster the patches. We ran experiments with two different standard clustering methods: k-means clustering and spectral clustering. Both methods have been used very successfully in many different kinds of applications, and we found that the difference in performance is not very substantial. We evaluated both methods on our data using the V-measure [15], which is defined as the harmonic mean of homogeneity and completeness of the clustering algorithm. In these experiments, the spectral clustering was slightly better, and it has the further advantage that it does not necessarily require the number of clusters specified as a parameter. The reason is that it is based on the eigen decomposition of the graph Laplacian of the data, and that a method called the *eigen gap heuristic* can be used to determine a good value for the number of clusters. For more details on spectral clustering, we refer to the work of Luxburg [16].

3.3   Querying Object Labels

The next step in our proposed method is to receive class label information from a human supervisor for the patches that have been clustered beforehand. To perform this label query, some important considerations need to be taken into account: On one side, the algorithm should ask the user as few times as possible to give a label input, because this is one of the main motivations of this work. Thus, we want to ask only once for each cluster. On the other side, we need to make sure that the data we provide as training samples to the semi-supervised learning method is as *pure* as possible, i.e. ideally there should be no instances of different objects labelled by the human with the same label. Unfortunately, no clustering algorithm can guarantee complete purity, neglecting of course the trivial clustering that assigns every data point to its own cluster. Therefore, we propose to use a quality measure q for all patches within a cluster, which is based on the similarities s computed earlier. Concretely, for every patch A of a given cluster $\mathcal{C}$, we compute q as the sum of similarities *within the cluster*:

$$q(A) = \sum_{B \in \mathcal{C}} s(A, B). \tag{4}$$

Note that this is different from the scores computed in Eq. (3), because here, our goal is to find the best cluster representatives. After computing the q-values, we sort all elements within a cluster in descending order of q and ask one common label from the user for the first m such elements of each cluster. This policy gives a good trade-off between the two opposing objectives of generating few label queries and providing pure training data. Of course, this method does not guarantee that there are no instances of different object classes that receive the same label from the supervisor. However, from our experience, the number of cases where queried data points are inconsistent can be reduced substantially using this method.

To illustrate this step, Fig. 3 shows an example result of the clustering step, where each row corresponds to a different cluster and only the first 3 elements according to the quality measure q are shown. As we can see, in two out of four cases the first three cluster elements only contain objects of the same class, and in the other two cases the mistakes made by the algorithm are completely comprehensible. We also note that the clustering result yields more clusters than there are actual classes, i.e. we have an over-clustering. This is only a problem in the sense that it requires the user to give more class labels than actually needed, but this effect was only minor in our experiments.

3.4 Training a Classifier

As a final step in our approach, we use the labelled data obtained from the previous step to learn a classifier for the objects discovered in the environment. Here, we considered three different strategies. First, we investigated the use of a standard supervised learning method using a linear Support Vector Machine (SVM). Then, we evaluated two semi-supervised learning techniques, where the first was a simple nearest neighbour rule, i.e. each unlabelled sample was assigned the label of the closest labelled sample according to our similarity measure. And finally, we used a transductive SVM [5] with an RBF kernel. Thus, in addition to the labelled training set $\mathcal{D}$ of size l, the algorithm is also given an unlabelled set $\mathcal{D}^{\star} = \{\mathbf{x}_i^{\star} \in \mathbb{R}^p\}_{i=1}^{k}$ of test examples to be classified. Formally, a transductive SVM is defined by the following primal optimization problem:

Find $(\mathbf{y}_1^{\star}, \mathbf{y}_2^{\star}, \dots, \mathbf{y}_n^{\star}, \mathbf{w}, b)$ so that

$$\min \frac{1}{2} \|\mathbf{w}\|^2$$
$$\text{subject to} \quad y_i[\mathbf{w} \cdot \mathbf{x}_i - b] \geq 1, \quad y_j^{\star}[\mathbf{w} \cdot \mathbf{x}_j^{\star} - b] \geq 1, \tag{5}$$
$$y_j^{\star} \in \{-1, 1\} \quad \forall i = 1, \dots l, \forall j = 1, \dots, k$$

Fig. 3. Examples of clusters obtained from the clustering algorithm (every row corresponds to a different cluster). For each cluster, we show the first three elements according to the quality measure defined in (4).

where $(\mathbf{x}_i, \mathbf{y}_i)$ are the training examples, $\mathbf{y}_i^\star$ are the predicted labels for the unlabelled test example and $\mathbf{w}$ is the weight vector. This means, that the transductive SVM learns from both the labelled and the unlabelled examples, and it returns label predictions for the unlabelled ones. In that sense, the training and the inference step are contained within the same common procedure.

From these three methods the worst in our experiments was the standard supervised SVM, and we did not consider this further. The highest classification performance was obtained with the transductive SVM, and we give more details in the experimental section. As feature vectors for training, we compute for every patch the Hierarchical Matching Pursuit (HMP) descriptor introduced by Bo *et al.* [17]. The HMP features are calculated in a multi-layer process where each layer is computed on a different scale, containing the same three steps: Matching Pursuit, Pyramid Max Pooling and Contrast Normalization. The key element in this process is the Matching Pursuit step, which is based on a sparse coding algorithm known as K-SVD. Given a set of h-dimensional observations $Y = [y^1, ..., y^n] \in R^{h \times n}$ (image patches in our case), K-SVD learns a dictionary $D = [d^1, ..., d^n] \in R^{h \times m}$, and an associate sparse code matrix $X = [x^1, ..., x^n] \in R^{m \times n}$ by minimizing the following reconstruction error,

$$\min_{x_i} \|y_i - Dx_i\|^2 \text{ s.t. } \|x_i\|_0 \leq K, \tag{6}$$

where x_i are the columns of X, the zero-norm $\|x_i\|_0$ counts the non-zero entries in the sparse code x_i, and K is the sparsity level, which bounds the number of the non-zero entries. The Matching Pursuit step finds an approximate solution to the optimization problem mentioned above using a greedy approach. Pyramid Max Pooling is a non-linear operator that generates higher level representations from sparse codes of local patches which are spatially close. And Contrast Normalization turns out to be essential for good recognition performance, since the magnitude of sparse codes varies over a wide range due to local variations in illumination and foreground-background contrast. Bo *et al.* [17] used a linear SVM in combination with HMP features and reported very good classification results. We verified these results using data from the Caltech 101 benchmark, and we show them in the results section. From this, we conclude that HMP features exhibit a high amount of expressiveness, because they give very good classification results for a comparably simple classifier such as the linear SVM.

In practice, the use of HMP features consists of two phases: one where the dictionaries are learned from some given training data, and one where feature vectors are computed for new test data based on the sparse codes with respect to the learned dictionaries. While the first phase can require huge computation time, as it usually uses a large training data set, the online phase is comparably fast, as it only requires the computation of a sparse representation for a given dictionary. We note however, that the dictionary learning step is completely unsupervised, as it does not require any human-labelled data.

4 Experiments and Results

To measure the performance of our approach, we performed several experiments. First, we evaluated our method to detect regions of interest. Then, we evaluated two different semi-supervised learning methods on a benchmark and on our own data. And finally, we verified experimentally the benefits of using our adaptive, semi-supervised learning method over a standard non-adaptive supervised strategy. More details about all experiments are given in the following.

4.1 Evaluating the ROI Detector

As mentioned above, our ROI detector finds patches that occur often with high similarity across images. Therefore, to assess this method quantitatively, we first created ground truth data for the objects that occurred most frequently in our data. Concretely, we labelled those ROIs as correct detections, which contained chairs, monitors or telephones. Results on 7 different images in terms of precision and recall are given in table 1. We see that our detector tends to find more ROIs than there actually are, and the recall is much better than the precision. However, for ROI detection we are actually more interested in recall than in

Table 1. Evaluation of the ROI detector on 7 input images. While the precision is comparably low, recall is good, which is the main purpose of this step.

	Image 1	Image 2	Image 3	Image 4	Image 5	Image 6	Image 7
Actual ROIs	2	3	2	1	1	2	2
Predicted ROIs	4	4	2	3	3	4	4
Recall	1	0.67	1	1	1	1	1
Precision	0.5	0.5	1	0.33	0.33	0.5	0.5

precision, because missing a candidate for classification is worse than reporting a background patch as a ROI, as the latter can be handled by the classifier.

For a qualitative evaluation, we show an example result of the ROI detector in Fig. 4. As we can see here, the detector found the two regions of actual interest, i.e. the chair and the monitor, and it only returned one false positive.

4.2   Comparison of Adaptive Semi-supervised Learning and Standard Supervised Learning

To measure the performance of our adaptive semi-supervised learning method, we ran experiments on a subset of the standard benchmark data set Caltech 101, and on our own data. The subset consisted of 10 classes (see Fig. 5), for the Caltech 101 and 3 classes for our data. For both experiments, we used dictionaries for the HMP features that were learned from 10 images per class from the benchmark set. For the Caltech 101 we did not employ the ROI detector, because these images already contain one major object and not much background. Thus, we only clustered the data, computed HMP features for each image and trained a semi-supervised learner on a mixture of labeled and unlabeled images, where the labels were obtained from querying the best 3 representatives of each cluster. The results for the k-nn method and the transductive SVM with RBF kernel are given in the left column of Table 2. As we can see, the transductive SVM performs much better than the k-nn approach, and the final accuracy is comparably high, given that only very few data samples used for training were actually labeled.

Fig. 4. Example result of our ROI detector. The ground-truth ROIs are shown on the left and the predicted ROIs on the right.

Fig. 5. Examples from each of the 10 classes in the Caltech 101 data set which were used for the experiments

The same conclusion we can draw for our indoor office data set (see right column of Table 2). Here, we used 25 ROIs for evaluation, consisting of 6 chairs, 13 monitors and 6 telephones. Again, the transductive SVM performs better than the naive k-nn approach. Also, it is interesting to see that supervised learning works well when trained and tested on the same kind of data, but when tested on data from a different environment, it may fail as in our example. To overcome such problems our adaptive SSL method seems to be an appropriate approach.

Note that our adaptive TSVM approach gives somewhat worse results than the standard SVM method on Caltech101. This is because the clustering step for this data set had to be done using the HMP features and not SIFT, as for our own data: the appearances of the objects in Caltech 101 are simply too diverse to compare them using SIFT. However, we experienced that spectral clustering works worse on HMP features, which means that for Caltech 101 the training data provided to TSVM was of less quality than if we had chosen standard supervised learning. For our evaluation, this is however of little importance, as our method anyhow aims at adapting to a given environment with no previously labelled data where objects of the same class are not very diverse. An application of our method to an environment-independent, pre-labelled data set such as Caltech101 is therefore not very meaningful.

4.3   Number of Generated Label Queries

In another experiment, we investigated the correspondence of the number of label queries made by the algorithm and the classification accuracy. There are two parameters that can be set: the number of clusters c and the number m of patches per cluster, which receive a label after the query (see above). On one side, we want to have few clusters, i.e. c should be low. However, if there are more clusters, then the clusters are smaller and therefore *purer*, i.e. there are more elements that agree on the true class label. Purer clusters means that we can increase m, without assigning wrong labels to patches, thus we obtain better training data. This relationship is shown in Fig. 6. If the number of clusters is

Table 2. Classification accuracy of standard SVM learning and adaptive SSL methods on different data sets. The standard SVM was trained on a subset of Caltech 101 in both cases. Thus, while standard supervised learning gives good results when training and test data are similar, it can perform badly when they are dissimilar. However, our adaptive SSL performs much better, because it queries the relevant class labels from the data before learning the classifier. From the two considered methods, transductive SVMs perform better than the k-nearest neighbour method.

Learning method	Caltech 101	Our data
standard SVM	95.25%	52.00%
adaptive k-nn SSL	55.86%	58.00%
adaptive TSVM	81.43%	88.00%

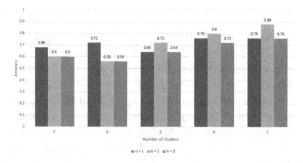

Fig. 6. Accuracy vs. number of clusters and number m (m = 1, 2, 3) of patches receiving a label from the query. More clusters lead to a higher cluster purity. Then, higher values of m are more effective, because the tSVM receives better training data.

small, we get the best accuracy for $m = 1$. But for more clusters, $m = 2$ is better, because by assigning the same label to the first m elements of each cluster, we get fewer wrong labels. In general we found that having less labels for training is better than having more, but wrong labels.

5   Discussion and Conclusions

Our proposed approach for adaptive semi-supervised learning for object detection in indoor environments has two major advantages over standard supervised learning methods: first, it is able to select informative data to learn from and to adapt to a given environment by only querying labels for currently observed, situation-relevant data and using them to train a classifier. And second, it reduces the number of required user interactions by making more informed questions about the data based on a pre-clustering step. Our experiments show that the proposed approach can outperform standard non-adaptive supervised learning when applied to environment-dependent data.

Acknowledgment. This work was funded by the EU project SPENCER (ICT-2011-600877).

References

1. Zhu, X.: Semi-supervised learning literature survey. Computer Sciences, University of Wisconsin-Madison, Tech. Rep. 1530 (2005)
2. Zhu, X.: Semi-supervised learning with graphs. Ph.D. dissertation, Carnegie Mellon University (2005)
3. Lawrence, N.D., Platt, J.C., Jordan, M.I.: Extensions of the informative vector machine. In: Winkler, J.R., Niranjan, M., Lawrence, N.D. (eds.) Machine Learning Workshop. LNCS (LNAI), vol. 3635, pp. 56–87. Springer, Heidelberg (2005)
4. Saffari, A., Leistner, C., Bischof, H.: Regularized multi-class semi-supervised boosting. In: Conf. on Comp. Vision & Patt. Recog., CVPR (2009)
5. Joachims, T.: Transductive inference for text classification using support vector machines, pp. 200–209 (1999)
6. Triebel, R., Paul, R., Rus, D., Newman, P.: Parsing outdoor scenes from streamed 3D laser data using online clustering and incremental belief updates. In: Robotics Track of AAAI Conference on Artificial Intelligence (2012)
7. Guillaumin, M., Verbeek, J., Schmid, C.: Multimodal semi-supervised learning for image classification. In: Conf. on Comp. Vision & Patt. Recog., CVPR (2010)
8. Ebert, S., Larlus, D., Schiele, B.: Extracting structures in image collections for object recognition. In: Daniilidis, K., Maragos, P., Paragios, N. (eds.) ECCV 2010, Part I. LNCS, vol. 6311, pp. 720–733. Springer, Heidelberg (2010)
9. Budvytis, I., Badrinarayanan, V., Cipolla, R.: Semi-supervised video segmentation using tree structured graphical models. Trans. on Pattern Analysis and Machine Intelligence 35(11), 2751–2764 (2013)
10. Settles, B.: Active learning literature survey. Tech. Rep. (2010)
11. Kapoor, A., Grauman, K., Urtasun, R., Darrell, T.: Gaussian processes for object categorization. Intern. Journal of Computer Vision 88(2), 169–188 (2010)
12. Triebel, R., Grimmett, H., Paul, R., Posner, I.: Driven learning for driving: How introspection improves semantic mapping. In: The International Symposium on Robotics Research, ISRR (2013)
13. Lowe, D.G.: Object recognition from local scale-invariant features. In: Proc. of the Intern. Conf. on Computer Vision (ICCV), pp. 1150–1157 (1999)
14. Achanta, R., Shaji, A., Smith, K., Lucchi, A., Fua, P., Susstrunk, S.: Slic superpixels compared to state-of-the-art superpixel methods. Trans. on Pattern Analysis and Machine Intelligence 34(11), 2274–2282 (2012)
15. Rosenberg, A., Hirschberg, J.: V-measure: A conditional entropy-based external cluster evaluation measure. In: Proc. of the Joint Conf. on Empirical Methods in Natural Language Proc. and Comp. Natural Language Learning (EMNLP-CoNLL), pp. 410–420 (2007)
16. Luxburg, U.: A tutorial on spectral clustering. Statistics and Computing 17(4), 395–416 (2007)
17. Bo, L., Ren, X., Fox, D.: Hierarchical matching pursuit for image classification: Architecture and fast algorithms. In: NIPS (2011)

Fast Semantic Segmentation of RGB-D Scenes with GPU-Accelerated Deep Neural Networks

Nico Höft, Hannes Schulz, and Sven Behnke

Rheinische Friedrich-Wilhelms-Universität Bonn,
Institut für Informatik VI, Friedrich-Ebert-Allee 144
{hoeft@cs,schulz@ais,behnke@cs}@uni-bonn.de

Abstract. In semantic scene segmentation, every pixel of an image is assigned a category label. This task can be made easier by incorporating depth information, which structured light sensors provide. Depth, however, has very different properties from RGB image channels. In this paper, we present a novel method to provide depth information to convolutional neural networks. For this purpose, we apply a simplified version of the histogram of oriented depth (HOD) descriptor to the depth channel. We evaluate the network on the challenging NYU Depth V2 dataset and show that with our method, we can reach competitive performance at a high frame rate.

Keywords: Deep learning, neural networks, object-class segmentation.

1 Introduction

Semantic scene segmentation is a major challenge on the way to functional computer vision systems. The task is to label every pixel in an image with surface category it belongs to. Modern depth cameras can make the task easier, but the depth information needs to be incorporated into existing techniques. In this paper, we demonstrate how depth images can be used in a convolutional neural network for scene labeling by employing a simplified version of the histogram of oriented gradients (HOG) descriptor to the depth channel (HOD). We train and evaluate our model on the challenging NYU Depth dataset and compare its classification performance and execution time to state of the art methods.

2 Network Architecture

We train a four-stage convolutional neural network, which is illustrated in Fig. 1, for object-class segmentation. The network structure, proposed by Schulz and Behnke [1], is derived from traditional convolutional neural networks, but has inputs at multiple scales. In contrast to classification networks, there are no fully connected layers at the top—the output maps are also convolutional.

The first three stages $s = \{0, 1, 2\}$ have input, hidden convolutional, and output maps I_s, C_s, O_s, respectively. Pooling layers P_s, P'_s between the stages

C. Lutz and M. Thielscher (Eds.): KI 2014, LNCS 8736, pp. 80–85, 2014.

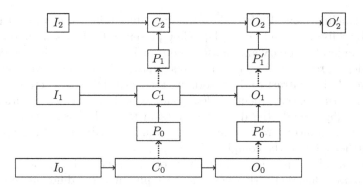

Fig. 1. Network structure used in this paper. On stage s, I_s is input, C_s a convolution, O_s the output, and P_i a pooling layer. Outputs of stage s are refined in stage $s + 1$, final outputs are refined from O_2 to O_2'. Solid and dashed arrows denote convolution and max-pooling operations, respectively. Every stage corresponds to a scale at which inputs are provided and outputs are evaluated.

reduce the resolution of the map representations. The output layer O_2' is the last stage. The network differs from common deep neural networks, as it is trained in stage-wise supervised manner and the outputs of the previous stage are supplied to the next stage to be refined. Thus, the lower stages provide a prior for the higher stages, while the simultaneous subsampling allows for the incorporation of a large receptive field into the final decision.

Every layer consists of multiple maps. Input layers have three maps for ZCA-whitened RGB channels, as well as five maps for histograms of oriented gradients and depth each (detailed in Section 4). Intermediate layers contain 32 maps. Convolutions extract local features from their source maps. Following Schulz and Behnke [1], all convolution filters have a size of 7×7, except for the last filter. The last filter has a size of 11×11 and only re-weights previous classification results, taking into account a larger receptive field. Also note that there are no fully connected layers—the convolutional output layers have one map for every class, and a pixel-wise multinomial logistic regression loss is applied. In contrast to Schulz and Behnke [1], we use rectifying non-linearities $\sigma(x) = \max(x, 0)$ after convolutions. This non-linearity improves convergence [2] and results in more defined boundaries in the output maps than sigmoid non-linearities. When multiple convolutions converge to a map, their results are added before applying a non-linearity.

3   Related Work

Our work builds on the architecture proposed in Schulz and Behnke [1], which (in the same year as Farabet et al. [3]) introduced neural networks for RGB scene segmentation. We improve on their model by employing rectifying non-linearities, recent learning algorithms, online pre-processing, and providing depth information to the model.

Scene labeling using RGB-D data was introduced with the NYU Depth V1 dataset by Silberman and Fergus [4]. They present a CRF-based approach and provide handcrafted unary and pairwise potentials encoding spatial location and relative depth, respectively. These features improve significantly over the depth-free approach. In contrast to their work, we use learned filters to combine predictions. Furthermore, our pipeline is less complex and achieves a high framerate. Later work [5] extends the dataset to version two, which we use here. Here, the authors also incorporate additional domain knowledge into their approach, which further adds to the complexity.

Couprie et al. [6] present a neural network for scene labeling which is very close to ours. Their network processes the input at three different resolutions using the same network structure for each scale. The results are then upsampled to the original size and merged within superpixels. Our model is only applied once to the whole image, but uses inputs from multiple scales, which involves less convolutions and is therefore faster. Outputs are also produced at all scales, but instead of a heuristic combination method, our network learns how to use them to improve the final segmentation results. Finally, the authors use raw depth as input to the network, which cannot be exploited easily by a convolutional neural network, e.g., absolute depth is less indicative of object boundaries than are relative depth changes.

A common method for pixel-wise labeling are random forests [7, 8], which currently provide the best results for RGB-D data [9, 10]. These methods scale feature size to match the depth for every image position. Our convolutional network does not normalize the feature computation by depth, which makes it easy to reuse lower-level features for multiple higher-level computations.

4   Pre-processing

Since our convolution routines[1] only support square input images, we first extend the images with mirrored margins. To increase generalization, we generate variations of the training set. This is performed online on the CPU while the GPU evaluates the loss and the gradient, at no cost of speed. We randomly flip the image horizontally, scale it by up to $\pm 10\%$, shift it by up to seven pixels in horizontal and vertical direction and rotate by up to $\pm 5°$. The depth channel is processed in the same way. We then generate three types of input maps.

From random patches in the training set, we determine a whitening filter that decorrelates RGB channels as well as neighboring pixels. Subtracting the mean and applying the filter to an image yields three zero phase (ZCA) whitened image channels.

On the RGB-image as well as on the depth channel, we compute a computationally inexpensive version of histograms of oriented gradients (HOG [11]) and histogram of oriented depth (HOD [12]) as follows.

For every pixel p, we determine its gradient direction α_p and magnitude n_p. The absolute value of $|\alpha_p|$ is then quantized by linear interpolation into two of

---

[1] We employ convolutions from the cuda-convnet framework of Alex Krizhevsky.

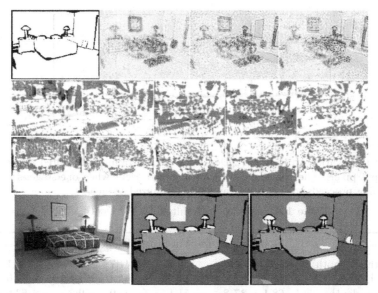

Fig. 2. Network maps, inputs and outputs. First row, ignore mask and ZCA-whitened RGB channels. Second and third row, HOG and HOD maps, respectively. Fourth row, original image, ground truth and network prediction multiplied by ignore mask for reference. Mirrored margins are removed for presentation to save space. Note that HOG and HOD encode very different image properties with similar statistics.

five bins at every image location, and weighted by n_p. To produce histograms of the orientation strengths present at all locations, we apply a Gaussian blur filter to all quantization images separately. Finally, the histograms are normalized with the L_2-hys norm.

The main difference to the standard HOG descriptor is that no image *cells* are combined into a single descriptor. This leaves it to the network to incorporate long-range dependencies and saves space, since our descriptor contains only five values per pixel.

All maps are normalized to have zero mean and unit variance over the training set. The process is repeated for every scale, where the size is reduced by a factor of two. For the first scale, we use a size of 196×196. The teacher maps are generated from ground truth by downsampling, rotating, scaling, and shifting to match the network output. We use an additional ignore map, which sets the loss to zero for pixels which were not annotated or where we added a margin to the image by mirroring. Sample maps and segmentations are shown in Fig. 2.

5   Experiments

We split the training data set into 796 training and 73 validation images. In a stage s, we use the RMSProp learning algorithm with an initial learnrate 10^{-4}, to train the weights of all stages below or equal to s. The active stage is automatically switched once the validation error increases or fails to improve. The pixel mean of the classification error over training is shown in Fig. 3. During

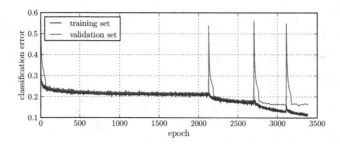

Fig. 3. Classification error on NYU Depth V2 during training, measured as the mean over output pixels. The peaks and subsequent drops occur when one stage is finished and learning proceeds to the next—randomly initialized—stage.

Table 1. Classification Results on NYU Depth V2

Method	Floor	Structure	Furniture	Props	Pixel Acc.	Class Acc.
Ours without depth	69.1	57.8	55.7	41.7	56.2	56.1
Ours with depth	77.9	65.4	**55.9**	**49.9**	61.1	62.0
[6] without depth	68.1	**87.8**	51.1	29.9	59.2	63.0
[6] with depth	**87.3**	86.1	45.3	35.5	63.5	64.5

the first two stages, training and validation error behave similarly, while in the final stages the network capacity is large enough to overfit.

Classification Performance. To evaluate performance on the 580 image test set, we crop the introduced margins, determine the pixel-wise maximum over output maps and scale the prediction to match the size of the original image. There are two common error metrics in the literature, the average pixel accuracy and the average accuracy over classes, both of which are shown in Table 1. Our network benefits greatly from the introduction of depth maps, as apparent in the class accuracy increase from 56.1 to 62.0. We compare our results with the architecture of Couprie et al. [6], which is similar but computationally more expensive. While we do not reach their overall accuracy, we outperform their model in two of the four classes, *furniture* and, interestingly, the rather small *props*—despite our coarser output resolution.

Prediction Speed. We can also attempt to compare the time it takes to process an image by the network. Couprie et al. [6] report 0.7 s per image on a laptop. We process multiple images in parallel on a GPU. With asynchronous pre-processing, our performance saturates at a batch size of 64, where we are able to process 52 frames per second on a 12 core Intel Xeon at 2.6 GHz and a NVIDIA GeForce GTX TITAN GPU. Note that this faster than the frame rate of the sensor collecting the dataset (30 Hz). While the implementation of Couprie et al. [6] could certainly also profit from a GPU implementation, it requires more convolutions as well as expensive superpixel averaging and upscaling operations. Our network is also faster than random forests on the same task (30.3 fps [10], hardware similar to ours).

6 Conclusion

We presented a convolutional neural network architecture for RGB-D semantic scene segmentation, where the depth channel is provided as feature maps representing components of a simplified histogram of oriented depth (HOD) operator. We evaluated the network on the challenging NYU Depth V2 dataset and found that introducing depth significantly improved the performance of our model, resulting in competitive classification performance. In contrast to other published results of neural network and random-forest based methods, our GPU implementation is able to process images at a high framerate of 52 fps.

References

[1] Schulz, H., Behnke, S.: Learning object-class segmentation with convolutional neural networks. In: Eur. Symp. on Art. Neural Networks (2012)

[2] Krizhevsky, A., Sutskever, I., Hinton, G.: Imagenet classification with deep convolutional neural networks. In: Adv. in Neural Information Processing Systems (2012)

[3] Farabet, C., Couprie, C., Najman, L., LeCun, Y.: Scene parsing with multiscale feature learning, purity trees, and optimal covers. arXiv preprint arXiv:1202.2160 (2012)

[4] Silberman, N., Fergus, R.: Indoor scene segmentation using a structured light sensor. In: Int. Conf. on Computer Vision (ICCV) Workshops (2011)

[5] Silberman, N., Hoiem, D., Kohli, P., Fergus, R.: Indoor Segmentation and Support Inference from RGBD Images. In: Fitzgibbon, A., Lazebnik, S., Perona, P., Sato, Y., Schmid, C. (eds.) ECCV 2012, Part V. LNCS, vol. 7576, pp. 746–760. Springer, Heidelberg (2012)

[6] Couprie, C., Farabet, C., Najman, L., LeCun, Y.: Indoor Semantic Segmentation using depth information. CoRR abs/1301.3572 (2013)

[7] Sharp, T.: Implementing decision trees and forests on a GPU. In: Forsyth, D., Torr, P., Zisserman, A. (eds.) ECCV 2008, Part IV. LNCS, vol. 5305, pp. 595–608. Springer, Heidelberg (2008)

[8] Shotton, J., Sharp, T., Kipman, A., Fitzgibbon, A., Finocchio, M., Blake, A., Cook, M., Moore, R.: Real-time human pose recognition in parts from single depth images. Communications of the ACM (2013)

[9] Stückler, J., Waldvogel, B., Schulz, H., Behnke, S.: Dense real-time mapping of object-class semantics from RGB-D video. Journal of Real-Time Image Processing (2013)

[10] Müller, A.C., Behnke, S.: Learning Depth-Sensitive Conditional Random Fields for Semantic Segmentation of RGB-D Images. In: Int. Conf. on Robotics and Automation, ICRA (2014)

[11] Dalal, N., Triggs, B.: Histograms of oriented gradients for human detection. In: Computer Vision and Pattern Recognition, CVPR (2005)

[12] Spinello, L., Arras, K.O.: People detection in RGB-D data. In: Int. Conf. on Intelligent Robots and Systems (IROS). IEEE (2011)

Energy-Efficient Routing:
Taking Speed into Account

Frederik Hartmann and Stefan Funke

Institut für Formale Methoden der Informatik
Universität Stuttgart

Abstract. We introduce a novel variant of the problem of computing energy-efficient and quick routes in a road network. In contrast to previous route planning approaches we do not only make use of variation of the routes to save energy but also allow variation of driving speed along the route to achieve energy savings. Our approach is based on a simple yet fundamental insight about the optimal velocities along a fixed route and a reduction to the constrained shortest path problem.

1 Introduction

Taking energy consumption into account when planning a road trip becomes more and more of an issue. While in the old days, gasoline was cheap, today fuel prices are constantly increasing and due to the limited supply of fossil fuels probably always will be. While in this case taking energy consumption into account is mostly a means of saving money and reducing carbon dioxide emissions, in the context of electric vehicles (EVs) energy-aware route planning might even make the difference between reaching the destination and getting stranded halfway due to a depleted battery. In the medium term, EVs (in particular when recharged using renewable energies, e.g. from solar or wind power) are to replace fossil fuel driven vehicles, but currently the limited energy reservoir (typically around or less than 200 km cruising range) as well as the sparsity of battery reloading/switch stations makes energy awareness mandatory for EVs.

Artmeier et al. in [2] formalized one variant of energy-constrained route planning, taking into account special characteristics of EVs like energy recuperation. They essentially use a variant of the Bellman-Ford algorithm to compute the most energy-efficient route for an EV. Later Eisner et al. in [3] showed how to transform the problem instance such that Dijkstra's algorithm as well as the speedup technique of contraction hierarchies [6] apply. This resulted in data structures that can be precomputed in few minutes even on country-sized road networks like that of Germany allowing for query times several orders of magnitude faster than Bellman-Ford or Dijkstra. There is a fundamental disadvantage of this approach, though: it only aims at minimizing the energy consumption not taking into account travel time or length of the respective route. In particular, since the models in [2] and [3] always assume that road segments are used with their typical maximum speed (e.g. residential roads at 30 km/h, inner city

C. Lutz and M. Thielscher (Eds.): KI 2014, LNCS 8736, pp. 86–97, 2014.

roads 50 km/h, country roads 100 km/h, autobahns 130 km/h), applying these approaches often leads to routes which excessively use residential and inner city roads since at these lower speeds the energy consumption is minimal – routes of this type are hardly useful in practice.

In [7] Storandt considered the *constrained shortest path* (CSP) problem in the energy-aware routing context: for a given bound T on the travel time the goal is to compute the most energy-efficient path from some node s to some node t in the road network not exceeding travel time T (alternatively, one could also bound the energy-consumption and optimize the travel time). Typically one would query with a bound T which is – let's say – 10% above the time of the quickest path from s to t takes. The resulting paths are considerably more useful in practice since nobody is willing to take a route which takes twice as long as the quickest route just for some minuscule energy savings. One difficulty with this approach is the hardness of the CSP problem in general, even though for real-world problem instances, a carefully tuned implementation like the one in [7] can compute probably optimal results in reasonable time. A similar result in the context of bicycle routes has been presented in [8]. The approach by Funke and Storandt [5] on the other hand allows to optimize a conic combination of two or more criteria, e.g., energy consumption and travel time. While excluding some Pareto-optimal solutions, the preprocessing and the query – in contrast to the CSP approach – can be performed in polynomial time. Still, [7] and [5] assume that road segments are always traversed at their typical maximum speed, ignoring the fact that it is well possible to save some energy e.g. on an autobahn by going 100 km/h instead of 140 km/h.

Our Contribution

In this paper we introduce a novel variant of the problem of computing energy-efficient yet quick routes in a road network. In contrast to previous route planning approaches we do not only deliberately choose the routes to save energy but also allow variation of the driving speed along the route to achieve energy savings. The main insight which our approach is based upon is the fact that for *a fixed route and travel time* it is most energy-efficient to drive with uniform speed if possible. We propose efficient solution strategies to obtain solutions to the problem via reduction to several constrained shortest path (CSP) problem instances. In spite of CSP being NP-hard we can compute exact solutions for real-world problem instances within a reasonable amount of time.

2 Fundamentals and Basic Techniques

Before we can talk about actual algorithms we first need to introduce our mobility model. We assume the road network is given as a directed acyclic graph $G(V, E)$ with a straightline embedding in the plane. Each edge $e \in E$ has a road type $type(e) \in R$. Each road type $r \in R$ has an associated upper bound $v_{max}(r)$ on the allowed speed on a road of that respective type. For example, for the road type 'autobahn', we might have $v_{\max}(autobahn) = 150$; often we directly write $v_{\max}(e) = 150$ for an edge e of type 'autobahn'. By $|e|$ we denote the Euclidean length of an edge in the given straightline embedding.

Obviously, when travelling at speed v, it takes $|e|/v$ time to traverse a road segment e of length $|e|$. The energy consumption along a road segment has a more complicated dependence on the speed, though.

2.1   Energy Model

Air resistance is the main factor that influences energy/fuel consumption when the speed increases. This essentially leads to a quadratic dependence on the speed. We use the following function as proposed in [4]

$$f(v)[ml/m] : v \rightarrow c_1v^2 - c_2v + c_3 + \frac{c_4}{v}$$

where $c_1 = 0.00625968$, $c_2 = 0.11736$, $c_3 = 2.1714$, $c_4 = 18\frac{1}{3}$, see Figure 1. The speed v is expected to be given as $[m/s]$, the fuel consumption as $[ml/m]$. Above 54 km/h, this function is non-negative, convex and strictly increasing (in the E-mobility context, the minimum is already at a lower speed). Observe that it never pays off to drive more slowly than 54 km/h, and in case of edges e with $v_{\max}(e) < 54$km/h, it is most beneficial to use them at that maximum speed.

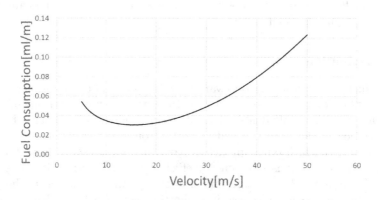

Fig. 1. Energy/Fuel Consumption dependent on velocity

2.2   Crucial Insight: Varying Speed Does Not Pay Off

Let us first examine how speed can be varied in different parts of a route if the travel time is to be kept constant. To that end consider without loss of generality a route section of unit length (not necessarily contiguous!) that is traversed in one unit of time and divide the route section into two halves of length 1/2 each.

Lemma 1. *If a unit length route section is traversed such that the speed in the first half is $v^{(l)}$, in the second half $v^{(r)}$, and the total travel time is one time unit, then for $v^{(l)} \leq v^{(r)}$ we have*

$$v^{(r)} = \frac{v^{(l)}}{2v^{(l)} - 1}$$

Proof. We have that $\frac{1/2}{v^{(l)}} + \frac{1/2}{v^{(r)}} = 1$, the above inequality follows.   □

The following lemma essentially states that if we go 1 km/h slower on the first half, we have to go faster by more than 1 km/h in the second half:

Lemma 2. *If a unit length route section is traversed in one unit of time, once with speeds $v_1^{(l)}$ ($v_1^{(r)}$) in the left (right) half, once with speeds $v_2^{(l)}$ ($v_2^{(r)}$), and $1/2 < v_1^{(l)} < v_2^{(r)} \leq 1$, then we have $v_1^{(l)} + v_1^{(r)} > v_2^{(l)} + v_2^{(r)}$*

Proof. Lemma 1 implies that the dependence of $v^{(r)}$ from $v^{(l)}$ behaves like $x \mapsto \frac{x}{2x-1}$ for $x \in (0.5, 1]$ which has slope less or equal to 1. The lemma follows.   □

We use the above two lemmas to prove the main theorem of this section.

Theorem 1. *Assume a unit length route section is traversed in one unit of time, once with speeds $v_1^{(l)}$ ($v_1^{(r)}$) in the left (right) half, once with speeds $v_2^{(l)}$ ($v_2^{(r)}$), and $1/2 < v_1^{(l)} < v_2^{((l))} \leq 1$. Then, the energy consumption of traversing the route section with speeds $v_1^{(l)}$, $v_1^{(r)}$ is strictly greater than the energy consumption of traversing the route section with speeds $v_2^{(l)}$, $v_2^{(r)}$ for strictly monotone and convex energy functions.*

Proof. Lemma 2 implies $v_1^{(l)} < v_2^{(l)} \leq 1 \leq v_2^{(r)} < v_1^{(r)}$. The energy consumptions to compare are $E_1 := (f(v_1^{(l)}) + f(v_1^{(r)}))/2$ and $E_2 := (f(v_2^{(l)}) + f(v_2^{(r)}))/2$.

Let $p_i^{(l)} := (v_i^{(l)}, f(v_i^{(l)})) \in \mathbb{R}^2$ and $p_i^{(r)} := (v_i^{(r)}, f(v_i^{(r)})) \in \mathbb{R}^2$. By convexity of f we know that the segment $p_2^{(l)} p_2^{(r)}$ lies below the segment $p_1^{(l)} p_1^{(r)}$ between $v_2^{(l)}$ and $v_2^{(r)}$. Lemma 2 also implies that $(v_2^{(l)} + v_2^{(r)})/2 < (v_1^{(l)} + v_1^{(r)})/2$, hence with the monotonicity of f we obtain $E_1 > E_2$.   □

Essentially this theorem states that if a route section is to be traversed within a certain time, it is most energy-efficient to do so at a uniform speed if possible. This leads to the following corollary which lies at the very heart of our routing approach.

Corollary 1. *If for a route section s that has to be traversed in time t it is possible to traverse it at uniform speed $v := |s|/t$, this is the most energy efficient way of traversal.*

Proof. Assume the most energy efficient way of traversal is not at uniform speed. Then we can identify a subsection (potentially infinitesimally small) where the first half is traversed at speed $v^{(l)}$, the second half at speed $v^{(r)}$, w.l.o.g.

$v^{(l)} < v^{(r)}$. Increasing $v^{(l)}$ a bit and hence being able to decrease $v^{(r)}$ without affecting the travel time for this subsection, we obtain a more energy efficient way of traversal according to our Theorem, contradicting the assumption that we started with the most energy efficient way of traversal.   □

This corollary immediately implies that on road sections of the same type (uniform speed-limit, not necessarily contiguous), we should always drive with uniform speed.

Furthermore, if we have a route composed of different road sections (with differing maximum speeds), the energy-optimal traversal strategy if a fixed travel time t has to be met is the following:

- along the route the maximum speed of travel is v^*
- for all road sections e with $v_{\max}(e) < v^*$, we travel at speed $v_{\max}$
- for all road sections e with $v_{\max}(e) \geq v^*$ we travel at speed v^*

Again, correctness follows from the fact that for road sections (even non-contiguous) with the same maximum speed limit it is most beneficial to drive at uniform speed. If, there is some route section e where we drive at speed $v' < v_{\max(e)}$ and $v' < v^*$, it is more economical to drive slightly slower than v^* on some other route section and slightly faster on e according to our Theorem.

In summary, the above discussion implies that once we fix a maximum speed in our search for an energy-optimal s-t path with time bound T, the speeds on all edges (and hence both time-consumption as well as energy consumption) are uniquely determined, hence turning our problem into an 'ordinary' constrained shortest path problem where for two fixed metrics we are to compute the optimal path with respect to one metric satisfying a constraint on the second.

Furthermore observe that due to the fact that road sections of the same type have to be traversed at the same speed, the energy/travel time characteristics of a path are solely determined by the aggregated lengths of the different road type sections (e.g. 20 km inner-city road, 80 km country road, 400 km autobahn).

2.3   Contraction Hierarchies (CH)

Our proposed algorithms make use of a very elegant yet effective speedup technique for shortest path queries which we will sketch briefly in the following. The CH preprocessing technique as introduced by Geisberger et al. in [6] augments the graph $G(V, E)$ with a set E' of so called shortcuts, which span (large) sections of shortest paths and hence allow for a reduction of edge relaxations and node settling steps in a Dijkstra run. During the CH-construction nodes are contracted one-by-one in some suitable order, thereby assigning a label $l : V \to \mathbb{N}$ to each node. An edge (v, w) is referred to as upwards if $l(v) < l(w)$ and downwards otherwise, a path is called upwards/downwards if it consists exclusively of edges of that type. Shortcuts are inserted in such a way, that for each source-target pair $s, t \in V$ a shortest path exists in $G' = G(V, E \cup E')$ which can be decomposed into an upward section starting at s followed by a downward section ending in t. This property allows to restrict a bidirectional Dijkstra run to $G_{out}^{\uparrow}(s)$ and $G_{in}^{\downarrow}(t)$ which refer to the subgraphs of G' containing only all upwards paths starting in s or all downwards paths ending in t respectively. For 'normal' shortest path queries, the restriction to $G_{out}^{\uparrow}(s)$ and $G_{in}^{\downarrow}(t)$ improves query times by several orders of magnitude.

2.4 The Constrained Shortest Path Problem

The two-criteria Constrained Shortest Path problem (CSP) can be defined as follows: We are given a (di)graph $G(V, E)$ ($|V| = n, |E| = m$), a cost function $c : E \to \mathbb{R}^+$ and a resource consumption function $r : E \to \mathbb{R}^+$ on the edges. A query is specified by a source and a target node $s, t \in V$ as well as a resource bound $R \in \mathbb{R}^+$. The goal is to determine the minimum cost path from s to t whose resource consumption does not exceed R.

In our context of energy-efficient routing, the cost function equals energy consumption, and the resource consumption equals travel time. It is important to note, though, that CSP assumes *scalar values* for the cost and resource values of individual edges, whereas in our case part of the problem is determining the optimum speed for each road segment.

Typical solutions to the CSP problem enumerate Pareto-optimal solutions by for example label setting [1]. In spite of NP-hardness of the CSP problem in general, these approaches are somewhat feasible for real-world data, in particular when combined with speedup techniques like contraction hierarchies, e.g. [7].

Our approach of taking into account speed variations into the energy-optimization problem will use (CH-accelerated) CSP as a basic building block.

2.5 The General Energy-Efficient Routing Problem

With our insights from Section 2.2 we are now ready to formally define the *General Energy-Efficient Routing Problem (GEERP)*:

Definition 1 (GEERP). *Given the straightline embedding of a directed graph $G(V, E)$, maximum speeds $v_{\max} : E \to \mathbb{R}$ on the edges, and an energy consumption function $f : \mathbb{R} \to \mathbb{R}$, the goal is to determine for a query (s, t, T) a path π from s to t as well as a speed value v^* such that*

– travel time along π does not exceed the time bound T:

$$\sum_{e \in \pi} \frac{|e|}{\min(v_{\max}(e), v^*))} \leq T$$

– the energy consumption

$$\sum_{e \in \pi} |e| \cdot f(\min(v_{\max}(e), v^*))$$

is minimal over all possible paths and speed values.

The assumption that one drives either at speed v^* or $v_{\max}(e)$ on an edge e of the path seems to be restrictive at first, but the above discussion has hopefully made clear that an optimal solution to the problem must have this special structure, so in fact we are also taking care of the general problem where arbitrary speeds are allowed on the road segments along the path π.

3   Algorithms

In the following we will describe algorithms to solve GEERP using the insights of the previous Section. For simplicity let us first assume that the possible speed values are *discrete*. We will come back to that issue later again.

3.1   Simple Reduction to CSP

If we have a discrete set of speeds $\{v_1, v_2, \ldots v_k\}$, we can 'simply' solve GEERP by considering k CSP instances; the i-th CSP instance is constructed by setting the travel times and energy consumption according to a speed of v_i (or the respective maximum speed if that lies below v_i). Among the at most k feasible CSP solutions we pick the one with minimum energy consumption.

Note, though, that binary search over the set of feasible speeds is not possible, since the minimum energy consumption to get from s to t within a certain time limit does not depend monotonically on the speed, see Figure 2.

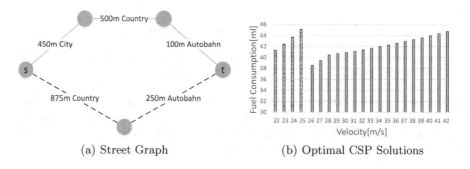

(a) Street Graph   (b) Optimal CSP Solutions

Fig. 2. Non-monotonical energy consumption with two alternative routes and a time constraint of 55 seconds (speed limits as in Table 1). Up to 25 m/s the lower path yields the optimal fuel consumption.

3.2   SpeedUp Using CH

The running times to solve the CSP problem on real-world roadmap data can be drastically improved by employing the speedup technique of contraction hierarchies. For example in [8], a contraction hierarchy is constructed which guarantees to preserve all Pareto-optimal paths. The crucial operation in the course of the CH construction is a *node contraction*. In [8], whenever a node v with neighbors u, w and $(u, v) \in E$, $(v, w) \in E$ is to be contracted, a shortcut (u, w) (with cost/resource consumption of the path uvw) has to be created if uvw is a Pareto-optimal path (note that this – in contrast to the single-metric case – typically leads to multi-edges between nodes). We could transfer this idea in a straightforward manner by constructing for each speed v_i a respective contraction hierarchy and use this for answering of the respective CSP instance. This seems ineffective, though, since we expect a lot of correlation between 'good' paths in the different contraction hierarchy graphs in particular for only slight variations of the speed. The space consumption of this approach is prohibitive: essentially we would need to store k times the CH-augmented road network (here k is the number of different velocities to be considered) – unrealistic for county-sized networks like that of Germany.

Instead our approach is to construct *one* contraction hierarchy that can be used for all CSP instances to be solved during the course of our algorithm. Again, the crucial operation is the node contraction step. When contracting a node v with neighbors u, w and $(u, v) \in E$ and $(v, w) \in E$, we need to create a shortcut uw if there exists a velocity s^* for which uvw is Pareto optimal. So we have to compare the velocity-dependent functions associated with paths(which have the same source and target) to decide on the creation of a shortcut. In Figure 3, left, we have depicted two paths with their velocity/fuel-consumption dependency. Each of the paths W1 and W2 is optimal for some choices of velocity. On the other hand, Figure 3, right, depicts three paths W1, W2, W3, where W1 is dominated by W2 and W3 since there is no speed value where W3 is on the boundary of the lower envelope. To decide whether a shortcut replacing uvw has to be created, we need to determine for all possible velocities the most energy-efficient paths from u to w; if uvw is amongst them the shortcut is necessary. We do this by explicitly computing the lower envelope of the speed-vs-energy function of all paths from u to w. Note that while the complexity of the speed-vs-energy function of a single route is constant (due to constantly many road types only), the lower envelope might exhibit almost arbitrary complexity. If during the CH construction the complexity of the lower envelope for some u, w-pair explodes, we refrain from contracting node v. In general – as for example in [8] – we only contract about 99.3% of all nodes leaving the remaining uncontracted.

In our experimental Section we will see that while we are far away from the speedups possible for 'ordinary' shortest path queries (see [6]), our CH constructed on edge cost functions still yields an order of magnitude improvement compared to unaccelerated CSP constructions.

3.3   Heuristic Solutions

Even the fastest exact solution is bound by the possibly exponential-sized Pareto-optimal solution sets, therefore a fast and simple solution to the CSP instances (and hence GEERP) cannot be expected. For many real world applications like

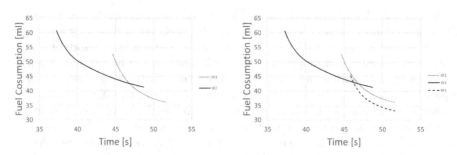

(a) Pareto-optimal Set after Insertion of W1 and W2

(b) Set after Insertion of Path W3 with now obsolete Path W1

Fig. 3. Two dimensional Example for combined Domination of Paths

the energy efficient routing a really optimal solution is not required, since a good approximation will already lead to a substantial improvement.

If we only consider a solution to be Pareto-optimal if it improves the target function by at least $x\%$ we are able to reduce the size of the solution sets substantially in real world applications. Even though the theoretical approximation guarantee is only $(1 + x)^{(i-1)}$ with i being the edge count in the optimal path, in practice, the resulting solutions are very close to optimal.

3.4   Further Remarks

At the very beginning we have restricted ourselves to a *discrete* set of velocities. Intuitively, this should not make a big difference, but we need to convince ourselves that this is indeed the case. Consider our energy cost function and an optimal path π^* from s to t with maximum velocity v^*. Clearly, we can also traverse the same path with the 'next' velocity $v' > v^*$ present in our discrete set of velocities using at most a factor of $\frac{f(v')}{f(v^*)}$ more energy. If we discretize the velocities at a granularity of at most 1 m/s, the respective difference cannot exceed 5.1%; a finer discretization, of course, leads to a reduction of the provable error (e.g. 0.5m/s yields at most 2.1%).

4   Experimental Results

To validate our approach and obtain approximation estimates, several real world graphs from OpenStreetMap were chosen as test instances. We used Java 7 as programming language with OpenJDK 7 as runtime environment. The contraction hierarchy was computed on a server with two AMD Opteron 6172 CPUs and 96 GB RAM. All queries were performed on a workstation with one Core i7 4770K CPU and 16GB RAM.

4.1 Benchmark Instances

The edge types shown in Table 1 represent the main types of streets found in Germany with their usual speed limitations. Note that our observations in Section 2.2 can easily be extended to the case where minimum speeds are given. In this case, if v^* is smaller than $v_{\min}(e)$, e is traversed at speed $v_{\min}(e)$.

Table 1. Used Street Types

	City	Country	Autobahn
v_{min}[km/h]	50	80	100
v_{max}[km/h]	50	100	150
v_{min}[m/s]	14	22	28
v_{max}[m/s]	14	28	42

Table 2. Size and Area of used Graphs

Graph	Area	Nodes	Edges
DE	Germany	$19,478,240$	$39,454,253$
BW	Baden-Württ.	$2,911,711$	$5,903,801$
ST	Stuttgart	$924,688$	$1,876,030$

We created the graphs shown in Table 2 by mapping the OSM edge types to their closest representative. Edge types that can't be used by motorized vehicles or requiring special permits have been removed.

4.2 CH-Creation

Table 3 shows the statistics for the CH construction. As can be seen, the number of edges has increased by less than factor of 2 after contraction of 99.3% of the nodes, the remaining 0.7% *peak nodes* were left uncontracted. As observed previously, e.g. in [7], contracting all nodes typically leads to a huge number of shortcuts and even worse query performance.

Table 3. Size and preprocessing Time of CH Creation (using 20 cores on our server)

Graph	Nodes	Edges	Peak Nodes	Preprocessing Time[s]
DE-CH	$19,478,240$	$70,128,496$	$154,856$ (0.7%)	$11,174$
BW-CH	$2,911,711$	$10,972,106$	$20,317$ (0.7%)	$4,767$
ST-CH	$924,688$	$3,452,011$	$2,743$ (0.7%)	$2,408$

4.3 CH-Accelerated CSP Queries – Exact and Approximate

We compared the runtime and number of priority queue pulls of the standard label-setting CSP algorithm with the CH-label-setting algorithm. As to be expected we observe an improvement by an order of magnitude, see Table 4.

With these query times being considerably above the response times desirable for route planning, we applied the heuristic proposed in Section 3.3 to reduce the runtime while preserving a good solution quality. As shown in Table 5, the runtime improves dramatically while keeping the average error below the required minimal Pareto difference. If we accept an average error of 0.4%, a CSP Query in BW can be answered in about 700 ms. Even on a country-sized road network like that of Germany, we achieve query times of few seconds.

Table 4. Query times for label-setting und CSP-CH at 42 m/s for the most energy-efficient path using at most 20% more time than the quickest path. Average of 1,000 (100 for BW/BW-CH) queries.

Graph	label-setting		CSP-CH	
	Query[ms]	Pulls	Query[ms]	Pulls
BW / BW-CH	331,143	$6.3 \cdot 10^8$	17,911	$1.8 \cdot 10^7$
ST / ST-CH	27,010	$8.2 \cdot 10^7$	1,730	$2.4 \cdot 10^6$

Table 5. Heuristic CSP solution; pruning ratio for Pareto sets, average (ΔE) and maximum $(\Delta E_{\max})$ deviation from energy consumption of optimal solution. 'Unused' time budget (ΔT). 42 m/s; at most 20% above quickest path.

	ST-CH				BW-CH				DE-CH
Pruning ratio	query time (ms)	ΔE	ΔE_{max}	ΔT	query time (ms)	ΔE	ΔE_{max}	ΔT	query (ms)
1	1,500	-	-	-	25,900 (100%)	-	-	-	570,691
1.001	416	0.009%	0.06%	−0.017%	4,100 (16%)	0.015%	0.08%	−0.016%	77,300
1.005	146	0.114%	0.91%	−0.174%	1,200 (5%)	0.152%	0.85%	−0.136%	20,200
1.01	103	0.300%	1.512%	−0.321%	692 (3%)	0.375%	1.83%	−0.405%	8,900

4.4 Solving GEERP

To solve the actual GEERP instance, we proceed as follows: First, we compute for every possible speed a rough solution using a rather coarse pruning rule for the Pareto sets. We start with the highest possible speed decreasing as long as feasible (i.e. within the given time bound T) solutions are found. This initial run identifies a smaller set of velocities where a more fine-grained approximation is computed. Table 6 lists the results.

Table 6. Heuristic GEERP solution results for DE-CH with total query time, preselection time and average cardinality of the preselected velocity set. The preselected velocity set was obtained by performing a coarse approximation and selecting velocities around the best solution. Average of 100 queries.

Fine-Grained Approximation	Preselection Pruning Rule	Query Time[s] (including Preselection)	Preselected Velocities
1.005	1.05	106.7 (30.3)	7.6
1.005	1.025	80.7 (49.1)	4.4
1.005	1.01	126.2 (109.6)	2.1
1.005	-	196.0	-
1.001	1.05	327.2 (30.3)	7.6
1.001	1.025	175.6 (49.1)	4.4
1.001	1.01	325.3 (109.6)	2.1
1.001	-	1,009.8	-

In summary, we can compute a very good approximation to the most energy-efficient route for given source and target within Germany meeting a hard time constraint within a few minutes. As an example, we considered a source-target pair in Germany with a minimum travel time of $3,815$ seconds and a fuel consumption of $9,025$ml. If we accepted a travel time of $4,570$ seconds, a path could be found by using a maximum speed CSP that required $6,825$ml of fuel. By applying our GEERP solution, a path could be found that only required $6,098$ml fuel, an improvement of about 25% compared to the shortest path and an additional improvement of 10% compared to the CSP path.

References

1. Aggarwal, V., Aneja, Y., Nair, K.: Minimal spanning tree subject to a side constraint. In: 32nd ACM Symposium on Theory of Computing (STOC), pp. 286–295 (1982)
2. Artmeier, A., Haselmayr, J., Leucker, M., Sachenbacher, M.: The shortest path problem revisited: Optimal routing for electric vehicles. In: Dillmann, R., Beyerer, J., Hanebeck, U.D., Schultz, T. (eds.) KI 2010. LNCS, vol. 6359, pp. 309–316. Springer, Heidelberg (2010)
3. Eisner, J., Funke, S., Storandt, S.: Optimal route planning for electric vehicles in large networks. In: AAAI Conference on Artificial Intelligence (2011), http://www.aaai.org/ocs/index.php/AAAI/AAAI11/paper/view/3637
4. Freie Universität Berlin, Institut für Chemie und Biochemie: Kfz energetisch betrachtet (January 2009), http://www.chemie.fu-berlin.de/chemistry/general/kfz-energetisch.html
5. Funke, S., Storandt, S.: Polynomial-time construction of contraction hierarchies for multi-criteria objectives. In: Algorithm Engineering and Experiments (ALENEX), pp. 41–54 (2013)
6. Geisberger, R., Sanders, P., Schultes, D., Delling, D.: Contraction hierarchies: Faster and simpler hierarchical routing in road networks. In: McGeoch, C.C. (ed.) WEA 2008. LNCS, vol. 5038, pp. 319–333. Springer, Heidelberg (2008), http://portal.acm.org/citation.cfm?id=1788888.1788912
7. Storandt, S.: Quick and energy-efficient routes: Computing constrained shortest paths for electric vehicles. In: Proceedings of the 5th ACM SIGSPATIAL International Workshop on Computational Transportation Science, IWCTS 2012, pp. 20–25. ACM, New York (2012)
8. Storandt, S.: Route planning for bicycles - exact constrained shortest paths made practical via contraction hierarchy. In: 22nd Int. Conf. on Automated Planning and Scheduling, ICAPS (2012)

CDCL Solver Additions: Local Look-Ahead, All-Unit-UIP Learning and On-the-Fly Probing

Norbert Manthey

Knowledge Representation and Reasoning Group,
Technische Universität Dresden

Abstract. Many applications can be tackled with modern CDCL SAT solvers. However, most of todays CDCL solvers guide their search with a simple, but very fast to compute decision heuristic. In contrast to CDCL solvers, SAT solvers that are based on look-ahead procedures spend more time for decisions and with their local reasoning. This paper proposes three light-weight additions to the CDCL algorithm, *local look-ahead*, *all-unit-UIP learning* and *on-the-fly-probing* which allow the search to find unit clauses that are hard to find by unit propagation and clause learning alone. With the additional reasoning steps of these techniques the resulting algorithm is able to solve SAT formulas that cannot be solved by the original algorithm.

1 Introduction

Complex search problems arise from various domains, ranging from logic puzzles over scheduling problems like railway scheduling [11] to large industrial problems like verification [6]. All these problems can be solved natively with a special domain solver, or the problem can be translated into satisfiability testing (SAT) [6]. Where randomly generated SAT formulas can be solved well with *stochastic local search* solver [17], SAT instances from applications are usually solved with solvers rooted in the DPLL procedure [7, 26], which perform a search that can be described as a depth-first-search. The best improvement of the DPLL algorithm is *clause learning* [22, 27]. This algorithm is known as the *conflict driven clause learning* (CDCL) algorithm, and adds *learned clauses* to the formula during search.

With this algorithm, modern SAT solvers can process a huge search space in a short amount of time. Reasons are for example the *Two-Watched-Literal* data structure [28], which is a slim data structure for the major inference technique, or the *VSIDS heuristic* [9,28], which leads to cheap to compute, but good decisions. With the help of *restarts* of the search [10, 18, 32], and frequently removing learned clauses from the formula again [1] the efficiency of the algorithm is increased even more.

The simplification of the formula is performed before the actual search of a SAT solver is started in a *preprocessing* step [2, 9, 24] with tools like SATELITE [8] or CO-PROCESSOR [25]. There are only a few SAT solvers, like for example LINGELING [5], that interleave the search with simplification (*inprocessing*). Hence, by the way the CDCL algorithm works, the majority of modern solvers miss a more global reasoning.

This paper proposes three simple and cheap to compute additions to the CDCL architecture that can be efficiently embedded without decreasing the speed of the CDCL

C. Lutz and M. Thielscher (Eds.): KI 2014, LNCS 8736, pp. 98–110, 2014.

algorithm. Furthermore, the proposed techniques add only unit clauses, which are never redundant.

The first addition proposes to perform a look-ahead step, which is capable of finding *backbones* [29] (also known as *necessary assignments* [15]), by performing look-ahead with up to five literals whenever five search decision have been made. By intersecting the 2^5 sets of implied literals, the literals in the intersection can be added as unit clauses to the formula. Typically, these unit clauses are hard to find for the CDCL algorithm. The motivation for the second addition is the following fact: When the CDCL algorithm learns a unit clause C_1, the procedure is stopped and the clause is added. The second addition proposes to continue the learning procedure in case the learned clause is a unit clause, because the next learned clause C_2 can be another unit clause as well. Interestingly, the clause C_2 cannot necessarily be found by unit propagation after C_1 is learned. Hence, adding C_2 to the formula prunes the search space. Finally, the third technique performs *probing* [23] with a learned clause C by finding the set of literals that is commonly implied by all literals of that clause. This probing is done on the binary implication graph of the formula to approximate costly operations on the formula, similarly to the work of Heule et al. [16]. With each technique instances can be solved that were not solved with the default setup of the solver, while the number of totally solved instances does not decrease significantly.

The paper is structured as follows: first, basic notations for satisfiability testing are given in Section 2. There, the algorithm of modern CDCL solvers is discussed as well. Next, the proposed additions are presented in Section 3 and after the proposed algorithms are compared to related work in Section 4, an empirical evaluation is presented in Section 5. Section 6 concludes the paper.

2 Preliminaries

Let $\mathcal{V}$ be a fixed infinite set of Boolean *variables*. A *literal* is a variable v (*positive literal*) or a negated variable $\overline{v}$ (*negative literal*). The *complement* $\overline{x}$ of a positive (negative, resp.) literal x is the negative (positive, resp.) literal with the same variable as x. In SAT, *formulas* are finite clause sets. Each clause C is a finite set of literals. A clause $\{x_1, \ldots, x_n\}$ is also written as disjunction $(x_1 \vee \ldots \vee x_n)$ and a formula $\{C_1, \ldots, C_n\}$ as a conjunction $(C_1 \wedge \ldots \wedge C_n)$. The empty clause is denoted with $\bot$, the empty formula is denoted with $\top$. The set of all variables occurring in a formula F (in positive or negative literals) is denoted by $\mathrm{vars}(F)$. Moreover, the set of all literals occurring in a formula F is denoted with $\mathrm{lits}(F)$.

The semantic of formulas is built on interpretations. An *interpretation* J is a set of literals where for all variables $v \in \mathcal{V}$ it holds that either $v \in J$ or $\neg v \in J$. A literal that is present in the interpretation J is called *satisfied*, and if the complement $\overline{l}$ is present in the interpretation, then the literal l is said to be *falsified*. As usual, the satisfaction relation $\models$ is defined as follows: $J \models \top$, $J \not\models \bot$, $J \models (x_1 \vee \ldots \vee x_n)$ iff $J \models x_i$ for some $i \in \{1, \ldots, n\}$, and $J \models (C_1 \wedge \ldots \wedge C_n)$ iff $J \models C_i$ for all $i \in \{1, \ldots, n\}$. The interpretation J is a *model* for the formula F if and only if $J \models F$. In the case that a formula F has a model, the formula F is *satisfiable* and otherwise the formula F is *unsatisfiable*. The *satisfiability problem* (SAT) then asks whether a given formula F

is satisfiable. This problem is solved with so called *SAT solvers*. An interpretation can also be *partial*. In this case, not all variables of V are present in the interpretation. Still, partial interpretations can satisfy formulas with the above definition.

The *reduct of the formula F w.r.t. the interpretation J* [14], in symbols $F|_J$ is computed as follows: First, all satisfied clauses are removed from F and in the second step, every falsified literal in F is removed. Intuitively, the reduct operator expresses the state of a DPLL-based SAT solver, where the formula F is the *working formula* and J is the *working assignment*.

In modern SAT solvers, the main deduction technique is *unit propagation* [2,5,9,24]. Given a formula F, and a partial interpretation J, then if there is a unit clause $C = x$ present in the reduct, $C \in F|_J$, then this clause can be satisfied only by assigning x to true. This assignment can only be achieved by adding the literal x to J. Such an extension is denoted as a procedure UP, which returns the extended interpretation: $\mathsf{UP}(F, J) = Jx$. Since there can be many unit clauses present in a formula, unit propagation is executed until a fixed point is reached. This execution is denoted with $J' = \mathsf{UP}(F, J)^{\square}$.

Finally, to approximate unit propagation of a formula F, only the binary clauses of the formula can be considered separately, and then unit propagation is performed only on this subset of clauses. This approximation is build on the *binary implication graph* (BIG) of the formula. A BIG is a graph (V, E), where V is the set of literals of the formula F, in symbols $V = \mathsf{lits}(F)$, and the set of edges E is build on the implications that are present as binary clauses: $E = \{(x, y), (\overline{y}, \overline{x}) \mid C \in F, C = (\overline{x} \vee y)\}$. To approximate unit propagation for a literal $x \in F$, a depth-first-search can be run in the BIG starting with node x. The set J' of literals of all the nodes that are visited during this search are implied by x with respect to F, in symbols: $(F \wedge x) \models J'$.

3   Finding Backbone Literals on the Fly

This section first discusses the CDCL algorithm that is used in modern SAT solvers. Then, three additions are presented, which enable the algorithm to perform more global reasoning.

3.1   The CDCL Algorithm

For applications, the satisfiability problem is solved best with the *conflict driven clause learning* (CDCL) algorithm [26, 27]. The CDCL algorithm takes a formula F as argument and returns either SAT or UNSAT as result, in case the formula is satisfiable or unsatisfiable. The algorithm starts with an empty partial interpretation J, and then extends this interpretation by adding search decisions, and implied literals. The implied literals are added by *unit propagation*, which is the major forward deduction technique of modern SAT solvers. With the help of specialized data structures, like the *two-watched literal* data structure, unit propagation can handle a large amount of clauses [28].

Search decisions are performed with so called decision heuristics. Such a heuristic selects the variable that should be used for the decision, and decides whether this variable should be bound to $\top$ or $\bot$. The number of decision variables in an interpretation define the *decision level* of all following variables in that interpretation. A widely used heuristic is the VSIDS heuristic [28] to select variables. A polarity is usually selected by *phase-saving* [31], which tries to assign the variable its most recent polarity, or the *Jeroslow-Wang* heuristic [21], which chooses the more frequent polarity. All these heuristics have in common that their computation is very cheap. This way, the heuristic decision might not be optimal, but the processing speed of the algorithm is kept high.

Another reason for the fast computation of the decision heuristic is the fact that as soon as a conflicting state is reached, the CDCL algorithm might undo all decisions that have been made so far. The reason is the *conflict analysis* procedure [27, 28, 34]. Let C be a clause of the current formula F, and J be the current partial interpretation that has been constructed by decisions and unit propagation. When the clause C is mapped to $\perp$ by J, then there is no extension of J that could satisfy C. Hence, literals are removed from J. These literals are determined by creating a new clause D with resolution. This clause D is also mapped to $\perp$ by J. Hence, J is reduced, such that the clause D can still be satisfied. Next, D is added to the formula, and then the algorithm continues with unit propagation and search. Since the clause D can be a unit clause, all literals of J might be removed, so that all decisions are undone. There is no information available, when the next conflict will be found, and how large the reduction of J might be. Thus, in current SAT solvers it pays off to spend little time on search decisions, because the quality of the current decision heuristics seems to be good enough.

Two more additions have been added to the CDCL algorithm: *Restarts* [10] are another technique that helps to search in the right place, or at least to stop searching in the wrong place. When the search is restarted, all learned clauses are kept, but all literals are removed from J. Modern solvers perform quite frequent restarts [18, 32]. By keeping the decision heuristic information and learned clauses, solvers do not loose too much information about their previous search focus, but by performing a restart, they can escape hard sub formulas [10].

The second addition is manage the added learned clauses. As there are exponentially many clauses that may be learned, SAT solvers aggressively remove clauses again to keep the deduction of all technique quick [1]. For the performance of CDCL solvers this step is crucial, because by removing irrelevant clauses, the current speed of the search can be kept high.

The widely used version of CDCL has a few weaknesses. First, only unit propagation is used as a deduction technique. Although with unit propagation implied literals can be computed fast, there exists reasoning techniques that deduce more literals. Another drawback is that only a single learned clause is generated from a conflict.[1] By generating multiple *good* clauses, the search space is pruned without introducing significant overhead. Finally, learned clauses can be used not only for unit propagation, but also for probing based techniques [23]. In the following sections for each of these weaknesses a solution is provided.

---

[1] An exception is the solver in [20], which generates multiple clauses to reduce the conflict graph.

3.2   Local Look Ahead

Given the current formula F and the current interpretation J, then the decision heuristic of CDCL solvers selects a single literal x and next this literal is used for unit propagation. Differently, look-ahead solvers test the immediate implications $J' = \mathsf{UP}(F, Jx)$ and $J'' = \mathsf{UP}(F, J\overline{x})$ before using x as a decision literal. The literals in the intersection of J' and J'' are known to be implied by the current reduct, $F|_J \models (J' \cap J'')$, so that these literals are added to J before x is used. Since CDCL solvers backjump and undo multiple decisions in one step, this kind of reasoning might introduce overhead compared to its contribution. However, as long as the interpretation J does not contain any decision literal, then the literals of the intersection $(J' \cap J'')$ are entailed by the formula F directly, and hence these literals can be added as unit clauses to the formula.

A first extension is to use two literals for the propagation, to be able to infer more literals during unit propagation, known as *double-look-ahead* [15]: For two literals L_1 and L_2, and for the four combinations $L_1 L_2$, $L_1 \overline{L_2}$, $\overline{L_1} L_2$ and $\overline{L_1 L_2}$ unit propagation is executed and the intersection of the four resulting sets of immediate implications is used. Since double-look-ahead cannot be executed for all variables of modern formulas, look-ahead solver preselect a set of literals and perform the double-look-ahead only based on these literals [15].

A similar idea can be used to run a more expensive look-ahead procedure dynamically during search. Let n be a fixed number of look-ahead literals. When the n-th decision literal L_n is added to the current interpretation J, the n decision literals are used to collect 2^n sets of immediate implications by performing unit propagation with the 2^n possible combinations of the literal L_1 to L_n and their complements. Finally, by building the intersection of all collected sets, a set of unit clauses that is entailed by the current formula F can be obtained.

The algorithm in Figure 1 illustrates this procedure. For the given set S of $n = |S|$ decision literals, the look-ahead procedure is executed. The intersection of all immediate implications J' is updated iteratively, and hence this intersection is initialized with the set of all the literals of the formula F (line 1). Next, for all combinations of the variables in S, where for each variable a polarity can be chosen (lines 2–6), the actual combination of literals M is created (line 2), and with this combination unit propagation is performed to collect the immediate implications J' (line 3). If this interpretation J' leads to a conflict with respect to the formula F, then the intersection I is not updated, because a conflict implies all literals. Otherwise, the intersection I is reduced J' (lines 4–5). The procedure is interrupted as soon as the intersection I becomes empty(line 6), because in this case no additional literals can be added. If the intersection contains literals after collecting all immediate implications, these literals are added to the formula (line 7).

As already explained, the first n decision literals of the interpretation J can be used for this procedure. Hence, the proposed algorithm executes local look-ahead as soon as the n-th decision literal is added to J. After the look-ahead procedure has been executed, the search should continue with the empty interpretation J.

Since n decisions will be reached soon again, and furthermore at least the first decision literal will be the same as before, the proposed look-ahead procedure should not be executed again as soon as the next n-th decision literal is added. Therefore, the set of

LocalLookAhead (CNF formula F, set of literals S)	
1 $I := \text{lits}(F)$	// initialize intersection
2 **for each** $M \in \text{complementPermutations}(S)$	// all combinations to negate literals
3 $J' := \text{UP}(F, M)^{\square}$	// execute unit propagation
4 **if** $\bot \notin F\vert_{J'}$ **then**	// if there is no conflict
5 $I := I \cap J'$	// update intersection
6 **if** $I = \emptyset$ **then break**	// early abort
7 $F := F \cup I$	// add the entailed unit clauses

Fig. 1. Pseudo code of the *LocalLookAhead* procedure

used decision literals S is stored as a tabu list. Only if the variables of this tabu list do not contain any of the current n decision literals, the look-ahead procedure is executed again, and the tabu list is updated. Furthermore, the presented algorithm is executed only right after adding the n-th decision literal, (and not after some number m of decisions greater n is added). This way, an additional disturbance of the search deeper in the search tree is avoided. In general the number n can be chosen arbitrarily. Since the number of combinations grows exponentially, the value $n = 5$ is proposed. Then, the intersection I can be computed efficiently, because this way a single 64 bit integer can store the truth value of a variable for all the 32 combinations, by using two bits per variable assignment to represent $\top$, $\bot$ or whether the variable is not assigned.

3.3 Learning Multiple Unit Clauses

Modern SAT solvers learn a single clause when a conflict is obtained, usually by resolution according to the *first-UIP* scheme [28]. In case a unit clause $C = x$ is learned, then all decision literals are removed from the current interpretation J, the unit clause (x) is added and then unit propagation is performed. As illustrated in the following example, the standard learning procedure might miss learning additional unit clauses which can be collected easily by a slight modification of the learning procedure. Given the formula

$$F = \begin{matrix} (\overline{a} \vee b) & \wedge & (\overline{b} \vee \overline{c} \vee d) & \wedge & (\overline{d} \vee e) & \wedge & (\overline{e} \vee f) \\ \wedge & (\overline{e} \vee g) & \wedge & (\overline{f} \vee \overline{g} \vee i) & \wedge & (\overline{i} \vee j) \\ \wedge & (\overline{i} \vee k) & \wedge & (\overline{i} \vee l) & \wedge & (\overline{j} \vee \overline{k} \vee m) & \wedge & (\overline{j} \vee \overline{l} \vee \overline{m}) \end{matrix}$$

and let J be the interpretation of the form $J = \dot{a}\dot{b}\dot{c}def\,gijlkm$ after the two decisions a and c. Then, the clause $(\overline{j} \vee \overline{l} \vee \overline{m})$ is the empty clause under the interpretation J.

The *conflict graph* in Figure 2 illustrates the interpretation J with respect to the clauses in the formula F. Each node in the graph represents a literal of the interpretation, or in case of $\overline{m}$ the complement of a literal in the interpretation. Furthermore, each literal is labeled with its decision level. The light grey nodes m and $\overline{m}$ mark the conflicting literal on the right side of the graph. The black nodes a and c on the left side of the graph represent the decision literals of J. Finally, the dark grey literals d, e and j represent the *unique implication points* (UIPs) of the conflict graph [28]. Each solid

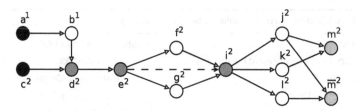

Fig. 2. A conflict graph that motivates all-unit-UIP learning

incoming arc shows for a literal which literal assignments led to the propagation of the current literal. Hence, the arc from f to i, and from g to i show that by assigning f and g to $\top$, the literal i has to be assigned to $\top$ as well. For each node with incoming edges and the corresponding literal there is a clause in the formula F that is responsible for the assignment of the literal. These clauses are called *reason clause*. For the literal i, the clause $(\overline{f} \vee \overline{g} \vee i)$ is the reason clause. The dashed arc from e to i in the graph show the implication $e \rightarrow i$, which is present in the formula F implicitly, meaning that the clause $(\overline{e} \vee i)$ is not present in the formula.

Typically, modern CDCL search learns first UIP clauses only [2, 5, 9, 24]. Such a clause is obtained by first resolving the reason clauses for the conflict literals m and $\overline{m}$. Then, resolution is performed with the reason clauses along the arcs of the conflict graph until only a single literal of the current decision level is left in the resolvent [27, 28]. The order of reason clauses to choose for resolution is obtained by traversing the interpretation J from its back to the front. When a variable is found in the interpretation J that is also present in the current resolvent, then this variable is used for resolution. Otherwise the next variable in J is considered [9].

In the above example, the unit clause $(\overline{i})$ is the first UIP clause. The *second UIP* is the clause $(\overline{e})$, the third UIP clause is the clause $(\overline{d})$, and the fourth and last UIP clause is the binary clause $(\overline{b} \vee \overline{c})$. Although all mentioned unit clauses could be learned from the given conflict graph, and thus are entailed by the underlying formula, the first UIP scheme generates only the clause $(\overline{i})$. Note that, based on the given formula, the unit clause $(\overline{i})$ does not find the other unit clauses unit propagation.

This weakness of the first UIP scheme can be overcome by continuing resolution along the arcs in the conflict graph, in case the learned clause is a unit clause. This addition is called *all-unit-UIP learning*. Hence, the proposed addition to the usual CDCL algorithm is to continue the learning procedure in case a unit clause C is learned. In the above example, the continued conflict analysis detects the other unit clauses $(\overline{e})$ and $(\overline{d})$, and also adds them to the formula.[2] Note that the presented situation can occur on any decision level, because missing all the unit clauses during conflict analysis is independent of the first decision level.

---

[2] Another way to resolve this issue would be to use *(lazy) hyper binary resolution* (LHBR), and to generate the clause $(i \vee \overline{e})$ by resolving the clauses $(\overline{e} \vee f)$ and $(\overline{e} \vee g)$ with $(\overline{f} \vee \overline{g} \vee i)$. However, LHBR checks have to be performed during unit propagation, whereas the proposed addition is necessary only during conflict analysis, and only if the learned clause is a unit clause. Therefore, the introduced overhead of multi-unit learning is considered to be lower.

3.4   Performing Probing During Search

After a clause is learned in the CDCL algorithm, this clause is added to the formula. Most of the learned clauses are removed again after a short time [1, 9]. By using an approximation of unit propagation and probing, additional knowledge can be inferred from the formula by testing each learned clause further.

Given a learned clause $C = (x_1 \lor \ldots \lor x_k)$, then unit propagation on each literal can be performed with the formula F to collect a set of intermediate implications: $J_i = \mathsf{UP}(F, (x_i))^{\square}$, $1 \leq i \leq k$. As already shown by Lynce et al. in [23], the intersection of these sets J_i is entailed by the formula F, in symbols $F \models \bigcap_{1 \leq i \leq k} J_i$, so that the units of the intersection can be added to the formula. Since, this algorithm is considered expensive [23] an approximation is proposed.

Similarly to the ideas of Heule et al. in [16], the *binary implication graph* (BIG) can be used to cheaply approximate unit propagation. The approximation collects only the literals that are implied by the current literal x_i in the BIG of the formula F. A further approximation is to not compute the transitive closure of the implied literals in the BIG, but only considering the adjacency list of the literal x_i. This adjacency list stores exactly those literals that appear in a binary clause with the literal $\overline{x_i}$. This way, the overhead of this technique is reduced. However, when building the intersection of the sets of the immediate implications J_i, this approximation yields another benefit. By sorting the adjacency lists in the BIG, the intersection of all sets $\bigcap_{1 \leq i \leq k} J_i$ can be computed in a single merging routine.

Treating Binary Clauses Specially. For special clause sizes extra inferences can be used. For unit clauses no deduction is necessary, because all immediate implications will be added by unit propagation. For learned binary clauses $C = (a \lor b)$, literals x have to be found, which are implied by both a and b, in symbols $a \rightarrow x$ and $b \rightarrow x$. This check can be performed with the approximation presented by Heule et al. in [16]. They traverse the BIG in a depth first manner and label each literal with two time stamps *start* and *end*. The time stamp *start* is assigned when the literal is seen the first time in the search, and the time stamp *end* is set when the depth first search finished the sub tree of the literal. The value of the stamp is increased whenever a new literal is visited, or when a visiting a literal finished. Let `start` be the function that returns that *start* time stamp for a literal, and let `end` be the function that returns the *end* time stamp for a literal. Then, a literal l is implied by another literal a in the BIG, if $\mathsf{start}(a) < \mathsf{start}(l)$ and $\mathsf{end}(l) < \mathsf{end}(a)$. Unfortunately, this check is incomplete, as also argued by Heule et al. Still, such a check enables adding more literals to the set of commonly implied literals for binary clauses, because literals can be added even when they are not present in the adjacency list of both literals a and b.

In general, for binary learned clauses, all literals of the formula could be tested with the above approximation. However, since such an exhaustive check is expensive, the literals for the check are limited to the literals x that are present in the adjacency lists of the two literals a and b. A literal x can be added to the set J' of commonly implied literals, if x is present in both adjacency lists, or if x is present in the adjacency list of one literal, and is implied by the other literal – checked with the approximation above.

Table 1. Empirical evaluation on the full benchmark

	AUIP	LLA	PLAIN	OTFP
Solved	1594	1588	**1615**	1604
Unique	13	**53**	22	11
SAT	917	916	**935**	925
UNSAT	677	672	**680**	679
conflicts / s	**13338**	11101	12123	11681

4   Related Work

There are additional techniques that help to simplify the formula during search or that infer additional knowledge. A technique that leads to similar effects as the all-unit-UIP learning is *lazy hyper-binary-resolution*(LHBR) [4], that checks for binary resolvents during propagation. By adding these binary resolvents, the missing implication is added to the formula. However, the computation of LHBR is more expensive than the computation of all-unit-UIP learning, because LHBR is tested for a clause during propagation whereas all-unit-UIP learning is only executed if the first UIP clause is a unit clause. Similarly to LHBR, the *dominator analysis* [12] analyzes clauses during propagation, and infers additional literals during conflict analysis.

Another technique that uses learned clauses for more deduction than unit propagation is *on-the-fly self subsumption* [13]. During the conflict analysis it is checked whether the resolvent D of the previous resolvent C_1 and the reason clause C_2 subsumes the reason clause C_2. In this case, C_2 is replaced in the formula by D, effectively removing one literal from that clause. This technique is enhanced by the *concurrent clause strengthening* of Wieringa [33]. By running the *clause vivification* algorithm [30] on the learned clauses in a separate solver environment, the size of learned clauses can be reduced.

Finally, the most powerful extra deduction during search can be achieved by using a complex CNF simplifier during search, as done for example in LINGELING [5]. This way, hyper binary resolution and clause strengthening can be executed to cover for example all-unit-UIP learning, however, implementing a full CNF simplifier is non-trivial. On the contrary, implementing the proposed additions to a CDCL solver requires the addition only a few lines of code. Furthermore, inprocessing could miss some relevant learned clauses, because the removal heuristic can delete these clauses before the next inprocessing step is scheduled.

5   Empirical Evaluation

The presented algorithm additions are implemented into the SAT solver RISS [24], which is an extension of the SAT solver GLUCOSE 2.2 mainly by incorporating the CNF simplifier COPROCESSOR [25].[3] To stay as close as possible to GLUCOSE, GLU-COSE's simplification algorithms are used. The evaluation is performed on all industrial

---

[3] RISS 4.27 with the additions is available at
  http://tools.computational-logic.org.

instances and all crafted instances that have been used in the SAT Race 2010, the SAT Competitions 2011 and 2013, and the SAT Challenge 2012. Furthermore, the unselected instances of these competitions 2011 and 2012 are added. The CPU time limit is set to 3600 seconds and the memory limit is 3.5 GB. The used CPU is an AMD Opteron 6274 with 2 MB level 2 cache that is shared by two cores. The experiment uses one out of four cores for a SAT solver to achieve stable results. The following abbreviations are used for the configurations: local look-ahead (LLA), all-unit-UIP learning (AUIP), on-the-fly-probing (OTFP) and PLAIN for the default configuration.

Table 1 shows the data for all the proposed additions to the algorithm, as well as running the plain algorithm on the full benchmark. Besides the number of solved instances, the number of *unique contributions* are presented – this number shows how many instances can be solved by the given configuration only – as well as the number of solved satisfiable and unsatisfiable instances. Interestingly the configuration with the highest number of unique contributions, namely LLA, solves the least number of instances. Another interesting fact is that the configuration AUIP cannot solve more instances than the configuration PLAIN, although it generates more conflicts per second, indicating that the search of this solver is faster. The solver seems to be tuned highly, so that any small change decreases its performance. The number of less solved instances can be explained better for the two remaining configurations: both LLA and OTFP produce less conflicts per second than the configuration PLAIN. The unique solver contribution of each solver gives a hint how well a portfolio of the four configurations would perform, by simply summing up the number of solved instances of the configuration PLAIN, with the unique solver contributions of the other configurations – with this calculation 1692 instances could be solved. The actual number of solved instances of all the configurations, also known as the *virtual best solver*, is 1726 solved instances.

The number of revealed additional unit clauses varies for each technique and each instance. Most unit clauses can be found with LLA, followed by OTFP and some unit clauses can be found by AUIP. For more than half of the formulas of the benchmark no additional unit clauses are found with a technique. For the formulas where unit clauses can be found, up to 10% of the variables of the formula can be found. When all three techniques are enabled together, then the performance of the solver does not improve, but the median run time decreases due to the overhead of all techniques. The number

Table 2. Empirical evaluation on crafted competition benchmark

Category (instances)	AUIP	LLA	PLAIN	OTFP
CRAFTED2011 (300)	**85**	83	**85**	**85**
SAT	58 (0)	57 (**6**)	**60** (0)	**60** (0)
UNSAT	**27** (**1**)	26 (1)	25 (0)	25 (0)
CRAFTED2012 (600)	286	291	**294**	290
SAT	180 (0)	183 (**13**)	**186** (2)	183 (0)
UNSAT	106 (0)	**108** (2)	**108** (1)	107 (1)
CRAFTED2013 (300)	**118**	116	115	108
SAT	84 (3)	**86** (**7**)	85 (1)	80 (0)
UNSAT	**34** (**4**)	30 (1)	30 (0)	28 (0)

Table 3. Empirical evaluation on industrial competition benchmark

Category (instances)	AUIP	LLA	PLAIN	OTFP
INDUSTRIAL2010 (100)	**65**	**65**	**65**	**65**
SAT	14 (0)	**15** (2)	14 (0)	**15** (1)
UNSAT	**51** (0)	50 (0)	**51** (0)	50 (0)
INDUSTRIAL2011 (300)	157	155	158	**159**
SAT	75 (0)	74 (**1**)	75 (**1**)	**76** (0)
UNSAT	82 (0)	81 (0)	**83** (2)	**83** (1)
INDUSTRIAL2012 (600)	434	437	440	**444**
SAT	205 (1)	204 (**5**)	**208** (3)	207 (1)
UNSAT	229 (1)	233 (**7**)	232 (3)	**237** (4)
INDUSTRIAL2013 (300)	112	107	**120**	115
SAT	66 (1)	65 (**4**)	**72** (4)	68 (2)
UNSAT	46 (**2**)	42 (**2**)	**48** (**2**)	47 (1)

of revealed unit clauses also increases for some formulas, so that different techniques reveal different unit clauses. However, this additional number of unit clauses does not improve the solver to solve more formulas than the configuration PLAIN.

Next, Table 2 shows the results on crafted competition instances. On this kind of instances, the additional reasoning helps solving more instances. Especially on unsatisfiable instances, this effect is visible. An effect that can be seen is that the performance of a configuration is not stable over the different benchmark sets. The 2011 benchmark can be solved equally well by all configurations, for 2012 PLAIN solves most instances, and the 2013 benchmark can be solved best by AUIP. Industrial benchmarks show a similar picture (Table 3). The number of solved instances is again different for each year. In the 2012 benchmark the additionally solved unsatisfiable instances of the configuration OTFP result in the highest number of total solved instances. Similarly, the configuration PLAIN solves the most instances of 2013.

As in the instance sets before, the configuration LLA usually solves less instances, but has more unique contributions. This effect might be explained as follows: The underlying solver RISS is already tuned on existing benchmark sets based on the number of totally solved instances. Hence, any addition to the algorithm usually results in decreasing the number of instances, since the default configuration resulted in a local minimum. The configuration LLA seems to push the algorithm configuration into an interesting direction, so that the solver is able to solve different instances, however, at the same time other instances cannot be solved any more in the time limit. By tuning the complete solver configuration with a tool like PARAMILS or SMAC [19], a setup might be found that can solve many instances, and furthermore provides a higher number of unique contributions. This step is considered as future work.

6   Conclusion

Modern CDCL solvers are very important for solving many industrial applications, as well as academic problems. The used algorithm is optimized to process a huge search space in a short amount of time. This paper proposes three additions to this algorithm that aim at finding backbone literals on the fly during search without significant overhead. The three techniques *local look-ahead*, *all-unit-UIP* learning and *on-the-fly-probing* allow to solve instances that cannot be solved with the plain algorithm, but the total number of solved instance of the benchmark does not increase due to the fact that the used SAT solver is already highly tuned. This drawback can be weakened by two additions that are considered as future work. First, by tuning the parameters of the solver with the new techniques a configuration might be found that outperforms the current setup. Furthermore, by combining the different techniques as a portfolio may also result in a higher performance.

Acknowledgments. The author thanks the ZIH of TU Dresden for providing the computational resources to produce the experimental data for the empirical evaluation and the reviewers for the helpful comments.

References

1. Audemard, G., Simon, L.: Predicting learnt clauses quality in modern SAT solvers. In: Boutilier, C. (ed.) IJCAI 2009, pp. 399–404. Morgan Kaufmann Publishers Inc., Pasadena (2009)
2. Audemard, G., Simon, L.: Glucose 2.3 in the SAT 2013 competition. In: Balint, et al. (eds.) [3], pp. 42–43
3. Balint, A., Belov, A., Heule, M.J., Järvisalo, M. (eds.): Proceedings of SAT Challenge 2013, Department of Computer Science Series of Publications B, vol. B-2013-1. University of Helsinki, Helsinki, Finland (2013)
4. Biere, A.: PrecoSAT system description (2009), http://fmv.jku.at/precosat/ preicosat-sc09.pdf
5. Biere, A.: Lingeling, Plingeling and Treengeling entering the SAT competition 2013. In: Balint, et al. (eds.) [3], pp. 51–52
6. Biere, A., Heule, M., van Maaren, H., Walsh, T. (eds.): Handbook of Satisfiability. IOS Press, Amsterdam (2009)
7. Davis, M., Logemann, G., Loveland, D.: A machine program for theorem-proving. Commun. ACM 5(7), 394–397 (1962)
8. Eén, N., Biere, A.: Effective preprocessing in SAT through variable and clause elimination. In: Bacchus, F., Walsh, T. (eds.) SAT 2005. LNCS, vol. 3569, pp. 61–75. Springer, Heidelberg (2005)
9. Eén, N., Sörensson, N.: An extensible SAT-solver. In: Giunchiglia, E., Tacchella, A. (eds.) SAT 2003. LNCS, vol. 2919, pp. 502–518. Springer, Heidelberg (2004)
10. Gomes, C.P., Selman, B., Crato, N., Kautz, H.: Heavy-tailed phenomena in satisfiability and constraint satisfaction problems. J. Autom. Reason. 24(1-2), 67–100 (2000)
11. Großmann, P., Hölldobler, S., Manthey, N., Nachtigall, K., Opitz, J., Steinke, P.: Solving periodic event scheduling problems with SAT. In: Jiang, H., Ding, W., Ali, M., Wu, X. (eds.) IEA/AIE 2012. LNCS, vol. 7345, pp. 166–175. Springer, Heidelberg (2012)
12. Han, H.J., Jin, H.S., Somenzi, F.: Clause simplification through dominator analysis. In: DATE, pp. 143–148. IEEE (2011)
13. Han, H., Somenzi, F.: On-the-fly clause improvement. In: Kullmann, O. (ed.) SAT 2009. LNCS, vol. 5584, pp. 209–222. Springer, Heidelberg (2009)

14. van Harmelen, F., Lifschitz, V., Porter, B.: Handbook of Knowledge Representation. Elsevier Science, San Diego (2007)
15. Heule, M., van Maaren, H.: Look-ahead based SAT solvers. In: Biere, et al. (eds.) [6], pp. 155–184
16. Heule, M.J.H., Järvisalo, M., Biere, A.: Efficient CNF simplification based on binary implication graphs. In: Sakallah, K.A., Simon, L. (eds.) SAT 2011. LNCS, vol. 6695, pp. 201–215. Springer, Heidelberg (2011)
17. Hoos, H., Sttzle, T.: Stochastic Local Search: Foundations & Applications. Morgan Kaufmann Publishers Inc., San Francisco (2004)
18. Huang, J.: The effect of restarts on the efficiency of clause learning. In: IJCAI, pp. 2318–2323 (2007)
19. Hutter, F., Hoos, H.H., Leyton-Brown, K.: Sequential model-based optimization for general algorithm configuration. In: Coello Coello, C.A. (ed.) LION 2011. LNCS, vol. 6683, pp. 507–523. Springer, Heidelberg (2011)
20. Jabbour, S., Lonlac, J., Saïs, L.: Adding new bi-asserting clauses for faster search in modern sat solvers. In: Frisch, A.M., Gregory, P. (eds.) SARA. AAAI (2013)
21. Jeroslow, R.G., Wang, J.: Solving propositional satisfiability problems. Annals of Mathematics and Artificial Intelligence 1, 167–187 (1990)
22. Katebi, H., Sakallah, K.A., Marques-Silva, J.P.: Empirical study of the anatomy of modern SAT solvers. In: Sakallah, K.A., Simon, L. (eds.) SAT 2011. LNCS, vol. 6695, pp. 343–356. Springer, Heidelberg (2011)
23. Lynce, I., Marques-Silva, J.P.: Probing-based preprocessing techniques for propositional satisfiability. In: ICTAI 2003, pp. 105–110. IEEE Computer Society (2003)
24. Manthey, N.: The SAT solver RISS3G at SC 2013. In: Balint, et al. (eds.) [3], pp. 72–73
25. Manthey, N.: Coprocessor 2.0 – A flexible CNF simplifier - (tool presentation). In: Cimatti, A., Sebastiani, R. (eds.) SAT 2012. LNCS, vol. 7317, pp. 436–441. Springer, Heidelberg (2012)
26. Marques-Silva, J.P., Lynce, I., Malik, S.: Conflict-driven clause learning SAT solvers. In: Biere, et al. (eds.) [6], ch. 4, pp. 131–153
27. Marques Silva, J.P., Sakallah, K.A.: GRASP: A search algorithm for propositional satisfiability. IEEE Transactions on Computers 48(5), 506–521 (1999)
28. Moskewicz, M.W., Madigan, C.F., Zhao, Y., Zhang, L., Malik, S.: Chaff: Engineering an efficient SAT solver. In: DAC 2001, pp. 530–535. ACM, New York (2001)
29. Parkes, A.J.: Clustering at the phase transition. In: AAAI 1997/IAAI 1997, pp. 340–345. AAAI Press (1997)
30. Piette, C., Hamadi, Y., Sais, L.: Vivifying propositional clausal formulae. In: ECAI. Frontiers in Artificial Intelligence and Applications, vol. 178, pp. 525–529 (2008)
31. Pipatsrisawat, K., Darwiche, A.: A lightweight component caching scheme for satisfiability solvers. In: Marques-Silva, J., Sakallah, K.A. (eds.) SAT 2007. LNCS, vol. 4501, pp. 294–299. Springer, Heidelberg (2007)
32. van der Tak, P., Ramos, A., Heule, M.: Reusing the assignment trail in cdcl solvers. JSAT 7(4), 133–138 (2011)
33. Wieringa, S., Heljanko, K.: Concurrent clause strengthening. In: Järvisalo, M., Van Gelder, A. (eds.) SAT 2013. LNCS, vol. 7962, pp. 116–132. Springer, Heidelberg (2013)
34. Zhang, L., Madigan, C.F., Moskewicz, M.W., Malik, S.: Efficient conflict driven learning in boolean satisfiability solver. In: International Conference on Computer-Aided Design, pp. 279–285 (2001)

Formula Simplifications as DRAT Derivations

Norbert Manthey and Tobias Philipp

Knowledge Representation and Reasoning Group,
Technische Universität Dresden, 01062 Dresden, Germany
tobias.philipp@tu-dresden.de

Abstract. Many real world problems are solved with satisfiability testing (SAT). However, SAT solvers have documented bugs and therefore the answer that a formula is unsatisfiable can be incorrect. Certifying algorithms are an attractive approach to increase the reliability of SAT solvers. For unsatisfiable formulas an unsatisfiability proof has to be created. This paper presents certificate constructions for various formula simplification techniques, which are crucial to the success of modern SAT solvers.

1 Introduction

The complexity class NP is one of the mostly studied classes in artificial intelligence. Due to the improvement of SAT solving technology in the last two decades, translating NP problems into Boolean satisfiability problem (SAT) became a successful and attractive approach. SAT solving is now widely applied to many applications in software verification [6], planning [24, 35], bioinformatics [27] or scheduling [12]. This success is also due to formula simplification that became an important part of SAT solvers and increase the robustness of the solver [8, 13, 14, 17, 18, 21, 26, 28, 29, 36, 37].

However, SAT solvers have documented bugs and therefore the answer of the solver can be incorrect. Certifying algorithms [7, 32] are an attractive approach to increase the reliability of SAT solvers. For satisfiable formulas, a model serves as a certificate for satisfiability; for unsatisfiable formulas, a proof of unsatisfiability is constructed: Van Gelder introduced *resolution graph proofs* in [10], which trace the clauses that have been used for deriving the learned clause. When the empty clause is derived, the formula is unsatisfiable and the trace can be easily verified. However, it requires significant effort to modify the SAT solver to emit resolution graph proofs and these proofs require a significant amount of space. Therefore, Goldberg et al. proposed *reverse unit propagation* (RUP) [11], which is more compact: If unit propagation on the formula together with the negated literals from the clause results in a conflict, the clause follows from the formula. In particular, learned clauses are RUP inferences [5]. Consequently, the sequence of learned clauses of CDCL-based SAT solvers is a RUP-proof. The verification of RUP proofs is more complex than for resolution graph proofs, but the RUP proof size is much smaller. Clause deletion is an important improvement of RUP proofs [15] (DRUP) and captures *clause forgetting* [2, 3, 9] in SAT solvers. Since DRUP cannot verify the addition of clauses that are not entailed by the formula, the format *deletion resolution asymmetric tautology* (DRAT) was proposed [16], that combines *clause deletion*, *reverse unit propagation* [11], and the redundancy property *resolution asymmetric tautology* [22].

C. Lutz and M. Thielscher (Eds.): KI 2014, LNCS 8736, pp. 111–122, 2014.

Järvisalo et al. have shown in [22] that many important techniques, such as *pure literals*, *blocked clauses* [21] are resolution asymmetric tautologies. For *bounded variable addition* [29] and *extended resolution* [37], it is stated how to construct DRAT derivations in [16]. Unfortunately, the general structure of DRAT derivations for general resolution-based techniques is not explicitly stated in the literature, and for some techniques such as *covered clause elimination*, a short DRAT derivation is not known.

Our Contributions. This paper presents various DRAT constructions. In particular:

- We develop a general structure for DRAT derivations for resolution-based simplification techniques, and apply the structure to obtain short derivations for hyper binary resolution, common direct implication, variable elimination, self-subsuming resolution, equivalent literal elimination, vivification and 2SAT-based reasoning. To the best our knowledge, the DRAT construction for covered clause elimination, and a variation of bounded variable addition are new.
- We discuss the novel simplification technique *covered literal elimination* and show that this technique is covered with DRAT.
- We extend the preprocessor `Coprocessor`[1] to emit DRAT derivations.

Structure. Section 2 presents preliminaries about propositional logic. Thereafter, in Sect. 3 we present DRAT derivations as certificates of unsatisfiability. Our contributions are then presented in Sect. 4, where we construct DRAT derivations for various formula simplifications, and proof various properties. We conclude in Sect. 5.

2   Preliminaries

We assume the reader familiar with propositional logic. We consider a fixed infinite set $\mathcal{V}$ of Boolean *variables*. A *literal* is a variable v (*positive literal*) or a negated variable $\overline{v}$ (*negative literal*). The set of all literals is denoted by $\mathcal{L}$. The *complement* $\overline{x}$ of a positive (negative, resp.) literal x is the negative (positive, resp.) literal with the same variable as x. In SAT, we deal with finite clause multisets, called *formulas*. Each clause C is a finite set of literals. Multiset operators are denoted as set operators, but marked with a dot. The set of variables occuring in a formula F is denoted by vars(F). An *interpretation* is a mapping from the set of truth values $\{\top, \bot\}$ and interprets clauses as disjunctions and a multiset of clauses as a conjunction under the usual semantics. A clause is a *tautology*, if it contains x and $\overline{x}$ for some variable $x \in \mathcal{V}$. If $I(F) = \top$, then I is a *model* of F and F is called *satisfiable* In the case that there is no model of a formula F, it is *unsatisfiable*. We use $\models$ to denote logical entailment. Two formulas F and F' are *equisatisfiable*, if they are both satisfiable or both unsatisfiable. Replacing all occurrences of the variable v with the variable w in the formula F is denoted by $F[v \mapsto w]$. The set of all variables occurring in a formula F (in positive or negative literals) is denoted by vars(F). Moreover, we denote the set of all literals occurring in a formula F as elements in a clause by lits(F).

---

[1] Available at http://tools.computational-logic.org/

Let $x \in C_1$ and $\overline{x} \in C_2$. Then the clause $(C_1 \setminus \{x\}) \cup (C_2 \setminus \{\overline{x}\})$, denoted by $C_1 \otimes_x C_2$, is the *resolvent of the clauses C and D upon the literal x*. A *linear resolution derivation from the clause C to the clause D in the formula F* is a finite sequence of clauses $(C_i \mid 1 \leq i \leq n)$ such that $C_1 = C$, $C_n = D$ and C_i is a resolvent of the clause C_{i-1} and some clause in the formula F for all $i \in \{2, \ldots, n\}$. A *resolution derivation in the formula F to the clause D* is a finite sequence $(C_i \mid 1 \leq i \leq n)$ of clauses such that $D = D_n$, $C_i \in F$ or C_i is a resolvent of two clauses C_j and C_k, where $1 \leq j < i \leq n$, and $1 \leq k < i \leq n$.

3 DRAT as a Certificate for Unsatisfiability

Given a formula F and a literal set S, *asymmetric literal addition* is the function $\mathsf{ALA} : 2^{\mathcal{L}} \mapsto 2^{\mathcal{L}}$ where

$$\mathsf{ALA}_F(S) = S \cup \{\overline{x} \mid \{x_1, \ldots, x_n, x\} \in F \text{ and } x_i \in S \text{ for all } 1 \leq i \leq n\}.$$

A clause C is an *asymmetric tautology* (AT) in the formula F, if $\mathsf{ALA}_F^n(C)$ is a tautology for some $n \in \mathbb{N}$. If the context is clear, we will sometimes drop the index F. The following example illustrate the definitions:

Example 1. Consider the formula $F = \{\{x_1, x_2\}, \{x_1, \overline{x_2}, x_3\}, \{\overline{x_3}, \overline{x_2}\}\}$. We have the following: *(i)* the clause $\{x_1\}$ is an asymmetric tautology w.r.t. the formula F, because $\mathsf{ALA}_F(\{x_1\}) = \{x_1, \overline{x_2}\}$ and $\mathsf{ALA}_F(\{x_1, \overline{x_2}\}) = \{x_1, \overline{x_2}, x_3, \overline{x_3}\}$, *(ii)* the clause $\emptyset$ is not an asymmetric tautology because $\mathsf{ALA}_F(\emptyset) = \emptyset$, and *(iii)* the clause $\{x_2\}$ is not an asymmetric tautology because $\mathsf{ALA}_F(\{x_2\}) = \{x_2, \overline{x_1}\}$ is a fixed point. In fact, the clause $\{x_1\}$ is the single, subset minimal asymmetric tautology in the formula F.

The clause C is a *resolution asymmetric tautology* (RAT) w.r.t F, if there is a literal x such that all resolvents of the clause C and clauses $D \in F$ with $\overline{x} \in D$ upon x are asymmetric tautologies.

Example 2. Consider the formula from the previous example. We have the following: *(i)* the clause $\{x_1\}$ is a RAT because there is no clause $D \in F$ with $\overline{x_1} \in D$, *(ii)* the clause $\{x_2\}$ is a RAT, because there is only one resolvent $\{x_1\}$ which is an AT, *(iii)* the clause $\{x_3\}$ is a RAT, because there is only one resolvent $\{x_1, \overline{x_2}\}$, which is an AT because it is subsumed by the AT $\{x_1\}$, and *(iv)* the clause $\{x_2, x_3\}$ is a RAT w.r.t. the literal x_2 because the resolvent $\{x_1, x_3\}$ is an AT and the resolvent $\{x_3, \overline{x_3}\}$ is an AT.

Järvisalo et al. have shown two nice properties in [22]: the addition of asymmetric tautologies and resolution asymmetric tautologies preserve satisfiability. We will now present DRAT derivations, that were introduced by Heule at. al. in [16].

A *labelled clause* is a pair (C, L), where C is a clause and $L \in \{\mathsf{d}, \mathsf{at}, \mathsf{rat}\}$. To ease our notation, we write C^L instead of (C, L). We consider finite sequences of labelled clauses, where the empty sequence is denoted by Λ. The associated formula of a sequence of labelled clauses $(C_i \mid 1 \leq i \leq n)$ w.r.t. the formula F is recursively defined as follows: $F_0 = F$, and $F_i = F_{i-1} \dot{\cup} \{C\}$, if $C_i = C^{\mathsf{at}}$ or $C_i = C^{\mathsf{rat}}$, and $F_i = F_{i-1} \setminus \{C\}$ if $C_i = C^{\mathsf{d}}$ for all $i \in \{1, \ldots, n\}$. A sequence of labelled clauses

Method	Structure of the Resulting Formula
Clause Elimination	$F \setminus \{C\}$
Clause Addition	$F \cup \{C\}$
Literal Elimination	$(F \setminus \{C\}) \cup \{C \setminus D\}$
Literal Addition	$(F \setminus \{C\}) \cup \{C \cup D\}$
Resolution-based	$(F \setminus G) \cup \{C_1, \ldots, C_n\}$
2SAT-based	$(F \setminus G) \cup \{D_1, \ldots, D_n\}$

Fig. 1. Categorization of formula simplification methods. F, G denote (possibly empty) formulas, C, D non-empty clauses, and the clauses C_i are obtained by a general resolution derivation in $F \cup G$, and D_i denote clauses that are logically entailed by the binary clauses in $F \cup G$.

$(C_i \mid 1 \leq i \leq n)$ is a *deletion resolution asymmetric tautology (DRAT) derivation* in the formula F if and only if for all $1 \leq i \leq n$ it holds that *1.* if $C_i = C^{\text{at}}$, then C is an asymmetric tautology in the associated formula F_{i-1}, and *2.* if $C_i = C^{\text{rat}}$, then C is a resolution asymmetric tautology in the associated formula F_{i-1}. A *DRAT refutation for the formula F* is a DRAT derivation $(C_i \mid 1 \leq i \leq n)$ w.r.t. F such that $\emptyset \in F_n$. If a DRAT refutation for the formula F exists, then the empty clause can be inferred from which we conclude that the formula F is unsatisfiable.

4   Formula Simplification Techniques

A *formula simplification technique* T is a mapping $T : \mathcal{F} \mapsto \mathcal{F}$ from the set of formulas $\mathcal{F}$ into the set of formulas $\mathcal{F}$. We investigate the question whether we can construct a short, corresponding DRAT derivation for formula simplification techniques:

Definition 1. *A technique T has* short DRAT-derivations, *if there is a polynomial p such that for every formula F there is a DRAT-derivation $(C_i \mid 1 \leq i \leq n)$ w.r.t. F such that $F_n = T(F)$ and $n \leq p(|F| + |T(F)|)$.*

We distinguish between clause elimination methods, resolution-based methods, clause addition methods, literal elimination, 2SAT-based and addition techniques (see Fig 1).

4.1   Clause Elimination and Literal Addition Techniques

First, we consider clause elimination and literal addition techniques. For instance, *subsumption elimination*, *tautology elimination*, *hidden tautology elimination* [17] and *blocked clause elimination* [21], *covered clause elimination* [18] belong to the first category, while techniques such as *hidden literal addition* [19] and *covered literal addition* [18] belong to literal addition techniques.

Proposition 1. *Clause elimination and literal addition techniques have short DRAT-derivations.*

Proof. Consider a clause elimination technique T_{CE}, the polynomial $p(s) = 2$, and a formula F. Then $T_{\text{CE}}(F) = F \setminus \{C\}$ for some clause C, and the labelled clause sequence C^d is a DRAT derivation of length $1 < p(|F| + |T(F)|)$. Hence, clause elimination techniques have short DRAT-derivations. Consider a literal addition technique T_{LA}. Then, $T_{\text{LA}}(F) = (F \setminus \{C\}) \cup \{C \cup \{x\}\}$ for some clause C and literal x. Note that the clause $C \cup \{x\}$ is an asymmetric tautology in F, because $C \in F$ and therefore $\{y, \overline{y}\} \subseteq \text{ALA}_F(C)$ for some literal $y \in C$. Hence, the labelled clause sequence $(C \cup \{x\})^{\text{at}} C^d$ is a DRAT derivation w.r.t. F of length $2 \leq p$. $\qquad\square$

Hence, if a technique removes a clause C from a formula, we can add C^d to the DRAT derivation, and if a techniques adds the literal x to a clause C, we add $(C \cup \{x\})^{\text{at}} C^d$ to the DRAT derivation.

4.2 Resolution-Based Simplification Techniques

We proceed with resolution-based techniques. In fact, many important techniques such as *variable elimination* [8, 36] *self-subsuming resolution* [13, 14] and *equivalent literal substitution* [26] are resolution-based techniques. Before we study these techniques, we first proof various properties of resolution in general. We start with the proof that resolvents are asymmetric tautologies:

Lemma 1. *Let C be the resolvent of the clauses $D \in F$ and $E \in F$ upon the variable v. Then the clause C is an asymmetric tautology in F.*

Proof. Follows straightforward since $\{v, \overline{v}\} \subseteq \text{ALA}_F(C)$. Hence, resolvents in the formula F are asymmetric tautologies in F. $\qquad\square$

The above Lemma allows us to add a resolvent in the formula F to a DRAT derivation in F as C^{at}. However, this is not the case when the added clause is the result of multiple resolution steps, as the following example demonstrates:

Example 3. Consider the formula $F = \{\{x, y, z\}, \{\overline{z}, y\}, \{x, \overline{y}, z\}, \{\overline{y}, \overline{z}\}\}$. The resolvent of the clauses $\{x, y, z\}$ and $\{\overline{z}, y\}$ upon z is $C = \{x, y\}$, and the resolvent of the clauses $\{x, \overline{y}, z\}$ and $\{\overline{y}, \overline{z}\}$ upon z is the clause $D = \{x, \overline{y}\}$. However, the resolvent $\{x\}$ of the clauses C and D upon y is not an asymmetric tautology, since $\text{ALA}_F(\{x\}) = \{x\}$.

To add the result of multiple resolution steps D to a DRAT derivation, we need to add *auxiliary clauses* before we add D^{at} to the derivation. Note that not all intermediate resolution steps need to be added:

Lemma 2. *Let C and D be asymmetric tautologies w.r.t. F with $x \in C$ and $\overline{x} \in D$. Then the resolvent E of C and D upon x is an asymmetric tautology in the formula $F \cup \{C\}$ and in the formula $F \cup \{D\}$.*

Proof. Consider the first formula. We then know that $E \cup \{\overline{x}\} \subseteq \text{ALA}_{F \cup \{C\}}(E)$. Since $D = E \cup \{\overline{x}\}$ and D is an asymmetric tautology, there is $n \in \mathbb{N}$ such that $\text{ALA}_F^n(D)$ contains a complementary pair of literals. Then, $\text{ALA}_G^{n+1}(E)$ contains a complementary pair of literals.

This means that the clauses C and D are not required to be *both* in the formula F. Instead, it is sufficient to just add one of these clauses to the formula, to add their resolvent. If we consider linear resolvents, we do not need to add auxiliary clauses.

Lemma 3. *If there is a linear resolution derivation to the clause C in the formula F, then the clause C is an asymmetric tautology in the formula F. [5]*

Proof. We proof the claim by induction on the length of the derivation. For the base case, $n = 1$, we know that $C = D$ and then $D \in F$. Every clause in a formula F is an asymmetric tautology in F. For the induction step, assume that C_i is an asymmetric tautology and the resolution candidate $D_i \in F$. Then, there is m such that $\mathsf{ALA}_F^m(C_i)$ is a tautology. Then $C_{i+1} = C_i \otimes_x D_i$ for some literal $x \in C_i$ and $\overline{x_i} \in D_i$, where $C_i \otimes_x D_i = (C_i \setminus \{x\}) \cup (D_i \setminus \{\overline{x}\})$. Then, $x \in \mathsf{ALA}_F(C_i \otimes_x D_i)$ and because $\mathsf{ALA}_F^m(C_i)$ is a tautology we conclude that $\mathsf{ALA}_F^{m+1}(C_i \otimes_x D_i)$ is a tautology.   □

In particular, this means that all resolution-based techniques, i.e. formula simplification methods that add resolvents and delete some clauses, have corresponding DRAT-derivations. The result of a resolution-based technique is $(F \setminus G) \dot{\cup} \{C_1, \dots, C_n\}$. Let $G = \{D_1, \dots, D_n\}$. Recall that there is a resolution derivation $(C_{i,j} \mid 1 \leq j \leq k)$ in the formula $F \dot{\cup} G$ to the clause C_i for each $i \in \{1, \dots, m\}$ by definition of resolution-based techniques. We construct the proof derivation $P_1 P_2 P_3$. Intuitively, the derivation P_1 adds all intermediate resolvents and the clauses C_i, the derivation P_2 deletes all intermediate resolvents but not the clauses C_i, and the derivation P_3 removes all clauses in G. Formally,

$$P_1 = C_{1,1}^{\mathsf{at}} C_{1,2}^{\mathsf{at}} \dots C_{1,k}^{\mathsf{at}} C_{2,1}^{\mathsf{at}} \dots C_{m,k}^{\mathsf{at}}$$
$$P_2 = C_{1,1}^{\mathsf{d}} \dots C_{1,k-1}^{\mathsf{d}} C_{2,1}^{\mathsf{d}} \dots C_{2,k-1}^{\mathsf{d}}$$
$$P_3 = D_1^{\mathsf{d}} \dots D_n^{\mathsf{d}}$$

Then the labelled clause sequence $P_1 P_2 P_3$ is a DRAT derivation in $F \dot{\cup} G$. In the rest of this subsection, we present the DRAT derivation for some important resolution-based formula simplification techniques.

Hyper Binary Resolution [4]. Given an input formula F with $\{y, x_1, \dots, x_n\} \in F$ and $\{\overline{x_i}, z\} \in F$ for all $i \in \{1, \dots, n\}$. Then, the clause $\{y, z\}$ is a *hyper binary resolvent* w.r.t. the formula F, and the result of applying hyper binary resolution is the formula $F' = F \dot{\cup} \{\{y, z\}\}$. A hyper binary resolvent C in the formula F is an asymmetric tautology in the formula F. In fact, the hyper binary resolvent can be obtained by the finite linear resolution derivation $(C_i \mid 1 \leq i \leq n + 1)$, where $C_1 = \{y, x_1, \dots, x_n\}$, and the resolution candidate in the formula is $D_i = \{\overline{x_i}, z\}$. Then, $C_i = \{y, z, x_i, x_{i+1}, \dots, x_n\}$ for $i \in \{2, \dots, n + 1\}$. Consequently, hyper binary resolvents are asymmetric tautologies in the formula F. Then, the addition of hyper binary resolvents has the corresponding short DRAT-derivation C^{at}.

Common Direct Implication [23]. A literal x is a common direct implication, if there is a clause $\{x_1, \dots, x_n\} \in F$ and $\{\overline{x_i}, x\} \in F$ for all $i \in \{1, \dots, n\}$. There is a linear resolution derivation $(C_i \mid 1 \leq i \leq n + 1)$ from the clause $\{x_1, \ldots, x_n\}$ to the clause $\{x\}$, where $C_i = \{x, x_i, x_{i+1}, \ldots, x_n\}$ for all $i \in \{2, \ldots, n + 1\}$. Hence, the clause $\{x\}$ is an asymmetric tautology in the formula F. Consequently, the addition of direct implications has a short and corresponding DRAT-derivation C^{at}.

Variable Elimination [8, 36]. For two formulas F_1, F_2 and a variable v, the multiset of all non-tautological resolvents of a clause in the formula F_1 with a clause in the formula F_2 upon the variable v is denoted by $F_1 \otimes_v F_2$. The multiset of clauses in the formula F that contain the literal x is denoted by F_x. Given an input formula F and a variable $v \in \mathcal{V}$, variable elimination adds all resolvents of the input formula F upon the variable v, and afterwards deletes all clauses containing the literals v or $\overline{v}$. Formally, the result of applying variable elimination is the formula

$$F' = (F \, \dot{\cup} \, (F_v \otimes_v F_{\overline{v}})) \setminus (F_v \, \dot{\cup} \, F_{\overline{v}}).$$

Let $F_v \, \dot{\cup} \, F_{\overline{v}} = \{D_1, \ldots, D_m\}$. By Lemma 3, the clauses $F_v \otimes F_{\overline{v}} = \{C_1, \ldots, C_n\}$ are asymmetric tautologies in the formula F, and therefore the labelled clause sequence $C_1^{\mathrm{at}} \ldots C_n^{\mathrm{at}} D_1^{\mathrm{d}} \ldots D_m^{\mathrm{d}}$ is a DRAT derivation. Moreover, it is short, because $n \leq |F|^2$ and $m \leq |F|$.

Self-Subsuming Resolution [13, 14]. Given a formula F with $C \in F$ and $D \in F$. Suppose that $C \otimes D$ subsumes the clause C, i.e. $C \otimes D \subseteq C$, self-subsuming resolution produces the formula $(F \setminus \{C\}) \, \dot{\cup} \, \{C \otimes D\}$. By Lemma 1, the clause C is an asymmetric tautology and consequently, $(C \otimes D)^{\mathrm{at}} C^{\mathrm{d}}$ is a short DRAT derivation.

Equivalent Literal Elimination [26]. Two variables x and y are equivalent in the formula F, if the formula F logically entails the equivalence of the two literals. We assume that the equivalence is stated in the formula, i.e. $\{\{\overline{x}, y\}, \{x, \overline{y}\}\} \dot{\subseteq} F$. Typically equivalent literals are obtained by reasoning in the binary causes of the formula F and therefore are asymmetric tautologies (see Sect. 4.3). Equivalence elimination produces the formula F' that is obtained by F by replacing each occurrence of x with y. Formally,

$$G_1 = \{C \in F \mid x \in C \text{ or } \overline{x} \in C\} = \{C_1, \ldots, C_n\}$$
$$G_2 = \{(C \setminus \{x\}) \cup \{y\} \mid x \in C \text{ and } C \in F\}$$
$$G_3 = \{(C \setminus \{\overline{x}\}) \cup \{\overline{y}\} \mid \overline{x} \in C \text{ and } C \in F\}$$
$$F' = (F \setminus G_1) \, \dot{\cup} \, G_2 \, \dot{\cup} \, G_3$$

Note that $(C \setminus \{x\}) \cup \{y\} = C \otimes_x \{\overline{x}, y\}$ if $x \in C$ and consequently, the introduced clauses $\{D_1, \ldots, D_m\} = G_2 \, \dot{\cup} \, G_3$ are asymmetric tautologies by Lemma 1. Then, $D_1^{\mathrm{at}} \ldots D_m^{\mathrm{at}} C_1^{\mathrm{d}} \ldots C_n^{\mathrm{d}}$ is the corresponding DRAT-derivation. Moreover, it is short, because $n \leq |F|$ and $m \leq |F|$.

Vivification, Asymmetric Branching [34]. Vivification shortens clauses in the formula F by replacing the clause $C = \{x_1, \ldots, x_n\}$ with the clause $D = \{x_1, \ldots, x_{n-1}\}$ if unit propagation in $F \, \dot{\cup} \, \{\{\overline{x_1}\}, \ldots, \{\overline{x_{n-1}}\}\}$ leads to a conflict. i.e. C' is an asymmetric tautology. Hence, $D^{\mathrm{at}} C^{\mathrm{d}}$ is the corresponding, short DRAT derivation.

4.3 2SAT-Based Simplifications

2SAT-based simplification methods are very attractive in theory as reasoning in 2SAT can be done in polynomial time. Reasoning uses the implication graph of the binary clauses in a formula F. Formally, the *binary implication graph* of the formula F is $\mathsf{BIG}(F) = (V, E)$, where $V = \{x, \overline{x} \mid x \in \mathsf{vars}(F)\}$ are the vertices and the set of edges is $E = \{(\overline{x}, y), (x, \overline{y}) \mid \{x, y\} \in F\}$. We consider the *extended* graph $\mathsf{BIG}_*(F)$ that also contains the edge $(x, \overline{x})$ for each literal $x \in \mathcal{L}$.

Lemma 4. $x \in \mathsf{ALA}_F^n(\{x_1, \ldots, x_n\})$ *if and only if there is a path of length smaller than n from x_i to $\overline{x}$ in $\mathsf{BIG}_*(F)$ for some $i \in \{1, \ldots, n\}$.*

Proof. We show the claim by induction on n. For the induction base $n = 0$: The "only-if" part follows immediately because whenever $x \in \{x_1, \ldots, x_n\}$, then $x = x_i$. Hence, it is trivially contained in BIG_*. Likewise, the "if"-part follows immediately from the monotonicity of the ALA function. We proceed to the induction step: Consider the "only-if" part. Let $x \in \mathsf{ALA}(\mathsf{ALA}_F^n(\{x_1, \ldots, x_m\}))$. If $x \in \mathsf{ALA}_F^n(\{x_1, \ldots, x_m\})$ holds, we apply inductive arguments. Otherwise, there is the clause $\{x_j, \overline{x}\} \in F$ and $x_j \in \mathsf{ALA}_F^n(C)$. By induction, there is a path from x_i to x_j of length smaller than n. Then, there is a path from x_j to x. Hence, there is a path from x_i to x of length smaller than $n + 1$. Consider the "if"-part. Suppose there is a path from x_i to $\overline{x}$ of length smaller than $n + 1$. Then, there is a path from x_i to z of length smaller than n and $(z, \overline{x})$. Then, $\overline{z} \in \mathsf{ALA}_F^n(C)$ and $\{x, z\} \in F$. Then $\overline{x} \in \mathsf{ALA}_F^{n+1}(C)$. ∎

Proposition 2. *Let F be a binary formula. Then the clause $\{x, y\}$ is an asymmetric tautology in F iff there is a path from x to $\overline{y}$ in $\mathsf{BIG}_*(F)$.*

Proof. Straightforward from Lemma 4. ∎

2SAT-based techniques have short DRAT-derivations, i.e. whenever the binary clauses entail a clause C, it is an asymmetric tautology. We now consider *common implications* in the general setting and in the 2SAT-setting.

Common Implications. Suppose that there are $n, m \in \mathbb{N}$ such that $x \in \mathsf{ALA}_F^n(\{y\})$ and $x \in \mathsf{ALA}_F^m(\{\overline{y}\})$. Then, the literal $\overline{x}$ is a *common implication* of the literal y. It is clear that the clauses $\{\overline{y}, \overline{x}\}$ and $\{y, \overline{x}\}$ are asymmetric tautologies. Therefore, $\{x\}$ is an asymmetric tautology in $F \cup \{\{\overline{y}, \overline{x}\}\}$ and in $F \cup \{y, \overline{x}\}$. However, the clause $\{x\}$ is not in general an asymmetric tautology in the formula F in general (see Example 4). Therefore, we use the clause $\{\overline{y}, \overline{x}\}$ or the clause $\{y, \overline{x}\}$ as an auxiliary clause (see Lemma 2). Hence, $\{\overline{y}, \overline{x}\}^{\mathsf{at}}\{x\}^{\mathsf{at}}\{\overline{y}, \overline{x}\}^{\mathsf{d}}$ is a short DRAT derivation.

Example 4. Consider the formula $F = \{\{y, z\}, \{y, \overline{z}, x\}, \{\overline{y}, z\}, \{\overline{y}, \overline{z}, x\}\}$. Then, the literal x is a common implication of the variable x, but the clause (x) is no AT.

Common Implications in 2SAT Reasoning. Consider the case that $\overline{x}$ is a common implication of the literal y w.r.t. the binary clauses of a formula F. Then the clauses $\{\overline{x}, y\}$ and $\{x, \overline{y}\}$ are asymmetric tautologies w.r.t. the binary clauses in the formula F. But then there is path from y to x and a path from y to $\overline{x}$ by Lemma 4. Then we can conclude by Lemma 4 that $\{x.\overline{x}\} \subseteq \mathsf{ALA}^n(\{y\})$ for some $n \in \mathbb{N}$. Hence, $\{y\}$ is an asymmetric tautology, i.e. we can add common implications in 2SAT case.

4.4 Literal Elimination Techniques

Given a formula F, general clause addition techniques produce the formula $F \cup \{C\}$ such that the formulas F and $F \cup \{C\}$ are equisatisfiable. We will now consider some important techniques that are used in state-of-the-art SAT solvers and that are under active research. For *blocked clause addition [22,25]*, the technique is the dual technique of blocked clause elimination, it is shown that the introduced clause is a resolution asymmetric tautology. Hence, the technique has short DRAT derivations.

Extended Resolution [37]. A variable v is fresh in a certain context, if the variable v does not occur in a formula. This technique adds a definition of a fresh variable v to the formula, i.e. given an input formula F, two literals $x, y \in \mathsf{lits}(F)$ and the fresh variable v, the technique produces the formula $F' = F \cup \{\{\overline{v}, x, y\}, \{\overline{x}, v\}, \{\overline{y}, v\}\}$. It is easy to see that $\{\overline{v}, x, y\}$ is a RAT in F w.r.t. $\overline{v}$, $\{\overline{x}, v\}$ is a RAT in $F \cup \{\{\overline{v}, x, y\}\}$ w.r.t. v, and $\{\overline{x}, v\}$ is a RAT in $F \cup \{\{\overline{v}, x, y\}, \{\overline{x}, v\}\}$ w.r.t. v. We therefore conclude that $\{\overline{v}, x, y\}^{\mathsf{rat}} \{\overline{x}, v\}^{\mathsf{rat}} \{\overline{y}, v\}^{\mathsf{rat}}$ is the corresponding short DRAT derivation [16].

Bounded Variable Addition (BVA-OR) [29]. This technique adds a partial definition of a fresh variable v to the formula: First, a fresh variable v is introduced like in extended resolution, resulting in the formula $G = F \cup \{\{v, \overline{x}, \overline{y}\}, \{\overline{v}, x\}, \{\overline{v}, y\}\}$, where $x, y \in \mathsf{lits}(F)$. Next, all clauses $C, D \in F$, which have a common subclause E such that $C = E \cup \{x\}$ and $D = E \cup \{y\}$ are replaced by the new clause $\{v\} \cup E$, resulting in the formula H. Finally, the formula F', the result of applying bounded variable addition, is obtained from the formula H by removing the clause $\{v, \overline{x}, \overline{y}\}$. We construct the corresponding DRAT derivation as follows: First, note that the clause $\{v, \overline{x}, \overline{y}\}$ is a RAT in F w.r.t. v, the clause $\{\overline{v}, x\}$ is a RAT in $F \cup \{\{v, \overline{x}, \overline{y}\}\}$ w.r.t. x, and that the clause $\{\overline{v}, y\}$ is a RAT in $F \cup \{\{v, \overline{x}, \overline{y}\}, \{\overline{v}, x\}\}$ w.r.t. x. Consider some clause pair C, D with the common subclause E. Then the clause $E \cup \{v\}$ is an asymmetric tautology in $F \cup \{\{v, \overline{x}, \overline{y}\}, \{\overline{v}, x\}, \{\overline{v}, y\}\}$, because $\{x, y\} \in \mathsf{ALA}(E \cup \{v\})$ and then $\{v, \overline{v}\} \in \mathsf{ALA}^2(E \cup \{v\})$. Finally, the clauses C, D can be removed. Hence, $\{v, \overline{x}, \overline{y}\}^{\mathsf{rat}} \{\overline{v}, x\}^{\mathsf{rat}} \{\overline{v}, y\}^{\mathsf{rat}} (\{v\} \cup E)^{\mathsf{at}} C^{\mathsf{d}} D^{\mathsf{d}} \{v, \overline{x}, \overline{y}\}^{\mathsf{d}}$ is a short DRAT derivation [16].

Bounded Variable Addition with XOR Gates (BVA-XOR). The idea of bounded variable can be adapted in the sense that we define XOR gates: Given a fresh variable x, BVA-XOR adds the clauses $\{\{x, y, z\}, \{x, \overline{y}, \overline{z}\}, \{\overline{x}, y, \overline{z}\}, \{\overline{x}, \overline{y}, z\}\}$, that encode $x \leftrightarrow \mathsf{xor}(y, z)$. Afterwards, we replace all subformulas in the intermediate formula of the form $\{\{y, z\} \cup C, \{\overline{y}, \overline{z}\} \cup C\}$ with $\{\{x\} \cup C\}$. Note that the clause $\{x\} \cup C$ is not an asymmetric tautology. However, the clause $\{x, y\} \cup C$ is an asymmetric tautology and acts as an auxiliary clause. The resulting DRAT derivation is then $P_1 P_2$, where

$$P_1 = \{x, y, z\}^{\mathsf{rat}} \{x, \overline{y}, \overline{z}\}^{\mathsf{rat}} \{\overline{x}, y, \overline{z}\}^{\mathsf{rat}} \{\overline{x}, \overline{y}, z\}^{\mathsf{rat}} (\{x, y\} \cup C)^{\mathsf{at}} (\{x\} \cup C)^{\mathsf{at}}$$
$$P_2 = (\{x, y\} \cup C)^{\mathsf{d}} (\{y, z\} \cup C)^{\mathsf{d}} (\{\overline{y}, \overline{z}\} \cup C)^{\mathsf{d}}$$

4.5 Literal Elimination

Literal elimination techniques remove a literal x from a clause C. Usually, literals are removed by a two-stage process: First, a shorter clause is constructed and afterwards subsumption elimination is applied. Often, the shorter clause can be constructed by resolution as for example with strengthening or vivification.

Hidden Literal Elimination. This technique is clause strengthening with a resolvent that can be obtained in the binary implication graph. From Prop. 2 we know that the clause is an asymmetric tautology. Hence, $C^{at}D^d$ is a short DRAT derivation.

Covered Literal Elimination. Covered literal elimination is the reverse direction of covered clause addition [18]. Consider a formula F and the clause $C \in F$ where $x \in C$. Suppose there is a literal $y \in C$ with $x \neq y$. Then, covered literal elimination replaces the clause C with $C \setminus \{x\}$, if $x \in ((C \setminus \{x\}) \otimes_y D)$ or $((C \setminus \{x\}) \otimes_y D)$ is a tautology for all $D \in F$ with $\overline{y} \in D$. We need to show that the clause $C \setminus \{x\}$ is a resolution asymmetric tautology w.r.t. y: Consider a clause $D \in F$ with $\overline{y} \in D$. Then, $y \in \mathsf{ALA}_F((C \setminus \{x\}) \otimes_y D)$ follows immediately. Because $x \in (C \setminus \{x\}) \otimes_y D$ and ALA_F is a monotone, we know that $x \in \mathsf{ALA}_F((C \setminus \{x\}) \otimes_y D)$. We then know that $C \subseteq \mathsf{ALA}_F((C \setminus \{x\}) \otimes_y D)$. Moreover, we know that $C \in F$, and conclude that $\mathsf{ALA}_F^2((C \setminus \{x\}) \otimes_y D)$ is a tautology. Hence, covered literal elimination has short DRAT-derivations of the form $(C \setminus \{x\})^{rat}C^d$.

5 Conclusion and Future Work

Boolean satisfiability testing is an important field in artificial intelligence and receives a lot of attention due to the enormous performance improvements of SAT solvers. Many formula simplifications were proposed to speed up SAT solvers. Formalizations of SAT solvers [1, 20, 30, 31, 33] are necessary tools to study soundness of various systems, but they do not guarantee the absence of bugs. For solving this issue, the DRAT proof format was developed such that SAT solvers can emit a witness of unsatisfiability which can be easily verified [16, 38].

In this paper, we considered the straight-forward techniques: clause elimination, literal addition, resolution, 2SAT reasoning, general clause addition, probing as well as literal elimination techniques. We have formally proven that clause elimination, literal addition and 2SAT-based techniques have short DRAT-derivations. Furthermore, we have presented a general structure of how DRAT derivations can be constructed for resolution-based methods.

As future work, we are interested in DRAT proof construction for parallel SAT solvers and for complex reasoning systems like the Fourier-Motzkin procedure.

Acknowledgements. We want to thank the reviewers for the proposed improvements and advises.

References

1. Arnold, H.: A linearized DPLL calculus with clause learning. Tech. rep., Universität Potsdam. Institut für Informatik (2009)
2. Audemard, G., Lagniez, J.-M., Mazure, B., Saïs, L.: On freezing and reactivating learnt clauses. In: Sakallah, K.A., Simon, L. (eds.) SAT 2011. LNCS, vol. 6695, pp. 188–200. Springer, Heidelberg (2011)
3. Audemard, G., Simon, L.: Predicting learnt clauses quality in modern SAT solvers. In: Boutilier, C. (ed.) IJCAI 2009, pp. 399–404. Morgan Kaufmann Publishers Inc., Pasadena (2009)
4. Bacchus, F., Winter, J.: Effective preprocessing with hyper-resolution and equality reduction. In: Giunchiglia, E., Tacchella, A. (eds.) SAT 2003. LNCS, vol. 2919, pp. 341–355. Springer, Heidelberg (2004)
5. Beame, P., Kautz, H., Sabharwal, A.: Towards understanding and harnessing the potential of clause learning. Journal of Artificial Intelligene Research 22(1), 319–351 (2004)
6. Biere, A., Cimatti, A., Clarke, E.M., Fujita, M., Zhu, Y.: Symbolic model checking using SAT procedures instead of BDDs. In: DAC 1999, pp. 317–320 (1999)
7. Blum, M., Kannan, S.: Designing programs that check their work. In: Johnson, D.S. (ed.) STOC 1989, pp. 86–97. ACM (1989)
8. Eén, N., Biere, A.: Effective preprocessing in SAT through variable and clause elimination. In: Bacchus, F., Walsh, T. (eds.) SAT 2005. LNCS, vol. 3569, pp. 61–75. Springer, Heidelberg (2005)
9. Eén, N., Sörensson, N.: An extensible SAT-solver. In: Giunchiglia, E., Tacchella, A. (eds.) SAT 2003. LNCS, vol. 2919, pp. 502–518. Springer, Heidelberg (2004)
10. Gelder, A.V.: Extracting (easily) checkable proofs from a satisfiability solver that employs both preorder and postorder resolution. In: ISAIM 2002 (2002)
11. Goldberg, E., Novikov, Y.: Verification of proofs of unsatisfiability for CNF formulas. In: DATE 2003, pp. 10886–10891. IEEE Computer Society, Washington, DC (2003)
12. Großmann, P., Hölldobler, S., Manthey, N., Nachtigall, K., Opitz, J., Steinke, P.: Solving periodic event scheduling problems with SAT. In: Jiang, H., Ding, W., Ali, M., Wu, X. (eds.) IEA/AIE 2012. LNCS, vol. 7345, pp. 166–175. Springer, Heidelberg (2012)
13. Hamadi, Y., Jabbour, S., Sais, L.: Control-based clause sharing in parallel SAT solving. In: Boutilier, C. (ed.) IJCAI 2009, pp. 499–504. Morgan Kaufmann Publishers Inc., Pasadena (2009)
14. Han, H., Somenzi, F.: On-the-fly clause improvement. In: Kullmann, O. (ed.) SAT 2009. LNCS, vol. 5584, pp. 209–222. Springer, Heidelberg (2009)
15. Heule, M., Hunt Jr., W.A., Wetzler, N.: Trimming while checking clausal proofs. In: Jobstman, B., Ray, S. (eds.) FMCAD 2013, pp. 181–188. IEEE (2013)
16. Heule, M.J.H., Hunt Jr., W.A., Wetzler, N.: Verifying refutations with extended resolution. In: Bonacina, M.P. (ed.) CADE 2013. LNCS, vol. 7898, pp. 345–359. Springer, Heidelberg (2013)
17. Heule, M., Järvisalo, M., Biere, A.: Clause elimination procedures for CNF formulas. In: Fermüller, C.G., Voronkov, A. (eds.) LPAR-17. LNCS, vol. 6397, pp. 357–371. Springer, Heidelberg (2010)
18. Heule, M., Järvisalo, M., Biere, A.: Covered clause elimination. In: Fermüller, C.G., Voronkov, A. (eds.) LPAR 2010. LNCS, vol. 6397, pp. 41–46. Springer, Heidelberg (2010)
19. Heule, M.J.H., Järvisalo, M., Biere, A.: Efficient CNF simplification based on binary implication graphs. In: Sakallah, K.A., Simon, L. (eds.) SAT 2011. LNCS, vol. 6695, pp. 201–215. Springer, Heidelberg (2011)

20. Hölldobler, S., Manthey, N., Philipp, T., Steinke, P.: Generic CDCL – A formalization of modern propositional satisfiability solvers. In: POS 2014 (accepted, 2014)
21. Järvisalo, M., Biere, A., Heule, M.: Blocked clause elimination. In: Esparza, J., Majumdar, R. (eds.) TACAS 2010. LNCS, vol. 6015, pp. 129–144. Springer, Heidelberg (2010)
22. Järvisalo, M., Heule, M.J.H., Biere, A.: Inprocessing rules. In: Gramlich, B., Miller, D., Sattler, U. (eds.) IJCAR 2012. LNCS, vol. 7364, pp. 355–370. Springer, Heidelberg (2012)
23. Kaufmann, M., Kottler, S.: Beyond unit propagation in SAT solving. In: Pardalos, P.M., Rebennack, S. (eds.) SEA 2011. LNCS, vol. 6630, pp. 267–279. Springer, Heidelberg (2011)
24. Kautz, H., Selman, B.: Planning as satisfiability. In: Neumann, B. (ed.) ECAI 1992, pp. 359–363. John Wiley & Sons, Inc., New York (1992)
25. Kullmann, O.: On a generalization of extended resolution. Discrete Applied Mathematics 96-97, 149–176 (1999)
26. Li, C.M.: Integrating equivalency reasoning into davis-putnam procedure. In: Kautz, H.A., Porter, B.W. (eds.) IAAI 2000, pp. 291–296. AAAI Press, Menlo Park (2000)
27. Lynce, I., Marques-Silva, J.: Efficient haplotype inference with Boolean satisfiability. In: AAAI 2006, pp. 104–109. AAAI Press, Menlo Park (2006)
28. Lynce, I., Marques-Silva, J.P.: Probing-based preprocessing techniques for propositional satisfiability. In: ICTAI 2003, pp. 105–110. IEEE Computer Society, Sacramento (2003)
29. Manthey, N., Heule, M.J.H., Biere, A.: Automated reencoding of Boolean formulas. In: Biere, A., Nahir, A., Vos, T. (eds.) HVC. LNCS, vol. 7857, pp. 102–117. Springer, Heidelberg (2013)
30. Manthey, N., Philipp, T., Wernhard, C.: Soundness of inprocessing in clause sharing SAT solvers. In: Järvisalo, M., Van Gelder, A. (eds.) SAT 2013. LNCS, vol. 7962, pp. 22–39. Springer, Heidelberg (2013)
31. Marić, F.: Formalization and implementation of modern SAT solvers. Journal of Automated Reasoning 43(1), 81–119 (2009)
32. McConnell, R.M., Mehlhorn, K., Näher, S., Schweitzer, P.: Certifying algorithms. Computer Science Review 5(2), 119–161 (2011)
33. Nieuwenhuis, R., Oliveras, A., Tinelli, C.: Abstract DPLL and abstract DPLL modulo theories. In: Baader, F., Voronkov, A. (eds.) LPAR 2004. LNCS (LNAI), vol. 3452, pp. 36–50. Springer, Heidelberg (2005)
34. Piette, C., Hamadi, Y., Sais, L.: Vivifying propositional clausal formulae. In: Ghallab, M., Spyropoulos, C.D., Fakotakis, N., Avouris, N.M. (eds.) ECAI 2008, pp. 525–529. IOS Press (2008)
35. Rintanen, J.: Engineering efficient planners with SAT. In: Raedt, L.D., Bessière, C., Dubois, D., Doherty, P., Frasconi, P., Heintz, F., Lucas, P.J.F. (eds.) ECAI 2012. Frontiers in Artificial Intelligence and Applications, vol. 242, pp. 684–689. IOS Press (2012)
36. Subbarayan, S., Pradhan, D.K.: NiVER: Non-increasing variable elimination resolution for preprocessing SAT instances. In: Hoos, H.H., Mitchell, D.G. (eds.) SAT 2004. LNCS, vol. 3542, pp. 276–291. Springer, Heidelberg (2005)
37. Tseitin, G.S.: On the complexity of derivation in propositional calculus. In: Siekmann, J.H., Wrightson, G. (eds.) Automation of Reasoning. Symbolic Computation, pp. 466–483. Springer, Heidelberg (1983)
38. Wetzler, N., Heule, M.J.H., Hunt Jr., W.A.: Mechanical verification of SAT refutations with extended resolution. In: Blazy, S., Paulin-Mohring, C., Pichardie, D. (eds.) ITP 2013. LNCS, vol. 7998, pp. 229–244. Springer, Heidelberg (2013)

A More Compact Translation of Pseudo-Boolean Constraints into CNF Such That Generalized Arc Consistency Is Maintained

Norbert Manthey, Tobias Philipp, and Peter Steinke

Knowledge Representation and Reasoning Group,
Technische Universität Dresden, 01062 Dresden, Germany
peter.steinke@tu-dresden.de

Abstract. In this paper we answer the open question for the existence of a more compact encoding from Pseudo-Boolean constraints into CNF that maintains generalized arc consistency by unit propagation, formalized by Bailleux et al. in [21]. In contrast to other encodings our approach is defined in an abstract way and we present a concrete instantiation, resulting in a space complexity of $\mathcal{O}(n^2 \log^2(n) \log(w_{\mathsf{max}}))$ clauses in contrast to $\mathcal{O}(n^3 \log(n) \log(w_{\mathsf{max}}))$ clauses generated by the previously best known encoding that maintains generalized arc consistency.

1 Introduction

Many applications benefit from the fast developments in the area of SAT solving by translating the high level description into rather simple conjunctive normal form (CNF) formulas. With the help of the Tseitin-translation, it is possible to solve many problems like hardware verification and model checking [5,26,22] as a SAT problem. However, for pseudo-Boolean (PB) constraints, that frequently occur in problems like scheduling, planning, and translations of problems from languages like CSP, ASP or integer programming, there is no straight-forward translation into CNF [13,14,23,7]. Being provided with a good translation is also relevant to solve optimization problems like MaxSAT, or to solve minimal set problems like the extraction of minimal unsatisfiable cores or maximal satisfying subformulas, or PB optimization itself [18,4,16,20,6].

Much effort has been put in finding good translations for PB constraints into CNF, because many problems can be expressed as conjunction of clauses and require only a few PB constraints. This fact can be illustrated by the distribution of PB constraints in recent PB competitions: only 11.6 % of all constraints are PB constraints, and the majority of 88.4 % are clauses [18]. Proposed encodings differ in the number of required clauses, auxiliary variables and the properties the translation guarantees. It is widely assumed that *generalized arc consistency* (GAC), known from constraint programming [23], is an important property, which is used to cut off the search space as soon as possible. An encoding of a PB constraint is considered better, if unit propagation (UP) in the encoding

C. Lutz and M. Thielscher (Eds.): KI 2014, LNCS 8736, pp. 123–134, 2014.
© Springer International Publishing Switzerland 2014

maintains GAC. A weaker property than GAC is that an encoding detects inconsistent variable assignments. Furthermore, SAT solvers are assumed to achieve a higher performance when the number of clauses is rather small [25,10,17].

Given a PB constraint of the form $\sum_{i=1}^{n} w_i x_i \leq k$, where w_i and k are positive integers, and x_i Boolean literals, the following encodings are known: *binary decision diagrams* (BDD), which maintain GAC, and require $\mathcal{O}(n \cdot k)$ clauses in the worst case [11,1,2]. In particular, this means that BDDs produce exponential many clauses, since k can be exponential in the size of n. However, BDDs are very competitive, since due to their construction they simplify the PB constraint implicitly. *Sorting networks* do not maintain GAC, nor detect inconsistent assignments, but produce only $\mathcal{O}(N \log^2(N))$ clauses, where N is bounded by $\lceil \log w_1 \rceil + \cdots + \lceil \log w_n \rceil$. Similarly, *adder networks* neither maintain GAC nor detect inconsistencies, but produce only $\mathcal{O}(n \log k)$ clauses. Sorting networks are assumed to provide a better performance for current SAT solvers, since adder networks are based on XOR-constraints [11]. The only non-exponential encoding that maintains GAC is the *local watchdog* encoding with $\mathcal{O}(n^3 \log n \log w_{\mathsf{max}}))$ clauses.

Our contribution in this paper is twofold: First we introduce the *Binary Merger* encoding that is strongly related to the known watchdog encoding [21]. We present this encoding in a more abstract way, based on an extended propositional logic formula. We prove that it is possible to translate the sorters and mergers – the fundamental parts of these encodings – into CNF with any sound translation that holds certain conditions. Second, with another CNF translation of these sorters and mergers as in the watchdog encoding, it is possible to answer an open question from Bailleux et al. [21]. They ask for a more compact encoding of PB constraints that maintains GAC. The *Binary Merger* encoding requires $\mathcal{O}(n^2 \log^2 n \log w_{\mathsf{max}}))$ clauses. If GAC should not be maintained, our encoding requires only $\mathcal{O}(n \log^2 n \log w_{\mathsf{max}}))$ clauses. Since the Binary Merger encoding is defined in an abstract way, it is also possible to find an instantiation that results in the watchdog encoding. Hence both encodings are strongly related.

In Section 2 we will describe basic concepts, notation of PB constraint and CNF encodings, as well as some bit operations. We will outline the idea of the encoding in Section 3 and present the abstract Binary Merger encoding and its properties in Section 4. Section 5 concludes the paper.

2   Preliminaries

We assume a fixed infinite set $\mathcal{V}$ of Boolean *variables*. A *literal* is a variable v (*positive literal*) or a negated variable $\overline{v}$ (*negative literal*). The *complement* $\overline{x}$ of a positive (negative, resp.) literal x is the negative (positive, resp.) literal with the same variable as x. For a set of literals J the complement of J, denoted with $\overline{J}$, is defined as $\overline{J} = \{\overline{x} \mid x \in J\}$. We deal with finite constraint sets called *formulas*. Each *constraint* is either

– a clause $(x_1 \vee \ldots \vee x_n)$, where x_i is a literal or a truth value $\top, \bot$,

- a *PB constraint* $\sum_{i=1}^{n} w_i \cdot x_i \lhd k$, where x_i is either a literal or one of the truth values $\top, \bot$, $w_i \in \mathbb{Z}$ are the associated weights for the literal x_i for every $i \in \{1, \ldots, n\}$, $k \in \mathbb{Z}$ and $\lhd \in \{=, \leq, <, >, \geq\}$,
- a *sorter constraint* $\mathsf{sort}(X, Y)$ where X and Y are finite sequences of literals and truth values, or
- a *merger constraint* $\mathsf{merge}(X, Y, Z)$ where X, Y, Z are finite sequences of literals and truth values.

To address an specific element x_i in the sequence $X = (x_1, x_2, \cdots, x_n)$, we will write X_i and the length n of a sequence X is denoted with $|X| = n$.

We write a formula $\{C_1, \ldots, C_n\}$ also as a conjunction $(C_1 \wedge \ldots \wedge C_n)$. The replacement of a variable v with a truth value $t \in \{\top, \bot\}$ in a constraint C is denoted with $C[v \mapsto t]$. *CNF formulas* are formulas that consist only of clauses. The set of all variables occurring in a formula F (in positive or negative literals) is denoted by $\mathsf{vars}(F)$ and the set of all variables F and their complement is $\mathsf{lits}(F) := \mathsf{vars}(F) \cup \overline{\mathsf{vars}(F)}$.

An *interpretation* I is a set of literals that contains for all variables v exactly one of v or $\overline{v}$. An interpretation $I[x]$ denotes the interpretation which is like the interpretation I except that $I[x]$ maps the literal x to true, that is $I[x] = (I \setminus \{\overline{x}\}) \cup \{x\}$. Likewise, $I[J]$ denotes the interpretation which is like the interpretation I, but maps every literal in the literal set J to true, that is $I[J] = (I \setminus \overline{J}) \cup J$.

Intuitively, an interpretation I satisfies a formula F, if it satisfies every constraint in F. Such interpretations are *models* of F. If a formula has at least one model, the formula is called *satisfiable* and otherwise *unsatisfiable*. The satisfaction relation $\models$ for the standard proposition logic concepts is defined in the usual way: Let x_i be literals, C_i clauses, F a formula, $w_i, k \in \mathbb{Z}$ and $\lhd \in \{=, \leq, <, >, \geq\}$, then $I \models \top$, $I \not\models \bot$, $I \models x$ iff $x \in I$, $I \models (x_1 \vee \ldots \vee x_n)$ iff $I \models x_i$ for some $i \in \{1, \ldots, n\}$, $I \models (C_1 \wedge \ldots \wedge C_n)$ iff $I \models C_i$ for all $i \in \{1, \ldots, n\}$, $I \models \overline{F}$ iff $I \not\models F$ and $I \models x_1 \rightarrow x_2$ iff $I \models (\overline{x_1} \vee x_2)$. We also introduce some non standard concepts:

$I \models \Sigma_{i=1}^{n} w_i x_i \lhd k$	iff $\sum \{w_i \mid x_i \in I \text{ and } 1 \leq i \leq n\} \lhd k$.
$\mathsf{unary}(X, I) = k$	iff $k = |\{X_i \mid X_i \in I \text{ and } 1 \leq i \leq n\}|$.
$I \models \mathsf{sort}(X)$	iff $I \models (X_{i+1} \rightarrow X_i)$ for all $1 \leq i < n$.
$I \models \mathsf{sort}(X, Y)$	iff $I \models \mathsf{sort}(Y)$ and $\mathsf{unary}(Y, I) = \mathsf{unary}(X, I)$.
$I \models \mathsf{merge}(X, Y, Z)$	iff $(I \models \mathsf{sort}(X)$ and $I \models \mathsf{sort}(Y))$ implies that $(I \models \mathsf{sort}(Z)$ and $\mathsf{unary}(Z, I) = \mathsf{unary}(X, I) + \mathsf{unary}(Y, I))$

F *entails* the G, in symbols $F \models G$ iff every model of F is a model G. F and G are *equivalent*, in symbols $F \equiv G$, iff F entails G and G entails F.

Encodings and Generalized Arc Consistency. Formally, the formula F *encodes* the formula G iff i) $F \models G$ and ii) for every model I of the formula G there is an interpretation I' with $I' \models F$ and $I' \cap \mathsf{vars}(G) \subseteq I$. The first condition states that we can use every model of the encoding as a model for the original formula, whereas the second condition states that we can construct a model of the encoding from a model of the original formula by changing the interpretation of auxiliary variables.

Encodings can have certain kinds of structural properties. Generalized arc consistency (GAC) is an important inference rule in constraint programming and can significantly reduce the search space [23]. As in [21], we describe the notions of GAC and inconsistency detection in terms of the entailment relation. An *assignment* J is a set of literals that may contain a literal and its complement, where J is inconsistent w.r.t. a constraint C iff the formula $(\bigwedge_{x \in J} x) \wedge C$ is unsatisfiable. Informally, GAC refers to the property that we cannot extend an assignment with further entailed literals. Formally, the *assignment* J *is GAC w.r.t. the constraint* C iff for every literal $y \in \mathsf{lits}(C)$ holds that $(\bigwedge_{x \in J} x) \wedge C \models y$ implies $y \in J$.

Unit propagation is the main inference rule in SAT solving [9,8,19,12]. Formally, unit propagation is defined as follows: $\mathsf{UP}^0(F, J) = J$, $\mathsf{UP}^{n+1}(F, J) = \mathsf{UP}^n(F, J) \cup \{x \mid (x \vee x_1 \vee \ldots x_n) \in F$ and $\overline{x_i} \in \mathsf{UP}^n(F, J)$ for every $1 \leq i \leq n\}$ and $\mathsf{UP}(F, J) = \mathsf{UP}^\infty(F, J)$. For convenience we write $\bot \in \mathsf{UP}(F, J)$ iff there is a propositional variable v such that $v \in \mathsf{UP}(F, J)$ and $\overline{v} \in \mathsf{UP}(F, J)$. A *formula* F *detects inconsistencies of the constraint* C iff for every inconsistent assignments J of the constraint C we find that $\bot \in \mathsf{UP}(F, J)$, i.e. unit propagation is powerful enough to find an inconsistency in the formula F if the current variable assignment is inconsistent w.r.t the constraint C. A *formula* F *maintains GAC of the constraint* C iff $\mathsf{UP}(F, J)$ is GAC w.r.t. the constraint C for every assignment J. That is, unit propagation infers every literal that is entailed by the constraint C and assignment J.

Bit Operations. In this paper, we intensively exploit the properties of the binary representation of numbers. We denote the binary representation of a number with a b as a suffix, e.g. $19 = 10011b$. The symbol $\mathsf{bits}(n) = \lceil \mathrm{ld}(n-1) \rceil$ denotes the number of bits without leading zeros in the binary representation of the number $n \in \mathbb{N}$. Let $n, p \in \mathbb{N}$ and $p \geq 1$. Then the symbol $\mathsf{bit}(n, p)$ denotes the p'th least significant bit in the binary representation of the number n. For instance, $\mathsf{bit}(19, 1) = 1$, $\mathsf{bit}(19, 2) = 1$ and $\mathsf{bit}(19, 3) = 0$, with $19 = 10011b$. The *binary cut* of a number n up to the p'th bit, in symbols $\mathsf{bcut}(n, p)$, is $\mathsf{bit}(n, 1) \cdot 2^0 + \mathsf{bit}(n, 2) \cdot 2^1 + \ldots + \mathsf{bit}(n, p) \cdot 2^{p-1}$. For instance, the binary cut of the number 19 up to the third bit is $\mathsf{bcut}(19, 3) = 011b = 3$. A *bit bucket* B^a of a PB constraint $\sum_{i=1}^n w_i x_i \lhd k$ is a sequence of propositional variables in arbitrary but fixed order, such that $x_i \in B^a$ iff $\mathsf{bit}(w_i, a) = 1$. For instance, the bit bucket B^1 of the PB constraint $3x_1 + 5x_2 + 3x_3 + 6x_4 < 12$ is (x_1, x_2, x_3) and $B^2 = (x_1, x_3, x_4)$. For a sequence of propositional variables $B = (b_1, b_2, \ldots, b_n)$, we construct the sequence $\widetilde{B} = (b_2, b_4, \ldots, b_{2 \cdot \lfloor n/2 \rfloor})$, to denote the sequences that contain only the elements of B with even indices.

Normalization of Pseudo-Boolean Constraints. We consider PB constraints in *normal-form*, i.e. they are of the form $\sum_{i=1}^n w_i x_i < q \cdot 2^{m-1}$ where $w_i \geq 0$, $m = \mathsf{bits}(w_{\mathsf{max}})$ and $w_{\mathsf{max}} = \max\{w_i \mid 1 \leq i \leq n\}$ is the largest weight w_i in the constraint. Every PB constraint can be translated into a set of normalized

PB constraints (in fact at most two PB constraints with at most n literals each) by the rules given in [24] and with $\sum_{i=1}^{n} w_i x_i < k \equiv w\top + \sum_{i=1}^{n} w_i x_i < k + w$ to adjust $k = q \cdot 2^{m-1}$.

Example Normalization:

$$3x_1 + 5x_2 + 3x_3 \geq 6 \equiv -3x_1 - 5x_2 - 3x_3 < -5$$
$$\equiv 3\overline{x_1} + 5\overline{x_2} + 3\overline{x_3} < 6$$
$$\equiv 2\top + 3\overline{x_1} + 5\overline{x_2} + 3\overline{x_3} < 8$$

---

3 Encoding Idea

The idea of the encoding is related to the calculation of the sum of multiple binary numbers, which is done with additional natural numbers for the sum of the bits of a certain significance S^j, the carry of the previous sum C^j and the sum of both M^j (the merge). Formally, given a set W of natural numbers, the sum over the numbers W, represented in binary in $r^z r^{z-1} \cdots r^1$, is computed as follows: Let $r^j(W) = M^j(W) \bmod 2$ for every $j \geq 0$, where $M^j(W) = C^j(W) + S^j(W)$ for $j > 0$, $M^0(W) = 0$, $S^j(W) = \sum_{w \in W} \text{bit}(w, j)$ for every $j \geq 0$, and $C^j(W) = \lfloor M^{j-1}(W)/2 \rfloor$.

An example of the computation of the sum of the numbers $\{7, 2, 3\}$ is presented in Fig. 1 as well as an illustration of the general algorithm.

							b_n^m	$\cdots$	b_n^2	b_n^1
							$\vdots$		$\vdots$	$\vdots$
1 1 1		1 1 1		1 1 1			b_2^m	$\cdots$	b_2^2	b_2^1
0 1 0		0 1 0		0 1 0			$+\, b_1^m$	$\cdots$	b_1^2	b_1^1
$+\,0\,1\,1$		$+\,0\,1\,1$		$+\,0\,1\,1$			S^m	$\cdots$	S^2	S^1
sum of bits		1 3 2		1 3 2	C^z	$\cdots$	C^m	$\cdots$	C^2	
carry		carry		1 2 1						
sum of both		sum of both		3 4	M^z	$\cdots$	M^m	$\cdots$	M^2	
result		result		1 1 0 0	r^z	$\cdots$	r^m	$\cdots$	r^2	r^1

Fig. 1. Calculation of the sum of multiple binary numbers in general on the right side, where $m := max\{bits(w_i) \mid 1 \leq i \leq n\}$. The example $111b + 010b + 011b$ is illustrated on the left.

In the proposition below we relate the value $M^p(W)$ and the sum over the binary cuts up to the $p'th$ bit of the set W. If the sum of all bits in W up to the position p is greater equal $a \cdot 2^{p-1}$ then $M^p(W)$ is greater equal a as well and vice versa.

Proposition 1. Let $W \in \mathcal{P}(\mathbb{N})$, $a, p \in \mathbb{N}$ then $\sum\{\text{bcut}(w, p) \mid w \in W\} \geq a \cdot 2^{p-1}$ iff $M^p(W) \geq a$.

Proof. We prove the statement by induction over p. For the induction base $p = 1$, we know that $\sum\{\mathsf{bcut}(w, 1) \mid w \in W\} = \sum\{\mathsf{bit}(w, 1) \mid w \in W\} = S^1(W) = M^1(W)$. Consequently, the claim follows since $2^0 = 1$. For the induction step, assume that the claim holds for an arbitrary p, and we now prove the claim for $p + 1$:

$$
\begin{array}{ll}
\sum\{\mathsf{bcut}(w, p + 1) \mid w \in W\} \geq a \cdot 2^p & \text{iff} \\
\sum\{\mathsf{bcut}(w, p) \mid w \in W\} + \sum\{\mathsf{bit}(w, p + 1) \mid w \in W\} \cdot 2^p \geq a \cdot 2^p & \text{iff} \\
\sum\{\mathsf{bcut}(w, p) \mid w \in W\} + S^{p+1}(W) \cdot 2^p \geq a \cdot 2^p & \text{iff} \\
\sum\{\mathsf{bcut}(w, p) \mid w \in W\} \geq a \cdot 2^p - S^{p+1}(W) \cdot 2^p & \text{iff} \\
\sum\{\mathsf{bcut}(w, p) \mid w \in W\} \geq (a - S^{p+1}(W)) \cdot 2^p & \text{iff} \\
\sum\{\mathsf{bcut}(w, p) \mid w \in W\} \geq 2 \cdot (a - S^{p+1}(W)) \cdot 2^{p-1} &
\end{array}
$$

We consider the $\Rightarrow$ direction: By induction, we can conclude that $M^p(W) \geq 2 \cdot (a - S^{p+1}(W))$. By the definition of the function $M^{p+1}(W) = C^{p+1}(W) + S^{p+1}(W) = \lfloor M^p(W)/2 \rfloor + S^{p+1}(W)$ we conclude that $M^{p+1}(W) \geq a - S^{p+1}(W) + S^{p+1}(W) \geq a$. The converse $\Leftarrow$ can be proven analog. $\qquad\square$

The idea of the encoding is to introduce propositional variables S_a^p and M_b^p, which are true if $S^p(W) \geq a$ and $M^p(W) \geq b$ respectively, where W are the weights of the currently satisfied literals.

4   The Abstract Binary Merger Encoding

In this section, we present the *abstract binary merge encoding* for normalized PB constraints. In particular, we prove correctness of the encoding and show that the encoding detects inconsistencies, if the used sorters and mergers maintain GAC. Finally, we prove that the encoding with support clauses maintain GAC.

Definition 1 (Binary Merger). *Let $C = \sum_{i=1}^{n} w_i x_i < q \cdot 2^{m-1}$ be a normalized PB constraint. Then, the formula $\mathsf{BinaryMerger}(C)$ is defined as:*

$$
\overline{M_q^m} \wedge \bigwedge_{i=1}^{m} \mathsf{sort}(B^i, S^i) \wedge \mathsf{merge}(S^i, \overrightarrow{M^{i-1}}, M^i)
$$

where $w_{\mathsf{max}} = \max\{w_1, \ldots, w_n\}$ is the largest weight, $m = \mathsf{bits}(w_{\mathsf{max}})$, M^0 is the empty sequence and M^i, S^i are sequences of propositional variables and B^i is the sequence of literals in the bit bucket i w.r.t. C, with $1 \leq i \leq m$, with $|S^i| = |B^i|$ and $|M^i| = |S^i| + |\overrightarrow{M^{i-1}}|$.

We illustrate the encoding of the PB constraint $3x_1 + 5x_2 + 3x_3 + 6x_4 < 12$ in Fig. 2. The bit buckets are $B^1 := (x_1, x_2, x_3)$, $B^2 := (x_1, x_3, x_4)$ and $B^3 := (x_2, x_4)$. The sorters are on the top and the mergers at the bottom in the figure, where the inputs are on the left half of a sorter and merger box and the output is on the right side. The mapping of the literals under the interpretation $I \supseteq \{x_1, x_2, \overline{x_3}, x_4\}$ is shown in the right part in the figure. The encoding contains the clause $(\overline{M_3^3})$ since $k = q \cdot 2^{m-1} = 3 \cdot 2^2 = 12$. Hence the interpretation I is inconsistent w.r.t. the considered PB constraint, since $3 + 5 + 0 + 6 \geq 12$.

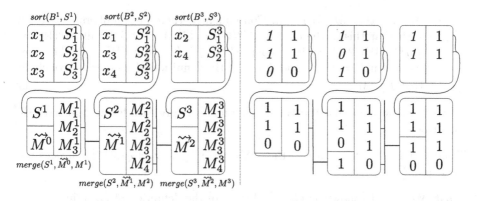

Fig. 2. Binary Merger for the PB constraint $3x_1 + 5x_2 + 3x_3 + 6x_4 < 12$. On the left side there is the generic overview of the sorters and mergers and on the right side there is the literal mapping under the interpretation $I \supseteq \{x_1, x_2, \overline{x_3}, x_4\}$. The mapping for the x_1, x_2, x_3, x_4 is set into italic numbers and the auxiliary variables S_j^i and M_j^i are mapped by I such that I is a model for $\mathsf{BinaryMerger}(C) \setminus [\overline{M_3^3}]$.

4.1 The Binary Merger Encodes Pseudo-Boolean Constraints

We proceed with the proof that the binary merger formula encodes normalized PB constraints. First, we derive a meaning for the variables S_b^p and M_a^p, where a and b are the positions in the sequences S^p and M^p.

Proposition 2 (Semantic Invariants). *Let* $I \models \mathsf{BinaryMerger}(\sum_{i=1}^{n} w_i x_i <$ $q \cdot 2^{m-1})$ *and let* $W = \{w_i \mid x_i \in I \text{ and } 1 \leq i \leq n\}$. *Then the following holds:*

(i) $I \models S_b^p$ *iff* $S^p(W) \geq b$ *for every* $b \in \{1, \dots, m\}$,
(ii) $I \models \mathsf{sort}(S^p)$ *and* $I \models \mathsf{sort}(M^p)$, *and*
(iii) $I \models M_a^p$ *iff* $M^p(W) \geq a$ *for every* $a \in \{1, \dots, m\}$.

Proof. We prove the claims separately.

(i) follows straightforward from the definition of the binary merger constraint and the definition of the sort constraint: $I \models S_b^p$ iff $\sum\{\mathsf{bit}(w, p) \mid x_i \in I\} \geq b$ iff $S^p(W) \geq b$.
(ii) can be easily shown by induction over p.
(iii) is shown by induction over p: For the induction base $p = 1$. We know that $I \models M_a^1$ iff $I \models S_a^1$ by the definition of the encoding. By (i) this is the case iff $S^1(W) \geq a$ and since $M^1(W) = S_1(W)$ we know that $M^p(W) \geq a$. For the induction step, assume that the claim (iii) holds for $p - 1$. We show both directions:

  $\Rightarrow$ Let $I \models M_x^p$. By the definition of the merger constraint, we conclude that there are numbers a, b such that $x = a + b$ and 1) $I \models M_{2 \cdot a}^{p-1}$ and 2) $I \models S_b^p$. Then by induction we know that $M^{p-1}(W) \geq 2 \cdot a$ and by (i) we know that $S^p(W) \geq b$. Then by definition of M^p we conclude that $M^p \geq a$.

$\Leftarrow$ Assume that $M^p(W) \geq x$. Consequently, there are numbers $x = a + b$ such that this is the case iff $M^p(W) = C^j(W) + S^j(W)$ iff $M^p(W) = \lfloor M^{p-1}(W)/2 \rfloor + S^j(W)$. Then $M^{p-1} \geq a/2$ and $S^j(W) \geq b$. Then by induction $I \models M^{p-1}_{a/2}$ and $I \models S^p_b$. By definition of merger we conclude that $I \models M^p_a$. $\square$

We can now show that the Binary Merger correctly encodes normalized PB-constraints.

Theorem 1. *The formula* $F = \mathsf{BinaryMerger}(\sum_{i=1}^{n} w_i x_i < q \cdot 2^{m-1})$ *encodes the constraint* $\sum_{i=1}^{n} w_i x_i < q \cdot 2^{m-1}$.

Proof. We have to show the two conditions of the definition of encoding.

i) Let I be a model of F. Since $\overline{M^m_q} \in F$ we know that $I \not\models M^m_q$. By Prop. 2 (iii) we conclude that $M^m(W) < q$. By Prop. 1 we conclude that $\sum\{\mathsf{bcut}(w, m) \mid w \in W\} = \sum W < q \cdot 2^{m-1}$. Hence $I \models \sum w_i x_i < q \cdot 2^{m-1}$.

ii) Assume that I is a model of $\sum w_i x_i < q \cdot 2^{m-1}$. Then, we construct a model I' for the formula F by assigning the auxiliary variables S^p_a and M^p_b as stated in Prop. 2. We can then show in a straight-forward way that $I' \models F$. $\square$

4.2   The Binary Merger Detects Inconsistencies

In the following, we consider instantiations of the Binary Merger encoding, where unit propagation maintains GAC for the sorter and merger constraints. Formally, the formula F is a *suitable Binary Merger encoding* of the PB constraint $\sum_{i=1}^{n} w_i x_i < k$ if the formula F encodes $\mathsf{BinaryMerger}(\sum_{i=1}^{n} w_i x_i < k)$ and the formula F maintains GAC for the used sorters and mergers. We prove that the propositional variables S^p_b and M^p_a are inferred by unit propagation.

Proposition 3 (Propagation Properties). *Let* $C = \sum_{i=1}^{n} w_i x_i < k$ *be a normalized PB-constraint,* J *be a variable assignment, and* $W = \{w_i \mid x_i \in J \text{ and } 1 \leq i \leq n\}$ *is the set of weights of all satisfied literals* x_i *w.r.t.* J. *For every suitable Binary Merger encoding* F *of the constraint* C *holds that:*

i) $S^p_b \in \mathsf{UP}(F, J)$, *if* $S^p(W) \geq b$, *and*
ii) $M^p_a \in \mathsf{UP}(F, J)$, *if* $M^p(W) \geq a$.

Proof. (i) follows straightforward from the assumption that the sorter maintains GAC: If more than b input variables of the sorter are assigned to true in J, then output sequence must start necessarily with at least b true literals. (ii) is shown by induction over p. For the induction base $p = 1$, the argumentation is analog to the proof of (i) since $M^1(W) = S^1(W)$. For the induction step, assume that the claim holds for p and we prove it now for $p + 1$. Suppose that $M^{p+1}(W) \geq x$. By the definition of the function M, there are numbers a and b such that $x = a + b$ and $a = \lfloor M^p(W)/2 \rfloor$ and $b = S^{p+1}(W)$. By induction we conclude that $M^p_{2 \cdot a} \in \mathsf{UP}(F, J)$ and $S^{p+1}_b \in \mathsf{UP}(F, J)$. Since the merger is assumed to maintain GAC, we then know that $M^{p+1}_{a+b} = M^{p+1}_x \in \mathsf{UP}(F, J)$. $\square$

We can now prove the claim in this section that suitable Binary Merger encodings detect inconsistencies.

Theorem 2. *Every suitable Binary Merger encoding of $\sum_{i=1}^{n} w_i x_i < k$ detects inconsistencies by unit propagation.*

Proof. Assume that the assignment J is inconsistent with the PB constraint $C = \sum_{i=1}^{n} w_i x_i < q \cdot 2^{m-1}$. We now prove that $\perp \in \mathsf{UP}(J, E)$. Since J is inconsistent, we know that $(\bigwedge_{x \in J} x) \wedge C$ is unsatisfiable. Consequently, $\sum \{w_i \mid x \in J$ and $1 \leq i \leq n\} \geq q \cdot 2^{m-1}$. By Prop 3, we know that $M_q^m \in \mathsf{UP}(F, J)$ and we know that $\overline{M_q^m} \in \mathsf{UP}(F, J)$ since $\overline{M_q^m} \in F$. Consequently, $\perp \in \mathsf{UP}(F, J)$. Hence, the formula F detects inconsistencies by unit propagation for the constraint C.   □

We require that suitable Binary Merger encodings maintain GAC for the sorters and mergers. Intuitively, if we consider instantiations of the Binary Merger that detects inconsistencies but do not maintain GAC for the sorters and mergers, then we cannot detect inconsistencies of the PB constraint. The reason is that the notion of inconsistency detection is too weak to infer the y literals in the sorter.

Note that we cannot prove this property for PB constraints of the form $\sum_{i=1}^{n} w_i x_i = k$, since we split the constraint up into two normalized PB constraints and the propagation property only holds for a individual normalized PB constraint.

4.3   The Binary Merger and Support Clauses Maintain GAC

We now proceed with a technique makes the Binary Merger encoding GAC-maintaining by adding support clauses.

Proposition 4. *Let $E(C)$ denote a formula that detects inconsistencies of the normalized PB constrain C. Consider $C = \sum_{i=1}^{n} w_i x_i < k$, where V is the set $\mathsf{vars}(C) \cup \overline{\mathsf{vars}(C)}$ Then the following holds:*

(i) $(\bigwedge_{x_i \in V}(E(C[x_i \mapsto \top]) \vee \overline{x_i}))$ encodes the constraint C, and
(ii) $(\bigwedge_{x_i \in V}(E(C[x_i \mapsto \top]) \vee \overline{x_i}))$ maintains GAC, and
(iii) $|F| = 2 \cdot \mathsf{vars}(C) \cdot |E(C)|$.

Proof. We show each statement separately:

(i) We have to show that the formula $F = (\bigwedge E(C[x_i \mapsto \top]) \vee \overline{x_i})$ satisfies the two conditions in the definition of encodings.

   1 Assume that the interpretation I is a model of the formula F. Consequently we know that either $I \models x_i$ or $I \models \overline{x_i}$ holds. We consider the first case, and the second can be analogously treated. Then it follows that $I \models E(C[x_i \mapsto \top])$ since $I \models x_i$ and $I \models E(C[x_i \mapsto \top]) \vee \overline{x_i}$. By the fact that the formula $E(C)$ encodes the constraint C we can then conclude that $I \models C[x_i \mapsto \top]$. Since $I \models x_i$, we know that $I \models C$.

2 Assume that the interpretation I is a model of the constraint C. Consequently, we know that either $I \models x_i$ or $I \models \overline{x_i}$. Consider the first case, as the second can be treated analogy. Since $E(C[x_i \mapsto \top])$ is an encoding, we construct I' over the auxiliary variables of this encoding. Then we know that $I' \models E(C[x_i \mapsto \top])$. Since the encoding use pairwise disjunct sets of auxiliary variables, we can continue the construction in the sketched way. Finally, we obtain that $I' \models F$.

(ii) Suppose that the formula F does not maintain GAC. Then there is an assignment J and literal x such that $J \wedge F \models x$, but $x \notin \mathsf{UP}(F, J)$. It is easy to see that J is inconsistent w.r.t. the constraint $C[x \mapsto \bot]$ Since $E(C[x \mapsto \bot])$ detects inconsistencies, we conclude that $x \in \mathsf{UP}(F, J)$ since $x \vee E(C[x \mapsto \bot]) \in F$. But this is a contradiction.

(iii) Follows directly from the definition of the encoding. □

4.4 Complexity of the Binary Merger

In this paper, we do not present encodings of the merger and sorter constraint, and instead want to refer the reader to *cardinality networks* [3].

Proposition 5. *The Binary Merger formula can be encoded with a space complexity of $\mathcal{O}(n \log^2(n) \log(w_{max}))$ clauses and variables.*

Proof. For the encoding of the sorter and merger we use the cardinality networks as presented in [3], that maintain GAC using $\mathcal{O}(n \log^2(n))$ clauses and variables, where n is the number of literals in the sequence that is sorted. Note that an encoding for a sorter can be used as an encoding for a merger as well since $merge(X, Y, Z) \equiv sort(X \cdot Y, Z)$ since X and Y are sorted in every model and where $X \cdot Y$ is the concatenation of two sequences.

Each S^i contains at most n literals and since the input for the merger is $|S^i| + |M^i|$ we have at most $n(1 + 1/2 + 1/4 + 1/8 \ldots 1/m) < 2n$ literals as input for the merger. Hence each sorter and merger results in $\mathcal{O}(n \log^2 n)$ clauses and variables. With m mergers and sorters we result in $\mathcal{O}(n \log^2(n) \log(w_{max}))$ clauses and variables. □

Theorem 3. *Pseudo-Boolean constraints can be encoded with a space complexity of $\mathcal{O}(n^2 \log^2(n) \log(w_{max}))$ clauses and variables such that unit propagation maintains GAC.*

Proof. Follows directly from Propositions 4 and 5. □

Hence with the Binary Merger encoding it is possible to encode a PB constraint with less then $\mathcal{O}(n^3 \log(n) \log(w_{max}))$ clauses and a bit more than the $\mathcal{O}(n^2 \log(n) \log(w_{max}))$ variables used in the polynomial watchdog encoding, the previously best known encoding for PB constraint that maintains GAC.

5   Conclusion

Pseudo-Boolean constraints of the form $\sum_{i=1}^{n} w_i \cdot x_i < k$ frequently arise in real world problems and are translated into CNF to use the strength of modern SAT reasoning systems. This paper presents the novel Binary Merger encoding for PB constraints. It uses $\mathcal{O}(n \log^2(n) \log(w_{max}))$ clauses, where w_{max} is the largest weight in the PB constraint. The addition of support clauses makes the Binary Merger GAC-maintaining and, to the best of our knowledge, the Binary Merger with support clauses is the asymptotically smallest encoding that maintains GAC, i.e. uses $\mathcal{O}(n^2 \log^2(n) \log(w_{max}))$ clauses. In particular, this answers the open question by Bailleux et al. in [21] for a more compact encoding.

References

1. Abío, I., Nieuwenhuis, R., Oliveras, A., Rodríguez-Carbonell, E.: BDDs for pseudo-Boolean constraints – revisited. In: Sakallah, K.A., Simon, L. (eds.) SAT 2011. LNCS, vol. 6695, pp. 61–75. Springer, Heidelberg (2011)
2. Abío, I., Nieuwenhuis, R., Oliveras, A., Rodríguez-Carbonell, E., Mayer-Eichberger, V.: A new look at BDDs for pseudo-Boolean constraints. JAIR 45, 443–480 (2012)
3. Asín, R., Nieuwenhuis, R., Oliveras, A., Rodríguez-Carbonell, E.: Cardinality networks and their applications. In: Kullmann (ed.) [15], pp. 167–180
4. Belov, A., Janota, M., Lynce, I., Marques-Silva, J.: On computing minimal equivalent subformulas. In: Milano, M. (ed.) CP 2012. LNCS, vol. 7514, pp. 158–174. Springer, Heidelberg (2012)
5. Biere, A., Heule, M., van Maaren, H., Walsh, T. (eds.): IOS Press, Amsterdam (2009)
6. Boros, E., Hammer, P.L.: Pseudo-boolean optimization. DAM 123(1-3), 155–225 (2002)
7. Brewka, G., Eiter, T., Truszczyński, M.: Answer set programming at a glance. CACM 54(12), 92–103 (2011)
8. Davis, M., Logemann, G., Loveland, D.: A machine program for theorem-proving. CACM 5(7), 394–397 (1962)
9. Davis, M., Putnam, H.: A computing procedure for quantification theory. JACM 7(3), 201–215 (1960)
10. Eén, N., Biere, A.: Effective preprocessing in SAT through variable and clause elimination. In: Bacchus, F., Walsh, T. (eds.) SAT 2005. LNCS, vol. 3569, pp. 61–75. Springer, Heidelberg (2005)
11. Eén, N., Sörensson, N.: Translating pseudo-Boolean constraints into SAT. JSAT 2, 1–26 (2006)
12. Hölldobler, S., Manthey, N., Saptawijaya, A.: Improving resource-unaware SAT solvers. In: Fermüller, C.G., Voronkov, A. (eds.) LPAR-17. LNCS, vol. 6397, pp. 519–534. Springer, Heidelberg (2010)
13. Kautz, H., Selman, B.: Planning as satisfiability. In: Neumann, B. (ed.) ECAI 1992, pp. 359–363. John Wiley & Sons, Inc., New York (1992)
14. Kautz, H., Selman, B.: Pushing the envelope: Planning, propositional logic, and stochastic search. In: AAAI 1996, pp. 1194–1201. MIT Press (1996)
15. Kullmann, O. (ed.): SAT 2009. LNCS, vol. 5584. Springer, Heidelberg (2009)
16. Liffiton, M.H., Sakallah, K.A.: Algorithms for computing minimal unsatisfiable subsets of constraints. JAR 40(1), 1–33 (2008)

17. Manthey, N., Heule, M.J.H., Biere, A.: Automated reencoding of Boolean formulas. In: Biere, A., Nahir, A., Vos, T. (eds.) HVC 2012. LNCS, vol. 7857, pp. 102–117. Springer, Heidelberg (2013)
18. Manthey, N., Steinke, P.: npSolver – A SAT based solver for optimization problems. In: POS 2012 (2012)
19. Moskewicz, M.W., Madigan, C.F., Zhao, Y., Zhang, L., Malik, S.: Chaff: Engineering an efficient SAT solver. In: DAC 2001, pp. 530–535. ACM, New York (2001)
20. Nadel, A.: Boosting minimal unsatisfiable core extraction. In: Bloem, R., Sharygina, N. (eds.) FMCAD 2010, pp. 121–128 (2010)
21. Bailleux, O., Boufkhad, Y., Roussel, O.: New encodings of pseudo-Boolean constraints into CNF. In: Kullmann (ed.) [15], pp. 181–194
22. Plaisted, D.A., Greenbaum, S.: A structure-preserving clause form translation. Journal of Symbolic Computation 2(3), 293–304 (1986)
23. Rossi, F., Beek, P.v., Walsh, T.: Handbook of Constraint Programming. Elsevier Science Inc., New York (2006)
24. Roussel, O., Manquinho, V.: Pseudo-Boolean and cardinality constraints. In: Biere, et al. (eds.) [5]
25. Subbarayan, S., Pradhan, D.K.: NiVER: Non-increasing variable elimination resolution for preprocessing SAT instances. In: Hoos, H.H., Mitchell, D.G. (eds.) SAT 2004. LNCS, vol. 3542, pp. 276–291. Springer, Heidelberg (2005)
26. Tseitin, G.S.: On the complexity of derivation in propositional calculus. In: Automation of Reasoning. Symbolic Computation, pp. 466–483. Springer, Heidelberg (1983)

Matching with Respect to General Concept Inclusions in the Description Logic $\mathcal{EL}$

Franz Baader and Barbara Morawska*

Theoretical Computer Science, TU Dresden, Germany
{baader,morawska}@tcs.inf.tu-dresden.de

Abstract. Matching concept descriptions against concept patterns was introduced as a new inference task in Description Logics (DLs) almost 20 years ago, motivated by applications in the Classic system. For the DL $\mathcal{EL}$, it was shown in 2000 that matching without a TBox is NP-complete. In this paper we show that matching in $\mathcal{EL}$ w.r.t. general TBoxes (i.e., finite sets of general concept inclusions, GCIs) is in NP by introducing a goal-oriented matching algorithm that uses non-deterministic rules to transform a given matching problem into a solved form by a polynomial number of rule applications. We also investigate some tractable variants of the matching problem w.r.t. general TBoxes.

1 Introduction

The DL $\mathcal{EL}$, which offers the constructors conjunction ($\sqcap$), existential restriction ($\exists r.C$), and the top concept ($\top$), has recently drawn considerable attention since, on the one hand, important inference problems such as the subsumption problem are polynomial in $\mathcal{EL}$, even in the presence of general concept inclusions (GCIs) [12]. On the other hand, though quite inexpressive, $\mathcal{EL}$ can be used to define biomedical ontologies, such as the large medical ontology SNOMED CT.[1]

Matching of concept descriptions against concept patterns is a non-standard inference task in Description Logics, which was originally motivated by applications of the Classic system [9]. In [11], Borgida and McGuinness proposed matching as a means to filter out the unimportant aspects of large concept descriptions appearing in knowledge bases of Classic. Subsequently, matching (as well as the more general problem of unification) was also proposed as a tool for detecting redundancies in knowledge bases [8] and to support the integration of knowledge bases by prompting interschema assertions to the integrator [10].

All three applications have in common that one wants to search the knowledge base for concepts having a certain (not completely specified) form. This "form" can be expressed with the help of so-called *concept patterns*, i.e., concept descriptions containing variables (which stand for descriptions). For example, assume that we want to find concepts that are concerned with individuals having a son and a daughter sharing some characteristic. This can be expressed

---

* Supported by DFG under grant BA 1122/14-2.

[1] See http://www.ihtsdo.org/snomed-ct/

C. Lutz and M. Thielscher (Eds.): KI 2014, LNCS 8736, pp. 135–146, 2014.

by the pattern $D := \exists$has-child.(Male $\sqcap X$) $\sqcap \exists$has-child.(Female $\sqcap X$), where X is a variable standing for the common characteristic. The concept description $C := \exists$has-child.(Tall $\sqcap$ Male) $\sqcap \exists$has-child.(Tall $\sqcap$ Female) matches this pattern in the sense that, if we replace the variable X by the description Tall, the pattern becomes *equivalent* to the description. Thus, the substitution $\sigma := \{X \mapsto$ Tall$\}$ is a *matcher modulo equivalence* of the matching problem $C \equiv^? D$ since $C \equiv \sigma(D)$.

The original paper by Borgida and McGuinness actually considered matching modulo subsumption rather than matching modulo equivalence: such a problem is of the form $C \sqsubseteq^? D$, and a matcher is a substitution σ satisfying $C \sqsubseteq \sigma(D)$. Obviously, any matcher modulo equivalence is also a matcher modulo subsumption, but not vice versa. For example, the substitution $\sigma_\top := \{X \mapsto \top\}$ is a *matcher modulo subsumption* of the matching problem $C \sqsubseteq^? D$, but it is not a matcher modulo equivalence of $C \equiv^? D$. For both cases of matching, the original definitions were formulated for concept descriptions without any TBox, i.e., the subsumption or equivalence that has to be achieved by an application of the matcher does not take a TBox into account. The reason was that at that time TBoxes were usually acyclic, and thus could be reduced away by unfolding.

The first results on matching in DLs were concerned with sublanguages of the Classic description language, which does not allow for existential restrictions of the kind used above. A polynomial-time algorithm for computing matchers modulo subsumption for a rather expressive DL was introduced in [11]. The main drawback of this algorithm was that it required the concept patterns to be in structural normal form, and thus it was not able to handle arbitrary matching problems. In addition, the algorithm was incomplete, i.e., it did not always find a matcher, even if one existed. For the DL $\mathcal{ALN}$, a polynomial-time algorithm for matching modulo subsumption and equivalence was presented in [6]. This algorithm is complete and it applies to arbitrary patterns. In [5], matching in DLs with existential restrictions was investigated for the first time. In particular, it was shown that in $\mathcal{EL}$ the matching problem (i.e., the problem of deciding whether a given matching problem has a matcher or not) is polynomial for matching modulo subsumption, but NP-complete for matching modulo equivalence.

Unification is a generalization of matching where both sides of the problem are patterns and thus the substitution needs to be applied to both sides. In [8] it was shown that the unification problem in the DL $\mathcal{FL}_0$, which offers the constructors conjunction ($\sqcap$), value restriction ($\forall r.C$), and the top concept ($\top$), is ExpTime-complete. In contrast, unification in $\mathcal{EL}$ is "only" NP-complete [7]. In the results for matching and unification mentioned until now, there was no TBox involved, i.e., equivalence and subsumption was considered with respect to the empty TBox. For unification in $\mathcal{EL}$, first attempts were made to take *general TBoxes*, i.e., finite sets of general concept inclusions (GCIs), into account. However, the results obtained so far, which are again NP-completeness results, are restricted to general TBoxes that satisfy a certain restriction on cyclic dependencies between concepts [2,3].

For matching, we solve the general case in this paper: we show that matching in $\mathcal{EL}$ w.r.t. general TBoxes is NP-complete by introducing a goal-oriented matching algorithm that uses non-deterministic rules to transform a given matching problem into a solved form by a polynomial number of rule applications. The matching problems considered in this paper are actually generalizations of matching modulo equivalence and matching modulo subsumption. For the special case of matching modulo subsumption, we show that the problem is tractable also in the presence of GCIs. The same is true for the dual problem where the pattern is on the side of the subsumee rather than on the side of the subsumer.

Due to space constraints, we cannot provide complete proofs of our results. They can be found in [1].

2   The Description Logics $\mathcal{EL}$

The expressiveness of a DL is determined both by the formalism for describing concepts (the concept description language) and the terminological formalism, which can be used to state additional constraints on the interpretation of concepts and roles in a so-called TBox.

The *concept description language* considered in this paper is called $\mathcal{EL}$. Starting with a finite set N_C of *concept names* and a finite set N_R of *role names*, $\mathcal{EL}$-concept descriptions are built from concept names using the constructors *conjunction* $(C \sqcap D)$, *existential restriction* $(\exists r.C$ for every $r \in N_R)$, and *top* $(\top)$. Since in this paper we only consider $\mathcal{EL}$-concept descriptions, we will sometimes dispense with the prefix $\mathcal{EL}$.

On the *semantic side*, concept descriptions are interpreted as sets. To be more precise, an *interpretation* $\mathcal{I} = (\Delta^{\mathcal{I}}, \cdot^{\mathcal{I}})$ consists of a non-empty domain $\Delta^{\mathcal{I}}$ and an interpretation function $\cdot^{\mathcal{I}}$ that maps concept names to subsets of $\Delta^{\mathcal{I}}$ and role names to binary relations over $\Delta^{\mathcal{I}}$. This function is inductively extended to concept descriptions as follows:

$$\top^{\mathcal{I}} := \Delta^{\mathcal{I}}, \quad (C \sqcap D)^{\mathcal{I}} := C^{\mathcal{I}} \cap D^{\mathcal{I}}, \quad (\exists r.C)^{\mathcal{I}} := \{x \mid \exists y : (x, y) \in r^{\mathcal{I}} \land y \in C^{\mathcal{I}}\}$$

A *general concept inclusion axiom (GCI)* is of the form $C \sqsubseteq D$ for concept descriptions C, D. An interpretation $\mathcal{I}$ *satisfies* such an axiom $C \sqsubseteq D$ iff $C^{\mathcal{I}} \subseteq D^{\mathcal{I}}$. A *general $\mathcal{EL}$-TBox* is a finite set of GCIs. An interpretation is a *model* of a general $\mathcal{EL}$-TBox if it satisfies all its GCIs.

A concept description C is *subsumed* by a concept description D w.r.t. a general TBox $\mathcal{T}$ (written $C \sqsubseteq_{\mathcal{T}} D$) if every model of $\mathcal{T}$ satisfies the GCI $C \sqsubseteq D$. We say that C is *equivalent* to D w.r.t. $\mathcal{T}$ ($C \equiv_{\mathcal{T}} D$) if $C \sqsubseteq_{\mathcal{T}} D$ and $D \sqsubseteq_{\mathcal{T}} C$. If $\mathcal{T}$ is empty, we also write $C \sqsubseteq D$ and $C \equiv D$ instead of $C \sqsubseteq_{\mathcal{T}} D$ and $C \equiv_{\mathcal{T}} D$, respectively. As shown in [12], subsumption w.r.t. general $\mathcal{EL}$-TBoxes is decidable in polynomial time.

An $\mathcal{EL}$-concept description is an *atom* if it is an existential restriction or a concept name. The atoms of an $\mathcal{EL}$-concept description C are the subdescriptions of C that are atoms, and the top-level atoms of C are the atoms occurring in the top-level conjunction of C. Obviously, any $\mathcal{EL}$-concept description is the conjunction of its top-level atoms, where the empty conjunction corresponds to $\top$. The atoms of a general $\mathcal{EL}$-TBox $\mathcal{T}$ are the atoms of all the concept descriptions occurring in GCIs of $\mathcal{T}$.

We say that a subsumption between two atoms is *structural* if their top-level structure is compatible. To be more precise, following [2] we define structural subsumption between atoms as follows: the atom C is *structurally subsumed* by the atom D w.r.t. $\mathcal{T}$ ($C \sqsubseteq_{\mathcal{T}}^s D$) iff one of the following holds:

1. $C = D$ is a concept name,
2. $C = \exists r.C'$, $D = \exists r.D'$, and $C' \sqsubseteq_{\mathcal{T}} D'$.

It is easy to see that subsumption w.r.t. $\emptyset$ between two atoms implies structural subsumption w.r.t. $\mathcal{T}$, which in turn implies subsumption w.r.t. $\mathcal{T}$. The matching algorithms presented below crucially depend on the following characterization of subsumption w.r.t. general $\mathcal{EL}$-TBoxes first stated in [2]:

Lemma 1. *Let $\mathcal{T}$ be an $\mathcal{EL}$-TBox and $C_1, \ldots, C_n, D_1, \ldots, D_m$ be atoms. Then $C_1 \sqcap \cdots \sqcap C_n \sqsubseteq_{\mathcal{T}} D_1 \sqcap \cdots \sqcap D_m$ iff for every $j \in \{1, \ldots, m\}$*

1. *there is an index $i \in \{1, \ldots, n\}$ such that $C_i \sqsubseteq_{\mathcal{T}}^s D_j$ or*
2. *there are atoms $A_1, \ldots, A_k, B$ of $\mathcal{T}$ ($k \geq 0$) such that*
   (a) *$A_1 \sqcap \cdots \sqcap A_k \sqsubseteq_{\mathcal{T}} B$,*
   (b) *for every $\eta \in \{1, \ldots, k\}$ there is $i \in \{1, \ldots, n\}$ with $C_i \sqsubseteq_{\mathcal{T}}^s A_\eta$, and*
   (c) *$B \sqsubseteq_{\mathcal{T}}^s D_j$.*

3 Matching in $\mathcal{EL}$

In addition to the set N_C of concept names (which must not be replaced by substitutions), we introduce a set N_V of concept variables (which may be replaced by substitutions). *Concept patterns* are now built from concept names and concept variables by applying the constructors of $\mathcal{EL}$. A *substitution* σ maps every concept variable to an $\mathcal{EL}$-concept description. It is extended to concept patterns in the usual way:

- $\sigma(A) := A$ for all $A \in N_C \cup \{\top\}$,
- $\sigma(C \sqcap D) := \sigma(C) \sqcap \sigma(D)$ and $\sigma(\exists r.C) := \exists r.\sigma(C)$.

An $\mathcal{EL}$-concept pattern C is *ground* if it does not contain variables, i.e., if it is a concept description. Obviously, a ground concept pattern is not modified by applying a substitution.

Definition 2. *Let $\mathcal{T}$ be a general $\mathcal{EL}$-TBox.[2] An $\mathcal{EL}$-matching problem w.r.t. $\mathcal{T}$ is a finite set $\Gamma = \{C_1 \sqsubseteq^? D_1, \ldots, C_n \sqsubseteq^? D_n\}$ of subsumptions between $\mathcal{EL}$-concept patterns, where for each $i, 1 \leq i \leq n$, C_i or D_i is ground. A substitution σ is a matcher of Γ w.r.t. $\mathcal{T}$ if σ solves all the subsumptions in Γ, i.e. if $\sigma(C_1) \sqsubseteq_{\mathcal{T}} \sigma(D_1), \ldots, \sigma(C_n) \sqsubseteq_{\mathcal{T}} \sigma(D_n)$. We say that Γ is matchable w.r.t. $\mathcal{T}$ if it has a matcher.*

---

[2] Note that the GCIs in $\mathcal{T}$ are built using concept descriptions, and thus do not contain variables.

Matching problems modulo equivalence and subsumption are special cases of the matching problems introduced above:

- The $\mathcal{EL}$-matching problem Γ is a *matching problem modulo equivalence* if $C \sqsubseteq^? D \in \Gamma$ implies $D \sqsubseteq^? C \in \Gamma$. This coincides with the notion of matching modulo equivalence considered in [6,5], but extended to a non-empty general TBox.
- The $\mathcal{EL}$-matching problem Γ is a *left-ground matching problem modulo subsumption* if $C \sqsubseteq^? D \in \Gamma$ implies that C is ground. This coincides with the notion of matching modulo subsumption considered in [6,5], but again extended to a non-empty general TBox.
- The $\mathcal{EL}$-matching problem Γ is a *right-ground matching problem modulo subsumption* if $C \sqsubseteq^? D \in \Gamma$ implies that D is ground. To the best of our knowledge, this notion of matching has not been investigated before.

We will show in the following that the general case of matching, as introduced in Definition 2, and thus also matching modulo equivalence, is NP-complete, whereas the two notions of matching modulo subsumption are tractable, even in the presence of GCIs.

4   Matching Modulo Subsumption

The case of *left-ground matching problems modulo subsumption* can be treated as sketched in [5] for the case without a TBox. Given a general $\mathcal{EL}$-TBox $\mathcal{T}$ and two substitutions σ, τ, we define: $\sigma \sqsubseteq_{\mathcal{T}} \tau$ iff $\sigma(X) \sqsubseteq_{\mathcal{T}} \tau(X)$ for all $X \in N_V$.

Consequently, if $\sigma_\top$ denotes the substitution satisfying $\sigma_\top(X) = \top$ for all $X \in N_V$, then $\sigma \sqsubseteq_{\mathcal{T}} \sigma_\top$ holds for all substitutions σ. Since the concept constructors of $\mathcal{EL}$ are monotonic w.r.t. subsumption, this implies $\sigma(D) \sqsubseteq_{\mathcal{T}} \sigma_\top(D)$ for all concept patterns D.

Lemma 3. *Let* $\Gamma = \{C_1 \sqsubseteq^? D_1, \ldots, C_n \sqsubseteq^? D_n\}$ *be a left-ground matching problem modulo subsumption. Then* Γ *has a matcher w.r.t.* $\mathcal{T}$ *iff* $\sigma_\top$ *is a matcher of* Γ *w.r.t.* $\mathcal{T}$.

Proof. The "if" direction is trivial. Conversely, assume that σ is a matcher of Γ w.r.t. $\mathcal{T}$. Then we have, for all $i, 1 \leq i \leq n$, that $\sigma_\top(C_i) = C_i = \sigma(C_i) \sqsubseteq_{\mathcal{T}} \sigma(D_i) \sqsubseteq_{\mathcal{T}} \sigma_\top(D_i)$, which shows that $\sigma_\top$ is a matcher of Γ w.r.t. $\mathcal{T}$.   □

The lemma shows that it is sufficient to test whether the substitution $\sigma_\top$ is a matcher of Γ, i.e., whether $\sigma_\top(C_i) \sqsubseteq_{\mathcal{T}} \sigma_\top(D_i)$ holds for all $i, 1 \leq i \leq n$. Since in $\mathcal{EL}$ subsumption w.r.t. general TBoxes is decidable in polynomial time, this yields a polynomial-time algorithm for left-ground matching modulo subsumption in $\mathcal{EL}$.

Theorem 4. *Let* Γ *be a left-ground $\mathcal{EL}$-matching problem modulo subsumption and* $\mathcal{T}$ *a general $\mathcal{EL}$-TBox. Then we can decide in polynomial time whether* Γ *has a matcher w.r.t.* $\mathcal{T}$ *or not.*

The case of *right-ground matching problems modulo subsumption* can be treated similarly. However, since $\mathcal{EL}$ does not have the bottom concept $\bot$ as a concept constructor, we cannot simply define $\sigma_\bot$ as the substitution satisfying $\sigma_\bot(X) = \bot$ for all $X \in N_V$, and then show that that the right-ground matching problems modulo subsumption, Γ, has a matcher w.r.t. $\mathcal{T}$ iff $\sigma_\bot$ is a matcher of Γ w.r.t. $\mathcal{T}$. Instead, we need to define $\sigma_\bot$ in a more complicated manner.

Given a general $\mathcal{EL}$-TBox $\mathcal{T}$ and a right-ground matching problems modulo subsumption $\Gamma = \{C_1 \sqsubseteq^? D_1, \ldots, C_n \sqsubseteq^? D_n\}$, we use $\bot(\Gamma, \mathcal{T})$ to denote the $\mathcal{EL}$-concept description that is the conjunction of all the atoms of $\mathcal{T}$ and of $D_1, \ldots, D_n$. We now define $\sigma_{\bot(\Gamma,\mathcal{T})}$ as the substitution satisfying $\sigma_{\bot(\Gamma,\mathcal{T})}(X) = \bot(\Gamma, \mathcal{T})$ for all $X \in N_V$.

Lemma 5. *Let $\Gamma = \{C_1 \sqsubseteq^? D_1, \ldots, C_n \sqsubseteq^? D_n\}$ be a right-ground matching problem modulo subsumption. Then Γ has a matcher w.r.t. $\mathcal{T}$ iff $\sigma_{\bot(\Gamma,\mathcal{T})}$ is a matcher of Γ w.r.t. $\mathcal{T}$.*

Proof. The "if" direction is trivial. To see the "only-if" direction, assume that σ is a matcher of Γ w.r.t. $\mathcal{T}$. We need to show that this implies the $\sigma_{\bot(\Gamma,\mathcal{T})}$ is also a matcher of Γ w.r.t. $\mathcal{T}$, i.e., that it satisfies $\sigma_{\bot(\Gamma,\mathcal{T})}(C) \sqsubseteq_\mathcal{T} D$ for every subsumption $C \sqsubseteq^? D \in \Gamma$.

More generally, we consider subsumptions $C \sqsubseteq^? D$ where C is a subpattern of a pattern occurring in Γ or $\mathcal{T}$ and D is an atom of $\mathcal{T}$ or $D_1, \ldots, D_n$. We show the following claim:

Claim: *For every such subsumption $C \sqsubseteq^? D$, it holds that $\sigma(C) \sqsubseteq_\mathcal{T} D$ implies $\sigma_{\bot(\Gamma,\mathcal{T})}(C) \sqsubseteq_\mathcal{T} D$.*

Before proving the claim, let us show that this implies that $\sigma_{\bot(\Gamma,\mathcal{T})}$ solves Γ w.r.t. $\mathcal{T}$. In fact, any subsumption in Γ is of the form $C \sqsubseteq^? E_1 \sqcap \ldots \sqcap E_k$ where C is a subpattern of a pattern occurring in Γ, and $E_1, \ldots, E_k$ are atoms of one of the D_i. In addition, a substitution solves $C \sqsubseteq^? E_1 \sqcap \ldots \sqcap E_k$ w.r.t. $\mathcal{T}$ iff it solves all the subsumptions $C \sqsubseteq^? E_i$ for $i = 1, \ldots, k$.

We prove the claim by induction on the size $|C|$ of the left-hand side C of the subsumption $C \sqsubseteq^? D$. Let $C = F_1 \sqcap \ldots \sqcap F_\ell$, where $F_1, \ldots, F_\ell$ are atoms. We distinguish the following three cases:

1. If there is an index $i \in \{1, \ldots, \ell\}$ such that F_i is a variable, then $\sigma_{\bot(\Gamma,\mathcal{T})}(F_i) \sqsubseteq D$ since D occurs as a conjunct in $\bot(\Gamma, \mathcal{T})$. This implies $\sigma_{\bot(\Gamma,\mathcal{T})}(C) \sqsubseteq_\mathcal{T} D$.
2. If there is an index $i \in \{1, \ldots, \ell\}$ such that F_i is ground and $\sigma(F_i) \sqsubseteq_\mathcal{T} D$, then $\sigma_{\bot(\Gamma,\mathcal{T})}(F_i) = F_i = \sigma(F_i) \sqsubseteq_\mathcal{T} D$. This again implies $\sigma_{\bot(\Gamma,\mathcal{T})}(C) \sqsubseteq_\mathcal{T} D$.
3. Assume that the above two cases do not hold. Using Lemma 1, we can distinguish two more cases, depending on whether the first or the second condition of the lemma applies.
   (a) If the first condition applies, then there is an index $i \in \{1, \ldots, \ell\}$ such that $F_i \sqsubseteq_\mathcal{T}^s D$. Since F_i is neither ground nor a variable, we know that F_i is a non-ground existential restriction. Thus, $F_i = \exists r.F'$, $D = \exists r.(D_1 \sqcap \ldots \sqcap D_m)$ with $D_1, \ldots, D_m$ atoms, and $\sigma(F') \sqsubseteq_\mathcal{T} D_i$ for all

$i \in \{1, \ldots, m\}$. Since F' is a subpattern of C, D_i are atoms of D, and $|F'| < |C|$, we can apply the induction hypothesis to the subsumptions $F' \sqsubseteq^? D_i$. This yields $\sigma_{\bot(\Gamma,\mathcal{T})}(F') \sqsubseteq_{\mathcal{T}} D_i$ for all $i \in \{1, \ldots, m\}$, and thus $\sigma_{\bot(\Gamma,\mathcal{T})}(C) \sqsubseteq_{\mathcal{T}} D$.

(b) If the second condition applies, then there are atoms $A_1, \ldots, A_k, B$ of $\mathcal{T}$ such that $A_1 \sqcap \cdots \sqcap A_k \sqsubseteq_{\mathcal{T}} B \sqsubseteq_{\mathcal{T}} D$ and for each $\eta \in \{1, \ldots, k\}$, there is $j \in \{1, \ldots, \ell\}$ such that

   i. F_j is a concept variable and $\sigma(F_j) \sqsubseteq_{\mathcal{T}} A_\eta$, or

   ii. F_j is ground and $F_j \sqsubseteq_{\mathcal{T}} A_\eta$, or

   iii. $F_j = \exists r.F'$, $A_\eta = \exists r.A'$ and $\sigma(F') \sqsubseteq_{\mathcal{T}} A'$.

It is sufficient to show that the subsumption relationships in 3(b)i and 3(b)iii also hold if we replace σ by $\sigma_{\bot(\Gamma,\mathcal{T})}$. For 3(b)i this can be shown as in 1 and for 3(b)iii as in 3a.

This completes the proof of the claim, and thus of the lemma. □

Since the size of $\bot(\Gamma, \mathcal{T})$ is polynomial in the size of Γ and $\mathcal{T}$, this lemma yields a polynomial-time decision procedure for right-ground matching modulo subsumption.

Theorem 6. *Let Γ be a right-ground $\mathcal{EL}$-matching problem modulo subsumption and $\mathcal{T}$ a general $\mathcal{EL}$-TBox. Then we can decide in polynomial time whether Γ has a matcher w.r.t. $\mathcal{T}$ or not.*

5 The General Case

NP-hardness for the general case follows from the known NP-hardness result for matching modulo equivalence without a TBox [5]. In the following, we show that matching in $\mathcal{EL}$ w.r.t. general TBoxes is in NP by introducing a goal-oriented matching algorithm that uses non-deterministic rules to transform a given matching problem into a solved form by a polynomial number of rule applications.

Let $\mathcal{T}$ be a general $\mathcal{EL}$-TBox and Γ_0 an $\mathcal{EL}$-matching problem. We can assume without loss of generality that all the subsumptions $C \sqsubseteq^? D$ in Γ_0 are such that either C or D is non-ground. In fact, if both C and D are ground, then the following holds:

- If $C \sqsubseteq_{\mathcal{T}} D$, then Γ_0 has a matcher w.r.t. $\mathcal{T}$ iff $\Gamma_0 \setminus \{C \sqsubseteq^? D\}$ has a matcher w.r.t. $\mathcal{T}$.
- If $C \not\sqsubseteq_{\mathcal{T}} D$, then Γ_0 does not have a matcher w.r.t. $\mathcal{T}$.

Consequently, we can either remove all the offending ground subsumptions without changing the solvability status of the problem, or immediately decide non-solvability. Using the fact that $C \sqsubseteq_{\mathcal{T}} D_1 \sqcap D_2$ iff $C \sqsubseteq_{\mathcal{T}} D_1$ and $C \sqsubseteq_{\mathcal{T}} D_2$, we can additionally normalize Γ_0 such that the right-hand side of each subsumption in Γ_0 is an atom. We call an $\mathcal{EL}$-matching problem *normalized* if $C \sqsubseteq^? D \in \Gamma_0$ implies that (i) either C or D is non-ground, and (ii) D is an atom.

Eager Solving (variable on the right):

> **Condition:** A subsumption $C \sqsubseteq^? X \in \Gamma$ where $X \in N_V$.
> **Action:**
> - If there is some subsumption of the form $X \sqsubseteq^? D \in \Gamma$ such that $C \not\sqsubseteq_{\mathcal{T}} D$, then the rule application fails.
> - Otherwise, mark $C \sqsubseteq^? X$ as "solved."

Eager Solving (variable on the left):

> **Condition:** A subsumption $X \sqsubseteq^? D \in \Gamma$ where $X \in N_V$.
> **Action:**
> - If there is some subsumption of the form $C \sqsubseteq^? X \in \Gamma$ such that $C \not\sqsubseteq_{\mathcal{T}} D$, then the rule application fails.
> - Otherwise, mark $X \sqsubseteq^? D$ as "solved."

Fig. 1. Eager Rules

Thus, assume that Γ_0 is a normalized $\mathcal{EL}$-matching problem. Our algorithm starts with $\Gamma := \Gamma_0$, and then applies non-deterministic rules to Γ. A non-failing application of a rule may add subsumptions to Γ. Note, however, that a subsumption is only added if it is not yet present. New subsumptions that are added are marked as "unsolved," as are initially all the subsumptions of Γ_0. A rule application may *fail*, which means that this attempt of solving the matching problem was not successful. A non-failing rule application marks one of the subsumptions in the matching problem as "solved." Rules are applied until all subsumptions are marked "solved" or an attempt to apply a rule has failed.

Our definition of the rules uses a function $Dec(\dots)$ on subsumptions of the form $C \sqsubseteq^? D$, where C and D are atoms and D is not a variable. A call of $Dec(C \sqsubseteq^? D)$ returns a (possibly empty) set of subsumptions or it fails:

1. $Dec(C \sqsubseteq^? D) := \{C \sqsubseteq^? D\}$, if C is a variable.
2. If $D_1, \dots, D_n$ are atoms, then $Dec(\exists r.C' \sqsubseteq^? \exists r.(D_1 \sqcap \cdots \sqcap D_n))$ fails if there is an $i \in \{1, \dots, n\}$ such that both sides of $C' \sqsubseteq^? D_i$ are ground and $C' \not\sqsubseteq_{\mathcal{T}} D_i$. Otherwise, $Dec(\exists r.C' \sqsubseteq^? \exists r.(D_1 \sqcap \cdots \sqcap D_n)) := \{C' \sqsubseteq^? D_i \mid 1 \leq i \leq n \text{ and } C' \text{ or } D_i \text{ is non-ground}\}$.
3. If $C = \exists r.C'$ and $D = \exists s.D'$ for roles $s \neq r$, then $Dec(C \sqsubseteq^? D)$ fails.
4. If $C = A$ is a concept name and $D = \exists r.D'$ an existential restriction, then $Dec(C \sqsubseteq^? D)$ fails.
5. If $D = A$ is a concept name and $C = \exists r.C'$ an existential restriction, then $Dec(C \sqsubseteq^? D)$ fails.
6. If both C and D are ground and $C \not\sqsubseteq_{\mathcal{T}} D$ then $Dec(C \sqsubseteq^? D)$ fails, and otherwise returns $\emptyset$.

Algorithm 7. Let Γ_0 be a normalized $\mathcal{EL}$-matching problem. Starting with $\Gamma := \Gamma_0$, apply the rules of Figure 1 and Figure 2 exhaustively in the following order:

Decomposition:

Condition: This rule applies to $\mathfrak{s} = C_1 \sqcap \cdots \sqcap C_n \sqsubseteq^? D \in \Gamma$.
Action: Its application chooses an index $i \in \{1, \ldots, n\}$ and calls $Dec(C_i \sqsubseteq^? D)$. If this call does not fail, then it adds the returned subsumptions to Γ, and marks $\mathfrak{s}$ as *solved*. If $Dec(C_i \sqsubseteq^? D)$ fails, it returns "failure."

Mutation :

Condition: This rule applies to $\mathfrak{s} = C_1 \sqcap \cdots \sqcap C_n \sqsubseteq^? D$ in Γ.
Action: Its application chooses atoms $A_1, \ldots, A_k, B$ of $\mathcal{T}$. If $A_1 \sqcap \cdots \sqcap A_k \sqsubseteq_{\mathcal{T}} B$ does not hold, then it returns "failure." Otherwise, it performs the following two steps:

- Choose for each $\eta \in \{1, \ldots, k\}$ an $i \in \{1, \ldots, n\}$ and call $Dec(C_i \sqsubseteq^? A_\eta)$. If this call does not fail, it adds the returned subsumptions to Γ. Otherwise, if $Dec(C_i \sqsubseteq^? A_\eta)$ fails, the rule returns "failure."
- If it has not failed before and $Dec(B \sqsubseteq^? D)$ does not fail, it adds the returned subsumptions to Γ. Otherwise, if $Dec(B \sqsubseteq^? D)$ fails, it returns "failure."

If these steps did not fail, then the rule marks $\mathfrak{s}$ as *solved*.

Fig. 2. Non-deterministic rules

(1) **Eager rule application:** If an eager rule from Figure 1 applies to an unsolved subsumption, apply it. If the rule application fails, stop and return "failure."

(2) **Non-deterministic rule application:** If no eager rule is applicable, let $\mathfrak{s}$ be an unsolved subsumption in Γ. Choose one of the non-deterministic rules of Figure 2, and apply it to $\mathfrak{s}$. If this rule application fails, then stop and return "failure."

If no more rule applies and the algorithm has not stopped returning "failure," then return "success."

In (2), the choice which unsolved subsumption to consider next is don't care non-deterministic. However, choosing which rule to apply to the chosen subsumption is don't know non-deterministic. Additionally, the application of a non-deterministic rules may require don't know non-deterministic choices to be made. If a non-deterministic rule is applied to a subsumption $\mathfrak{s}$, then neither its left-hand side nor its right-hand side is a variable. In fact, a subsumption that has a variable on one of its sides is solved by one of the eager rules, which have precedence over the non-deterministic rules.

It is easy to see that the subsumptions added by the non-deterministic rules satisfy the normalization conditions (i) and (ii), and thus all the sets Γ generated during a run of the algorithm are normalized $\mathcal{EL}$-matching problems. The next lemma states an important property ensured by the presence of the eager rules.

Lemma 8. *If Γ is a matching problem generated during a non-failing run of the algorithm, and both $C \sqsubseteq^? X \in \Gamma$ and $X \sqsubseteq^? D \in \Gamma$ are solved, then $C \sqsubseteq_{\mathcal{T}} D$.*

Proof. Obviously, one of the two subsumptions was solved after the other. This means that, when it was solved by the application of an eager rule, the other one was already present. Since we consider a non-failing run, the application of the eager rule did not fail, which yields $C \sqsubseteq_{\mathcal{T}} D$.   □

Any run of the algorithm *terminates after a polynomial number of steps.* The main reason for this is that there are only *polynomially many subsumptions* that can occur in the matching problems Γ generated during a run.

Lemma 9. *Let Γ be a matching problem generated during a run of Algorithm 7. Then any subsumption occurring in Γ is of one of the following forms:*

1. *A subsumption contained in the original input matching problem Γ_0.*
2. *A subsumption of the form $C \sqsubseteq^? D$ where C, D are subpatterns of concept patterns occurring in Γ_0.*
3. *A subsumption of the form $C \sqsubseteq^? A$ or $A \sqsubseteq^? C$ where A is an atom of $\mathcal{T}$ and C is a subpattern of a concept pattern occurring in Γ_0.*

Since any rule application either fails while trying to solve an unsolved subsumption (in which case the algorithm stops immediately) or actually solves an unsolved subsumption, there can be only polynomially many rule applications during a run. In addition, it is easy to see that each rule application can be realized in polynomial time, with a polynomial number of possible non-deterministic choices. This shows that Algorithm 7 is indeed an NP-algorithm. It remains to show that it is sound and complete.

To show *soundness*, assume that Γ is a matching problem obtained after termination of a non-failing run of the algorithm. Since the run terminated without failure, all the subsumptions in Γ are solved. We use the subsumptions of the form $X \sqsubseteq^? C \in \Gamma$ to define a substitution σ_Γ. Note that the fact that Γ is a normalized $\mathcal{EL}$-matching problem implies that C is a ground pattern, i.e., a concept description. For each variable $X \in N_V$, we define

$$S_X^\Gamma := \{C \mid X \sqsubseteq^? C \in \Gamma\},$$

and denote the conjunction of all the elements of S_X^Γ as $\sqcap S_X^\Gamma$, where the empty conjunction is $\top$. The substitution σ_Γ is now defined as

$$\sigma_\Gamma(X) := \sqcap S_X^\Gamma \text{ for all } X \in N_V.$$

Lemma 10. *σ_Γ is a matcher of Γ w.r.t. $\mathcal{T}$.*

Since the input matching problem Γ_0 is contained in Γ, this lemma shows that σ_Γ is a matcher also of Γ_0 w.r.t. $\mathcal{T}$. This completes the proof of soundness.

Regarding *completeness*, we can use a given matcher of Γ_0 w.r.t. $\mathcal{T}$ to guide the application of the non-deterministic rules such that a non-failing run is generated (see [1] for details).

Lemma 11. *Let σ be a matcher of Γ_0 w.r.t. $\mathcal{T}$. Then there is a non-failing and terminating run of Algorithm 7 producing a matching problem Γ such that σ is a matcher of Γ w.r.t. $\mathcal{T}$.*

This lemma provides the final step towards showing that Algorithm 7 is an NP-decision procedure for matching w.r.t. general TBoxes in $\mathcal{EL}$.

Theorem 12. *The problem of deciding whether a given $\mathcal{EL}$-matching problem has a matcher w.r.t. a given general $\mathcal{EL}$-TBox or not is NP-complete.*

Let us illustrate the working of the algorithm with a small example. We consider the TBox $\mathcal{T} := \{C \sqsubseteq A, C \sqsubseteq \exists s.C, \exists s.B \sqsubseteq \exists s.C\}$ and the matching problem $\Gamma := \{X \sqcap B \sqsubseteq^? \exists s.A, \exists s.B \sqsubseteq^? \exists s.X\}$. Obviously, this problem is neither left- nor right-ground, and thus we need to use Algorithm 7 to solve it. In the beginning, all the subsumptions in Γ are unsolved, and no eager rule is applicable.

In order to apply a non-deterministic rule, the algorithm chooses one of the unsolved subsumptions. Let us assume that this is the first one, i.e., $X \sqcap B \sqsubseteq^? \exists s.A$. Now, we have a (don't know non-deterministic) choice between applying *Decomposition* or *Mutation*. Consider the case where *Decomposition* is applied in such a way that it produces $Dec(X \sqsubseteq^? \exists s.A) = \{X \sqsubseteq^? \exists s.A\}$. The unsolved subsumption $X \sqsubseteq^? \exists s.A$ is then added to Γ, while $X \sqcap B \sqsubseteq^? \exists s.A$ is marked as "solved."

Now, the algorithm applies *Eager Solving (variable on the left)* to $X \sqsubseteq^? \exists s.A$. Since there are no subsumptions with right-hand side X, the rule application does not fail and $X \sqsubseteq^? \exists s.A$ is marked as "solved."

The algorithm then chooses the only unsolved subsumption left: $\exists s.B \sqsubseteq^? \exists s.X$. Again, there is the choice between applying *Decomposition* and *Mutation*. Let us assume that *Decomposition* is chosen, which yields $Dec(\exists s.B \sqsubseteq^? \exists s.X) = \{B \sqsubseteq^? X\}$. The subsumption $\exists s.B \sqsubseteq^? \exists s.X$ is marked as "solved" and the unsolved subsumption $B \sqsubseteq^? X$ is added to Γ.

Now *Eager Solving (variable on the right)* is applied to this subsumption, which leads to failure since $B \not\sqsubseteq_\mathcal{T} \exists s.A$.

Backtracking to the last choice point, the algorithm applies *Mutation* to $\exists s.B \sqsubseteq^? \exists s.X$. Let us assume that it chooses the atoms $\exists s.B, \exists s.C$ of $\mathcal{T}$, which is a good choice since $\exists s.B \sqsubseteq_\mathcal{T} \exists s.C$. *Mutation* then yields $Dec(\exists s.B \sqsubseteq^? \exists s.B) = \emptyset$ and $Dec(\exists s.C \sqsubseteq^? \exists s.X) = \{C \sqsubseteq^? X\}$. The subsumption $\exists s.B \sqsubseteq^? \exists s.X$ is then marked as "solved" and the unsolved subsumption $C \sqsubseteq^? X$ is added to Γ.

Finally, *Eager Solving (variable on the right)* is applied to this subsumption, which does not fail since $C \sqsubseteq_\mathcal{T} \exists s.A$.

Since now all subsumptions are solved, no more rules apply, and the algorithm returns "success." The matcher computed by this run of the algorithm (as defined in the proof of soundness) is $\{X \mapsto \exists s.A\}$.

6 Conclusion

We have extended the known results for matching in $\mathcal{EL}$ [5] to the case where subsumption and equivalence is considered w.r.t. a non-empty general TBox, i.e., a non-empty set of GCIs. For the DL $\mathcal{FL}_0$, matching without GCIs is polynomial, and this remains true even in the extension $\mathcal{ALN}$ of $\mathcal{FL}_0$. It would be interesting to see how one can solve matching problems w.r.t. general TBoxes in these DLs. Since already subsumption in $\mathcal{FL}_0$ w.r.t. general TBoxes is ExpTime-complete [4], the complexity of solving such matching problems is at least ExpTime-hard. Another interesting open problem is unification in $\mathcal{EL}$ w.r.t. general TBoxes.

References

1. Baader, F., Morawska, B.: Matching with respect to general concept inclusions in the description logic $\mathcal{EL}$. LTCS-Report 14-03, Chair of Automata Theory, Institute of Theoretical Computer Science, Technische Universität Dresden, Dresden, Germany (2014), http://lat.inf.tu-dresden.de/research/reports.html
2. Baader, F., Borgwardt, S., Morawska, B.: Extending unification in $\mathcal{EL}$ towards general TBoxes. In: Proc. of the 13th Int. Conf. on Principles of Knowledge Representation and Reasoning (KR 2012), pp. 568–572. AAAI Press (2012)
3. Baader, F., Borgwardt, S., Morawska, B.: A goal-oriented algorithm for unification in $\mathcal{ELH}_{R^+}$ w.r.t. cycle-restricted ontologies. In: Thielscher, M., Zhang, D. (eds.) AI 2012. LNCS, vol. 7691, pp. 493–504. Springer, Heidelberg (2012)
4. Baader, F., Brandt, S., Lutz, C.: Pushing the $\mathcal{EL}$ envelope. In: Kaelbling, L.P., Saffiotti, A. (eds.) Proc. of the 19th Int. Joint Conf. on Artificial Intelligence (IJCAI 2005), pp. 364–369. Morgan Kaufmann, Los Altos (2005)
5. Baader, F., Küsters, R.: Matching in description logics with existential restrictions. In: Proc. of the 7th Int. Conf. on Principles of Knowledge Representation and Reasoning (KR 2000), pp. 261–272 (2000)
6. Baader, F., Küsters, R., Borgida, A., McGuinness, D.L.: Matching in description logics. J. of Logic and Computation 9(3), 411–447 (1999)
7. Baader, F., Morawska, B.: Unification in the description logic $\mathcal{EL}$. Logical Methods in Computer Science 6(3) (2010)
8. Baader, F., Narendran, P.: Unification of concept terms in description logics. J. of Symbolic Computation 31(3), 277–305 (2001)
9. Borgida, A., Brachman, R.J., McGuinness, D.L., Alperin Resnick, L.: CLASSIC: A structural data model for objects. In: Proc. of the ACM SIGMOD Int. Conf. on Management of Data, pp. 59–67 (1989)
10. Borgida, A., Küsters, R.: What's not in a name? Initial explorations of a structural approach to integrating large concept knowledge-bases. Tech. Rep. DCS-TR-391, Rutgers University (1999)
11. Borgida, A., McGuinness, D.L.: Asking queries about frames. In: Proc. of the 5th Int. Conf. on the Principles of Knowledge Representation and Reasoning (KR 1996), pp. 340–349 (1996)
12. Brandt, S.: Polynomial time reasoning in a description logic with existential restrictions, GCI axioms, and—what else? In: de Mántaras, R.L., Saitta, L. (eds.) Proc. of the 16th Eur. Conf. on Artificial Intelligence (ECAI 2004), pp. 298–302 (2004)

Evaluating Practical Automated Negotiation Based on Spatial Evolutionary Game Theory

Siqi Chen[1], Jianye Hao[2], Gerhard Weiss[1], Karl Tuyls[3], and Ho-fung Leung[4]

[1] Dept. of Knowledge Engineering, Maastricht University, NL
siqi.chen@maastrichtuniversity.nl
[2] Massachusetts Institute of Technology, USA
[3] University of Liverpool, UK
[4] The Chinese University of Hong Kong, HK

Abstract. Over the past decade automated negotiation has developed into a subject of central interest in distributed artificial intelligence. For a great part this is because of its broad application potential in different areas such as economics, e-commerce, the political and social sciences. The complexity of practical automated negotiation – a multi-issue, incomplete-information and continuous-time environment – poses severe challenges, and in recent years many negotiation strategies have been proposed in response to this challenge. Traditionally, the performance of such strategies is evaluated in game-theoretic settings in which each agent "globally" interacts (negotiates) with all other participating agents. This traditional evaluation, however, is not suited for negotiation settings that are primarily characterized by "local" interactions among the participating agents, that is, settings in which each of possibly many participating agents negotiates only with its local neighbors rather than all other agents. This paper presents an approach to handle this type of local setting. Starting out from the traditional global perspective, the negotiations are also analyzed in a new fashion that negotiation locality (hence spatial information about the agents) is taken into consideration. It is shown how both empirical and spatial evolutionary game theory can be used to interpret bilateral negotiation results among state of the art negotiating agents in these different scenarios.

1 Introduction

As one of the most fundamental and powerful mechanisms for managing inter-agent dependencies, automated negotiation is central for resolving distributed conflicts between two or multiple parties [11]. Recent years have witnessed an increasing interest in developing negotiation models and strategies for a variety of problems, for example, its deployment in business process management, electronic commerce and markets, task and service allocation, etc. As a result, automated negotiation brings together research topics of artificial intelligence, machine learning, game theory, economics, and social psychology.

Although automated negotiation has been a very active topic for decades, most of the research efforts in this area focus either on theoretical negotiation models or on simplified models for practical negotiation applications. Owing to the growing popularity of

C. Lutz and M. Thielscher (Eds.): KI 2014, LNCS 8736, pp. 147–158, 2014.

the international agent-based negotiation competition ANAC [10], more recent research has concentrated on practical bilateral negotiation [3,8]. They together advance the state of the art of negotiation theory to a more realistic and complex stage. This kind of negotiation normally shares the following five features that are still poorly understood. (1) Negotiations occur in continuous time. (2) The behavior model[1] of the opposing party is not available and can only be observed indirectly through the exchange of offers. (3) There are multiple items under negotiation. (4) The achievable profit through an agreement decreases over time. Finally, (5) participants have a private reservation value, which is set as the agent's minimal benefit when no mutually acceptable agreement can be found. Since the negotiation strategies discussed here are all implemented in the form of (software) agents, in this paper no explicit distinction is made between the terms negotiation strategy and negotiating agent.

There exist a number of good examples of research on complex negotiation such as [4,5,8,16]. Williams et al. [16] employ Gaussian processes for optimizing an agent's own concession rate by predicting the maximal concession that the opponent is expected to make in the future. This strategy, known as IAMhaggler2011, made the third place in ANAC 2011. Another successful strategy based on Gaussian processes is described in [3], where Sparse Pseudo-input Gaussian processes are applied to alleviate the computational complexity of building an opponent model. Hao and Leung [8] propose a novel strategy, which was the winner of ANAC 2012. This method attempts at exploiting the opponent as much as possible by learning opponent behavior and also predicts the optimal offer for the opposing side to improve the acceptance probability of its own proposals, using a reinforcement-learning based approach. Chen et al. [5] adopt an approach called OMAC to complex negotiations that aims at learning an opponent's strategy by analyzing its behavior through discrete wavelet transformation and cubic smoothing spline. With the learnt opponent model, OMAC dynamically adjusts its concession rate in response to uncertainties in the environment. OMAC outperformed the five best agents of ANAC 2011 and was finally awarded the third place in ANAC 2012. To tackle the problem of limited experience available in a single negotiation, Chen et al. [4] then develop a strategy that is able to transfer knowledge efficiently from previous tasks on the basis of factored conditional restricted Boltzmann machines. In the latest edition of the negotiation competition, ANAC 2013 [1], agents can make use of their negotiation history to improve their performance in new encounters. According to the final results, the best-performing agent is Fawkes, which learns an opponent model by combining the two approaches proposed in [5,8].

Many new and novel strategies for complex negotiations have been proposed, but they are primarily evaluated in terms of their scores in fixed negotiation tournaments [7,14], where agents leave their strategies unchanged through tournaments, and which opponents an agent needs to interact with and when they encounter are both fixed. Even although some recent works [4,6] employ empirical game theory to investigate the fitness of the strategies (or so-called robustness in other research) in more open settings where agents are allowed to deviate to different strategies, it still suffers from the small number of possible involved players, and more importantly, the limitation of not con-

---

[1] Because both an agent's utility function and bidding strategy is hidden, we will often use the term behavior model to refer to both as the "joint forces" that govern its negotiating behavior.

sidering the location of individuals. Against this background, the contributions of this paper are as follows. We first provide a standard evaluation of state-of-the-art negotiating agents, which is still missing from current literature. These agents are tested in a number of tournament competitions, where the domains are adopted from the most recent international agent-based negotiation competition (i.e., ANAC 2013). The results are also used as a basis of further analysis. Second, dependent on a strategy-pair payoff matrix (which comes from results of previous tournament competitions), the fitness of the strategies is studied using empirical game theory in a setting where only a few agents globally negotiate with all others. Lastly, we extend this setting to a more interesting but complicated one in which the number of players can be very large and the interaction range of each involved agent is locally limited. Specifically, we consider negotiation settings in which the location of players may affect other agents' choices of new strategies. Spatial evolutionary game theory is applied to analyze the changes of each strategy share in the whole population. This allows to better understand the impact of different settings on negotiation strategies' fitness.

The remainder of this paper is organized as follows. Section 2 briefly introduces the negotiating agents analyzed in this work as well as the test domains and the negotiation simulation environment used for the analysis. Section 3 shows results of the performance of a number of state of the art negotiating agents in tournament experiments. Section 4 provides a thorough game-theoretic analysis of the fitness of negotiation strategies in different cases. Finally, Section 5 concludes the paper and identifies some important research lines opened by the described work.

2 Agents and Test Domains

To provide an extensive coverage of advanced negotiation agents, this work considers those agents which are ranked the first three places in ANAC 2011 – 2013 and whose sources can also be publicly accessed. They together result in a highly competitive negotiation setting. An overview of these ANAC agents is given in Table 1. Due to space limitation, here we do not discuss the technicalities of these agents. The interested reader is suggested to refer to [1,5,10] for a thorough discussion.

Table 1. Overview of top three agents of ANAC 2011 – 2013

Agent	Affiliation	Achievement
Fawkes	Delft University of Technology	1st in 2013
Meta Agent	Ben Gurion University of the Negev	2nd in 2013
TMF Agent	Ben Gurion University of the Negev	3rd in 2013
CUHKAgent	Chinese University of Hong Kong	1st in 2012
AgentLG	Bar-Ilan University	2nd in 2012
OMAC	Maastricht University	3rd in 2012
HardHeaded	Delft University of Technology	1st in 2011
Gahboninho	Bar Ilan University	2nd in 2011
IAMhaggler2011	University of Southampton	3rd in 2011

The test domain is another decision factor for the quality of evaluation results. On the contrary to previous work that only examines the efficiency of negotiating agents in a relatively small number of domains, for the sake of a high level of generality, we adopt the whole set of domains created for ANAC 2013 (18 domains in total). Moreover, to capture the influence of the discounting factor δ and the reservation value ϑ on the performance of agents, different values for these two parameters are considered. Thus, experiments are conducted with three discounting factors (i.e., $\delta = \{0.5, 0.75, 1.0\}$) and three reservation values (i.e., $\vartheta = \{0, 0.25, 0.5\}$), which produce nine ($3 \times 3$) different scenarios for each domain. In doing so, possible bias on domain selection can be avoided. The agents cannot get chances to optimize their strategies in such a circumstance; on the other hand, a good spread of domain characteristics is also ensured.

The performance evaluation on negotiating agents is done with the simulation environment – Genius [9]. It is the official testbed of the ANAC competition, which allows to evaluate intelligent agents employing different negotiation strategies across a variety of application domains under real-time constraints. Incorporating many key features to support and analyze automated negotiation, Genius facilitates the research on the field and provides a standard platform for people from the community to easily compare newly developed agents with those existing ones. For each scenario of every single domain, we run a tournament ten times to guarantee results with statistical confidence. In each tournament agents repeat negotiation against the same opponent with different negotiation roles (i.e., buyer and seller role) as well as the order in which they start with bidding. If a negotiation fails (e.g., no agreement is made before/at the end of an encounter), then the disagreement solution applies, which means that each agent merely receives its own reservation value ϑ.

3   Tournament Competition Results

Because of space limitation, the detailed negotiation settings are not presented here; the interested reader is suggested to refer to [3,6] for more information. As specified in the previous section, nine variants of each of these 18 domains with different discounting factors and reservation values were used, totalling up to 162 scenarios. This resulted in a total number of 524,880 negotiations in the experiments (with each scenario repeated 10 times).

The overall performance of the agents is summarized in Table 2 with the mean utility and standard deviation. The best performance came from CUHKAgent and AgentLG (1st and 2nd in ANAC 2012), followed by TMF-Agent (3rd in 2013) with a very small difference. Meta-Agent (2nd in 2013), OMAC (3rd in 2012) and Hardheaded (1st in 2011) then took the fourth and sixth place in the competition, respectively. As the latest edition of the competition focuses more on learning and adaption in negotiation, it is surprising to see that ANAC 2013 agents that are given negotiation history to aid their performance in new tasks still (on average) lag behind those 2012 agents. These findings revealed an important fact that the scope of the tournament pool has a significant impact on the experimental results, and illustrated the necessity of a wide range of state-of-the-art benchmarking agents when assessing a negotiation strategy.

According to the experimental results, the strategy-pair payoff matrix is set up and shown in Table 3 (which are averaged over all negotiation encounters considered in our

Table 2. Overall performance of all agents across all scenarios in descending order. The letter in bold of each strategy is taken as its identifier for the later game-theoretic analysis.

Agent	Mean utility	Standard deviation
CUHKAgent	0.656	0.0002
AgentLG	0.656	0.0003
TMF-Agent	0.648	0.0003
Meta-Agent	0.645	0.0004
OMAC	0.638	0.0002
HardHeaded	0.635	0.0002
Gahboninho	0.626	0.0002
Fawkes	0.619	0.0003
IAMhaggler2011	0.581	0.0001

work). The first letter of each strategy is used as its identifier. As the matrix is symmetric, we only present the row strategy's payoff. On the basis of this payoff matrix, in the subsequent sections we perform the game-theoretic analysis of repeated negotiation scenarios that is more open than those in this section.

Table 3. Strategy-pair payoff matrix, where the score pair in each entry is averaged over all domains, with the score representing the column player's payoff (as the matrix is symmetric). The first letter (**bold**) of each agent is used as the identifier.

Payoff	G	H	I	A	C	O	M	T	F
G	0.686	0.672	0.639	0.707	0.731	0.698	0.694	0.706	0.674
H	0.559	0.616	0.592	0.608	0.647	0.640	0.630	0.658	0.609
I	0.788	0.743	0.715	0.766	0.796	0.750	0.773	0.772	0.758
A	0.607	0.593	0.621	0.591	0.582	0.581	0.609	0.536	0.562
C	0.616	0.626	0.522	0.672	0.619	0.628	0.621	0.630	0.592
O	0.585	0.579	0.534	0.584	0.610	0.596	0.592	0.599	0.573
M	0.654	0.648	0.609	0.676	0.661	0.636	0.677	0.653	0.662
T	0.534	0.577	0.478	0.614	0.550	0.545	0.570	0.551	0.515
F	0.660	0.635	0.653	0.617	0.668	0.621	0.666	0.629	0.325

4   Game-Theoretic Analysis of Automated Negotiations

We have deeply studied the strategy performance from the competition perspective. As discussed before, there however exists a significant limitation of this performance measure because it cannot give any indication about the fitness of these strategies in a open environment. It is unclear, for instance, which strategy will become the winner of a competition when the players are allowed to deviate, i.e., to switch to another strategy for the sake of better individual profits, or when the mixture of opponent strategies changes. For the purpose of providing a broader view of the agents' performance, empirical game theory and spatial evolutionary game theory are both applied in this section

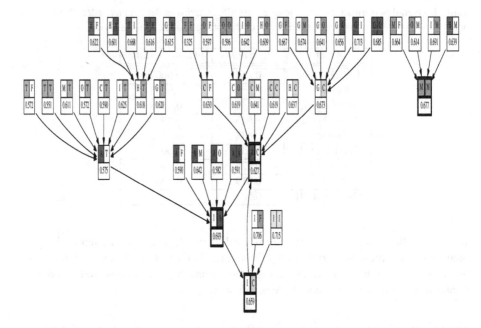

Fig. 1. Deviation analysis for the two-player negotiation. Each node shows a strategy profile and the average score of the two involved strategies with the higher scoring one marked by a color background. The arrow indicates the statistically significant deviation between strategy profiles. The equilibria are the nodes marked with a thicker border.

to analyze the fitness of the strategies in two distinct cases. The following analysis is performed based on the payoff matrix shown in Table 3.

4.1 Small Number of Players with Global Interaction

We start by studying strategy fitness in the case where several players negotiate with others. To appropriately address strategy fitness with global interaction, empirical game theory (EGT) analysis [12] is employed, which was initially developed to analyze the Trading Agent Competition (TAC). We consider the strategy deviations as discussed in [16], where there is an incentive for one agent to unilaterally change the strategy in order to statistically improve its own profit. The aim of using EGT is to search for pure Nash equilibria in which no agent has an incentive to deviate from its current strategy, or best reply cycle where there exists a set of profiles (i.e., the combination of strategies chosen by players) for which a path of deviations exists that connect them, with no deviation leading to a profile outside of the set. For convenience, these two types of states are both called empirical stable states.

We investigated strategy fitness with global interaction by means of EGT in the two different scenarios with increasing complexity below:

Scenario 1: a negotiation encounter between two players.
Scenario 2: the full tournament composed of nine players with nine strategies.

This is because the former represents the underlying bilateral negotiation, i.e., only two players participate in the game, and the other illustrates such kinds of negotiations in more complex tournaments. For brevity, we use the bold letters in Table 2 as the identifier for each strategy (e.g., **H** means Hardheaded, **C** means CUHKAgent). The set of strategies is given by $\Sigma = \{$**G, H, I, A, C, O, M, T, F**$\}$.

In the first scenario, the resulting graph under EGT analysis contains $\binom{|p|+|s|-1}{|p|} = \binom{10}{2} = 45$ distinct nodes, where $|p|$ means the number of players and $|s|$ the number of strategies. A *profile* is defined as the two strategies used by the players in the game (it is worth noting that the two players may use the same strategy). Furthermore, the score of a specific strategy in a particular profile is decided by the payoff matrix given in Table 3. The results are depicted in Figure 1. Each node represents a strategy profile being a mix of two strategies; an arrow indicates the statistically significant deviation to a different strategy profile. Please note that this figure only cares about the strategy mixture and therefore the player order is not taken into account. Under this EGT analysis, there exists one pure Nash equilibrium and a best reply cycle, highlighted by a thick border in Figure 1 as follows:

1. The players both use Meta-Agent, i.e., [**M|M**].
2. a best reply cycle consists of [**A|C**], [**I|C**] and [**I|A**].

The sole equilibrium is the strategy profile [**M|M**]. This stable state only attracts few profiles. For the remaining states, there exists a path of statistically significant deviations that leads to one state of the best reply cycle. This cycle has a basin of attraction[2] of 89% of the profiles. The results of repeated single negotiations (i.e., between two players) show that there are four empirical stable states including four robust strategies – Meta-Agent, CUHKAgent, IAMhaggler2011 and AgentLG; moreover, Meta-Agent, CUHKAgent and AgentLG are the winning strategies in one or more states (i.e., they gain a higher score). In addition, the analysis also indicates that high-scoring strategies (e.g., TMF-Agent and OMAC) do not necessarily perform well in repeated single encounters, or in other words, they are not robust. It is, however, worth pointing out that the repeated single encounter analysis, while useful, cannot tell anything about the strategy robustness when the setup gets more complicated. Next, we turn our attention to a more complex setting composed of more players with more strategies.

For scenario 2, we consider tournaments consisting of nine players, where each can select one of the nine strategies introduced in Table 2. The results are given in Figure 2. Here a *profile* is defined as the mixture of strategies used by players in a tournament. The nodes in this figure consist of two rows. The top row explains the set of strategies selected by agents in the tournament; the second means the number of agents choosing each strategy. As Figure 2 tells, there is one pure Nash equilibrium that only includes Meta-Agent; in other words, all the players switch to this strategy in the end. The basin of attraction of the equilibrium state includes 100% of the profiles. With that, the results of the second case suggest that in the setting of more complex tournaments, only

---

[2] The basin of attraction [2] of a stable state is the number of profile states which converge to a stable state. The likelihood of reaching that stable state can be measured on the basis of the size of the basin of attraction.

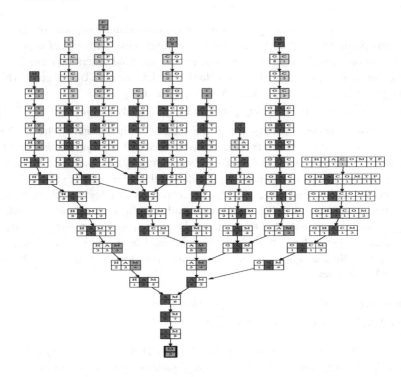

Fig. 2. Deviation analysis for nine-player tournaments composed of nine strategies. The equilibrium is the nodes with no outgoing arrow and a thicker border.

Meta-Agent remains robust, among the four stable strategies that we have found in the repeated single negotiations.

The EGT analysis proves good fitness of four strategies – Meta-Agent, CUHKAgent, AgentLG and IAMhaggler2011; especially Meta-Agent performs consistently well in both scenarios. It is very interesting to see that although not being the strongest agent in the competition results (refer to Table 2), Meta-Agent is more suitable for an open and competitive environment than others. A high performance in self-play and a fairly good relative advantage of this strategy over other competitors may account for its success.

4.2   Large Number of Players with Various Interaction Ranges

The EGT analysis is based on the assumption that each player interacts with all other involved players, that is, global interaction is assumed (e.g., [3,4,16]). This does not hold in many real-life cases; for instance, in diplomatic negotiations on a territorial dispute it is obvious that negotiation concerns only adjacent countries rather than all countries with which the disputing countries are in some relationship. As another example, the location of individuals is also of great importance for resources allocation in wireless sensor networks. Locality thus is an important factor in negotiation that has not been well studied so far. Moreover, the number of possible players is rather limited using the EGT approach; otherwise the resulting profiles/nodes would be extremely large to be

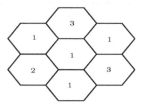

Fig. 3. A locality in a hexagon model

well analyzed. There naturally arises another question how the fitness of the strategies changes when the player size dramatically grows. For these two reasons, we investigate how a population of players or individuals behave by changing their negotiation strategies in the case of local and global interaction ranges. In contrast to global interaction where a player negotiates with all other players, local interaction takes into account the agents' local neighborhood. Toward this end, evolutionary game theory, more precisely spatial evolutionary game theory [13,15], is applied to the tournament results. This allows to analyze the impact on fitness (i.e., how well an individual is adapted to a dynamic environment) of each species (strategy) competing with others locally.

In the context of this research, an individual is assumed to be located at a certain environmental position (also called cell) and its fitness is determined by the average payoff of its strategy playing against its neighbors (refer to Table 3). Take a simple case with three strategies as a toy example, where the center cell choosing strategy 1 meets its neighbors as shown in Fig. 3. The fitness of the center cell is the average payoff of playing against three opponents using strategy 1, one opponent using strategy 2, and two opponents using strategy 3 (i.e., with the neighbor distribution $x=(\frac{3}{6},\frac{1}{6},\frac{2}{6})$), which is formally defined in Equation 1. The payoff matrix of the three strategies is given by matrix A below:

$$A = \begin{bmatrix} 4 & 10 & 0 \\ 1 & 4 & 9 \\ 3 & 7 & 4 \end{bmatrix}$$

where an entry A(i,j) is the payoff of strategy i against strategy j. Thus, the fitness (ρ) of the center cell is $\frac{22}{6}$, following the equation below.

$$\rho = e_i A x^T \tag{1}$$

where e_i denotes the i-th row of a unit matrix e with the size of the number of strategies and A denotes the payoff matrix.

In our analysis we assume that there is a population of players using the strategy set (Σ) consisting of the nine negotiation strategies, with a payoff matrix (see Table 3) suggesting utilities of any pair of strategies. Initially, every strategy has an equal population of 100 players randomly distributed over a 30×30 two-dimensional hexagon lattice Λ. Each cell (I) is occupied by a strategy and bordered with six other cells, that is to say, every single cell has six neighbors in its local scale. Calculating the fitness of each cell in the field is simultaneously performed. After this, each cell then imitates which one has the highest fitness of its neighborhood (including itself). In this way the natural se-

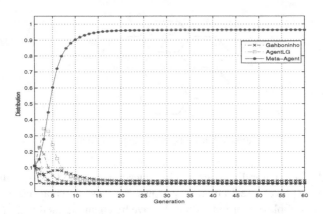

Fig. 4. Strategy distributions over generations when players interact with their direct neighbors

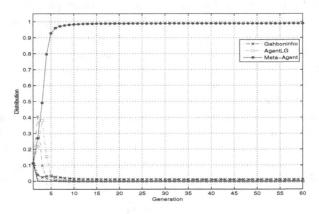

Fig. 5. Strategy distributions over generations when players interact with their neighbors and neighbors' neighbors

lection process (i.e., how to choose the new strategy of the cell for the next generation) is well defined.

To obtain results with high statistical significance, we ran the simulation 10,000 times with random initialization of the location arrangement of the nine strategies. Fig. 4 shows the strategy distributions over generations in the case of players interacting with others in their neighborhood. As can be seen, this spatial evolutionary game, after around 25 generations, ends up with a co-existence of three strategies – Meta-Agent, AgentLG and Gahboninho. Further, the strategy Meta-Agent plays a dominant role in population shares, attracting more than 96% of the individuals. In spite of being the best one in competitions (see Table 2), CUHKAgent is exterminated like other weak strategies. With a poor performance in competitions, the survival of Gahboninho as the second largest proportion (yet quite small) in the population is surprising.

However, if the natural selection process is modified such that a player's interaction range is extended to its neighbors' neighbors, then the difference between Meta-Agent and others would be enlarged. We show the result in Fig.5. In this case, only two strategies – Meta-Agent and Gahboninho exist, while Meta-Agent almost fully dominates the population share. Moreover, the time needed for players to converge to Meta-Agent also becomes shorter. As a matter of fact, when further extending agents' interaction range to all other players (i.e., global interaction), all individuals switch to Meta-Agent in just few generations.

When comparing the results depending on empirical game theory and spatial evolutionary game theory, we found that Meta-Agent was a very successful strategy in various scenarios. To summarize, the more players and larger agent-interaction range in the game, the better performance it delivers.

5   Conclusions

This paper presented a thorough review of the performance of practical negotiation strategies from the perspective of game theory. A wide range of high quality agents (using these strategies) from ANAC competitions were evaluated with respect to two different game-theoretic techniques. More importantly, this paper, as the very first work, studies the fitness of negotiation strategies in a repeated fashion where the number of participating players is large and the location of players serves as an important factor of how to decide their new strategies. The detailed analysis conducted in the work provided a number of valuable new insights into the efficacy of a negotiation strategy. First of all, competition performance, while important, does not serve as a good indicator for an agent in an open environment in which agents, having freedom to change their strategies, repeatedly negotiate with others. Recall that some high-scoring agents like CUHKAgent and OMAC perform disappointingly in the new settings. Then, for the negotiations where a small number of players are involved with global interaction, fitness of strategies may be qualitatively different in settings with different complexity. For instance, AgentLG is not robust anymore in the second scenario where more players and strategies are available. Last but not least, the results obtained from spatial evolutionary game-theoretic analysis illustrate that agent-interaction range indeed has an effect on the evolution process of strategies in terms of when to reach a stable state and what share a strategy can occupy in the population. Moreover, the range of interaction seemingly boosts the performance of leading strategies. They together confirm the necessity of considerations of both local and global interaction in the performance analysis of the strategies.

Regarding future work, we believe it is worth investing research efforts in exploring several interesting questions. For example, how would the evolution process change if the impact of neighbors is weighted by their distance (e.g., weighted influence of neighbors), or if a player is allowed to choose any strategy from Σ rather than merely from its neighborhood (e.g., by modifying the natural selection process). Another important avenue we see is to apply our method to the negotiation results between autonomous negotiating agents against human negotiators.

References

1. The Fourth International Automated Negotiating Agent Competition (ANAC 2013), `http://www.itolab.nitech.ac.jp/ANAC2013/`
2. Baarslag, T., Fujita, K., Gerding, E.H., Hindriks, K., Ito, T., Jennings, N.R., Jonker, C., Kraus, S., Lin, R., Robu, V., Williams, C.R.: Evaluating practical negotiating agents: Results and analysis of the 2011 international competition. Artificial Intelligence 198, 73–103 (2013)
3. Chen, S., Ammar, H.B., Tuyls, K., Weiss, G.: Optimizing complex automated negotiation using sparse pseudo-input Gaussian processes. In: Proceedings of the 12th Int. Joint Conf. on Automomous Agents and Multi-Agent Systems, pp. 707–714. ACM (2013)
4. Chen, S., Ammar, H.B., Tuyls, K., Weiss, G.: Using conditional restricted boltzmann machine for highly competitive negotiation tasks. In: Proceedings of the 23rd Int. Joint Conf. on Artificial Intelligence, pp. 69–75. AAAI Press (2013)
5. Chen, S., Weiss, G.: An Efficient and Adaptive Approach to Negotiation in Complex Environments. In: Proceedings of the 20th European Conference on Artificial Intelligence, pp. 228–233. IOS Press (2012)
6. Chen, S., Weiss, G.: An efficient automated negotiation strategy for complex environments. Engineering Applications of Artificial Intelligence 26(10), 2613–2623 (2013)
7. Fujita, K., Ito, T., Baarslag, T., Hindriks, K., Jonker, C., Kraus, S., Lin, R.: The Second Automated Negotiating Agents Competition (ANAC 2011). In: Ito, T., Zhang, M., Robu, V., Matsuo, T. (eds.) Complex Automated Negotiations. SCI, vol. 435, pp. 183–197. Springer, Heidelberg (2012)
8. Hao, J., Leung, H.: ABiNeS: An adaptive bilateral negotiating strategy over multiple items. In: Proceedings of WI/IAT 2012, pp. 95–102. IEEE Computer Society (2012)
9. Hindriks, K., Jonker, C., Kraus, S., Lin, R., Tykhonov, D.: Genius: negotiation environment for heterogeneous agents. In: Proceedings of the 8th International Joint Conference on Autonomous Agents and Multiagent Systems, pp. 1397–1398. ACM (2009)
10. Ito, T., Zhang, M., Robu, V., Fatima, S., Matsuo, T. (eds.): New Trends in Agent-Based Complex Automated Negotiations. SCI, vol. 383. Springer, Heidelberg (2012)
11. Jennings, N.R., Faratin, P., Lomuscio, A.R., Parsons, S., Sierra, C., Wooldridge, M.: Automated negotiation: prospects, methods and challenges. International Journal of Group Decision and Negotiation 10(2), 199–215 (2001)
12. Jordan, P.R., Kiekintveld, C., Wellman, M.P.: Empirical game-theoretic analysis of the tac supply chain game. In: Proceedings of AAMAS 2007, pp. 1188–1195. ACM (2007)
13. Killingback, T., Doebeli, M.: Spatial evolutionary game theory: Hawks and doves revisited. Proceedings of the Royal Society of London. Series B: Biological Sciences 263(1374), 1135–1144 (1996)
14. Marsa-Maestre, I., Lopez-Carmona, M.A., Ito, T., Zhang, M., Bai, Q., Fujita, K. (eds.): Novel Insights in Agent-based Complex Automated Negotiation. Springer (2014)
15. Szabó, G., Fáth, G.: Evolutionary games on graphs. Physics Reports 446(4), 97–216 (2007)
16. Williams, C., Robu, V., Gerding, E., Jennings, N.: Using gaussian processes to optimise concession in complex negotiations against unknown opponents. In: Proceedings of the 22nd Int. Joint Conf. on Artificial Intelligence, pp. 432–438. AAAI Press (2011)

Towards a New Semantics for Possibilistic Answer Sets

Julien Hué, Matthias Westphal, and Stefan Wölfl

Albert-Ludwigs-Universität Freiburg, Department of Computer Science, Germany
{hue,westpham,woelfl}@informatik.uni-freiburg.de

Abstract. Possibilistic Answer Set Programming is an extension of the standard ASP framework that allows for attaching degrees of certainty to the rules in ASP programs. In the literature, several semantics for such PASP-programs have been presented, each of them having particular strengths and weaknesses. In this work we present a new semantics that employs so-called iota-answer sets, a solution concept introduced by Gebser et al. (2009), in order to find solutions for standard ASP programs with odd cycles or auto-blocking rules. This is achieved by considering maximal subsets of a given ASP program for which answer sets exist. The main idea of our work is to integrate iota-semantics into the possibilistic framework in such a way that degrees of certainty are not only assigned to atoms mentioned in the answer sets, but also to the answer sets themselves. Our approach gives more satisfactory solutions and avoids counter-intuitive examples arising in the other approaches. We compare our approach to existing ones and present a translation into the standard ASP framework allowing the computation of solutions by existing tools.

1 Introduction

Answer Set Programming (ASP) [1] is a logic programming formalism which is nowadays one of the main paradigms for nonmonotonic reasoning. In view of application contexts, however, the framework has some limitations. Quite often, when a knowledge base is to be set up, the modeler is not only aware of the nonmonotonic nature of some general rules to be represented, but also considers some of these rules more plausible than others. Within the standard ASP framework it is not possible to order rules according to their certainty or plausibility in an explicit manner. Of course, the modeler can try to modify the knowledge base by introspecting which rules are applied under which conditions in order to obtain some expected solution to a reasoning task on the knowledge base (see, e.g., [2]). But if the problem instance has several solution candidates it is still not possible to rank them, i.e., to estimate which of them is (or should be considered) more plausible than others.

One way to remedy this deficiency is to consider knowledge bases equipped with probability distributions. In this context different strands of research can be found in the literature. For the more general context of equipping conditionals with probabilities we refer to [3], and [4]. But also in the context of logic and answer set programming, probabilistic approaches have been discussed (see., e.g., Poole [5], Lukasiewicz [6], Baral et al. [7]). The problem with such approaches is that most of the time exact probability values (and even lower or upper bounds of them) are not available or hard to

C. Lutz and M. Thielscher (Eds.): KI 2014, LNCS 8736, pp. 159–170, 2014.

argue for. A typical situation is that the modeler has just some qualitative ranking between the rules in the knowledge base in mind, and (maybe even more importantly) that she is also only interested in an ordinal-scale ranking of the possible solutions of the given problem.

In this situation, ideas from possibilistic logic [8] seem promising to deal with plausibility degrees of general rules. Possibilistic logic is a framework for representing uncertainty (in a propositional logic context) by using a pair of possibility and necessity measures. These measures are understood qualitatively and are used for rank-ordering interpretations. To combine the ideas of possibilistic logic and answer set programming (referred to as *possibilistic answer set programming*) several approaches have been proposed in the literature, for example, by Bauters et al. [9], and Nicolas et al. [10]. Each of these approaches has particular strengths and weaknesses, which will be discussed later in more detail. The reader might also consult [11] which presents a variation of stable semantics called pstable semantics associated with possibilistic logic.

In this paper, we present a new semantics that is based on so-called ι-answer sets. The ι-answer set semantics has been introduced by Gebser et al. [12] in order to solve problems arising in standard logic programs, e.g., with odd cycles or with auto-blocking rules. The main idea is to consider subsets of the program instead of the complete program to check whether it is possible to entail a set of atoms. The semantics we propose for possibilistic answer sets follows the ideas of ι-answer set semantics. As we will see, the proposed semantics naturally leads to not only associating a necessity value to each atom within a stable model, but also a possibility value to the stable models themselves. We argue that the new semantics, while still being NP-complete, is closer to the philosophy underlying both possibilistic logic and ASP than other semantics in the literature.

Structure of the paper. We start by presenting in the next section the necessary background and notations, and discuss in more detail the mentioned other semantic approaches for possibilistic logic programs. We then present our new semantics, and discuss its formal properties. Finally, we present a translation of possibilistic answer set programs into classic answer set programs which allows to use existing tools for computing solutions.

2   Background and Notations

2.1   Answer Set Programming

A logic program (or *normal logic program*) is a (finite) set of rules of the form

$$r \; : \; a \leftarrow b_1, \ldots, b_m, \text{not } c_1, \ldots, \text{not } c_n.$$

where a, b_i and c_j are propositional atoms. The keyword *not* denotes negation as failure. The atom a is called the head of the rule (denoted by $head(r)$) and $b_1, \ldots, b_m$, not $c_1, \ldots,$ not c_n is called the body of the rule. The set of all atoms b_i and c_j that make up the body of the rule is denoted by $body(r)$. The body can be divided into a positive and negative part. Atoms b_i represent the positive body, denoted by $body^+(r)$, and atoms

c_j represent the negative body, denoted by $body^-(r)$. Thus, $body(r) = body^+(r) \cup body^-(r)$ and we sometimes write r as $head(r) \leftarrow body^+(r)$, not $body^-(r)$. Further, we extend this notation to logic programs P in the obvious way: $body^+(P) = \{a \mid a \in body^+(r) \text{ for some } r \in P\}$ and $body^-(P) = \{a \mid a \in body^-(r) \text{ for some } r \in P\}$. We denote by $atoms(P)$ the set of atoms that occur in P.

Intuitively, a rule can be understood as follows: if each of the atoms b_i of the positive body of the rule is true and none of the atoms c_j of the negative body is true, then the head of the rule can be inferred. Given rule r, we denote by r^+ the rule $head(r) \leftarrow body^+(r)$. A rule r with empty head is called an *integrity constraint* (we often write such rules in the form $\perp \leftarrow \ldots$). Similarly, the body of a rule can be empty, thus stating that the head is a *fact*.

Atoms a as well as their default negation not a are called *literals*. A *basic program* is a logic program where all rules are of the form $r : a \leftarrow b_1, \ldots, b_m$, i.e., with an empty negative body and thus without negation as failure.

Definition 1. *A set of atoms A is said to be* closed under a basic program P *if for each rule $r \in P$, $head(r) \in A$ whenever $body(r) \subseteq A$. The smallest set closed under a basic program P is denoted by $CN(P)$, and referred to as the set of* consequences *of the program. For arbitrary programs we write $CN^+(P)$ for the set $CN(\{r^+ \mid r \in P\})$.*

A *stable model* of a program is a set of atoms that represents a set of consequences consistent with the beliefs expressed by the program, but also has the property that the presence of each of the atoms in the set is justified. In other words, a stable model is necessarily minimal with respect to set inclusion, that is, a proper subset of a stable model cannot be a stable model. More formally, stable models can be defined in terms of the so-called Gelfond-Lifschitz reduct [13]:

Definition 2. *The* Gelfond-Lifschitz reduct *of a program P by a set of atoms A is defined as the following set of rules: $P^A = \{r^+ \mid r \in P \text{ and } body^-(r) \cap A = \emptyset\}$. Given a logic program P, a set of atoms A is called a* stable model *of P if and only if $CN(P^A) = A$.*

In the literature, the terms answer set and stable model are mostly used in an equivalent way. For a more comprehensive introduction to answer set semantics we refer to [14,1].

2.2 ι-Answer Sets

Gebser et al. [12] introduce the notion of ι-answer sets. This concept allows for incrementally constructing solutions to a given normal logic program. Contrary to standard answer set semantics, the ι-answer set semantics has the advantage that we can always talk about solutions of a program, even when stable models do not exist.

Definition 3. *Let P be a logic program and A be a set of atoms. Then A is called an ι-answer set of P if $A = CN^+(Q)$ for some $\subseteq$-maximal $Q \subseteq P$ such that (i) $body^+(Q) \subseteq CN^+(Q)$ and (ii) $body^-(Q) \cap CN^+(Q) = \emptyset$.*

It is also possible to characterize the ι-answer sets in terms of applied rules.

Definition 4. *Let P be a logic program and A be a set of atoms. Then the set of applied rules of P for A is defined as:*

$$App_P(A) = \{r \in P \mid body^+(r) \subseteq A, body^-(r) \cap A = \emptyset, head(r) \in A\}.$$

It can be shown that a set of atoms A is an ι-answer set of P if and only if $A = CN^+(App_P(A))$ and if for each $r \in P \setminus App_P(A)$, at least one of the following conditions holds true: (i) $body^+(r) \not\subseteq A$, (ii) $body^-(r) \cap A \neq \emptyset$, or (iii) $head(r) \in body^-(App_P(A) \cup \{r\})$.

2.3 Possibilistic Logic

We consider a finite propositional language $\mathcal{L}$. The set of all interpretations over $\mathcal{L}$ is denoted by Ω. Possibilistic logic [8] is defined in terms of a possibility distribution $\pi \colon \Omega \to [0, 1]$ representing how plausible an interpretation is with regard to the available knowledge. For an interpretation $\omega \in \Omega$, $\pi(\omega) = 0$ means that ω is considered impossible and $\pi(\omega) = 1$ means that there is no contradiction with assuming ω to be true. The possibility distribution only represents a *preordering* over the interpretations, i.e., $\pi(\omega) > \pi(\omega')$ expresses that ω is considered more plausible than ω'. A possibility distribution allows to define two functions Π and N from the set of formulae over $\mathcal{L}$ to $[0, 1]$ as follows:

$$\Pi(\varphi) := \max\{\pi(\omega) \mid \omega \in \Omega, \omega \models \varphi\} \text{ and } N(\varphi) := 1 - \Pi(\neg\varphi).$$

The function Π is called *possibility measure* and N is called *necessity measure*: $\Pi(\varphi)$ measures to what extent the formula φ is compatible with the available knowledge, while $N(\varphi)$ measures to what extent it is entailed. Given a possibility distribution π, a formula φ is said to be a *consequence* of π if and only if $\Pi(\varphi) > \Pi(\neg\varphi)$. Intuitively, φ is a consequence of π if the best models of φ (namely the models of φ having a highest degree) are more plausible (or more preferred) than the best models of $\neg\varphi$.

A *possibilistic formula* is a tuple $\langle\varphi, \alpha\rangle$ where $\varphi \in \mathcal{L}$ and $\alpha \in (0, 1]$ expresses that φ is considered certain at least to the level α. Thus, given a necessity measure N, it holds $N(\varphi) \geq \alpha$. A *possibilistic knowledge base* is a set K of possibilistic formulas. The strict α-cut K_α of K is defined as $K_\alpha = \{\varphi \mid \langle\varphi, \beta\rangle \in K \text{ and } \beta > \alpha\}$. From the strict α-cut, we define the inconsistency value of K $Inc(K) = \max\{\alpha \mid K_\alpha$ is inconsistent or $\alpha = 0\}$ which is the necessity degree under which information is ignored. We thus define $Core(K) = K_{Inc(K)}$ and say that a formula is a *consequence* of K (denoted by $K \vdash_\pi \varphi$) if $Core(K) \vdash \varphi$.

3   Possibilistic Logic Programs

We define the possibilistic extension of classic logic programs following [10]. These are logic programs where each rule is augmented with a necessity value.

A *possibilistic rule* is a pair $r = \langle r^*, \alpha\rangle$ where r^* is some rule in the sense of ASP and α denotes the rule's necessity degree in the range $(0, 1]$. The ASP rule r^* is called the *projection* of the possibilistic rule r, i.e., the rule obtained by ignoring the attached necessity degree. A *possibilistic logic program* Q is a set of possibilistic rules. The projection of a possibilistic program Q^* is the set of rules $\{r^* \mid r \in Q\}$, i.e., a logic program in the sense of ASP.

Given a set A of propositional atoms, a *possibilistic atom* is a pair $p = \langle a, \alpha \rangle \in A \times (0, 1]$ where α denotes the necessity degree of a. A *possibilistic atom set* is a set of possibilistic atoms in which every propositional atom occurs in at most one possibilistic atom. Projections are defined as before, that is $p^* = a$ and $\{p_1, \dots\}^* = \{p_1^*, \dots\}$. Because stable models are sets of atoms, it seems intuitively appropriate to consider "possibilistic answer sets" of a possibilistic program as possibilistic atom sets. Indeed in [10] the projection of a possibilistic stable model of a possibilistic program is always a stable model of the projection of the program. However, in our opinion this is not adequate for reasons discussed in the following.

Before we introduce our new semantics of possibilistic logic programs we review the differnet semantics discussed in the literature.

Nicolas et al. [10]. Possibilistic answer sets are here defined as possibilistic atom sets whose projection is a classic answer set of the projection of the possibilistic program. The attached necessity values are determined according to the grounding sequence[1]. As a consequence, it does not capture all possible solutions of a possibilistic logic program with respect to possibilistic logic.

Example 1. Consider the possibilistic program $P_n = \{\langle \text{concert} \leftarrow \text{not canceled.}, 0.8\rangle,$ $\langle \text{canceled.}, 0.6\rangle\}$. The only possibilistic answer set (in the sense of [10]) of this program is $\{\langle \text{canceled}, 0.6\rangle\}$.

In this example the necessity value of *canceled* indicates that there exists some reason to believe it was not canceled. However, this is not reflected in the concept of possibilistic answer set by [10].

Moreover, Nicolas et al. define possibility distributions for possibilistic logic programs (although without providing an algorithm for computing it). The possibility of a set of atoms A given a logic program P is $\tilde{\pi}_P(A) = \pi_{P^A}(A)$ with $\pi_{P^A}(A)$ being defined as 0 if A is not grounded, 1 if it is a least model of the consequence operator applied to P^A, and $1 - \alpha$ otherwise (where α is the maximal possibility value among the non-satisfied rules).

Another issue with this semantics is the way how integrity constraints are treated. A violated integrity constraint prevents a set of atoms to be a possibilistic stable model independently of its necessity value, and a non-violated integrity constraint is ignored just as its necessity value. For example, the program $\{\langle \text{concert} \leftarrow \text{not canceled.}, 1\rangle,$ $\langle \perp \leftarrow \text{concert.}, \alpha\rangle\}$ has no solution for any $\alpha \in (0, 1]$ even if α is very low.

Bauters et al. [9]. This approach starts from a different paradigm in order to overcome the issue described above. Bauters et al. identify that the possibilistic answer sets in the sense of Nicolas et al. [10] are computed based on the Gelfond-Lifschitz reduct of the program, which excludes any information about the necessity or possibility value

---

[1] A grounding sequence is the ordered set of rules involved in the deduction of an answer set.

that could have been drawn from the negative atoms. Bauters et al. also use possibilistic atom sets, but propose to consider and enforce the equalities $N(a) = \Pi(\text{not } a)$ and thus $N(\text{not } a) = 1 - N(a)$. In our opinion, this leads to some counter-intuitive results. Let us consider two examples to illustrate this (the first one has already been discussed by Bauters et al. [9]).

Example 2. Consider the possibilistic logic program: $P_{b1} = \{ \langle a \leftarrow \text{not } a., 1 \rangle \}$. The only answer set in the sense of Bauters et al. [9] is $\{\langle a, 0.5 \rangle\}$.

The rule $a \leftarrow \text{not } a$. used in this example is a self-contradiction which carries the maximal necessity value and, in the classic possibilistic logic context, would bring the inconsistency value of the program to 1.

Example 3. Consider the following possibilistic logic programs:

$$P_{b2} = \{ \langle a \leftarrow \text{not } a., 1 \rangle, \langle b., 0.7 \rangle \} \quad P_{b3} = \{ \langle a \leftarrow \text{not } a., 1 \rangle, \langle b., 0.3 \rangle \}$$

The only answer set for P_{b2} is $\{\langle a, 0.5 \rangle, \langle b, 0.7 \rangle\}$ and for P_{b3} $\{\langle a, 0.5 \rangle, \langle b, 0.3 \rangle\}$. The rank-ordering of the atoms a and b in the answer set is no longer only governed by the rank-ordering of the grounding sequence allowing their deduction. Here b is considered more certain than a if the necessity of the rule b. is more than half the necessity of $a \leftarrow \text{not } a$.

We think that the point made in the last example is in opposition to the philosophy of possibilistic logic where the necessity values only define a preordering between the formulas. It seems that the definition by Bauters et al. [9] introduces some logarithmic scale within the semantics which is not suitable from our point of view.

Bauters et al. [15]. The same authors proposed another approach for dealing with possibilistic logic and answer sets which is based on subsets of a program. This work differs from our approach in several aspects: first they consider every possible subset of the program which is harmful for the complexity and entails a different semantics. Also they do not consider answer sets properly speaking but only the brave and cautious consequences of the program. Moreover, this approach has a higher complexity, at the second level of the polynomial hierarchy [16].

Discussion. All of the approaches presented so far have problems. One of them is the inability to give an overall possibility value of the answer set as the possibilities are only attached to atoms. They are, for example, unable to measure the certainty of the empty set as a solution, e.g, to make the difference between $\langle a \leftarrow \text{not } a., 0.1 \rangle$ and $\langle a \leftarrow \text{not } a., 1 \rangle$. The semantics presented in the next section addresses these issues.

4   A New Definition of Possibilistic Answer Sets

In the examples presented previously, and given the non-monotonicity of the language, we can see that we could deduce atoms by ignoring the deduction of others. Ignoring rules as part of a definition can be helpful in two ways:

- It allows for considering more efficiently the reason why some atoms have been overlooked and to measure how harmful it was.
- It allows for defining possibilistic answer sets based on ι-answer sets.

As we want to represent the fact that some rules might have been ignored, we can introduce an overall possibility value for sets of atoms from which we define the concept of possibilistic interpretation. The possibility value is deduced from the necessity of rules going against the set of atoms.

Definition 5. *Let X be a possibilistic atom set and $\alpha \in (0, 1]$. Then a* possibilistic interpretation *is a pair $\langle X, \alpha \rangle$ where α denotes the possibility degree of X.*

In this context, a possibilistic ι-answer set can be naturally defined with the help of an ι-answer set:

Definition 6. *Let P be a possibilistic logic program and $I = \langle X, \alpha \rangle$ be a possibilistic interpretation. Then I is a* possibilistic ι-answer set *of P if there exists some $Q \subseteq P$ such that the following holds:*

1. $X^* = CN^+(Q^*)$,
2. $body^+(Q^*) \subseteq CN^+(Q^*)$,
3. $body^-(Q^*) \cap CN^+(Q^*) = \emptyset$,
4. $\alpha = 1 - \max\{\beta \mid \langle r, \beta \rangle \in P \setminus Q\}$ *if $P \neq Q$, and $\alpha = 1$ otherwise,*
5. *for each $a \in atoms(Q^*)$ and $r^* \in Q^*$ such that $a = head(r^*)$, $\{b_1, \ldots, b_m\} = body^+(r^*) \subseteq X$, and $body^-(r^*) \cap X = \emptyset$, it holds $N(a) \geq \min\{\alpha, \beta_1, \ldots, \beta_n\}$, where $N(r) = \alpha$ and $N(b_i) = \beta_i$ and there exists some $r^* \in Q^*$ such that $N(a) = \min\{\alpha, \beta_1, \ldots, \beta_n\}$,*
6. *there is no Q' with $Q \subsetneq Q' \subseteq P$ satisfying conditions 2 to 4.*

On top of the necessity value of each atom, there is a possibility value for the overall possibilistic ι-answer set, which represents its plausibility as a solution. A possibilistic ι-answer set $I = \langle X, \alpha \rangle$ can thus be understood as follows: X can be accepted as a possibilistic ι-answer set but there exists a $1 - \alpha$ necessity against it; in case it is considered, the necessity of each atom is given in X.

With necessity being defined as a lower bound, classical possibilistic logic enforces formulas in a possibilistic knowledge base not to have a necessity degree of zero because otherwise they bring no information. For possibilistic ι-answer sets we enforce the same requirement.

Example 4. Consider the following possibilistic logic program:

$$P = \left\{ \begin{array}{ll} \langle rain \leftarrow not\ sun., 1 \rangle, & \langle umbrella \leftarrow rain., 1 \rangle, \\ \langle sun., 0.6 \rangle, & \langle glasses \leftarrow sun., 1 \rangle \end{array} \right\}$$

It has two possibilistic ι-answer set $\langle \{\langle sun., 0.6 \rangle, \langle glasses, 0.6 \rangle\}, 1 \rangle$ with $P = Q$ and $\langle \{\langle rain, 1 \rangle, \langle umbrella, 1 \rangle\}, 0.4 \rangle$ with $P \setminus Q = \{\langle sun., 0.6 \rangle\}$.

A parallel can be established between possibilistic ι-answer sets and answer sets.

Proposition 1. *Let P be a possibilistic logic program and $I = \langle X, \alpha \rangle$ be a possibilistic ι-answer set of P. Then $\alpha = 1$ if and only if X^* is an answer set of P^* in the classical sense.*

The previous proposition follows directly from Theorem 3.6 of [12]. Moreover, this immediately shows the NP-hardness of finding possibilistic ι-answer sets. Here, the NP-membership is trivial as one has to guess the set of atoms X from Definition 6 and from there one can polynomially compute the consequence. From these observations, we obtain the following result.

Theorem 1. *Let P be a possibilistic logic program. Deciding the existence of an possibilistic ι-answer set for P is NP-complete.*

Integrity Constraints. In the original definition of ι-answer sets, Gebser et al. had to treat integrity constraints separately from the other rules. This distinction is necessary because discarding a rule from the applied rules set comes with no penalty in the original context. If there is no penalty in ignoring integrity constraints, they become useless. For our possibilistic ι-answer sets, such a special treatment is not necessary. The possibility value of an answer set reflects the importance of the discarded rules. We illustrate this in the following.

Example 5. Consider the following classic logic program and its possibilistic variant:

$$P = \{a \leftarrow \text{not } b. \qquad b \leftarrow \text{not } a. \qquad \bot \leftarrow a.\}$$
$$P' = \{\langle a \leftarrow \text{not } b., 1 \rangle \qquad \langle b \leftarrow \text{not } a., 1 \rangle \qquad \langle \bot \leftarrow a., 0.5 \rangle\}$$

In P, there is one answer set here $\{b\}$ as $\{a\}$ is forbidden by the constraint. The constraint is considered part of the applied rules according to Definition 4. The necessity value attached to constraints can be used to rank-order the answer sets. Here we have, for example, $\langle \{\langle b, 1 \rangle\}, 1 \rangle$ and $\langle \{\langle a, 1 \rangle\}, 0.5 \rangle$ where the latter is considered less possible.

5   A Translation of Possibilistic Logic Programs into ASP

Gebser et al. [12] propose a translation, called ι-completion, from classical positive-order logic programs into SAT. We use this translation as a basis for encoding possibilistic logic programs into ASP.

Let P^* be a classical logic program, and P_C^* denote the set of self-blocking rules within P^* given by

$$P_C^* = \{r \mid r \in P^* \text{ and } head(r) \cap body^-(r) \neq \emptyset\}.$$

The set $sup(a)$ allows for identifying the necessary premisses to the deduction of a.

$$rule(a) = \{r \in P^* \setminus P_C^* \mid head(r) = a\}$$
$$sup(a) = \bigvee_{r \in rule(a)} \left(\bigwedge_{p^+ \in body^+(r)} p^+ \wedge \bigwedge_{p^- \in body^-(r)} \neg p^- \right)$$

The set $block(a)$ allows for identifying all the self blocking rules in which a is involved. $block(a)$ is true if one self-blocking rule is supposed to be fired in the answer set, which is impossible. Thus, the ι-completion forces $block(a)$ to be false.

$$neg(a) = \{r \in P^* \setminus P_C^* \mid a \in body^-(r)\}$$

$$block(a) = \bigvee_{r \in neg(a)} \left(head(r) \wedge \bigwedge_{p^+ \in body^+(r)} p^+ \wedge \bigwedge_{p^- \in body^-(r)} \neg p^- \right)$$

Let C^* denote the set of integrity constraints of P^*. The ι-completion is given by:

$$comp(P^*, C^*) = \{a \leftrightarrow sup(a) \wedge \neg block(a) \mid a \in atoms(P^*)\}$$

Because existing answer set solvers cannot handle floating point numbers, we assume in the following that both possibility and necessity values are given as integers in the range $\mathcal{V} = \{1, \ldots, 100\}$. For example, a necessity 0.8 is written as 80. This is not problematic as there are always only finitely many necessity values in a possibilistic program, and thus they can be accommodated on some finite integer scale.

The translation for ι-answer sets is done in four steps. The idea is close to the one introduced in [17]. The logic program checks for every possible interpretation whether it is a ι-answer set. After the checking is done, another part of the program finds the possibility value associated to the ι-answer set and to each of its atoms.

Step 1: Generating interpretations. In order to check every interpretation, we first have to assert that each atom is assigned true of false. To this end, we introduce for each atom $a \in atoms(P^*)$ an additional new atom na denoting not a, and the rules: $1\{l(a), l(na)\}1.$ and $\leftarrow l(a), l(na).$

Step 2: Checking for support. The second step is a translation of the completion given before. Namely, for each atom $a \in atoms(P^*)$ we introduce the rules:

$$l(a) \leftarrow sup(a), \text{not } block(a). \qquad l(na) \leftarrow \text{not } sup(a). \qquad l(na) \leftarrow block(a).$$

as well as the rules corresponding to $sup(a)$ and $block(a)$. They can easily be translated into ASP using labeling conversion.

Step 3: Computing necessity values. The third step computes the consequence of the reduct. An atom must be deduced under two conditions: it needs to have a rule allowing its deduction, and the atoms in this rule's positive body must be justified. To achieve this, we introduce the following for each rule $\langle r^*, v \rangle \in P$ and for each $N \leq v \in \mathcal{V}$.

$$vlip(head(r^*), N) \leftarrow l(head(r^*)), vlip(body^+(r^*), N), \text{not } body^-(r^*), N \leq v.$$

Here N represents the necessity value of the atom which has to be equal to the minimum amongst the necessity value of the atoms in the positive body and the rule itself. Thus, the head is deduced with a necessity v if all atoms in $body^+(r^*)$ have been deduced with at least a necessity v and the necessity of the rule is also at least v.

We need to compute the final necessity value for each of the atoms. For each $p \in atoms(P^*), \forall N, O \in \mathcal{V}$ we introduce the rules where L is a variable representing atoms.

$$negvli(L, N) \leftarrow vlip(L, N), vlip(L, O), N < O.$$
$$vli(L, N) \leftarrow vlip(L, N), \text{not } negvli(L, N).$$

Step 4: Computing the possibility value. For the possibility value, we need first to check rules that might have been ignored. We introduce the rule:

$$vasp(100 - v) \leftarrow \text{not } head(r^*), body^+(r^*), \text{not } body^-(r^*).$$

for each rule $\langle r^*, v \rangle \in P$. From all the rules ignored, the higher necessity value is the most relevant (and thus the smaller possibility $vasp(N)$). The first rule marks the values which are not minimal. Then the minimal value is the one that remains unmarked as computed by the second rule. For each $N \in \mathcal{V} \cup \{0\}$ this is achieved by the two rules:
$negvas(N) \leftarrow vasp(N), vasp(O), N > O. \qquad vas(N) \leftarrow vasp(N), \text{not } negvas(N).$
All these 4 steps together form the program $\tau(P)$.

Theorem 2. *The stable models of the translated program $\tau(P)$ are exactly the possibilistic ι-answer sets of P.*

The proof comes from the separation of the program in two parts. The first part (step 1 and 2) is exactly the translation proposed in [12] and the second part (step 3 and 4) cannot prevent a set to be a solution, but only computes the necessity and possibility values associated.

Example 6. We present an example to illustrate the translation process. Let P be the following possibilistic logic program:

$$P = \left\{ \begin{array}{lll} \langle a \leftarrow \text{not } b., 1 \rangle & \langle d \leftarrow a., 1 \rangle & \langle b \leftarrow \text{not } c., 0.8 \rangle \\ \langle e \leftarrow b., 1 \rangle & \langle c \leftarrow \text{not } a., 0.6 \rangle & \langle f \leftarrow c., 1 \rangle \end{array} \right\}$$

Program P leads to the final translation in ASP presented in Figure 1[2]. For the sake of space, the *sup* and *neg* rules are given only for the atom a. Only the atoms of the solutions which are relevant for understanding are given. This translation has 3 solutions partially exhibited here:

$$\left\{ \begin{array}{l} \{l(a), l(nb), l(nc), l(d), l(ne), l(nf), vas(20), vli(d, 100), vli(a, 100)\}, \\ \{l(na), l(b), l(nc), l(nd), l(e), l(nf), vas(40), vli(e, 80), vli(b, 80)\}, \\ \{l(na), l(nb), l(c), l(nd), l(ne), l(f), vas(0), vli(f, 60), vli(c, 60)\} \end{array} \right\}$$

The last solution should be ignored because its possibility is equal to zero.

Experimental Results. In order to evaluate the usability of our approach we ran a series of tests[3] with clingo [18] on an Intel Pentium with 2 GHz. The tests were performed on randomly generated instances with two parameters: the number of rules *nbr* and the number of atoms *nba*. The average running times over 1000 instances for a pair (*nbr,nba*) were (500,250) in 0.34s, (1000,500) in 0.97s, (5000,2500) in 15.84s and (10000,5000) in 58.03s. For comparison, a normal ASP (10000,5000) instance is solved in 0.280s on average. This suggests that finding possibilistic ι-answer sets can be performed on instances of acceptable size.

---

[2] The statement $1\{a_1, ..., a_n\}1$ stands for "exactly one atom in $\{a_1, ..., a_n\}$ is true".

[3] The script used is available at http://www.informatik.uni-freiburg.de/ hue/translate.tar.gz

$$1\{l(a), l(na)\}1 \quad 1\{l(b), l(nb)\}1 \quad 1\{l(c), l(nc)\}1 \quad 1\{l(d), l(nd)\}1$$
$$1\{l(e), l(ne)\}1 \quad 1\{l(f), l(nf)\}1$$

$negvli(L, N) \leftarrow vlip(L, N), vlip(L, O), N < O.$ $vli(L, N) \leftarrow vlip(L, N), \text{not } negvli(L, N).$
$vlip(a, N) \leftarrow l(a), l(nb), N <= 100.$ $vlip(b, N) \leftarrow l(b), l(nc), N <= 80.$
$vlip(c, N) \leftarrow l(c), l(na), N <= 60.$ $vlip(d, N) \leftarrow l(d), vlip(a, N), N <= 100.$
$vlip(e, N) \leftarrow l(e), vlip(b, N), N <= 100.$ $vlip(f, N) \leftarrow l(f), vlip(c, N), N <= 100.$
$negvas(N) \leftarrow vasp(N), vasp(O), N > O.$ $vas(N) \leftarrow vasp(N), \text{not } negvas(N).$

$vasp(0) \leftarrow l(na), l(nb).$ $vasp(20) \leftarrow l(nb), l(nc).$ $vasp(40) \leftarrow l(nc), l(na).$
$vasp(0) \leftarrow l(nd), l(a).$ $vasp(0) \leftarrow l(ne), l(b).$ $vasp(0) \leftarrow l(nf), l(c).$
$sup(a) \leftarrow suprule(a, r_0).$ $suprule(a, r_0) \leftarrow l(nb).$ $neg(a) \leftarrow negrule(a, r_0).$
$negrule(a, r_0) \leftarrow l(c), l(na).$ $l(a) \leftarrow sup(a), \text{not } neg(a).$ $l(na) \leftarrow \text{not } sup(a).$
    $l(na) \leftarrow neg(a).$

Fig. 1. ASP translation of Example 6

6   Conclusion

In this paper we considered an extension of ASP that involves possibilistic rules. Such possibilistic logic programs allows for concisely expressing degrees of possibility and giving a rank-ordering of the program's rules. While the concept of possibilistic logic programs has been considered before, previous semantics of the resulting possibilistic answer sets are in our opinion contrary to the intuition behind possibilistic logic and lack several expected properties.

We have here provided a new semantics for possibilistic programs based on the existing concept of ι-answer sets. Our semantics extends the original definition by Nicolas et al. [10], overcoming its shortcomings and providing a reasonable concept of possibilistic solution that is not limited to the classic stable models of a logic program. Moreover, our definition handles inconsistencies and integrity constraints much more gracefully than alternative suggestions put forward by Bauters et al. [9]. The new semantics is in line with and respects the original philosophy of possibilistic logic in the sense of rank-ordering rules. This is in contrast to Bauters et al. [9] who require computations on necessity values exceeding a pure rank-ordering.

Our definition of possibilistic answer sets allows for computing them using existing answer set tools by transforming possibilistic logic programs into classic logic programs. Thus, possibilistic rules can be easily applied in existing application scenarios based on modeling only without requiring new tools.

Acknowledgements. We thank the anonymous reviewers of this paper and a previous version for helpful suggestions and comments. J.H. and M.W. acknowledge support by the DFG Transregional Collaborative Research Center *SFB/TR 8 Spatial Cognition* (project: R4-[LogoSpace]). S.W. acknowledges support by the DFG priority program *SPP 1516: New Frameworks of Rationality* (project: Models of human non-monotonic reasoning).

References

1. Lifschitz, V.: Thirteen definitions of a stable model. In: Blass, A., Dershowitz, N., Reisig, W. (eds.) Fields of Logic and Computation. LNCS, vol. 6300, pp. 488–503. Springer, Heidelberg (2010)
2. Brewka, G., Eiter, T.: Preferred answer sets for extended logic programs. Artif. Intell. 109(1-2), 297–356 (1999)
3. Bacchus, F., Grove, A.J., Halpern, J.Y., Koller, D.: From statistical knowledge bases to degrees of belief. Artificial Intelligence 87(1-2), 75–143 (1996)
4. Thimm, M., Kern-Isberner, G.: On probabilistic inference in relational conditional logics. Logic Journal of the IGPL 20(5), 872–908 (2012)
5. Poole, D.: Logic programming, abduction and probability. In: Proceedings of the International Conference on Fifth Generation Computer Systems (FCGS), pp. 530–538 (1992)
6. Lukasiewicz, T.: Probabilistic logic programming. In: ECAI, pp. 388–392 (1998)
7. Baral, C., Gelfond, M., Rushton, J.N.: Probabilistic reasoning with answer sets. Theory and Practice of Logic Programming 9(1), 57–144 (2009)
8. Dubois, D., Lang, J., Prade, H.: Possibilistic logic. In: Handbook of Logic in Artificial Intelligence and Logic Programming, vol. 3, pp. 439–513 (1994)
9. Bauters, K., Schockaert, S., De Cock, M., Vermeir, D.: Possibilistic answer set programming revisited. In: Proceedings of the 26th Conference on Uncertainty in Artificial Intelligence (UAI). AUAI Press (2010)
10. Nicolas, P., Garcia, L., Stéphan, I.: Possibilistic stable models. In: IJCAI, pp. 248–253. Morgan Kaufmann Publishers (2005)
11. Osorio, M., Nieves, J.C.: PStable semantics for possibilistic logic programs. In: Gelbukh, A., Kuri Morales, Á.F. (eds.) MICAI 2007. LNCS (LNAI), vol. 4827, pp. 294–304. Springer, Heidelberg (2007)
12. Gebser, M., Gharib, M., Mercer, R.E., Schaub, T.: Monotonic answer set programming. Journal of Logic and Computation 19(4), 539–564 (2009)
13. Gelfond, M., Lifschitz, V.: The stable model semantics for logic programming. In: Proceedings of the 5th International Conference on Logic Programming (ICLP), pp. 1070–1080 (1988)
14. Baral, C., Kreinovich, V., Lifschitz, V.: Introduction: Logic programming, non-monotonic reasoning and reasoning about actions. Annals of Mathematics and Artificial Intelligence 21(2-4), 129 (1997)
15. Bauters, K., Schockaert, S., Cock, M.D., Vermeir, D.: Possible and necessary answer sets of possibilistic answer set programs. In: ICTAI, pp. 836–843. IEEE (2012)
16. Bauters, K., Schockaert, S., De Cock, M., Vermeir, D.: Answer set programs with optional rules: a possibilistic approach. Working papers of the IJCAI 2013 Workshop on Weighted Logics for Artificial Intelligence, WL4AI 2013, pp. 2–9 (2013)
17. Hué, J., Papini, O., Würbel, E.: Removed sets fusion: Performing off the shelf. In: ECAI, pp. 94–98 (2008)
18. Gebser, M., Kaminski, R., Kaufmann, B., Ostrowski, M., Schaub, T., Schneider, M.: Potassco: The Potsdam answer set solving collection. AICOM 24(2), 107–124 (2011)

Reasoning in $\mathcal{ALC}$ with Fuzzy Concrete Domains

Dorian Merz[3], Rafael Peñaloza[1,2,*], and Anni-Yasmin Turhan[1,**]

[1] Institute for Theoretical Computer Science, TU Dresden
[2] Center for Advancing Electronics Dresden
[3] Department of Computer Science, University of Erlangen-Nuremberg, Erlangen

Abstract. In the context of Description Logics (DLs) concrete domains allow to model concepts and facts by the use of concrete values and predicates between them. For reasoning in the DL $\mathcal{ALC}$ with general TBoxes concrete domains may cause undecidability. Under certain restrictions of the concrete domains decidability can be regained. Typically, the concrete domain predicates are crisp, which is a limitation for some applications. In this paper we investigate crisp $\mathcal{ALC}$ in combination with fuzzy concrete domains for general TBoxes, devise conditions for decidability, and give a tableau-based reasoning algorithm.

1 Introduction

Concrete domains were introduced in [2] as an extension to DLs, which allows to model DL concepts based on objects that come from a specified, i.e. concrete, domain and by a set of predicates on that domain, which constrain the set of objects. For example, the natural numbers could be used as a concrete domain to model sizes, or regions together with the RCC relations can be used to model geo-spatial domains.

In order to allow for reasoning a concrete domain $\mathcal{D}$ needs to satisfy some conditions. A concrete domain is called *admissible*, if it contains a predicate for domain membership, the set of predicates is finite and closed under negation, and testing for finite conjunctions of predicates is decidable. In [2] these conditions and a tableaux-based reasoning algorithm for testing concept satisfiability w. r. t. terminologies were given. Concept satisfiability w. r. t. general TBoxes easily becomes undecidable for admissible concrete domains [6]. In [7] Lutz and Miličić give a condition for concrete domains under which decidability can be regained. Essentially, these condition of ω-admissibility ensures that a model for all constraints expressed in the DL knowledge base can be constructed from locally consistent parts.

In this paper we consider fuzzy concrete domains (CDs), where objects from the concrete domain can be related to one another to some degree. This allows for a more fine-grained modelling for vague information as, for instance, in situation recognition in context-aware systems or even to model fuzzy spatial relations for

---

* Partially supported by DFG within the Cluster of Excellence 'cfAED'.
** Partially supported by DFG in the CRC 912 HAEC.

C. Lutz and M. Thielscher (Eds.): KI 2014, LNCS 8736, pp. 171–182, 2014.

image recognition. The combination of DLs and fuzzy concrete domains has been investigated already in a number of settings [11,3,9,8]. However, fuzzy DLs can easily turn out to be undecidable [4]. In our approach, we consider a crisp DL language, with a fuzzy concrete domain. Since our underlying DL is crisp, while the concrete domain is not, the fuzzy values from the fuzzy concrete domain need to be discretized at some point. A natural question is whether the fuzzy CD can be (easily) encoded in a crisp one. In principle this can be done, however, the approach in [7] uses relational networks to represent a set of constraints imposed on the concrete domain objects. The predicates used in relational networks are required to be jointly exhaustive and pairwise disjoint. In a fuzzy setting, where all tuples of concrete domain objects are related to each other via *all* predicates (possibly by degree zero), this is no longer a natural requirement. Moreover, a translation of the fuzzy constraints to crisp ones can lead to an exponential blow-up of the knowledge base as shown in Section 4.

This finding motivates our direct reasoning algorithm for $\mathcal{ALC}$ (with functional roles) and fuzzy concrete domains, since it allows for a more succinct representation of the TBox. To this end we transfer the notion of ω-admissibility to fuzzy concrete domains and give a tableaux-based reasoning procedure for concept satisfiability in the presence of general TBoxes for the new DL $\mathcal{ALC}(\mathbb{D})$ in Section 3. We show soundness, completeness and termination for our procedure. For the full detail of the proofs, we refer the reader to [10].

We give the definition of the basic notions of DLs, (fuzzy) concrete domains and the DL $\mathcal{ALC}(\mathbb{D})$ in Section 2. In Section 3 we devise a tableau algorithm for $\mathcal{ALC}(\mathbb{D})$ with ω-admissible concrete domains. Afterwards we investigate the translation-based approach to handle fuzzy concrete domains by crisp ones in Section 4. We end the paper with conclusions and considerations for future work.

2   Preliminaries

We give only a short introduction to the basic notions of DLs—for a more thorough presentation see [1]. Starting from countable and disjoint sets N_C of concept names and N_R of role names, *concept constructors* are used to build complex concepts. In the DL $\mathcal{ALC}$ complex concepts are formed using the concept constructors listed in Table 1.

The semantics of this logic is given by means of interpretations. An *interpretation* $\mathcal{I} = (\Delta^{\mathcal{I}}, \cdot^{\mathcal{I}})$ is a pair consisting of an *interpretation domain* $\Delta^{\mathcal{I}}$ and a function $\cdot^{\mathcal{I}}$ that maps concept names to subsets of $\Delta^{\mathcal{I}}$ and role names to binary relations on $\Delta^{\mathcal{I}}$. This function is extended to complex $\mathcal{ALC}$-concepts as shown in the last column of Table 1. As usual in DLs, we use $\perp$ to denote any contradictory concept (e.g. $A \sqcap \neg A$) and $\top$ to denote a tautology ($A \sqcup \neg A$).

Concepts are related to each other by *general concept inclusions* (GCIs), which are statements of the form $C \sqsubseteq D$. The interpretation $\mathcal{I}$ *satisfies* the GCI $C \sqsubseteq D$, if $C^{\mathcal{I}} \subseteq D^{\mathcal{I}}$. A finite set of GCIs is called a *TBox* $\mathcal{T}$. If a TBox $\mathcal{T}$ contains only GCIs, with concept names as left-hand sides, each concept name appears at most once on the left-hand side of a GCI and the concept names in the left-hand sides

Table 1. Syntax and semantics of $\mathcal{ALC}$-concepts

Constructor	Syntax	Semantics
concept name	A	$A^{\mathcal{I}} \subseteq \Delta^{\mathcal{I}}$
negation	$\neg C$	$(\neg C)^{\mathcal{I}} = \Delta^{\mathcal{I}} \setminus C^{\mathcal{I}}$
conjunction	$C \sqcap D$	$(C \sqcap D)^{\mathcal{I}} = C^{\mathcal{I}} \cap D^{\mathcal{I}}$
disjunction	$C \sqcup D$	$(C \sqcup D)^{\mathcal{I}} = C^{\mathcal{I}} \cup D^{\mathcal{I}}$
existential restriction	$\exists r.C$	$(\exists r.C)^{\mathcal{I}} = \{d \mid \exists e \in \Delta^{\mathcal{I}}.(d,e) \in r^{\mathcal{I}} \text{ and } e \in C^{\mathcal{I}}\}$
value restriction	$\forall r.C$	$(\forall r.C)^{\mathcal{I}} = \{d \mid \forall e \in \Delta^{\mathcal{I}}.(d,e) \in r^{\mathcal{I}} \Rightarrow e \in C^{\mathcal{I}}\}$

of GCIs do neither directly nor indirectly refer to themselves, then the TBox $\mathcal{T}$ is called a *terminology*. An interpretation is a *model* of a TBox $\mathcal{T}$, if it satisfies each GCI in $\mathcal{T}$.

We consider here the reasoning task of testing satisfiability of concepts with respect to the TBox. Given the concept C and a TBox $\mathcal{T}$, C is *satisfiable* w.r.t. $\mathcal{T}$ iff $\mathcal{T}$ has a model $\mathcal{I}$ such that $C^{\mathcal{I}} \neq \emptyset$.

2.1 Concrete Domains

We extend the approach of Lutz and Miličić in [7] to the fuzzy setting and thus adopt their way of introducing concrete domains. They use constraint systems as concrete domains that have binary predicates which are interpreted as jointly exhaustive and pairwise disjoint (JEPD) relations. This does not limit the expressiveness of the concrete domain, since any concrete domain with a finite set of predicates can be translated into one with binary JEPD relations, e.g. see [10]. Before introducing constraint systems, we introduce the class of structures they describe.

Definition 1. *Let V be a countably infinite set of variables and Rel a finite set of binary relations. A Rel-constraint is a tuple of the form (t, R), where t is a pair over V and $R \in Rel$. A Rel-network N is a (possibly infinite) set of Rel-constraints. For a given Rel-network N, the set of its variables is denoted by V_N and the set of its relations by Rel_N. A Rel-network N is in normal form, if for all $x, y \in V_N$, there is exactly one constraint $((x, y), R) \in N$.*

Let τ be a mapping from variables to variables, then τ is extended to pairs by $\tau((v, w)) = (\tau(v), \tau(w))$, to constraints by $\tau((t, R)) = (\tau(t), R)$, and to Rel-networks by $\tau(N) = \{\tau(c) \mid c \in N\}$. A Rel-network N' in normal form is a model of network N, if there is a total mapping $\tau : V_N \to V_{N'}$ such that $\tau(N) \subseteq N'$.

Intuitively, a constraint system defines a set of Rel-networks that are satisfiable.

Definition 2. *A constraint system $\mathbf{D} = (V, Rel, \mathcal{M})$ is a tuple consisting of the sets of variables V, relations Rel and $\mathcal{M}$, a set of models of $\mathbf{D}$, which are* *complete Rel-networks. A Rel-network N is* satisfiable *in **D**, if there is a model $M \in \mathcal{M}$ and a total mapping $\tau : V_N \rightarrow V_M$ from the variables of N to those of M, such that $\tau(N) \subseteq M$.*

The notion of ω-admissible constraint systems was introduced in [7]. We refer the reader to this paper for the definition of this notion and only give its variant for the case of fuzzy concrete domains here.

2.2 Fuzzy Concrete Domains

While in the classical notion of concrete domains a predicate for elements holds completely or not at all, fuzzy concrete domains can express that a predicate holds for elements *to some extent*, i.e., with a membership degree from the real unit interval. The requirement to allow for a tuple of variables to be related exclusively via a single relation is not well-defined for fuzzy concrete domains, since variables are always related via all relations of the same arity—possibly only by degree 0. For that reason, we drop the requirement of JEPD relations in the fuzzy setting.

It is not hard to show that fuzzy relations of arbitrary arity can be represented by binary ones, see [10]. Thus relations of higher arity can be handled by our approach, but for the ease of presentation, we only use binary relations here. To allow for a general notion of fuzzy constraints, we use membership degree *sets* defined over a domain $\mathbf{1} \subseteq [0, 1]$. We consider a class of *membership degree sets* such that $\mathbf{1}$ is a membership degree set and for every two membership degree sets σ, σ', (i) σ has a finite representation, and (ii) $\sigma \cap \sigma'$ and $\mathbf{1} \setminus \sigma$ are membership degree sets, too.

Definition 3. *Let V and Rel be as before and $\mathbf{1} \subseteq [0, 1]$. A* fuzzy Rel-constraint *is a triple (t, R, σ) with $t \in V^2$, $R \in Rel$, and $\sigma \subseteq \mathbf{1}$. A* fuzzy Rel-network $\mathbb{N}$ *is a set of fuzzy Rel-constraints. For $\mathbb{N}$ the set of its variables is indicated by $V_{\mathbb{N}}$ and the one for its relations by $Rel_{\mathbb{N}}$.*

A fuzzy constraint system $\mathbb{D} = (V, Rel, \mathbf{1}, \mathfrak{M})$ *consists of the sets of variables V, of relations Rel, and of models $\mathfrak{M}$, a set of fuzzy Rel-networks.*

Intuitively, a fuzzy concrete domain represents a set of *Rel*-networks that are satisfiable in a fuzzy constraint system $\mathbb{D}$.

Definition 4. *Let $\mathbb{N}$ be a fuzzy Rel-network. An* interpretation *of $\mathbb{N}$ is a function $\mathbb{I} : V^2 \times Rel \rightarrow \mathbf{1}$ that maps pairs of variables and relations to a fuzzy degree. An interpretation $\mathbb{I}$ satisfies a constraint (t, R, σ) if $\mathbb{I}(t, R) \in \sigma$. If $\mathbb{I}$ satisfies all constraints in a fuzzy Rel-network $\mathbb{N}$, then $\mathbb{I}$ satisfies $\mathbb{N}$.*

$\mathbb{N}$ is satisfiable *in a fuzzy constraint system $\mathbb{D} = (V, Rel, \mathbf{1}, \mathfrak{M})$, if there exists a model $\mathbb{M} \in \mathfrak{M}$, a mapping $\tau : V_{\mathbb{N}} \rightarrow V_{\mathbb{M}}$ and an interpretation that satisfies $\mathbb{M}$ and $\tau(\mathbb{N})$.*

The idea is that the interpretation $\mathbb{I}$ assigns to each relation R a membership degree function $\mu_R : V^2 \rightarrow \mathbf{1}$ such that $\mu_R(t) = d$, if $\mathbb{I}(t, R) = d$. In case the elements in t are not related via R, the membership degree assigned is 0.

A fuzzy *Rel*-network is in *normal form*, if it contains exactly one fuzzy constraint for each pair of variables and relation $R \in Rel$. It is shown in [10] that every fuzzy *Rel*-network $\mathbb{N}$ can be transformed into a normalized one that is satisfied by the same interpretations. Essentially, the two constraints (t, R, σ) and (t, R, σ') can be equivalently replaced by the constraint $(t, R, \sigma \cap \sigma')$, which is well defined, since the class of membership degree sets is closed under intersection.

A fuzzy *Rel*-network $\mathbb{N}$ contains a *Rel-clash*, if for a relation $R \in Rel$ and a tuple t there is a subset of *Rel*-constraints $\{(t, R, \sigma_i) \mid i \in I\} \subseteq \mathbb{N}$, such that $\bigcap_{i \in I} \sigma_i = \emptyset$, with an arbitrary index set I. In other words, this fuzzy *Rel*-network contains a clash iff after transforming it into normal form, it contains a constraint of the form $(t, R, \emptyset)$. Otherwise it is *clash-free*.

It is well-known that extending $\mathcal{ALC}$ with concrete domains leads to undecidability of reasoning w.r.t. TBoxes. To regain decidability of reasoning in the presence of TBoxes, conditions need to be imposed on the concrete domain or on a constraint system, respectively. In the crisp case, the concrete domain is required to be ω-admissible by Lutz and Miličić in [7]. We transfer this condition now to the case of fuzzy constraint systems.

Definition 5. *Given a fuzzy constraint system* $\mathbb{D} = (V, Rel, \mathbf{1}, \mathfrak{M})$. $\mathbb{D}$ *has the*

- patchwork property *if for two finite, satisfiable fuzzy Rel-networks* $\mathbb{N}_1$ *and* $\mathbb{N}_2$ *holds: if* $\mathbb{N}_1 \cup \mathbb{N}_2$ *is clash-free, then* $\mathbb{N}_1 \cup \mathbb{N}_2$ *is satisfiable in* $\mathbb{D}$.
- compactness property *if it holds that any infinite fuzzy Rel-network* $\mathbb{N}$ *in normal form is satisfiable iff for all finite* $U \subseteq V$ *the fuzzy Rel-network* $\mathbb{N}_U = \{((x, y), R, \sigma) \in \mathbb{N} \mid x, y \in U\}$ *is satisfiable.*

$\mathbb{D}$ *is* ω-admissible *if (1) satisfiability of finite fuzzy Rel-networks in* $\mathbb{D}$ *is decidable, (2)* $\mathbb{D}$ *has the patchwork property, and (3)* $\mathbb{D}$ *has the compactness property.*

The condition of ω-admissibility ensures decidability of reasoning when combining $\mathcal{ALC}$ and fuzzy constraint systems.

2.3   A DL with Fuzzy Concrete Domains: $\mathcal{ALC}(\mathbb{D})$

To define the DL $\mathcal{ALC}(\mathbb{D})$ we need to introduce *features*, which are functional roles. Let N_{aF} be an infinite countable set of *abstract feature names* and N_{cF} be an infinite countable set of *concrete feature names* and $N_{aF} \cap N_{cF} = \emptyset$. A *feature path* P is either a concrete feature f or a pair of an abstract and a concrete feature: $P = a\, f$ with $a \in N_{aF}$ and $f \in N_{cF}$.

Definition 6. *Let* $\mathbb{D} = (V, Rel, \mathbf{1}, \mathfrak{M})$ *be a fuzzy constraint system,* r *a role in* $N_R \cup N_{aF}$, $R \in Rel$, *and* $\sigma \subseteq \mathbf{1}$. *Complex* $\mathcal{ALC}(\mathbb{D})$-*concepts are formed using the concept constructors of* $\mathcal{ALC}$ *listed in Table 1, where in existential or value restrictions abstract features can be used instead of roles. Additionally,* $\mathcal{ALC}(\mathbb{D})$ *allows for* fuzzy constraint restrictions, *which are expressions of the form* $\exists(P_1, P_2, R, \sigma)$ *or* $\forall(P_1, P_2, R, \sigma)$, *where* $R \in Rel$, *and* $\sigma \subseteq \mathbf{1}$ *and* P_i *are feature paths.*

For the semantics of $\mathcal{ALC}(\mathbb{D})$-concepts, we need to extend the notion of an interpretation to fuzzy constraint restrictions and thus accommodate Rel-networks.

Definition 7. *An* interpretation *is a tuple* $\mathcal{I} = (\Delta^{\mathcal{I}}, \cdot^{\mathcal{I}}, \mathsf{N}_{\mathcal{I}})$ *consisting of a domain* $\Delta^{\mathcal{I}}$, *a mapping* $\cdot^{\mathcal{I}}$, *and a fuzzy Rel-network in normal form* $\mathsf{N}_{\mathcal{I}}$. *The function* $\cdot^{\mathcal{I}}$ *maps names from* $N_C \cup N_R$ *as for* $\mathcal{ALC}$; *abstract features* $a \in N_{aF}$ *are interpreted as partial functions over* $\Delta^{\mathcal{I}}$, *and concrete features* $f \in N_{cF}$ *are partial functions from* $\Delta^{\mathcal{I}}$ *to* $\mathsf{N}_{\mathcal{I}}$. *The interpretation of a feature path* $P = a\, f$ *is the function that maps* $d \in \Delta^{\mathcal{I}}$ *to* $P(d)^{\mathcal{I}} = f^{\mathcal{I}}(a^{\mathcal{I}}(d))$, *when this is well-defined. The semantics of the new concept constructors are:*

$$\left(\exists(P_1, P_2, R, \sigma)\right)^{\mathcal{I}} = \big\{d \in \Delta^{\mathcal{I}} \mid \exists v, w \in V_{\mathsf{N}_{\mathcal{I}}}, \exists \sigma' \subseteq \underline{\mathbf{1}} : P_1^{\mathcal{I}}(d) = v \wedge$$
$$P_2^{\mathcal{I}}(d) = w \wedge (v, w, R, \sigma') \in \mathsf{N}_{\mathcal{I}} \wedge \sigma' \subseteq \sigma\big\}$$

$$\left(\forall(P_1, P_2, R, \sigma)\right)^{\mathcal{I}} = \big\{d \in \Delta^{\mathcal{I}} \mid \forall v, w \in V_{\mathsf{N}_{\mathcal{I}}}, \forall \sigma' \subseteq \underline{\mathbf{1}} : \big(P_1^{\mathcal{I}}(d) = v \wedge$$
$$P_2^{\mathcal{I}}(d) = w \wedge (v, w, R, \sigma') \in \mathsf{N}_{\mathcal{I}}\big) \implies \sigma' \subseteq \sigma\big\}.$$

The classical DL $\mathcal{ALC}(\mathcal{D})$ is a special case of $\mathcal{ALC}(\mathbb{D})$, where $\sigma = \{0, 1\}$ and only the constraint restrictions with $\sigma = \{1\}$ are mentioned.

Let $r \in N_R \cup N_{aF}$. An $\mathcal{ALC}(\mathbb{D})$-concept is in *negation normal form* (NNF), if negation only appears in front of concept names. It is easy to see that every $\mathcal{ALC}(\mathbb{D})$-concept can be transformed into NNF by exhaustive application of the following rules.

$$\neg\neg C \to C$$
$$\neg(\exists r.C) \to (\forall r.\neg C)$$
$$\neg(\forall r.C) \to (\exists r.\neg C)$$

$$\neg(C \sqcap D) \to (\neg C \sqcup \neg D)$$
$$\neg(C \sqcup D) \to (\neg C \sqcap \neg D)$$
$$\neg(\exists(P_1, P_2, R, \sigma)) \to (\forall(P_1, P_2, R, \underline{\mathbf{1}} \setminus \sigma))$$
$$\neg(\forall(P_1, P_2, R, \sigma)) \to (\exists(P_1, P_2, R, \underline{\mathbf{1}} \setminus \sigma))$$

3   A Tableau Algorithm for Concept Satisfiability

We show that satisfiability of $\mathcal{ALC}(\mathbb{D})$-concepts w.r.t. $\mathcal{ALC}(\mathbb{D})$-TBoxes is decidable for any ω-admissible fuzzy constraint system $\mathbb{D}$ by describing a tableau-based algorithm for this problem. For the rest of this section we consider a fixed concept C in NNF and a TBox $\mathcal{T}$ containing exactly one GCI $\top \sqsubseteq C_{\mathcal{T}}$ with normalized Rel-networks. These assumptions are w.l.o.g., since every GCI $D \sqsubseteq E$ can be equivalently rewritten as $\top \sqsubseteq \neg D \sqcup E$, and every concept can be transformed into NNF in linear time using the rules introduced above.

The algorithm keeps as data structure a *completion system* $\mathcal{S} = (\mathfrak{T}, \mathsf{N}, \Sigma)$, where N is a finite fuzzy Rel-network, Σ is a finite set of subsets of $\underline{\mathbf{1}}$ that describes the membership degrees relevant for reasoning, and $\mathfrak{T}$ is a labeled tree $\mathfrak{T} = (V, E, \mathcal{L})$ such that V is partitioned into two sets V_A and V_C, $E \subseteq V_A \times V$ and $\mathcal{L}$ labels every node $v \in V_A$ with a set of concepts $\mathcal{L}(v) \subseteq \mathsf{sub}(C) \cup \mathsf{sub}(C_{\mathcal{T}})$,[1]

---

[1] Here $\mathsf{sub}(C)$ denotes the set of subconcepts of a concept C, consider e.g. [1].

Table 2. Tableau rules for $\mathcal{ALC}(\mathbb{D})$

$\mathbf{R_{\sqcap}}$	if $D_1 \sqcap D_2 \in \mathcal{L}(v)$ and $\{D_1, D_2\} \nsubseteq \mathcal{L}(v)$, then add D_1, D_2 to $\mathcal{L}(v)$
$\mathbf{R_{\sqcup}}$	if $D_1 \sqcup D_2 \in \mathcal{L}(v)$ and $\{D_1, D_2\} \cap \mathcal{L}(v) \neq \emptyset$, then add D_1 or D_2 to $\mathcal{L}(v)$
$\mathbf{R_{\exists}}$	if $\exists r.D \in \mathcal{L}(v)$, v is not blocked, and there is no r-successor w of v such that $D \in \mathcal{L}(w)$, then **extend** $\mathfrak{T}$ with a fresh r-successor x of v and add D to $\mathcal{L}(x)$
$\mathbf{R_{\forall}}$	if $\forall r.D \in \mathcal{L}(v)$ and there is an r-successor w of v such that $D \notin \mathcal{L}(w)$, then add D to $\mathcal{L}(w)$
$\mathbf{R_{\ominus}}$	if $\exists (P_1, P_2, R, \sigma) \in \mathcal{L}(v)$, v is not blocked, and there are no $c_1, c_2 \in V_C, \sigma' \in \Sigma$ with $P_i(v) = c_i, i \in \{1, 2\}$, $(c_1, c_2, R, \sigma') \in \mathbb{N}$ and $\sigma' \subseteq \sigma$, then **extend** $\mathfrak{T}$ with fresh P_i-successors x_i of $v, i \in \{1, 2\}$ and add (x_1, x_2, R, σ) to $\mathbb{N}$ and σ to Σ
$\mathbf{R_{\ominus}}$	if $\forall (P_1, P_2, R, \sigma) \in \mathcal{L}(v)$ and there are $c_1, c_2 \in V_C, \sigma' \in \Sigma$ with $P_i(v) = c_i$, $i \in \{1, 2\}$ and $(c_1, c_2, R, \sigma') \notin \mathbb{N}$ for all $\sigma' \subseteq \sigma$, then add (c_1, c_2, R, σ) to $\mathbb{N}$ and σ to Σ

every edge $(v, w) \in V_A \times V_A$ with a role name $\mathcal{L}(v, w) \in N_R \cup N_{aF}$, and each edge $(v, c) \in V_A \times V_C$ with a concrete feature $\mathcal{L}(v, c) \in N_{cF}$. $\mathfrak{T}$ is called a *tableau tree*, which intuitively describes a (partial) tree-shaped interpretation. The nodes in V_A correspond to the abstract domain elements, and V_C contains concrete domain elements. Each abstract element $x \in V_A$ is labeled with the set of concepts that it satisfies. Similarly, edges are labeled with the role or feature that associates its endpoints. The *Rel*-network $\mathbb{N}$ stores the set of constraints that must be satisfied among the concrete domain elements appearing in $\mathfrak{T}$. For each node $v \in V_A$, we define the *local network*

$$\mathbb{N}(v) := \{((a, b), R, \sigma) \in \mathbb{N} \mid (v, a) \in E \text{ or } (v, b) \in E\};$$

that is, $\mathbb{N}(v)$ contains all the fuzzy *Rel*-constraints that are related to the abstract element v. We say that the local networks of two nodes $v, w \in V_A$ are *isomorphic*, denoted as $\mathbb{N}(v) \sim \mathbb{N}(w)$, if there exists a bijective function $\mu : V_{\mathbb{N}(v)} \to V_{\mathbb{N}(w)}$ such that $\mathbb{N}(w) = \mu(\mathbb{N}(v))$. Finally, the component Σ in a completion system $\mathcal{S} = (\mathfrak{T}, \mathbb{N}, \Sigma)$ keeps track of all relevant sets of fuzzy degrees that may be used for satisfying $\mathbb{N}$.

The completion system is initialized to the tuple $\mathcal{S} = (\mathfrak{T}_0, \emptyset, \{\underline{1}\})$, where $\mathfrak{T}_0 = (\{v_0\}, \emptyset, \mathcal{L})$ is the tableau tree containing only one node v_0 labeled as $\mathcal{L}(v_0) = \{C, C_{\mathcal{T}}\}$. The idea is to try to build a model for $\mathcal{T}$ that makes the interpretation of C non-empty. Thus, we start with one single domain element, namely v_0, that is considered to belong to this concept C. Since the interpretation must be a model of $\mathcal{T}$, v_0 must also belong to $C_{\mathcal{T}}$.

The completion system is then extended by application of the rules from Table 2. Each rule application extends the system and never removes information from it. Only the rule $\mathbf{R_{\sqcup}}$ allows for a non-deterministic choice, which corresponds to deciding which disjunct is used to satisfy the concept $D_1 \sqcup D_2$. Additionally, the two rules for handling existential restrictions $\mathbf{R_{\exists}}$ and $\mathbf{R_{\ominus}}$ have a special pre-condition as they are the only ones that add new nodes to the tree $\mathfrak{T}$. Specifically, these rules are only applicable if the node v is *not blocked*, and their application *extends* $\mathfrak{T}$ with either a new r-successor, for r a role or feature name, or P-successor, for P a feature path.

Since the GCIs in the TBox may contain cycles, termination needs to be ensured by detecting cycles in the construction of the model. This can be done by the well-known blocking technique, which is a detection of repetitions in partially constructed models. In *anywhere blocking* [5] an element v in $\mathfrak{T}$ is blocked, if there is another node w that has been introduced before v and that requires the same conditions in the model as v does—in case of $\mathcal{ALC}(\mathbb{D})$ additionally isomorphism of their local *Rel*-networks is required. In that case, it suffices to use the node w as a template to extend v into a model. Hence, there is no need to explicitly extend v during the execution of the tableau algorithm.

The extension of the tree depends on the kind of roles used. Essentially, the idea is that one or more new nodes are added to the tree in order to satisfy the existential restriction. However, recall that abstract and concrete features are restricted to be functional; that is, if g is a feature, then there is at most one g-successor of any given node v. When extending the tree $\mathfrak{T}$, we need to ensure that this functionality is preserved. If there exists already a g-successor, then it must be reused. Formally, let $\mathfrak{T}$ be a tableau tree. For $r \in N_R$, the *extension* of $\mathfrak{T}$ with a fresh r-successor x of v is the tree $\mathfrak{T}'$ obtained from $\mathfrak{T}$ such that:

- if $r \in N_R$ or $r \in N_{aF}$, but v has no r-successors, then $\mathfrak{T}'$ contains a new abstract node $x \in V_A$ and the edge $(v, x) \in E$ with $\mathcal{L}(x) = \{C_{\mathcal{T}}\}$ and $\mathcal{L}(v, x) = r$;
- otherwise, i.e., if $r \in N_{aF}$ and v has an r-successor w, rename w to x.

Similarly, for a concrete feature f, the *extension* of $\mathfrak{T}$ with a fresh f-successor x is the tree where:

- if v has no f-successors, then $\mathfrak{T}'$ contains a new concrete node $x \in V_C$ and the edge $(v, x) \in E$ with $\mathcal{L}(v, x) = f$;
- otherwise, i.e., if v has an f-successor w, rename w to x.

Given a feature path $P = a\,f$, the extension of $\mathfrak{T}$ with a fresh P-successor of v is obtained by extending $\mathfrak{T}$ with an a-successor x of v, and an f-successor of x. If at some point the completion system is *saturated*, i.e., no tableau rule is applicable to it, then the algorithm decides satisfiability of C by searching for an obvious contradiction, or clash. The completion system $\mathcal{S} = (\mathfrak{T}, \mathbb{N}, \Sigma)$ contains a *clash* if $\mathbb{N}$ is unsatisfiable or there exist a node $v \in V_A$ and a concept $D \in \mathsf{sub}(C) \cup \mathsf{sub}(C_{\mathcal{T}})$ such that $\{D, \neg D\} \subseteq \mathcal{L}(v)$. Starting from the initial completion system $(\mathfrak{T}_0, \emptyset, \{\underline{1}\})$, the algorithm applies the completion rules in any order until a saturated system $\mathcal{S}$ is found. If $\mathcal{S}$ contains a clash, then the algorithm answers that the concept C is *unsatisfiable* w.r.t. $\mathcal{T}$; otherwise, i.e., if there is no clash in $\mathcal{S}$, then C is *satisfiable*. We show that this tableau algorithm is indeed a decision procedure for concept satisfiability, i.e., we show that it is sound, complete, and terminating.

We first show that the algorithm is sound. To show this, we will construct, given a finite completion system $\mathcal{S} = (\mathfrak{T}, \mathsf{N}, \Sigma)$, a model $\mathcal{I}_{\mathcal{S}}$ of $\mathcal{T}$ that satisfies C. The idea is to use $\mathfrak{T}$ as a template for building this model, and when a blocked node is reached, iterate using copies of the blocking node and its successors. A $\mathfrak{T}$-*chain* is a sequence $\chi = \frac{v_1}{w_1} \cdots \frac{v_n}{w_n}$ such that for every $i, 1 \le i < n, v_i, w_i \in V_A$, $(v_i, w_{i+1}) \in E$, and either (i) v_{i+1} is not blocked and $w_{i+1} = v_{i+1}$, or (ii) v_{i+1} is blocked by w_{i+1}. In this case, we say that $\frac{v_n}{w_n}$ is the *tail* of χ, written $\mathsf{tl}(\chi)$. We also express as $f(\chi)$, for a concrete feature f, the concrete element $f(w)$ where $\mathsf{tl}(\chi) = \frac{v}{w}$. We denote as chains the set of all chains in $\mathfrak{T}$ that start with $\frac{v_0}{v_0}$.

Let $\mathcal{I}_{\mathcal{S}} = (\Delta^{\mathcal{I}_{\mathcal{S}}}, \cdot^{\mathcal{I}_{\mathcal{S}}}, \mathsf{N}_{\mathcal{I}_{\mathcal{S}}})$ be the interpretation where $\Delta^{\mathcal{I}_{\mathcal{S}}} = $ chains, for every $A \in N_C$, $A^{\mathcal{I}_{\mathcal{S}}} = \{\chi \mid \mathsf{tl}(\chi) = \frac{v}{w}, A \in \mathcal{L}(v)\}$, and for every role name $r \in N_R$, $r^{\mathcal{I}_{\mathcal{S}}} = \{(\chi, \chi\frac{v'}{w'}) \mid \mathsf{tl}(\chi) = \frac{v}{w}, (v, w') \in E, \mathcal{L}(v, w') = r, v' \in V_A\}$. The network $\mathsf{N}_{\mathcal{I}_{\mathcal{S}}}$ is defined over the variables $V_{\mathcal{I}_{\mathcal{S}}} = \{f(\chi) \mid \chi \in \text{chains}\}$ and contains all constraints

$$((f_1(\chi_1), f_2(\chi_2)), R, \sigma)$$

where for $i \in \{1, 2\}$:

$$\mathsf{tl}(\chi_i) = \frac{v_i}{w_i}, (f_1(w_1), f_2(w_2), R, \sigma) \in \mathsf{N}, v_i \in V_A.$$

Notice that $\mathcal{I}_{\mathcal{S}}$ is infinite, and also contains an infinite fuzzy *Rel*-network $\mathsf{N}_{\mathcal{I}_{\mathcal{S}}}$. However, this network is built using copies of a satisfiable *Rel*-network N. The patchwork property guarantees that each finite union of these copies remains satisfiable, and hence, by compactness, the whole system is satisfiable. It can thus be shown by induction on the structure of the concepts, and using the properties of ω-admissibility that if $\mathcal{S}$ does not contain a clash, then $\mathcal{I}_{\mathcal{S}}$ is a model of $\mathcal{T}$ and $v_0 \in C^{\mathcal{I}_{\mathcal{S}}}$.

Lemma 8. *Let S be a saturated completion system obtained by application of the tableau rules to $(\mathfrak{T}_0, \emptyset, \{\underline{1}\})$ where $\mathcal{L}(v_0) = \{C, C_{\mathcal{T}}\}$. If S contains no clash then C is satisfiable w.r.t. $\mathcal{T}$.*

Suppose now that C is satisfiable w.r.t. $\mathcal{T}$. To prove that the algorithm is complete, we need to show that it can produce a clash-free completion system $\mathcal{S}$. Since C is satisfiable, there exists a model $\mathcal{I}$ of $\mathcal{T}$ such that $C^{\mathcal{I}} \neq \emptyset$. We use this model to guide the construction of the completion system through rule applications. The idea is to identify, for each node of the tree $\mathfrak{T}$, an element in $\Delta^{\mathcal{I}}$ that will serve as its *pattern*. The root node is associated to an arbitrary element in $C^{\mathcal{I}}$. When the rule requires a non-deterministic choice ($\mathbf{R}_{\sqcup}$) or the insertion of new elements ($\mathbf{R}_{\exists}, \mathbf{R}_{\partial}$), the choice is made based on the properties of the associated node from $\mathcal{I}$. Since $\mathcal{I}$ is a model, the completion system built this way is guaranteed to be clash-free. This is shown using a variant of relatively standard proof techniques for tableau algorithms, see [7,10] for full details.

Lemma 9. *If every saturated completion system obtained by the application of tableau rules to $(\mathfrak{T}_0, \emptyset, \{\underline{1}\})$ contains a clash, then C is not satisfiable w.r.t. $\mathcal{T}$.*

These two lemmas show that the tableau algorithm is sound and complete. The only remaining issue is to show that it terminates on every input, which is a consequence of the following observations. First, every concrete node in the tree $\mathfrak{T}$ is labeled with a set $\mathcal{L}(v) \subseteq \mathsf{sub}(C) \cup \mathsf{sub}(C_\mathcal{T})$. Similarly, every edge is labeled with a role name appearing in C or $C_\mathcal{T}$. Since $\mathsf{sub}(C)$ and $\mathsf{sub}(C_\mathcal{T})$ are both finite, there are finitely many different such labels. Second, the fuzzy Rel-network N only contains constraints of the form $((c_1, c_2), R, \sigma)$ where R and σ appear explicitly in C or $\mathcal{T}$. Hence, there are finitely many pairs (R, σ) appearing in N. Third, every rule application adds at least one concept to the label of a node, or a constraint to N, but never deletes any previous assertions. Thus, to prove termination it suffices to show that the tree $\mathfrak{T}$ has finitely many nodes.

Notice that new nodes are introduced to the tree $\mathfrak{T}$ only through applications of the rules $\mathbf{R}_\exists$ and $\mathbf{R}_\ominus$. Each application of any of these rules adds at most two abstract and at most two concrete nodes. Thus, the number of successors of any node is bounded linearly by the number of existential restrictions in $\mathsf{sub}(C) \cup \mathsf{sub}(C_\mathcal{T})$, which is finite. In other words, $\mathfrak{T}$ has finite branching. As described before, the number of different node labels $\mathcal{L}(v)$ is bounded by the number of sets of subconcepts of C and $C_\mathcal{T}$; call this number n_C. Similarly, each local network $\mathsf{N}(v)$ is finite, bounded by the number n_N of combinations of concrete features f, relations R and membership degrees Σ allowed. It thus follows that every path of length greater than $n_C \cdot n_\mathsf{N}$ must contain at least one directly blocked node. Since the rules $\mathbf{R}_\exists$ and $\mathbf{R}_\ominus$ are only applicable to nodes that are not blocked, the depth of the tree $\mathfrak{T}$ is also finite. Overall, this implies that $\mathfrak{T}$ must be finite, which yields the following result.

Lemma 10. *The tableau algorithm terminates.*

Summarizing, we showed that our tableau algorithm always terminates, is sound and complete for testing whether a concept C is satisfiable w.r.t. a TBox $\mathcal{T}$.

Theorem 11. *The tableau algorithm is a decision procedure for $\mathcal{ALC}(\mathbb{D})$ concept satisfiability.*

Thus, the problem is decidable. A more fine-grained analysis of the bounds used to prove termination reveals that this algorithm applies exponentially many rules, in the worst case, until the completion system is saturated. At this point, the Rel-network N contains exponentially many constraints and needs to be checked for satisfiability. This satisfiability check for the Rel-network is only sufficient for concrete domains that are ω-admissible. Assuming a constant-time oracle for testing N and since the algorithm is non-deterministic, due to $\mathbf{R}_\sqcup$, overall we obtain that concept satisfiability in $\mathcal{ALC}(\mathbb{D})$ is in $\mathrm{NExpTime}$, with an oracle for $\mathbb{D}$. Next, we show that reasoning in $\mathcal{ALC}(\mathbb{D})$ can be reduced to reasoning in $\mathcal{ALC}(\mathcal{D})$ for some, well-chosen (crisp) constraint system $\mathcal{D}$.

4   Translating Fuzzy to Crisp Constraints

The extension of $\mathcal{ALC}$ with fuzzy concrete domains with membership degree sets, which are closed under intersection and negation, is not more expressive than

$\mathcal{ALC}$ with (crisp) concrete domains. To be more precise, for any fuzzy constraint system $\mathbb{D}$ and $\mathcal{ALC}(\mathbb{D})$-TBox $\mathbb{T}$, we can effectively construct a constraint system $\mathbf{D}_{\mathbb{T}}$ and an $\mathcal{ALC}(\mathbf{D}_{\mathbb{T}})$-TBox $\mathcal{T}$ that preserves the consequences of $\mathbb{T}$. In this section, we assume that $\mathbb{D}$ is an arbitrary, but fixed, fuzzy constraint system. Given an $\mathcal{ALC}(\mathbb{D})$-TBox $\mathbb{T}$, let $\Sigma_{\mathbb{T}}$ be the set of all sets $\sigma \subseteq \mathbf{1}$ such that σ appears in $\mathbb{T}$, extended with $\mathbf{1}$. Since $\mathbb{T}$ is finite, so is $\Sigma_{\mathbb{T}}$, and its closure under complementation and intersection $\Lambda_{\mathbb{T}}$. Moreover, the $|\Lambda_{\mathbb{T}}|$ is bounded exponentially by $\Sigma_{\mathbb{T}}$ and is in the worst case exponential on the size of $\mathbb{T}$.

Let $\Pi_{\mathbb{T}}$ be the set of all relation names appearing in $\mathbb{T}$. Obviously, $|\Pi_{\mathbb{T}}|$ is linear in $|\mathbb{T}|$. Finally, let $R_1, \ldots, R_m$ be an arbitrary, but fixed, enumeration of the elements of $\Pi_{\mathbb{T}}$. We define the set of binary relations containing every sequence of length m of elements of $\Lambda_{\mathbb{T}}$ as $\mathsf{Rel} := \{\lambda_1 \cdots \lambda_m \mid \lambda_i \in \Lambda_{\mathbb{T}}, 1 \leq i \leq m\}$. Clearly, Rel has $|\Lambda_{\mathbb{T}}|^m$ relation names.

Intuitively, the relation $\lambda_1 \cdots \lambda_m$ is interpreted to include all the pairs (a, b) of elements of the constraint model such that $R_i(a, b) \in \lambda_i$, for all i, $1 \leq i \leq m$. That is, each of these relations describes, in a crisp manner, the degrees to which the pair belongs to all the relevant fuzzy relations. Following this intuition, we denote as $\sigma^{(i)}$ the relation in Rel that has σ in its i-th position, and $\mathbf{1}$ in all other positions. It is interpreted as all pairs of individuals that are related via R_i with a degree in σ, regardless of the degrees associated with the other fuzzy relations.

Our translation function ν maps $\mathcal{ALC}(\mathbb{D})$ concepts to $\mathcal{ALC}(\mathbf{D})$ concepts, such that all consequences from $\mathbb{T}$ are preserved by $\nu(\mathbb{T})$. This translation is defined inductively over the structure of concepts. Let C, D be $\mathcal{ALC}(\mathbb{D})$-concepts and $r \in N_R \cup N_{aF}$, $R_i \in \Pi_{\mathbb{T}}$, $\sigma \in \Lambda_{\mathbb{T}}$, and P_1, P_2 two feature paths, the translation ν of the fuzzy constraint restrictions is defined by:

$$\nu(A) := A \quad \text{for } A \in N_C \cup \{\top, \bot\}, \qquad \nu(\exists r.C) := \exists r.\nu(C),$$
$$\nu(\neg C) := \neg\nu(C), \qquad\qquad\qquad\quad \nu(\forall r.C) := \forall r.\nu(C),$$
$$\nu(C \sqcap D) := \nu(C) \sqcap \nu(D), \qquad \nu(\exists(P_1, P_2, R_i, \sigma)) := \exists(P_1, P_2, \sigma^{(i)}),$$
$$\nu(C \sqcup D) := \nu(C) \sqcup \nu(D) \text{ and} \qquad \nu(\forall(P_1, P_2, R_i, \sigma)) := \forall(P_1, P_2, \sigma^{(i)}).$$

We define $\nu(\mathbb{T}) := \{\nu(C) \sqsubseteq \nu(D) \mid C \sqsubseteq D \in \mathbb{T}\}$. Obviously, this construction preserves all consequences of the original TBox. Additionally, $|\nu(\mathbb{T})|$ is linear in $|\mathbb{T}|$. The main difference is that the crisp constraint system $\mathbf{D}$ obtained has exponentially many more relation functions than $\mathbb{D}$. This is not problematic for reasoning, since the system of constraints is solved by an external oracle. However, it must be noted that these relations are not JEPD as assumed in [7]. To obtain a constraint system satisfying this condition, a rewriting of each concrete domain restriction into a possibly exponential disjunction of restrictions is needed, which causes a blow-up in $|\mathbb{T}|$.

Observe, that the translation presented depends on the specific sets of degrees σ that appear in $\mathbb{T}$. Indeed, to produce one constraint system that can be used for any arbitrary $\mathcal{ALC}(\mathbb{D})$-TBox, we would need to be able to handle arbitrary subsets of $\mathbf{1}$.

5   Conclusions

We introduced the DL $\mathcal{ALC}(\mathbb{D})$ that extends $\mathcal{ALC}$ with fuzzy concrete domain restrictions. These in turn introduce fuzzy relations between elements of the concrete domain, i.e., functions that map tuples of concrete elements to a membership degree in $[0, 1]$. We extended the approach from [7] for regaining decidability of reasoning in the presence of general TBoxes, to the fuzzy setting. The required conditions on the concrete domain are the *patchwork property* and *compactness*, which together yield ω-admissibility. Decidability of concept satisfiability w.r.t. TBoxes is proven by a sound, complete and terminating tableau-based algorithm which builds a finite representation of an infinite tree-like model of the TBox and the concept. We show that this algorithm requires (non-deterministic) exponential time, if the constraint systems can be solved in constant time. Our proofs of correctness depend strongly on the notion of ω-admissibility. Thus, it is an open question whether relaxed conditions would still guarantee decidability.

References

1. Baader, F., Calvanese, D., McGuinness, D., Nardi, D., Patel-Schneider, P.F. (eds.): The Description Logic Handbook: Theory, Implementation, and Applications. Cambridge University Press (2003)
2. Baader, F., Hanschke, P.: A schema for integrating concrete domains into concept languages. In: Proc. of the 12th Int. Joint Conf. on Artificial Intelligence (IJCAI 1991), Sydney, pp. 452–457 (1991)
3. Bobillo, F., Straccia, U.: fuzzydl: An expressive fuzzy description logic reasoner. In: In Proceedings of the IEEE International Conference on Fuzzy Systems (FUZZ-IEEE 2008), pp. 923–930. IEEE (2008)
4. Borgwardt, S., Peñaloza, R.: Undecidability of fuzzy description logics. In: Proceedings of the 13th International Conference on Principles of Knowledge Representation and Reasoning (KR 2012), pp. 232–242. AAAI Press (2012)
5. Glimm, B., Horrocks, I., Motik, B.: Optimized description logic reasoning via core blocking. In: Giesl, J., Hähnle, R. (eds.) IJCAR 2010. LNCS, vol. 6173, pp. 457–471. Springer, Heidelberg (2010)
6. Lutz, C.: Description logics with concrete domains—a survey. In: Advances in Modal Logic 2002 (AiML 2002), Toulouse, France (2002)
7. Lutz, C., Miličić, M.: A Tableau Algorithm for DLs with Concrete Domains and GCIs. Journal of Automated Reasoning 38(1-3), 227–259 (2007)
8. Mailis, T., Peñaloza, R., Turhan, A.-Y.: Conjunctive query answering in finitely-valued fuzzy description logics. In: Kontchakov, R., Mugnier, M.-L. (eds.) RR 2014. LNCS, vol. 8741, pp. 124–139. Springer, Heidelberg (2014)
9. Mailis, T.P., Stoilos, G., Simou, N., Stamou, G.B., Kollias, S.D.: Tractable reasoning with vague knowledge using fuzzy $\mathcal{EL}^{++}$. Journal of Intelligent Information Systems 39(2), 399–440 (2012)
10. Merz, D.: Decidability of reasoning in $\mathcal{ALC}$ with fuzzy concrete domains. Diplomarbeit, Technische Universität Dresden (2013), http://lat.inf.tu-dresden.de/research/mas/
11. Straccia, U.: Description logics with fuzzy concrete domains. In: Proc. of the 21st Conf. in Uncertainty in AI (UAI 2005), pp. 559–567. AUAI Press (2005)

A Stream-Temporal Query Language
for Ontology Based Data Access[*]

Özgür Lütfü Özçep, Ralf Möller, and Christian Neuenstadt

Institute for Softwaresystems (STS)
Hamburg University of Technology
Hamburg, Germany
{oezguer.oezcep,moeller,christian.neuenstadt}@tu-harburg.de

Abstract. The paper contributes to the recent efforts on temporalizing
and streamifiying ontology based data access (OBDA) by discussing aspects of rewritability, i.e., compilability of the TBox into ontology-level
queries, and unfoldability, i.e., transformability of ontology-level queries
to queries on datasource level, for the new query-language framework
STARQL. The distinguishing feature of STARQL is its general stream
windowing and ABox sequencing strategy which allows it to plugin well-
known query languages such as unions of conjunctive queries (UCQs)
in combination with TBox languages such as DL-Lite and do temporal
reasoning with a sorted first-order logic on top of them. The paper discusses safety aspects under which STARQL queries that embed UCQs
over DL-Lite ontologies can be rewritten and unfolded to back-end relational stream query languages such as CQL. With these results, the
adoption of description logic technology in industrially relevant application areas such as industrial monitoring is crucially fostered.

Keywords: streams, OBDA, monitoring, unfolding, safety.

1   Introduction

The work described in this paper is part of recent efforts on streamifiying OBDA
[11,6,17] and, to some extent, also temporalizing OBDA [5,4]. Streams, as potentially infinite sequences of elements, cannot be processed as a whole. Hence
blocking operators such as the classical grouping operator and aggregation operators cannot be applied to it. The simple but fundamental idea of circumventing
this problem is to apply on streams a (small) window the content of which is
updated as new elements from the stream arrive at the query answering system.

Stream window operators play an important role also in the new query language framework STARQL (Streaming and Temporal ontology Access with a
Reasoning-based Query Language, pronounced Star-Q-L, [16,15]). Its framework
character relies on the facts that 1) it can embed queries of various query languages, 2) refer to ontologies in various DL languages, and 3) use a first-order

---

[*] This work has been supported by the European Commission as part of the FP7
project Optique.

C. Lutz and M. Thielscher (Eds.): KI 2014, LNCS 8736, pp. 183–194, 2014.
© Springer International Publishing Switzerland 2014

logic (FOL) fragment for temporal reasoning over ABox sequences constructed within the query. In this paper, we focus on the latter aspect assuming for the first two unions of conjunctive queries (UCQs) w.r.t DL-Lite ontologies.

In STARQL, the idea of processing over windows is pushed further by extending these with sequencing operators that set up at every time point a finite sequence of ABoxes on which temporal reasoning can be applied. STARQL does not assume a stream of ABoxes which hold universally but rather modifies/exploits the given ABox streams to build its own stream of finite ABox sequences. This sequencing strategy, among other things, distinguishes STARQL from the approaches in [11,6,17]. It is a natural addition to the window operators that sets up at every time point a context in which temporal reasoning can be applied.

In this paper, we consider an instantiation of STARQL where Intra-ABox reasoning within sequences is handled by answering UCQs over DL-Lite ontologies w.r.t. the certain answer semantics. Within Inter-ABox reasoning certain answers from the different ABoxes are related and constrained with an outer temporal FOL formula. This is challenging if one allows in the FOL template negation, disjunction and all quantifiers in combination with concrete domains, as these, if not constrained, would immediately lead to infinite sets of answers, in particular w.r.t. concrete domain values.

STARQL uses a new adornment technique for variables to guarantee safeness. We demonstrate the safety mechanism which will guarantee that the FOL template language is domain independent [1] and as such can be rewritten as SQL query. This opens the door for (rewriting and) unfolding STARQL queries into queries of domain independent languages such as the relational stream query language CQL [3]. Based on CQL, practical systems have been developed. Thus, this paper provides the foundation for expressive ODBA stream querying.

2   The STARQL Framework

We describe the syntax and the semantics for a fragment of STARQL, ignoring a.o. macro definitions, aggregators etc. (see [16] for the full version; but note that here we use a different, more SPARQL like syntax). We assume familiarity with the description logic DL-Lite [7].

Our running example for illustration purposes is a measurement scenario in which there is a (possibly virtual) stream S_{Msmt} of ABox assertions. Its initial part, called $S_{Msmt}^{\leq 5s}$ here, contains timestamped ABox assertions giving the value of a temperature sensor s_0 at 6 time points starting with $0s$.

$$S_{Msmt}^{\leq 5s} = \{val(s_0, 90°)\langle 0s\rangle, val(s_0, 93°)\langle 1s\rangle, val(s_0, 94°)\langle 2s\rangle$$
$$val(s_0, 92°)\langle 3s\rangle, val(s_0, 93°)\langle 4s\rangle, val(s_0, 95°)\langle 5s\rangle\}$$

Assume further, that a static ABox contains knowledge on sensors telling, e.g., which sensor is of which type. In particular, let $BurnerTipTempSens(s_0)$ be in the static ABox. Moreover, let there be a pure DL-Lite TBox with additional information such as $BurnerTipTempSens \sqsubseteq TempSens$ saying that all burner tip temperature sensors are temperature sensors.

We want to formalize the following information need: Starting with time point 0s, output every second those temperature sensors whose value grew monotonically in the last 2 seconds. A possible STARQL representation of the information is illustrated in the following listing.

```
CREATE STREAM S_out AS
CREATE PULSE AS START = 0s, FREQUENCE = 1s
CONSTRUCT  GRAPH NOW { ?s rdf:type MonInc }
FROM S_Msmt [NOW-2s, NOW]->1s , STATIC ABOX <http://Astatic>,
        TBOX <http://TBox>
WHERE { ?s rdf:type TempSens }
SEQUENCE BY StdSeq AS SEQ
HAVING FORALL i < j IN SEQ,?x,?y:
  IF (GRAPH i { ?s val ?x }  AND GRAPH j { ?s  val ?y }) THEN
     ?x <= ?y
```

Though the monotonicity condition seems simple, it should be noted that recent approaches for temporal DL-lite logics as that of [5] cannot express it.

Syntax. The example demonstrates much of the syntactical possibilities within STARQL whose grammar is sketched in Fig. 1. The rules for the HAVING clause are not given there but are discussed in more detail in the following sections.

After the create expressions for the stream and the output frequency the queries' main contents are captured by the CONSTRUCT expressions. The head of the construct expression describes the output format of the stream, using the named-graph notation of SPARQL for fixing a basic graph pattern (BGP) and attaching a time expression, here NOW, for the evolving time. The general motivation for this approach is similar to the CONSTRUCT operator in the SPARQL query language. So the actual result in the monotonicity example (in DL notation) is a stream of ABox assertions of the form $MonInc(s_0)\langle t\rangle$.

$$S_{out}^{\leq 5s} = \{MonInc(s_0)\langle 0s\rangle, MonInc(s_0)\langle 1s\rangle, MonInc(s_0)\langle 2s\rangle, MonInc(s_0)\langle 5s\rangle\}$$

Within the WHERE clause one can bind variables w.r.t. the non-streaming sources (ABox, TBox) mentioned in the FROM clause by using (unions) of BGPs. We assume an underlying DL-Lite logic for the static ABox, the TBox and the BGP (considered as unions of conjunctive queries UCQs) which allows for concrete domain values, e.g., DL-Lite$_A$ [7]. In this example, instantiations of the sensors ?s are fixed w.r.t. a static ABox and a TBox given by URIs.

The heart of the STARQL queries is the window operator in combination with the sequencing mechanism. In the example, the operator [NOW-2s, NOW]->1s describes a sliding window operator, which collects the timestamped ABox assertions in the last two seconds and then slides 1s forward in time. Every temporal ABox produced by the window operator is converted to a sequence of (pure) ABoxes. At every time point, one has a sequence of ABoxes on which temporal (state-based) reasoning can be applied. This is realized in STARQL by a sorted

$$createExp \longrightarrow \texttt{CREATE STREAM } name \texttt{ AS } [pulseExp]\ constrExp\ |\ pulseExp$$
$$pulseExp \longrightarrow \texttt{CREATE PULSE AS START } = startTime, \texttt{ FREQUENCE } = freq$$
$$constrExp \longrightarrow \texttt{CONSTRUCT } constrHead(\boldsymbol{x}, \boldsymbol{y})$$
$$\texttt{FROM } listWinStreamExp\ [\ ,\ listOfRessources]$$
$$\texttt{WHERE } whereClause(\boldsymbol{x})$$
$$\texttt{SEQUENCE BY } seqMethod\ [\texttt{HAVING } safeHavingClause(\boldsymbol{x}, \boldsymbol{y})]$$
$$constrHead(\boldsymbol{x}, \boldsymbol{y}) \longrightarrow \texttt{GRAPH } timeExp\ BGP(\boldsymbol{x}, \boldsymbol{y})\ [\ ,\ constrHead]$$
$$listWinStreamExp \longrightarrow (name\ |\ constrExp)windowExp[\ ,\ listWinStreamExp]$$
$$windowExp \longrightarrow \texttt{[} timeExp_1, timeExp_2\ \texttt{]->}sl$$
$$listOfRessources \longrightarrow typedRessourceList[\ ,\ listOfRessources]$$
$$typedRessourceList \longrightarrow \texttt{STATIC ABOX } listofURIstoStaticABoxes\ |$$
$$\texttt{TEMPORAL ABOX } listofURIstoTemporalABoxes\ |$$
$$\texttt{TBOX } listofURIstoTBoxes$$
$$whereClause(\boldsymbol{x}) \longrightarrow \Psi(\boldsymbol{x})\quad (\Psi(\boldsymbol{x})\ \text{a union of BGPs with distinguished variables } \boldsymbol{x})$$
$$seqMethod \longrightarrow StdSeq\ |\ SeqMethod(\sim)$$

Fig. 1. Syntax for STARQL (without HAVING clauses)

first-order logic template in which state stamped UCQs conditions are embedded. We use here again the GRAPH notation from SPARQL. In the example above, the HAVING clause expresses a monotonicity condition stating that for all values $?x$ that are values of sensor $?s$ w.r.t the ith ABox (subgraph) and for all values $?y$ that are values of the same sensor $?s$ w.r.t. the $j^{t}h$ ABox (subgraph), it must be the case that $?x$ is less than or equal to $?y$.

Semantics. STARQL queries have streams of ABox assertions (RDF triples) as input and output. So, the semantics for STARQL has to explicate how the output stream of ABox assertions is computed from the input streams. Using compositionality, the semantics definition for STARQL can be accomplished by defining the semantic denotations for the substructures of the query and then by composing them to the denotation of the whole query. We sketch the semantics of the window operator, of the sequencing, and of the HAVING clause.

A stream of ABox assertions is an infinite set of timestamped ABox assertions of the form $ax\langle t\rangle$. The timestamps stem from a flow of time $(T, \leq)$ where T may even be a dense set and where $\leq$ is a linear order. Let S be a stream name with its denotation $[\![S]\!]$ being such a stream of timestamped ABox assertions. We declare the denotation of the windowed stream $ws = S\ winExp = S\ [timeExp_1, timeExp_2]\texttt{->}sl$ as a stream of temporal ABoxes, where a temporal ABox is a set of timestamped assertions.

Let $\lambda t.g_1(t) = [\![timeExp_1]\!]$ and $\lambda t.g_2(t) = [\![timeExp_2]\!]$ be the functions corresponding to the time expressions. The pulse declaration defines a subset $T' \subseteq T$

of the time domain. T' is the set of timestamps of the stream of temporal ABoxes $[\![ws]\!]$. Let T' be represented by the increasing sequence of timestamps $(t_i)_{i \in \mathbb{N}}$, where t_0 is the starting point fixed in the pulse declaration.

Now, one defines for every t_i the temporal ABox $\tilde{\mathcal{A}}_{t_i}$ such that $(\tilde{\mathcal{A}}_{t_i}, t_i) \in [\![wS]\!]$. If $t_i < sl - 1$, then $\tilde{\mathcal{A}}_{t_i} = \emptyset$. Else set first $t_{start} = \lfloor t_i/sl \rfloor \times sl$ and $t_{end} = max\{t_{start} - (g_2(t_i) - g_1(t_i)), 0\}$, and define on that basis

$$\tilde{\mathcal{A}}_{t_i} = \{(ass, t) \mid (ass, t) \in [\![S]\!] \text{ and } t_{end} \leq t \leq t_{start}\}$$

In our example, $timeExp_1 = NOW - 2s$ (so $[\![timeExp_1]\!] = \lambda t.t - 2$), $timeExp_2 = NOW$ and $sl = 1s$; the example's results for second 4s and 5s are the following.

Time	Temporal ABox
4s	$\{val(s_0, 94°)\langle 2s \rangle, val(s_0, 92°)\langle 3s \rangle, val(s_0, 93°)\langle 4s \rangle\}$
5s	$\{val(s_0, 92°)\langle 3s \rangle, val(s_0, 93°)\langle 4s \rangle, val(s_0, 95°)\langle 5s \rangle\}$

If the STARQL query refers to more than one stream, then these are joined by time-wise union of the temporal ABoxes of the windowed streams, which is possible as the pulse declaration synchronizes all streams of temporal ABoxes.

The stream of temporal ABoxes is the input for the sequencing operator which produces for every time point of the pulse a sequence of (pure) ABoxes. The sequencing methods used in STARQL refer to an equivalence relation $\sim$ to specify which assertions go into the same ABox. The equivalence classes $[x]_\sim$ for $x \in T$ form a partition of T. We restrict the class of admissible equivalence relations to those $\sim$ that respect the time ordering, i.e., the equivalence classes under $\sim$ should be intervals on the time domain.

Now, we define the sequence of ABoxes generated by $seqMethod(\sim)$ on the stream of temporal ABoxes as follows: Let $(\tilde{\mathcal{A}}_t, t)$ be the temporal ABox at t. Let $T' = \{t_1, \ldots, t_l\}$ be the time points occurring in $\tilde{\mathcal{A}}_t$ and let k the number of equivalence classes generated by the time points in T'. Then define the sequence at t as $(\mathcal{A}_0, \ldots, \mathcal{A}_k)$ where for every $i \in \{0, \ldots, k\}$ the pure ABox $\mathcal{A}_i$ is

$$\mathcal{A}_i = \{ax\langle t' \rangle \mid ax\langle t' \rangle \in \tilde{\mathcal{A}}_t \text{ and } t' \text{ in } i^{th} \text{ equivalence class}\}$$

In the example above, the equivalence is the identity (keyword StdSeq for standard sequencing), so that the resulting sequence of ABoxes at time point 5s is trivial as there are no more than two ABox assertions with the same timestamp: $\{val(s_0, 92°)\}\langle 0 \rangle, \{val(s_0, 93°)\}\langle 1 \rangle, \{val(s_0, 95°)\}\langle 2 \rangle$.

STARQL's semantics for the HAVING clauses relies on the certain answer semantics (see [7]) for the embedded UCQs. The idea is to view the tuples in the certain answer sets as members of a sorted FOL structure $\mathcal{I}_t$. Assume that the sequence of ABoxes at some given time point t is $seq = (\mathcal{A}_0, \ldots, \mathcal{A}_k)$. Then the domain of $\mathcal{I}_t$ consists of the index set $\{0, \ldots, k\}$ as well as the set of all individual constants and all value constants of the signature. Now, if the HAVING clause contains, for example, the state tagged condition query $val(s, x)\langle i \rangle$ (with embedded UCQ $val(s, x)$), then we introduce for it a ternary relation symbol R and replace $val(s, x)\langle i \rangle$ by $R(s, x, i)$ in the HAVING clause. This symbol is denoted in $\mathcal{I}_t$ by the certain answers of the embedded query extended with the index i:

$R^{\mathcal{I}_t} = \{(a, b, i) \mid (a, b) \in cert(val(s, x), \mathcal{A}_i \cup \mathcal{A}_{static} \cup \mathcal{T})\}$. Constants are denoted by themselves in $\mathcal{I}_t$. This already fixes a structure $\mathcal{I}_t$ with finite denotations of its relation symbols. The evaluation of the HAVING clause is then nothing more than evaluating the FOL formula (after the substitutions) on the structure $\mathcal{I}_t$.

3   A Safe Fragment for HAVING Clauses

As demonstrated with the monotonicity example, STARQL allows a sorted FOL to reason on the ABox sequences. The semantics for the HAVING clauses rests on the structure $\mathcal{I}_t$ whose domain $\Delta^{\mathcal{I}_t}$ does not consist only of the individual and value constants in the interpretations of the relations, the so called *active domain* according to database terminology [1], but the whole set *Dom* of individual constants, value constants and the indices produced in the sequencing. With a safety mechanism on the HAVING clauses it can be guaranteed that the evaluation of the HAVING clause on the ABox sequence depends only on the active domain, i.e., HAVING clauses are domain independent (d.i.). Formally, a query q is d.i. iff for all interpretations $\mathcal{I}_1, \mathcal{I}_2$ having domains $\Delta^{\mathcal{I}_1}, \Delta^{\mathcal{I}_2} \subseteq Dom$ and identical denotation functions $(\cdot)^{\mathcal{I}_1} = (\cdot)^{\mathcal{I}_2}$, the answers for q in $\mathcal{I}_1$ is the same as the answers for q in $\mathcal{I}_2$. Without a safety mechanism, a HAVING clause of the form $y > 3$, with free concrete domain variable y, would be allowed: the set of bindings for y would be infinite, namely, the set of all real number bigger than 3. In particular, $y > 3$ is not d.i.

Figure 2 contains the grammar for the HAVING clauses with its safety mechanism realized by variable guards/adornments. The safe HAVING clauses (denoted by the start symbol *safeHavingClause*) contain only those variables for individuals that have guard status +. We illustrate the meaning of the rules with Rule (1) for the OR case and then go in more detail w.r.t. adornments.

$$hCl(z^{g^1 \vee g^2}) \longrightarrow hCl(z^{g^1}) \text{ OR } hCl(z^{g^2}) \tag{1}$$

A having clause hCl may be constructed as (produces) a disjunction of two having clauses under some conditions on the variables occurring in them. If during production a clause $hCl(z^g)$ with variables z and some adornment g for them is reached, then Rule (1) justifies the production of $hCl(z^{g^1})$ OR $hCl(z^{g^2})$ if the adornment g can be represented as $g = g^1 \vee g^2$, i.e., if g is the result of applying a function $\vee$ on the adornment lists g^1, g^2.

The adornments $g = g_1, \ldots, g_n$ are lists of guard status g_i (g-status for short), where $g_i \in \{+, -, --, \emptyset\}$. We use z^g as an abbreviation for $z_1^{g_1}, \ldots, z_n^{g_n}$ where $z = z_1, \ldots, z_n$ and $g = g_1, \ldots, g_n$. We assume the ordering $\emptyset \preceq -- \preceq - \preceq +$ on the guards. This ordering is relevant for the calculation of g_{max} in the rule of Fig. 2 where the clause is constructed from an arbitrary clause hCl and an identity atom. The special case of $g_i = \emptyset$ is a convenience notation meaning for $x^{\emptyset}$ that x does not occur at all in the formula.

The meanings of the functions $\neg, \vee, \wedge, \rightarrow$ over vectors of g-status are fixed by the tables in Figure 3. Combinations with the g-status $\emptyset$ is handled in

$$safeHavingClause(\boldsymbol{z}) \longrightarrow hCl(\boldsymbol{z}^+) \quad \text{(for } \boldsymbol{z} \in Var_{val} \cup Var_{ind})$$

$$term(i^+) \longrightarrow i$$

$$term() \longrightarrow \texttt{max} \mid \texttt{0} \mid \texttt{1}$$

$$stateAtom(\boldsymbol{y}^+, i^+) \longrightarrow \Psi(\boldsymbol{x}, \boldsymbol{y}) \texttt{ <i>}$$
$$\text{(for a UCQ } \Psi(\boldsymbol{x}, \boldsymbol{y}) \text{ and}$$
$$\boldsymbol{x} \subseteq X, \boldsymbol{y} \subseteq Var_{ind} \cup Var_{val} \setminus X)$$

$$stateAtom(x^{--}, y^{--}) \longrightarrow x = y \quad \text{(for } y, x \notin X \cup Var_{val})$$

$$stateAtom(x^+) \longrightarrow x = a \mid a = x$$
$$\text{(for } a \in (X \cap Var_{ind}) \cup Const_{const}, \, x \in Var_{ind} \setminus X)$$

$$vAtom(z_1^+) \longrightarrow z_1 = v \mid v = z_1$$
$$\text{(for } z_1 \in Var_{val} \setminus X \text{ and } v \in Const_{val})$$

$$vAtom(z_1^+) \longrightarrow z_1 = z_2 \mid z_2 = z_1$$
$$\text{(for } z_1 \in Var_{val} \setminus X, \text{ and } z_2 \in X \cap Var_{val})$$

$$vAtom(z_1^{--}, z_2^{--}) \longrightarrow z_1 \; op \; z_2$$
$$\text{(for } op \in \{\texttt{<,<=, >, >=, =}\}; z_1, z_2 \in Var_{val} \setminus X)$$

$$vAtom(z_1^{--}) \longrightarrow z_1 \; op \; z_2 \quad \text{(for } op \in \{\texttt{<,<=, >, >=}\}, z_1 \in Var_{val} \setminus X,$$
$$z_2 \in Val_{const} \cup (X \cap Val_{var}))$$

$$stateArithAtom(i_1^{g_1}, i_2^{g_2}) \longrightarrow term_1(i_1^{g_1}) \; op \; term_2(i_2^{g_2})$$
$$\text{(for } op \in \{\texttt{<,<=, =, >, >=}\})$$

$$stateArithAtom(i_1^{g_1}, i_2^{g_2}, i_3^{g_3}) \longrightarrow \texttt{plus}\,(term_1(i_1^{g_1}), term_2(i_2^{g_2}), term_3(i_3^{g_3}))$$

$$hCl(\boldsymbol{z}^g) \longrightarrow stateAtom(\boldsymbol{z}^g) \mid vAtom(\boldsymbol{z}^g) \mid stateArithAtom(\boldsymbol{z}^g)$$

$$hCl(\boldsymbol{z}^{g^1 \vee g^2}) \longrightarrow hCl(\boldsymbol{z}^{g^1}) \; \texttt{OR} \; hCl(\boldsymbol{z}^{g^2})$$

$$hCl(\boldsymbol{z}^{g^1 \wedge g^2}) \longrightarrow hCl(\boldsymbol{z}^{g^1}) \; \texttt{AND} \; hCl(\boldsymbol{z}^{g^2}) \quad \text{(both conjuncts are}$$
$$\text{not of form } x = y \text{ for } x, y \in Var_{ind} \cup Var_{val})$$

$$hCl(z_1^{g_{max}}, z_2^{g_{max}}, \boldsymbol{z_3}^{g_3}) \longrightarrow hCl(z_1^{g_1}, z_2^{g_2}, \boldsymbol{z_3}^{g_3}) \; \texttt{AND} \; z_1^{h_1} = z_2^{h_2}$$
$$\text{(for } g_{max} = max\{g_1, g_2, h_1, h_2\})$$

$$hCl(\boldsymbol{z}^{\neg g}) \longrightarrow \texttt{NOT} \; hCl(\boldsymbol{z}^g)$$

$$hCl(\boldsymbol{z}^{g^1 \rightarrow g^2}) \longrightarrow \texttt{IF} \; hCl(\boldsymbol{z}^{g^1}) \; \texttt{THEN} \; hCl(\boldsymbol{z}^{g^2})$$

$$hCl(\boldsymbol{z}^{g^1 \rightarrow g^2}) \longrightarrow \texttt{FORALL} \; y \; \texttt{IF} \; hCl(\boldsymbol{z}^{g^1}, y^+) \; \texttt{THEN} \; hCl(\boldsymbol{z}^{g^2}, y^g)$$

$$hCl(\boldsymbol{z}^{g^1 \wedge g^2}) \longrightarrow \texttt{EXISTS} \; y \; hCl(\boldsymbol{z}^{g^1}, y^+) \; \texttt{AND} \; hCl(\boldsymbol{z}^{g^2}, y^g)$$

Fig. 2. Grammar for HAVING clauses (the set of variables X is the set of variables that are bounded by the WHERE clause in the STARQL query)

an extra table 3b. So for example, assume that one has produced a HAVING clause $F(x_1^{--}, x_2^{+}, x_3^{-})$, where x_1 has g-status $--$, x_2 has g-status $+$, and x_3 has g-status $-$. Then rule (1) and the tables allow, e.g., the production of $F_1(x_1^{--}, x_2^{+}, x_3^{-})$ OR $F_2(x_1^{+}, x_2^{+}, x_3^{0})$. Let us verify this for the variable x_1: Its g-status $--$ in F_1 and its g-status $+$ in F_2 combines to the g-status $-- = -- \vee +$ in F—according to the entry for the pair $(--, +)$ in the table of $\vee$.

g_1	g_2	$\neg g_1$	$g_1 \wedge g_2$	$g_1 \vee g_2$	$g_1 \to g_2$
$--$	$--$	$--$	$--$	$--$	$--$
$--$	$-$	$--$	$--$	$-$	$-$
$--$	$+$	$--$	$+$	$--$	$--$
$-$	$--$	$+$	$--$	$-$	$--$
$-$	$-$	$+$	$-$	$-$	$-$
$-$	$+$	$+$	$+$	$-$	$+$
$+$	$--$	$-$	$+$	$--$	$-$
$+$	$-$	$-$	$+$	$-$	$-$
$+$	$+$	$-$	$+$	$+$	$-$

g_1	g_2	$g_1 \wedge g_2$	$g_1 \vee g_2$	$g_1 \to g_2$
$--$	$\emptyset$	$--$	$--$	$--$
$-$	$\emptyset$	$-$	$-$	$--$
$+$	$\emptyset$	$+$	$--$	$-$
$\emptyset$	$--$	$--$	$--$	$--$
$\emptyset$	$-$	$-$	$-$	$-$
$\emptyset$	$+$	$+$	$--$	$--$

(a) Variables existent in both subformulas   (b) Variable missing in one subformula

Fig. 3. Combination of Guards

Now, we will show how to transform HAVING clauses to SQL. In particular this shows that the HAVING clause language is d.i. as SQL is d.i.For a formula F let $SRNF(F)$ be the formula in *safe range normal form (SRNF)* [1, S.85] resulting from applying the following normalization steps: Rename variables such that no variable symbol occurrence is bound by different quantifiers and such that no variable occurs bound and free; rewrite IF F THEN G to NOT F OR G; eliminate double negations; rewrite FORALLz with NOT EXISTS z NOT; push NOT through using de Morgan rules. These steps are applied in some order until they cannot be applied anymore. A formula F is said to be in SRNF iff $F = SRNF(F)$.

Domain independence for formulas in SRNF is handled in the literature [1] also by a guard concept. This is realized by a function rr as follows.

1. $rr(r(t_1, \ldots, t_n)) = $ variables in $t_1, \ldots, t_n$.
2. $rr(x \ op \ y) = \emptyset$ for $x, y \in Var_{val}, op \in \{<, >, \leq, \geq\}$
3. $rr(x \ op \ v) = rr(x \ op \ v) = \emptyset$ for $x \in Var_{val}, v \in Const_{val}, op \in \{<, >, \leq, \geq\}$
4. $rr(x = a) = rr(a = x) = \{x\}$ (for $x \in Var, a \in Const$)
5. $rr(F \ \text{AND} \ G) = rr(F) \cup rr(G)$
6. $rr(F \ \text{AND} \ (x = y)) = \begin{cases} rr(F) \cup \{x, y\} & \text{if } rr(F) \cap \{x, y\} \neq \emptyset \\ rr(F) & \text{else} \end{cases}$
7. $rr(F \ \text{OR} \ G) = rr(F) \cap rr(G)$
8. $rr(\text{NOT} \ F) = \emptyset$
9. $rr(\text{EXISTS} \ xF) = \begin{cases} rr(F) \setminus x & \text{if } x \subseteq rr(F) \\ \text{return } \bot & \text{else} \end{cases}$

The definition of rr in [1] are simpler than our adornment technique used in the grammar because of two main reasons: the authors in [1] assume that the formula is already in SRNF form, whereas we do not. Moreover, we define the HAVING clause grammar in the context of the grammar for STARQL queries. So, we have to take care of variables X that are already bounded by the WHERE clause. This leads to many sub-cases in our grammar.

A formula F in SRNF is called *range restricted* iff $free(F) = rr(F)$ and no subformula returns $\perp$. A well-known theorem states that range restricted formulas in SRNF are exactly as expressive as relational algebra—which is known to be d.i. Hence it is well-known that safe range formulas are d.i. (in particular all sets of answers are finite).

Relating our set of g-status with the set of g-status used in [1] leads to the desired theorem.

Theorem 1. *All safe HAVING clauses (considered as queries on the DB $\mathcal{I}_t$ of certain answers within the actual ABox sequence at t) are d.i.*

Let $safehCl(u^+)$ be a safe HAVING clause. Let $safehClNF(u)$ be the formula resulting from applying the SRNF normalization rules. The status of all the guards are not changed by the rules. Now, we see that for all subformulas $G(x^+, y^-, z^{--})$ in $safehClNF(u)$ we have

(*) $rr(G) = x$ (= all variables in G with g-status +)

The proof of (*) is by structural induction on construction of the formula $safehcLNF(u)$. Let $G(x^+, y^-, z^{--})$ be an atomic clause. Then $rr(G) = x$ follows from looking at the adornments of the atomic clauses G in Fig. 2 and checking that only those with g-status + are in $rr(G)$. Hereby, variables $x \in X$, where X is defined in the grammar, are treated as constants in the definition of $rr(\cdot)$. The case of conjunction is clear too as any + g-status combines with any other g-status to +. Now take negation $G = \text{NOT } F(x^+, y^-, z^{--})$. The definition of rr for the negation case says $rr(G) = \emptyset$. Actually we know that F is an atomic formula. Looking at all variables for these formulas in the grammar we see that no one of these as g-status $-$, hence actually $y = \emptyset$ and we have $G(x^-, z^{--})$, so there is no variable in G with g-status +, hence indeed we get that $rr(G) = \emptyset =$ the variables in G with g-status +. The case for disjunction is clear as a positive g-status results for a variable in a disjunction only if both variables exists in the disjuncts and are labelled +. Now the last case is that of the existential quantifier $G = \text{EXISTS } xF(x^+, y^-, z^{--})$. According to induction assumption $rr(F) = x$. G may result from a transformation of an exists subformula $\text{EXISTS } xhCl(x^+, \dots)$ AND F' in $hcl(u^+)$. So the variable x is by definition in the set x of variables in F with g-status +, hence $rr(G) = rr(F) \setminus \{x\}$. But G does not occur as free variable in G, hence the set of variables in G with g-status + is actually x without x, which proves the induction claim. Now G may also result from applying somewhere the rule $\text{FORALL} \equiv \text{NOT EXISTS NOT}$. But again, there is a formula with variables that have g-status + and are bounded by the all quantifier so that one gets again a formula of the form $\text{EXISTS } xhCl(x^+, \dots)$ AND F'.

4   Unfolding STARQL into CQL

Having shown domain independence for the HAVING clause language is the main
step towards using STARQL for OBDA in the classical sense according to which
queries on the ontology level are rewritten and unfolded into queries over the
data source. The general procedure is illustrated below.

```
Input: STARQL Query SQ, Mappings M      Output: CQL query OQ
SQ1 = Rewrite(SQ, TBox(SQ))
SQ2 = SRNF(SQ1)
OQ = Unfold(SQ2, M)
```

Rewriting is done locally w.r.t. every embedded UCQ, using the TBox of the
STARQL query SQ. The result SQ1 is transformed to a query SQ2 in (range-
restricted) SRNF, which can be unfolded to an SQL like streaming language
query OQ. In the following we illustrate the unfolding process into CQL queries.

CQL [3] is one of the early relational stream query languages having served
as a blue print for many stream query languages even on the ontological level
(e.g., [11],[6],[17]). CQL window operators get as input a stream and produce a
temporal relation, which is a function over the time domain T giving for every t
an ordinary (instantaneous) relation R_t. The operator $RStream$ gets a temporal
relation R as input and produces a stream of tuples $d\langle t\rangle$ such that $d \in R_t$.

Following the classical OBDA approach we assume that the streams to which
STARQL refers are produced by mappings. In our example, let be given a
CQL stream of measurements $Msmt$ with schema Msmt(MID, MtimeStamp,
SID, Mval). A mapping takes a CQL query over this stream and produces a
stream of assertions of the form $val(x,y)\langle t\rangle$.

$$val(x,y)\langle z\rangle \longleftarrow \text{SELECT Rstream(f(SID) as x, Mval as y,}$$
$$\text{MtimeStamp as z) FROM Msmt[NOW]}$$

We assume that the STARQL queries use the standard sequencing only, so
that from every state i in the sequence associated with t_{NOW} one can reconstruct
the timestamps of the tuples occurring in the ABox $\mathcal{A}_i$.

The following listing shows the unfolded CQL pendant of the STARQL query.
The outer WHERE clause is the pendant (in SRNF form) of the monotonicity
formula expressed in the HAVING clause.

```
CREATE VIEW windowRelation as
SELECT *   FROM Msmt[RANGE 2s Slide 1s];
SELECT Rstream(sensor, timestamp)
FROM windowRel, sensorRel
WHERE sensorRel.type = ''BurnerTipTempSens'' AND
NOT EXISTS (
 SELECT * FROM
 (SELECT timestamp as i, value as x FROM windowRelation),
 (SELECT timestamp as j, value as y FROM windowRelation)
 WHERE   i < j AND x > y );
```

5   Related Work

Much of the relevant work on stream processing has been done in the context of data stream management systems (DSMSs), mainly with SQL-like stream query languages such as CQL [3] or the ones used in TelegraphCQ [8], Aurora/Borealis [12], or PIPES [14]. Nevertheless, the stream community is far from having a query standard for DSMS (see [13] for some ideas).

First steps towards streamified OBDA are C-SPARQL [11], SPARQLstream [6], and CQELS [17]. These approaches extend SPARQL with a window operator whose content is a multi-set of variable bindings for the open variables in the query. This solution is not without problems. It presupposes mixed interim states in which the constraints/consequences of the ontologies are not accounted for out. In particular, the window operator's forgetfulness w.r.t. time stamps lead to inconsistencies that are not in the input streams.

The semantical foundation of evaluating HAVING clauses is similar to that of [5], one of the recent approaches to temporalizing OBDA. (Another one is [4]). The difference is that [5] uses an LTL based language with embedded CQs not a sorted FOL language. For engineering applications with information needs as in the monotonicity example the LTL framework is not sufficient, as it does not provide existential quantifiers on top of the embedded CQs.

Safety conditions are considered in the classical DB literature [1] but also specifically for temporal DBs [9]. We do not claim novelty w.r.t. safety aspects but only w.r.t. the new adornment technique which directly operates on the FOL formulas without transforming them to some normal form.

Though not directly related to OBDA, other relevant work stems from the field of *complexed event processing*. For example, EP-SPARQL/ETALIS [2] uses also a sequencing constructor; and T-REX with the event specification language TESLA [10] uses an FOL language for identifying patterns.

6   Conclusion

The paper has presented a query framework lying in the intersection of classical OBDA and stream processing. The query language (necessarily) extends the sliding window concepts, which are known from many languages for relational stream data management systems as well as recent systems for RDFS, with ABox sequencing constructors. The advantage of using a sequence based methodology over other approaches are, first, that the sequence sets up a (nearly) standard context in which standard OBDA reasoning services can be applied, and second, that the query language can be equipped with a neat semantics based on the certain answer semantics for pure DL-Lite ABoxes (see [16]).

STARQL's combination of sufficient expressiveness on the conceptual level with high expressiveness w.r.t. arithmetical, and statistical computations as well as event specifications can be implemented in a safe manner in order to reach domain independence. This lays the ground for a complete and correct transformation to streaming query languages on the backend data sources.

References

1. Abiteboul, S., Hull, R., Vianu, V.: Foundations of Databases. Addison-Wesley (1995)
2. Anicic, D., Rudolph, S., Fodor, P., Stojanovic, N.: Stream reasoning and complex event processing in ETALIS. Semantic Web 3(4), 397–407 (2012)
3. Arasu, A., Babu, S., Widom, J.: The CQL continuous query language: semantic foundations and query execution. The VLDB Journal 15, 121–142 (2006)
4. Artale, A., Kontchakov, R., Wolter, F., Zakharyaschev, M.: Temporal description logic for ontology-based data access. In: Proceedings of the Twenty-Third International Joint Conference on Artificial Intelligence, IJCAI 2013, pp. 711–717 (2013)
5. Borgwardt, S., Lippmann, M., Thost, V.: Temporal query answering in the description logic *DL-Lite*. In: Fontaine, P., Ringeissen, C., Schmidt, R.A. (eds.) FroCoS 2013. LNCS, vol. 8152, pp. 165–180. Springer, Heidelberg (2013)
6. Calbimonte, J.P., Jeung, H., Corcho, O., Aberer, K.: Enabling query technologies for the semantic sensor web. Int. J. Semant. Web Inf. Syst. 8(1), 43–63 (2012)
7. Calvanese, D., De Giacomo, G., Lembo, D., Lenzerini, M., Poggi, A., Rodriguez-Muro, M., Rosati, R.: Ontologies and databases: The *DL-Lite* approach. In: Tessaris, S., Franconi, E., Eiter, T., Gutierrez, C., Handschuh, S., Rousset, M.-C., Schmidt, R.A. (eds.) Reasoning Web. LNCS, vol. 5689, pp. 255–356. Springer, Heidelberg (2009)
8. Chandrasekaran, S., Cooper, O., Deshpande, A., Franklin, M.J., Hellerstein, J.M., Hong, W., Krishnamurthy, S., Madden, S., Raman, V., Reiss, F., Shah, M.A.: TelegraphCQ: Continuous dataflow processing for an uncertain world. In: CIDR (2003)
9. Chomicki, J., Toman, D.: Temporal databases. In: Handbook of Temporal Reasoning in Artificial Intelligence, vol. 1, pp. 429–467. Elsevier (2005)
10. Cugola, G., Margara, A.: TESLA: A formally defined event specification language. In: Proceedings of the Fourth ACM International Conference on Distributed Event-Based Systems, DEBS 2010, pp. 50–61. ACM, New York (2010)
11. Della Valle, E., Ceri, S., Barbieri, D.F., Braga, D., Campi, A.: A first step towards stream reasoning. In: Domingue, J., Fensel, D., Traverso, P. (eds.) FIS 2008. LNCS, vol. 5468, pp. 72–81. Springer, Heidelberg (2009)
12. Hwang, J.H., Xing, Y., Çetintemel, U., Zdonik, S.B.: A cooperative, self-configuring high-availability solution for stream processing. In: ICDE, pp. 176–185 (2007)
13. Jain, N., Mishra, S., Srinivasan, A., Gehrke, J., Widom, J., Balakrishnan, H., Çetintemel, U., Cherniack, M., Tibbetts, R., Zdonik, S.: Towards a streaming SQL standard. Proc. VLDB Endow. 1(2), 1379–1390 (2008)
14. Krämer, J., Seeger, B.: Semantics and implementation of continuous sliding window queries over data streams. ACM Trans. Database Syst. 34(1), 1–49 (2009)
15. Özçep, O.L., Möller, R., Neuenstadt, C.: Obda stream access combined with safe first-order temporal reasoning. Techn. report, Hamburg Univ. of Technology (2014)
16. Özçep, Ö.L., Möller, R., Neuenstadt, C., Zheleznyakov, D., Kharlamov, E.: Deliverable D5.1 – a semantics for temporal and stream-based query answering in an OBDA context. Deliverable FP7-318338, EU (October 2013)
17. Le-Phuoc, D., Dao-Tran, M., Parreira, J.X., Hauswirth, M.: A native and adaptive approach for unified processing of linked streams and linked data. In: Aroyo, L., Welty, C., Alani, H., Taylor, J., Bernstein, A., Kagal, L., Noy, N., Blomqvist, E. (eds.) ISWC 2011, Part I. LNCS, vol. 7031, pp. 370–388. Springer, Heidelberg (2011)

Towards Large-Scale Inconsistency Measurement

Matthias Thimm

Institute for Web Science and Technologies
Universität Koblenz-Landau, Germany

Abstract. We investigate the problem of inconsistency measurement on large knowledge bases by considering *stream-based inconsistency measurement*, i. e., we investigate inconsistency measures that cannot consider a knowledge base as a whole but process it within a stream. For that, we present, first, a novel inconsistency measure that is apt to be applied to the streaming case and, second, stream-based approximations for the new and some existing inconsistency measures. We conduct an extensive empirical analysis on the behavior of these inconsistency measures on large knowledge bases, in terms of runtime, accuracy, and scalability. We conclude that for two of these measures, the approximation of the new inconsistency measure and an approximation of the *contension* inconsistency measure, large-scale inconsistency measurement is feasible.

1 Introduction

Inconsistency measurement [1] is a subfield of Knowledge Representation and Reasoning (KR) that is concerned with the quantitative assessment of the severity of inconsistencies in knowledge bases. Consider the following two knowledge bases $\mathcal{K}_1$ and $\mathcal{K}_2$ formalized in propositional logic:

$$\mathcal{K}_1 = \{a, b \vee c, \neg a \wedge \neg b, d\} \qquad \mathcal{K}_2 = \{a, \neg a, b, \neg b\}$$

Both knowledge bases are classically inconsistent as for $\mathcal{K}_1$ we have $\{a, \neg a \wedge \neg b\} \models \bot$ and for $\mathcal{K}_2$ we have, e. g., $\{a, \neg a\} \models \bot$. These inconsistencies render the knowledge bases useless for reasoning if one wants to use classical reasoning techniques. In order to make the knowledge bases useful again, one can either use non-monotonic/paraconsistent reasoning techniques [2,3] or one revises the knowledge bases appropriately to make them consistent [4]. Looking again at the knowledge bases $\mathcal{K}_1$ and $\mathcal{K}_2$ one can observe that the *severity* of their inconsistency is different. In $\mathcal{K}_1$, only two out of four formulas (a and $\neg a \wedge \neg b$) are *participating* in making $\mathcal{K}_1$ inconsistent while for $\mathcal{K}_2$ all formulas contribute to its inconsistency. Furthermore, for $\mathcal{K}_1$ only two propositions (a and b) participate in a conflict and using, e. g., paraconsistent reasoning one could still infer meaningful statements about c and d. For $\mathcal{K}_2$ no such statement can be made. This leads to the assessment that $\mathcal{K}_2$ should be regarded *more* inconsistent than $\mathcal{K}_1$. Inconsistency measures can be used to quantitatively assess the inconsistency of knowledge bases and to provide a guide for how to repair them, cf. [5]. Moreover, they can be used as an analytical tool to assess the quality of knowledge representation. For example, one simple inconsistency measure is to take the number of *minimal inconsistent subsets*

C. Lutz and M. Thielscher (Eds.): KI 2014, LNCS 8736, pp. 195–206, 2014.

(MIs) as an indicator for the inconsistency: the more MIs a knowledge base contains, the more inconsistent it is. For $\mathcal{K}_1$ we have then 1 as its inconsistency value and for $\mathcal{K}_2$ we have 2.

In this paper, we consider the computational problems of inconsistency measurement, particularly with respect to scalable inconsistency measurement on large knowledge bases, as they appear in, e. g., Semantic Web applications. To this end we present a novel inconsistency measure $\mathcal{I}_{hs}$ that approximates the η-inconsistency measure from [6] and is particularly apt to be applied to large knowledge bases. This measure is based on the notion of a *hitting set* which (in our context) is a minimal set of classical interpretations such that every formula of a knowledge base is satisfied by at least one element of the set. In order to investigate the problem of measuring inconsistency in large knowledge bases we also present a stream-based processing framework for inconsistency measurement. More precisely, the contributions of this paper are as follows:

1. We present a novel inconsistency measure $\mathcal{I}_{hs}$ based on hitting sets and show how this measure relates to other measures and, in particular, that it is a simplification of the η-inconsistency measure [6] (Section 3).
2. We formalize a theory of inconsistency measurement in streams and provide approximations of several inconsistency measures for the streaming case (Section 4).
3. We conduct an extensive empirical study on the behavior of those inconsistency measures in terms of runtime, accuracy, and scalability. In particular, we show that the stream variants of $\mathcal{I}_{hs}$ and of the *contension* measure $\mathcal{I}_c$ are effective and accurate for measuring inconsistency in the streaming setting and, therefore, in large knowledge bases (Section 5).

We give necessary preliminaries for propositional logic and inconsistency measurement in Section 2 and conclude the paper with a discussion in Section 6. Proofs of technical results are omitted but can be found in an extended version of this paper[1].

2   Preliminaries

Let At be a propositional signature, i. e., a (finite) set of propositions, and let $\mathcal{L}(\mathsf{At})$ be the corresponding propositional language. We use the symbol $\bot$ to denote contradiction. Then a knowledge base $\mathcal{K}$ is a finite set of formulas $\mathcal{K} \subseteq \mathcal{L}(\mathsf{At})$. Let $\mathbb{K}(\mathsf{At})$ be the set of all knowledge bases. We write $\mathbb{K}$ instead of $\mathbb{K}(\mathsf{At})$ when there is no ambiguity regarding the signature. Semantics to $\mathcal{L}(\mathsf{At})$ is given by *interpretations* $\omega : \mathsf{At} \to \{\mathsf{true}, \mathsf{false}\}$. Let $\mathsf{Int}(\mathsf{At})$ denote the set of all interpretations for At. An interpretation ω *satisfies* (or is a *model* of) an atom $a \in \mathsf{At}$, denoted by $\omega \models a$ (or $\omega \in \mathsf{Mod}(a)$), if and only if $\omega(a) = \mathsf{true}$. Both $\models$ and $\mathsf{Mod}(\cdot)$ are extended to arbitrary formulas, sets, and knowledge bases as usual.

Inconsistency measures are functions $\mathcal{I} : \mathbb{K} \to [0, \infty)$ that aim at assessing the severity of the inconsistency in a knowledge base $\mathcal{K}$, cf. [5]. The basic idea is that the larger the inconsistency in $\mathcal{K}$ the larger the value $\mathcal{I}(\mathcal{K})$. However, inconsistency is a concept that is not easily quantified and there have been a couple of proposals for

---

[1] http://www.mthimm.de/misc/thimm_inc_ki2014_extended.pdf

inconsistency measures so far, see e. g. [6,7,8,1,9,10]. There are two main paradigms for assessing inconsistency [9], the first being based on the (number of) formulas needed to produce inconsistencies and the second being based on the proportion of the language that is affected by the inconsistency. Below we recall some popular measures from both categories but we first introduce some necessary notations. Let $\mathcal{K} \in \mathbb{K}$ be some knowledge base.

Definition 1. *A set $M \subseteq \mathcal{K}$ is called* minimal inconsistent subset *(MI) of $\mathcal{K}$ if $M \models \perp$ and there is no $M' \subset M$ with $M' \models \perp$. Let $\mathsf{MI}(\mathcal{K})$ be the set of all MIs of $\mathcal{K}$.*

Definition 2. *A formula $\alpha \in \mathcal{K}$ is called* free formula *of $\mathcal{K}$ if there is no $M \in \mathsf{MI}(\mathcal{K})$ with $\alpha \in M$. Let $\mathsf{Free}(\mathcal{K})$ denote the set of all free formulas of $\mathcal{K}$.*

We adopt the following definition of a (basic) inconsistency measure from [5].

Definition 3. *A basic inconsistency measure is a function $\mathcal{I} : \mathbb{K} \to [0, \infty)$ that satisfies the following three conditions: 1.) $\mathcal{I}(\mathcal{K}) = 0$ if and only if $\mathcal{K}$ is consistent, 2.) if $\mathcal{K} \subseteq \mathcal{K}'$ then $\mathcal{I}(\mathcal{K}) \leq \mathcal{I}(\mathcal{K}')$, and 3.) for all $\alpha \in \mathsf{Free}(\mathcal{K})$ we have $\mathcal{I}(\mathcal{K}) = \mathcal{I}(\mathcal{K} \setminus \{\alpha\})$.*

For the remainder of this paper we consider the following selection of inconsistency measures: the MI measure $\mathcal{I}_{\mathsf{MI}}$, the MI^c measure $\mathcal{I}_{\mathsf{MI}^c}$, the contension measure $\mathcal{I}_c$, and the η measure $\mathcal{I}_\eta$, which will be defined below, cf. [5,6]. In order to define the contension measure $\mathcal{I}_c$ we need to consider three-valued interpretations for propositional logic [3]. A three-valued interpretation v on At is a function $v : \mathsf{At} \to \{T, F, B\}$ where the values T and F correspond to the classical true and false, respectively. The additional truth value B stands for *both* and is meant to represent a conflicting truth value for a proposition. The function v is extended to arbitrary formulas as shown in Table 1. Then, an interpretation v satisfies a formula α, denoted by $v \models^3 \alpha$ if either $v(\alpha) = T$

Table 1. Truth tables for propositional three-valued logic [3]

$\alpha\ \beta$	$\alpha \wedge \beta$	$\alpha \vee \beta$	$\neg\alpha$	$\alpha\ \beta$	$\alpha \wedge \beta$	$\alpha \vee \beta$	$\neg\alpha$	$\alpha\ \beta$	$\alpha \wedge \beta$	$\alpha \vee \beta$	$\neg\alpha$
T T	T	T	F	B T	B	T	B	F T	F	T	T
T B	B	T	F	B B	B	B	B	F B	F	B	T
T F	F	T	F	B F	F	B	B	F F	F	F	T

or $v(\alpha) = B$.

For defining the η-inconsistency measure [6] we need to consider probability functions P of the form $P : \mathsf{Int}(\mathsf{At}) \to [0, 1]$ with $\sum_{\omega \in \mathsf{Int}(\mathsf{At})} P(\omega) = 1$. Let $\mathcal{P}(\mathsf{At})$ be the set of all those probability functions and for a given probability function $P \in \mathcal{P}(\mathsf{At})$ define the probability of an arbitrary formula α via $P(\alpha) = \sum_{\omega \models \alpha} P(\omega)$.

Definition 4. *Let $\mathcal{I}_{\mathsf{MI}}, \mathcal{I}_{\mathsf{MI}^c}, \mathcal{I}_c,$ and $\mathcal{I}_\eta$ be defined via*

$$\mathcal{I}_{\mathsf{MI}}(\mathcal{K}) = |\mathsf{MI}(\mathcal{K})|, \qquad \mathcal{I}_\eta(\mathcal{K}) = 1 - \max\{\xi \mid \exists P \in \mathcal{P}(\mathsf{At}) : \forall \alpha \in \mathcal{K} : P(\alpha) \geq \xi\},$$

$$\mathcal{I}_{\mathsf{MI}^c}(\mathcal{K}) = \sum_{M \in \mathsf{MI}(\mathcal{K})} \frac{1}{|M|}, \quad \mathcal{I}_c(\mathcal{K}) = \min\{|v^{-1}(B)| \mid v \models^3 \mathcal{K}\}$$

All these measures are basic inconsistency measures as defined in Definition 3.

Example 1. For the knowledge bases $\mathcal{K}_1 = \{a, b \lor c, \neg a \land \neg b, d\}$ and $\mathcal{K}_2 = \{a, \neg a, b, \neg b\}$ from the introduction we obtain $\mathcal{I}_{\mathsf{MI}}(\mathcal{K}_1) = 1$, $\mathcal{I}_{\mathsf{MI}^c}(\mathcal{K}_1) = 0.5$, $\mathcal{I}_c(\mathcal{K}_1) = 2$, $\mathcal{I}_\eta(\mathcal{K}_1) = 0.5$, $\mathcal{I}_{\mathsf{MI}}(\mathcal{K}_2) = 2$, $\mathcal{I}_{\mathsf{MI}^c}(\mathcal{K}_2) = 1$, $\mathcal{I}_c(\mathcal{K}_2) = 2$, $\mathcal{I}_\eta(\mathcal{K}_2) = 0.5$.

For a more detailed introduction to inconsistency measures see e. g. [1,5,6] and for some recent developments see e. g. [8,11].

As for computational complexity, the problem of computing an inconsistency value wrt. any of the above inconsistency measures is at least FNP-hard[2] as it contains a satisfiability problem as a sub problem.

3   An Inconsistency Measure Based on Hitting Sets

The basic idea of our novel inconsistency measure $\mathcal{I}_{hs}$ is inspired by the measure $\mathcal{I}_\eta$ which seeks a probability function that maximizes the probability of all formulas of a knowledge base. Basically, the measure $\mathcal{I}_\eta$ looks for a minimal number of models of parts of the knowledge base and maximizes their probability in order to maximize the probability of the formulas. By just considering this basic idea we arrive at the notion of a *hitting set* for inconsistent knowledge bases.

Definition 5. *A subset $H \subset \mathsf{Int}(\mathsf{At})$ is called a* hitting set *of $\mathcal{K}$ if for every $\alpha \in \mathcal{K}$ there is $\omega \in H$ with $\omega \models \alpha$. H is called a* **card***-minimal hitting set if it is minimal wrt. cardinality. Let $h_{\mathcal{K}}$ be the cardinality of any* **card***-minimal hitting set (define $h_{\mathcal{K}} = \infty$ if there does not exist a hitting set of $\mathcal{K}$).*

Definition 6. *The function $\mathcal{I}_{hs} : \mathbb{K} \to [0, \infty]$ is defined via $\mathcal{I}_{hs}(\mathcal{K}) = h_{\mathcal{K}} - 1$ for every $\mathcal{K} \in \mathbb{K}$.*

Note, that if a knowledge base $\mathcal{K}$ contains a contradictory formula (e. g. $a \land \neg a$) we have $\mathcal{I}_{hs}(\mathcal{K}) = \infty$. In the following, we assume that $\mathcal{K}$ contains no such contradictory formulas.

Example 2. Consider the knowledge base $\mathcal{K}_3$ defined via

$$\mathcal{K}_3 = \{a \lor d, a \land b \land c, b, \neg b \lor \neg a, a \land b \land \neg c, a \land \neg b \land c\}$$

Then $\{\omega_1, \omega_2, \omega_3\} \subset \mathsf{Int}(\mathsf{At})$ with $\omega_1(a) = \omega_1(b) = \omega_1(c) = \mathsf{true}$, $\omega_2(a) = \omega_2(c) = \mathsf{true}$, $\omega_1(b) = \mathsf{false}$, and $\omega_3(a) = \omega_3(b) = \mathsf{true}$, $\omega_3(c) = \mathsf{false}$ is a **card**-minimal hitting set for $\mathcal{K}_3$ and therefore $\mathcal{I}_{hs}(\mathcal{K}_3) = 2$. Note that for the knowledge bases $\mathcal{K}_1$ and $\mathcal{K}_2$ from Example 1 we have $\mathcal{I}_{hs}(\mathcal{K}_1) = \mathcal{I}_{hs}(\mathcal{K}_2) = 1$.

Proposition 1. *The function $\mathcal{I}_{hs}$ is a (basic) inconsistency measure.*

The result below shows that $\mathcal{I}_{hs}$ also behaves well with some more properties mentioned in the literature [9,10]. For that, we denote with $\mathsf{At}(F)$ for a formula or a set of formulas F the set of propositions appearing in F. Furthermore, two knowledge bases $\mathcal{K}_1, \mathcal{K}_2$ are *semi-extensionally equivalent* ($\mathcal{K}_1 \equiv^\sigma \mathcal{K}_2$) if there is a bijection $\sigma : \mathcal{K}_1 \to \mathcal{K}_2$ such that for all $\alpha \in \mathcal{K}_1$ we have $\alpha \equiv \sigma(\alpha)$.

---

[2] FNP is the generalization of the class NP to functional problems.

Proposition 2. *The measure* $\mathcal{I}_{hs}$ *satisfies the following properties:*

- *If* $\alpha \in \mathcal{K}$ *is such that* $\text{At}(\alpha) \cap \text{At}(\mathcal{K} \setminus \{\alpha\}) = \emptyset$ *then* $\mathcal{I}_{hs}(\mathcal{K}) = \mathcal{I}_{hs}(\mathcal{K} \setminus \{\alpha\})$ *(safe formula independence).*
- *If* $\mathcal{K} \equiv^{\sigma} \mathcal{K}'$ *then* $\mathcal{I}_{hs}(\mathcal{K}) = \mathcal{I}_{hs}(\mathcal{K}')$ *(irrelevance of syntax).*
- *If* $\alpha \models \beta$ *and* $\alpha \not\models \bot$ *then* $\mathcal{I}_{hs}(\mathcal{K} \cup \{\alpha\}) \geq \mathcal{I}_{hs}(\mathcal{K} \cup \{\beta\})$ *(dominance).*

The measure $\mathcal{I}_{hs}$ can also be nicely characterized by a consistent *partitioning* of a knowledge base.

Definition 7. *A set* $\Phi = \{\Phi_1, \ldots, \Phi_n\}$ *with* $\Phi_1 \cup \ldots \cup \Phi_n = \mathcal{K}$ *and* $\Phi_i \cap \Phi_j = \emptyset$ *for* $i, j = 1, \ldots, n, i \neq j$, *is called a* partitioning *of* $\mathcal{K}$. *A partitioning* $\Phi = \{\Phi_1, \ldots, \Phi_n\}$ *is consistent if* $\Phi_i \not\models \bot$ *for* $i = 1, \ldots, n$. *A consistent partitioning* Φ *is called* **card**-*minimal if it is minimal wrt. cardinality among all consistent partitionings of* $\mathcal{K}$.

Proposition 3. *A consistent partitioning* Φ *is a* **card**-*minimal partitioning of* $\mathcal{K}$ *if and only if* $\mathcal{I}_{hs}(\mathcal{K}) = |\Phi| - 1$.

As $\mathcal{I}_{hs}$ is inspired by $\mathcal{I}_{\eta}$ we go on by comparing these two measures.

Proposition 4. *Let* $\mathcal{K}$ *be a knowledge base. If* $\infty > \mathcal{I}_{hs}(\mathcal{K}) > 0$ *then*

$$1 - \frac{1}{\mathcal{I}_{hs}(\mathcal{K})} < \mathcal{I}_{\eta}(\mathcal{K}) \leq 1 - \frac{1}{\mathcal{I}_{hs}(\mathcal{K}) + 1}$$

Note that for $\mathcal{I}_{hs}(\mathcal{K}) = 0$ we always have $\mathcal{I}_{\eta}(\mathcal{K}) = 0$ as well, as both are basic inconsistency measures.

Corollary 1. *If* $\mathcal{I}_{\eta}(\mathcal{K}_1) \leq \mathcal{I}_{\eta}(\mathcal{K}_2)$ *then* $\mathcal{I}_{hs}(\mathcal{K}_1) \leq \mathcal{I}_{hs}(\mathcal{K}_2)$.

However, the measures $\mathcal{I}_{\eta}$ and $\mathcal{I}_{hs}$ are not equivalent as the following example shows.

Example 3. Consider the knowledge bases $\mathcal{K}_1 = \{a, \neg a\}$ and $\mathcal{K}_2 = \{a, b, \neg a \vee \neg b\}$. Then we have $\mathcal{I}_{hs}(\mathcal{K}_1) = \mathcal{I}_{hs}(\mathcal{K}_2) = 1$ but $\mathcal{I}_{\eta}(\mathcal{K}_1) = 0.5 > 1/3 = \mathcal{I}_{\eta}(\mathcal{K}_2)$.

It follows that the order among knowledge bases induced by $\mathcal{I}_{\eta}$ is a refinement of the order induced by $\mathcal{I}_{hs}$. However, $\mathcal{I}_{hs}$ is better suited for approximation in large knowledge bases than $\mathcal{I}_{\eta}$, cf. the following section.

The idea underlying $\mathcal{I}_{hs}$ is also similar to the contension inconsistency measure $\mathcal{I}_c$. However, these measures are not equivalent as the following example shows.

Example 4. Consider the knowledge bases $\mathcal{K}_1 = \{a \wedge b \wedge c, \neg a \wedge \neg b \wedge \neg c\}$ and $\mathcal{K}_2 = \{a \wedge b, \neg a \wedge b, a \wedge \neg b\}$. Then we have $\mathcal{I}_{hs}(\mathcal{K}_1) = 2 < 3 = \mathcal{I}_{hs}(\mathcal{K}_2)$ but $\mathcal{I}_c(\mathcal{K}_1) = 3 > 2 = \mathcal{I}_c(\mathcal{K}_2)$.

4 Inconsistency Measurement in Streams

In the following, we discuss the problem of inconsistency measurement in large knowledge bases. We address this issue by using a stream-based approach of accessing the formulas of a large knowledge base. Formulas of a knowledge base then need to be processed one by one by a stream-based inconsistency measure. The goal of this formalization is to obtain stream-based inconsistency measures that approximate given inconsistency measures when the latter would have been applied to the knowledge base as a whole. We first formalize this setting and, afterwards, provide concrete approaches for some inconsistency measures.

4.1 Problem Formalization

We use a very simple formalization of a stream that is sufficient for our needs.

Definition 8. *A* propositional stream $\mathcal{S}$ *is a function* $\mathcal{S} : \mathbb{N} \to \mathcal{L}(\text{At})$. *Let* $\mathbb{S}$ *be the set of all propositional streams.*

A propositional stream models a sequence of propositional formulas. On a wider scope, a propositional stream can also be interpreted as a very general abstraction of the output of a linked open data crawler (such as LDSpider [12]) that crawls knowledge formalized as RDF *(Resource Description Framework)* from the web, enriched, e. g. with OWL semantics. We model large knowledge bases by propositional streams that indefinitely repeat the formulas of the knowledge base. For that, we assume for a knowledge base $\mathcal{K} = \{\phi_1, \dots, \phi_n\}$ the existence of a *canonical enumeration* $\mathcal{K}^c = \langle \phi_1, \dots, \phi_n \rangle$ of the elements of $\mathcal{K}$. This enumeration can be arbitrary and has no specific meaning other than to enumerate the elements in an unambiguous way.

Definition 9. *Let* $\mathcal{K}$ *be a knowledge base and* $\mathcal{K}^c = \langle \phi_1, \dots, \phi_n \rangle$ *its canonical enumeration. The* $\mathcal{K}$-*stream* $\mathcal{S}_\mathcal{K}$ *is defined as* $\mathcal{S}_\mathcal{K}(i) = \phi_{(i \bmod n)+1}$ *for all* $i \in \mathbb{N}$.

Given a $\mathcal{K}$-stream $\mathcal{S}_\mathcal{K}$ and an inconsistency measure $\mathcal{I}$ we aim at defining a method that processes the elements of $\mathcal{S}_\mathcal{K}$ one by one and approximates $\mathcal{I}(\mathcal{K})$.

Definition 10. *A* stream-based inconsistency measure $\mathcal{J}$ *is a function* $\mathcal{J} : \mathbb{S} \times \mathbb{N} \to [0, \infty)$.

Definition 11. *Let* $\mathcal{I}$ *be an inconsistency measure and* $\mathcal{J}$ *a stream-based inconsistency measure. Then* $\mathcal{J}$ approximates *(or is an approximation of)* $\mathcal{I}$ *if for all* $\mathcal{K} \in \mathbb{K}$ *we have* $\lim_{i \to \infty} \mathcal{J}(\mathcal{S}_\mathcal{K}, i) = \mathcal{I}(\mathcal{K})$.

4.2 A Naive Window-Based Approach

The simplest form of implementing a stream-based variant of any algorithm or function is to use a window-based approach, i. e., to consider at any time point a specific excerpt from the stream and apply the original algorithm or function on this excerpt. For any propositional stream $\mathcal{S}$ let $\mathcal{S}^{i,j}$ (for $i \leq j$) be the knowledge base obtained by taking the formulas from $\mathcal{S}$ between positions i and j, i. e., $\mathcal{S}^{i,j} = \{\mathcal{S}(i), \dots, \mathcal{S}(j)\}$.

Definition 12. *Let* $\mathcal{I}$ *be an inconsistency measure,* $w \in \mathbb{N} \cup \{\infty\}$, *and* g *some function* $g : [0, \infty) \times [0, \infty) \to [0, \infty)$ *with* $g(x, y) \in [\min\{x, y\}, \max\{x, y\}]$. *We define the naive window-based measure* $\mathcal{J}_\mathcal{I}^{w,g} : \mathbb{S} \times \mathbb{N} \to [0, \infty)$ *via*

$$\mathcal{J}_\mathcal{I}^{w,g}(\mathcal{S}, i) = \begin{cases} 0 & \textit{if } i = 0 \\ g(\mathcal{I}(\mathcal{S}^{\max\{0, i-w\}, i}), \mathcal{J}_\mathcal{I}^{w,g}(\mathcal{S}, i - 1)) & \textit{otherwise} \end{cases}$$

for every $\mathcal{S}$ *and* $i \in \mathbb{N}$.

The function g in the above definition is supposed to be an aggregation function that combines the new obtained inconsistency value $\mathcal{I}(\mathcal{S}_\mathcal{K}^{\max\{0, i-w\}, i})$ with the previous value $\mathcal{J}_\mathcal{I}^{w,g}(\mathcal{S}, i - 1)$. This function can be, e. g., the maximum function max or a smoothing function $g_\alpha(x, y) = \alpha x + (1 - \alpha)y$ for some $\alpha \in [0, 1]$ (for every $x, y \in [0, \infty)$).

Proposition 5. *Let $\mathcal{I}$ be an inconsistency measure, $w \in \mathbb{N} \cup \{\infty\}$, and g some function $g : [0, \infty) \times [0, \infty) \to [0, \infty)$ with $g(x, y) \in [\min\{x, y\}, \max\{x, y\}]$.*

1. *If w is finite then $\mathcal{J}_{\mathcal{I}}^{w,g}$ is* not *an approximation of $\mathcal{I}$.*
2. *If $w = \infty$ and $g(x, y) > \min\{x, y\}$ if $x \neq y$ then $\mathcal{J}_{\mathcal{I}}^{w,g}$ is an approximation of $\mathcal{I}$.*
3. *$\mathcal{J}_{\mathcal{I}}^{w,g}(\mathcal{S}_{\mathcal{K}}, i) \leq \mathcal{I}(\mathcal{K})$ for every $\mathcal{K} \in \mathbb{K}$ and $i \in \mathbb{N}$.*

4.3 Approximation Algorithms for $\mathcal{I}_{hs}$ and $\mathcal{I}_c$

The approximation algorithms for $\mathcal{I}_{hs}$ and $\mathcal{I}_c$ that are presented in this subsection are using concepts of the programming paradigms of *simulated annealing* and *genetic programming* [13]. Both algorithms follow the same idea and we will only formalize the one for $\mathcal{I}_{hs}$ and give some hints on how to adapt it for $\mathcal{I}_c$.

The basic idea for the stream-based approximation of $\mathcal{I}_{hs}$ is as follows. At any processing step we maintain a candidate set $C \in 2^{\mathsf{Int}(\mathsf{At})}$ (initialized with the empty set) that approximates a hitting set of the underlying knowledge base. At the beginning of a processing step we make a random choice (with decreasing probability the more formulas we already encountered) whether to remove some element of C. This action ensures that C does not contain superfluous elements. Afterwards we check whether there is still an interpretation in C that satisfies the currently encountered formula. If this is not the case we add some random model of the formula to C. Finally, we update the previously computed inconsistency value with $|C| - 1$, taking also some aggregation function g (as for the naive window-based approach) into account. In order to increase the probability of successfully finding a minimal hitting set we do not maintain a single candidate set C but a (multi-)set $Cand = \{C_1, \ldots, C_m\}$ for some previously specified parameter $m \in \mathbb{N}$ and use the average size of these candidate hitting sets.

Definition 13. *Let $m \in \mathbb{N}$, g some function $g : [0, \infty) \times [0, \infty) \to [0, \infty)$ with $g(x, y) \in [\min\{x, y\}, \max\{x, y\}]$, and $f : \mathbb{N} \to [0, 1]$ some monotonically decreasing function with $\lim_{n \to \infty} f(n) = 0$. We define $\mathcal{J}_{hs}^{m,g,f}$ via*

$$\mathcal{J}_{hs}^{m,g,f}(\mathcal{S}, i) = \begin{cases} 0 & \text{if } i = 0 \\ \mathtt{update}_{hs}^{m,g,f}(\mathcal{S}(i)) & \text{otherwise} \end{cases}$$

for every $\mathcal{S}$ and $i \in \mathbb{N}$. The function $\mathtt{update}_{hs}^{m,g,f}$ is depicted in Algorithm 1.

At the first call of the algorithm $\mathtt{update}_{hs}^{m,g,f}$ the value of *currentValue* (which contains the currently estimated inconsistency value) is initialized to 0 and the (mulit-)set $Cand \subseteq 2^{\mathsf{Int}(\mathsf{At})}$ (which contains a population of candidate hitting sets) is initialized with m empty sets. The function f can be any monotonically decreasing function with $\lim_{n \to \infty} f(n) = 0$ (this ensures that at any candidate C reaches some stable result). The parameter m increases the probability that at least one of the candidate hitting sets attains the global optimum of a **card**-minimal hitting set.

As $\mathcal{J}_{hs}^{m,g,f}$ is a random process we cannot show that $\mathcal{J}_{hs}^{m,g,f}$ is an approximation of $\mathcal{I}_{hs}$ in the general case. However, we can give the following result.

Proposition 6. *For every probability $p \in [0, 1)$, g some function $g : [0, \infty) \times [0, \infty) \to [0, \infty)$ with $g(x, y) \in [\min\{x, y\}, \max\{x, y\}]$ and $g(x, y) > \min\{x, y\}$ if $x \neq y$, a monotonically decreasing function $f : \mathbb{N} \to [0, 1]$ with $\lim_{n \to \infty} f(n) = 0$, and*

Algorithm 1 update$_{hs}^{m,g,f}(form)$

1: Initialize $currentValue$ and $Cand$
2: $N = N + 1$
3: $newValue = 0$
4: **for all** $C \in Cand$ **do**
5:      $rand \in [0, 1]$
6:      **if** $rand < f(N)$ **then**
7:          Remove some random ω from C
8:      **if** $\neg \exists \omega \in C : \omega \models form$ **then**
9:          Add random $\omega \in \mathsf{Mod}(form)$ to C
10:      $newValue = newValue + (|C| - 1)/|Cand|$
11: $currentValue = g(newValue, currentValue)$
12: **return** $currentValue$

$\mathcal{K} \in \mathbb{K}$ *there is* $m \in \mathbb{N}$ *such that with probability greater or equal* p *it is the case that* $\lim_{i \to \infty} \mathcal{J}_{hs}^{m,g,f}(\mathcal{S}_\mathcal{K}, i) = \mathcal{I}_{hs}(\mathcal{K})$.

This result states that $\mathcal{J}_{hs}^{m,g,f}$ indeed approximates $\mathcal{I}_{hs}$ if we choose the number of populations large enough. In the next section we will provide some empirical evidence that even for small values of m results are satisfactory.

Both Definition 13 and Algorithm 1 can be modified slightly in order to approximate $\mathcal{I}_c$ instead of $\mathcal{I}_{hs}$, yielding a new measure $\mathcal{J}_c^{m,g,f}$. For that, the set of candidates $Cand$ contains three-valued interpretations instead of sets of classical interpretations. In line 7, we do not remove an interpretation from C but flip some arbitrary proposition from B to T or F. Similarly, in line 9 we do not add an interpretation but flip some propositions to B in order to satisfy the new formula. Finally, the inconsistency value is determined by taking the number of B-valued propositions. For more details see the implementations of both $\mathcal{J}_{hs}^{m,g,f}$ and $\mathcal{J}_c^{m,g,f}$, which will also be discussed in the next section.

5   Empirical Evaluation

In this section we describe our empirical experiments on runtime, accuracy, and scalability of some stream-based inconsistency measures. Our **Java** implementations[3] have been added to the *Tweety Libraries for Knowledge Representation* [14].

5.1   Evaluated Approaches and Experiment Setup

For our evaluation, we considered the inconsistency measures $\mathcal{I}_{\mathsf{MI}}$, $\mathcal{I}_{\mathsf{MI}^c}$, $\mathcal{I}_\eta$, $\mathcal{I}_c$, and $\mathcal{I}_{hs}$. We used the SAT solver *lingeling*[4] for the sub-problems of determining consis-

---

[3] $\mathcal{I}_{\mathsf{MI}}, \mathcal{I}_{\mathsf{MI}^c}, \mathcal{I}_\eta, \mathcal{J}_\mathcal{I}^{w,g}$: http://mthimm.de/r?r=tweety-inc-commons
$\mathcal{I}_c, \mathcal{I}_{hs}$: http://mthimm.de/r?r=tweety-inc-pl
$\mathcal{J}_{hs}^{m,g,f}$: http://mthimm.de/r?r=tweety-stream-hs
$\mathcal{J}_c^{m,g,f}$: http://mthimm.de/r?r=tweety-stream-c
Evaluation framework: http://mthimm.de/r?r=tweety-stream-eval
[4] http://fmv.jku.at/lingeling/

Table 2. Runtimes for the evaluated measures; each value is averaged over 100 random knowledge bases of 5000 formulas; the total runtime is after 40000 iterations

Measure	RT (iteration)	RT (total)	Measure	RT (iteration)	RT (total)
$\mathcal{J}_{\mathcal{I}_{MI}}^{500,max}$	198ms	133m	$\mathcal{J}_{c}^{10,g_{0.75},f_1}$	0.16ms	6.406s
$\mathcal{J}_{\mathcal{I}_{MI}}^{1000,max}$	359ms	240m	$\mathcal{J}_{c}^{100,g_{0.75},f_1}$	1.1ms	43.632s
$\mathcal{J}_{\mathcal{I}_{MI}}^{2000,max}$	14703ms	9812m	$\mathcal{J}_{c}^{500,g_{0.75},f_1}$	5.21ms	208.422s
$\mathcal{J}_{\mathcal{I}_{MI^c}}^{500,max}$	198ms	134m	$\mathcal{J}_{hs}^{10,g_{0.75},f_1}$	0.07ms	2.788s
$\mathcal{J}_{\mathcal{I}_{MI^c}}^{1000,max}$	361ms	241m	$\mathcal{J}_{hs}^{100,g_{0.75},f_1}$	0.24ms	9.679s
$\mathcal{J}_{\mathcal{I}_{MI^c}}^{2000,max}$	14812ms	9874m	$\mathcal{J}_{hs}^{500,g_{0.75},f_1}$	1.02ms	40.614s

tency and to compute a model of a formula. For enumerating the set of MIs of a knowledge base (as required by $\mathcal{I}_{MI}$ and $\mathcal{I}_{MI^c}$) we used MARCO[5]. The measure $\mathcal{I}_\eta$ was implemented using the linear optimization solver *lp_solve*[6]. The measures $\mathcal{I}_{MI}$, $\mathcal{I}_{MI^c}$, and $\mathcal{I}_\eta$ were used to define three different versions of the naive window-based measure $\mathcal{J}_{\mathcal{I}}^{w,g}$ (with $w = 500, 1000, 2000$ and $g = $ max). For the measures $\mathcal{I}_c$ and $\mathcal{I}_{hs}$ we tested each three versions of their streaming variants $\mathcal{J}_c^{m,g_{0.75},f_1}$ and $\mathcal{J}_{hs}^{m,g_{0.75},f_1}$ (with $m = 10, 100, 500$) with $f_1 : \mathbb{N} \rightarrow [0,1]$ defined via $f_1(i) = 1/(i+1)$ for all $i \in \mathbb{N}$ and $g_{0.75}$ is the smoothing function for $\alpha = 0.75$ as defined in the previous section.

For measuring the runtime of the different approaches we generated 100 random knowledge bases in CNF (*Conjunctive Normal Form*) with each 5000 formulas (=disjunctions) and 30 propositions. For each generated knowledge base $\mathcal{K}$ we considered its $\mathcal{K}$-stream and processing of the stream was aborted after 40000 iterations. We fed the $\mathcal{K}$-stream to each of the evaluated stream-based inconsistency measures and measured the average runtime per iteration and the total runtime. For each iteration, we set a time-out of 2 minutes and aborted processing of the stream completely if a time-out occurred.

In order to measure accuracy, for each of the considered approaches we generated another 100 random knowledge bases with specifically set inconsistency values[7], used otherwise the same settings as above, and measured the returned inconsistency values.

To evaluate the scalability of our stream-based approach of $\mathcal{I}_{hs}$ we conducted a third experiment[8] where we fixed the number of propositions (60) and the specifically set inconsistency value (200) and varied the size of the knowledge bases from 5000 to 50000 (with steps of 5000 formulas). We measured the total runtime up to the point when the inconsistency value was within a tolerance of ± 1 of the expected inconsistency value.

The experiments were conducted on a server with two Intel Xeon X5550 QuadCore (2.67 GHz) processors with 8 GB RAM running SUSE Linux 2.6.

---

[5] http://sun.iwu.edu/~mliffito/marco/

[6] http://lpsolve.sourceforge.net

[7] The sampling algorithms can be found at http://mthimm.de/r?r=tweety-sampler

[8] We did the same experiment with our stream-based approach of $\mathcal{I}_c$ but do not report the results due to the similarity to $\mathcal{I}_{hs}$ and space restrictions.

5.2 Results

Our first observation concerns the inconsistency measure $\mathcal{I}_\eta$ which proved to be not suitable to work on large knowledge bases[9]. Computing the value $\mathcal{I}_\eta(\mathcal{K})$ for some knowledge base $\mathcal{K}$ includes solving a linear optimization problem over a number of variables which is (in the worst-case) exponential in the number of propositions of the signature. In our setting with $|At| = 30$ the generated optimization problem contained therefore $2^{30} = 1073741824$ variables. Hence, even the optimization problem itself could not be constructed within the timeout of 2 minutes for every step. As we are not aware of any more efficient implementation of $\mathcal{I}_\eta$, we will not report on further results for $\mathcal{I}_\eta$ in the following.

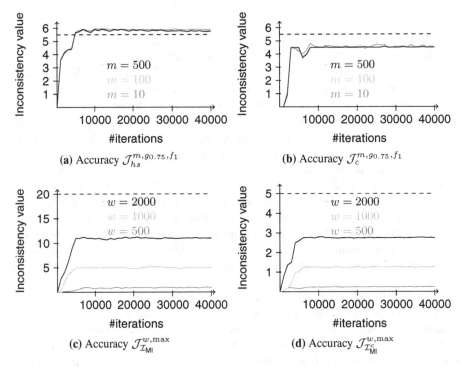

Fig. 1. Accuracy performance for the evaluated measures (dashed line is actual inconsistency value); each value is averaged over 100 random knowledge bases of 5000 formulas (30 propositions) with varying inconsistency values

As for the runtime of the naive window-based approaches of $\mathcal{I}_{MI}$ and $\mathcal{I}_{MI^c}$ and our stream-based approaches for $\mathcal{I}_c$ and $\mathcal{I}_{hs}$ see Table 2. There one can see that $\mathcal{J}_{\mathcal{I}_{MI}}^{w,g}$ and $\mathcal{J}_{\mathcal{I}_{MI^c}}^{w,g}$ on the one hand, and $\mathcal{J}_c^{m,g,f}$ and $\mathcal{J}_{hs}^{m,g,f}$ on the other hand, have comparable runtimes, respectively. The former two have almost identical runtimes, which is obvious as the determination of the MIs is the main problem in both their computations. Clearly,

---

[9] More precisely, our implementation of the measure proved to be not suitable for this setting

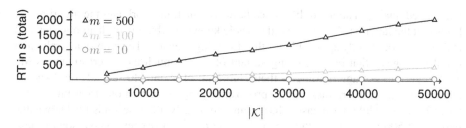

Fig. 2. Evaluation of the scalability of $\mathcal{J}_{hs}^{m,g_{0.75},f_1}$; each value is averaged over 10 random knowledge bases of the given size

$\mathcal{J}_c^{m,g,f}$ and $\mathcal{J}_{hs}^{m,g,f}$ are significantly faster per iteration (and in total) than $\mathcal{J}_{\mathcal{I}_{MI}}^{w,g}$ and $\mathcal{J}_{\mathcal{I}_{MI^c}}^{w,g}$, only very few milliseconds for the latter and several hundreds and thousands of milliseconds for the former (for all variants of m and w). The impact of increasing w for $\mathcal{J}_c^{m,g,f}$ and $\mathcal{J}_{hs}^{m,g,f}$ is expectedly linear while the impact of increasing the window size w for $\mathcal{J}_{\mathcal{I}_{MI}}^{w,g}$ and $\mathcal{J}_{\mathcal{I}_{MI^c}}^{w,g}$ is exponential (this is also clear as both solve an FNP-hard problem).

As for the accuracy of the different approaches see Figure 1. There one can see that both $\mathcal{J}_{hs}^{m,g,f}$ and $\mathcal{J}_c^{m,g,f}$ (Figures 1a and 1b) converge quite quickly (almost right after the knowledge base has been processed once) into a $[-1, 1]$ interval around the actual inconsistency value, where $\mathcal{J}_c^{m,g,f}$ is even closer to it. The naive window-based approaches (Figures 1c and 1d) have a comparable bad performance (this is clear as those approaches cannot *see* all MIs at any iteration due to the limited window size). Surprisingly, the impact of larger values of m for $\mathcal{J}_{hs}^{m,g,f}$ and $\mathcal{J}_c^{m,g,f}$ is rather small in terms of accuracy which suggests that the random process of our algorithm is quite robust. Even for $m = 10$ the results are quite satisfactory.

As for the scalability of $\mathcal{J}_{hs}^{m,g_{0.75},f_1}$ see Figure 2. There one can observe a linear increase in the runtime of all variants wrt. the size of the knowledge base. Furthermore, the difference between the variants is also linearly in the parameter m (which is also clear as each population is an independent random process). It is noteworthy, that the average runtime for $\mathcal{J}_{hs}^{10,g_{0.75},f_1}$ is about 66.1 seconds for knowledge bases with 50000 formulas. As the significance of the parameter m for the accuracy is also only marginal, the measure $\mathcal{J}_{hs}^{10,g_{0.75},f_1}$ is clearly an effective and accurate stream-based inconsistency measure.

6   Discussion and Conclusion

In this paper we discussed the issue of large-scale inconsistency measurement and proposed novel approximation algorithms that are effective for the streaming case. To the best of our knowledge, the computational issues for measuring inconsistency, in particular with respect to scalability problems, have not yet been addressed in the literature before. One exception is the work by Ma and colleagues [7] who present an anytime algorithm that approximates an inconsistency measure based on a 4-valued paraconsistent logic (similar to the contension inconsistency measure). The algorithm provides lower and upper bounds for this measure and can be stopped at any point in time with some guaranteed quality. The main difference between our framework and the algorithm of [7] is that the latter needs to process the whole knowledge base in each atomic step and is therefore not directly applicable for the streaming scenario. The empirical evaluation [7] also suggests that our streaming variant of $\mathcal{I}_{hs}$ is much more performant as Ma et al. report an average runtime of their algorithm of about 240 seconds on a knowledge base with 120 formulas and 20 propositions (no evaluation on larger knowledge bases is given) while our measure has a runtime of only a few seconds for knowledge bases with 5000 formulas with comparable accuracy[10]. A deeper comparison of these different approaches is planned for future work.

Our work showed that inconsistency measurement is not only a theoretical field but can actually be applied to problems of reasonable size. In particular, our stream-based approaches of $\mathcal{I}_{hs}$ and $\mathcal{I}_c$ are accurate and effective for measuring inconsistencies in large knowledge bases. Current and future work is about the application of our work on linked open data sets [12].

References

1. Grant, J., Hunter, A.: Measuring inconsistency in knowledgebases. Journal of Intelligent Information Systems 27, 159–184 (2006)
2. Makinson, D.: Bridges from Classical to Nonmonotonic Logic. College Publications (2005)
3. Priest, G.: Logic of Paradox. Journal of Philosophical Logic 8, 219–241 (1979)
4. Hansson, S.O.: A Textbook of Belief Dynamics. Kluwer Academic Publishers (2001)
5. Grant, J., Hunter, A.: Measuring consistency gain and information loss in stepwise inconsistency resolution. In: Liu, W. (ed.) ECSQARU 2011. LNCS, vol. 6717, pp. 362–373. Springer, Heidelberg (2011)
6. Knight, K.M.: A Theory of Inconsistency. PhD thesis, University of Manchester (2002)
7. Ma, Y., Qi, G., Xiao, G., Hitzler, P., Lin, Z.: An anytime algorithm for computing inconsistency measurement. In: Karagiannis, D., Jin, Z. (eds.) KSEM 2009. LNCS, vol. 5914, pp. 29–40. Springer, Heidelberg (2009)
8. Grant, J., Hunter, A.: Distance-Based Measures of Inconsistency. In: van der Gaag, L.C. (ed.) ECSQARU 2013. LNCS, vol. 7958, pp. 230–241. Springer, Heidelberg (2013)
9. Hunter, A., Konieczny, S.: On the measure of conflicts: Shapley inconsistency values. Artificial Intelligence 174(14), 1007–1026 (2010)
10. Thimm, M.: Inconsistency measures for probabilistic logics. Artificial Intelligence 197, 1–24 (2013)
11. Jabbour, S., Ma, Y., Raddaoui, B.: Inconsistency measurement thanks to mus decomposition. In: Proc. of the 13th Int. Conference on Autonomous Agents and Multiagent Systems (2014)
12. Isele, R., Umbrich, J., Bizer, C., Harth, A.: LDSpider: An open-source crawling framework for the web of linked data. In: Proceedings of 9th International Semantic Web Conference (ISWC 2010) Posters and Demos (2010)
13. Lawrence, D.: Genetic Algorithms and Simulated Annealing. Pitman Publishing (1987)
14. Thimm, M.: Tweety - A Comprehensive Collection of Java Libraries for Logical Aspects of Artificial Intelligence and Knowledge Representation. In: Proceedings of the 14th Int. Conference on Principles of Knowledge Representation and Reasoning, KR 2014 (2014)

---

[10] Although hardware specifications for these experiments are different this huge difference is significant.

On the Scope of Qualitative Constraint Calculi

Matthias Westphal, Julien Hué, and Stefan Wölfl

Department of Computer Science, University of Freiburg,
Georges-Köhler-Allee 52, 79110 Freiburg, Germany
{westpham,hue,woelfl}@informatik.uni-freiburg.de

Abstract. A central notion in qualitative spatial and temporal reasoning is the concept of qualitative constraint calculus, which captures a particular paradigm of representing and reasoning about spatial and temporal knowledge. The concept, informally used in the research community for a long time, was formally defined by Ligozat and Renz in 2004 as a special kind of relation algebra — thus emphasizing a particular type of reasoning about binary constraints. Although the concept is known to be limited it has prevailed in the community. In this paper we revisit the concept, contrast it with alternative approaches, and analyze general properties. Our results indicate that the concept of qualitative constraint calculus is both too narrow and too general: it disallows different approaches, but its setup already enables arbitrarily hard problems.

1 Introduction

The research area of qualitative spatial and temporal reasoning considers reasoning about qualitative descriptions of space and time. For example, in the case of linear time one can abstract from concrete time points by restricting a formal language to the set of binary relations *before*, *equals*, and *after*. This disallows specifying exact time points of events, but expresses the relations between them.

Ligozat and Renz [1] generalized on examples of finite relation algebras to form a definition of what constitutes a qualitative constraint calculus. Often research focuses on their algebraic properties (e.g. [2, 3]). The unique feature of these calculi was supposed to be their underlying domains, which are usually infinite (e.g. time and space) rather than finite as often assumed in the context of constraint satisfaction. At first glance, such a demarcation sounds plausible, but there are approaches to constraint satisfaction not limited to finite domains by employing model-theoretical concepts of first-order (FO) logic (e.g. [4–6]).

Qualitative calculi are based on abstractions by means of so-called partition schemes which induce relation algebras. However, each partition scheme can easily be conceived of as a relational structure. Considering FO sentences over this structure gives a well-defined satisfiability problem without committing to a particular reasoning approach. Thus one can consider alternatives such as, e.g., FO theories, rule-based approaches, or structure-specific algorithms.

In this paper we revisit the definition of qualitative constraint calculi. The aim is to provide an analysis and formal comparison to relation algebras, relational structures, and constraint satisfaction. In doing so, we show that almost

C. Lutz and M. Thielscher (Eds.): KI 2014, LNCS 8736, pp. 207–218, 2014.

any constraint problem can be defined using finite partition schemes. Moreover, we point out that there are no guarantees of calculi having good properties and show a central theorem by Renz and Ligozat to be incorrect. Finally, for each qualitative calculus we define a unique FO structure that gives proper FO semantics.

2   Preliminaries

We assume the reader is familiar with the basics of FO logic. The following definitions are well-known in the literature, e.g. Hodges' book "Model Theory" [7].

A *relational signature* σ is a set of relation symbols each with an associated arity $n \in \mathbb{N}$. All signatures herein are at most countable. For a relational signature $\sigma = \{R_1, \dots\}$ a *relational σ-structure* Γ is a tuple $\langle D \, ; R_1^\Gamma, \dots \rangle$ where D is the domain of the structure and R_i^Γ is the interpretation of the symbol R_i, i.e., $R_i^\Gamma \subseteq D^n$ for an n-ary R_i. When the interpretation of symbols is clear from context, we often simply write the structure as $\langle D \, ; R_1, \dots \rangle$. By $\bar{a}$ we denote a tuple $a_1, \dots, a_n$. A *homomorphism* h from Γ to a σ-structure Γ', written $h \colon \Gamma \to \Gamma'$, is a map from D^Γ to $D^{\Gamma'}$ that satisfies $\bar{a} \in R^\Gamma \Rightarrow (h(a_1), \dots, h(a_n)) \in R^{\Gamma'}$ for each relation symbol $R \in \sigma$. An *embedding* of Γ in Γ' is an injective homomorphism $e \colon \Gamma \to \Gamma'$ that satisfies $\bar{a} \in R^\Gamma \Leftrightarrow (e(a_1), \dots, e(a_n)) \in R^{\Gamma'}$ for each relation symbol $R \in \sigma$. Although we focus on relational structures, we also work with *algebraic structures*, which simply are structures built on *function* and *constant* symbols instead of relation symbols. Here the structure assigns to each constant symbol an element of the domain, and to each n-ary function symbol an n-ary function $f \colon D^n \to D$.

A FO σ-formula is a formula using only FO logic symbols and symbols in σ. Sentences are formulas without free variables. A FO formula is *primitive positive* (short pp) if it is purely conjunctive with at most existential quantification. An n-ary relation $X \subseteq D^n$ is *pp definable* in Γ iff there exists a pp σ-formula $\varphi(\bar{x})$ with free variables $\bar{x} = x_1, \dots, x_n$ such that $X = \{ \bar{a} \mid \Gamma \models \varphi(\bar{a}) \}$.

A structure is *finite* if its domain D is finite (analogously for *infinite* and *countable*). A special kind of structures are ω-categorical structures. A countable structure Γ is *ω-categorical* (or countably categorical) iff for each $n \in \mathbb{N}, n \geq 1$ there exist only finitely many inequivalent FO formulas with n free variables over Γ.

Let σ, σ' be two relational signatures and $d \in \mathbb{N}, d \geq 1$. A *$d$-dimensional syntactic interpretation* π of σ' in σ is defined by (i) a FO σ-formula (the *domain formula*) $\partial_\pi(x_1, \dots, x_d)$ with d free variables and (ii) a map assigning to each relation symbol $R \in \sigma'$ of arity n a FO σ-formula (the *defining formula*) $\varphi_\pi(R)(\bar{x}_1, \dots, \bar{x}_n)$ where the $\bar{x}_i$ are disjoint d-tuples of distinct variables.

Let Γ' be a relational σ'-structure and Γ be a relational σ-structure. We say that Γ' has a *d-dimensional FO interpretation* in Γ if there is a d-dimensional syntactic interpretation π of σ' in σ and a surjective map $f_\pi \colon \partial_\pi(\Gamma^d) \to D^{\Gamma'}$ (the *coordinate map*) such that for each $R \in \sigma'$ of some arity n and all d-tuples $\bar{a}_i \in \partial_\pi(\Gamma^d)$ it holds $\Gamma' \models R(f_\pi(\bar{a}_1), \dots, f_\pi(\bar{a}_n)) \Leftrightarrow \Gamma \models \varphi_\pi(R)(\bar{a}_1, \dots, \bar{a}_n)$.

A fundamental theorem in this context is the *reduction theorem* and its associated *reduction map* [7]: For any FO σ'-formula $\psi(x_1, \ldots, x_n)$ there exists an inductively defined FO σ-formula $\varphi_\pi(\psi)(\overline{x}_1, \ldots, \overline{x}_n)$ such that for all d-tuples $\overline{a}_i \in \partial_\pi(\Gamma^d)$ it holds

$$\Gamma' \models \psi\big(f_\pi(\overline{a}_1), \ldots, f_\pi(\overline{a}_n)\big) \iff \Gamma \models \varphi_\pi(\psi)(\overline{a}_1, \ldots, \overline{a}_n).$$

For our purposes it suffices to note that given a syntactic interpretation the reduction map yields pp formulas if the syntactic interpretation consists of pp formulas only and that it only polynomially increases the size of a formula.

2.1 Constraint Satisfaction Problems

Let Γ be a relational structure with signature σ. The problem of deciding the satisfiability of any given pp σ-sentence ψ in Γ, i.e., to test whether $\Gamma \models \psi$, is called the *constraint satisfaction problem for Γ*. We denote it by CSP(Γ). In this context Γ is often called a *constraint language*. For $\psi = \exists \overline{x}\, \varphi(\overline{x})$ with a quantifier-free φ, we call φ an instance of CSP(Γ). A *solution* of the instance is a map $h: \{x_1, \ldots, x_n\} \to D^\Gamma$ that satisfies the formula φ in Γ. This is equivalent to reading φ as a finite relational σ-structure I on domain $D^I = \{x_1, \ldots, x_n\}$ and h as a homomorphism $h: I \to \Gamma$ (see e.g. [6]).

Example 1 ([4]). The constraint language

$$\Gamma := \big\langle\, \mathbb{Z}\,;\, \big\{\, (x,y,z) \in \mathbb{Z}^3 \,\big|\, x+y+z = 1 \,\big\},\, \big\{\, (x,y,z) \in \mathbb{Z}^3 \,\big|\, x \cdot y = z \,\big\} \,\big\rangle$$

has an *undecidable* CSP(Γ) as it allows to formulate diophantine equations.

2.2 From Boolean Algebras to Relation Algebras

A *Boolean algebra* $\mathcal{B}$ is an algebraic structure $\langle\, B\,;\, \wedge, \vee, -, 0, 1\,\rangle$ on the domain B with two binary functions $\wedge, \vee$ (*conjunction* and *disjunction*), a unary function $-$ (*negation*) and distinguished constants $0, 1 \in B$ (*zero* and *universal* elements). The functions $\wedge$ and $\vee$ are associative and commutative, and $\wedge$ distributes over $\vee$ and vice-versa. For each $a \in B$: $a \vee 0 = a$, $a \wedge 1 = a$, and $a \wedge -a = 0$, $a \vee -a = 1$. The *Boolean ordering* $\leq$ on B is defined by $a \leq b$ iff $a \vee b = b$. An *atom* a of $\mathcal{B}$ is a non-zero element that is $\leq$-minimal. A Boolean algebra $\mathcal{B}$ is *atomic* if for every non-zero element b there exists an atom a such that $a \leq b$. The *set of all atoms of $\mathcal{B}$* is denoted by At($\mathcal{B}$).

Simple examples of Boolean algebras are given by algebras of sets. In fact, any Boolean algebra is isomorphic to one given by a *field of sets*. A *representation of a Boolean algebra* is a pair (D, i) where i is maps each element of the algebra to subsets of D such that i is isomorphic with regard to the functions of the algebra. An expansion of Boolean algebras are relation algebras.

A *weakly associative relation algebra* (short WA) [8] $\mathcal{A}$ is an algebraic structure $\langle\, A\,;\, \wedge, \vee, -, 0, 1, \mathrm{id}, \diamond, \cdot^{-1}\,\rangle$ where id is a constant (*identity*), $\diamond$ is a binary function (*composition*), $\cdot^{-1}$ is a unary function (*converse*), such that its reduct

$\diamond$	id	$R_{\neq}$
id	id	$R_{\neq}$
$R_{\neq}$	$R_{\neq}$	1

$\cdot^{-1}$	
id	id
$R_{\neq}$	$R_{\neq}$

Fig. 1. Composition and converse function of the relation algebra in Example 2

$\langle A\,;\wedge,\vee,-,0,1\rangle$ is a Boolean algebra, and the structure satisfies the following axioms for all $a,b,c \in A$: $\mathrm{id}\diamond a = a\diamond\mathrm{id} = a$, $\left(a^{-1}\right)^{-1} = a$, $(a\vee b)^{-1} = a^{-1}\vee b^{-1}$, $(-a)^{-1} = -(a^{-1})$, $a\diamond(b\vee c) = (a\diamond b)\vee(a\diamond c)$, $(a\diamond b)^{-1} = b^{-1}\diamond a^{-1}$, $(a\diamond b)\wedge c^{-1} = 0$ iff $(b\diamond c)\wedge a^{-1} = 0$, and *weak associativity* $(\mathrm{id}\wedge a)\diamond(1\diamond 1) = \left((\mathrm{id}\wedge a)\diamond 1\right)\diamond 1$.

A WA $\mathcal{A}$ is *integral* if the identity is an atom, and *associative* if composition is associative. Further $\mathcal{A}$ is called *atomic* if its Boolean algebra is atomic — in this case the atoms of $\mathcal{A}$ are simply the atoms of its Boolean algebra. Note, if a relation algebra is finite it is atomic and further all its operations are completely determined by the operations on its atoms.

In the context of WAs a *representation* is a map i from the elements of the algebra to *binary* relations over a domain D such that i is isomorphic with respect to the algebra's functions. Note, any WA that has a representation is associative. Unlike Boolean algebras, it is not even the case that every finite associative relation algebra has a representation (see e.g. [9]).

Example 2. The relation algebra $\mathcal{A} := \langle A\,;\wedge,\vee,-,0,1,\mathrm{id},\diamond,\cdot^{-1}\rangle$ on domain $A := \{0,\mathrm{id},R_{\neq},1\}$ with functions as in Fig. 1 is atomic and integral. A representation over $D := \{a,b,c\}$ is given by $i(\mathrm{id}) = \{(a,a),(b,b),(c,c)\}, i(R_{\neq}) = D^2 \setminus i(\mathrm{id})$.

We recall a convenient way of defining WAs by expanding Boolean algebras. The definition is in principle the same as the "notion of consistency" in the sense of Hodkinson [10], but we restrict ourselves to finite algebras. Let $\mathcal{B}$ be a finite Boolean algebra on domain B. A *notion of consistency* for $\mathcal{B}$ is a triple $\langle\mathrm{id},\cdot^{-1},\mathcal{T}\rangle$ consisting of an element $\mathrm{id}\in B$, a Boolean algebra automorphism $\cdot^{-1}$ of $\mathcal{B}$ satisfying (i) $\mathrm{id}^{-1} = \mathrm{id}$, (ii) $\left(a^{-1}\right)^{-1} = a$ for all $a\in B$, and a set $\mathcal{T}\subseteq B^3$ of "inconsistent triangles" satisfying the following axioms:

- for all pairs of elements $a,b \in B$ it holds $(a,b,\mathrm{id})\in\mathcal{T}$ iff $a\wedge b^{-1} = 0$,
- for each $(a,b,c)\in\mathcal{T}$ it holds $(b,c^{-1},a^{-1})\in\mathcal{T}$ and $(c,b^{-1},a)\in\mathcal{T}$, and
- for each set of elements $A\subseteq B$ and pair of elements $a,c\in B$ it holds $(a,\bigvee A,c)\in\mathcal{T}$ iff $(a,b,c)\in\mathcal{T}$ for each $b\in A$.

According to Hodkinson: Given a notion of consistency $\langle\mathrm{id},\cdot^{-1},\mathcal{T}\rangle$ for some finite Boolean algebra $\mathcal{B} = \langle B\,;\wedge,\vee,-,0,1\rangle$ where id is an atom, we can define $l_{a,b} := \{c\in B\mid(a,b,c)\in\mathcal{T}\}$ and if $\bigvee l_{a,b}$ exists, then $a\diamond b := -(\bigvee l_{a,b})$ yields a weakly associative composition function. Together with $\cdot^{-1},\mathrm{id}$ this forms a WA.

Example 3. Consider the finite Boolean algebra $\mathcal{B}$ on domain B with atoms $\{\mathrm{id},R,S,R',S'\}$ and composition and converse on atoms as given in Fig. 2. This is an integral WA as $(R\diamond R')\diamond S = \mathrm{id}\diamond S = S\neq 0 = R\diamond 0 = R\diamond(R'\diamond S)$.

$\diamond$	id	R	R'	S	S'
id	id	R	R'	S	S'
R	R	0	id	0	0
R'	R'	id	0	0	0
S	S	0	0	0	id
S'	S'	0	0	id	0

$\cdot^{-1}$	
id	id
R	R'
R'	R
S	S'
S'	S

Fig. 2. Composition and converse functions on atoms for Example 3

We close with an observation discussed by Hodkinson. For a given Boolean algebra $\mathcal{B}$ on an at most countable domain B with a representation (D, i), we can define a relational signature σ_B denoting the elements of B such that $\Gamma :=$ $\langle D \, ; \sigma_B \rangle$ is a relational structure with $b^\Gamma := i(b)$ for each $b \in B$. The same can be applied to Boolean algebra reducts of WAs. In particular if the Boolean algebra has a representation on D^2, a structure with binary relations on D can be defined.

3   Qualitative Constraint Calculi

We define the framework of qualitative constraint calculi [1]. For the sake of simplicity, we give the definition in the terminology we have introduced so far. The only minor difference to [1] is that we restrict ourselves to finite algebras.

A *finite partition scheme* Γ is a relational structure on some domain D with a finite signature σ consisting only of binary relation symbols, such that (1) each relation symbol has a non-empty interpretation, (2) D^2 is the disjoint union of all relations, (3) the relations are closed under converse (i.e., for each $R_i \in \sigma$ there exists an $R_j \in \sigma$ such that $R_i(x, y) \equiv R_j(y, x)$ in Γ), and (4) one of the relations is the identity on D^2. Due to property (2) partition schemes are called jointly exhaustive and pairwise disjoint.

Every finite partition scheme Γ with signature $\{R_1, \ldots, R_k\}$ induces a finite Boolean algebra $\mathcal{B}$ on atoms $\{R_1, \ldots, R_k\}$. As the algebra consists of all disjunctions of atoms, a representation of the algebra is given by an expansion of Γ, denoted by $\Gamma_\vee$, to all elements of the algebra. Naturally, here we have for each symbol S of $\Gamma_\vee$ with $S = \bigvee_{i \in I} R_i$ that $S^{\Gamma_\vee} = \bigcup_{i \in I} R_i^\Gamma$.

A *qualitative constraint calculus* (QCC) is the finite integral WA $\mathcal{A}$ given by $\mathcal{B}$ and the "notion of consistency" defined by the identity in Γ, the converse operation on relations, and the following set of inconsistent triangles

$$\mathcal{T} := \big\{ (R, S, T) \in \mathcal{B}^3 \, \big| \, \Gamma_\vee \not\models \exists xyz \big(R(x, y) \wedge S(y, z) \wedge T(x, z) \big) \big\}.$$

We note that by construction these calculi are atomic and weakly associative (the latter property was not observed by Ligozat and Renz). Further, Ligozat and Renz define QCC as the tuple $(\mathcal{A}, \Gamma)$ — we here differentiate between the two to have one symbolic and one semantic object. This enables a clear distinction between symbolic and semantic level, but has otherwise no bearing on the presented material.

The definition of QCC does not require them to be induced by a partition scheme with an *infinite* domain. Arguably we do not have to resort to abstract algebras if the original structure is finite. However, it is easy to construct examples from finite cases. Note here, for each such example, we can easily produce an example based on a partition scheme with infinite domain by using the direct product of the given QCC with a simple one defined on an infinite domain (consider $\langle \mathbb{N}; =, \neq \rangle$) — the resulting QCC can be conceived of as being induced by the direct product of their partition schemes which then has an infinite domain.

The term calculus here refers to the operations of the algebra. In standard mathematical notation these are rules of the form

$$\frac{R(x,y)}{R^{-1}(y,x)} \qquad \frac{\begin{array}{c} R(x,y) \\ S(x,y) \end{array}}{(R \wedge S)(x,y)} \qquad \frac{\begin{array}{c} R(x,z) \\ S(z,y) \end{array}}{(R \diamond S)(x,y)}$$

which allows for deriving new facts. Consider as our input an instance I on the same signature: as it is primitive positive, it is a set of facts. With the rules new facts can be deduced until a fixpoint is reached. If $0(x,y)$ is derived for some pair of variables x, y, then we know the instance is unsatisfiable. This is usually achieved with the help of a *path consistency* algorithm, e.g. PC2 [11], which has a time complexity $O(n^3)$ where n is the number of variables in the instance.

Instances where $0(x,y)$ is not derived for any pair x, y are those that are *consistent* with regard to the calculus — they adhere to the "notion of consistency".[1] Note, this is *not* the same as being satisfiable or k-consistent. For a QCC $\mathcal{A}$ induced by a finite partition scheme Γ, it is common to say that $\mathcal{A}$ solves $\mathrm{CSP}(\Gamma)$ iff the consistent instances of $\mathrm{CSP}(\Gamma)$ are exactly the satisfiable ones.

Which instances satisfy the "notion of consistency"? Primarily we consider the most refined structures, the so-called atomic networks [9].[2]

A *partial atomic network* over $\mathcal{A}$ is a relational structure N on a finite domain V with a binary signature denoting the atoms of $\mathcal{A}$ such that the following conditions are satisfied for all $a, b, c \in V$:

- If for some symbol $R \in \mathrm{At}\,(\mathcal{A})$ it holds $(a,b) \in R^N$, then there is no distinct $R' \in \mathrm{At}\,(\mathcal{A})$ such that $(a,b) \in R'^N$. We write $N(a,b)$ for this (unique) relation symbol R.
- $N(a,a)$ exists and $N(a,a) \leq \mathrm{id}$.
- If $N(a,b)$ exists, then $N(b,a)$ exists.
- If $N(a,b)$, $N(b,c)$, and $N(a,c)$ exist, then $N(a,c) \leq N(a,b) \diamond N(b,c)$.

A (complete) *atomic network* is then a partial atomic network where for each tuple $(a,b) \in V$, $N(a,b)$ exists, i.e., there is a symbol R with $(a,b) \in R^N$.

---

[1] Unlike previous work (e.g. [9, 12]), we strictly differentiate between consistency wrt. to given calculus rules and satisfiability in Γ.

[2] Note, there are different notions of networks in the literature. Here, we restrict ourselves to networks on atomic relations that are already *consistent* wrt. the calculus.

For a given WA $\mathcal{A}$, we denote by $\text{Net}(\mathcal{A})$ the class of all finite atomic networks and by $\text{PNet}(\mathcal{A})$ the class of all partial finite atomic networks. Clearly, we have $\text{Net}(\mathcal{A}) \subsetneq \text{PNet}(\mathcal{A})$. We introduce some standard FO terminology for these classes as also considered by Hirsch and Hodkinson [9]. Let K be a class of relational structures. We say that K has the

- *Joint embedding property* (JEP), if for all $A, B \in K$ there exists a C such that A and B embed into C;
- *Amalgamation property* (AP), if for all $A, B, C \in K$ and embeddings $e \colon A \to B$ and $f \colon A \to C$, there exists an $X \in K$ with embeddings $g \colon B \to X$ and $h \colon C \to X$ such that $g \circ e = h \circ f$.

From Hirsch and Hodkinson we know that both $\text{Net}(\mathcal{A})$ and $\text{PNet}(\mathcal{A})$ are closed under substructures and here AP always implies JEP (we allow the empty network). Further, $\text{PNet}(\mathcal{A})$ trivially has JEP and AP.

Both JEP and AP can be motivated by practical questions: Given an instance that consists of disjoint subproblems can you glue their solutions? Can you make use of the instance's graph structure for faster reasoning (e.g. [5])?

4   Properties of Qualitative Constraint Calculi

In this section we take a look at QCC from the viewpoint of relation algebras and the CSP. Given the setting of infinite domains, QCC prove here to be a limited framework. We are not aware that the results discussed here have been explicitly pointed out before.

4.1   QCC and WAs

In the previous section we have stated that, by construction, every QCC is a finite integral WA. Observe, that the converse does not hold as not every finite integral WA can be obtained from a partition scheme.

Proposition 1. *The class of qualitative constraint calculi QCC is a proper subclass of the class of finite integral weakly associative relation algebras.*

Proof (idea). To show proper parthood consider the algebra $\mathcal{A}$ in Example 3. Assuming $\mathcal{A} \in \text{QCC}$, its Boolean algebra must have a representation as an expansion $\Gamma_\vee$ of a finite partition scheme which supports the notion of consistency. A proof by contradiction shows that $\Gamma_\vee$ does not exist.

The fact that each QCC is integral can be detrimental as is shown next.

Example 4. Let $\mathcal{A}$ be the QCC induced by the partition scheme $\langle \{0,1\}; <,=,> \rangle$. We observe that $\mathcal{A}$ is not associative, as $(< \diamond <) \diamond >$ is equal to the zero element, but $< \diamond (< \diamond >)$ is $<$. Clearly, the calculus has no representation. Further, $\text{Net}(\mathcal{A})$ does not have the AP. For example, the instance $b = b$ embeds into both $a = a < b = b$ and $b = b < c = c$, but there is no large network that accommodates both as it would contain a part $a' < b = b < c'$ for some a', c' where composition would derive the zero element.

However, splitting $=$ into two atoms $=_0, =_1$ results in a non-integral associative relation algebra $\mathcal{A}'$ on atoms $\{ <, =_0, =_1, > \}$ where $\mathrm{Net}(\mathcal{A}')$ has the AP. A representation of $\mathcal{A}'$ is given by the intended structure Γ' on $D^{\Gamma'} := \{0,1\}$: $<^{\Gamma'} := \{(0,1)\}$, $=_0^{\Gamma'} := \{(0,0)\}$, etc. Yet, $\mathcal{A}'$ is not a QCC as it is not integral.

We just showed that the notion of QCC is too narrow within the general theory of WAs. Altogether, QCC being defined amongst integral WAs seems overly restrictive in many aspects.

4.2   Relation to CSPs

So far we have seen QCC as an abstraction on finite partition schemes that form algebras. If we use the algebras for reasoning complete atomic networks are the most-refined relational structures that are consistent with regard to the calculus operations. For a QCC $\mathcal{A}$ induced by a finite partition scheme Γ the networks in $\mathrm{Net}(\mathcal{A})$ can all be conceived of as instances of $\mathrm{CSP}(\Gamma)$. The (old) important question is whether all instances in $\mathrm{Net}(\mathcal{A})$ are indeed satisfiable in Γ. In general, the answer is known to be negative (see e.g. [9] for relation algebras). We start by revisiting the calculus given in Example 4.

Example 4 (continued). Let Γ be the partition scheme $\langle \{0,1\}; <, =, > \rangle$ and $\mathcal{A}$ be the QCC induced by Γ. Then every structure in $\mathrm{Net}(\mathcal{A})$ homomorphically maps to Γ. To prove this, we can define an equivalence relation $\sim$ on elements of a structure $I \in \mathrm{Net}(\mathcal{A})$ by $v \sim w$ iff $(v, w) \in =^I$ (as in e.g. [9]). If there were more than two equivalence classes, composition would derive the zero element.

This example demonstrates that although the QCC is unrepresentable and the complete atomic networks do not enjoy the AP, they all homomorphically map to the partition scheme. Although this may seem encouraging, we now switch our attention to the general question which types of constraint satisfaction problems can be formulated with a finite partition scheme. As we will see, it is almost all of them.

Theorem 1. *Let Γ' be a constraint language with finite signature. Then there exists a finite partition scheme Γ such that Γ' has a FO interpretation in Γ based on a primitive positive syntactic interpretation.*

Proof (sketch). W.l.o.g. let Γ' be the σ'-structure $\langle D'; R'_1, \ldots, R'_k \rangle$ where each relation is n-ary. We construct Γ with $D^\Gamma := (D'^n) \times \mathbb{N}$. The first n elements of $\bar{a} \in D^\Gamma$ are used to define the relations of Γ' and the last element is used to guarantee pairwise disjointness. For each $R'_l \in \sigma'$ we define $R_l^\Gamma := \left\{ (\bar{a}, \bar{b}) \in D^\Gamma \times D^\Gamma \,\middle|\, a_1, \ldots, a_n \in R_l'^{\Gamma'}, a_{n+1} = 0, b_{n+1} = l \right\}$ and a converse relation for each. Adding the identity relation and some additional relations that establish equality on elements of tuples one can ensure the claimed FO interpretation properties. Assigning unused tuples to a fresh relation makes Γ jointly exhaustive.

This theorem shows any constraint language Γ' on a finite signature can be wrapped inside a finite partition scheme Γ. Moreover, the syntactic interpretation is existential such that the associated reduction map allows each instance of CSP(Γ') to be cast as an instance of CSP(Γ). This suffices to show that the computational complexity of the CSP for finite partition schemes is not well-behaved in the general case — we consider examples listed in [4]: the structure in Example 1 (undecidable decision problem) and relational structures constructed by Bauslaugh [13] (decision problem with arbitrary time complexity).

The grand question remains: When do qualitative constraint calculi solve the CSP of the partition scheme? Renz and Ligozat [12] claim to have characterized these cases by the notion of being "closed under constraints":

Let Γ be a finite partition scheme and R^Γ one of its relations. Then R^Γ can be refined to a "subrelation" $X \neq \emptyset$ if $X \subsetneq R^\Gamma$ and X is pp definable in Γ with a formula $\varphi(x, y)$. We say Γ is "closed under constraints" if for each of its relations R^Γ all "subrelations" that R^Γ can be refined to have a non-empty intersection.

The main claim of Renz and Ligozat [12] is as follows.

Claim (Theorem 1 in [12]). Let $\mathcal{A}$ be a qualitative constraint calculus induced by a finite partition scheme Γ. Then $\mathcal{A}$ solves CSP(Γ) iff Γ is "closed under constraints".

We argue that the claim is wrong by showing that the implication does not hold in either direction.

Proposition 2. *Let $\mathcal{A}$ be a qualitative constraint calculus induced by a finite partition scheme Γ. Whether $\mathcal{A}$ solves CSP(Γ) is independent of whether Γ is "closed under constraints".*

Proof (sketch). First consider 3-colorability. The QCC for this problem was given in Example 2 with a representation that serves as a finite partition scheme Γ. Any instance I of CSP(Γ) with $(v, w) \in R_{\neq}^I$ for each distinct pair $v, w \in D^I$ and $(v, v) \in \mathrm{id}^I$ for each $v \in D^I$ is a complete atomic network. Such instances are however never satisfiable for $|D^I| \geq 4$. To show that Γ is "closed under constraints" consider that all permutations on D^Γ are automorphisms of Γ. As automorphisms preserve solutions of all FO formulas over the structure, X must be invariant under these permutations, and thus it cannot be a subrelation.

Now consider the QCC and partition scheme Γ given in Example 4. For any instance of CSP(Γ) the calculus easily completes the atomic network of any connected component and those homomorphically map to Γ. Thus it solves CSP(Γ). However, we can pp define the relation $\{(0,0)\}$ by $\exists c\,(a < c \wedge b < c)$ and $\{(1,1)\}$ by $\exists c\,(a > c \wedge b > c)$. Thus Γ is not "closed under constraints".

From the first part of the proof, we can also see that the original claim by Renz and Ligozat implies that 3-colorability is in **P** and thus **P** = **NP**.

Proposition 3. *There is a finite partition scheme Γ that induces a qualitative constraint calculus $\mathcal{A}$ where $\mathrm{Net}(\mathcal{A})$ does not have the JEP.*

The proof consists of constructing a counterexample based on a suitable finite structure Γ. Unfortunately, we do not have the space to give the example here.

We state some simple observations regarding consistency and satisfiability.

Proposition 4. *Let $\mathcal{A}$ be a qualitative constraint calculus induced by a finite partition scheme Γ. The following holds for $\mathrm{CSP}(\Gamma)$ and the class of complete atomic networks $\mathrm{Net}(\mathcal{A})$.*

(a) *If I is an instance of $\mathrm{CSP}(\Gamma)$ where for $a, b \in D^I$ there is exactly one symbol R with $(a, b) \in R^I$, then $I \in \mathrm{Net}(\mathcal{A})$ iff for every $V' \subseteq D^I, |V'| \leq 3$ there is a homomorphism from the substructure $I|_{V'}$ to Γ.*

(b) *For each satisfiable instance I of $\mathrm{CSP}(\Gamma)$ there is a network $I' \in \mathrm{Net}(\mathcal{A})$ on the same domain with $R^I \subseteq R^{I'}$ for each $R \in \mathrm{At}(\mathcal{A})$.*

(c) *If $\mathcal{A}$ solves $\mathrm{CSP}(\Gamma)$, then each complete atomic network homomorphically maps to Γ.*

(d) *If each complete atomic network homomorphically maps to Γ, then $\mathrm{Net}(\mathcal{A})$ has the JEP.*

As we see here, qualitative constraint calculi are a very restricted setting of relational FO structures and in particular of reasoning. Bodirsky and Dalmau [5] already criticize relation algebras for their limitations, in particular, the limitation to binary relations with a particular kind of disjunction. They also show that the operations of the algebra correspond to a Datalog program.

4.3   Countably Categorical Representations

We shift the perspective to the CSP and the class of complete atomic networks. In the following we "forget" the original partition scheme. This is interesting mainly because a QCC is the algebra, not the partition scheme. For reasoning tools the algebra and thus the notion of complete atomic networks is all that is available. We previously stressed that QCC are purely symbolic objects. So, given such an object what can we salvage from the calculus in terms of interpretation? In the following, we *build* an interpretation of the relation symbols in a QCC in which all complete atomic networks are satisfiable. It is already known due to Hirsch and Hodkinson [9] that *every* atomic and at most countable WA has a "relativized" representation. We apply the same argument to the QCC here, where the result can be strengthened because the considered algebras are finite.

Proposition 5. *Let $\mathcal{A}$ be a qualitative constraint calculus. Then the Fraïssé limit [7] of the class $\mathrm{PNet}(\mathcal{A})$ exists. The Fraïssé limit $\mathbb{A}$ is ω-categorical and embeds all structures of $\mathrm{PNet}(\mathcal{A})$. In particular, $D^{\mathbb{A}}$ is countable, $\mathbb{A}$ is ultrahomogenous and determined up to isomorphism. We call $\mathbb{A}$ the relativized model of the algebra $\mathcal{A}$.*

Using the class of partial networks is in general a necessity, as the class of complete atomic networks might not have AP which is necessary for the construction of the Fraïssé limit. In case the class of complete atomic networks has AP one can build a representation of the complete networks by the same method — as considered before in, e.g. [4, 6, 9, 14].

With the relativized model $\mathbb{A}$ we obtain a well-defined constraint problem CSP($\mathbb{A}$) for every QCC. Solving these problems is now *not* limited to the path consistency algorithm. As $\mathbb{A}$ is ω-categorical the results by Bodirsky and Dalmau [5] on the ω-categorical approach to constraint satisfaction are applicable.

If $\mathbb{A}$ has signature σ naming the atoms, we naturally have the augmented signature $\sigma_\vee$ denoting the disjunction of atoms. For this let $\mathbb{A}_\vee$ be the expansion of $\mathbb{A}$ to disjunctive symbols where the new symbols have the natural FO definition $\varphi(R_1 \vee \cdots \vee R_n)(v, w) = R_1(v, w) \vee \cdots \vee R_n(v, w)$. By construction we have the following result.

Proposition 6. *Let $\mathcal{A}$ be a qualitative constraint calculus, $\mathbb{A}$ its relativized model and $\mathbb{A}_\vee$ its expansion to all elements of the algebra $\mathcal{A}$. Then*

(a) *any instance I of $\mathrm{CSP}(\mathbb{A})$ can be solved in time $O(n^3)$ for $n = |D^I|$,*
(b) *$\mathrm{CSP}(\mathbb{A}_\vee)$ is in $\mathbf{NP}$.*

In particular, for CSP($\mathbb{A}_\vee$) every partial atomic network is globally consistent and path consistency implies strong 3-consistency. It is important to note that this ignores the original finite partition scheme — which, as we have seen, might not have much connection with $\mathbb{A}$. Further, even if all *complete* atomic networks are satisfiable over the original partition scheme, it is usually not the case that *partial* networks are. However, we can state connectedness in each instance: We can easily add $1(a, b)$ for each pair of variables a, b to force complete networks.

We summarize the relation between CSP($\mathbb{A}_\vee$) and CSP(Γ) in the following.

Proposition 7. *Let $\mathcal{A}$ be a qualitative constraint calculus induced by a finite partition scheme Γ, $\mathbb{A}$ its relativized model, $\Gamma_\vee, \mathbb{A}_\vee$ their disjunctive expansions, and I an instance of $\mathrm{CSP}(\Gamma_\vee)$.*

(a) *If I homomorphically maps to $\Gamma_\vee$, then I homomorphically maps to $\mathbb{A}_\vee$.*
(b) *If for each $a, b \in D^I$ there is at least one symbol R with $(a, b) \in R^I$, I homomorphically maps to $\mathbb{A}_\vee$, and each complete atomic network over $\mathcal{A}$ homomorphically maps to Γ, then I homomorphically maps to $\Gamma_\vee$.*

The relativized model $\mathbb{A}$ allows us to define many more relations. Unlike WAs and networks which are limited to binary relations and only disjunctions built on atoms, $\mathbb{A}$ allows to consider arbitrary disjunctions of relations.

5   Conclusion

In this paper we discussed the framework of qualitative constraint calculi for reasoning with binary constraints. We contrasted these calculi with relation algebras, first-order logic, and constraint satisfaction. In the process we showed that almost any constraint satisfaction problem falls within the scope of the framework and that the central theorem of "closure under constraints" characterizing satisfiability of instances on atoms is wrong. We conclude that qualitative calculi as defined by Ligozat and Renz [1] are on one hand too narrow as they always provide only one fixed type of calculus rules and too general on the other as they attempt to cover too many constraint satisfaction problems.

Further, we have defined the relativized model for the symbolic formalism which provides the necessary background for applying the theoretic and practical results of Bodirsky and Dalmau [5] on constraint satisfaction with ω-categorical structures. In particular, this link enables us to consider well-defined k-consistencies from the constraint satisfaction literature instead of being limited to the operations of a qualitative calculus. Alternative less restrictive approaches for constraint satisfaction that clearly separate the syntax, semantics, and reasoning algorithms have a lot to offer for qualitative reasoning.

Acknowledgements. We thank the anonymous reviewers for helpful suggestions and comments. This work was supported by DFG (Transregional Collaborative Research Center *SFB/TR 8 Spatial Cognition*, project R4-[LogoSpace]).

References

1. Ligozat, G., Renz, J.: What is a qualitative calculus? A general framework. In: Zhang, C., Guesgen, H.W., Yeap, W.K. (eds.) PRICAI 2004. LNCS (LNAI), vol. 3157, pp. 53–64. Springer, Heidelberg (2004)
2. Ligozat, G.: Categorical methods in qualitative reasoning: The case for weak representations. In: Cohn, A.G., Mark, D.M. (eds.) COSIT 2005. LNCS, vol. 3693, pp. 265–282. Springer, Heidelberg (2005)
3. Dylla, F., Mossakowski, T., Schneider, T., Wolter, D.: Algebraic properties of qualitative spatio-temporal calculi. In: Tenbrink, T., Stell, J., Galton, A., Wood, Z. (eds.) COSIT 2013. LNCS, vol. 8116, pp. 516–536. Springer, Heidelberg (2013)
4. Bodirsky, M.: Constraint satisfaction problems with infinite templates. In: Creignou, N., Kolaitis, P.G., Vollmer, H. (eds.) Complexity of Constraints. LNCS, vol. 5250, pp. 196–228. Springer, Heidelberg (2008)
5. Bodirsky, M., Dalmau, V.: Datalog and constraint satisfaction with infinite templates. Journal of Computer and System Sciences 79(1), 79–100 (2013)
6. Bodirsky, M., Chen, H.: Qualitative temporal and spatial reasoning revisited. Journal of Logic and Computation 19(6), 1359–1383 (2009)
7. Hodges, W.: Model Theory. Encyclopedia of Mathematics and its Applications. Cambridge University Press (1993)
8. Maddux, R.: Some varieties containing relation algebras. Transactions of the American Mathematical Society 272(2) (1982)
9. Hirsch, R., Hodkinson, I.M.: Step by step - building representations in algebraic logic. The Journal of Symbolic Logic 62(1), 225–279 (1997)
10. Hodkinson, I.M.: Atom structures of relation algebras (1995), retrieved from his homepage: http://www.doc.ic.ac.uk/~imh/
11. Mackworth, A.K., Freuder, E.C.: The complexity of some polynomial network consistency algorithms for constraint satisfaction problems. Artificial Intelligence 25(1), 65–74 (1985)
12. Renz, J., Ligozat, G.: Weak composition for qualitative spatial and temporal reasoning. In: van Beek, P. (ed.) CP 2005. LNCS, vol. 3709, pp. 534–548. Springer, Heidelberg (2005)
13. Bauslaugh, B.L.: The complexity of infinite h-coloring. Journal of Combinatorial Theory, Series B 61(2), 141–154 (1994)
14. Bodirsky, M., Wölfl, S.: RCC8 is polynomial on networks of bounded treewidth. In: Walsh, T. (ed.) IJCAI, pp. 756–761. IJCAI/AAAI (2011)

From Intelligibility to Debuggability in Context-Aware Systems

Daniel Moos, Sebastian Bader, and Thomas Kirste

MMIS, Computer Science, University of Rostock
first.last@uni-rostock.de
https://mmis.informatik.uni-rostock.de

Abstract. Intelligibility is a design principle for context-aware systems which focuses on providing information about context acquisition and interpretation to its users. In this paper we present existing approaches to provide intelligibility and identify a common shortcoming. Explanations starting on the context level are insufficient to help users in finding and understanding why their system is not working. Debuggability for context-aware systems is introduced as a means to assist users in debugging the cause of a failure. To achieve this we adapt an information exchange approach from explanatory debugging. Furthermore we discuss open problems of debuggability and provide a possible solution.

Keywords: intelligibility, debuggability, explanation generation.

1 Introduction and Motivation

In our lab we build and analyze context-aware systems that are able to provide proactive assistance. Our use cases are smart meeting rooms and multi-display environment and therefore the lab is equipped with multiple projection screens and projectors. Also we have multiple conference tables and a video/audio matrix switch to connect the video port from a table to every projector. One day we connected a notebook using a Mini DisplayPort adapter, but the projector did not show the notebooks' output. After several hours of debugging we swapped the adapter and finally saw the notebook on the screen. This whole process was done without any assistance and we were wondering if a context-aware system can provide assistance for debugging itself.

Users of single computer environments have experienced these kinds of problems in the past and solutions has been developed to ease the use of computers in faulty situations, like network failures. Examples include help functions in programs or the network diagnostics assistant. The shift towards ubiquitous computing raises the need for new solutions, as now hundreds of computers are surrounding the user. This has been acknowledged by other researchers and lead to the proposition of two design principles for context-aware systems: *intelligibility* and *control* [2]. In order to achieve these principles a system has to inform its users what context is acquired and how it is interpreted, and to provide means to correct taken actions.

C. Lutz and M. Thielscher (Eds.): KI 2014, LNCS 8736, pp. 219–224, 2014.

Intelligibility is concerned about what kind of information goes into the system, how it is interpreted, and why certain decisions are taken. So a context-aware system with support for intelligibility is not a black box as it can provide explanations about its details to users. In this paper we argue that the sole focus on context for intelligibility is not sufficient. The underlying infrastructure remains a black box and the system cannot answer questions about its working parts. A dynamic integration of components and the usage of different sensor sources increases the complexity of context-aware systems and also increases the chance of failures. As argued below, existing systems cannot provide the required assistance for debugging if the cause of the failure is unrecognizable with sensors. Though the system can guide the user to gather the required information to detect the cause.

The contribution of this paper is threefold: (a) we review different approaches to intelligibility, (b) we categorize them with respect to an extended classification scheme, and (c) we identify the open problem of *debuggability* in context-aware systems and present an approach for a solution.

2   Related Work

In the last years various efforts were made to provide intelligibility. One approach is to provide middlewares with capabilities to track the acquirement and usage of context. For example the Context Toolkit [5] has been extended with Situations [6]. Situations expose application logic as they enable a declarative, rule-based way to implement context-aware systems. The system automatically handles the underlying details that are required to gather the context data and to perform the specified actions. The information contained in a Situation and its current state are used to build interfaces that provide intelligibility and also allow the collection of application traces to support developers in debugging context rules.

A more sophisticated extension of the Context Toolkit is the Intelligibility Toolkit [11]. It provides support for the four most popular models to build context-aware systems and for eight out of the ten explanation types that have been identified by Lim & Dey [10]. Explanation types express a desire for a certain kind of information from the application and intelligibility is realized by providing answers. The explanations are generated in disjunctive normal form with conditionals (e.g. temperature ≤ 23) as atomic unit and Presenters can be provided for a visualization. Therefore a separation between the developer of the context-aware system and the (intelligibility) interface designer is possible, while the toolkit handles the explanation generation. A shortcoming is the lack of support for the infrastructure, so the toolkit cannot generate explanations for unexpected behavior like connectivity issues or missing components in the environment.

Based on the ten types of explanations that are desired by users, other researchers focused on ways to generate explanations for users' questions. PervasiveCrystal focuses on why and why not questions, and is based on event-condition-action rules [15]. A way is presented how graphical user interfaces can be built to support users in asking the environment why (not) a certain action has been taken, and to provide an interface to manually override or trigger this action.

To show the feasibility of intelligibility in a dynamic setting, an existing assistance system for smart environments has been extended to provide explanations [1]. The developed system supports goal-based interaction [8] and is able to answer how-to and why questions, and also provide hints to users how they could optimize their usage of the environment. Instead of a disjunctive normal form or a graphical user interface, an explanation is generated in natural language.

These solutions differ in aspects like the form of explanations and represent different points in the design space of intelligibility. Different dimensions for this design space have been proposed, e.g. six dimensions in [14]: I. timing (*before*, *during*, or *after* an interaction), II. generality (human-computer interaction via *general* or *domain-specific* interfaces), III. degree of co-location (intelligibility is *embedded* in the system or *external* and needs to be switched), IV. initiative (intelligibility is manually triggered by the *user* or automatically by the *system*), V. modality (interaction modality, e.g. *visual*, *auditory*, *haptic*), and VI. level of control (varies between *intelligibility* with no additional control, *counteract* to undo actions of the system, *configuration* to tweak parameters of the system, and *programmability* to change how the system works); or three dimensions in [4]: I. timing (same as before), II. syntax (complies with modality), and III. degree of user expertise (new dimension; different users have different requirements and capabilities).

3   Explaining Unexpected Behavior

In the last section we have presented different solutions that provide intelligibility to end-users. All have in common that they provide only information for designed functionality, they can explain what context information has been used and present the result of the internal reasoning process. Various surveys have been performed with inhabitants of smart homes and users expressed "discomfort with her inability to fix their system" [3] and that they "want to understand the house. . . my home, how it works, so that I will learn [to fix] it myself" [13]. So far these users have to rely on consultants and technicians to get problems in their home resolved. This problem has already been identified by Edwards & Grinter as one of the seven challenges for ubiquitous computing [7]. They mention that home environments are not designed from the ground to contain a variety of devices, but are piecemeal equipped with additional ones and inhabitants are facing the challenge of understanding the interaction between the changing set of devices in their home (they call it the "accidentally" smart home). Intelligibility provides only a partial solution as it focuses on context and not on the underlying infrastructure that is needed to acquire and process the context information. As explanations about the behavior of a context-aware system result in a stronger feeling of trust towards the system [12], we assume that explanations about causes of malfunctions will also increase the trust.

The creation of explanations for debugging purposes for end-users has been discussed outside the fields of context-aware systems. For example a solution has been developed for machine-learned programs and *explanatory debugging* is described as "a two-way exchange of information, introducing new facts along the way and using descriptions both parties understand" [9].

In this work we focus on causes of unexpected behavior that the context-aware system cannot detect on its own, otherwise the system could either fix them itself or instruct the user how to fix them. Without the ability to detect the problem itself, the system is dependent on the user and an exchange of information is required to assist the user in debugging her environment. We call this *debuggability*.

4   Extending the Design Space of Intelligibility

In Sec. 2 seven different dimensions for the design space of intelligibility were gathered from the literature. To capture the *level of explanation* (infrastructure, context, assistance) we propose this as an additional dimension. We distinguish between *context* to provide details about what context information are used, *assistance* to provide explanations how the context is interpreted and what actions are issued, and *infrastructure* to provide inner details of a context-aware system that are needed for a proper functionality. So the infrastructure level is concerned with details below the other two levels.

As mentioned in Sec. 3, we do only consider problems that the system cannot detect itself. This results in an exchange of roles, because now the context-aware system has to ask questions and the user provides explanations to enable the system to find the cause of a problem. This poses two new challenges:

1. What does the system have to ask the user to determine the cause of the problem?
2. How have explanations to be formulated to be understandable by the system?

To the best of our knowledge all existing solutions for intelligibility generate explanations on the context and assistance level only. Also they do not support the exchange of roles that gives the end-user the possibility to provide explanations to the system. A classification of approaches from Sec. 2 into the eight dimensions of the design space of intelligibility is shown in Tab. 1.

The two challenges raise several sub-problems, discussed below:

How is the environment described? A problem is the knowledge about the environment, because the system requires to explicitly know what devices are present, how they are connected to each other, and what is the cooperation between them to reach emergent behavior. To work across different devices from different vendors and enable subsequent usage a formal model is needed.

What is the reasoning process? With an explicit and formal description the system is able to identify possible causes for failures. Abductive reasoning is a suitable approach for this.

Table 1. Solutions for intelligibility from Sec. 2 classified within the eight dimensions of the design space. (a) = after, (as) = assistance, (ca) = counteract, (cf) = configuration, (co) = context, (d) = developer, (e) = end-user, (em) = embedded, (ex) = external, (g) = general, (in) = intelligibility, (s) = system, (u) = user, and (v) = visual.

	timing	generality	degree of co-location	initiative	modality	level of control	degree of user expertise	level of explanation
Situations [6]	(a)	(g)	(em)	(u)	(v)	(in), (cf)	(d), (e)	(co), (as)
Intelligibility Toolkit [11]	(a)	(g)	(em)	(u)	(v)	(in)	(d), (e)	(co), (as)
PervasiveCrystal [15]	(a)	(g)	(ex)	(u)	(v)	(ca), (cf)	(e)	(co), (as)
unnamed [1]	(a)	(g)	(em)	(u), (s)	(v)	(in)	(e)	(co), (as)

How does the system find the correct reason? In a complex setting abduction can find many hypotheses for a failure. The system has to choose questions that help to eliminate them, in order to identify the correct reason. This requires the system to select questions optimal with respect to cost, weight, or probability.

What is the form of interaction? Yet it is unclear how the system can guide the user. The questions have to be understandable and informative in order to get valuable feedback and the system needs the ability to understand the answers of the user. So the concrete form of questions and the mode of interaction has to be chosen according to the current situation.

5   Conclusions

In this paper we presented a short overview of existing solutions for providing intelligibility in context-aware systems. We extended existing classification schemes with another dimension (level of explanation) to describe that a system provides information about the infrastructure, context, or assistance level. Also we showed that debugging the infrastructure level requires an exchange of roles, the system provides the questions and the user generates the explanations. And we summarized open problems that we are going to investigate in future work.

In our future research we focus on systems which help users to identify infrastructure problems. As mentioned in Sec. 4, this includes solving various problems ranging from natural language processing, abduction, cost-optimal planing, and others. Debuggability for the infrastructure level is necessary to close the existing gap in former systems for intelligibility and thus necessary to solve one of the seven challenges for ubiquitous computing [7].

Acknowledgements This work is supported by the german research foundation (DFG) within research training group 1424 MuSAMA.

References

1. Bader, S.: Generating explanations for pro-active assistance from formal action descriptions. In: Augusto, J.C., Wichert, R., Collier, R., Keyson, D., Salah, A.A., Tan, A.-H. (eds.) AmI 2013. LNCS, vol. 8309, pp. 19–31. Springer, Heidelberg (2013)
2. Bellotti, V., Edwards, K.: Intelligibility and accountability: human considerations in context-aware systems. Human–Computer Interaction 16, 193–212 (2001)
3. Brush, A., Lee, B., Mahajan, R., Agarwal, S., Saroiu, S., Dixon, C.: Home automation in the wild: challenges and opportunities. In: Proc. of the SIGCHI Conference on Human Factors in Computing Systems, pp. 2115–2124. ACM (2011)
4. Bucur, D.: Embedded-system support for user intelligibility. In: Workshop on Pervasive Intelligibility (2012)
5. Dey, A., Abowd, G., Salber, D.: A conceptual framework and a toolkit for supporting the rapid prototyping of context-aware applications. Hum.-Comput. Interact. 16(2), 97–166 (2001)
6. Dey, A., Newberger, A.: Support for context-aware intelligibility and control. In: Proc. of the SIGCHI Conference on Human Factors in Computing Systems, CHI 2009, pp. 859–868. ACM (2009)
7. Edwards, W.K., Grinter, R.E.: At home with ubiquitous computing: Seven challenges. In: Abowd, G.D., Brumitt, B., Shafer, S. (eds.) UbiComp 2001. LNCS, vol. 2201, pp. 256–272. Springer, Heidelberg (2001)
8. Heider, T., Kirste, T.: Supporting goal-based interaction with dynamic intelligent environments. In: ECAI, pp. 596–600 (2002)
9. Kulesza, T., Stumpf, S., Burnett, M., Wong, W.-K., Riche, Y., Moore, T., Oberst, I., Shinsel, A., McIntosh, K.: Explanatory debugging: Supporting end-user debugging of machine-learned programs. In: 2010 IEEE Symposium on Visual Languages and Human-Centric Computing (VL/HCC), pp. 41–48. IEEE (2010)
10. Lim, B., Dey, A.: Assessing demand for intelligibility in context-aware applications. In: Proc. of Ubicomp 2009, pp. 195–204. ACM (2009)
11. Lim, B., Dey, A.: Toolkit to support intelligibility in context-aware applications. In: Proc. of Ubicomp 2010, pp. 13–22. ACM (2010)
12. Lim, B., Dey, A., Avrahami, D.: Why and why not explanations improve the intelligibility of context-aware intelligent systems. In: Proc. of SIGCHI Conference on Human Factors in Computing Systems, pp. 2119–2128. ACM (2009)
13. Mennicken, S., Huang, E.M.: Why can't i have both? The tension between comfort and control in smart homes. Workshop Paper presented at Pervasive Intelligibility Workshop at Pervasive 2012 (2012)
14. Vermeulen, J.: Improving intelligibility and control in ubicomp. In: Adj. Proc. of Ubicomp 2010, pp. 485–488. ACM (2010)
15. Vermeulen, J., Vanderhulst, G., Luyten, K., Coninx, K.: Pervasivecrystal: asking and answering why and why not questions about pervasive computing applications. In: 2010 Sixth International Conference on Intelligent Environments (IE), pp. 271–276. IEEE (2010)

Towards a Trace Index
Based Workflow Similarity Function

Pol Schumacher and Mirjam Minor

Goethe Universität Frankfurt - Institut für Informatik*
D-60325 Frankfurt am Main, Germany
{schumacher,minor}@cs.uni-frankfurt.de

Abstract. In this paper we present first steps towards an index based workflow similarity function. Classical approaches on workflow similarity perform a pairwise comparison of workflows, thus the workflow similarity function presented in this paper can speedup the calculation as the comparison is performed on the index.

Keywords: Knowledge representation and reasoning, case-based reasoning, workflow reasoning.

1 Introduction

Similarity is a subjective concept, suited for approximate rather than exact reasoning [1]. Similarity functions are used in a manifold of applications for example to retrieve similar cases of a case-base in a case-based reasoning scenario. *Workflows* are "the automation of a business process, in whole or part, during which documents, information or tasks are passed from one participant to another for action, according to a set of procedural rules" [2]. Multiple different similarity functions for workflows have been presented in the past [3–6]. There is a need for improvement of the computational performance of workflow similarities. The similarity function which we present in this paper employs an index to calculate the similarity between two workflows. The similarity computation of two workflows based on this novel index is much more efficient than the existing approaches which perform a pairwise comparison on the workflow structure. A workflow instructs a user to perform certain activities in a certain order. The workflow index which we present in this paper is based on the precedence relation for activities. The comparison of two workflows is done by comparing the indices of the workflows. The index can determine multiple categories of differences between workflows. It can detect missing activities, it gathers differences in the positioning of activities, it incorporates discrepancies of control-flow nodes and it includes the importance of certain activities into the similarity computation. This paper is organized as follows. In the next section we introduce our index

* This work was funded by the German Research Foundation, project number BE 1373/3-1.

C. Lutz and M. Thielscher (Eds.): KI 2014, LNCS 8736, pp. 225–230, 2014.

and how it is used to determine the similarity of two workflows. It includes a running example illustrating the index creation. After that we are going to present some related work on workflow similarity functions and discuss the differences to our approach. Finally, we draw a short conclusion and provide an outlook on our future work.

2 Workflow Similarity

This section begins with the presentation of our workflow description language. Then we are going to recapitulate some basic definitions on multisets which are necessary for the workflow similarity calculation. After that we present the construction of the index and finally we are going to employ the presented index to calculate workflow similarities. We have chosen an XML-based language [7] for workflow descriptions that is part of the CAKE[1] system. It is a block-oriented workflow description language: The control-flow can contain sequences, XOR-, AND-, LOOP-blocks. These building blocks cannot be interleaved but they can be nested. Sequences contain at least an activity, XOR-, AND or, LOOP-block. XOR- and AND-blocks contain at least two sequences. In the case of an XOR-block one sequence is chosen which is executed. In the case of AND-blocks both sequences are executed. Fig. 1 contains on the top a sample for a workflow in BPMN. Activities are represented by rounded rectangles and control-flow nodes by the diamond with "X" for XOR-nodes and an "+" for AND-nodes. The arrows between the elements represent the control-flow.

We are going to recapitulate some basic definitions of multisets [8] as our similarity function uses multisets. Multisets are sets which can contain multiple occurrences of the same element.

Definition 1 (Multiset). *Let D be a set. A multiset over D is a pair $\langle D, f \rangle$, where D is a set and $f : D \to \mathbb{N}$. is the function.*

Definition 2 (Multiset operations). *Suppose that $\mathcal{A} = \langle A, f \rangle$, $\mathcal{B} = \langle A, g \rangle$ and $\mathcal{C} = \langle A, h \rangle$ are multisets then multiset operations cardinality, sum and intersection are defined as follows:*

$$card(\mathcal{A}) = \sum_{a \in A} f(a) .$$

$$\mathcal{A} \uplus \mathcal{B} = \mathcal{C}, with\ h(a) = f(a) + g(a) .$$

$$\mathcal{A} \cap \mathcal{B} = \mathcal{C}, with\ h(a) = \min\big(f(a), g(a)\big) .$$

The index creation is illustrated in Fig. 1. The index for a workflow is created using its executions traces depicted in the middle layer of Fig. 1. A workflow execution trace is a sequence of activities which represents the order of execution of activities, as it follows a workflow model. An activity cannot occur multiple

---

[1] Collaborative Agile Knowledge Engine.

times in a trace. If a workflow model contains an AND-, XOR- or LOOP-block it can produce multiple different workflow execution traces. For a given workflow model it is possible to produce the set of possible execution traces by traversing every possible path through the workflow. Please note that workflows containing AND-blocks can produce a large (exponential growth) number of different traces. The large number of traces is only a problem during the offline creation of the index. We expect that this problem can be overcome in future by modifying the trace creation process. Two workflows can be compared using their trace set. A similarity function based on the trace sets could be derived from the cardinality of the intersection of the sets. Unfortunately this would result in a very pessimistic similarity function as one missing activity in a trace compared to another trace is sufficient that the traces are regarded as unequal. Therefore it is necessary to split the traces into smaller chunks. A trace of a workflow can be used to derive a precedence relation of that particular trace. The precedence relation of two activities is the information that an activity must be performed before another activity. Due to control-flow nodes a workflow can contain multiple different, even conflicting precedence relations for two activities. For example sequences of an AND-block can produce conflicting relations, as the order of execution between the two sequences in the block is not defined. This conflicting precedence relations are not a problem for our similarity function as it does not rely on a single relation but it does collect all relations for a workflow in an index. A set of traces induces a set of precedence relations. The participants of the precedence relations are collected by a multiset sum. The resulting multiset is used as index. It is important that we are using multisets instead of normal sets. If the index would use normal sets, it would lose a lot of distinctiveness. Fig. 1 illustrates the creation of the index for a sample workflow.

Definition 3 (Trace precedence relation). *Let W be a workflow. Let A be the set of activities a_i of W. Let the sequence of activities $w = (a_m, ..., a_n)$ with $a_m, ..., a_n \in A$ be an execution trace of W. Then $(<_w, A, A)$ is the precedence relation within a trace w. $a_q <_w a_s$ if a_q has an earlier position in w than a_s.*

Definition 4 (Trace index). *Let W be a workflow and let T_W be the set of all trace precedence relations which can be produced by the workflow W, then the trace index of W denoted index(W) is defined as:*

$$index(W) = \underset{\forall t_i \in T_W}{\uplus} <_{t_i} .$$

The similarity between two workflows can be calculated by means of their index. The index can be precomputed , thus the actual similarity computation is very fast. The similarity of two indices is computed with a similarity measure which is an extension of the Dice coefficient [9]. The Dice coefficient is a well-known similarity measure for normal sets, for two sets A and B $Dice(A, B) = \frac{2\,|A \cap B|}{|A| + |B|}$ [9].

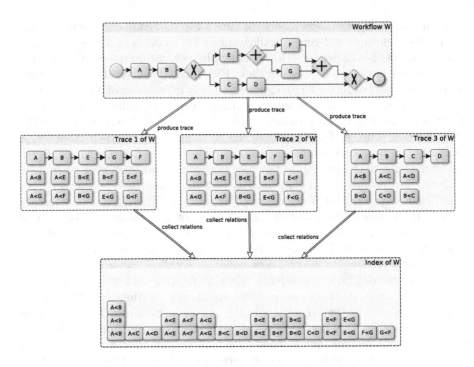

Fig. 1. Illustration of index creation of a workflow

Definition 5 (Workflow similarity). *Let W and G be workflows then their similarity denoted sim(W, G) is defined as:*

$$sim(W, G) = \frac{2\ card(index(W) \cap index(G))}{card(index(W) \uplus index(G))} \ .$$

Fig. 2 shows how different types of differences between workflows are covered by the trace index. The first example shows how the similarity functions takes into account missing activities. In the right workflow, the activity B is missing and the trace index of the right workflow has only one precedence relation element in common with the trace index of the left workflow. The example in middle shows how the similarity function penalizes a misplaced activity. In the sample workflows the last two activities swapped the position. The trace index of the left and the right workflow contain one precedence relation element which is not contained in the trace index of the other workflow. The higher the difference in positioning of the activities is, the more precedence relation elements differ and thus the lower similarity is. The last example illustrates how different control-flow nodes are taken into account. The trace index does not contain control-flow nodes explicitly but the semantics of the control-flow nodes are used during the trace index creation therefore the trace index of the left workflow does only contain two precedence relation elements while the right one does contain four precedence relation elements.

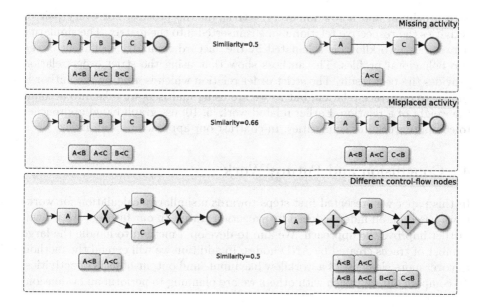

Fig. 2. Illustration of the use of the index for the detection of differences between workflows

3 Related Work

Multiple workflow similarity functions have been presented in the past. Wombacher and Li represent workflows based on its finite set of states [4]. In their representation states are n-grams, i.e. a sequence of n transition labels ending in that state. To calculate the distance of two workflows, they calculate the sum of the minimal distance of the states of a workflow with the states of the other workflow. The distance of two states is the string edit-distance of the n-grams. They use multiplicity of the state multisets to weight the distances of the states. The idea to use state n-grams is similar to our idea of the trace relations and they too use the multiplicity of multisets as means of weighting. The main difference to our approach is that they need to calculate the minimal edit-distance for every state for every pair of workflows in the repository while in our approach workflows are compared based on their relation-fingerprint. Eshuis and Grefen define relations between activities of a BPEL process [3]. Based on these relations and the activities of the workflow a graph can be defined. The authors define different exact and inexact matchings on that graph. The main advantage of that approach is that it ignores irrelevant syntactic differences and that it can be computed in an efficient way too. Our approach takes into account more details (e.g. the number of occurrences of an activity) and can be computed efficiently too. Kunze et al. calculate the similarity of two processes based on their behavioral profile [5]. For the profile they define the relations strict order, exclusiveness and interleaving order. The profile is built by creating a matrix with a column and a row for every activity in the process. For every pair of activities the respective relation name is inserted into the matrix. The similarity between two workflows is calculated by the Jaccard similarity coefficient of the two behavioral profiles. The authors show that using the strict order relation provides the best result. The strict order relation which is used by the author is similar to our trace relation, but as we are using multisets we take into account the weight of a relation. Earlier related work [6, 10] use graph based approaches to compute workflow similarities. In contrast our approach uses an index.

4   Conclusion and Future Work

In this paper we presented first steps towards a similarity calculation for work-flows based on an index induced by execution traces. In our future work we will further improve the approach. We aim to develop a method to handle the large number of traces created by AND-nodes. In addition we will extend the method to cover more elements of a workflow like input- and output-objects of activities. To compare our approach with others we are planning to perform an evaluation.

References

1. Richter, M.M., Weber, R.O.: Case-Based Reasoning - A Textbook. Springer (2013)
2. Workflow Management Coalition: Workflow management coalition glossary & terminology (1999) (last access May 23, 2007)
3. Eshuis, R., Grefen, P.: Structural matching of BPEL processes. In: Fifth European Conference on Web Services, ECOWS 2007, pp. 171–180. IEEE (2007)
4. Wombacher, A., Li, C.: Alternative approaches for workflow similarity. In: 2010 IEEE International Conference on Services Computing (SCC), pp. 337–345. IEEE (2010)
5. Kunze, M., Weidlich, M., Weske, M.: Behavioral similarity – A proper metric. In: Rinderle-Ma, S., Toumani, F., Wolf, K. (eds.) BPM 2011. LNCS, vol. 6896, pp. 166–181. Springer, Heidelberg (2011)
6. Bergmann, R., Gil, Y.: Similarity assessment and efficient retrieval of semantic workflows. Inf. Syst. 40, 115–127 (2014)
7. Minor, M., Schmalen, D., Bergmann, R.: XML-based representation of agile work-flows. In: Bichler, M., Hess, T., Krcmar, H., Lechner, U., Matthes, F., Picot, A., Speitkamp, B., Wolf, P. (eds.) Multikonferenz Wirtschaftsinformatik 2008, pp. 439–440. GITO-Verlag, Berlin (2008)
8. Syropoulos, A.: Mathematics of multisets. In: Calude, C.S., Pun, G., Rozenberg, G., Salomaa, A. (eds.) Multiset Processing. LNCS, vol. 2235, pp. 347–358. Springer, Heidelberg (2001)
9. Carullo, M., Binaghi, E., Gallo, I.: An online document clustering technique for short web contents. Pattern Recognition Letters 30(10), 870–876 (2009)
10. Minor, M., Tartakovski, A., Schmalen, D.: Agile workflow technology and case-based change reuse for long-term processes. IJIIT 4(1), 80–98 (2008)

Local Feature Extractors Accelerating HNNP
for Phoneme Recognition

Ruth Janning, Carlotta Schatten, and Lars Schmidt-Thieme

Information Systems and Machine Learning Lab (ISMLL), University of Hildesheim,
Marienburger Platz 22, 31141 Hildesheim, Germany
{janning,schatten,schmidt-thieme}@ismll.uni-hildesheim.de
http://www.ismll.uni-hildesheim.de

Abstract. Artificial neural networks are fast in the application phase
but very slow in the training phase. On the other hand there are state-of-
the-art approaches using neural networks, which are very efficient in image classification tasks, like the hybrid neural network plait (HNNP) approach for images from signal data stemming for instance from phonemes.
We propose to accelerate HNNP for phoneme recognition by substituting
the neural network with the highest computation costs, the convolutional
neural network, within the HNNP by a preceding local feature extractor and a simpler and faster neural network. Hence, in this paper we
propose appropriate feature extractors for this problem and investigate
and compare the resulting computation costs as well as the classification performance. The results of our experiments show that HNNP with
the best one of our proposed feature extractors in combination with a
smaller neural network is more than two times faster than HNNP with
the more complex convolutional neural network and delivers still a good
classification performance.

Keywords: image classification, phoneme recognition, artificial neural
network, convolutional neural network, hybrid neural network plait, local
feature extraction.

1 Introduction

Artificial neural networks with multiple layers and complex connections are fast
in the application phase but need a long time for the training phase compared
to other classification approaches. That may be acceptable in approaches where
just one training phase takes place before the system is used. In areas where
periodically plenty of new data is available and has to be integrated so that
the system has to be retrained frequently, a very long training time becomes
unacceptable. On the other hand there are very strong and often used state-
of-the-art neural networks like convolutional neural networks which are mainly
used for image classification tasks like digit or face recognition (see e.g. [12],
[14]), but also for problems like phoneme recognition as in [1]. In former works
([4], [5]) we developed HNNP, a hybrid neural network plait for improving the

C. Lutz and M. Thielscher (Eds.): KI 2014, LNCS 8736, pp. 231–242, 2014.
© Springer International Publishing Switzerland 2014

classification performance of single neural networks applied to images gained from signal data like for instance Ground Penetrating Radar data (see [2], [3]), Synthetic Aperture Radar data ([10]) or phoneme data ([13]). HNNP is able to improve the classification performance significantly, but the time for training HNNP is proportional to the training time of the integrated convolutional neural network. Hence, the question arises if there is a way to profit still from the property of HNNP to improve the classification performance and to reduce the training time at the same time. In this paper we propose and investigate a strategy to simulate the convolutional neural network within the HNNP by replacing it by a combination of a preceding local feature extraction method and a simpler and faster neural network for the classification within HNNP. The main contributions of this paper are: (1) proposal of a new approach for accelerating HNNP, (2) presentation of three different feature extractors for this acceleration, and (3) investigation of computation costs and performance of the accelerated HNNP. In the following we will describe some related work in section 2 and the HNNP approach in section 3. In section 4 we will explain our proposed feature extractors. Before we conclude we will present the experiments in section 5.

2   Related Work

The most famous problems convolutional neural networks are used for are handwritten digit classification and face recognition. Convolutional neural networks for face recognition and gender classification are presented e.g. in [9] and [14]. The well known LeNet-5 convolutional neural network for digits recognition is presented in [7]. A further convolutional neural network for digit recognition with a simpler and shallower architecture is proposed e.g in [12]. However, convolutional neural networks are also used for problems like phoneme recognition which can be considered as an image classification problem. In [1] a convolutional neural network for phoneme recognition is described. We use a version of this network within HNNP for the comparison with our approach of HNNP with preceding local feature extractors and simpler neural networks instead.

Common approaches for feature extraction in image processing are methods like edge detection (see e.g. [15], [11]), Hough transform (see e.g. [6]) or Scale-invariant feature transform (SIFT, [8]). However, in this work we consider images stemming from Mel Frequency Cepstral Coefficients of phonemes, representing speech frequencies. In these images we do not search for certain shapes but for combinations of extreme frequencies. Hence, the mentioned image feature extraction methods are not appropriate for this kind of data and we will propose in section 4 three other local feature extractors. Two of them simulate the behavior of a certain part of a convolutional neural network, whereas the third one uses some background information about the considered data. Before we will describe these feature extractors, in the next section we will explain HNNP.

3   HNNP

The hybrid neural network plait (HNNP) approach integrates on the one hand different information sources delivering different feature sets and requiring different learning models, and retrains on the other hand these learning models interactively within one common structure. The different information sources are the normalized pixel values of the input image and additional side information like statistical information or domain information. The learning model for the image pixels is, according to state-of-the-art approaches (see sec. 2), a convolutional neural network (cnn). For the training of the feature sets of the other information sources fully connected multilayer perceptrons are used. The plait (see fig. 1) is

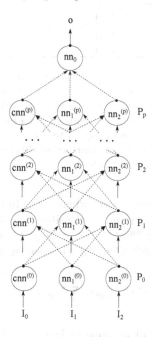

Fig. 1. Architecture of the hybrid neural network plait (HNNP). The plait is composed of $p+1$ layers $P_0, P_1, \ldots, P_p$. Each layer contains $k+1$ different neural networks (here $k = 2$) according to the $k+1$ different information sources $I_0, I_1, \ldots, I_k$ for the input. I_0 corresponds to the input image and the appropriate learning model is a convolutional neural network (cnn). The learning models for the other information sources $I_1, \ldots, I_k$ are multilayer perceptrons ($nn_1, nn_2, \ldots, nn_k$). In every layer from P_1 on the neural networks are retrained with additional input from the former layer. After the last layer P_p a further multilayer perceptron (nn_0) is attached to achieve one common output vector **o** delivering the final classification result.

composed of several layers in each of which the networks are retrained by considering the classification decisions of the other networks from the former layer. The cnn used for HNNP for phoneme recognition is pictured in fig. 2. In these kind of networks the input layer (L_0), convolution layer (L_1) and the maxpooling layer

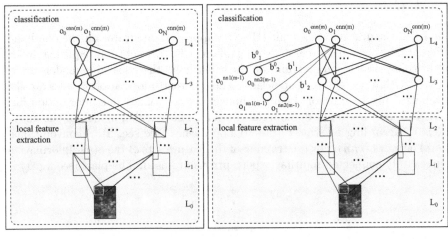

Fig. 2. Left: Architecture of a *cnn* for phoneme recognition. It is composed of 5 layers L_0, L_1, L_2, L_3, L_4, where L_0 is the input layer fed with the image, L_1 is a convolution layer followed by a maxpooling layer (L_2). L_0, L_1, L_2 build the local feature extractor. The fully connected layer (L_3) and the output layer L_4 instead build the trainable classifier. Right: Architecture of the *cnn* adapted to the plait structure with 3 information sources. In contrast to left the output neurons of this *cnn* get additional input from the other networks of the plait layer before.

(L_2) serve as a local feature extractor, whereas the fully connected layer (L_3) and output layer (L_4) serve as a trainable classifier. The output layer of such a *cnn* delivers an output vector $\hat{\mathbf{o}}^{\mathbf{cnn}} := (\hat{o}_0^{cnn}, \ldots, \hat{o}_N^{cnn}), -1 \leq \hat{o}_i^{cnn} \leq 1, i = 0, \ldots, N$, where the actual output $\hat{o}_i^{cnn}$ of the ith neuron in output layer n corresponds to

$$\hat{o}_i^{cnn} = \tanh\left(\sum_{l=0}^{N_{n-1}} w_n^{il} x_{n-1}^l \right), \tag{1}$$

with N_{n-1} as the number of neurons in layer $n-1$, w_n^{il} as the weight of the lth connection between neuron i and the neurons in layer $n-1$, x_{n-1}^l as the output of the lth neuron in layer $n-1$ and tanh (hyperbolic tangent) as activation function with an output within the interval $[-1, 1]$. Each neuron of the output layer is assigned to one class in $\{C_0, \ldots, C_N\}$. The classification result $C_{\arg\max_i \hat{o}_i^{cnn}}$ corresponds to the class C_i assigned to the output neuron with maximum output value $\hat{o}_i^{cnn}$. In opposite to the *cnn*, fully connected multilayer perceptrons fulfill only a role as classifier (without local feature extraction) but use the same formulas for $\hat{\mathbf{o}}^{\mathbf{nni}}$.

cnns and multilayer perceptrons are interweaved within the HNNP structure like in a plait (fig. 1), which is enabled by adapting their architectures. In these new architectures (fig. 2) – using the example of the *cnn* – every neuron $o_i^{cnn^{(m)}}$ of the output layer L_n of a *cnn* in plait layer P_m is additionally connected to the outputs $\hat{o}_i^{nn_1^{(m-1)}}, \hat{o}_i^{nn_2^{(m-1)}}, \ldots, \hat{o}_i^{nn_k^{(m-1)}}$ of the k other networks $nn_1, nn_2, \ldots, nn_k$

from the previous plait layer P_{m-1}. This leads to new output formulas for the neural networks within the plait. In the case of k information sources for additional side information, the new output formulas for the $k+1$ adapted networks cnn and $nn_x, x = 1, \ldots, k$ are as follows:

$$\hat{o}_i^{cnn^{(m)}} = \tanh(\sum_{l=0}^{N_{n-1}} w_n^{il} x_{n-1}^l + \sum_{j=1}^{k} b_j^i \hat{o}_i^{nn_j^{(m-1)}}) , \qquad (2)$$

$$\hat{o}_i^{nn_x^{(m)}} = \tanh(\sum_{l=0}^{N_{n-1}} w_n^{il} x_{n-1}^l + b_0^i \hat{o}_i^{cnn^{(m-1)}} + \sum_{j=1,j\neq x}^{k} b_j^i \hat{o}_i^{nn_j^{(m-1)}}) . \qquad (3)$$

In this way each neural network learns to which degree it should consider the classification decisions of all other networks from the previous plait layer. The number $p + 1$ of plait layers is a hyper parameter.

A further improvement of HNNP can be reached by using within HNNP automatically estimated subclasses like shown in [5]. The results of applying HNNP to 400 examples of phonemes 'iy' and 'n' of the TIMIT data set ([13]) with 10 automatically estimated subclasses are shown in table 1 (see also [5]). In this paper we propose to substitute the cnn within HNNP by a preceding

Table 1. Results of [5] of a 5-fold cross validation for 400 examples of phonemes 'iy' and 'n' of the TIMIT data set: Classification test errors (%) of the 5 baselines cnn, nn_1, nn_2, *majority ensemble* and *stacking ensemble* and the HNNP (standard deviations in brackets) with 10 automatically estimated subclasses

cnn	nn_1	nn_2	majority	stacking	HNNP
27.88	35.75	30.88	26.38	22.13	**12.50**
(4.32)	(4.04)	(1.86)	(1.90)	(1.69)	(0.99)

local feature extraction and a simpler and faster neural network to accelerate the HNNP. Hence, in the following section we will present the proposed local feature extractors for this purpose.

4   Local Feature Extractors for HNNP

As mentioned above, we want to substitute the cnn within the HNNP by a preceding local feature extraction and a simpler and faster neural network. This is reasonable as in the cnn the convolution layer and the maxpooling layer serve as a local feature extractor and the fully connected layer as a trainable classifier (see fig. 2 and sec. 3). The mentioned simpler and faster neural network shall adopt the rule of the trainable classifier and is realized by a fully connected multilayer perceptron equivalent to the second part of the cnn (see the *classification* part in fig. 2). For the preceding local feature extraction we propose 3 different feature extractors, which will be described in the following subsections: (1)

$tanh_{amd}$, (2) amd^2 and (3) max_{iv}. $tanh_{amd}$ and amd^2 are inspired by the *cnn*, i.e. $tanh_{amd}$ and amd^2 simulate the local feature extractor of the *cnn*, however without learning weights, or without a training respectively, but by means of the maximum, minimmum and average functions. max_{iv} instead is inspired by the data, i.e. it considers certain characteristics of the input data.

4.1 $tanh_{amd}$

$tanh_{amd}$ (hyperbolic tangent and **a**verage, **m**aximum, **d**istance) is composed of two parts (see also fig. 3). The first part applies a convolution similar to

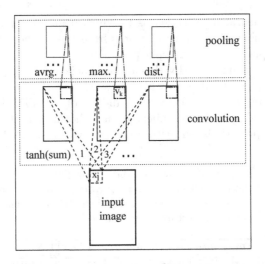

Fig. 3. Approach of $tanh_{amd}$, as well as of amd^2 if tanh(sum) is replaced by average (1), maximum (2) and distance (3)

the convolution layer of the *cnn* but without weights to learn. $tanh_{amd}$ creates 3 equal maps with values y_j stemming from applying to every possible 8×8 window x_j of the input image a summation and the hyperbolic tangent (cp. eq. (1)):

$$y_j = tanh\left(\sum_{i=1}^{64} x_j^{(i)}\right). \tag{4}$$

The $x_j^{(i)}, i = 1,\ldots,64$, correspond to the pixel values, normalized according to [7], of the input image in the appropriate 8×8 window and have a value between -0.15 and 1.175 depending on their intensity (the darkest pixels have value -0.15 and the brightest pixels have value 1.175). That means that if there are a few very bright pixels in the considered window, then y_j converges rather to 1 and if there are many very dark pixels y_j converges rather to -1.

The second part of $tanh_{amd}$ applies to one of the 3 convolution maps the same maxpooling as the *cnn* does. That is the maximum value w_k of each second 6×6

window v_k of the considered convolution map is inserted into one of the 3 pooling maps:

$$w_k = \max_i(v_k^{(i)}) \, . \tag{5}$$

For the two other pooling maps instead the average value w_k' and the value w_k'' of the distance between maximal and minimal value of each second 6×6 window v_k' and v_k'' of the considered convolution maps are inserted into the appropriate pooling maps:

$$w_k' = \frac{\sum_{i=1}^{36} v'_k{}^{(i)}}{36} \, , \quad w_k'' = \left(\max_i(v''_k{}^{(i)}) - \min_i(v''_k{}^{(i)})\right) \, . \tag{6}$$

The final output is a feature vector containing all values of the three pooling maps.

4.2 amd^2

amd^2 (average, maximum and distance twice) is similar to $tanh_{amd}$ but it uses instead of the hyperbolic tangent applied to the sum already in the convolution part the average, maximum and distance functions:

$$y_j' = \frac{\sum_{i=1}^{64} x'_j{}^{(i)}}{64} \, , \quad y_j = \max_i(x_j^{(i)}) \, , \quad y_j'' = \left(\max_i(x''_j{}^{(i)}) - \min_i(x''_j{}^{(i)})\right) \, . \tag{7}$$

That is y_j' is put into the first of the 3 convolution maps (see label '1' in fig. 3), y_j is put into the second convolution map (label '2' in fig. 3) and y_j'' is put into the third convolution map (label '3' in fig. 3).

The second part of amd^2 is the same as in the case of $tanh_{amd}$ and hence it also uses formula (5) and (6). Similar to $tanh_{amd}$, the final output of amd^2 is a feature vector containing all values of the three pooling maps.

4.3 max_{iv}

max_{iv} (maximum index and value) is different to $tanh_{amd}$ and amd^2 as it does not directly simulate the behavior of the cnn, but it is more oriented to the data. The data we are considering in this work are phonemes. More explicitly, as usual in phoneme recognition the input are matrices consisting of several consecutive feature vectors with Mel Frequency Cepstral Coefficients (MFCC), which are gained from the spectrograms of certain time segments of the speech input. The input images for our approach contain these matrices but the values are normalized. That means that the rows of the input images correspond to values of certain frequencies and the columns correspond to MFCC vectors of consecutive time segments. The characteristics of such data are that for different instances there are different extreme frequencies at different positions. By means of these extreme frequency values we try to distinguish the different phonemes (see also fig. 4). max_{iv} uses this side information to apply a feature extraction by extracting from every input image for each row and each column the maximum value (extreme frequency) and its position. As there could be more than one pixel in a row with this maximum value, max_{iv} searches from left to right as well as from right to left for the maximum in a row and stores besides the maximum value the most left and the most right position of the maximum. Correspondingly, it searches from top to bottom and from bottom to top in a column for the maximum and stores besides the maximum value the topmost position and the position closest to the bottom. Accordingly, a feature vector extracted by max_{iv} from an image with c columns and r rows consists of $3*(c+r)$ values, as there is one triple composed of the maximum value and two indexes for each row and each column.

5   Experiments

In the preceding sections we described three different feature extractors for realizing our aim to accelerate the HNNP approach by substituting the cnn by a preceding feature extraction without weights to learn and a simpler neural network, namely a fully connected multilayer perceptron. However, the question arises how this approach influences the classification performance of HNNP, as it leads to a trade-off between computation costs and classification performance. Hence, we investigated two different aspects: (1) the different computation costs for the training of HNNP with the cnn on the one hand and with the three different preceding feature extractors $tanh_{amd}$, amd^2, max_{iv} plus a multilayer perceptron on the other hand, and (2) the different classification performances of HNNP in the different cases. Aspect (1) is discussed in section 5.2 and aspect (2) in section 5.3. But first we will introduce the data used for the experiments in the following section 5.1.

5.1   Data Set and Experimental Settings

For our experiments we applied HNNP with 10 automatically estimated subclasses to a real data set of phonemes, or of the MFCC vectors of speech signals interpreted as images (of 19×43 pixels, see fig. 4) by combining several chronologically subsequent vectors respectively (see also [1]). The data are gained from the TIMIT data set ([13]) by choosing 400 examples of each of two different phonemes ('iy','n'). We applied the following experimental settings: the HNNP approach uses $k + 1 = 3$ information sources and accordingly 3 neural networks in every plait layer (of $p + 1 = 3$ plait layers). Two of them are fully connected multilayer perceptrons (nn_1 and nn_2) with input feature sets coming from appropriate additional side information. More explicitly, nn_1 is fed with 4 histograms of 16 gray values, each of which represents one quarter of the input image. nn_2 is fed with the number of pixels with a light gray value (a value within the upper quarter of all gray values of the image) per area, where an area is one of 105 areas of the image (partitioned by a 7×15 grid). The third neural network is either a cnn fed with the normalized pixel values of the images to classify, or a fully connected multilayer perceptron which is fed with the output of one of the presented feature extractors $tanh_{amd}$, amd^2 and max_{iv}. The performance of HNNP in the different settings is additionally compared to the three baselines $fcnn$, $majority\ ensemble$ and $stacking\ ensemble$. $fcnn$ is a standalone fully connected multilayer perceptron with input from $tanh_{amd}$, amd^2 or max_{iv} outside of HNNP. $Majority\ ensemble$ classifies according to the majority vote of the three networks nn_1, nn_2 and cnn or $fcnn$. $Stacking\ ensemble$ learns to combine the classification decisions of nn_1, nn_2 and cnn or $fcnn$ by using the subsequent multilayer perceptron nn_0. For every different setting we conducted a 5-fold cross validation.

Fig. 4. Examples of the data set (phoneme 'iy' left, 'n' right)

5.2 Computation Costs

In neural networks the main effort is the training of the network, or learning the weights respectively. During the training for every iteration for every training instance every weight is updated. In our experiments we used for each network the same number of iterations and the same number of training instances, hence the only one of these numbers which differs is the number of weights to learn. For this reason we consider for the comparison of the computation costs the numbers of weights to learn within the considered neural networks. As the training within one plait layer can be parallelized in the HNNP, the time complexity for the training of the HNNP is proportional to the training time complexity of the one neural network nn^{max} within the plait which has the highest time complexity for training (see also [4]). In table 2 one can see that cnn corresponds to nn^{max}, as it has the largest number of weights to learn. The numbers in table 2 are gained by the following computations:

- **nn_1:** nn_1 is fully connected and has $4 \cdot 16$ neurons in its input layer, 64 neurons in a hidden layer and 10 neurons in the output layer as well as a bias weight for every neuron, resulting in $(64 \cdot 64) + (64 \cdot 10) + 64 + 10 = 4,810$ weights to learn.

Table 2. Numbers of weights to learn for nn_1, nn_2, cnn and $fcnn$ with $tanh_{amd}$ (amd^2) or max_{iv}. The last column reports the speedup factor of $fcnn$ compared to cnn.

	nn_1	nn_2	cnn	$fcnn$	$\frac{cnn}{fcnn}$
$tanh_{amd}$ amd^2	4,810	12,190	44,190	20,310	2.18
max_{iv}	4,810	12,190	44,190	19,710	2.24

- **nn_2:** The only difference to nn_1 is that the input is of size 105, resulting in 12,190 weights to learn.
- **cnn:** In the convolution layer there are 6 maps of size 12×36 and each neuron of them has weighted connections to a 8×8 window of the input image, but the weights are shared within the maps. Furthermore, every neuron possesses an additional bias weight. The 100 neurons of the fully connected layer are connected with a weight to every neuron in the maxpooling layer which consists of 6 maps of size 4×16. Finally, each of the 10 output neurons has a weighted connection to each of the 100 neurons in the fully connected layer. The addition of all weights of every layer results in 44,190 weights to learn.
- **fcnn with $tanh_{amd}$ or amd^2:** $fcnn$ corresponds to the classification part of the cnn, i.e. each of the 10 output neurons has a weighted connection to each of the 100 neurons in the fully connected layer and each of the 100 neurons in the fully connected layer is connected with a weight to each of the input neurons. The input comes from $tanh_{amd}$ or amd^2, which deliver a feature vector containing all 192 values of the 3 pooling maps of size 4×16. If one considers finally the bias weights, this results in $(192 \cdot 100) + (100 \cdot 10) + 100 + 10 = 20,310$ weights to learn.
- **fcnn with max_{iv}:** The only difference to $fcnn$ with $tanh_{amd}$ is, that max_{iv} delivers a feature vector with $3 \cdot (19 + 43) = 186$ values (3 values for each column and row) resulting in 19,710 weights to learn.

Table 2 and figure 5 show that for the $fcnn$ with $tanh_{amd}$, amd^2 or max_{iv} there are less then half of the number of weights of the cnn to learn, i.e. $fcnn$ is more than two times faster to train than the cnn.

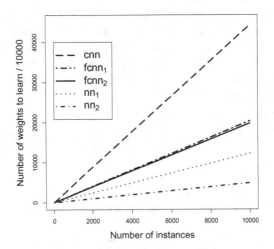

Fig. 5. Numbers of weights to learn $\cdot \frac{1}{10,000}$ for different numbers of training instances for nn_1, nn_2, cnn and $fcnn$ with $tanh_{amd}$ or amd^2 (both represented by $fcnn_1$) or max_{iv} ($fcnn_2$).

Table 3. Results of the 5-fold cross validation for 400 examples of phonemes 'iy' and 'n' of the TIMIT data set: Classification test errors (%) for each proposed feature extraction of the baselines *fcnn*, *majority ensemble* and *stacking ensemble* and the HNNP (standard deviations in brackets) with 10 automatically estimated subclasses.

feature extraction	$fcnn$	majority	stacking	HNNP
$tanh_{amd}$	31.50	25.00	22.25	18.25
	(4.91)	(3.03)	(1.69)	(0.81)
amd^2	30.50	24.63	21.25	17.25
	(2.18)	(2.52)	(4.53)	(0.84)
max_{iv}	26.25	23.50	19.75	**16.00**
	(1.98)	(1.69)	(2.44)	(1.14)

5.3   Classification Performance

In the section before we investigated the computation costs, but we also have to consider the classification performances of the accelerated HNNP versions. In table 3 the results of the 5-fold cross validation of $fcnn$, the ensemble methods and HNNP with $fcnn$ are presented. As one can see, HNNP with $fcnn$ with $tanh_{amd}$, amd^2 or max_{iv} outperforms the single $fcnn$ as well as the ensemble methods. The best classification result delivers HNNP with $fcnn$ with max_{iv}. However, as mentioned it is a trade-off between computation costs and classification performance and – as expected – HNNP with $fcnn$ with max_{iv} is not able to outperform HNNP with cnn in terms of classification performance (cp. tab. 1). But the classification performance improvement of HNNP with $fcnn$ with max_{iv} is still significant and it is more than two times faster than HNNP with cnn (see sec. 5.2).

6   Conclusions

We proposed an approach for accelerating HNNP for phoneme recognition by replacing the neural network within the HNNP with the highest computation costs by a preceding local feature extraction and a simpler and faster network. For this purpose we proposed three different appropriate feature extractors. We investigated the computation costs and classification performance of HNNP with the presented feature extractors and showed that these HNNP versions are more than two times faster than HNNP with the more complex convolutional neural network and deliver still a significant classification performance improvement.

Acknowledgments. This work is co-funded by the EU project iTalk2Learn (http://www.italk2learn.eu) under grant agreement no. 318051.

References

1. Abdel-Hamid, O., Mohamed, A., Jiang, H., Penn, G.: Applying Convolutional Neural Networks concepts to hybrid NN-HMM model for speech recognition. In: IEEE International Conference on Acoustics, Speech and Signal Processing (ICASSP), pp. 4277–4280 (2012)
2. Janning, R., Horváth, T., Busche, A., Schmidt-Thieme, L.: GamRec: A Clustering Method Using Geometrical Background Knowledge for GPR Data Preprocessing. In: Iliadis, L., Maglogiannis, I., Papadopoulos, H. (eds.) AIAI 2012. IFIP AICT, vol. 381, pp. 347–356. Springer, Heidelberg (2012)
3. Janning, R., Busche, A., Horváth, T., Schmidt-Thieme, L.: Buried Pipe Localization Using an Iterative Geometric Clustering on GPR Data. Artificial Intelligence Review (2013), doi:10.1007/s10462-013-9410-2
4. Janning, R., Schatten, C., Schmidt-Thieme, L.: HNNP – A Hybrid Neural Network Plait for Improving Image Classification with Additional Side Information. In: Proceedings of the IEEE International Conference on Tools with Artificial Intelligence (ICTAI 2013), Washington DC, USA, pp. 24–29 (2013)
5. Janning, R., Schatten, C., Schmidt-Thieme, L.: Automatic Subclasses Estimation for a Better Classification with HNNP. In: Andreasen, T., Christiansen, H., Cubero, J.-C., Raś, Z.W. (eds.) ISMIS 2014. LNCS, vol. 8502, pp. 93–102. Springer, Heidelberg (2014)
6. Kälviäinen, H., Hirvonen, P., Xu, L., Oja, E.: Probabilistic and non-probabilistic Hough transforms: overview and comparisons. Image and Vision Computing 13(4), 239–252 (1995)
7. LeCun, Y., Bottou, L., Bengio, Y., Haffner, P.: Gradient-Based Learning Applied to Document Recognition. Proceedings of the IEEE 86(11), 2278–2324 (1998)
8. Lowe, D.: Distinctive image features from scale-invariant keypoints. International Journal of Computer Vision 60(2), 91–110 (2004)
9. Matsugu, M., Mori, K., Mitari, Y., Kaneda, Y.: Subject independent facial expression recognition with robust face detection using a convolutional neural network. Neural Networks 16, 555–559 (2003)
10. Pettengill, G.H., Ford, P.G., Johnson, W.T.K., Raney, R.K., Soderblom, L.A.: Magellan: Radar Performance and Data Products. Science 252, 260–265 (1991)
11. Senthilkumaran, N., Rajesh, R.: Edge Detection Techniques for Image Segmentation – A Survey of Soft Computing Approaches. International Journal of Recent Trends in Engineering 1(2), 250–254 (2009)
12. Simard, P.Y., Steinkraus, D., Platt, J.: Best Practices for Convolutional Neural Networks Applied to Visual Document Analysis. In: External Link International Conference on Document Analysis and Recognition (ICDAR), pp. 958–962. IEEE Computer Society, Los Alamitos (2003)
13. TIMIT Acoustic-Phonetic Continuous Speech Corpus, http://www.ldc.upenn.edu/Catalog/CatalogEntry.jsp?catalogId=LDC93S1
14. Tivive, F.H.C., Bouzerdoum, A.: A Shunting Inhibitory Convolutional Neural Network for Gender Classification. In: 18th International Conference on Pattern Recognition 2006 (ICPR 2006), pp. 421–424. IEEE (2006)
15. Ziou, D., Tabbone, S.: Edge Detection Techniques - An Overview. International Journal of Pattern Recognition and Image Analysis 8, 537–559 (1998)

Parallel Fitting of Additive Models for Regression

Valeriy Khakhutskyy[1] and Markus Hegland[2]

[1] Institute for Advanced Study, Technische Universität Munchen,
Lichtenbergstrasse 2a, D-85748 Garching, Germany
khakhutv@in.tum.de
[2] Centre for Mathematics and Its Applications, Mathematical Sciences Institute
Australian National University, Canberra, ACT 0200, Australia

Abstract. To solve big data problems which occur in modern data mining applications, a comprehensive approach is required that combines a flexible model and an optimisation algorithm with fast convergence and a potential for efficient parallelisation both in the number of data points and the number of features.

In this paper we present an algorithm for fitting additive models based on the basis expansion principle. The classical backfitting algorithm that solves the underlying normal equations cannot be properly parallelised due to inherent data dependencies and leads to a limited error reduction under certain circumstances. Instead, we suggest a modified BiCGStab method adapted to suit the special block structure of the problem. The new method demonstrates superior convergence speed and promising parallel scalability.

We discuss the convergence properties of the method and investigate its convergence and scalability further using a set of benchmark problems.

Keywords: backfitting, additive models, parallelisation, regression.

1   Introduction

Approximation of high-dimensional functions from data is an important area of machine learning research. With increasing interest in data mining and increasing computational power more effort is spent on collecting and analysing data and, hence, data mining applications continuously grow in size and dimensionality.

Some algorithms, e.g. sparse grids [1], show linear complexity with respect to the amount of data points for storage and computation. This result is already optimal, as we cannot process data without looking at least once at every data point, although the multiplicative complexity constants for different models and algorithm implementations could lead to significant differences in actual runtime. Hence, further development is focused on minimising complexity constants by improving implementation efficiency, by parallelising, or by developing sub-sampling heuristics [2–4].

Dimensionality of the approximation problem poses a more difficult challenge. In 1961 Richard Bellman coined the term "curse of dimensionality", which refers

C. Lutz and M. Thielscher (Eds.): KI 2014, LNCS 8736, pp. 243–254, 2014.
© Springer International Publishing Switzerland 2014

to the observation that the costs for computation and storage of an approximation for a d-dimensional function and a pre-defined accuracy ε have the complexity $\mathcal{O}\left(\varepsilon^{-d/r}\right)$ [5]. The constant r depends on the properties of the problem, e.g.
smoothness, separability, etc., as well as on the kind of approximation method
and its implementation.

The exponential dependency of the cost on the dimensionality is inherent in
the nature of the problem. Research in information-based complexity suggests
that the curse of dimensionality can be avoided only if a problem possesses a
special structure that algorithms exploit, e.g. sufficiently fast converging ANOVA
decomposition [6–10].

To solve big data problems which occur in modern data mining applications,
a comprehensive approach is required that combines a flexible model and an
optimisation algorithm with fast convergence and a potential for efficient parallelisation both in data size and dimensionality. In this paper we discuss such
a comprehensive approach based on additive models and a parallel BiCGStab
algorithm for optimisation.

Additive models are well established in statistics and thoroughly studied in
the literature [11, 12]. The concept with somewhat different model requirements,
is popular in the machine learning community. For example, recent developments
apply new optimisation methods [13] and a parallelisation paradigm [14].

Moreover, estimation of additive models is an integral part of generalised
additive models – a more powerful but also more computationally demanding
representation concept [11].

We begin with a revision of the original formulation of additive model estimation proposed by Buja, Hastie, and Tibshirani [12] and show how beside
smoothing problems (Section 2), many current regression methods can be cast
into this form (Section 3). In Section 4 we then suggest a Krylov-space method
for solution of normal equations and show how the problem structure can be
exploited for efficiency and parallelisation. We illustrate convergence and scalability of the new method using benchmark problems in Section 5. Finally, we
conclude with a discussion of the results and provide an overview of future work
in Section 6.

2   Theoretical Background

We consider a dataset of the form $(\mathbf{t}^{(1)}, y^{(1)}), \ldots, (\mathbf{t}^{(N)}, y^{(N)})$ with input variables
$\mathbf{t}^{(i)}$ and target variables $y^{(i)}$ and make a basic assumption about the existence
of an underlying function $f(\mathbf{t})$ that generates the data and some additive model
error and measurement noise summarised in the term $\epsilon(\mathbf{t})$. Then the input-target
relationship can be represented as

$$y = f(\mathbf{t}) + \epsilon(\mathbf{t}).$$

Different methods to find an approximation of f in a functional space V often lead to a penalised least squares problem

$$\min_{f \in V} \frac{1}{N} \sum_{i=1}^{N} (f(\mathbf{t}^{(i)}) - y^{(i)})^2 + \lambda \|Df\|_2^2 \tag{1}$$

with a positive regularisation parameter λ and some smoothness operator D.

As mentioned above, (1) suffers from the curse of dimensionality so that only the problems with moderate dimensionality can be handled. Approaches that do not face the curse, e.g. additive models or ANOVA [15], are based on decomposition of the space V into a sum of simpler function spaces

$$V = V_1 + \ldots + V_n. \tag{2}$$

For example, in the context of ANOVA the decomposition of a function f with a d-dimensional input has the form

$$f(\mathbf{t}) = f_0 + \sum_{j=1}^{d} f_j(t_j) + \sum_{1 \le i < j \le d} f_{i,j}(t_i, t_j) + \sum_{1 \le i < j < k \le d} f_{i,j,k}(t_i, t_j, t_k) + \ldots,$$

where t_j stands for the j-th component of the data point $\mathbf{t}$.

For tractability we drop the higher-order interaction terms. This corresponds to an assumption that the structure of the problem admits reasonably accurate representation which utilises only low-order interaction terms. In the following we consider only the 1-dimensional terms f_j. However, the extension to first-order interaction terms $f_{i,j}$ is straightforward.

While it is not assumed that the V_j are linearly independent, we assume that the penalty term is consistent with the decomposition of V, such that $f_j, j = 0, \ldots, d$, solve the optimisation problem

$$\min_{f_0 \in \mathbb{R}, f_1 \in V_1, \ldots, f_d \in V_d} \frac{1}{N} \sum_{i=1}^{N} \left(f_0 + \sum_{j=1}^{d} f_j(t_j^{(i)}) - y^{(i)} \right)^2 + \sum_{j=1}^{d} \lambda_j \|D_j f_j\|_2^2. \tag{3}$$

As discussed in the next section, many models for representation of f_j can be cast in terms of linear algebra. Denote $\mathbf{x}$ as the vector of components of $f(\mathbf{t})$ with respect to some generating system, e.g. coefficients of a polynomial model. Furthermore, let $\mathbf{Ax}$ be a vector of function values $f(\mathbf{t}^{(i)})$ and $\mathbf{y}$ the vector of data values $y^{(i)}$. Taking into account the residual $\mathbf{r}$ we obtain

$$\underbrace{[\mathbf{A}_1 \ldots \mathbf{A}_d]}_{\mathbf{A}} \underbrace{\begin{bmatrix} \mathbf{x}_1 \\ \vdots \\ \mathbf{x}_d \end{bmatrix}}_{\mathbf{x}} = \mathbf{y} - \mathbf{r} \tag{4}$$

with $\mathbf{x}_j \in \mathbb{R}^{m_j}$, $\mathbf{A}_j \in \mathbb{R}^{N \times m_j}$, $\mathbf{y}, \mathbf{r} \in \mathbb{R}^N$, $\mathbf{x} \in \mathbb{R}^m$, $\mathbf{A} \in \mathbb{R}^{N \times m}$, and $m := m_1 + \ldots + m_d$. The problem (3) can now be written as

$$\min_{\mathbf{x}} \|\mathbf{Ax} - \mathbf{y}\|_2^2 + \lambda \mathbf{x}^T \mathbf{Dx} \tag{5}$$

with $\mathbf{D}$ a block diagonal matrix, which can be partitioned such that its block structure is compatible with that of $\mathbf{x}$. Often $\mathbf{D}$ will just be an identity matrix.

In order to minimise (5) one needs to solve the normal equations

$$(\mathbf{A}^T\mathbf{A} + \lambda\mathbf{D})\mathbf{x} = \mathbf{A}^T\mathbf{y} \tag{6}$$

If we substitute (4) into (6) we obtain an $m \times m$ system

$$\begin{bmatrix} \mathbf{A}_1^T\mathbf{A}_1 + \lambda\mathbf{D}_1 & \mathbf{A}_1^T\mathbf{A}_2 & \cdots & \mathbf{A}_1^T\mathbf{A}_d \\ \mathbf{A}_2^T\mathbf{A}_1 & \mathbf{A}_2^T\mathbf{A}_2 + \lambda\mathbf{D}_2 & \cdots & \mathbf{A}_2^T\mathbf{A}_d \\ \vdots & & \ddots & \vdots \\ \mathbf{A}_d^T\mathbf{A}_1 & \mathbf{A}_d^T\mathbf{A}_2 & \cdots & \mathbf{A}_d^T\mathbf{A}_d + \lambda\mathbf{D}_d \end{bmatrix} \begin{bmatrix} \mathbf{x}_1 \\ \mathbf{x}_2 \\ \vdots \\ \mathbf{x}_d \end{bmatrix} = \begin{bmatrix} \mathbf{A}_1^T\mathbf{y} \\ \mathbf{A}_2^T\mathbf{y} \\ \vdots \\ \mathbf{A}_d^T\mathbf{y} \end{bmatrix}. \tag{7}$$

We are particularly interested in problems where (7) is used to determine the predicted values $\hat{\mathbf{f}} = \mathbf{A}\mathbf{x} = \mathbf{y} - \mathbf{r}$, which in view of (4) can be written as

$$\hat{\mathbf{f}} := \mathbf{f}_1 + \ldots + \mathbf{f}_d, \text{ with } \mathbf{f}_i = \mathbf{A}_i\mathbf{x}_i, i = 1,\ldots,d. \tag{8}$$

If we multiply every row block i of (7) by $\mathbf{A}_i(\mathbf{A}_i^T\mathbf{A}_i + \lambda\mathbf{D}_i)^{-1}$ from the left and introduce

$$\mathbf{S}_i := \mathbf{A}_i(\mathbf{A}_i^T\mathbf{A}_i + \lambda\mathbf{D}_i)^{-1}\mathbf{A}_i^T \quad (i = 1,\ldots,d), \tag{9}$$

we obtain equations of the form

$$\underbrace{\begin{bmatrix} \mathbf{I} & \mathbf{S}_1 & \mathbf{S}_1 & \ldots & \mathbf{S}_1 \\ \mathbf{S}_2 & \mathbf{I} & \mathbf{S}_2 & \ldots & \mathbf{S}_2 \\ \mathbf{S}_3 & \mathbf{S}_3 & \mathbf{I} & \ldots & \mathbf{S}_3 \\ \vdots & \vdots & & \ddots & \vdots \\ \mathbf{S}_d & \mathbf{S}_d & \mathbf{S}_d & \ldots & \mathbf{I} \end{bmatrix}}_{\mathbf{S}} \underbrace{\begin{bmatrix} \mathbf{f}_1 \\ \mathbf{f}_2 \\ \mathbf{f}_3 \\ \vdots \\ \mathbf{f}_d \end{bmatrix}}_{\mathbf{f}} = \begin{bmatrix} \mathbf{S}_1\mathbf{y} \\ \mathbf{S}_2\mathbf{y} \\ \mathbf{S}_3\mathbf{y} \\ \vdots \\ \mathbf{S}_d\mathbf{y} \end{bmatrix}. \tag{10}$$

Following the tradition from statistics we call matrices $\mathbf{S}_i$ *smoothing matrices*. The normal equation (10) is the one we are interested in solving. In Section 5 we discuss why we prefer it over (7).

3   Regression Models

Problem (7) arises naturally in a number of regression models which utilise the basis expansion [16]

$$f_j(t_j) = \sum_{l=1}^{m_j} \beta_l\phi_l(t_j) \tag{11}$$

with functions ϕ_l being a basis of a function space V_j and β_l being model parameters.

The matrix $\mathbf{A}_j$ has the components

$$\{\mathbf{A}_j\}_{kl} = \phi_l(t_j^{(k)}), k = 1,\ldots,N, l = 1,\ldots,m_j.$$

We illustrate this on the example of regression splines. The derivation for other basis expansion models, e.g. linear and polynomial regression or sparse grids, is analogous.

Regression splines form piecewise-polynomials of order M (for cubic splines $M = 4$) with knots ξ_j, $j = 1, \ldots, K$. The general form for the truncated-power basis set would be [16]

$$\phi_j(t) = t^{j-1}, j = 1, \ldots, M,$$
$$\phi_{M+l}(t) = \max\{0, (X - \xi_l)^{M-1}\}, l = 1, \ldots, K.$$

The cubic spline regression solves the problem (5) with $\mathbf{D}$ having the components $\{\mathbf{D}\}_{kl} = \int \phi_k''(t)\phi_l''(t)dt$.

Buja et al. have shown the existence of at least one solution for the normal equations (10) for symmetric smoothers with eigenvalues in [0,1] and so this result also applies for other additive models that fit the requirements [12]. Furthermore, the Gauss-Seidel and related procedures would always converge to some solution of (10).

It can be shown that for any Hermitian positive definite matrix $\mathbf{D}_j$ and $\mathbf{A}_j$ resulting from our basis expansion the corresponding smoothing matrix $\mathbf{S}_j$ has its spectrum in $[0, 1)$ as well and hence all convergence results apply.

Problem (10) arises naturally from the models based on reproducing kernel Hilbert spaces, such as Nadaraya-Watson kernel regression.

Nadaraya-Watson kernel regression is another popular non-parametric regression method from statistics. The estimator function describes the conditional expectation of the target variable relative to the input variable:

$$f(t) = \frac{\sum_{i=1}^{N} \phi_h(t - t^{(i)})y^{(i)}}{\sum_{i=1}^{N} \phi_h(t - t^{(i)})}, \tag{12}$$

where ϕ is a kernel function with a bandwidth h.

The smoothing matrix in this case can be expressed explicitly as

$$\{\mathbf{S}_j\}_{kl} = \frac{\phi_h(\mathbf{t}_j^{(k)} - \mathbf{t}_j^{(l)})}{\sum_{i=1}^{N} \phi_h(\mathbf{t}_j^{(k)} - \mathbf{t}_j^{(i)})}, k = 1, \ldots, N, l = 1, \ldots, N \tag{13}$$

Convergence theory for this type of models is currently an area of active research [17].

4   Fitting Methods

As mentioned in the previous section, the convergence of many algorithms for solving (10) depends on properties of the spectrum of $\mathbf{S}_j$. However, while the convergence can be established, the convergence rate of the algorithms would depend on the magnitude and distribution of the system matrix eigenvalues.

A popular method to solve (10) is the Backfitting Algorithm 1. The main principle of the algorithm is a blocked Gauss-Seidel method.

Buja et al. show that the convergence rate of the backfitting algorithm heavily depends on the magnitude of the eigenvalues that are significantly smaller than

---

Algorithm 1 Backfitting Algorithm

Input: $\mathbf{S}_1, \ldots, \mathbf{S}_d$ smoothing matrices, $\mathbf{y}$ target vector
Output: $\mathbf{f}^T := (\mathbf{f}_1^T, \ldots, \mathbf{f}_d^T)^T$ predictions of the additive models
while not converged **do**
    for $j = 1$ to d **do**
$$\mathbf{f}_j = \mathbf{S}_j \left(\mathbf{y} - \sum_{k \neq j} \mathbf{f}_k \right)$$
    end for
end while

---

1. This means that the error terms corresponding to the eigenvectors with eigenvalues near 1 (e.g. constant, linear and low-frequency) would not be eliminated at all by the algorithm.

Figure 1 illustrates a typical distribution of the eigenvalues of the matrix $\mathbf{S}$. The matrix has a single large eigenvalue that is equal to the d, followed by a cluster of eigenvalues in the range $[0, 1.37)$.

At this point we suggest to use a BiCGStab-based Krylov method [18] instead of Gauss-Seidel iteration for solving Equation (10) to improve the convergence. Not only is it better suited for system matrices with clustered eigenvalues, it also eliminates the error components that are problematic for backfitting and have to be handled separately, e.g. using modified backfitting [12].

Algorithm 2 shows the original formulation of the BiCGStab algorithm without preconditioning. It is not well suited for parallelisation as it requires synchronisation in lines 9, 10, 13, and 14.

Algorithm 2 BiCGStab Algorithm

---

1. **Input:** $\mathbf{S}, \mathbf{S}_1, \ldots, \mathbf{S}_d$ smoothing matrices, $\mathbf{y}$ target vector
2. **Output:** $\mathbf{f}$ predictions of the additive models
3. $\mathbf{r}^T = (\mathbf{r}^0)^T = (\mathbf{S}_1\mathbf{y}, \mathbf{S}_2\mathbf{y}, \ldots, \mathbf{S}_d\mathbf{y})$
4. $\mathbf{f} = \mathbf{t} = \mathbf{v} = \mathbf{s} = \mathbf{0}$
5. $\alpha = \omega = 1$; $\rho^{old} = \rho^{new} = \beta = \mathbf{r}^T\mathbf{r}$
6. **while** not converged **do**
7. $\beta = \rho^{new}/\rho^{old} \cdot \alpha/\omega$; $\rho^{old} = \rho^{new}$
8. $\mathbf{p} = \beta(\mathbf{p} - \omega\mathbf{v}) + \mathbf{r}$
9. $\mathbf{v} = \mathbf{S}\mathbf{p}$ {synchronisation}
10. $\alpha = \rho^{old}/\mathbf{v}^T\mathbf{r}_0$ {synchronisation}
11. $\mathbf{s} = \mathbf{r} - \alpha\mathbf{v}$
12.   check convergence
13. $\mathbf{t} = \mathbf{S}\mathbf{s}$ {synchronisation}
14. $\omega = \frac{\mathbf{t}^T\mathbf{s}}{\mathbf{t}^T\mathbf{t}}$; $\rho^{new} = -\omega\mathbf{t}^T\mathbf{r}_0$ {synchronisation}
15. $\mathbf{r} = \mathbf{s} - \omega\mathbf{t}$
16. $\mathbf{f} = \mathbf{f} + \omega\mathbf{s} + \alpha\mathbf{p}$
17.   check convergence
18. **end while**

To reduce the communication we postpone the calculation of the scalar products until the aggregation of the results of matrix-vector multiplications is necessary. We can do this because the system matrix has a very specific structure and its application on a vector requires only minimal communication:

$$\mathbf{v}_j = \mathbf{p}_j + \mathbf{S}_j(\sum_{i \neq j} \mathbf{p}_j) = \mathbf{p}_j + \mathbf{S}_j(\sum_{i=1}^{d} \mathbf{p}_i - \mathbf{p}_j),$$

$$\mathbf{t}_j = \mathbf{s}_j + \mathbf{S}_j(\sum_{i \neq j} \mathbf{s}_j) = \mathbf{s}_j + \mathbf{S}_j(\sum_{i=1}^{d} \mathbf{s}_i - \mathbf{s}_j)$$

with $\mathbf{v}_j, \mathbf{p}_j, \mathbf{t}_j, \mathbf{s}_j$ denoting the subvectors, similar to $\mathbf{x}_j$.

Furthermore, to reduce communication we found it more convenient to aggregate the sum of vectors $\mathbf{t}_i$ and $\mathbf{v}_i$ instead of $\mathbf{p}_i$ and $\mathbf{s}_i$

Algorithm 3 presents the final algorithm. Vectors with the subscript "Σ", e.g. $\mathbf{t}_\Sigma$, represent the results of the sum of individual vectors, e.g. $\sum_i \mathbf{t}_i$. The scalar products in the second argument of the `Allreduce` functions in lines 10 and 20 stand for variables containing the corresponding scalar products. In these calls a vector and scalar products are joined into a single memory segment to reduce communication.

We illustrate the scalability of the algorithm in the next section.

5   Results

To motivate the use of the smoothing matrix formulation and normal equations of the form (10) instead of (7), we begin by illustrating the convergence speed of the same problem in these two formulations.

A synthetic dataset used for this experiment was generated from a linear model with random coefficients. This dataset has 100-dimensions whereas only 10 dimensions are informative. The targets were obfuscated by additive noise term with $\mathcal{N}(0, 0.01)$:

$$y = \beta_0 + \beta_1 t_1 + \ldots + \beta_{10} t_{10} + 0 t_{11} + \ldots + 0 t_{100} + \varepsilon,$$
$$\beta_0, \beta_1, \ldots, \beta_{10} \sim \mathcal{U}(0, 100), \varepsilon \sim \mathcal{N}(0, 0.01). \tag{14}$$

Altogether 1000 points were used to generate the results. To model the function we used regression cubic splines described in Section 3 with 10 basis functions per dimension and regression parameter $\lambda = 10^{-7}$.

Figure 2 illustrates the norm of the residual and the prediction error. We normalise the measurements by the norm of the residual/error at iteration 0, so that at the beginning the residual/error norm is always 1. Equation (7) is solved using MINRES method [19], while Equation (10) is solved once using backfitting and once using BiCGStab method.

One can easily see the superiority of the problem formulation (10) both by using the classical backfitting algorithm and by the BiCGStab method. While

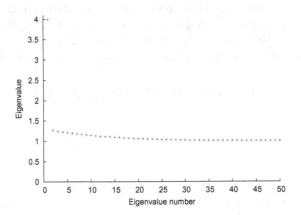

Fig. 1. Distribution of the 50 largest eigenvalues of the matrix **S** from a 4-dimensional Friedman 2 dataset with cubic spline regressors

---

Algorithm 3 Parallel BiCGStab Algorithm: code for processor $j, 0 \le j \le n-1$

1. **Input:** S_j smoothing matrix, **y** target vector
2. **Output:** $\mathbf{f}_j$ predictions of the function $f_j(x)$ at the data points
3. $\mathbf{r}_j^0 = S_j \mathbf{y}; \mathbf{r}_j = \mathbf{r}_j^0$
4. $\texttt{Allreduce}([\mathbf{r}_j, \mathbf{r}_j^T \mathbf{r}_j], [\mathbf{r}_\Sigma, \rho^{\text{new}}], \text{SUM})$
5. $\alpha = \omega = 1; \rho^{\text{old}} = \beta = \rho^{\text{new}}$
6. $\mathbf{f}_j = \mathbf{t}_j = \mathbf{v}_j = \mathbf{v}_\Sigma = \mathbf{p}_j = \mathbf{p}_\Sigma = \mathbf{s}_j = \mathbf{s}_\Sigma = \mathbf{0}$
7. **while** not converged **do**
8.   **if** iteration > 0 **then**
9. $\rho^{\text{old}} = \rho^{\text{new}}$
10. $\texttt{Allreduce}([\mathbf{s}_j^T \mathbf{r}_j^0, \mathbf{t}_j^T \mathbf{s}_j, \mathbf{t}_j^T \mathbf{t}_j, \mathbf{t}_j^T \mathbf{r}_j^0, \mathbf{t}_j], [\mathbf{s}^T \mathbf{r}^0, \mathbf{t}^T \mathbf{s}, \mathbf{t}^T \mathbf{t}, \mathbf{t}^T \mathbf{r}^0, \mathbf{t}_\Sigma], \text{SUM})$
11. $\omega = \frac{\mathbf{t}^T \mathbf{s}}{\mathbf{t}^T \mathbf{t}}; \rho^{\text{new}} = \mathbf{s}^T \mathbf{r}^0 - \omega \mathbf{t}^T \mathbf{r}^0; \beta = \frac{\rho^{\text{new}}}{\rho^{\text{old}}} \cdot \frac{\alpha}{\omega}$
12. $\rho^{\text{old}} = \rho^{\text{new}}$
13. $\mathbf{r}_j = \mathbf{s}_j - \omega \mathbf{t}_j; \mathbf{r}_\Sigma = \mathbf{s}_\Sigma - \omega \mathbf{t}_\Sigma$
14. $\mathbf{f}_j = \mathbf{f}_j + \omega \mathbf{s}_j$
15.   check convergence on **r**
16.   **end if**
17. $\mathbf{p}_j = \beta(\mathbf{p}_j - \omega \mathbf{v}_j) + \mathbf{r}_j$
18. $\mathbf{p}_\Sigma = \beta(\mathbf{p}_\Sigma - \omega \mathbf{v}_\Sigma) + \mathbf{r}_\Sigma$
19. $\mathbf{v}_j = \mathbf{p}_j + S_j(\mathbf{p}_\Sigma - \mathbf{p}_j)$
20. $\texttt{Allreduce}([\mathbf{v}_j^T \mathbf{r}_j^0, \mathbf{v}_j], [\mathbf{v}^T \mathbf{r}^0, \mathbf{v}_\Sigma], \text{SUM})$
21. $\alpha = \rho^{\text{old}} / \mathbf{v}^T \mathbf{r}^0$
22. $\mathbf{s}_j = \mathbf{r}_j - \alpha \mathbf{v}_j; \mathbf{s}_\Sigma = \mathbf{r}_\Sigma - \alpha \mathbf{v}_\Sigma$
23. $\mathbf{f}_j = \mathbf{f}_j + \alpha \mathbf{p}_j$
24.   check convergence on **s**
25. $\mathbf{t}_j = \mathbf{s}_j + S_j(\mathbf{s}_\Sigma - \mathbf{s}_j)$
26. **end while**

the residual in the formulation (7) decreases, it does not seem to significantly reduce the error of the resulting additive model which is our main goal.

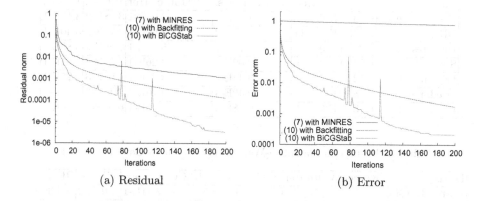

(a) Residual   (b) Error

Fig. 2. Comparison of problem formulations (7) solved with MINRES and (10) solved with backfitting and BiCGStab for minimisation of residual and error of a synthetic 100-dimensional dataset from model (14)

Figure 2 also gives an impression of the convergence comparison between backfitting and BiCGStab. Backfitting shows more stable, but slower convergence even on this simple example.

We extend the numerical comparison by a number of benchmark datasets (see Table 1 for description). Tables 2 and 3 compare the final normalised residual and error for a number of problems. As our main focus is the solution of Equation (10) we do not discuss the selection of optimal learning parameters and confine to setting the same parameters for the backfitting and BiCGStab.

Table 1. Summary description of the benchmark datasets

Dataset	Samples	Dimensions	Source
Boston Housing	506	13	[20]
DR 5	10000	6	[21]
Diabetes	442	10	[22]
Spam	3064	16	[16]
Friedman 1	2000	10	[23]
Friedman 2	1000	4	[23]
Friedman 3	1000	4	[23]

The BiCGStab method is at least as good and in many cases clearly superior to the backfitting algorithm. We also observed that, depending on the problem, backfitting would catch up with more iterations allowed or stagnate with a higher error.

Table 2. Results for cubic spline regression

Dataset	m_j	λ	Iter.	BiCGStab res.	BiCGStab error	BF res.	BF err.
Boston Housing	20	1E-4	6	1.87E-2	3.08E-1	3.48E-2	3.17E-1
DR 5	50	1E-6	11	1.77E-2	4.60E-1	4.74E-2	5.40E-1
Diabetes	25	1E-10	5	7.75E-2	5.46E-1	1.20E-1	5.85E-1
Spam	100	1E-10	6	2.09E-2	4.26E-1	3.27E-2	4.31E-1
Friedman 1	12	1E-7	3	3.44E-4	3.25E-1	1.04E-3	3.25E-1
Friedman 2	8	1E-7	2	9.49E-4	4.76E-1	7.17E-3	4.76E-1
Friedman 3	8	1E-7	2	6.48E-4	4.49E-1	6.98E-3	4.49E-1

Table 3. Results for Nadaraya-Watson regressor with Gaussian kernel

Dataset	Kernel Width	Iter.	BiCGStab res.	BiCGStab err.	BF. res.	BF. err.
Boston Housing	10	6	9.33E-3	2.81E-1	3.03E-2	2.88E-1
DR 5	10	12	1.61E-2	4.21E-1	4.27E-2	4.96E-1
Diabetes	10	4	1.00E-2	5.45E-1	5.53E-2	5.48E-1
Spam	10	5	1.43E-2	3.91E-1	4.00E-2	3.97E-1
Friedman 1	10	5	5.95E-3	2.53E-1	6.90E-3	2.53E-1
Friedman 2	10	3	2.27E-3	4.40E-1	7.67E-3	4.40E-1
Friedman 3	10	3	2.21E-3	4.23E-1	7.39E-3	4.28E-1

To study the scalability of the Algorithm 3 we implemented it in C++ using `MPI_Allreduce` function for data aggregation. Every processor j is responsible for one $\mathbf{S}_j$ smoothing matrix so that increasing number of processors corresponds to fitting an additive model approximation problem with more dimensions or interaction terms. We focus on the study of weak scaling of the Algorithm 3 since our primary goal is parallelisation as a mean to solve higher-dimensional problems.

In our experiment every processor j generates a random full-rank symmetric positive definite matrix of a given size with spectrum in $[0, 1]$ to use as the matrix $\mathbf{S}_j$. As, obviously, the number of synchronisation steps would usually increase if we solve a higher-dimensional problem, we limit the runs to 50 iterations in every case. Figure 3 illustrates the weak scaling results. The total time slightly increases as the communication time grows logarithmically with the number of processors. This growth however is marginal.

It is straightforward to parallelise matrix-vector and scalar products on a shared memory (MKL, OpenBLAS) and distributed memory (PBLAS) architectures for solving problems with more data. This would allow one to study strong scaling properties and is a topic for future work.

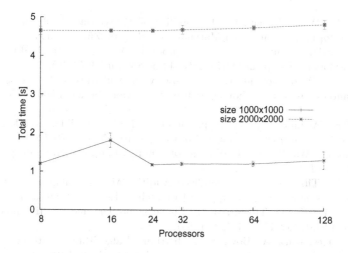

Fig. 3. Weak scaling results for Algorithm 3. Time measurements were performed after 50 iterations with individual matrices $\mathbf{S}_j$ of sizes 1000×1000 and 2000×2000. Median of 7 trials was used in the diagram, while bars indicate the standard deviation.

6   Conclusion

We presented a new approach for fitting additive models using BiCGStab algorithm that, besides smoothing, can be used for larger regression problems. This approach overcomes the shortcomings of the classical backfitting algorithm.

While the convergence of the BiCGStab method cannot be proved theoretically, it usually works well in practice. It converges fast and can be efficiently parallelised for distributed computer architectures.

Our future work will include parallelisation of the data-intensive operations as well as development of preconditioning methods to stabilise and accelerate the convergence.

References

1. Garcke, J., Griebel, M., Thess, M.: Data mining with sparse grids. Computing 67(3), 225–253 (2001)
2. Pflüger, D.: Spatially Adaptive Sparse Grids for High-Dimensional Problems. Verlag Dr. Hut, München (2010)
3. Heinecke, A., Pflüger, D.: Emerging architectures enable to boost massively parallel data mining using adaptive sparse grids. International Journal of Parallel Programming, 1–43 (July 2012)
4. Xu, W.: Towards optimal one pass large scale learning with averaged stochastic gradient descent. CoRR, abs/1107.2490 (2011)
5. Bellman, R., Bellman, R.: Adaptive Control Processes: A Guided Tour. Rand Corporation. Research studies, Princeton University Press (1961)

6. Novak, E., Wozniakowski, H.: Tractability of Multivariate Problems, Volume I: Linear Information. European Mathematical Society, Zürich (2008)
7. Novak, E.: Tractability of multivariate problems, Volume II: Standard Information for Functionals. European Mathematical Society, Zürich (2010)
8. Novak, E., Wozniakowski, H.: Tractability of Multivariate Problems, Volume III: Standard Information for Operators. European Mathematical Society, Zürich (2012)
9. Novak, E., Woźniakowski, H.: Approximation of infinitely differentiable multivariate functions is intractable. Journal of Complexity 25, 398–404 (2009)
10. Hegland, M., Wasilkowski, G.W.: On tractability of approximation in special function spaces. J. Complex. 29, 76–91 (2013)
11. Hastie, T., Tibshirani, R.: Generalized Additive Models. Chapman & Hall/CRC Monographs on Statistics & Applied Probability. Taylor & Francis (1990)
12. Buja, A., Hastie, T., Tibshirani, R.: Linear smoothers and additive models. The Annals of Statistics 17, 453–510 (1989)
13. Chu, E., Keshavarz, A., Boyd, S.: A distributed algorithm for fitting generalized additive models. Optimization and Engineering 14, 213–224 (2013)
14. Hsu, D., Karampatziakis, N., Langford, J., Smola, A.: Parallel online learning, ch. 14. Cambridge University Press (2011)
15. Stone, C.J.: The dimensionality reduction principle for generalized additive models. The Annals of Statistics 14, 590–606 (1986)
16. Hastie, T., Tibshirani, R., Friedman, J.: The Elements of Statistical Learning: Data Mining, Inference, and Prediction, 2nd edn. Springer Series in Statistics. Springer (2011)
17. Xia, Y.: A note on the backfitting estimation of additive models. Bernoulli 15, 1148–1153 (2009)
18. van der Vorst, H.: Bi-cgstab: A fast and smoothly converging variant of bi-cg for the solution of nonsymmetric linear systems. SIAM Journal on Scientific and Statistical Computing 13(2), 631–644 (1992)
19. Paige, C., Saunders, M.: Solution of sparse indefinite systems of linear equations. SIAM Journal on Numerical Analysis 12(4), 617–629 (1975)
20. Harrison, D.J., Rubinfeld, D.L.: Hedonic housing prices and the demand for clean air. Journal of Environmental Economics and Management 5(1), 81–102 (1978)
21. Adelman-McCarthy, J.K., et al.: The fifth data release of the sloan digital sky survey. The Astrophysical Journal Supplement Series 172(2), 634 (2007)
22. Efron, B., Hastie, T., Johnstone, I., Tibshirani, R.: Least angle regression. The Annals of Statistics 32, 407–499 (2004)
23. Friedman, J.H.: Multivariate adaptive regression splines. The Annals of Statistics 19, 1–67 (1991)

Multi-stage Constraint Surrogate Models for Evolution Strategies

Jendrik Poloczek and Oliver Kramer

Computational Intelligence Group
Department of Computing Science
University of Oldenburg, Germany
{jendrik.poloczek,oliver.kramer}@uni-oldenburg.de

Abstract. Real-parameter blackbox optimization using evolution strategies (ES) is often applied when the fitness function or its characteristics are not explicitly given. The evaluation of fitness and feasibility might be expensive. In the past, different surrogate model approaches have been proposed to address this issue. In our previous work, local feasibility surrogate models have been proposed, which are trained with already evaluated individuals. This tightly coupled interdependency with the optimization process leads to complex side effects when applied with meta-heuristics like the covariance matrix adaption ES (CMA-ES). The objective of this paper is to propose a new type of constraint surrogate model, which uses the concept of active learning in multiple stages for the estimation of the constraint boundary for a stage-depending accuracy. The underlying linear model of the constraint boundary is estimated in every stage with binary search. In the optimization process the pre-selection scheme is employed to save constraint function calls. The surrogate model is evaluated on a simple adaptive $(1 + 1)$-ES as well as on the complex $(1 + 1)$-CMA-ES for constrained optimization. The results of both ES on a linearly-constrained test bed look promising.

1 Introduction

Real-parameter black box optimization includes problems, in which neither the fitness nor the constraint function and their mathematical characteristics are explicitly given. Due to the nature of meta-heuristic search in the space of possible solutions, a relatively large amount of fitness function calls (FFC) and constraint function calls (CFC) is required. Both types of evaluations are expensive in terms of computation power. Hence, it is desirable to reduce the amount of FFC and CFC without hindering the convergence of the optimization process. In the past, various surrogate models (SM) have been proposed to solve this issue for fitness and constraint evaluations. The latter is by now relatively unexplored, nevertheless for practical applications worth to investigate.

The objective of this paper is to propose a new kind of constraint surrogate model, which uses the concept of active learning in multiple stages for the estimation of the constraint boundary for a stage-depending accuracy. The linear model is estimated in every stage with binary search and total least squares regression. An important aspect of this approach is the loosely-coupled interdependency with the ES, which allows the training of the SM nearly independent from the optimization process, s.t. the optimizer

C. Lutz and M. Thielscher (Eds.): KI 2014, LNCS 8736, pp. 255–266, 2014.

can almost be considered as black box. The feasibility and performance of this approach is evaluated with a simple (1 + 1)-ES and the complex (1 + 1)-CMA-ES for constrained optimization, see [2]. While the simplicity of the first allows an easy integration of a tightly-coupled SM as in [11], the covariance matrix adaptation of the latter clearly requires a loosely-coupled SM. The approach is employed in each case with a pessimistic and an optimistic variant. The problem test bed includes sphere functions with linear constraint boundaries.

The remainder of this paper is organized as follows. In Section 2 an overview of related work is given, the constrained real-parameter optimization problem is defined and ES are briefly introduced. In Section 3 the SM management algorithm with multiple-stages and the SM training algorithm with binary search and total least squares regression are described. In Section 4 an experimental evaluation of the integrated SM is conducted and the results are interpreted. Last, in Section 5 the results of this paper are discussed.

2   Optimization with Evolution Strategies

A constrained continuous optimization problem is defined as follows: In the n-dimensional search space $\mathscr{X} \subseteq \mathbb{R}^n$ the task is to find the global optimum $\mathbf{x}^* \in \mathscr{X}$, which minimizes the fitness function $f(\mathbf{x})$ with subject to inequalities $g_i(\mathbf{x}) \geq 0, i = 1, \ldots, n_1$ and equalities $h_j(\mathbf{x}) = 0, j = 1, \ldots, n_2$. The function $f : \mathbb{R}^n \to \mathbb{R}$ is referred to as the objective function. The functions $g_i : \mathbb{R}^n \to \mathbb{R}$ are the constraint functions. The constraints g_i and h_i divide the search space $\mathscr{X}$ into a feasible subspace $\mathscr{F}$ and an infeasible subspace $\mathscr{I}$. Whenever the search space is restricted due to additional constraints, a constraint handling methodology is required. In [3], different approaches are discussed. In the last decade, various approaches for fitness and constraint SMs have been proposed to decrease the amount of FFC and CFC. An overview of the recent developments is given in [8] and [13]. As stated in [8], the computationally most efficient way for estimating fitness is the use of machine learning models.

The first ES used for experiments and integration of the SM is a simple (1 + 1)-ES. The (1 + 1)-ES uses uncorrelated Gaussian mutation, see Figure 1(a) and plus selection. For the adjustment of the mutation step-size Rechenberg's original 1/5-th success rule is employed, which was first proposed in [12]. The global step-size σ is adjusted according to the probability of generating offspring with a better fitness. If the probability is greater than 1/5, the step-size is increased. Increasing the step-size allows the ES to approximate the optimum faster. If it is exactly 1/5, the step-size is left untouched. If the probability is lower than 1/5, the step-size is decreased to allow convergence. An offspring is generated by the following equation:

$$\mathbf{c} \leftarrow \mathbf{x_b} + \sigma \cdot X \quad \text{s.t.} \quad X \sim \mathscr{N}(0, 1), \tag{1}$$

where $\mathbf{c}$ is the offspring candidate, $\mathbf{x}_b$ is the currently best individual, σ is the global mutation step-size and X is a random variable distributed according to the normal distribution $\mathscr{N}$ with a mean of 0 and a standard deviation of 1.

The (1 + 1)-CMA-ES for constrained optimization used in this paper is introduced in [2]. The idea of this algorithm is to introduce exponentially fading constraint vectors which estimate linear constraint boundaries when generating infeasible candidates,

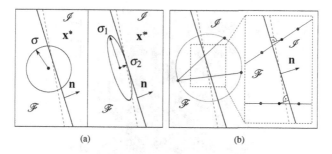

Fig. 1. (a) Two scenerarios are illustrated: The uncorrelated mutation ellipsoid of a (1 + 1)-ES with a global σ (b) and the correlated mutation ellipsoid of a (1 + 1)-CMA-ES. Right: The two steps of the SM training: First, estimation of the closest mean points to the constraint boundary with binary search. Second, total least squares for an estimation of the constraint boundary hyperplane

and use these records to reduce the variance of the distribution of offspring in the direction of normal of the linear constraint boundary, see Figure 1(b). The approach is based on the (1 + 1)-CMA-ES proposed by [7], which includes an efficient covariance matrix adaption via Cholesky decomposition and an improved implementation of the 1/5-th success rule for step-size adaption[1]. In [15], an analogous efficient matrix update is shown. Additionally, the active covariance matrix improvements of [1] are incorporated, which in addition to successful steps uses also unsuccessful steps to update the distribution of offspring candidate solutions. An offspring solution is generated by the following equation:

$$\mathbf{c} \leftarrow \mathbf{x}_b + \sigma \cdot \mathbf{A} \cdot X \quad \text{s.t.} \quad X \sim \mathcal{N}(0,1), \tag{2}$$

where $\mathbf{c}$ is the offspring candidate, $\mathbf{x}_b$ is the currently best individual, σ is the global mutation step-size, $\mathbf{A}$ is a Cholesky factor of the covariance matrix $\mathbf{C}$ and X is a random variable with standard normally distributed components. If an infeasible offspring is generated the corresponding constraint vector is updated according to:

$$\mathbf{v}_j \leftarrow (1 - c_c) \cdot \mathbf{v} + c_c \cdot \mathbf{c}, \tag{3}$$

where $\mathbf{v}_j \in \mathbb{R}^n$ is the fading record, $c_c \in (0,1)$ is a fading factor and $\mathbf{c} \in \mathcal{X}$ is the infeasible solution. The fading factor determines how fast the past information in the vector fades. The fading factor is heuristically determined by parameter tuning on a test bed of multiple problems, see [2]. The constraint vectors $\mathbf{v}_j$ are used to reduce the variance of the distribution of offspring candidate solutions in the direction of the (estimated) normal of the linear constraint boundary. The update is executed in those generations where the offspring candidate solution is infeasible. The Cholesky factor $\mathbf{A}$ of the covariance matrix $\mathbf{C}$ is adjusted according to:

$$\mathbf{A} \leftarrow \mathbf{A} - \frac{\beta}{\sum_{j=1}^{m} \mathbb{1}_{g_j(y)>0}} \frac{\mathbf{v}_j \cdot \mathbf{w}_j^T}{\mathbf{w}_j^T \cdot \mathbf{w}_j}, \tag{4}$$

---

[1] This replaces the commonly used cumulation path length control, which was used in the original CMA-ES approaches.

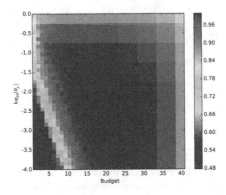

Fig. 2. The accuracy of the binary classification depending on the standard deviation and the budget of CFC invested

where $\mathbf{w}_j = \mathbf{A}^{-1} \cdot \mathbf{v}_j$ and $\mathbb{1}_{g_j(c)>0}$ equals one if the j-th constraint is active and otherwise zero. The parameter β adjusts the impact of the update and is heuristically determined by parameter tuning on a test bed of multiple problems. In the remainder of this paper the $(1 + 1)$-CMA-ES for constrained optimization, proposed in [2], is referred to as $(1 + 1)$-CMA-ES. In the following section, the SM management, training and the integration of the SM in the ES are described.

3   Algorithm

In the following, important considerations are outlined, which motivate the desired properties of the proposed SM. Further, the underlying heuristics are described. Last, it is shown how the loosely-coupled SM is trained and integrated into the ES.

3.1   Considerations

In our previous studies, it has been shown that the SM management is a crucial choice. This includes design choices like which information is used to train the SM, when to update the SM or when to make use of the SM. In our previous work [11], a tightly-coupled SM is employed, which only uses already evaluated solutions to train the SM. The results of this pre-selection strategy are quite satisfying for self-adaptive ES. However, in the case of the CMA-ES a tightly-coupled SM is inappropriate: On the one hand, the CMA-ES uses the covariance matrix adaption to adapt the offspring distribution towards better fitness while simultaneously avoiding infeasible solutions. On the other hand, the offspring is used to estimate the constraint boundary. The latter goal ideally requires feasible as well as infeasible solutions with the highest information gain. Nevertheless, due to the former goal mostly feasible solutions are evaluated. A solution for this dilemma is a separation of the SM and the ES. These loosely-coupled SM only use the latest feasible and infeasible solutions with the highest information gain as a starting position. Independently, the SM estimates the constraint boundary by generating new offspring candidates and evaluating their feasibility.

From a machine learning perspective the estimation of the constraint boundary (hyperplane) can be seen as an active learning scenario, where a huge amount of unlabeled patterns is given and where labeled instances can be obtained via CFC. This scenario implies an advantage over typical supervised machine learning scenarios. Instead of learning a data set which minimizes the empirical risk, the SM can estimate the linear constraint boundary by querying the feasibility of the solutions with the highest information gain. In [9] a pre-sampling strategy is employed which uses the closest feasible and infeasible solutions, obtained by binary search, to estimate the linear constraint boundary. Similarly, in [4], a support vector machine with a radial basis function (RBF) kernel function is used to iteratively sample points and train points which lie close to the hard margin hyperplane. Using an RBF kernel function allows the estimation of non-linear constraint boundaries.

Even though the approaches in [4,9] are loosely-coupled, a pre-sampling strategy is employed, which only allows an estimation of the constraint boundary at the beginning for a fixed CFC budget. The downside of these approaches is clear: If the ES converges to solutions with an accuracy which is not reached by the pre-sampling SM, the SM is uncertain if the solutions are feasible or not. Based on the SM management, the SM is not used in the future if it reaches this lower bound accuracy, or false positive classifications[2] misleadingly allow infeasible solutions to be the optimum.

3.2 Learning

The proposed SM of this paper uses binary search and total least squares regression to estimate the constraint boundary hyperplane. The following descriptions require a basic understanding how the constraint boundary is estimated. For the sake of a better understanding, Figure 1(a) illustrates the estimation. For an estimation of the constraint boundary in an n-dimensional search space, one feasible and n infeasible points (or vice versa) are required. For each pair of the feasible and one infeasible solution a binary search on the line between the two points is employed. In an uncertainty sampling manner, the binary search calculates the mean of the feasible and infeasible solution and evaluates it. If it is feasible, the closest feasible solution record is updated to the calculated mean. Otherwise, the closest infeasible solution record is updated to the mean. After the CFC budget is exhausted, for each pair of closest feasible and infeasible solution, the mean points are calculated. The mean points are points on the estimated constraint boundary hyperplane. The centroid $\mathbf{c}$ of the mean points can be used as a position vector of the hyperplane. The normal of the hyperplane is calculated by the total least squares regression method given the means and the centroid. For an introduction into total least squares regression, we refer to [5]. The resulting estimated hyperplane is used to classify the feasibility of a solution by the decision function $d(\mathbf{x})$:

$$d(\mathbf{x}) = (\mathbf{x} - \mathbf{c}) \cdot \mathbf{n}, \tag{5}$$

where $\mathbf{x} \in \mathcal{X}$ is the test solution, $\mathbf{c} \in \mathcal{X}$ is the centroid of the estimated hyperplane and $\mathbf{n} \in \mathcal{X}$ is the estimated normal of the hyperplane, where n points to the direction of the feasible subspace $\mathcal{F}$. A solution $\mathbf{x}$ is predicted as feasible if $d > 0$ and infeasible otherwise.

---

[2] This is the case, when true infeasibles are by mistake classified as feasible solutions.

3.3 Budget Heuristic

The proposed new kind of constraint surrogate model uses binary search and total least squares regression for an estimation of the linear constraint in multiple stages. A stage is defined as an interval of generations between two accuracies. Similar to the approaches in [9,4], a fixed budget of CFC needs to be specified. In the following, an experimentally determined heuristic for CFC budget per accuracy is proposed.

The heuristic is based on the assumption that binary search and total least squares regression are employed to estimate the linear constraint boundary, see Section 3.2. In an experiment, the constraint boundary is placed at the origin of the search space. At the beginning, the search space is sampled normally distributed given a mean of zero and a standard deviation of 10^{σ_c} to find one feasible and n infeasible solutions, where n is the dimension of the search space $\mathscr{X}$. In the experiment, given a fixed current accuracy exponent $\sigma_c = -1$, the accuracy of this hyperplane is measured depending on the CFC budget and the goal accuracy exponent σ_g of the test solutions. The result of this experiment is shown in Figure 2. Two important observations are the basis of the proposed heuristic. First, even if $\sigma_g \geq \sigma_c$, a budget smaller than 15 results in inaccurate classification. This implies that a budget of roughly 15 CFC is needed to predict in the same or lower accuracy. The second key observation is, that the budget required to reach a good classification for a given σ_g increases linearly between $\sigma_c = -1$ and σ_g on a $\log_{10}$-scale. These observations are invariant to the choice of σ_c. The SM should save as much CFC as possible, but still spend enough CFC for a proper classification with a goal accuracy. Hence, given the resulting visualization in Figure 2, the optimal parameter choice, given a fixed $\sigma_c = -1$ and variable σ_g and budget, lies on the left margin of the red area. A linear function, which maps CFC budget to σ_g is given by:

$$\sigma_g = -\left(\frac{\sigma_2 - \sigma_1}{b_2 - b_1}\right) \cdot b + \sigma_c. \tag{6}$$

with parameters b, b_1, and b_2. As already stated, the optimal parameter choice lies in the left margin of the red area. Hence, the gradient of the linear function is chosen s.t. an overlapping with the red area while saving as most CFC as possible. An appropriate heuristically determined gradient is $-(1/10)$. The linear function is equivalent to the linear function expressing the amount of CFC budget needed from σ_c to σ_g:

$$b(\sigma_c, \sigma_g) = (\sigma_g - \sigma_c) \cdot -\frac{(b_2 - b_1)}{\sigma_2 - \sigma_1} = -(\sigma_g - \sigma_c) \cdot \frac{10}{1}. \tag{7}$$

In the following, the factor resulting from the heuristically determined gradient is referred to as budget factor $b_f \approx 10$. In the next step, the first observation of the experiment has to be incorporated into the CFC budget function B. As already mentioned, a constant CFC budget of roughly 15 has to be spent on estimation to assert a proper classification of solutions of a current accuracy exponent σ_c or higher. Therefore, the heuristically determined constant $b_0 \approx 15$ is added to the linear CFC budget function b:

$$B(\sigma_c, \sigma_g) = -(\sigma_g - \sigma_c) \cdot b_f + b_0 = -(\sigma_g - \sigma_c) \cdot 10 + 15. \tag{8}$$

The overall CFC budget function $B(\sigma_c, \sigma_g)$ is employed when the SM has to estimate the constraint boundary for the next stage.

Algorithm 1.1. $(1 + 1)$-ES with Pessimistic SM

```
1   σc, σg ← log₁₀(σ), log₁₀(σ) − σstep;
2   while |F| < 1 and |I| < n do
3       c ← xs + σ · N(0,1);
4       if feasible (c) then F.append(c);
5       xb ← c;
6       ;
7       else I.append(c);
8       ;
9   end
10  mm.train (F, I, σc, σg);
11  σlb = log₁₀(σ) − σstep;
12  while |f(xb) − f(x*)| < ε do
13      c ← xs + σ · N(0,1);
14      if mm.feasible (c) then
15          if feasible (c) then
16              if fitness (c) < fitness (x) then
17                  xb ← c;
18                  F.append(xb);
19              end
20          else
21              I.append(c);
22          end
23      end
24      adjust_sigma ();
25      σc, σg ← log₁₀(σ), log₁₀(σ) − σstep;
26      if σc < σlb then
27          mm.train (F, I, σc, σg);
28          σlb ← log₁₀(σ) − σstep;
29      end
30  end
```

3.4   General Integration

In the previous sections, considerations have been outlined which were taken into account for the design of the SM and the estimation of the constraint boundary and the proposed CFC budget heuristic has been explained. In the following, the multi-stage approach and its integration with ES are clarified. As already stated, the main idea of the multi-stage SM is to estimate the constraint boundary in multiple stages for a stage-depending accuracy. The approach makes use of the additional variables: the current accuracy exponent $\sigma_c \in \mathbb{N}$, the goal accuracy exponent $\sigma_g \in \mathbb{N}$ and the lower bound accuracy exponent $\sigma_{lb} \in \mathbb{N}$. Additionally, the σ-step parameter is introduced, where $\sigma_{step} \in \mathbb{R}$ and $\sigma_{step} > 0$. The parameter σ-step defines the interval length for which the SM for a certain stage should be able to properly predict the feasibility. The SM is explained along the simple $(1 + 1)$-ES in Algorithm 1. In the algorithm a pessimistic SM is employed, which uses the SM as a pre-selection for feasible solutions, but still verifies the feasibility with the actual constraint function. Parameter ε specifies a fitness threshold for the termination condition. The abbreviation *mm* denotes meta-model.

First, the current accuracy exponent σ_c and the goal accuracy exponent σ_g are assigned. Before the optimization, an initial SM is trained, given a feasible and n infeasible sampled solutions. The estimation of the constraint hyperplane via binary search and total least squares regression is explained in Section 3.2. The CFC budget is determined by the CFC budget heuristic proposed in Section 3.3. After training, the lower bound accuracy exponent σ_{lb} is updated to the goal accuracy exponent σ_g. The

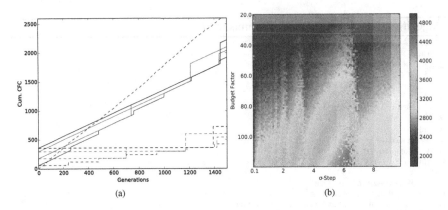

Fig. 3. (a) The cumulated amount of CFC depending on the generations with a (1 + 1)-ES: without SM (dashed blue and nearly linear), with a pessimistic SM (colored solid) and with an optimistic SM (dashed colored step functions). (b) The total amount of CFC depending on the budget factor and the parameter σ-step for the (1 + 1)-ES on test problem S1.

variable σ_{lb} stores the accuracy which is still properly predictable by the SM in the current stage. In the while-loop an offspring is generated. Its feasibility is predicted by the SM of the current stage. The SM filters in a pre-selection manner only feasible-predicted solutions. As already stated, due to the pessimistic variant the feasibility is verified by the actual constraint function. The latest truly feasible and truly infeasible solutions can be exploited as starting points for the SM in the next stage. After adjusting the mutation step size σ, the variables σ_c and σ_g are updated. If the current accuracy exponent σ_c is smaller than the lower bound accuracy exponent σ_{lb}, a new SM is trained for the next stage is trained and the new lower bound accuracy exponent is set accordingly. The optimistic variant relies on the SM without verifying the feasibility with the actual constraint function. Hence, in the optimistic variant the latest feasible and the latest n infeasible are used to sample truly feasible and infeasible starting points every time the SM needs to be trained.

The interdependency between the total amount of CFC and the budget and the σ-step parameter with the (1 + 1)-ES is visually shown in Figure 3(b). In this parameter study experiment, the mean of 10 runs is measured. Clearly, it can be observed that a budget factor below 20 results in wasted CFC. The leaps in the plot correspond to late CFC investments, where the optimum is near and a lower budget would be more appropriate.

3.5   Integration with (1 + 1)-CMA-ES

Because of a lack of space, the complex (1 + 1)-CMA-ES with SM is not described in this paper. Nevertheless, the integration with the SM is analogous, except an important modification to the σ_c update. The mutation step-size is contained in the global step size σ as well as in the Cholesky factor **A**. Therefore, the following equation is used to update the current accuracy exponent:

$$\sigma_c \leftarrow \log_{10}(\|\sigma \cdot \mathbf{A} \cdot \mathbf{1}\|). \tag{9}$$

with In this equation the euclidean norm of the scaled and transformed one vector is used to approximate the current accuracy.

4   Experimental Evaluation

In this section, the experimental evaluation of the proposed SM is described. The proposed loosely-coupled multi-stage SM is evaluated by comparing the cumulated amount of CFC as well as the cumulated amount of FFC of ES with SM to original ES without the SM. The total amount of FFC is taken into account, because the use of the SM might prevent convergence, which might lead to an increase in FFC. In the following, the experimental settings are outlined.

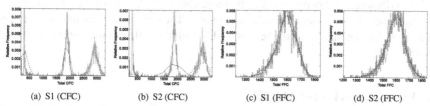

| (a) S1 (CFC) | (b) S2 (CFC) | (c) S1 (FFC) | (d) S2 (FFC) |

Fig. 4. Distributions of total FFC and CFC on both problems with (1 + 1)-ES depending on surrogate model: no meta model (dashed green), pessimistic meta model (solid blue), optimistic meta model (solid black)

4.1   Experiment Design

The experimental evaluation includes the comparison of FFC and CFC between the ES with SM and the ES without SM. A one-factor experiment design is employed, where the cumulated amount of FFC and the cumulated amount of CFC with different settings are compared. Because the optimization is a stochastic process, 500 runs are simulated per setting. In the evaluation, the simple (1 + 1)-ES and the complex (1 + 1)-CMA-ES, proposed in [2] are employed. Further, the two variants of SM use are examined: the pessimistic and the optimistic multi-stage SM. The test bed problems are based on the Sphere function

$$\text{minimize}\quad f(\mathbf{x}) := x_1^2 + x_2^2 \tag{10}$$

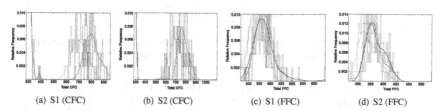

| (a) S1 (CFC) | (b) S2 (CFC) | (c) S1 (FFC) | (d) S2 (FFC) |

Fig. 5. Distributions of total FFC and CFC on both problems with (1 + 1)-CMA-ES depending on surrogate model: no meta model (dashed green), pessimistic meta model (solid blue), optimistic meta model (solid black)

subject to (S1) constraint $x_1 + x_2 \geq 0$ and (S2) constraint $x_1 \geq 0$. The start position in both experiments is $(1.0, 1.0)^T$ and the initial global σ is 1.0. The parameter σ-step of the multi-stage SM is 3.

4.2 Experiment: (1 + 1)-ES

The results of the experiment are shown visually in Figure 4. The distribution of cumulated FFC and CFC is estimated with a Parzen window kernel density estimation, see [10], where the kernel bandwidth is set according to Silverman's rule, see [14]. The characteristic numbers are presented in Table 1. When the total amount of FFC is compared, the different SM uses do not differ. Hence, the cumulated amount of CFC can be compared, because the SM use does not affect the cumulated amount of FFC. When the CFC are compared, it can be observed that a pessimistic SM saves CFC. Nevertheless, the optimistic SM saves significantly more CFC. The cumulated amount of CFC depending on the generations with the (1 + 1)-ES with the different uses of SM is shown in Figure 3(a).

4.3 Experiment: (1 + 1)-CMA-ES

The results of the experiment are shown in Figure 5. Like in the previous experiment, the distributions are estimated with a Parzen window kernel density estimation. The characteristic numbers are presented in Table 2. When the total amount of FFC is compared, the different uses of SM do not differ. Hence, analogous to the previous experiment, the cumulated amount CFC can be compared, because the use of SM does not affect the total amount of FFC. In the comparison of CFC, it is observed that a pessimistic SM requires more CFC than the original (1 + 1)-CMA-ES. A possible reason might be that the internal SM of the (1 + 1)-CMA-ES, the covariance matrix adaption and the constraint vector is sufficient and the external multi-stage SM spends CFC for redundant information. Nevertheless, the optimistic SM case saves significantly more cumulated CFC on both problems.

Table 1. FFC and CFC with (1 + 1)-ES

	FFC				CFC			
	Min.	Mean	Max.	Std.	Min.	Mean	Max.	Std.
without								
S1	1260.00	1586.75	1798.00	74.90	2293.00	2903.15	9113.00	245.51
S2	1197.00	1593.83	1838.00	75.51	2195.00	2933.81	22279.0	632.32
pessimistic								
S1	1286.00	1589.88	1831.00	70.62	1475.00	1885.14	3741.00	123.53
S2	1206.00	1586.84	1827.00	78.37	1390.00	1917.89	31539.0	1027.53
optimistic								
S1	1223.00	1586.18	1840.00	77.90	188.00	323.07	14850.0	506.55
S2	1252.00	1590.91	1807.00	76.32	188.00	309.37	1969.00	113.55

Table 2. FFC and CFC with (1 + 1)-CMA-ES

	FFC				CFC			
	Min.	Mean	Max.	Std.	Min.	Mean	Max.	Std.
without								
S1	264.00	337.17	411.00	33.98	592.00	709.35	924.00	61.64
S2	260.00	342.23	591.00	43.03	575.00	708.00	1115.00	73.75
pessimistic								
S1	285.00	371.70	475.00	36.70	677.00	805.68	952.00	55.17
S2	270.00	361.61	455.00	34.60	560.00	773.36	902.00	53.44
optimistic								
S1	283.00	371.78	652.00	51.41	283.00	306.51	394.00	18.89
S2	308.00	367.78	454.00	33.66	282.00	292.12	318.00	7.37

5   Discussion and Future Work

The SM proposed in Section 3.1 suggests that a loosely-coupled SM clearly is required when the ES also has an internal SM, like the CMA-ES. Therefore, the focus of this paper lies on the adoption of a possible loosely-coupled SM and its assumptions and heuristics. In the experimental analysis, it is found that the optimistic SM is superior to all other uses of SM. The experimental evaluation is arguable in its robustness given other test problems. Nevertheless, it can be observed that the multi-stage approach is compatible even with the complex (1 + 1)-CMA-ES. This paper proposes a working loosely-coupled SM, however, different implementation of loosely-coupled SM might be useful depending on the use case. For example, the SM proposed in [4] is able to estimate the non-linear constraint boundary using a support vector machine with an RBF kernel and an active learning approach, but the integration in ES is missing. A promising future work might be to incorporate the multi-stage approach with a non-linear boundary estimation to save CFC in reset strategies to find the global optimum.

References

1. Arnold, D.V., Hansen, N.: Active Covariance Matrix Adaptation for the (1+1)-CMA-ES. In: Proceedings of the 12th Annual Conference on Genetic and Evolutionary Computation, Portland, United States, pp. 385–392 (2010)
2. Arnold, D.V., Hansen, N.: A (1+1)-CMA-ES for constrained optimisation. In: Proceedings of the Fourteenth International Conference on Genetic and Evolutionary Computation Conference, GECCO 2012, pp. 297–304. ACM, New York (2012)
3. Coello, C.A.C.: Constraint-handling techniques used with evolutionary algorithms. In: Soule, T., Moore, J.H. (eds.) GECCO (Companion), pp. 849–872. ACM (2012)
4. Gieseke, F., Kramer, O.: Towards non-linear constraint estimation for expensive optimization. In: Esparcia-Alcázar, A.I. (ed.) EvoApplications 2013. LNCS, vol. 7835, pp. 459–468. Springer, Heidelberg (2013)
5. de Groen, P.P.N.: An introduction to total least squares (1998)
6. Hansen, N.: The CMA evolution strategy: A comparing review. In: Lozano, J., Larrañaga, P., Inza, I., Bengoetxea, E. (eds.) Towards a New Evolutionary Computation. STUDFUZZ, vol. 192, pp. 75–102. Springer, Heidelberg (2006)

7. Igel, C., Suttorp, T., Hansen, N.: A computational efficient covariance matrix update and a (1+1)-CMA for evolution strategies. In: Proceedings of the 8th Annual Conference on Genetic and Evolutionary Computation, GECCO 2006, pp. 453–460. ACM, New York (2006)

8. Jin, Y.: Surrogate-assisted evolutionary computation: Recent advances and future challenges. Swarm and Evolutionary Computation 1(2), 61–70 (2011)

9. Kramer, O., Barthelmes, A., Rudolph, G.: Surrogate constraint functions for CMA evolution strategies. In: Mertsching, B., Hund, M., Aziz, Z. (eds.) KI 2009. LNCS, vol. 5803, pp. 169–176. Springer, Heidelberg (2009)

10. Parzen, E.: On estimation of a probability density function and mode. The Annals of Mathematical Statistics 33(3), 1065–1076 (1962)

11. Poloczek, J., Kramer, O.: Local SVM constraint surrogate models for self-adaptive evolution strategies. In: Timm, I.J., Thimm, M. (eds.) KI 2013. LNCS, vol. 8077, pp. 164–175. Springer, Heidelberg (2013)

12. Rechenberg, I.: Evolutionsstrategie: Optimierung technischer Systeme nach Prinzipien der biologischen Evolution. PhD thesis, TU Berlin (1973)

13. Santana-Quintero, L.V., Montaño, A.A., Coello, C.A.C.: A review of techniques for handling expensive functions in evolutionary multi-objective optimization. In: Tenne, Y., Goh, C.-K. (eds.) Computational Intelligence in Expensive Optimization Problems. Adaptation, Learning, and Optimization, vol. 2, pp. 29–59. Springer, Heidelberg (2010)

14. Silverman, B.W.: Density Estimation for Statistics and Data Analysis. Chapman & Hall, London (1986)

15. Suttorp, T., Hansen, N., Igel, C.: Efficient Covariance Matrix Update for Variable Metric Evolution Strategies. Machine Learning (2009)

Evolutionary Turbine Selection
for Wind Power Predictions

Nils André Treiber and Oliver Kramer

Department of Computer Science
University of Oldenburg, Germany
{nils.andre.treiber,oliver.kramer}@uni-oldenburg.de

Abstract. Statistical methods have shown great success in short-term prediction of wind power in the recent past. A preselection of turbines is presented that is based on the segmentation of the area around the target turbine with a specific radius. Small problem instances allow a rigorous comparison of different input sets employing various regression techniques and motivate the application of evolutionary algorithms for finding adequate features. The optimization problem turns out to be difficult to solve, while strongly depending on the target turbine and the prediction technique.

1 Introduction

For balancing the electrical grid, the precise prediction of wind power has an important part to play. In the taxonomy of wind prediction models, one can differentiate between two main classes of methods, i.e., numerical weather simulations [1] and statistical models that derive functional dependencies directly from the observations. The latter are well appropriate for short-term prediction horizons in the range of minutes to few hours and are now in focus. In the past, we developed prediction models that are exclusively based on wind power time series measurements [4] and formulated the prediction task as multivariate regression problem considering the time series of neighboring turbines for a specific target turbine. We could show that our model significantly outperforms the persistence model, which is a naive and hard to beat method for comparison in short-term prediction assuming that the wind does not change, see Wegley *et al.* [9]. In this paper, we focus on improving the forecast accuracy of our spatio-temporal model by selecting an adequate subset of neighboring turbines as inputs (features) of the regression model. As this task is a complex combinatorial optimization problem, we propose to employ evolutionary algorithms (EAs) for turbine selection.

1.1 Related Work

EAs in data mining are often employed for feature selection. In the field of wind power prediction, Jursa and Rohrig [3] introduced a method, based on the application of EAs for the automated specification of two well-known time series

C. Lutz and M. Thielscher (Eds.): KI 2014, LNCS 8736, pp. 267–272, 2014.

prediction models with particle particle swarm optimization and differential evolution. This paper presents a very comprehensive model. But a detailed analysis of features measured at different places around the target is desirable from our point of view. Many papers with a focus on wind energy prediction use EAs to tune certain parameters of their introduced methods. For example, Kusiak *et al.* [5] employ EAs to determine the parameters for a nonlinear modeling of wind farm power curves. Shi *et al.* [7] provide a model that uses a genetic algorithm to find appropriate parameters of a *piecewise* support vector machine, based on the power curves of the wind turbine generators. In addition, evolutionary strategies are used in the wind community to optimize the placement of turbines, see e.g. [8] and [2].

1.2   Wind Data Set and Prediction Model

The experiments in this paper are based on the National Renewable Energy Laboratory (NREL) western wind resources data set [6], which is part of a large integration study. The data set has been designed to perform temporal and spatial comparisons like load correlation or estimation of production from hypothetical i.e., simulated wind turbines for demand analysis and planning of storage based on wind variability. It consists of ten-minute wind speed and wind power time series of 32,043 turbines for three years based on numerical simulations and real-world wind measurements. In this paper, we predict the power output of three arbitrarily selected wind turbines near Casper (WY, ID: 23167), Comanche (WY, ID:8419), and Tehachapi (CA, ID: 4155).

We formulate the prediction task as regression problem. Let us first assume we want to predict the power production of a turbine only with its time series. The wind power measurement $\mathbf{x} = p(t)$ (pattern) is mapped to the power production at target time $y = p(t + \lambda)$ (label). For our regression model, we assume to have N of such pattern label pairs $(\mathbf{x}^i, y^i)$ that are basis of our training set $T = \{(\mathbf{x}^1, y^1), \ldots, (\mathbf{x}^N, y^N)\}$ and allow the prediction of the label for unknown patterns via regression. One can assume, that this model generates better predictions, if more information of the times series will be used. For this reason, we extend the patterns by appending past measurements $p(t-1), \ldots, p(t-\mu)$ with $\mu \in \mathbb{N}^+$. To consider some spatio-temporal effects we additionally extend the pattern by extra features x_j of m neighboring turbines $j = 1, 2, \ldots, m$ that are generated in the same way as for the target turbine. In the end, one has a pattern with a dimension $d = (1 + m)(1 + \mu)$, which is mapped to the power output of the target turbine. Generally, the goal is now to find a function f that provides good predictions to unseen patterns $\mathbf{x}$. In our experiments, we employ linear regression, support vector regression (SVR), and k-nearest neighbors (kNN).

2   Segmentation and Combinatorial Prestudies

In this section, we compare the regression methods for short-term predictions of the selected target turbines. We use a small number of turbines that allows to test all possible combinations of inputs. In the following experiments, we employ a feature window size of one, i.e., it holds $\mu = 0$ and no past measurements are taken into account for constructing pattern $\mathbf{x}$.

2.1 Segmentation

First of all, we have to choose a radius, in which the neighboring turbines should be located. Instead of a random selection of turbines, which would prefer locations with large aggregations, we aim at a uniform, radial distribution. For this sake, we divide the area in a particular radius into 12 segments and choose the turbines that are closest to the center of each segment. With given mean wind speeds in the interval of 8.2-9.2 m/s and the assumption that wind propagates linearly, we decide to focus on a one-hour-ahead prediction resulting in an average distance between the target and other turbines of about 30 km. Figure 1 shows the neighboring turbines of the three target turbines.

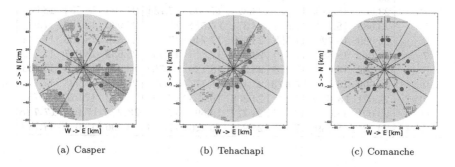

(a) Casper   (b) Tehachapi   (c) Comanche

Fig. 1. Segmentation of the neighborhood of the three target turbines for a finite number of additional inputs. Available turbines are shown in blue, while the selected ones are shown in red.

2.2 Combinatorial Tests

The question comes up, which subset of the 12 available turbines (plus the target itself) leads to the best prediction accuracy. Due to the small solution space size ($\sum_{j=0}^{12} \binom{12}{j} = 4096$ possible solutions), we can evaluate the complete search space, i.e., all turbine combinations with $0, 1, 2, \ldots, 12$ additional turbines. We train the model with data from 2004 and evaluate the mean square error (MSE) $\delta = \frac{1}{M} \sum_{i=1}^{M} (f(\mathbf{x}^i) - y^i)^2$ for $i = 1, \ldots, M$ predictions $f(\mathbf{x}^i)$ of 2005. For the parameter tuning of the nonlinear regression techniques, we employ a 2-fold cross-validation on 2004. For kNN regression, we test various numbers of neighbors, i.e., $k = 10, 20, \ldots, 130$. For reasons of efficiency of the SVR training process, we narrow the grid search for optimal parameters settings of C and γ to the following intervals, i.e., $C \in [500, 1000, 2000]$ for regularization and $\gamma \in [10^{-3}, 10^{-6}]$ for the RBF kernel bandwidth, which turned out to be appropriate in preliminary experiments. To speed up the training process, only every fifth time step is taken into account. In this smaller training set, still varying wind conditions of different seasons are included. The results are shown in Table 1. An important observation is that not the maximum number of input achieves

Table 1. Best MSE of a one-hour-ahead prediction for a varying numbers of inputs. The values represent the MSE of the best combination of each input size. The whole space of turbines is shown in Figure 1. The errors of the persistence model are 26.066 [MW^2] for Casper (CS), 20.715 [MW^2] for Tehachapi (TC), and 24.274 [MW^2] for Comanche (CM).

add. inputs	linear CS	linear TC	linear CM	kNN CS	kNN TC	kNN CM	SVR CS	SVR TC	SVR CM
univariate	24.755	20.072	22.700	24.884	20.006	22.869	25.724	20.574	23.566
1	23.472	19.278	19.654	23.422	18.708	19.748	24.839	19.800	20.154
2	23.185	19.089	18.697	**23.258**	17.989	18.710	24.537	19.404	19.123
3	23.116	18.948	18.119	23.308	17.655	18.121	24.296	19.061	18.477
4	23.098	18.823	17.777	23.325	17.595	17.734	24.155	18.754	18.065
5	23.085	18.761	17.644	23.371	**17.588**	17.633	23.930	18.480	17.925
6	23.069	18.726	17.553	23.609	17.749	17.563	23.813	18.266	17.844
7	**23.061**	18.686	17.489	23.726	17.815	17.552	23.632	18.067	17.782
8	23.062	18.678	17.475	23.969	18.120	**17.501**	23.607	17.968	17.763
9	23.069	18.673	**17.473**	24.172	18.777	17.554	23.574	17.928	17.754
10	23.071	**18.670**	17.481	24.388	19.225	17.601	23.513	17.926	17.738
11	23.091	18.689	17.497	24.772	19.692	17.645	**23.477**	**17.926**	**17.738**
12	23.121	18.739	17.502	24.948	20.226	17.673	23.496	18.049	17.749

the best prediction accuracy, but a certain subset of turbines. If too few or too many turbines are taken into account, the predictions are getting worse.

A conclusion we can draw from the experiments is that there is no superior regression technique in general. The optimization problem turns out to be data set- and method-specific and is hence not trivial to solve, which motivates the application of evolutionary methods. For the following experiments, we focus on kNN regression, since it achieves the best results in mean. However, the evolutionary feature selection approach is independent of the employed regression technique.

3   Evolutionary Turbine Selection

Now, we introduce an evolutionary approach to automatically determine the optimal subset of turbines (size and combination) to achieve a high prediction accuracy for a particular target turbine given a regression method. EAs are heuristic search methods that mimic the process of natural evolution.

3.1 Modeling

Let ϕ be the number of neighboring turbines the segmentation pre-processing step selects, see Section 2. The objective is to find an optimal subset Ω of turbines that minimizes the prediction accuracy in terms of MSE, see Section 2.2. The fitness function $\hat{f}(\cdot)$ the EA has to optimize, determines the prediction accuracy of a regression model given index set Ω of considered turbines. For this sake, a training and a test set of patterns are constructed, the regression model is trained with cross-validation and evaluated on an independent test set. We choose the following representation for a candidate solution. A bit string $\mathbf{z} = (z_1, \ldots, z_\phi)$ of length ϕ defines, which turbines are taken into account. If z_i is One, turbine $i \in \phi$ is taken into account as feature in the regression model. If z_i is Zero, turbine with index i is not considered. This representation automatically allows an adaptation of the number of turbines.

At the beginning, the EA generates μ individuals by initializing μ bit strings $\mathbf{z}_1, \ldots, \mathbf{z}_\mu$ with elements z_i that are set to One with a probabilty p_{set}. In the evolutionary loop, the EA generates λ children based on μ parents with 1-point crossover. Consequently, each child carries the genetic material of two parents. As mutation operator, bit flip mutation is employed with mutation strength $p = 1/\phi$. The fitness $\hat{f}(\cdot)$ of all λ individuals is determined by computing the MSE and is the basis for selecting the μ best individuals as parents for the following generation. Plus selection selects the μ best solutions from the union $\mathcal{P} \cup \mathcal{P}'$ of the best parental population $\mathcal{P}$ and the current offspring population $\mathcal{P}'$ and is denoted by $(\mu + \lambda)$-EA. In contrast, comma selection chooses the parents exclusively from the offspring population, even if the parents have a superior fitness, and is denoted by (μ, λ)-EA.

3.2 Comparison of Selection Operators

We compare the number of generations of the kNN regression model for a (μ, λ)-EA and a $(\mu + \lambda)$-EA. Previous experiments have shown that the population size choices $\mu = 5$ and $\lambda = 10$ led to a good compromise between the number of fitness function evaluations and solution quality. In our implementation, we choose the initial probability $p_{set} = 0.5$ of a turbine to be selected. The results are shown in Table 2. The statistics are based on 30 runs for each approach. Since we assume unequal variances, we employ the Welch test for checking the significance of the results. With a p-value of $p = 0.028$ for Tehachapi and a value of $p = 0.034$ for Comanche, there is strong evidence against the null hypothesis. Therefore,

Table 2. Number of generations with standard deviation until best inputs are found for the (5, 10) and (5 + 10) EA

turbine	(5, 10)-EA	(5 + 10)-EA
Casper	12.0 ± 8.2	10.9 ± 5.1
Tehachapi	15.4 ± 8.4	11.4 ± 4.7
Comanche	20.1 ± 13.0	13.4 ± 7.6

we conclude that plus selection leads to a faster convergence. For Casper, no statistical difference between both selection variants can be observed.

4 Conclusion

Prediction is an important task for the integration of wind power. In this work, we focused on the selection of turbines with EAs for an improvement of prediction accuracies. In particular, we have shown that the accuracy of kNN regression prediction benefits greatly from an appropriate set of features. The implemented EA shows a good performance by identifying the best subset of input turbines for small problem instances with a relatively small number of regression calls.

In the future, we concentrate on mutation rate control methods to improve the evolutionary search. A further effect of the turbine selection is a speedup of training and prediction time due to a reduction of the feature space. We plan to investigate the tradeoff between EA runtime and expected prediction accuracies for a setup with more available turbines after the segmentation.

References

1. Costa, A., Crespo, A., Navarro, J., Lizcano, G., Madsen, H., Feitosa, E.: A review on the young history of the wind power short-term prediction. Renewable and Sustainable Energy Reviews 12(6), 1725–1744 (2008)
2. Grady, S.A., Hussaini, M.Y., Abdullah, M.M.: Placement of wind turbines using genetic algorithms. Renewable Energy 30(2), 259–270 (2005)
3. Jursa, R., Rohrig, K.: Short-term wind power forecasting using evolutionary algorithms for the automated specification of artificial intelligence models. International Journal of Forecasting 24(4), 694–709 (2008)
4. Kramer, O., Gieseke, F.: Short-term wind energy forecasting using support vector regression. In: Corchado, E., Snášel, V., Sedano, J., Hassanien, A.E., Calvo, J.L., Ślęzak, D. (eds.) SOCO 2011. AISC, vol. 87, pp. 271–280. Springer, Heidelberg (2011)
5. Kusiak, A., Zheng, H., Song, Z.: Models for monitoring wind farm power. Renewable Energy 34, 583–590 (2009)
6. Potter, C.W., Lew, D., McCaa, J., Cheng, S., Eichelberger, S., Grimit, E.: Creating the dataset for the western wind and solar integration study (U.S.A.). Wind Engineering 32(4), 325–338 (2008)
7. Shi, J., Yang, Y., Wang, P., Liu, Y., Han, S.: Genetic algorithm-piecewise support vector machine model for short term wind power prediction. In: Proceedings of the 8th World Congress on Intelligent Control and Automation, pp. 2254–2258 (2010)
8. Wagner, M., Veeremachaneni, K., Neumann, F., O'Reilly, U.-M.: Optimizing the layout of 1000 wind turbines. In: European Wind Energy Association Annual Event, pp. 205–209 (2011)
9. Wegley, H., Kosorok, M., Formica, W.: Subhourly wind forecasting techniques for wind turbine operations. Technical report, Pacific Northwest Lab, Richland, WA, USA (1984)

Planning in the Wild: Modeling Tools for PDDL

Volker Strobel and Alexandra Kirsch

Department of Informatics
Eberhard Karls Universität Tübingen

Abstract. Even though there are sophisticated AI planning algorithms, many integrated, large-scale projects do not use planning. One reason seems to be the missing support by engineering tools such as syntax highlighting and visualization. We propose MYPDDL— a modular toolbox for efficiently creating PDDL domains and problems. To evaluate MYPDDL, we compare it to existing knowledge engineering tools for PDDL and experimentally assess its usefulness for novice PDDL users.

1   Introduction

A large community of researchers dedicate their efforts to AI planning. However, the progress made in this community is often ignored when it comes to developing complete AI systems. Planning is a fundamental cognitive function that is useful for most systems claiming to be intelligent, such as autonomous robots or decision support systems.

The basics of AI planning are taught in any AI course and there are many planners readily available, also due to the International Planning Competition[1]. So why is planning not used in more systems? We believe that one reason is the gap between modeling textbook toy problems and modeling complex, real-world problems. The standard AI planning language PDDL differentiates between domain files with definitions of types, predicates and actions, and problem files with definitions of objects and goals. Realistic domains contain hundreds of objects, different agents with different capabilities, able to perform a large variety of actions. Modeling such domains soon gets confusing: object and action definitions depend on the type hierarchy, goals have to be compatible with predicate and action definitions, etc.

This problem is not specific to planning, but poses a challenge to software engineering in general. As projects grow in size, developers have to be supported with appropriate tools in order to keep track of the overall structure. We think that it is time to move AI planning from a purely scientific discipline into the direction of *Planning Task Engineering* in the sense that planning becomes a standard component of AI systems, readily usable for anyone wishing to build intelligent systems.

In this paper we propose MYPDDL, a set of tools for modeling large domains and associated problems. After a review of existing tools for PDDL, we introduce

---

[1] `http://ipc.icaps-conference.org/`

C. Lutz and M. Thielscher (Eds.): KI 2014, LNCS 8736, pp. 273–284, 2014.

the MYPDDL modules. We then compare MYPDDL to the other existing tools and present a user test for two MYPDDL modules. We conclude with an outlook on further steps necessary to improve the availability of planning for intelligent system development.

2   Existing Tools

There have been some attempts to provide modeling tools for PDDL. We introduce the three most sophisticated tools we found and use those as a benchmark for MYPDDL in Section 4.1.

PDDL STUDIO[2] [13] is an application for creating and managing PDDL projects, i.e. a collection of PDDL files. The PDDL STUDIO integrated development environment (IDE) was inspired by Microsoft Visual Studio and imperative programming paradigms. Its main features are syntax highlighting, error detection, context sensitive code completion, code folding, project management, and planner integration. PDDL STUDIO's error detection can recognize both syntactic (missing keywords, parentheses, etc.) and semantic (wrong type of predicate parameters, misspelled predicates, etc.) errors.

A major drawback of PDDL STUDIO is that it is not updated regularly and only supports PDDL 1.2. Later PDDL versions contain several additional features such as durative actions, numeric fluents, and plan-metrics [6].

ITSIMPLE [20] follows a graphical approach using Unified Modeling Language (UML) [3] diagrams. In the process leading up to ITSIMPLE, UML.P (UML in a Planning Approach) was proposed, a UML variant specifically designed for modeling planning domains and problems [19].

ITSIMPLE's modeling workflow is unidirectional as changes in the PDDL domain do not affect the UML model and UML models have to be modeled manually, meaning that they cannot by generated from PDDL. However, [18] present a translation process from a PDDL domain specification to an object-oriented UML.P model as a possible integration for ITSIMPLE. This translation process makes extensive semantic assumptions for PDDL descriptions. For example, the first parameter in the :parameters section of an action is automatically declared as a subclass of the default class *Agent*, and the method is limited to predicates with a maximum arity of two. The currently version of ITSIMPLE does not include the translation process from PDDL to UML.

Starting in version 4.0 [21] ITSIMPLE expanded its features to allow the creation of PDDL projects from scratch (i.e. without the UML to PDDL translation process). Thus far, the PDDL editing features are basic. A minimal syntax highlighting feature recognizes PDDL keywords, variables, and comments. ITSIMPLE also provides templates for PDDL constructs, such as requirement specifications, predicates, actions, initial state, and goal definitions.

Both PDDL STUDIO and ITSIMPLE do not build on existing editors and therefore cannot fall back on refined implementations of features that have been modified and improved many times throughout their existence.

---

[2] http://amis.mff.cuni.cz/PDDLStudio/

The PDDL-mode for the widely used Emacs editor [17] builds on the sophisticated features of Emacs and uses its extensibility and customizability. It provides syntax highlighting by way of basic pattern matching of keywords, variables, and comments. Additional features are automatic indentation and code completion as well as bracket matching. Code snippets for the creation of domains, problems, and actions are also available. Finally, the PDDL-mode keeps track of action and problem declarations by adding them to a menu and thus intending to allow for easy and fast code navigation.

PDDL-mode for Emacs supports PDDL versions up to 2.2, which includes derived predicates and timed initial predicates [5], but does not recognize later features like object-fluents.

In sum, there is currently no tool available supporting all features of PDDL 3.1, nor all the steps in the modeling process.

3   MyPDDL

MYPDDL is designed as a modular framework. We first introduce the implemented modules and then explain their details with respect to design guidelines for knowledge engineering tools.

3.1   Modules

MYPDDL-IDE is an integrated development environment for the use of MYPDDL in Sublime Text[3]. Since MYPDDL-SNIPPET and -SYNTAX are devised explicitly for Sublime Text, their integration is implicit. The other tools can be used independently of Sublime Text with the command-line interface and any PDDL file, but were also integrated into the editor.

MYPDDL-SYNTAX is a context-aware syntax highlighting feature for Sublime Text. It distinguishes all PDDL constructs up to version 3.1. Using regular expressions that can recognize both the start and the end of code blocks by means of a sophisticated pattern matching heuristic, MYPDDL-SYNTAX identifies PDDL code blocks and constructs and divides them into so called *scopes*, i.e. named regions. Sublime Text colorizes the code elements via the assigned scope names and in accordance with the current color scheme. These scopes allow for a fragmentation of the PDDL files, so that constructs are only highlighted if they appear in the correct context. Thus missing brackets, misplaced expressions and misspelled keywords are visually distinct and can be identified (see Figure 1).

MYPDDL-NEW helps to organize PDDL projects by generating the following folder structure:

---

[3] http://www.sublimetext.com/

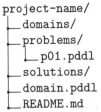

Fig. 1. Syntax highlighting in the MYPDDL-IDE in the Sublime Text editor. White text contains errors.

```
project-name/
  └─domains/
  └─problems/
      └─p01.pddl
  └─solutions/
  └─domain.pddl
  └─README.md
```

The domain file `domain.pddl` and the problem file `p01.pddl` initially contain corresponding PDDL skeletons which can also be customized. All problem files that are associated with one domain file are collected in the folder `problems/`. `README.md` is a Markdown file, which is intended for (but not limited to) information about the author(s) of the project, contact information, informal domain and problem specifications, and licensing information. Markdown files can be converted to HTML by various hosting services (like GitHub or Bitbucket).

MYPDDL-SNIPPET provides code skeletons, i.e. templates for often used PDDL constructs such as domains, problems, type and function declarations, and actions. They can be inserted by typing a triggering keyword.

MYPDDL-CLOJURE provides a preprocessor for PDDL files to bypass PDDL's limited mathematical capabilities, thus reducing modeling time without overcharging planning algorithms. We decided to use Clojure [7], a modern Lisp dialect that runs on the Java Virtual Machine (JVM) [9], facilitating input and output of the Lisp-style PDDL constructs. MYPDDL-CLOJURE is the basis for MYPDDL-DISTANCE and MYPDDL-DIAGRAM.

MYPDDL-DISTANCE provides special preprocessing functions for distance calculations. For domains with spatial components, the distance of objects is often important and should not be omitted in the domain model. However, calculating distances from coordinates requires the square root function, which

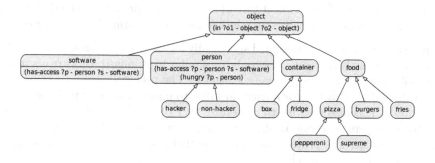

Fig. 2. Type diagram generated by MYPDDL-DIAGRAM

is not supported by PDDL (it only supports the four basic arithmetic operators). More sophisticated calculations can be achieved with the supported operators, but the solutions are rather inefficent and inelegant [12]. By calculating the distances offline and including them as additional predicates in the problem file using MYPDDL-DISTANCE, the distances between objects are given to the planner as part of the problem description.

MYPDDL-DIAGRAM generates a png image from a PDDL domain file as shown in Figure 2. The diagrammatic representation of textual information helps to quickly understand the connection of hierarchically structured items and should thus be able to simplify the communication and collaboration between developers. In the process of generating the diagrams, a copy of the PDDL file is created, so that a simple version control is also included.

3.2 Design Principles

As guidelines for design decisions, we used the seven criteria for knowledge engineering tools proposed by Shah et al. [16] as well as general usability principles.

Operationality asks whether the generated models can improve the planning performance. This is not a design principle for MYPDDL, because we assume that MYPDDL does not improve the quality (with respect to planning performance) of the resulting PDDL specifications. Therefore, we replaced this criterion with *functional suitability* from the ISO/IEC 25010 standard, which is defined as "the degree to which the software product provides an appropriate set of functions for specified tasks and user objectives" (ISO 25010 6.1.1). MYPDDL supports the current version 3.1 of PDDL. It encompasses and exceeds most of the functionality of the existing tools. It specifically supports basic editor features with a high customizability as well as visualization support.

Collaboration: With the growing importance of team work and team members not necessarily working in the same building, or in the same country, there is an increasing need for tools supporting the collaboration effort. In developing MYPDDL, this need was sought to be met by MYPDDL-DIAGRAM. Complex type hierarchies can be hard to overlook, especially if they were constructed by someone else. Therefore, a good way of tackling this problem seemed to be by providing a means to visualize such hierarchies in the form of type diagrams.

Experience: MYPDDL was designed specifically for users with a background in AI, but not necessarily in PDDL. The tools are similar to standard software engineering tools and should thus be easily learnable. The user evaluation (Section 4.2) confirms that MYPDDL helps novices in PDDL to master planning task modeling. In addition, it is also possible to customize MYPDDL so as to adapt its look and feel to other programs one is already familiar with, or simply to make it more enjoyable to use. The project site[4] provides MYPDDL video introductions and a manual to get started quickly.

Efficiency: All MYPDDL tools are intended to increase the efficiency with which PDDL files are created. MYPDDL-SNIPPET enables the fast creation of large and correct code skeletons that only need to be complemented. MYPDDL-SYNTAX can reduce the time spent on searching errors. Code folding allows users to hide currently irrelevant parts of the code and automatic indentation increases its readability. To easily keep track of all the parts of a project, folders are automatically created and named with MYPDDL-NEW. MYPDDL-CLOJURE and -DISTANCE allow for a straightforward inclusion of numerical values in the problem definition.

Debugging: MYPDDL-SYNTAX highlights all syntactically correct constructs and leaves all syntactical errors non-highlighted. In contrast, PDDL-mode for Emacs and ITSIMPLE only provide basic syntax highlighting for emphasizing the structure. PDDL STUDIO explicitly detects errors, but the user is immediately prompted when an error is detected. Often, such error messages are premature, for example, just because the closing parenthesis was not typed yet, does not mean it was forgotten. MYPDDL indicates errors in a more subtle way: syntactic errors are simply not highlighted, while all correct PDDL code is. The colors are customizable, so that users can choose how prominently the highlighting sticks out.

Maintenance: The possibility to maintain PDDL files is a key aspect of MYPDDL. The automatically generated type diagram (MYPDDL-DIAGRAM) gives an overview of the domain structure and thereby serves as a continuous means of documentation. Helping to understand foreign code, though, it follows logically that MYPDDL-DIAGRAM also helps in coming back and changing one's own models if some time has elapsed since they were last edited. The basic revision control feature of MYPDDL-DIAGRAM keeps track of changes, making it easy to revert to a previous domain version. Furthermore, MYPDDL-NEW encourages adhering to an organized project structure and stores corresponding files at the same location. The automatically created readme file can induce the user to provide further information and documentation about the PDDL project.

Support: MYPDDL-IDE can be installed using Sublime Text's Package Control [2]. This allows for an easy installation and staying up-to-date with future versions. In order to provide global access and with it the possibility for developing an

---

[4] http://pold87.github.io/myPDDL/

active community, the project source code is hosted on GitHub[5]. Additionally, the project site provides room for discussing features and reporting bugs.

4   Validation and Evaluation

To assess the utility of MYPDDL, we used the criteria listed in Section 3.2. We show the functional suitability in a benchmark validation, comparing MYPDDL's functionality with the tools described in Section 2. The criteria collaboration, experience, efficiency and debugging were evaluated in a user test. The MYPDDL components supporting maintenance are the same that are used in the user test, but their long-term usage is difficult to evaluate. The support criterion depends primarily on the infrastructure, which has been established as explained in Section 3.2.

4.1   Benchmark Validation

Functional suitability encompasses the set of functions to meet the user objectives. The tools of Section 2 basically all follow the same objectives as MYPDDL: creating PDDL domains and problems. They intend to support this process in general and the various stages of the design cycle to different degrees. The features offered by each tool are summarized in Table 1.

Besides supporting the latest PDDL version, a strength of MYPDDL is its high customizability, which comes with the Sublime Text editor. Being the only one of the four tools capable of visualizing parts of the PDDL code, it must be understood as complementary to ITSIMPLE, which takes the opposite approach of transforming UML diagrams into PDDL files. The fact that MYPDDL does not check for semantic errors is not actually a drawback as planners will usually detect semantic errors. All in all, MYPDDL combines the most useful tools of PDDL STUDIO, ITSIMPLE, and PDDL-mode for Emacs and strives to support the planning task engineer during all phases of the modeling process. Additionally, it features some unique tools, such as domain visualization. It can therefore be concluded that MYPDDL provides an appropriate set of functions for developing PDDL files and is thus functionally suitable.

4.2   User Evaluation

The two most central modules of MYPDDL are MYPDDL-SYNTAX and MYPDDL-DIAGRAM, since they support collaboration, efficiency and debugging independently of the user's experience with PDDL.

Procedure. We invited eight participants[6] to a user test (three female, average age 22.9, standard deviation 0.6), who had some basic experience with at least

---

[5] https://github.com/Pold87/myPDDL

[6] In Usability Engineering, a typical number of participants for user tests is five to ten. Studies have shown that even such small sample sizes identify about 80% of the usability problems [10,8]. Our study design required at least eight participants.

Table 1. Comparison of knowledge engineering tools and their features

Feature	PDDL STUDIO	ITSIMPLE	PDDL-mode	MYPDDL
latest supported PDDL version	1.2	3.1	2.2	3.1
syntax highlighting	yes	basic	basic	yes
semantic error detection	yes	no	no	no
automatic indentation	no	no	yes	yes
code completion	yes	no	yes	yes
code snippets	no	yes	yes	yes
code folding	yes	no	yes	yes
domain visualization	no	planned	no	yes
project management	yes	yes	no	yes
UML to PDDL code translation	no	yes	no	no
planner integration	basic	yes	no	basic
plan visualization	no	yes	no	no
dynamic analysis	no	yes	no	no
declaration menu	no	no	yes	no
interface with programming language	no	no	no	yes
customization features	basic	no	yes	yes

one Lisp dialect (in order not to be confused with the many parentheses), but no experience with PDDL or AI planning in general.

No earlier than 24 hours before the experiment was to take place, participants received the web link to a 30-minute interactive video tutorial on AI planning and PDDL[7]. This method was chosen in order not to pressure the participant with the presence of an experimenter when trying to understand the material.

We defined four tasks: two debugging tasks and two type hierarchy tasks asking for details of a given domain (e.g. "Can a Spleus be married to a Schlok?"). As a within-subjects design was considered most suited (to control for individual differences within such a small sample), it was necessary to construct two tasks (matched in difficulty) for each of these two types to compare the effects of having the tools available. The two tasks to test syntax highlighting presented the user with domains that were 54 lines in length, consisted of 1605 characters and contained 17 errors each. Errors were distributed evenly throughout the domains and were categorized into different types. The occurrence frequencies of these types were matched across domains as well, to ensure equal difficulty for both domains. To test the type diagram generator, two fictional domains with equally complex type hierarchies consisting of non-words were designed (five and six layers in depth, 20 and 21 types). The domains were also matched in length and overall complexity (five and six predicates with approximately the same distribution of arities, one action with four predicates in the precondition and two and three predicates in the effect).

Each participant started either with a debugging or type hierarchy task and was given the MYPDDL tools either in the first two tasks or the second two

---

[7] http://www.youtube.com/playlist?list=PL3CZzLUZuiIMWEfJxy-G6OxYVzUrvjwuV

tasks, so that each participant completed each task type once with and once without MYPDDL. This results in 2 (first task is debugging or hierarchy) × 2 (task variations for debugging and hierarchy) × 2 (starting with or without MYPDDL) = 8 individual task orders, one per participant.

For the debugging tasks, participants were given six minutes[8] to detect as many of the errors as possible. They were asked to record each error in a table (pen and paper) with the line number and a short comment and to immediately correct the errors in the code if they knew how to, but not to dwell on the correction otherwise. For the type hierarchy task, participants were asked to answer five questions concerning the domains, all of which could be facilitated with the type diagram generator, but one of which also required looking into the code. Participants were told that they should not feel pressured to answer quickly, but to not waste time either. Also they were asked to say their answer out loud as soon as it became evident to them. They were not told that the time it took them to come up with an answer was recorded, since this could have made them feel pressured and thus led to more false answers. At the end of the usability test they were asked to evaluate the perceived usability of MYPDDL using the system usability scale [4].

Results.

1. Debugging Tasks
   As shown in Figure 3(a), on average participants found 7.6 errors without syntax highlighting and 10.3 errors with syntax highlighting (i.e. approximately 36 % more errors were found with syntax highlighting).
   Two participants remarked that the syntax highlighting colors confused them and that they found them more distracting than helpful. One of them mentioned that the contrast of the colors used was so low that they were hard for her to distinguish. She found the same number of errors with and without syntax highlighting. The other of the two was the only participant who found fewer errors with syntax highlighting than without it. With MYPDDL-SYNTAX, two participants found all errors in the domain, while none achieved this without syntax highlighting.
2. Type Hierarchy Tasks
   Figure 3(b) shows the geometric mean[9] of the completion time of successful tasks for each question with and without the type diagram generator.
   With the type diagram generator participants answered all questions (except Question 4) on average nearly twice as fast. The fact that the availability of tools did not have a positive effect on task completion times for Question 4 can probably be attributed to the complexity of this question. In contrast to the other four questions, to answer Question 4 correctly, the participants were required to look at the actions in the domain file in addition to the type diagram. Most participants were confused by this, because they had

---

[8] A reasonable time frame tested on two pilot tests.

[9] The geometric mean is a more accurate measure of the mean for small sample sizes as task times have a strong tendency to be positively skewed [15].

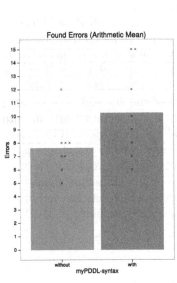

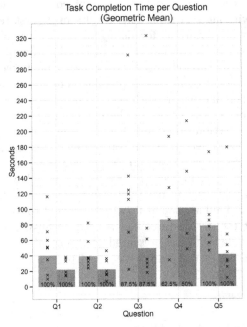

(a) Comparison of detected errors with and without the syntax highlighting feature. The bars display the arithmetic mean.

(b) Task completion time for the type hierarchy tasks. The bars display the geometric mean. The percent values at the bottom of the bars show the the percentage of users that completed the task successfully.

Fig. 3. Results of the user test. The crosses (×) represent single participants. red: with MYPDDL, blue: without MYPDDL.

assumed that once having the type diagram available, it alone would suffice to answer all questions. This initial confusion cost some time, thus negatively influencing the time on the task.

3. System Usability Scale

   MYPDDL reached a score of 89.6 on the system usability scale [10], with a standard deviation of 3.9. Since the overall mean score of the system usability scale has an approximate value of 68 with a standard deviation of 12.5 [14], the score of MYPDDL is well above average with a small standard deviation. A score of 89.6 is usually attributed to superior products [1]. Furthermore, 89.6 corresponds approximately to a percentile rank of 99.8 %, meaning that it has a better perceived ease-of-use than 99.8 % of the products in the database used by Sauro [14].

Discussion. The user test shows that overall MYPDDL provides very useful tools for novices in AI planning and PDDL. It also shows that customizability is im-

---

[10] The range of possible values for the system usability scale is 0 to 100.

portant, as not all users prefer the same colors or syntax highlighting at all and their personal preferences seem to correlate with the effectiveness of the tools.

Visualization tools such as MYPDDL-DIAGRAM can improve the understanding of unknown PDDL code and thus support collaboration. But users may be unaware of the limitations of such tools. A possible solution is to extend MYPDDL-DIAGRAM to display actions, but this can overload the diagram and especially for large domains render it unreadable. Different views for different aspects of the domain or dynamically displayed content could integrate more data, but this also hides functionality, which is generally undesired for usability [11].

5   Conclusion

MYPDDL was designed with the goal to support plan engineers in modeling domains and planning problems as well as in understanding, modifying, extending, and using existing planning domains. This was realized with a set of tools comprising code editing features, namely syntax highlighting and code snippets, a type diagram generator, and a distance calculator. To also have all tools accessible from one place, they were made available in the Sublime Text editor. The different needs and requirements of knowledge engineers are met by the modular, extensible, and customizable architecture of the toolkit and Sublime Text. The evaluation of MYPDDL has shown some initial evidence that it allows a faster understanding of the domain structure, which could be beneficial for the maintenance and application of existing task specifications and for the communication between engineers. Users perceive it as easy and enjoyable to use, and the increase in their performance when using MYPDDL underpins their subjective impressions.

Despite MYPDDL already providing a rich modeling environment, there are still numerous features that could be added in the future. Especially MYPDDL-CLOJURE offers multiple interesting further research directions: It provides a basis for dynamic planning scenarios. Applications could be the modeling of learning and forgetting (by adding facts to or retracting facts from a PDDL file) or the modeling of an ever changing real world via dynamic predicate lists. Another way of putting the interface to use would be by making the planning process more interactive, allowing for the online interception of planning software in order to account for the needs and wishes of the end user.

We hope that MYPDDL will be accepted in the planning community, but especially that it will be used by people who create integrated AI systems and are not necessarily planning experts. We are looking forward to feedback for continual improvements.

Project website: http://pold87.github.io/myPDDL/

References

1. Bangor, A., Kortum, P.T., Miller, J.T.: An empirical evaluation of the system usability scale. Intl. Journal of Human - Computer Interaction 24, 574–594 (2008)
2. Bond, W.: (2013), https://sublime.wbond.net/about

3. Booch, G., Rumbaugh, J., Jacobson, I.: The Unified Modeling Language User Guide. Pearson Education, India (1999)
4. Brooke, J.: SUS — a quick and dirty usability scale. Usability Evaluation in Industry 189, 194 (1996)
5. Edelkamp, S., Hoffmann, J.: PDDL2.2: The language for the classical part of the 4th international planning competition. In: 4th International Planning Competition (IPC 2004), at ICAPS 2004 (2004)
6. Fox, M., Long, D.: PDDL2.1: An extension to PDDL for expressing temporal planning domains. J. Artif. Intell. Res.(JAIR) 20, 61–124 (2003)
7. Hickey, R.: The Clojure programming language. In: Proceedings of the 2008 Symposium on Dynamic Languages. ACM (2008)
8. Hwang, W., Salvendy, G.: Number of people required for usability evaluation: The 10±2 rule. Communications of the ACM 53(5), 130–133 (2010)
9. Lindholm, T., Yellin, F., Bracha, G.: Virtual machine specification. Java CardTM Platform, Version 2(2) (2011)
10. Nielsen, J.: Estimating the number of subjects needed for a thinking aloud test. International Journal of Human-Computer Studies 41(3), 385–397 (1994)
11. Norman, D.: The Design of Everyday Things. Basic Books, New York (1988)
12. Parkinson, S., Longstaff, A.P.: Increasing the numeric expressiveness of the planning domain definition language. In: Proceedings of the 30th Workshop of the UK Planning and Scheduling Special Interest Group (PlanSIG 2012). UK Planning and Scheduling Special Interest Group (2012)
13. Plch, T., Chomut, M., Brom, C., Barták, R.: Inspect, edit and debug PDDL documents: Simply and efficiently with PDDL studio. In: System Demonstrations and Exhibits at ICAPS 2012 (2012)
14. Sauro, J.: A Practical Guide to the System Usability Scale: Background, Benchmarks & Best Practices. Measuring Usability LCC (2011)
15. Sauro, J., Lewis, J.R.: Quantifying the User Experience: Practical Statistics for User Research. Elsevier (2012)
16. Shah, M., Chrpa, L., Jimoh, F., Kitchin, D., McCluskey, T., Parkinson, S., Vallati, M.: Knowledge engineering tools in planning: State-of-the-art and future challenges. In: Knowledge Engineering for Planning and Scheduling, p. 53 (2013)
17. Singhi, S.: Emacs mode for PDDL (2005),
http://rakaposhi.eas.asu.edu/planninglist-mailarchive/msg00085.html
18. Tonidandel, F., Vaquero, T.S., Silva, J.R.: Reading PDDL, writing an object-oriented model. In: Sichman, J.S., Coelho, H., Rezende, S.O. (eds.) IBERAMIA-SBIA 2006. LNCS (LNAI), vol. 4140, pp. 532–541. Springer, Heidelberg (2006)
19. Vaquero, T.S., Tonidandel, F., de Barros, L.N., Silva, J.R.: On the use of UML.p for modeling a real application as a planning problem. In: International Conference on Automated Planning and Scheduling (ICAPS), pp. 434–437 (2006)
20. Vaquero, T.S., Tonidandel, F., Silva, J.R.: The itSIMPLE tool for modeling planning domains. In: Proceedings of the First International Competition on Knowledge Engineering for AI Planning, Monterey, California, USA (2005)
21. Vaquero, T., Tonaco, R., Costa, G., Tonidandel, F., Silva, J.R., Beck, J.C.: itsimple4.0: Enhancing the modeling experience of planning problems. In: System Demonstration–Proceedings of the 22nd International Conference on Automated Planning & Scheduling, ICAPS 2012 (2012)

Monte-Carlo Tree Search
for 3D Packing with Object Orientation

Stefan Edelkamp, Max Gath, and Moritz Rohde

Universität Bremen, Germany
{edelkamp,mgath}@tzi.de, roh@biba.uni-bremen.de

Abstract. In this paper we look at packing problems that naturally arise in container loading. Given a set of 3D iso-oriented objects and a container, the task is to find a packing sequence of the input objects consisting of the ID, location, and orientation that minimizes the space wasted by the packing. Instead of the decision problem, we look at the packing optimization problem, minimizing the total height of a packing. Our solutions uses extreme points and applies Monte-Carlo tree search with policy adaptation, a randomized search technique that has been shown to be effective for solving single-agent games and, more recently, complex traveling salesman and vehicle routing problems. The implementation is considerably simple and conceptually different from mathematical programming branch-and-bound and local search approaches. Nonetheless, the results in solving 2D and 3D packing problems are promising.

1 Introduction

Industrial robots have eventually found their way into container packing and unpacking. Such intelligent packaging robots pack and unpack containers with loose packages fully automatically. Some companies have such systems already operating in their logistics centers.

A packing robot system (shown in Figure 1) consists of a chassis beneath the robot, a telescope conveyor, a 3D laser scanner and an interchangeable gripper system. The robot is positioned on the chassis, which is connected to the conveyor belt. This can be extended mechanically and transports robot and chassis into the container. That way the work envelope of the robot will be extended and the gripper arm of the robot can reach any point in the container. By use of the 3D laser scanner possible gripping positions for the pile of parcels can be analyzed and an optimal unloading sequence and collision-free trajectories can be computed. The removed packages are then transported by the conveyor belt until the container is completely empty. In this paper we look at the inverse problem of optimally packing 3D objects into a container to maximize its load. For loading the same hardware as outlined above can be used. Compared to the unloading the loading process is simpler in handling since the size of the goods and the depending positions for pick-up and drop-down are defined. But still there are big challenges especially for the loading of parcel with unequal sizes and weights in containers or swap-bodies.

In a study about the contents of containers arriving in European ports it was identified that 46,7% of the goods come in boxes of different size [8]. Another study [20] stated

C. Lutz and M. Thielscher (Eds.): KI 2014, LNCS 8736, pp. 285–296, 2014.

that for contract logistics the biggest amount of parcels have a weight of 5-15 kg. On average 1200 parcels fit in a 40'-container. With regard to this values the maximum payload of a 40'-container of approx. 30t can hardly be exploited by parcels. From the economical point of view for the full capacity of a container an optimal stacking is required with no or minimal gaps between the goods.

Whereas parcels are mostly imported in containers they are often distributed in swap-bodies. Here the maximum height of the pile is relevant. DHL for instance ordered a maximum stacking height of 2m to reduce accidents by dropping goods. Optimizing the loading process to achieve a compact and solid pile is a requirement for the effective and safe transport and subsequent unloading process.

In this paper we aim at packing rather than unpacking. The 3D packing problem is a true extension of the rectangle packing problem, already known to be a hard optimization problem. Even the bin packing problem is known to be NP-complete. While pseudo-polynomial time algorithms have been derived for the 1D packing problem, no such results have been derived for the 3D packing problem. We study the packing problem that maximizes the volume utility of a single container with and without orientation restrictions on the boxes. A solution is an ordering of (possibly oriented) objects together with a set of coordinates. We enforce objects to form a connected arrangement of objects. Objects are only stable if their center of mass rests on top of another object. We assume that unoccupied space can be filled with other material so stability is not an issue.

Fig. 1. Container packing scenario with mobile robot platform and conveyor belt

The paper is structured as follows. We start with a definition of the problem followed by an introduction to Monte-Carlo search with the concept of extreme points. We present the adaption of the concepts to the packing of iso-oriented objects, and analyze the time complexity of the most important method. The evaluation considers a benchmark for 2D square packing, and up to industry-sized random 3D problem instances. We conclude the paper with discussing related work and future research avenues.

2 Problem Specification

We are given a set of rectangular boxes $B = \{b_1, \ldots, b_n\}$ and a rectangular container C. Let x_i, y_i and z_i represent the three dimensions of the box b_i, and X, Y, and Z represent the three dimensions of the container. The objective of the problem is to select a subset $S \subseteq B$ and assign a position to each box $b_j \in S$, in the 3D space of container C such that $\sum_{b_j \in S} x_j \cdot y_j \cdot z_j$ is maximized subject to the constraints that all boxes must be totally contained in C, no two boxes intersect in 3D space and every edge of the packed box must be parallel or orthogonal to the container walls.

If oriented boxes are to considered, the values of triples (x_j, y_j, z_j) can be permuted. Given that for all j the values of x_j, y_j, and z_j are pairwise different, for the 2D problem we have $2! = 2$ possible orientations, while in 3D we have $3! = 6$ different orientations of an object (suppose an unoriented package has dimension 1x2x3; consequently, there are 6 different orientations that lead to the following rotated dimensions for this package: 1x2x3, 2x1x3, 1x3x2, 2x3x1, 3x1x2, 3x2x1). In the 3D *strip packing problem* that we consider in this paper, we are given a set of 3D rectangular items and a 3D open box B. The goal is to pack all the items in B such that the height of the packing is minimized. We consider the most basic version of the problem, where the items must be packed with their edges parallel to the edges of B. In the oriented case, we allow rotation. A trivial upper bound $X_{\max}$ for the height of the packing is $\sum_{i=1}^n x_i$. Of course, more effective bounds can be derived.

The problem of the center of mass of a box is apparent. It is dependent on the package weight distribution and whether additional support *bridges* can be inserted to support overhanging parts. The problem of packing many small boxes into a single larger box is part of a number of cutting, packing, scheduling, and transportation applications. There are a number of heuristic solvers, but the progress in exact solvers that can deal also with orientation, in general, and integer programming solvers, in particular, has been limited. Padberg (Math. Methods Oper. Res., 52(1):1 21, 2000) estimated his extension of the integer linear programming formulation of Chen et al. could cope with about 20 boxes.

3 Nested Monte-Carlo Search

Nested Monte-Carlo (NMC) [3] is a randomized search method that has been successfully applied to solve many challenging combinatorial problems, including Klondike Solitaire [2], Morpion Solitaire, and Same Game just to name a few. Recently, a large fraction of Traveling Salesman Problems with Time Windows benchmark set have been solved efficiently at or very close to the optimum [4]. Compared to other specialized heuristic methods that include much more information, a NMC solver is competitive. Algorithmic refinements to the solver [9] further improve the solution quality by reducing the time complexity and by biasing the probability distribution used in the search by prior knowledge.

The NMC algorithm is parametrized with the *level* of the search which denotes how deep the search is and with the number of *iterations*, that shows how strong the policy learning effect within the search is. At each leaf of the recursive search (Level 0), a

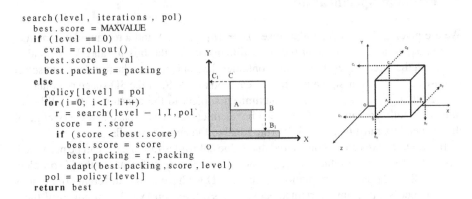

```
search(level, iterations, pol)
  best.score = MAXVALUE
  if (level == 0)
    eval = rollout()
    best.score = eval
    best.packing = packing
  else
    policy[level] = pol
    for(i=0; i<I; i++)
      r = search(level - 1,I,pol)
      score = r.score
      if (score < best.score)
        best.score = score
        best.packing = r.packing
        adapt(best.packing,score,level)
    pol = policy[level]
  return best
```

Fig. 2. NRPA (left), extreme points in 2D and 3D (right)

rollout is invoked. A rollout corresponds to a (possibly constraint violating) packing. A rollout performs and evaluates a random run to construct a packing. An example setting is a level-5 search with 50 iterations, which leads to 50^5 rollouts.

The state-of-the-art advancement to NMC is *policy adaptation*, that dynamically changes the probabilities of choosing the successor states in the rollout based on the success of previous experiences. Rather than navigating the tree directly the approach instead uses gradient ascent on the rollout policy at each level of the nested search. Its improved behavior has been documented on Crossword Puzzle and Morpion Solitaire problem instances.

A generic pseudo-code implementation of NMC with policy adaptation (aka Nested Rollout Policy Adaptation, NRPA) is shown in Fig 2 (left). NRPA is state-of-the-art in Monte Carlo Tree Search, since it broke a 30 year old record in Morpion Solitaire [21]. We see that the evaluation of a Level k search relies on the result obtained in Level $k-1$ search and that the results are propagated bottom up. A policy is a mapping from a state to the successor state in form of a probability distribution function.

4 Extreme Points

The basic idea of *extreme points* is that when an item j with sizes X_j, Y_j and Z_j is added to a given packing and is placed with the left-back-down corner in position (x_j, y_j, z_j) it generates a series of new extreme points, where additional objects can be placed. The new extreme points are generated by projecting the points with coordinates $(x_j + X_j, y_j, z_j)$, $(x_j, y_j + Y_j, z_j)$ $(x_j, y_j, z_j + Z_j)$ on the orthogonal axes of the container. In 2D this leads to at most 2 extreme points generated for each object being placed, while in 3D we have at most 6 extreme points (see Figure 2, right). Each point is projected on all items lying between item i and the wall of the container in the respective direction. If there is more than on item on which a point can be projected, the algorithm chooses the nearest one. Moreover, to avoid wasted space by additionally sliding the object we urge them to respect connectivity and gravity constraints.

If the container is empty, the first object is placed in position $(0, 0, 0)$ generating extreme points at $(X_j, 0,0)$, $(0, Y_j,0)$, $(0, 0,Z_j)$.

While the extreme point approach applies to floating-point size data, in our experiments we decided to discretize the domains of the object and container sizes to integers. This change supports operations in the integer range progressing a global layout of the objects. The test of intersection and the projection simplifies.

5 Packing

The most important function to be applied in NMC is the *rollout*. Code profiling shows that most time is spend in this function. In a rollout we randomly walk down the search tree from root to a leaf node to form a complete packing. The pseudo-code implementation of the rollout function for the packing is depicted in Fig. 3 (left). Using *visited*-flags, successors are eliminated from the set of all possible values, so that any generated solution necessarily has to be a permutation of boxes. Some parameters such as *visited*-flags, the set of successors found, the current assignement of packages to container cells, as well as the incrementally generated packing (including ID, location, and orientation) and the (layered) policy tables are kept globally in class member variables. The function *legal* places all remaining objects on all possible extreme points. The outcome is a list of successors m of (possibly oriented) objects together with their coordinates l and orientation o. In the following we describe one possible implementation.

Proposition 1. *The rollout branching factor for 3D packing is at most $O(n^2)$.*

Proof. In each level of the rollout at least one extreme point is consumed and 6 are generated, so that $5n + 1$ is the maximum number of extreme points. At each extreme point an object might be placed. For each of the remaining packages (at most n) there are 6 possible orientations, so that we have at most $6n(5n + 1) = O(n^2)$ children.

Proposition 2. *The time for updating all boxes is bounded by $O(XY_\square + YZ_\square + XZ_\square)$, where $XY_\square = \sum_{i=1}^{n} x_i y_i$, $YZ_\square = \sum_{i=1}^{n} y_i z_i$, and $XZ_\square = \sum_{i=1}^{n} x_i z_i$.*

Proof. If we incrementally add and delete objects by their surrounding surfaces, the number of cells updated in one rollout is bounded by $2XY_\square + 2YZ_\square + 2XZ_\square = O(XY_\square + YZ_\square + XZ_\square)$.

Proposition 3. *The time for all intersection tests is at most $O(n^2 \cdot (\sum_{i=1}^{n} x_i + y_i + z_i))$.*

Proof. At each of the at most $5n + 1$ extreme points a skeleton of at most n objects in any orientation is traversed, returning a false in case of an occupied cell. The incorrect placements with an already existing box piercing the skeleton are detected in updating the state followed by returning a very large cost value. (We do not have to test a box at an extreme point, where it previously did not fit.) The skeleton of box i has size $O(x_i + y_i + z_i)$, so that the cumulated size of all skeletons is $O(\sum_{i=1}^{n} x_i + y_i + z_i)$. All intersection tests, therefore, take time $O(n^2 \cdot (\sum_{i=1}^{n} x_i + y_i + z_i))$.

Theorem 1 (Time Complexity Rollout for 3D Packing with Orientation). *The time for one rollout is at most $O((XY_\square + YZ_\square + XZ_\square) + n^2 \cdot (\sum_{i=1}^{n} x_i + y_i + z_i))$.*

```
rollout ()
  cost = objectsSize = 0;
  nextreme = 1; extreme [0] = 0;
  for (j=0;j<N;j++) visited[j] = false;
  while (objectsSize < N) {
    successors = legal(nextreme);
    sum = 0;
    for (i=0; i<successors; i++)
      value[i] = exp(pol[code(l[i],o[i],m[i])]);
      sum += value[i];
    mrand=random(sum);
    i=0; sum = value[0];
    while (sum<mrand) sum += value[++i];
    object = m[i];
    location[objectsSize] = l[i];
    orientation[objectsSize] = twist[i];
    objects[objectsSize++] = object;
    place(object,twist[i],l[i]);
    visited[object] = true;
    nextreme =
      update(object,twist[i],l[i],nextreme);
    if (cost < x+sizes[object].x)
      cost = x+sizes[object].x;
  clear(cost);
  return 1000 * cost + nextreme;
```

```
adapt(packing, cost, level) {
  for (j=0;j<N;j++)
    visited[j] = false;
  object = 0;
  nextreme = 1;
  extreme [0] = 0;
  for(p=0; p<N; p++)
    successors = legal(nextreme);
    object = packing.objects[p];
    l = packing.location[p];
    o = packing.orientation[p];
    layer[level][code(l,o,object)] +=
      ALPHA;
    z = 0.0;
    for(i=0; i<successors; i++)
      z += exp(pol[code(l,o,m[i])]);
    for (i=0; i<successors; i++)
      layer[level][code(l,o,m[i])] -=
      ALPHA*
        exp(policy[code(l,o,m[i])])/z;
    place(object,o l);
    nextreme =
      update(object,l,o,nextreme);
    visited[object] = true;
  clear(cost);
```

Fig. 3. Rollout and policy adaptation functions for the container packing optimization problem

To avoid the generation of clearly dominated solutions it also slides objects (in turn) towards lower x-, y- and z coordinates. This ensures that the packing is connected and (to some extent) stable. As we do not expect knowledge on the weight distribution within an object, we do not compute the center of mass. This constraint can be added by the user or bypassed by adding additional *bridges*.

The number of violations to the enforced constraints can be included into the cost function evaluation that is returned to the NMC algorithm. The major objective of the cost function is to reduce the number of layers in x-direction. As a minor objective, the number of remaining extreme points are minimized. Our implementation features orientation of rectangles.

Objects are *placed* into a one-sided open container of cells. This is done by setting the respective cells to the id of the object. The resulting set of extreme points is computed in the *update* procedure. While objects have to fit wrt. the x- and y-dimension of the container, they are allowed to exceed the x-dimension. At the end of the rollout procedure, all cells of the container are *cleared*.

Furthermore, *packing* is a global variable or the parameter and includes the object, its location, and its orientation. Copying of *pol* and *policy* is already done in the search procedure Fig. 2. We need a temporary, which makes the code harder to read.

For the packing problem, similar to the finding in Morpion solitaire [21], adjacencies are less important compared to absolute coordinates. In an existing policy P rollouts children s' for a node s are chosen wrt. $e^{P(s,s')}$. The choice of successors is done using a roulette wheel fitness selection based on these values. Initially, the all policy values are set to 0. As the entire state-to-state table surely is too big, it is projected to an essential part to be learnt.

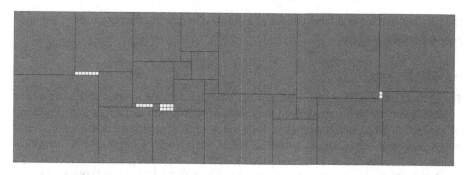

Fig. 4. Solutions to two square packing problems (for 25 objects). The 1×1 square is removed from the input and assumed to fit.

Given a packing that improves the current best cost value, policy adaptation (see Figure 3, right) performs gradient decent as follows. The sequence of children $s' = (s'_0, \ldots, s'_l)$ of states $s = (s_0, \ldots, s_l)$ with $s_{i+1} = s'_i$ has the probability $Prob(s, s') = \prod_{j=0}^{l} e^{P(s_j, s'_j)} / \sum_{i=0}^{l} e^{P(s_j, s'_i)}$. The gradient of the logarithm at j of this term is $1 - e^{P(s_j, s'_j)} / \sum_{i=0}^{l} e^{P(s_j, s_i)}$, so that we add α to the best chosen successor and subtract $\alpha \cdot e^{P(s_j, s'_j)} / \sum_{i=0}^{l} e^{P(s_j, s'_i)}$ from the others, where α is a factor for accelerating the learning process. This ensures that policy adaptation increases the probability of the solution sequence. The policy learned is a mapping from objects together with their orientation to the y- and z- coordinates.

Policies are copied top-down, adapted bottom-up, and improved while progressing from one successor to its sibling.

Solutions for packing the squares 1×1 to 22×22 into a box of size 31×69 problem and for packing squares 1×1 to 25×25 into a box of size 43×129 problem are shown Figure 4. In the discretization objects are represented by their boundary surfaces. This makes intersection tests easier.

6 Experiments

Our GNU C/C++ single-core implementation consist of less than 400 LOC[1]. It is generic and supports 2D and 3D non-oriented and oriented packings. (The support of higher dimensions would only require different projection and intersection functions.) Benchmarking is made possible by changing compiler-time options. For square packing we extracted a Java program with 200 LOC. (To our surprise it was competitive with the C/C++ implementation).

All experiments ran on an Intel(R) Core(TM) i5-2520M CPU at 2.5 GHz running Ubuntu 11.10 (oneiric). The computer was equipped with 8 GB RAM. The memory requirements of our NMC implementation are negligible and dominated by the size of the board and the policy. The objective (cost) function is to minimize the total height of

---

[1] This is only an indicator for the simplicity of the implementation (and maybe parallelization). Of course this does not imply much, nor is it a necessary property.

the packing. We included the number of extreme points to aid the optimizer to continue search for tight packings.

6.1 2D Packing

For 2D rectangle packing we look at Korf's square packing instances [15,16]. These combinatorial problems are defined as constraint satisfaction and not as a strip packing minimization problems. Nonetheless, with our general approach we could solve several benchmark problem instances within an NRPA search with 6 levels and 20 iterations. (namely – form $N : L \times B$ (time/rollouts) – 2 : 2 × 3 (0.1s/1), 3 : 3 × 5 (0.1s/1), 4 : 5 × 7 (0.1s/2), 5 : 5 × 12 (0.1s/13), 6 : 9 × 11 (0.1s/50), 7 : 11 × 14 (0.1/48), 8 : 14 × 15 (0.2s/3728), 9 : 15 × 20 (0.2s/8502), 10 : 15 × 27 (0.1s/97), 11 : 19 × 27 (55s/3520193), 12 : 23 × 29 (8s/329903), 13 : 22 × 38 (4s/8557), 14 : 23 × 45 (11s/335798), 15 : 23 × 55 (3s/1947), 16 : 28 × 54 (1m31s/1658002), 18 : 31 × 69 (31.4s/463297), 20 : 34 × 85 (23m15s/3483648), and 22 : 39 × 98 (49m26s/4418323)). We always took the larger container size value as being undefined. With this search we could not solve the instances 17 : 39 × 46 19 : 47 × 53, 23 : 64 × 68 24 : 56 × 88, and 25 : 43 × 129[2]. Korf's approach is based on heuristically guided depth-first branch-and-bound search with a lower bound for computing wasted space based on a reduction to bin packing. As we leave the container open, we do not rely on wasted space computations.

Alternative approaches for non-square problem have been addressed by [13] and high precision rectangles have been considered by [19,12].

6.2 3D Packing

For 3D packing we generated randomly sized 3D objects. The sizes of the objects were random choices in $[1..X_{max}/2] \times [1..Y_{max}/2] \times [1..Z_{max}/2]$. As X_{max} was unknown, we used Y_{max} instead. As the interpretation of an ASCII output of the solution is limited, we used gnuplot to visualize the three dimensional outcome of the NRPA optimization process. A simple packing example is shown in Fig. 5 (left).

In small to moderate benchmarks we tested the effect of varying the parameters of the search, namely the level and the iterations. Table 1 shows the obtained quality in terms of the cost function, and Table 2 provides the according runtimes. We see that a shallow search lead to smaller runtimes and still good results.

Table 1. Solution quality in terms of the cost function value obtained by NRPA search for the oriented packing problem with $Y_{max} = Z_{max} = 10$ averaged over 5 trials

n	10	15	20	25	30	35	40	45	50
5,7	4418.4	6629.0	8438.6	9853.0	11862.8	14267.8	15882.2	18283.4	20287.4
4,10	4420.6	6633.8	8639.6	9847.8	12659.8	14283.8	16082.8	18682.4	20694.8
3,22	3819.2	6027.6	8039.6	10044.4	11658.2	13672.6	15273.2	17886.4	20096.0
2,100	3819.0	5828.8	7831.4	9241.2	12459.6	12461.2	16271.6	16472.2	19290.8

---

[2] We found a typo in Korf's report as the first 21 square boxes exceed a container of size 38 × 85.

Table 2. Runtimes of NRPA search of the oriented packing problem with $Y_{max} = Z_{max} = 10$ averaged over 5 runs

n	10	15	20	25	30	35	40	45	50
5,7	16.4s	34.0s	1m3.0s	1m37.8s	2m24.6s	3m26.6s	4m37.8s	6m1.0s	7m50.8s
4,10	7.4s	17.0s	31.6s	53.4s	1m19.6s	1m55.8s	2m35.6s	3m26.0s	4m26.4s
3,22	5.6s	14.2s	29.0s	49.6s	1m16.8s	1m53.6s	2m33.6s	3m27.8s	4m33.0s
2,100	4.0s	11.8s	24.0s	44.4s	1m10.6s	1m44.2s	2m26.2s	3m18.2s	4m23.2s

In Fig. 5 (right) we show four learning curves of an NRPA search with 2 levels, 100 iterations, and up to 200 objects. The experiment with 100 iterations took 24m34s, the one with 150 68m10s, and the one with 200 152m21s.

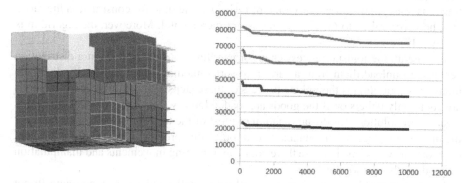

Fig. 5. Visualization of a sample 3D packing of a simple instance (left); learning curves for NRPA for a varying number of oriented objects (right, $n = 50, 100, 150, 200$ read from bottom to top). The x-axis is the number of rollouts, the y-axis denotes the obtained solution quality in terms of the cost function.

By reducing the number of rollouts, we could scale the algorithm to optimize packings of 1000-2000 boxes and more, and thus we can handle packing problems for industrial-sized containers. The time complexity for the rollout operation is substantial, so we can only run a smaller number of rollouts (depending on the time provided). However, this is already sufficient for first optimizations as NRPA is *anytime*.

7 Related Work

Recently, Monte-Carlo tree search has been applied to routing problems. For example, NRPA search has also applied to efficiently solve the well-known Traveling Salesman Problem with Time Windows (TSPTW) optimal or very close to the optimum for small problem instances with up to 50 cities [4]. For the TSP, the result of a rollout is a (possibly constraint violating) tour. The policy provides information of how good an adjacent pair of city and successor city performs in a tour. Good performing pairs are preferred in the rollout. If hard constraints such as time windows and capacity constraints are not satisfied within a tour, the costs increase significantly for each violation. Consequently, the algorithm minimizes constraint violations with highest priority. Algorithmic refinements to accelerate the search are provided by [9]. This approach has been extended to solve single-vehicle pickup and delivery problems with time windows and capacity constraints with up to 200 cities to be visited.

There are several heuristic approaches from operations research to solve variants of the container loading problems [1,22,7,18,14,10], but they often have difficulties to scale to a larger number of objects, and do not cover orientation.

2D rectangle intersection for n objects can be tested by a divide-and-conquer approach in $O(n \lg n)$ time [11]. The drawback is that intersections are detected only after all rectangles are placed leading to many invalid placements during the rollout. In 3D the axis-aligned bounding boxes (AABB-AABB) algorithm is practically fast, but requires $O(n^2)$ for the test. There is also the option of using range trees (with fractional cascading) for a query time of $O(\lg^2 n)$, the time for construction the range tree, however, raises to $O(n \lg^2 n)$ and is not incremental. Moreover, the algorithm is involved [6].

In general, the logistic process chain of handling consumer goods in a distribution center is to unload them from a carrier, to sort sometimes store and finally distribute them. Transportation is the linking process of these steps. Carrier of the arriving goods are commonly pallets or, if the goods are loaded loosely, containers or trucks. There is a variety of solutions for the automation of most of the tasks mentioned above, except the unloading process. The manual execution of this process, is a very tiring and not ergonomically activity, because there are many recurring movements and manipulation of goods with high weight.

In order to enable the automation of unloading palletized goods, the system Robot Cell Light3 might be used. The loaded pallet has to be put manually inside the system. After the process has been started, it unloads the goods independently of the packing pattern, layer by layer and separates them while they are dropped on a conveyor. The separation allows further logistics processes like label reading, measurement of its volumes or sorting. The goods that might be unloaded with this system have to have a closed and flat surface, like e.g. catalogues or parcels.

The unloading of loose and cubic goods is the mission of the system Parcel Robot4. This robot has an innovative kinematics that allows a higher performance than standard robots. Instead of gripping a parcel and transport around its own axis in order to drop it on a conveyor, this kinematics allows the system to drop a gripped parcel underneath itself. The parcels have to have a closed surface and a maximum weight of 31.5kg. Mounted on a steerable platform, which banks the system to the unloading position inside a truck or container, the system can unload up to 480 parcels per hour.

The work by Lim and Ying [17] proposes a new method for the 3D container packing problem that deviates from the traditional approach of wall building and layering. It uses the concept of *building growing* from multiple sides of the container. The idea of this 3D packing algorithm comes from the process of constructing a building. Boxes are placed on the wall of the container first as it builds the basement on the ground. After which, other boxes will be placed on top of the basement boxes. Following this process, boxes will be placed one on top of another. Every wall of the container can be treated as the ground for boxes to stack on. One drawback of the approach is that it does not consider gravity constraints.

Crainic et al. introduce the extreme point concept and present a new extreme point-based rule for packing items inside a three-dimensional container [5]. The extreme point rule is addressed independently of the particular packing problem and can handle additional constraints, such as fixing the position of the items. The extreme point rule is also used to derive new constructive heuristics for the three-dimensional bin-packing problem. This rule was used in the space defragmentation heuristic [23].

8   Conclusion

In this paper we have seen a novel approach to solve multi-dimensional packing problems by applying nested Monte-Carlo tree search with policy adaptation. Our optimization algorithm is based on a combination of random choice and machine learning and yields a trade-off between state space exploitation and exploration.

The implementation is flexible: It can handle additional placing constraints as well as alternative orientation. The obtained solution quality in a series of benchmarks is promising and calls for further refinements. One core advantage of the search is the anytime behavior: after the first random run a feasible packing is known. Another important feature are the low memory requirements. Only the amount of space for storing the packing and the policies at each level of the search and all container cells have to be present. As some rollouts can be executed in parallel, an implementation on a multi-core CPU and a many-core GPU appears to be possible. So far we worked on single-threaded implementation and experimented with several processes executed in parallel.

There are many interesting problems to be solved in container packing. Iso-oriented boxes and the restriction to six possible orientations might be too inflexible, so that different angles and placements based on a CAD model of the object are of interest. Here we can foresee the potential of the randomized search approach.

Especially the inclusion of dynamics is crucial. If only parts of the conveyor belt are accessible, we have an on-line instead of an off-line optimization problem for which an algorithm with a good competitive ratio has to be designed. Additionally to the packing there might also be ordering constraints, due to the partial delivery of products to the customers. If customer A is visited before customer B on a delivery tour, the objects should be placed in a way that it should be possible to unpack objects for A without moving packages for B.

In conclusion, our 3D packing approach is another example of successfully applying randomized combinatorial search to the domain of logistics. For the future, we expect to attack other optimization problems with Monte-Carlo tree search, where local search, branch-and-bound search, and mathematical programming together with several model-based and algorithmic improvements are currently the options of choice.

References

1. Bischoff, E.E., Marriott, M.D.: A comparative evaluation of heuristics for container loading. European Journal of Operational Research 44, 267–276 (1990)

2. Bjarnason, R., Fern, A., Tadepalli, P.: Lower bounding Klondike solitaire with Monte-Carlo planning. In: ICAPS (2009)
3. Cazenave, T.: Nested monte-carlo search. In: IJCAI
4. Cazenave, T., Teytaud, F.: Application of the nested rollout policy adaptation algorithm to the traveling salesman problem with time windows. In: Hamadi, Y., Schoenauer, M. (eds.) LION 2012. LNCS, vol. 7219, pp. 42–54. Springer, Heidelberg (2012)
5. Crainic, T.G., Perboli, G., Tadei, R.: Extreme point-based heuristics for three-dimensional bin packing. INFORMS Journal on Computing 20(3), 368–384 (2008)
6. de Berg, M., van Kreveld, M., Overmars, M., Schwarzkopf, O.: Computational Geometry: Algorithms and Applications, 2nd edn. Springer (2000)
7. Dowsland, W.B.: Three dimensional packing solution approaches and heuristic development. International Journal of Operational Research 29, 1637–1685 (1991)
8. Echelmeyer, W., Kirchheim, A., Lilienthal, A.L., Akbiyik, H., Bonini, M.: Performance indicators for robotics systems in logistics applications. In: IROS Workshop on Metrics and Methodologies for Autonomous Robot Teams in Logistics, MMARTLOG (2011)
9. Edelkamp, S., Gath, M., Cazenave, T., Teytaud, F.: Algorithm and knowledge engineering for the TSPTW problem. In: IEEE Symposium Series on Computational Intelligence, SSCI (2013)
10. George, J.A., Robinson, D.F.: A heuristic for packing boxes into a container. Computer and Operational Research 7, 147–156 (1980)
11. Gueting, R.H., Wood, D.: Finding rectangle intersections by divide-and-conquer. IEEE Transactions on Computers 33(7), 671–675 (1984)
12. Huang, E., Korf, R.E.: Optimal packing of high-precision rectangles. In: The International Symposium on Combinatorial Search, SOCS (2011)
13. Huang, E., Korf, R.E.: Optimal rectangle packing on non-square benchmarks. In: AAAI (2010)
14. Knott, K., Han, C.P., Egbelu, P.J.: A heuristic approach to the three-dimensional cargoloading problem. Int. J. Prod. Res. 27(5), 757–774 (1989)
15. Korf, R.E.: Optimal rectangle packing: Initial results. In: ICAPS, pp. 287–295 (2003)
16. Korf, R.E.: Optimal rectangle packing: New results. In: ICAPS, pp. 142–149 (2004)
17. Lim, A., Ying, W.: A new method for the three dimensional container packing problem. In: Proceedings of the 17th International Joint Conference on Artificial Intelligence, IJCAI 2001, vol. 1, pp. 342–347. Morgan Kaufmann Publishers Inc., San Francisco (2001)
18. Menschner, K., Gehring, H., Meyer, M.: A computer-based heuristic for packing pooled shipment containers. European Journal of Operational Research 1(44), 277–288 (1990)
19. Moffitt, M.D., Pollack, M.E.: Optimal rectangle packing: A Meta-CSP approach. In: ICAPS, pp. 93–102 (2006)
20. Rohde, M., Echelmeyer, W.: Cooperation possibilities between research and industry: Parcel-robot. Bremer Value Reports für Produktion und Logistik 3(1), 1–18 (2010)
21. Rosin, C.D.: Nested rollout policy adaptation for monte carlo tree search. In: IJCAI, pp. 649–654 (2011)
22. Wang, Y.: 3D container packing. PhD thesis, National University of Singapore (2001)
23. Zhang, Z., Guo, S., Zhu, W., Oon, W.-C., Lim, A.: Space defragmentation heuristic for 2D and 3D bin packing problems. In: IJCAI, pp. 699–704 (2011)

An Experimental Comparison of Classical, FOND and Probabilistic Planning

Andreas Hertle, Christian Dornhege, Thomas Keller,
Robert Mattmüller, Manuela Ortlieb, and Bernhard Nebel

University of Freiburg, 79110 Freiburg, Germany
{hertle,dornhege,tkeller,mattmuel,
ortlieb,nebel}@informatik.uni-freiburg.de

Abstract. Domain-independent planning in general is broadly applicable to a wide range of tasks. Many formalisms exist that allow the description of different aspects of realistic problems. Which one to use is often no obvious choice, since a higher degree of expressiveness usually comes with an increased planning time and/or a decreased policy quality. Under the assumption that hard guarantees are not required, users are faced with a decision between multiple approaches. As a generic model we use a probabilistic description in the form of Markov Decision Processes (MDPs). We define abstracting translations into a classical planning formalism and fully observable nondeterministic planning. Our goal is to give insight into how state-of-the-art systems perform on different MDP planning domains.

1 Introduction

Domain-independent planning is used to solve problems from various domains, including tasks from real-world robotics applications. Often, such tasks feature aspects that go beyond classical planning, such as nondeterministic or probabilistic effects, partial observability, etc. However, when modeling a problem, there is a tradeoff between modeling as many of these aspects as possible and finding solutions fast. Different existing planning formalisms capture different (combinations of) aspects of real-world problems. Modeling and abstracting away different aspects, they also induce different solution concepts. Which formalism is the best for a specific problem is not always obvious. As long as the application allows it, a less expressive formalism is chosen often in practice.

In this work, we study the question how to best deal with probabilistic action outcomes when modeling and solving a planning task. *Classical planning* formulations only model deterministic actions. They are often used by embedding the planner in an execution-monitoring-planning loop that replans on unexpected outcomes. *Fully observable nondeterministic (FOND)* planning explicitly considers nondeterministic actions and produces strategies that guarantee to reach a goal. *Probabilistic planning* additionally considers outcome probabilities and aims to maximize the expected accumulated reward.

C. Lutz and M. Thielscher (Eds.): KI 2014, LNCS 8736, pp. 297–308, 2014.

Since different formulations give different guarantees on the solution, an entirely fair comparison is impossible. We therefore compare classical planning, FOND planning and probabilistic planning experimentally and emphasize differences in solution quality, planning time and the ability to avoid deadend states of the considered algorithms. Since our planning systems [7,16,11] require different levels of abstraction regarding the input, we also provide abstracting translations between the planning formalisms.Our goal is to show how state-of-the-art planning systems cope with different problems in a realistic setting, a problem that users are commonly faced with when applying planning to solve actual tasks, which also sheds some light on claimed advantages in speed or solution quality.

We model three domains: one originally used in probabilistic planning, one from FOND planning, and a classical planning domain that is derived from a robotic planning scenario. Probabilistic action outcomes of the latter two are added in a first step, such that all domains are available as a Factored MDP [1]. These are then translated into corresponding FOND and classical planning formulations following the set of rules described in Sec. 4, and evaluated with three state-of-the-art planning systems in Sec. 5. Prior to that, we describe related work and give formal definitions for the used planning formalisms.

2   Related Work

Classical planners have been successfully integrated in robotic systems – a real-world domain known for unexpected outcomes. Kaelbling et al.[8] developed a robot planning system that integrates task and motion planning. This system uses a hierarchical regression planner where a refined prefix is executed directly. They argue that "there are few catastrophic or entirely irreversible outcomes". Following similar arguments, Nebel et al. [18] and Keller et. al [12] demonstrate how a classical planner embedded in a continual planning loop solves complex mobile manipulation tasks on a robot. Replanning is used to deal with execution failures and unexpected situations. In their KVP system, Gaschler et al. [4] combine the power of a symbolic planner with efficient geometric computations to create a framework for knowledge based planning in a real robot environment.

In recent years, nondeterministic planners have been improved in efficiency. Recently, compilation approaches that compute strong cyclic plans with classical planners became popular [14,3,17]. Mattmüller et al. [16] show how pattern database heuristics can be used in fully observable nondeterministic domains to guide the search more efficiently towards goal states. Little and Thiébaux [15] investigate the notion of probabilistic interestingness, where they investigate the effectiveness of replanning or compilation approaches to solve probabilistic planning tasks. Keller and Eyerich [11] developed PROST, a domain independent probabilistic planning system based on the UCT* algorithm [13], which is able to improve the quality of the solution policy by identifying unreasonable actions and actively searching for dead ends and goals in the MDP with a reward lock detection procedure.

3 Planning Formalisms

In this section, we describe the planning formalisms we use to specify classical, FOND, and probabilistic planning tasks.

3.1 Classical Planning

A *classical SAS*⁺ planning task is a tuple $\Pi = \langle \mathcal{V}, s_0, s_\star, \mathcal{O} \rangle$ consisting of the following components: $\mathcal{V}$ is a finite set of *state variables* v, each with a finite *domain* $\mathcal{D}_v$ and an *extended domain* $\mathcal{D}_v^+ = \mathcal{D}_v \uplus \{\bot\}$, where $\bot$ denotes the *undefined* or *don't-care* value. A *partial state* is a function s with $s(v) \in \mathcal{D}_v^+$ for all $v \in \mathcal{V}$. We say that s is *defined* for $v \in \mathcal{V}$ if $s(v) \neq \bot$. A *state* is a partial state s that is defined for all $v \in \mathcal{V}$. The set of all states s over $\mathcal{V}$ is denoted as $\mathcal{S}$. Depending on the context, a partial state s_p can be interpreted either as a *condition*, which is *satisfied* in a state s iff s agrees with s_p on all variables for which s_p is defined, or as an *update* on a state s, resulting in a new state s' that agrees with s_p on all variables for which s_p is defined, and with s on all other variables. The *initial state* s_0 of a problem is a state, and the *goal description* $s_\star$ is a partial state. A state s is a *goal state* iff $s_\star$ is satisfied in s. $\mathcal{O}$ is a finite set of *actions* of the form $a = \langle pre, eff \rangle$, where the *precondition* pre and the *effect* eff are partial states. The *application* of an outcome eff to a state s is the state $app(eff, s)$ that results from updating s with eff. An action is *applicable* in s iff its precondition is satisfied in s. The application of a to s is $app(a, s) = app(eff, s)$ if a is applicable in s, and undefined otherwise. Solutions to a *classical* planning task $\Pi = \langle \mathcal{V}, s_0, s_\star, \mathcal{O} \rangle$ are *plans*, i.e. sequences of $a_0, a_1, \ldots, a_n$, where $a_i \in \mathcal{O}$, $i = 0, \ldots, n$, a_i is applicable in s_i, $app(eff_i, s_i)$ results in s_{i+1} for $i = 0, \ldots, n-1$, and $s_\star$ is satisfied in s_{n+1}.

3.2 Nondeterministic Planning

A *fully observable nondeterministic (FOND) SAS*⁺ planning task is a tuple $\Pi = \langle \mathcal{V}, s_0, s_\star, \mathcal{O} \rangle$ with the same $\mathcal{V}$, s_0, and $s_\star$ as a classical planning task and *nondeterministic* actions $\mathcal{O}$ of the form $a = \langle pre, Eff \rangle$ with preconditions pre as before, but finite *sets* Eff of possible effects, the *nondeterministic outcomes* of a. Each $eff \in Eff$ is a partial state as before. The application of a set Eff to a state s is the set of states $app(Eff, s) = \{app(eff, s) \mid eff \in Eff\}$ that might be reached by applying a nondeterministic outcome from Eff to s. The application of a to s is $app(a, s) = app(Eff, s)$ if a is applicable in s, and undefined otherwise. Solutions to a planning task Π are now *strategies*, i.e., mappings $\pi : \mathcal{S}_\pi \to \mathcal{O} \cup \{\bot\}$ for a set of states $\mathcal{S}_\pi \subseteq \mathcal{S}$ such that $\pi(s) = \bot$ iff s is a goal state and that for all nongoal states s in $\mathcal{S}_\pi$, the action $\pi(s)$ is applicable in s and $\mathcal{S}_\pi$ contains all states in $app(\pi(s), s)$. A strategy π is a *strong cyclic plan* ("trial-and-error strategy") for a planning task Π iff $s_0 \in \mathcal{S}_\pi$ and for each state s reachable from state s_0 following strategy π, a goal state is reachable from s following strategy π.

3.3   Probabilistic Planning

A factored, finite-horizon MDP [1] with initial state and goal is a seven-tuple $\langle \mathcal{V}, \mathcal{O}, s_0, s_\star, P, R, H \rangle$, where the set of states $\mathcal{S}$ is induced by the set of *state variables* $\mathcal{V}$ and the *remaining steps* $h \in \{0, \ldots, H\}$ as $\mathcal{S} = 2^{\mathcal{V}} \times \{0, \ldots, H\}$. $\mathcal{O}$ is a finite set of *actions*, $s_0 \in \mathcal{S}$ is the *initial state*, $s_\star$ is a *goal description* as above, $P : \mathcal{S} \times \mathcal{O} \times \mathcal{S} \to [0, 1]$ is the *transition function* which gives the probability $P(s'|a, s)$ that applying action $a \in \mathcal{O}$ in state $s \in \mathcal{S}$ leads to state $s' \in \mathcal{S}$, $R : \mathcal{S} \times \mathcal{O} \to \mathbb{R}$ is the *reward function*, and $H \in \mathbb{N}$ is the *horizon* which specifies the number of decisions before each run terminates. For the purpose of this paper, we assume that the reward function has a special structure, specifically that the reward reflects (unit) action costs and numbers of unsatisfied goals. More formally, we let $unsat(s)$ be the number of variables v such that $s_\star(v)$ is defined and $s(v) \neq s_\star(v)$. Then, $R(s, a) = -(unsat(s) + 1)$, if s is not a goal state, and $R(s, a) = 0$, otherwise.

4   Translation between Planning Formalisms

Conversion from the probabilistic MDP formalism to the nondeterministic and classical planning formalism follows a set of rules that we present here. The conversion process could be completely automated and does therefore not require any domain-specific knowledge. However, in this paper we convert the domains manually following those rules.

All three planning formalisms work on the same finite set of states $\mathcal{S}$. Given the goal specification for an MDP is derived from a partial state $s_\star$ as described in Sec. 3.3, we use that same partial state $s_\star$ as the goal state for classical and FOND planning. The major differences in the formalisms now lie in how actions and action costs are derived from a given MDP.

4.1   Translating MDP to FOND Planning

An MDP action a is translated to a set of FOND actions. First, we compute all possible predecessors, in which a could have been applied.

$$Pre = \{s | P(s'|a, s) > 0; s, s' \in \mathcal{S}\} \qquad (1)$$

Each such state potentially can produce multiple outcomes. We obtain a set of effect states Eff_i for each state $pre_i \in Pre$.

$$Eff_i = \{s' | P(s'|a, pre_i) > 0; s' \in \mathcal{S}\} \qquad (2)$$

For each state $pre_i \in Pre$ we produce a FOND action with outcomes Eff_i, so that the MDP action a results in a set of FOND actions $\{\langle pre_i, Eff_i \rangle | pre_i \in Pre\}$. The actions obtained with these rules have full states as preconditions and effects. However, logical simplifications can drastically reduce the number of generated actions by summarizing the full states into partial states. In practice often one MDP action translates to one FOND action.

4.2   Translating MDP to Classical Planning

For converting MDP actions to classical actions we determine predecessors $pre_i \in Pre$ and effect outcomes Eff_i from an MDP action a analogously to the FOND translation. In contrast to FOND, classical actions allow only one deterministic effect eff. There are two commonly used determinizations: all-outcome determinization and most-likely determinization. Both assume that a specific effect can be chosen and plan accordingly.

An all-outcome determinization creates a separate classical action for each possible effect $eff \in Eff_i$. For each action in the MDP, we therefore obtain a set of actions with an entry for each predecessor $pre_i \in Pre$:

$$\{\langle pre_i, eff \rangle \,|\, eff \in Eff_i\} \tag{3}$$

Even though there are techniques that only lead to a polynomial blowup of the number of actions in the determinization [10], this can still be prohibitively large in practice. An alternative is the most-likely determinization, which only considers the effect with the highest probability. For a predecessor $pre_i \in Pre$ the most-likely effect eff_{max} is determined from all possible outcomes Eff_i.

$$eff_{max} = \underset{eff \in Eff_i}{\operatorname{argmax}} P(eff | a, pre_i) \tag{4}$$

Now for each predecessor $pre_i \in Pre$ only a single most-likely action is created as $\langle pre_i, eff_{max} \rangle$. Similarly to FOND we apply logical simplifications when possible to reduce the number of distinct actions for both determinizations.

As planners aim for minimal cost plans a meaningful action cost that considers the operator cost and probability $p = P(eff | a, pre_i)$ for an all-outcome operator, or $p = P(eff_{max} | a, pre_i)$ for a most-likely determinized operator is beneficial to improve the quality of resulting plans. Under the assumption that either that outcome happens with probability p or the state is unchanged with $1 - p$, we use the expected cost, when retrying an action with unit cost until the desired outcome is reached.

$$\sum_{i=1}^{\infty} (1 - p)^{i-1} \cdot p \cdot i = \frac{1}{p} \tag{5}$$

If action outcomes with unit cost have probability p we therefore use $\frac{1}{p}$ as the operator cost in the classical planning formulation. Other examples for combining operator cost and probability are to use the negative logarithm of p, which produces the most-likely plans (ignoring cost) or a weighted combination of $cost(a)$ and $-\log(p)$ [9].

4.3   Theoretical and Practical Properties of Translations and Planning Algorithms

Classical planning, FOND, and probabilistic planning differ both in their theoretical and their practical computational properties. On the theoretical side, classical planning with all-outcome determinization, FOND planning and probabilistic planning are guaranteed to preserve MDP goal paths in the translated model. For classical planning with most-likely determinization, this is not the case. All goal paths can be lost in the determinization. Classical planning with all-outcome determinization and probabilistic planning have the property that MDP plan existence implies that the translated models still have solutions. Classical planning with most-likely determinization and FOND planning do not have this property. The major advantage of probabilistic planning is the guarantee to find a *reward-optimal* solution in the limit of long deliberation time per step. None of the other approaches has the same guarantee. On the other hand, given that we usually do not compute optimal MDP policies online, offline FOND planning is the only approach that is guaranteed to *avoid dead-ends* at execution time. It does so at the expense of a significant amount of *offline planning time* that the other approaches avoid. Finally, at execution time, the high offline planning time is compensated for by fast state-action table lookups. Online planning speed (average response time) of classical (re-)planning and online probabilistic planning are incomparable, since the latter can use an arbitrary timeout for each step and return the best action so far, whereas classical planning has to expend at least the amount of time necessary to find *some* classical plan.

5 Evaluation

We use three different domains, each one originating from a different planning formalism to give a balanced evaluation. Each domain has been formulated as a factored MDP and was translated to classical and FOND planning.

5.1 Domains

MobileManipulation. In the MOBILEMANIPULATION domain, an autonomous service robot operates in a house. The robot is equipped with two arms and sensors to perceive the environment. There are multiple rooms with a number of objects located on tables. The goal is to tidy up the rooms, i.e. find all objects, pick them up and bring them to a specified destination table. In addition all tables should be wiped clean. Within a room, the robot can move freely between tables. Between rooms doors might need to be opened. The robot traverses through open doors with arms either close to the robot body or not. With retracted arms, success probabilities are higher (0.9 in comparison to 0.4). When close to a table the robot can choose to perceive object locations increasing the success probabilities for manipulation actions from 0.3 to 0.9. Objects can be picked up with either hand and brought to any table. Manipulation can go wrong, as the robot might be unable to grasp an object or might topple another object on the table. Should an object happen to fall to the floor, the robot will not be able to recover it. Only tables cleared of all objects can be wiped with a sponge.

TriangleTireworld. The TRIANGLETIREWORLD domain was introduced by Little and Thiébaux [15] and is a special case of the IPC TIREWORLD domain, in which a car has to drive from an initial to a goal location along directed edges. In each step, a tire can go flat probabilistically (we use $p = 0.2$). Before moving further, it has to be fixed, which is only possible if a spare tire is present in the current location. Only a subset of the locations contain a spare, so success is only guaranteed if the car follows a path such that every location along the path (except the goal) has a spare. The TRIANGLETIREWORLD domain is designed for offline planners to outperform replanners. This is achieved by requiring a particular structure of the roadmap graph: The locations form a triangle with corners A, B and C, the start is A, the goal is B, and the only safe path with spares in all locations is the maximal detour from A via C to B. Replanners trying to find shortest paths from A to B have a high probability of getting stuck, whereas offline planners should find and follow the only safe path. Instances of the TRIANGLETIREWORLD domain vary in their numbers of locations.

EarthObservation. The EARTHOBSERVATION domain models a satellite orbiting the earth. It can take pictures of the landscape below with a camera. The landscape is subdivided into square regions of interest forming a grid wrapped around a cylindrical projection of the earth surface. The camera focuses on one region at a time and can be shifted north or south. It can take a picture of the region currently in focus. The focus may not be shifted while taking a picture. Regardless whether the focus is shifted or a picture is taken, the satellite travels eastward around the earth, shifting the focus one grid cell to the east in addition to the other effects in each step. The objective is to take pictures of certain regions in a limited timeframe with as few shifts as possible. Taking a picture of a region does not guarantee good image quality: the worse the weather, the lower the chance of success. Over time the visibility in each region can change probabilistically, and changes between similar levels of visibility are more likely than vast changes. Apart from the weather change probabilities, which vary between 0.01 and 0.5, instances of the EARTHOBSERVATION domain differ in the numbers of grid cells and imaging objectives.

5.2   Planners

We use state-of-the-art planners from the field of classical planning (FAST DOWNWARD), fully observable nondeterministic planning (MYND) and probabilistic planning (PROST). We give a short overview of the underlying approaches.

FAST DOWNWARD. For classical planning, we use the FAST DOWNWARD planning system [7] in the LAMA 2011 configuration. In this setting, the planner first looks for a suboptimal plan with Greedy Best First search. When a plan is found, the search engine is switched to weighted A* to look for plans of higher quality. We let the planner search until an optimal plan is found or the timeout of 90 seconds is reached. Since we only produce classical plans for probabilistic problems, we have to deal with unexpected results when executing a plan on the plan simulator. Therefore, we wrap an execute-monitor-replan loop around FAST DOWNWARD. When monitoring determines that a plan is invalid, a new planning process is initiated for the current situation.

MYND. For offline planning, we use the FOND variant of the MYND planner [16] that uses LAO* search [5] guided by the canonical PDB heuristic [2,6]. We use the goal variables as singleton patterns for the pattern collection. The planner outputs strong cyclic plans in the form of state-action tables that are then interpreted by an execution simulator. For each single planning task, we set an offline planning time limit of 30 minutes. Lookup times during plan simulation are negligible.

PROST. We use the PROST planning framework [11] for MDP planning, equipped with the UCT* algorithm [13] as used in the configuration that won IPPC 2014. This search procedure combines dynamic programming, heuristic search and Monte-Carlo tree search to an algorithm that is asymptotically optimal in the limit, but which is also able to make decisions under tight time constraints in an online fashion. In our experiments, a time limit of one second per simulation step was used. The heuristic is the base heuristic of PROST [11], which is based on an iterative deepening search in the most-likely determinization.

Table 1. Average response time and rewards for the EARTHOBSERVATION domain, the average of 100 runs is shown. Time values for MYND include offline planning time.

	Response Time [s]		Reward		
	eff_{max}	MYND	eff_{max}	MYND	PROST
1	8 ± 4	1	-151 ± 72	-66 ± 8	-62 ± 17
2	1 ± 1	0	-9 ± 3	-11 ± 6	-9 ± 4
3	16 ± 3	1	-391 ± 103	-109 ± 34	-85 ± 25
4	124 ± 93	3	-1141 ± 24	-399 ± 56	-355 ± 65
5	75 ± 31	3	-894 ± 35	-294 ± 64	-283 ± 46
6	9 ± 4	0	-172 ± 80	-126 ± 29	-67 ± 14
7	6 ± 3	0	-86 ± 39	-46 ± 14	-48 ± 16
8	3 ± 2	0	-16 ± 8	-10 ± 5	-10 ± 6
9	41 ± 6	2	-908 ± 146	-290 ± 94	-172 ± 35
10	39 ± 33	156	-2203 ± 18	-885 ± 187	-677 ± 97
11	1 ± 1	0	-10 ± 5	-15 ± 8	-18 ± 15
12	57 ± 12	4	-1191 ± 93	-301 ± 54	-237 ± 45
13	163 ± 53	15	-1481 ± 146	-341 ± 74	-275 ± 47
14	38 ± 8	2	-614 ± 160	-179 ± 44	-165 ± 68
15	128 ± 100	40	-2717 ± 61	-1015 ± 277	-826 ± 148
16	3 ± 1	0	-24 ± 10	-20 ± 7	-18 ± 9
17	478 ± 192	102	-2316 ± 125	-646 ± 200	-416 ± 76
18	230 ± 78	15	-1807 ± 80	-527 ± 111	-394 ± 81
19	466 ± 154	90	-2038 ± 116	-604 ± 202	-497 ± 90
20	101 ± 74	52	-2871 ± 29	-1144 ± 219	-814 ± 151

Table 2. Average response time and rewards for the MOBILEMANIPULATION domain, the average of 100 runs is shown. Time values for MYND include offline planning time.

	Response Time [s]			Reward			
	$Eff\star$	eff_{max}	MYND	$Eff\star$	eff_{max}	MYND	PROST
1	3 ± 1	2 ± 0	1	-27 ± 1	-27 ± 1	-27 ± 1	-75 ± 44
2	16 ± 6	7 ± 3	1	-82 ± 7	-81 ± 4	-84 ± 4	-218 ± 92
3	109 ± 34	34 ± 9	143	-134 ± 11	-132 ± 8	-156 ± 7	-419 ± 18
4	125 ± 45	113 ± 54	3	-123 ± 7	-127 ± 6	-146 ± 6	-396 ± 72
5	367 ± 187	218 ± 88	4	-190 ± 13	-191 ± 9	-217 ± 10	-805
6	530 ± 195	335 ± 127	5	-283 ± 16	-279 ± 11	-286 ± 14	-1005
7	312 ± 165	223 ± 109	3	-187 ± 14	-184 ± 7	-240 ± 8	-805
8	470 ± 193	299 ± 132	11	-307 ± 32	-278 ± 11	-310 ± 8	-1505
9	613 ± 259	492 ± 175	14	-413 ± 18	-421 ± 18	-460 ± 17	-1805
10	1106 ± 244	611 ± 291	134	-604 ± 59	-967 ± 656	-645 ± 18	-2105

5.3   Experiments

In this paper we compare three planning paradigms that not only differ in their expressivity but also have unique plan representations. To find common ground to evaluate the quality of the produced plans we use Scott Sanner's rddlsim[1], the simulator of the International Probabilistic Planning Competition (IPPC). For each of the three planning domains we provide between 10 and 20 instances to be solved. Every instance is simulated 100 times with a timeout of 30 minutes per instance. For each domain and planning formulation we record the number of dead ends, the average response time and the average reward for each instance when no dead end was reached. The average response time is the accumulated time to produce an action for a simulation run. For the Classical formalization solved by FAST DOWNWARD we denote the all-outcome determinization as $Eff\star$ and the most-likely determinization by eff_{max} in tables.

The EARTHOBSERVATION domain does not have dead ends. The all-outcome determinization ran into memory limitations and thus was not applicable. Response times and rewards are given in Tab. 1. Since PROST is an online planner, its planning time per decision is a parameter and hence not illustrated in any of our Tables (we set it to one second per step). Classical and FOND planning are more dependent on the problem structure as they have to find a plan first. The most-likely determinization here suffers from the problem that the most likely result for taking an observation with bad weather is that no picture is taken. Thus as long as there is one patch with bad weather no proper plans are found. The rewards in Tab. 1 illustrate this clearly. MYND and PROST perform better than the most-likely determinization.

We see a different effect for the MOBILEMANIPULATION setting. Obviously, MYND never ends up in a dead-end (see Tab. 4), but the most-likely determinization is also well-suited to avoid this case. This is due to the fact that the most likely outcome of 'risky' actions always leads to a dead-end, so FAST

---

[1] https://code.google.com/p/rddlsim/

Table 3. Average response time and rewards for the TRIANGLETIREWORLD domain, the average of 100 runs is shown. Time values for MYND include offline planning time.

	Response Time [s]			Reward			
	$Eff\star$	eff_{max}	MYND	$Eff\star$	eff_{max}	MYND	PROST
1	0	0	0	-2	-2	-5	-5 ± 1
2	0	0	0	-4	-4	-12	-9 ± 1
3	1	1	0	-6	-6	-19 ± 2	-14 ± 1
4	1	1	2	-8	-8	-25 ± 1	-21 ± 2
5	2	1	5	-10	-10	-31 ± 2	-28 ± 2
6	2	1	10	-12	-12	-37 ± 1	-31 ± 2
7	5	2	78	-14	-14	-44 ± 2	-36 ± 2
8	16	2	n/a	-16	-16	n/a	-41 ± 3
9	60	3	n/a	-18	-18	n/a	-45 ± 2
10	94	3	n/a	-20	-20	n/a	-52 ± 3
11	97	5	n/a	-22	-22	n/a	-57 ± 3
12	99	7	n/a	-24	-24	n/a	-60 ± 3
13	100	8	n/a	-26	-26	n/a	-66 ± 3
14	102	10	n/a	-28	-28	n/a	-70 ± 3
15	103	13	n/a	-30	-30	n/a	-76 ± 3

Table 4. These tables show, how many deadends were reached in 100 iterations for the MOBILEMANIPULATION (left) and TRIANGLETIREWORLD (right) domains

	$Eff\star$	eff_{max}	MYND	PROST
1	0	0	0	0
2	29	0	0	0
3	56	0	0	0
4	68	0	0	0
5	88	0	0	0
6	67	0	0	0
7	20	0	0	0
8	52	0	0	0
9	76	0	0	0
10	78	0	0	0

	$Eff\star$	eff_{max}	MYND	PROST
1	15	15	0	0
2	41	41	0	0
3	62	62	0	0
4	79	79	0	0
5	86	86	0	1
6	90	90	0	2
7	95	95	0	0
8	96	96	n/a	4
9	97	97	n/a	0
10	98	98	n/a	20
11	99	99	n/a	9
12	99	99	n/a	9
13	99	99	n/a	2
14	99	99	n/a	2
15	99	99	n/a	10

DOWNWARD never considers this option. PROST performs comparably bad in the MOBILEMANIPULATION domain since its heuristic maximizes the reward in the next couple of steps rather than lead it to a goal state. Unlike the other domains, a large number of actions must be performed until there is a positive effect on the reward formula. Starting with instance five, it doesn't perform any meaningful actions. Response times in Tab. 2 show that the MYND planner is consistently faster besides problem three, while the rewards are similar for all planners but PROST.

For the TRIANGLETIREWORLD domain we observe that classical planning runs into dead-ends early on, while PROST solves most problems such that no or only a few runs end in a dead end state (see Tab. 4). The response times in Tab. 3 show the expected behavior on this domain for those runs not leading to a dead end. No FOND strategy could be found for problem instances eight and higher, while FAST DOWNWARD still produces optimistic plans and PROST still manages to find a safe path to the goal in most instances. FAST DOWNWARD is fastest finding optimal weak plans efficiently being extremely optimistic. The rewards in Tab. 3 show this explicitly. If a plan was produced the reward always was maximal. The FOND planner must be pessimistic and thus gains lower rewards and solves fewer instances. However, there are no dead ends for the solved problems. In this domain, the tradeoff between dead-end avoidance and planning time is most obvious.

6   Conclusion

We evaluated three different planning approaches on distinctly different domains with probabilistic outcomes. Our results indicate that more expressive planning formulations are not necessarily slower for realistic problem sizes. Each planner showed different behavior dependent on the specific domain. It should be noted that classical planning performs faster, when most actions are deterministic. However, in the presented challenging settings a clear advantage based on computation times cannot be seen. If more expressive features are desired a richer planning formalism does not need to be prohibitively slow; nondeterministic or probabilistic planning formalisms can show better overall performance.

Acknowledgements. This work was supported by the German Aerospace Center (DLR) as part of the Kontiplan project (50 RA 1010), by the German Research Foundation (DFG) as part of the Transregional Collaborative Research Centers SFB/TR 14 AVACS and SFB/TR 8 Project R7, and the PACMAN project within the HYBRIS research group (NE 623/13-1).

References

1. Boutilier, C., Dearden, R., Goldszmidt, M.: Stochastic Dynamic Programming with Factored Representations. Artificial Intelligence (AIJ) 121(1-2), 49–107 (2000)
2. Culberson, J.C., Schaeffer, J.: Searching with pattern databases. In: McCalla, G.I. (ed.) Canadian AI 1996. LNCS, vol. 1081, pp. 402–416. Springer, Heidelberg (1996)
3. Fu, J., Ng, V., Bastani, F.B., Yen, I.L.: Simple and fast strong cyclic planning for fully-observable nondeterministic planning problems. In: International Joint Conference on Artificial Intelligence (IJCAI), pp. 1949–1954 (2011)
4. Gaschler, A., Petrick, R.P.A., Kröger, T., Knoll, A., Khatib, O.: Robot task planning with contingencies for run-time sensing. In: ICRA Workshop on Combining Task and Motion Planning (2013)

5. Hansen, E.A., Zilberstein, S.: LAO*: A heuristic search algorithm that finds solutions with loops. Artificial Intelligence 129(1-2), 35–62 (2001)
6. Haslum, P., Botea, A., Helmert, M., Bonet, B., Koenig, S.: Domain-independent construction of pattern database heuristics for cost-optimal planning. In: AAAI Conference on Artificial Intelligence (AAAI), pp. 1007–1012 (2007)
7. Helmert, M.: The fast downward planning system. Journal of Artificial Intelligence Research (JAIR) 26, 191–246 (2006)
8. Kaelbling, L., Lozano-Perez, T.: Hierarchical task and motion planning in the now. In: IEEE Conference on Robotics and Automation, ICRA (2011)
9. Kaelbling, L., Lozano-Perez, T.: Integrated task and motion planning in belief space. International Journal of Robotics Research (2013)
10. Keller, T., Eyerich, P.: A Polynomial All Outcomes Determinization for Probabilistic Planning. In: International Conference on Automated Planning and Scheduling (ICAPS), pp. 331–334. AAAI Press (2011)
11. Keller, T., Eyerich, P.: PROST: Probabilistic Planning Based on UCT. In: International Conference on Automated Planning and Scheduling (ICAPS). pp. 119–127 (2012)
12. Keller, T., Eyerich, P., Nebel, B.: Task planning for an autonomous service robot. In: Dillmann, R., Beyerer, J., Hanebeck, U.D., Schultz, T. (eds.) KI 2010. LNCS, vol. 6359, pp. 358–365. Springer, Heidelberg (2010)
13. Keller, T., Helmert, M.: Trial-based Heuristic Tree Search for Finite Horizon MDPs. In: Proceedings of the 23rd International Conference on Automated Planning and Scheduling (ICAPS 2013), pp. 135–143 (2013)
14. Kuter, U., Nau, D.S., Reisner, E., Goldman, R.P.: Using classical planners to solve nondeterministic planning problems. In: Proceedings of the International Conference on Automated Planning and Scheduling (ICAPS), pp. 190–197 (2008)
15. Little, I., Thiébaux, S.: Probabilistic planning vs replanning. In: ICAPS Workshop on IPC: Past, Present and Future (2007)
16. Mattmüller, R., Ortlieb, M., Helmert, M., Bercher, P.: Pattern database heuristics for fully observable nondeterministic planning. In: International Conference on Automated Planning and Scheduling (ICAPS), pp. 105–112 (2010)
17. Muise, C.J., McIlraith, S.A., Beck, J.C.: Improved non-deterministic planning by exploiting state relevance. In: Proceedings of the 22nd International Conference on Automated Planning and Scheduling, ICAPS (2012)
18. Nebel, B., Dornhege, C., Hertle, A.: How much does a household robot need to know in order to tidy up your home? In: AAAI Workshop on Intelligent Robotic Systems (2013)

Minimizing Necessary Observations for Nondeterministic Planning

Robert Mattmüller, Manuela Ortlieb, and Erik Wacker

Research Group Foundations of AI, University of Freiburg, Germany
{mattmuel,ortlieb,wackere}@informatik.uni-freiburg.de

Abstract. Autonomous agents interact with their environments via sensors and actuators. Motivated by the observation that sensors can be expensive, in this paper we are concerned with the problem of minimizing the amount of sensors an agent needs in order to successfully plan and act in a partially observable nondeterministic environment. More specifically, we present a simple greedy top-down algorithm in the space of observation variables that returns an inclusion minimal set of state variables sufficient to observe in order to find a plan. We enhance the algorithm by reusing plans from earlier iterations and by the use of functional dependencies between variables that allows the values of some variables to be inferred from those of other variables. Our experimental evaluation on a number of benchmark problems shows promising results regarding runtime, numbers of sensors and plan quality.

Keywords: AI planning, nondeterministic planning, partial observability, observation actions.

1 Introduction

When an autonomous agent interacts with its environment, it does so via *sensors* and *actuators* [8]. We consider an agent acting in a partially observable nondeterministic environment and equipped with an appropriate offline planning component. In particular, we consider the *sensors* this agent needs to be fitted with. Assuming that sensors are expensive, e.g., regarding power consumption, weight, or financially, it can be worthwhile trying to minimize the set of sensors necessary to solve a certain planning task. For example, it might turn out that in some specific robotic application, an RGB-D camera can handle all the observations a laser scanner would be used for, thus obviating the latter. In this paper, we study the problem of minimizing the set of necessary sensors, *not* the problem of minimizing the number of occurrences of observations in a plan. This makes a difference, since, e.g., excluding a laser scanner from the set of sensors makes the robot cheaper, but may lead to more complicated behavior and more compensatory observations at runtime. We simplify the problem by assuming that the amount of sensors needed is proportional to the number of variables that may have to be observed. Given a planning domain, this reduces our problem to finding a minimal set of (schematic) state variables such

C. Lutz and M. Thielscher (Eds.): KI 2014, LNCS 8736, pp. 309–320, 2014.

that every possible planning task from that domain is solvable if those and only those (schematic) variables are observable. We further simplify our problem by searching for sufficient sets of (grounded) state variables on the level of planning tasks instead of the level of planning domains. Strictly speaking, the resulting set of state variables is only sufficient for one specific planning task. But if that task is reasonably chosen (featuring all interesting aspects of the underlying domain), the set of observation variables found for that task can again be lifted to the schematic level of the underlying planning domain. Moreover, searching for sufficient observation variables on the instantiated level has the advantage of being more fine-grained than searching on the schematic level. This can potentially show that some ground instances of a predicate are necessary observations, whereas other ground instances of the same predicate are not necessary, possibly leading to a more fine-grained choice of sensors. Consider for example a nondeterministic version of the BLOCKSWORLD domain where the PUTONBLOCK(A, B) actions can have the undesired outcome that the moved block A is dropped to the table. All other actions are deterministic. If the initial state is completely known, it turns out that it is sufficient to observe the values of the variables CLEAR(B) for all blocks B for which an action PUTONBLOCK(A, B) occurs in the plan for some other block A. This is because the initial belief state is a singleton belief state and whenever a nondeterministic action of the form PUTONBLOCK(A, B) is applied to a singleton belief state, the resulting belief state will contain exactly two world states (one with A on B, the other with A on the table) that can be distinguished by observing the variable CLEAR(B). Notice that depending on the initial and goal state, not all instances of the CLEAR predicate may have to be observed, but for all nontrivial tasks, at least one of them has to be. Lifting this back to the domain level shows that observing the schematic CLEAR predicate is sufficient to solve all tasks from this domain. Regarding sensors this means that it is sufficient to install an overhead camera that is only able to observe if blocks are clear, but not in which configurations they are stacked. To our knowledge, there is little previous work on this topic. Huang et al. [5] study the related problem of finding an approximately minimal set of observation variables for strong planning, given a set of observation variables $\mathcal{V}$ (including possibly derived variables) and a *fixed* strong plan π that works under the assumption that all variables from $\mathcal{V}$ are observable. Their algorithm then reduces $\mathcal{V}$ to a sufficient subset for π still to work by first identifying all state pairs that need to be distinguishable for π to work and then identifying all variables from $\mathcal{V}$ necessary to actually distinguish those. Unlike in their approach, here we retain flexibility regarding the choice of the plan and allow any (strong cyclic) plan to be found as long as the observation variables found along with it are sufficient for the plan to be executable.

2   Preliminaries

We formalize partially observable nondeterministic (POND) planning tasks using a *finite-domain representation* for the state variables similar to the formalization of Ortlieb and Mattmüller [6]. A *POND planning task skeleton* is a tuple $\Pi = \langle \mathcal{V}, B_0, B_\star, \mathcal{A}, \mathcal{W} \rangle$ consisting of the following components: $\mathcal{V}$ is a finite set of *state variables* v, each with a finite *domain* $\mathcal{D}_v$ and an *extended domain* $\mathcal{D}_v^+ = \mathcal{D}_v \uplus \{\bot\}$, where $\bot$ denotes the *undefined* or *don't-care* value. A *partial state* is a function s with $s(v) \in \mathcal{D}_v^+$ for all $v \in \mathcal{V}$. We say that s is *defined* for $v \in \mathcal{V}$ if $s(v) \neq \bot$. A *state* is a partial state s such that its *scope* $\text{scope}(s) = \{v \in \mathcal{V} \mid s(v) \neq \bot\}$ is $\mathcal{V}$. The set of all states s over $\mathcal{V}$ is denoted as $\mathcal{S}$, and the set of all *belief states* B over $\mathcal{V}$ is denoted as $\mathcal{B} = 2^\mathcal{S}$. Depending on the context, a partial state s_p can be interpreted either as a *condition*, which is *satisfied* in a state s iff s agrees with s_p on all variables for which s_p is defined, or as an *update* on a state s, resulting in a new state s' that agrees with s_p on all variables for which s_p is defined, and with s on all other variables. The *initial belief state* B_0 and the *goal description* $B_\star$ of a task skeleton are both belief states. A belief state B is a *goal belief state* iff $B \subseteq B_\star$. $\mathcal{A}$ is a finite set of *actions* of the form $a = \langle Pre, Eff \rangle$, where the *precondition Pre* is a partial state, and the *effect Eff* is a finite set of partial states *eff*, the *nondeterministic outcomes* of a. The *application* of a nondeterministic outcome *eff* to a state s is the state $app(eff, s)$ that results from updating s with *eff*. The application of an effect *Eff* to s is the set of states $app(Eff, s) = \{ app(eff, s) \mid eff \in Eff \}$ that might be reached by applying a nondeterministic outcome from *Eff* to s. An action is *applicable* in a state s iff its precondition is satisfied in s, and it is applicable in a belief state B if it is applicable in all $s \in B$. Actions are applied in belief states and result in belief states. The application of an action in a belief state B is undefined if the action is inapplicable in B. Otherwise, the application of an action $a = \langle Pre, Eff \rangle$ to B is the set $app(a, B) = \{ app(eff, s) \mid eff \in Eff, s \in B \}$. Finally, $\mathcal{W} \subseteq \mathcal{V}$ is the set of variables that are possibly observable.

A POND planning task skeleton still lacks observations, which we define next. An *observation* is simply a variable $o \in \mathcal{W}$. The application of an observation o to B is the set of nonempty belief states that result from splitting B according to possible values of o, i.e., $app(o, B) = \{\{ s \in B \mid s(o) = d \} \mid d \in \mathcal{D}_o \} \setminus \{\emptyset\}$. Now, a *POND planning task* is a tuple $\Pi[\mathcal{O}] = \langle \Pi, \mathcal{O} \rangle$ consisting of a POND planning task skeleton Π and a finite set of observations $\mathcal{O}$. All actions and observation applications have unit cost. We will sometimes abuse notation and refer to a planning task by Π as well. POND planning tasks as defined above induce nondeterministic transition systems where the nodes are the (reachable) belief states and where there is an arc from a belief state B to a belief state B' labeled with an action a (or observation o) iff a (or o) is applicable in B and $B' = app(a, B)$ (or $B' \in app(o, B)$). Given a POND planning task, we seek a strong cyclic plan [2] solving the task, i.e., a partial mapping π from belief states to applicable actions or observations such that for all belief states B reachable from the initial belief state B_0 following π, B is either a goal belief state, or π is defined for B (π *is closed*) and at least one goal belief state is reachable from B following π (π *is proper*). For a plan π, by $\mathcal{B}_\pi$ we denote the set of belief states for which π is defined, i.e., the set of non-goal belief states reachable following π, including the initial belief state.

3 Minimizing Necessary Observations

We can formalize the problem of finding minimal sets of observations sufficient to solve a planning task either in terms of cardinality minimality or of inclusion minimality. For cardinality minimality, we get the following search problem.

Problem 1 (OBSERVECARDMIN).
INPUT: A POND planning task skeleton $\Pi = \langle \mathcal{V}, B_0, B_\star, \mathcal{A}, \mathcal{W} \rangle$.
OUTPUT: A cardinality minimal set of observations $\mathcal{O} \subseteq \mathcal{W}$ for Π such that there exists a strong cyclic plan for $\Pi[\mathcal{O}]$, or NONE if no such set $\mathcal{O}$ exists.

To classify the problem OBSERVECARDMIN complexity theoretically, we need a theorem by Rintanen.

Theorem 1 (Rintanen, 2004 [7]). *The strong cyclic plan existence problem for POND planning, PLANEXPOND, is 2-EXPTIME-complete.* $\square$

Rintanen's formalism differs slightly from ours in that his variables are propositional instead of finite-domain, that he encodes initial and goal states symbolically using formulas, and that he allows conditional effects. Neither of those differences affects the 2-EXPTIME-completeness result. Using Rintanen's result, we can immediately prove the following theorem.

Theorem 2. OBSERVECARDMIN *is* 2-EXPTIME-*complete.*

Proof. To show that OBSERVECARDMIN is 2-EXPTIME-hard, we polynomially reduce PLANEXPOND to OBSERVECARDMIN. POND planning tasks in the sense of PLANEXPOND have exactly the same form as our POND planning tasks skeletons $\Pi = \langle \mathcal{V}, B_0, B_\star, \mathcal{A}, \mathcal{W} \rangle$. Viewing such a POND planning task Π as an input to OBSERVECARDMIN, we see that the output of OBSERVECARDMIN is different from NONE iff Π is a positive instance of PLANEXPOND. To see that OBSERVECARDMIN $\in$ 2-EXPTIME, we have to give a 2-EXPTIME algorithm solving the problem. The naïve algorithm that iterates over all (exponentially many) candidate subsets $\mathcal{O} \subseteq \mathcal{W}$, tests whether $\Pi[\mathcal{O}]$ is solvable, and returns a cardinality minimal set $\mathcal{O}$ for which this is the case, is such an algorithm, because each test if $\Pi[\mathcal{O}]$ is solvable is in 2-EXPTIME according to Theorem 1, and at most exponentially many such tests have to be performed. $\square$

For inclusion instead of cardinality minimality we get a similar result.

Problem 2 (OBSERVEINCLMIN).
INPUT: A POND planning task skeleton $\Pi = \langle \mathcal{V}, B_0, B_\star, \mathcal{A}, \mathcal{W} \rangle$.
OUTPUT: An inclusion minimal set of observations $\mathcal{O} \subseteq \mathcal{W}$ for Π such that there exists a strong cyclic plan for $\Pi[\mathcal{O}]$, or NONE if no such set $\mathcal{O}$ exists.

Theorem 3. OBSERVEINCLMIN *is* 2-EXPTIME-*complete.*

Proof. Similar to proof that OBSERVECARDMIN is 2-EXPTIME-complete. $\square$

Clearly, cardinality minimal solutions are also inclusion minimal, but not every inclusion minimal solution is also cardinality minimal. Although both OB-SERVECARDMIN and OBSERVEINCLMIN are 2-EXPTIME-complete, we expect OBSERVECARDMIN to be even more challenging in practice, since, in the worst case, the complete space of subsets of W has to be exhausted, whereas for OB-SERVEINCLMIN a greedy top-down or bottom-up search in the space of those subsets is sufficient. Therefore, in the following we restrict our attention to practically solving OBSERVEINCLMIN.

3.1 Greedy Top-Down Search

When looking for minimal sets of observations, we can restrict our attention to variables that may ever need to be observed because they are either unknown initially or for which there is an action that makes them unknown.

Definition 1. *Let B be a belief state, $v \in \mathcal{V}$ a variable, and $a = \langle Pre, Eff \rangle \in \mathcal{A}$ an action. Then*

1. *v is known in B iff there exists a value $d \in \mathcal{D}_v$ such that $s(v) = d$ for all states $s \in B$.*
2. *a makes v unknown iff there are two nondeterministic effects $eff, eff' \in Eff$ such that $eff(v) = d$ for some value $d \in \mathcal{D}_v$ with $d \neq Pre(v)$ and $eff'(v) \neq d$.*
3. *v may need to be observed iff v is not known in the initial belief state B_0 or there exists an action $a \in \mathcal{A}$ that makes v unknown.*

Since whenever $\Pi[\mathcal{O}]$ is solvable, also $\Pi[\mathcal{O}^*]$ is solvable, where $\mathcal{O}^*$ is the set of all $v \in \mathcal{O}$ that may need to be observed, for the rest of this paper we assume that all $v \in \mathcal{W}$ may need to be observed.

Algorithm 1 shows a simple greedy algorithm that solves OBSERVEINCLMIN.

Algorithm 1. Simple Greedy Algorithm for OBSERVEINCLMIN

```
 1: function SIMPLEGREEDYSEARCH(Π):
 2:     if Π[W] is unsolvable then
 3:         return NONE
 4:     Compute some plan π for Π[W]
 5:     Let O be the set of variables actually observed in π
 6:     Let O' = O
 7:     for all o ∈ O' do
 8:         if Π[O \ {o}] is solvable then
 9:             Set O to O \ {o}
10:     return O
```

It is obvious that Algorithm 1 runs in doubly exponential time. We can also prove correctness of the algorithm.

Theorem 4. *Algorithm 1 correctly solves problem OBSERVEINCLMIN.*

Proof. Clearly, Algorithm 1 returns NONE iff no set $\mathcal{O} \subseteq \mathcal{W}$ exists such that $\Pi[\mathcal{O}]$ admits a strong cyclic plan. If there is a solution, then to see that Algorithm 1 returns an inclusion minimal set $\mathcal{O} \subseteq \mathcal{W}$ such that $\Pi[\mathcal{O}]$ admits a strong cyclic plan, we have to show that $\Pi[\mathcal{O}]$ is solvable and that $\Pi[\mathcal{O}']$ is unsolvable for all proper subsets $\mathcal{O}' \subsetneq \mathcal{O}$. Let $\mathcal{O}_0$ be the set of observation variables computed in line 5 and $o_1, \ldots, o_n$ be the order in which $\mathcal{O}_0$ is traversed by the algorithm, and let $\mathcal{O}_i$ be the set $\mathcal{O}$ after the i-th iteration, $i = 1, \ldots, n$. The fact that $\Pi[\mathcal{O}]$ is solvable follows inductively from the fact that $\Pi[\mathcal{O}_0]$ is solvable and that $\mathcal{O}_{i+1} \neq \mathcal{O}_i$ only if $\Pi[\mathcal{O}_{i+1}]$ is still solvable. To see that $\Pi[\mathcal{O}']$ is unsolvable for all proper subsets $\mathcal{O}' \subsetneq \mathcal{O}_n$, let $o_i \in \mathcal{O}_n$. Then in the i-th iteration, o_i was not removed, because $\Pi[\mathcal{O}_{i-1} \setminus \{o_i\}]$ would have been unsolvable. But since $\mathcal{O}_n \subseteq \mathcal{O}_{i-1}$ and hence $\mathcal{O}_n \setminus \{o_i\} \subseteq \mathcal{O}_{i-1} \setminus \{o_i\}$, also $\Pi[\mathcal{O}_n \setminus \{o_i\}]$ would be unsolvable (since removing observations only reduces solvability). □

Algorithm 1 is simple, but quite inefficient. Specifically, when testing if the task remains solvable after deleting a variable (line 8), no plan information from the previous step is reused. In the next subsection, we investigate the reuse of portions of plans not affected by making a particular variable unobservable.

3.2 Plan Reuse

Suppose we know a plan π for $\Pi[\mathcal{O}]$ and want to test if there also exists a plan for $\Pi[\mathcal{O} \setminus \{o\}]$ for some $o \in \mathcal{O}$. Instead of replanning, we can try to reuse the portions of π *before the first splits of belief states with respect to* o.

Let $\pi : \mathcal{B}_\pi \to \mathcal{A} \cup \mathcal{O}$ be a plan for $\Pi[\mathcal{O}]$, and let $o \in \mathcal{O}$. Then by $knownpos(\pi, o)$ we refer to the set of all belief states $B \in \mathcal{B}_\pi \cup \{app(\pi(B'), B')) \mid B' \in \mathcal{B}_\pi\}$ such that v is known in B, and by $safepos(\pi, o)$ to the set of all belief states $B \in knownpos(\pi, o)$ that are reachable from B_0 following π along paths passing exclusively through belief states in $knownpos(\pi, o)$. By $gaps(\pi, o)$ we refer to those $B \in safepos(\pi, o)$ that (a) are not goal belief states, (b) for which the successor belief state $B' = app(\pi(B), B))$ following π is not in $knownpos(\pi, o)$, and (c) there exists a path from B to a goal belief state following π such that some action along that path is the observation of o. Intuitively, $gaps(\pi, o)$ is the set of belief states that form the fringe between the portion of the plan π that we can reuse and the portion we need to recompute. In Algorithm 2 we will iteratively fill those gaps, starting from shallow ones and working our way down to the deeper ones. To that end, we associate with each belief state $B \in gaps(\pi, o)$ a value $depth(B)$ that denotes the length of the shortest execution sequence of actions (and observations) leading from B_0 to B following π. By π_o we denote the part of π that lies before $gaps(\pi, o)$. More formally, we can view π as a set of pairs (B, a), where B is a belief state and $a = \pi(B)$ is an action or observation. Then such a pair from π is also contained in π_o if $B \in safepos(\pi, o) \setminus gaps(\pi, o)$. We call π_o the *plan* π *restricted to safe prefixes with respect to* o.

For all gap belief states $B \in gaps(\pi, o)$, in order to replan for B we need to solve the planning task that is like $\Pi[\mathcal{O} \setminus \{o\}]$, but with its initial belief state replaced by B. We refer to a planning task skeleton (or a planning task) Π with initial belief state replaced by B as $\Pi\langle B \rangle$. Therefore, the task we have to replan for is $\Pi[\mathcal{O} \setminus \{o\}]\langle B \rangle$. Algorithm 2 shows a greedy algorithm with plan reuse to (approximately) solve OBSERVEINCLMIN.

Algorithm 2. Greedy Algorithm with Plan Reuse for OBSERVEINCLMIN

1: **function** GREEDYSEARCHWITHPLANREUSE(Π):
2:    **if** $\Pi[\mathcal{W}]$ is unsolvable **then**
3:       **return** NONE
4:    Compute some plan π for $\Pi[\mathcal{W}]$
5:    Let $\mathcal{O}$ be the set of variables actually observed in π
6:    Let $\mathcal{O}' = \mathcal{O}$
7:    **for all** $o \in \mathcal{O}'$ **do**
8:       Let $\mathcal{G}$ be $gaps(\pi, o)$
9:       Let π_o be the plan π restricted to safe prefixes with respect to o
10:      Set $allGapsFillable$ to $true$
11:      **while** $\mathcal{G} \neq \emptyset$ and $allGapsFillable$ **do**
12:         Pick $B \in \mathcal{G}$ with minimal $depth(B)$ and remove it from $\mathcal{G}$
13:         **if** $\Pi[\mathcal{O} \setminus \{o\}]\langle B \rangle$ is solvable with plan π^B_{-o} **then**
14:            Merge π^B_{-o} into π_o (resulting in updated π_o)
15:            Trace π_o and retain in $\mathcal{G}$ only those belief states that are non-goal
16:               belief states reachable following π_o for which π_o is undefined.
17:            **if** $\mathcal{G} = \emptyset$ **then**
18:               Set $\mathcal{O}$ to $\mathcal{O} \setminus \{o\}$
19:               Set π to π_o
20:         **else**
21:            Set $allGapsFillable$ to $false$
22:    **return** $\mathcal{O}$

Like Algorithm 1, Algorithm 2 first tests for solvability, computes an initial plan, and then iteratively tries to remove variables from the observation set $\mathcal{O}$. Unlike Algorithm 1, when testing if o can be removed, it determines the gaps in π that arise if o is no longer observable and that need to be filled using new subplans. It also identifies the portion π_o of π that can be reused as it does not depend on o. If at least one gap cannot be filled, o is retained and the next observation variable is considered (line 21). In order to fill one gap B, a plan π^B_{-o} for $\Pi[\mathcal{O} \setminus \{o\}]\langle B \rangle$ is computed. This plan π^B_{-o} is then merged into π_o (line 14), which means that all entries from π^B_{-o} are added to π_o, and if both π_o and π^B_{-o} contain an entry for the same belief state B', then the entry from π^B_{-o} is used and that from π_o is overridden. More formally, in line 14 we set π_o to $\pi_o \oplus \pi^B_{-o}$, where $(\pi_o \oplus \pi^B_{-o})(B') = \pi^B_{-o}(B')$ if $\pi^B_{-o}(B')$ is defined, and $(\pi_o \oplus \pi^B_{-o})(B') = \pi_o(B')$, otherwise. In line 15/16, the algorithm removes from $\mathcal{G}$ all gaps that were "accidentally" *closed* by π^B_{-o} and need not be considered any longer, i.e., all gaps B' for which π^B_{-o} is defined, as well as all gaps "accidentally" *circumvented* by π^B_{-o} by a different choice further up in the plan. Finally, if no gaps are left, o is removed from $\mathcal{O}$, π is set to π_o, and the next observation variable is considered. Notice that traversing the gaps from shallow to deep is only used as a heuristic and not strictly necessary for the algorithm.

Regarding runtime, it is obvious that the POND planning steps that take doubly exponential time in the worst case still dominate the overall runtime, and that at most exponentially many such planning steps are necessary. All other computations are cheaper than 2-EXPTIME. Therefore, Algorithm 2 runs in doubly exponential time. We still need to show that the final plan π is really a strong cyclic plan for the task $\Pi[\mathcal{O}]$ with the final set $\mathcal{O}$, and we have to reason about inclusion minimality of $\mathcal{O}$. We first give an example showing that the returned set $\mathcal{O}$ is in general *not* inclusion minimal, and that the fact that we consider the removal of each observation variable only once is not the culprit. Instead, the reason is that some gap B might not be fillable without observing variable o, but completely replanning without observing o is possible and B simply does not occur in a completely replanned solution.

Example 1. Consider the planning task skeleton $\Pi = \langle \mathcal{V}, B_0, B_\star, \mathcal{A}, \mathcal{W} \rangle$ with $\mathcal{V} = \{a, b, c\}$ and $\mathcal{D}_v = \{0, 1\}$ for all $v \in \mathcal{V}$. For ease of notation, we write (belief) states and preconditions as Boolean formulas over $\mathcal{V}$, and nondeterministic effects as sets of such formulas. Furthermore, $B_0 = \neg a \wedge \neg b \wedge \neg c$, $B_\star = c$, $\mathcal{W} = \{b\}$, and $\mathcal{A} = \{a_1, a_2, a_3, a_4\}$, where $a_1 = \langle \neg a, \{a\}\rangle$, $a_2 = \langle \neg b, \{b, \top\}\rangle$, $a_3 = \langle b, \{c\}\rangle$, and $a_4 = \langle \neg a \wedge \neg b \wedge \neg c, \{c\}\rangle$. A solution π for $\Pi[\mathcal{W}]$ is depicted on the left below.

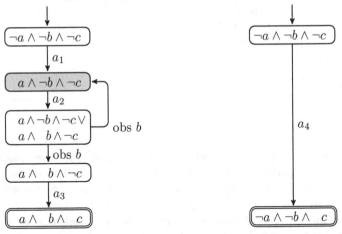

When b is made unobservable, we seek a plan for $\Pi[\emptyset]$. We can reuse the first two belief states from π up to the (only) gap state marked in gray. However, replanning with initial belief state $a \wedge \neg b \wedge \neg c$ without observing b will fail, since each action that makes c true needs b to be known or a to be false, neither of which can be accomplished from $a \wedge \neg b \wedge \neg c$ without observing b. Therefore, Algorithm 2 will return $\mathcal{O} = \{b\}$, whereas $\mathcal{O}^* = \emptyset$ would be an inclusion minimal solution, as witnessed by the plan in the right-hand part of the figure above.   □

Therefore, in order to find inclusion minimal observation sets, one would still have to run Algorithm 1 initialized with the output of Algorithm 2. Next, we show that Algorithm 2 returns a valid solution.

Theorem 5. *Assume $\Pi[\mathcal{W}]$ is solvable and let π and $\mathcal{O}$ be the plan and the set of observation variables at termination of Algorithm 2. Then π is a strong cyclic plan for $\Pi[\mathcal{O}]$.*

Proof. Let $\mathcal{O}_0$ be the set of observation variables used in the initial plan π^0, let $o_1, \ldots, o_n$ be the order in which $\mathcal{O}_0$ is traversed by the algorithm, let $\mathcal{O}_i$ be the set $\mathcal{O}$ after the i-th iteration, $i = 1, \ldots, n$, and π^i the corresponding plan.

We show the claim by induction over i. The induction base is obvious, since π^0 is a strong cyclic plan for $\Pi[\mathcal{O}_0]$ by construction. For the inductive step from i to $i + 1$, there are two cases. If $\mathcal{O}_{i+1} = \mathcal{O}_i$, then also $\pi^{i+1} = \pi^i$ and vice versa. Since π^i is a plan for $\Pi[\mathcal{O}_i]$, also π^{i+1} is a plan for $\Pi[\mathcal{O}_{i+1}]$. The more interesting case is the one where $\mathcal{O}_{i+1} = \mathcal{O}_i \setminus \{o_{i+1}\}$. We have to show that after all gaps are filled, the resulting composite plan solves $\Pi[\mathcal{O}_{i+1}]$. Let $B_i^1, \ldots, B_i^k \in \mathcal{G}$ be the set of all gaps that actually get filled, in that order (some gaps might be skipped if they are accidentally filled or avoided before the algorithm would explicitly take care of them). Let $\pi_j^i := \pi_{-o_{i+1}}^{B_i^j}, j = 1, \ldots, k$, be the corresponding plans to fill the gaps, and let $\pi_o^i := \pi_{o_{i+1}}^i$. Then the resulting plan π^{i+1} is $(\ldots (\pi_o^i \oplus \pi_1^i) \oplus \ldots) \oplus \pi_k^i$. We have to show that π^{i+1} is a strong cyclic plan for $\Pi[\mathcal{O}_{i+1}]$. It is clear that π^{i+1} does not observe any variable outside $\mathcal{O}_i$, and also it does not observe o_{i+1} by construction. What is left is showing that π^{i+1} is closed and proper. To see this, notice that by construction each execution of π^{i+1} starts out as an execution of π_o^i (for zero or more steps), then possibly executes π_1^i (for zero or more steps), then π_2^i and so on, with lower indices j of the executed subplan π_j^i only increasing. Eventually, it only follows π_o^i or π_j^i for some maximal $j \leq k$. Since π^i and all $\pi_j^i, j = 1, \ldots, k$, are closed and proper, the same holds for π^{i+1}. This concludes the proof. $\qquad\square$

3.3   Use of Functional Dependencies

We discuss one more way to speed up Algorithm 1 or 2, a preprocessing step that discards potential observation variables o whose value can be derived from the values of other observation variables. For our purpose, in order to discard o, it is sufficient that there are observation variables $o^1, \ldots, o^n$ that are not discarded and a function $f : \prod_{i=1}^n \mathcal{D}_{o^i} \to \mathcal{D}_o$ such that for all world states s in all belief states B encountered following π, $s(o) = f(s(o^1), \ldots, s(o^n))$. For states not encountered following the plan, this equality does not necessarily have to hold. We call a tuple $F = (o, \{o^1, \ldots, o^n\}, f)$ with this property a *functional dependency* in π, $head(F) = o$ the *head* of F, $body(F) = \{o^1, \ldots, o^n\}$ the *body* of F, and $fun(F) = f$ the *function* of F. We call a set of functional dependencies $\mathcal{F}$ *acyclic* if there are no $F_1, \ldots, F_k \in \mathcal{F}$ such that $head(F_i) \in body(F_{i+1})$ for all $i = 1, \ldots, k-1$ and $head(F_k) \in body(F_1)$. Given a plan π that observes only variables in $\mathcal{O}$ and an acyclic set of functional dependencies $\mathcal{F} = \{F_1, \ldots, F_m\}$ in π such that (a) for all $F, F' \in \mathcal{F}$, $head(F) \notin body(F')$ (if $\mathcal{F}$ is acyclic, this can be assumed without loss of generality), (b) for all $F \neq F' \in \mathcal{F}$, $head(F) \neq head(F')$, and (c) for all $F \in \mathcal{F}$, $body(F) \subseteq \mathcal{O}$, every occurrence of an observation o in π

such that $o = head(F)$ for some $F \in \mathcal{F}$ can be replaced by successive observations of (a subset of) the observation variables in $body(F)$. This produces a new plan $\pi_{\mathcal{F}}$ that observes only variables in $\mathcal{O} \setminus \{head(F) \mid F \in \mathcal{F}\}$.

We can extend Algorithms 1 and 2 accordingly as follows: After computing some plan π for $\Pi[\mathcal{W}]$, find an acyclic set of functional dependencies $\mathcal{F}$ in π with properties (a), (b) and (c) as above and replace π with $\pi_{\mathcal{F}}$. In our implementation, we use a simplified version of this idea: We only identify sets $\mathcal{X}$ of Boolean observation variables such that in each state reachable with π, exactly one $X \in \mathcal{X}$ is true. Each such set $\mathcal{X} = \{X_1, \ldots, X_k\}$ induces k functional dependencies $F_1, \ldots, F_k$, where $F_i = (X_i, \mathcal{X} \setminus X_i, f)$, $i = 1, \ldots, k$, where $f(x_1, \ldots, x_{k-1}) = 1$ if $x_1 = \cdots = x_{k-1} = 0$, and $f(x_1, \ldots, x_{k-1}) = 0$, otherwise. Regarding computation of such sets $\mathcal{X}_1, \ldots, \mathcal{X}_n$, for all subsets of Boolean variables we test whether they satisfy the desired mutex property. Candidate sets that obviously cannot satisfy it (after inspection of the reachable states) are not generated. From the functional dependencies induced by the remaining sets $\mathcal{X}$, we keep an acyclic (but not necessarily maximal) subcollection $\mathcal{F}$ as above.

4   Experiments

We implemented Algorithms 1 and 2 on top of the MYND planner [6] that uses LAO* search [3] guided the FF heuristic [4] applied to sampled world states of the belief state to be evaluated. Belief states and transitions between them are represented symbolically using BDDs [1]. Our benchmark domains are POND versions of the IPC domains BLOCKSWORLD and FIRSTRESPONDERS as well as the TIDYUP domain concerned with a robot tidying up a number of tables in a number of rooms.

Figure 1 shows the runtimes until the final set of observation variables has been found. We used a memory limit of 8 GB and a time limit of 30 minutes per task. The first six instances on the x-axis are our BLOCKSWORLD instances, the next 15 are from the FIRSTRESPONDERS domain, and the remaining ones are from the TIDYUP domain, sorted by difficulty per domain. We can see that the plan reuse from Algorithm 2 clearly pays off compared to the simple greedy algorithm. Use of functional dependencies leads to little extra time savings, except for some of the harder TIDYUP instances. Figure 2 shows the cardinalities of the sets of observation variables $|\mathcal{W}|$ before and $|\mathcal{O}|$ after minimization, with the x-axis as before. In principle, different inclusion minimal sets are incomparable cardinality-wise, but in our experiments the three configurations shown in the figure agreed on the sizes of the sets found. In particular, the problem from Example 1 does not occur here. The initial observation set cardinalities the algorithm starts with are 36 for all BLOCKSWORLD instances, between 7 and 39 for FIRSTRESPONDERS, and between 7 and 25 for TIDYUP.

We also conducted an experiment measuring the expected numbers of actions and observations necessary to reach a goal using the different intermediate plans π^i, expecting that plans with fewer allowed observations would tend to lead to longer execution sequences due to the need to replace simple, but forbidden

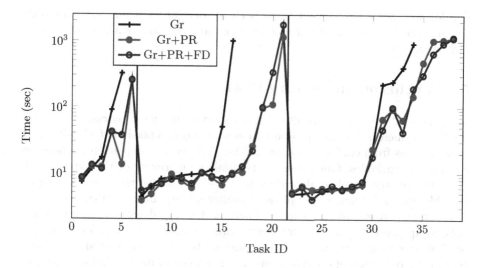

Fig. 1. Overall runtime needed for finding final observation set. Legend: Gr = greedy, PR = plan reuse, FD = functional dependencies.

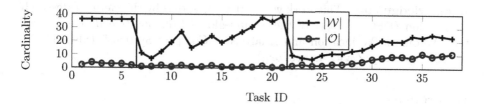

Fig. 2. Cardinalities of the observation sets before and after minimization

observations by longer observation sequences. In a few instances we saw evidence supporting this (e.g., in one of the BLOCKSWORLD instance, the expected plan steps increases from 34 to 65.5), but this is an exception, and across all instances expected execution steps mostly stay the same or increase only minimally.

Finally, it is interesting to see which sets of variables are typically left as observation variables having domain knowledge in mind: In BLOCKSWORLD, in most of the runs most of the remaining predicates are instances of the ONTABLE predicate, followed by occasional uses of the CLEAR predicate as predicted in the example in the Introduction. Both of these predicates on their own are sufficient. In FIRSTRESPONDERS, we get an even clearer picture: FIRES always need to be observed in order to make sure they are eventually extinguished. In all but one FIRSTRESPONDERS instance, nothing else but FIRE predicates are observed, the only exception being the only task in which there is no road from a victim's location to a hospital, which necessitates treating him on scene. For that, observing his VICTIMSTATUS is identified as being necessary. In the TIDYUP domain, we always get one sensing action for the status of the grippers, one for whether each relevant table is clean, one for each relevant door state (open or closed), one for the robot location, and one for each relevant cup on any of the tables.

5   Conclusion and Future Work

We presented an asymptotically optimal greedy top-down baseline algorithm for finding inclusion minimal observation sets and extended that algorithm by reusing plans from earlier iterations and using functional dependencies between observation variables. Our experiments showed superiority of the extended algorithm over the baseline algorithm in terms of runtime, whereas observation variable sets and strong cyclic plans of similar quality are generated.

For future work, we plan to complement the top-down procedure with a bottom-up procedure and to investigate variable ordering heuristics for the iteration over candidate variables for removal (based on an analysis of nondeterministic outcomes of operators, giving preference to more volatile variables). Moreover, we want to study the same problem on the domain instead of planning task level.

Acknowledgments. This work was partly supported by the German Research Foundation (DFG) as part of the Transregional Collaborative Research Center "Automatic Verification and Analysis of Complex Systems" (SFB/TR 14 AVACS, see http://www.avacs.org).

References

1. Bryant, R.E.: Graph-based algorithms for boolean function manipulation. IEEE Transactions on Computers 35(8), 677–691 (1986)
2. Cimatti, A., Pistore, M., Roveri, M., Traverso, P.: Weak, strong, and strong cyclic planning via symbolic model checking. Artificial Intelligence 147(1-2), 35–84 (2003)
3. Hansen, E.A., Zilberstein, S.: LAO*: A heuristic search algorithm that finds solutions with loops. Artificial Intelligence 129(1-2), 35–62 (2001)
4. Hoffmann, J., Nebel, B.: The FF planning system: Fast plan generation through heuristic search. Journal of Artificial Intelligence Research 14, 253–302 (2001)
5. Huang, W., Wen, Z., Jiang, Y., Wu, L.: Observation reduction for strong plans. In: Proc. 20th International Joint Conference on Artificial Intelligence (IJCAI 2007), pp. 1930–1935 (2007)
6. Ortlieb, M., Mattmüller, R.: Pattern-database heuristics for partially observable nondeterministic planning. In: Timm, I.J., Thimm, M. (eds.) KI 2013. LNCS, vol. 8077, pp. 140–151. Springer, Heidelberg (2013)
7. Rintanen, J.: Complexity of planning with partial observability. In: Proc. 14th International Conference on Automated Planning and Scheduling (ICAPS 2004), pp. 345–354 (2004)
8. Russell, S.J., Norvig, P.: Artificial Intelligence: A Modern Approach, 3rd edn. Pearson Education (2010)

Author Index